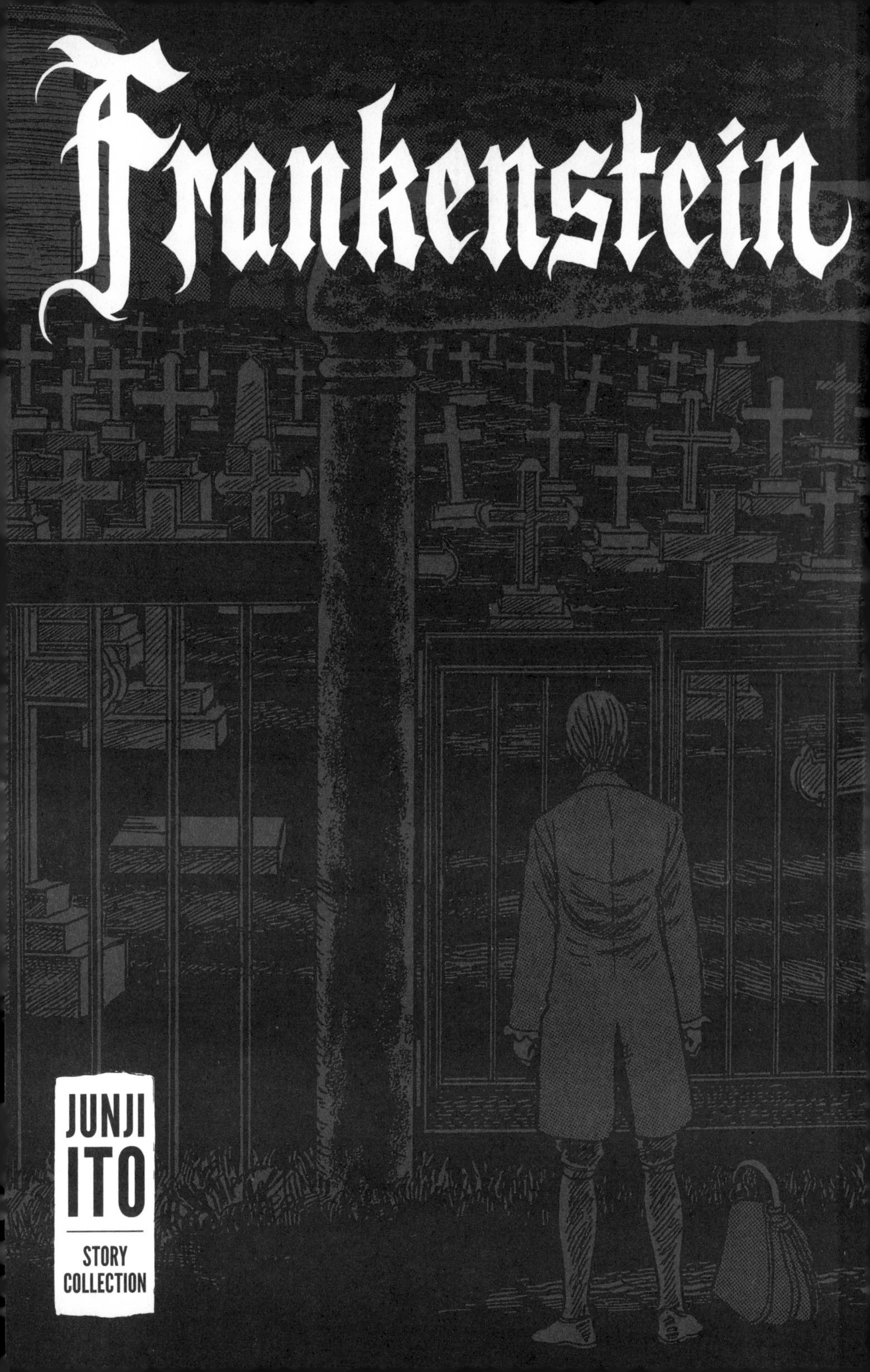
Frankenstein
JUNJI ITO
STORY COLLECTION

CONTENTS

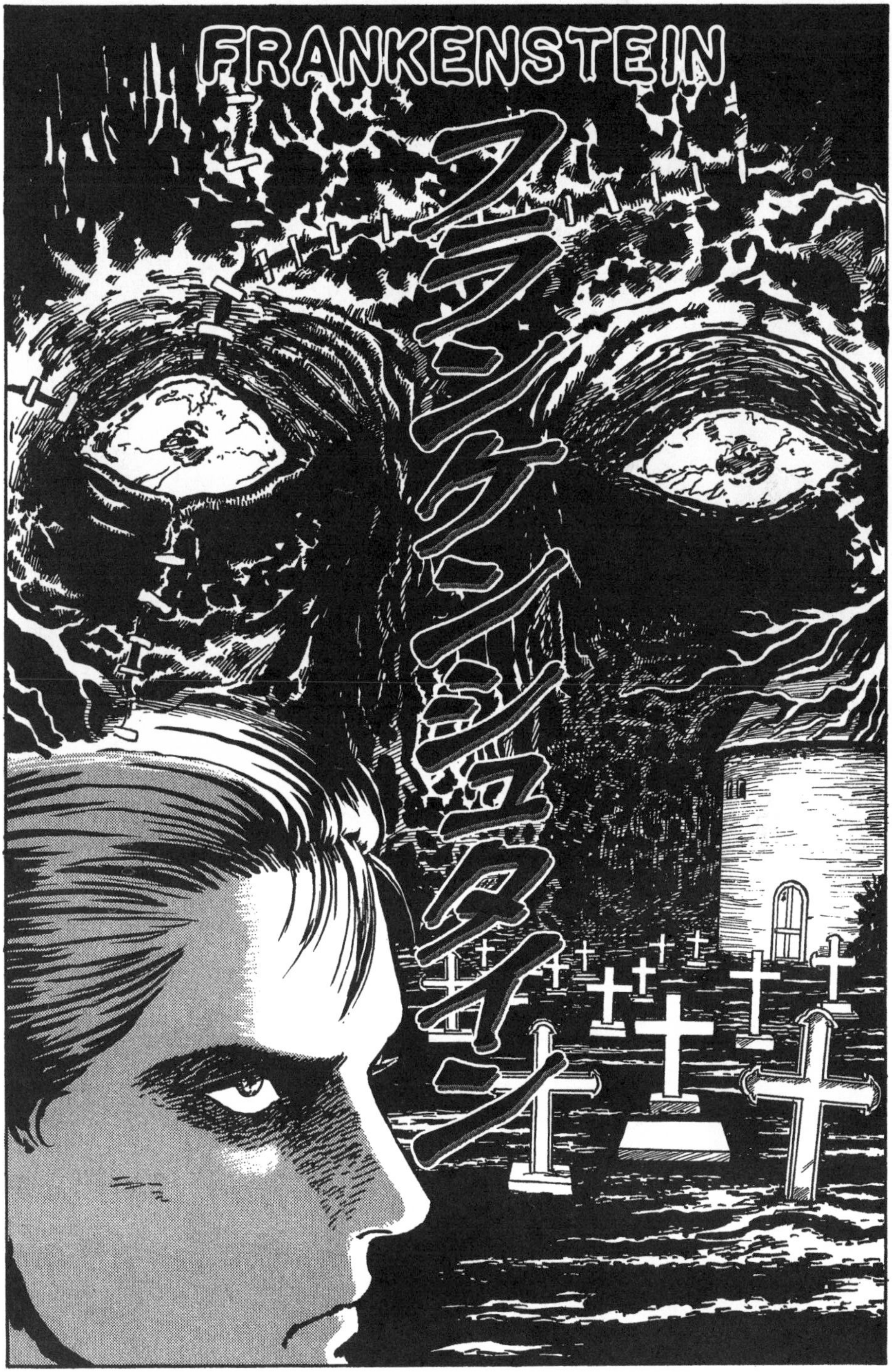
FRANKENSTEIN
フランケンシュタイン

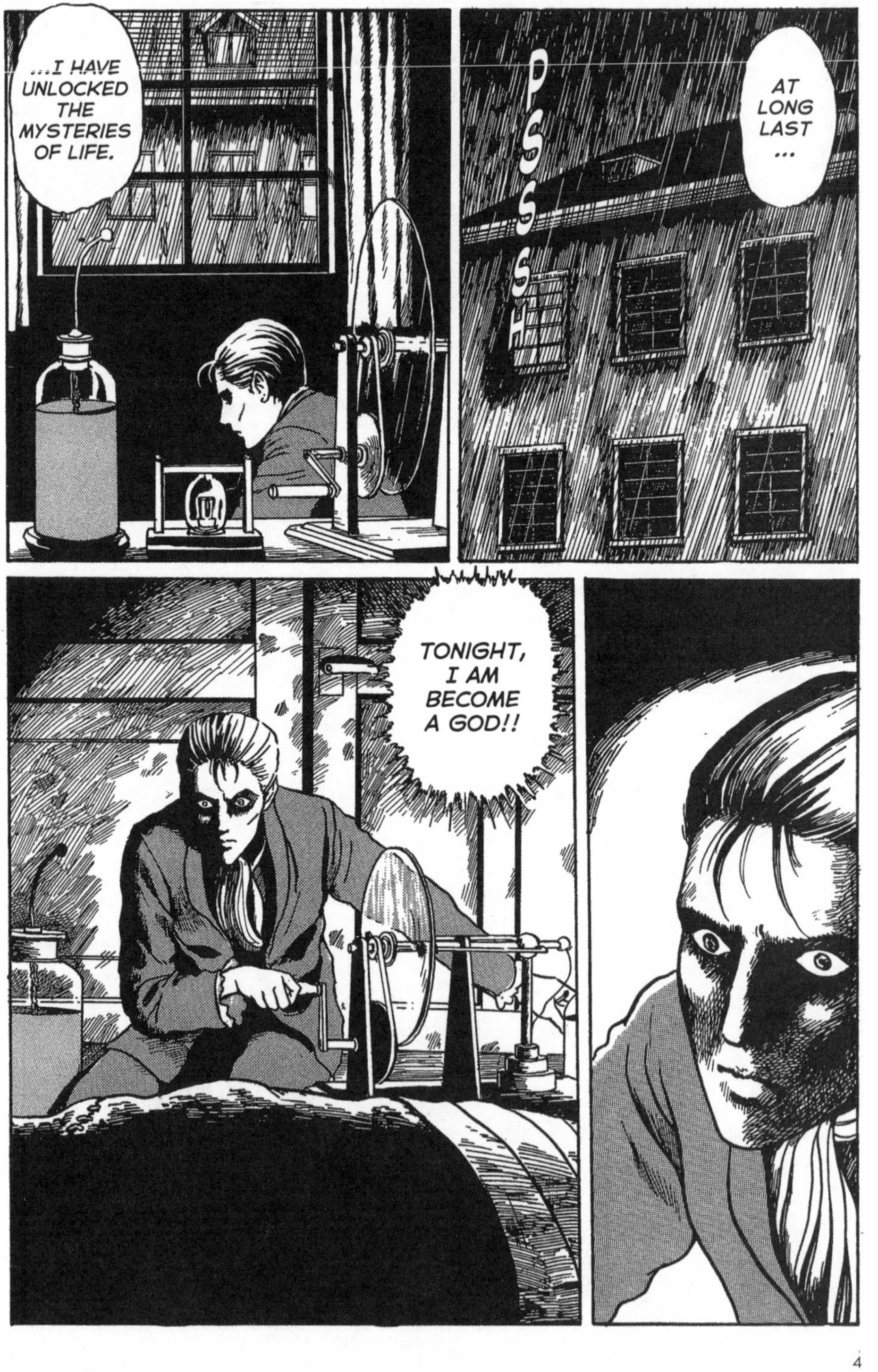
PSSSH
AT LONG LAST ...
...I HAVE UNLOCKED THE MYSTERIES OF LIFE.
TONIGHT, I AM BECOME A GOD!!

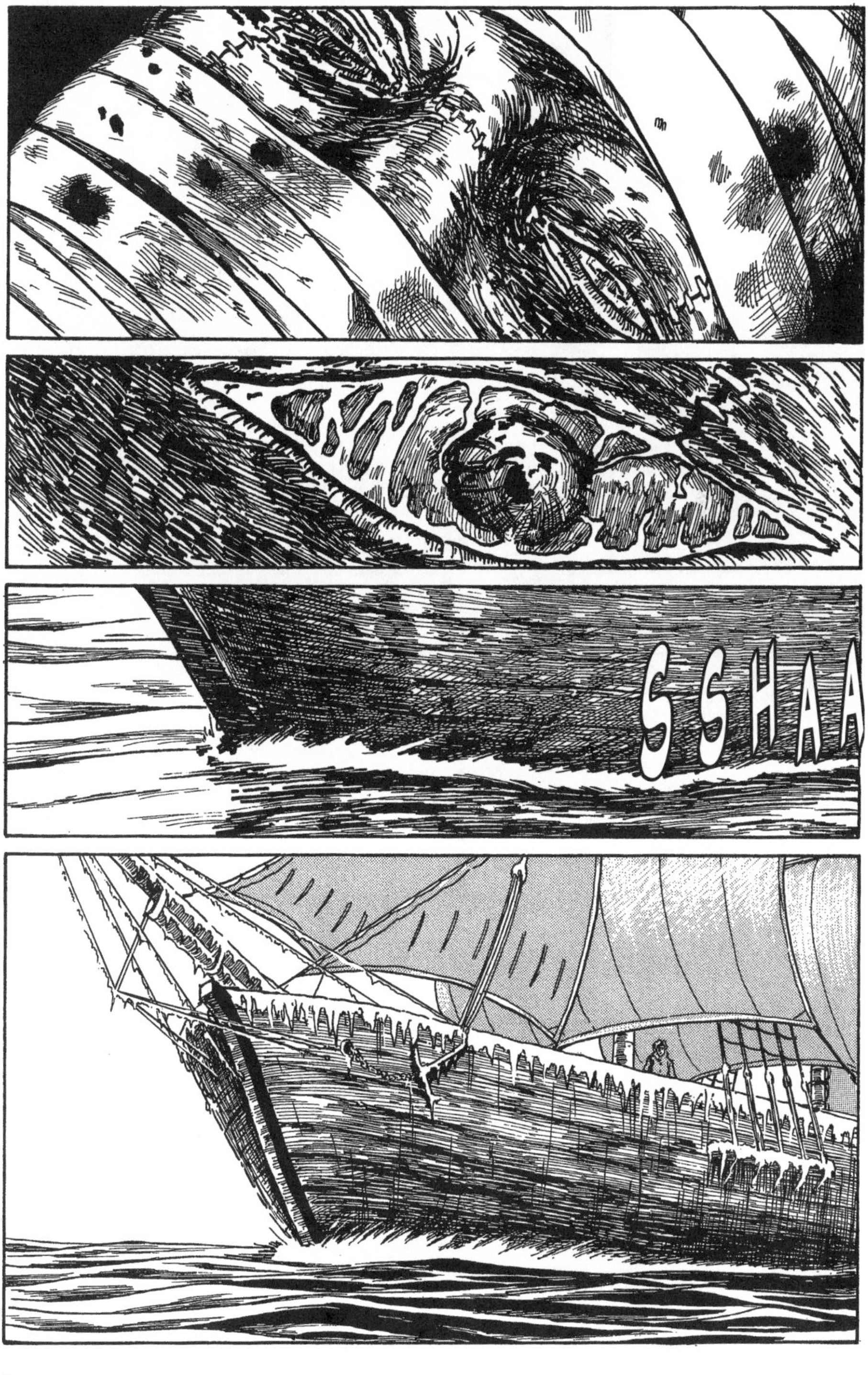
SSHAA

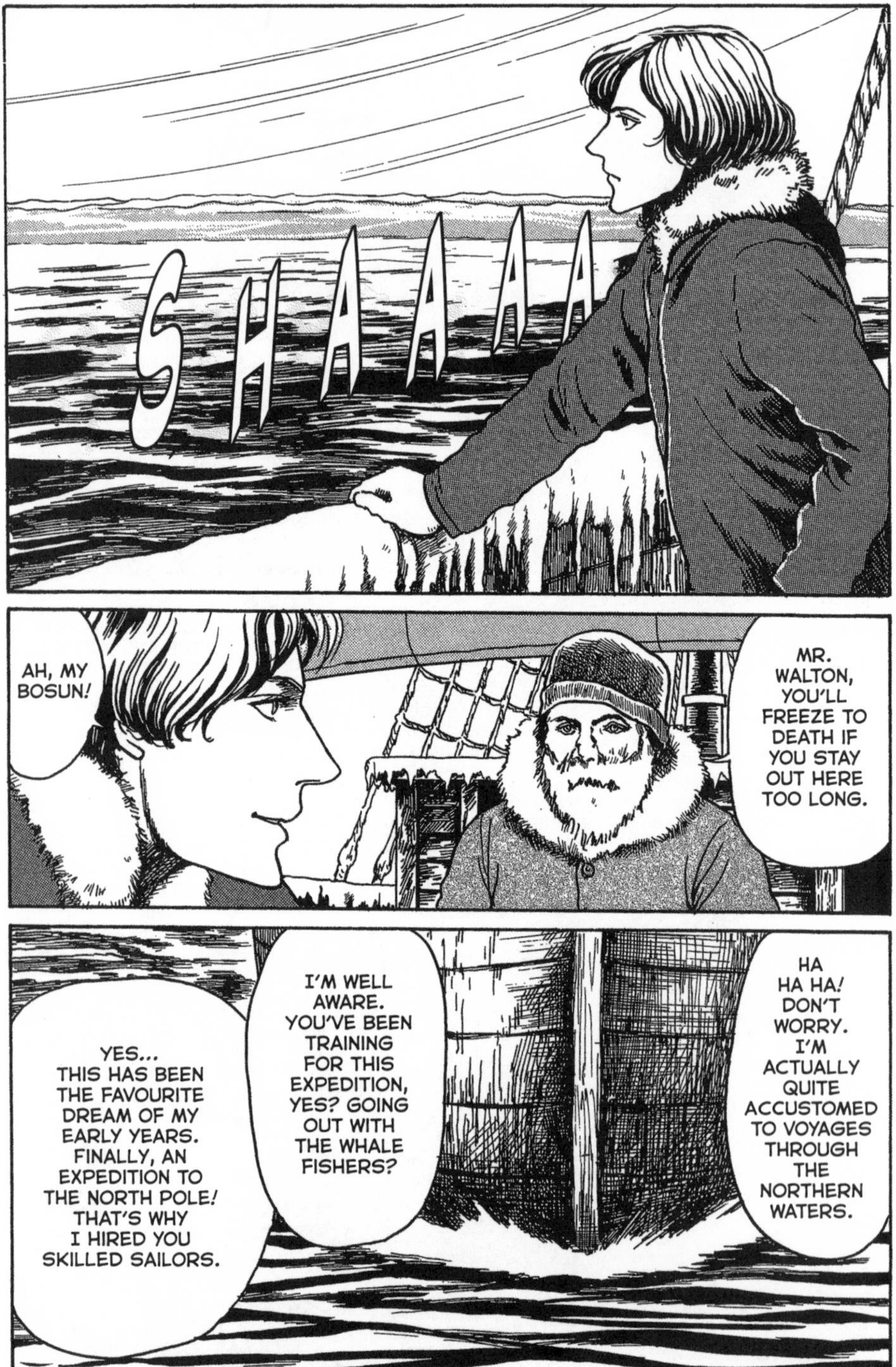
SHAAAA
MR. WALTON, YOU'LL FREEZE TO DEATH IF YOU STAY OUT HERE TOO LONG.
AH, MY BOSUN!
HA HA HA! DON'T WORRY. I'M ACTUALLY QUITE ACCUSTOMED TO VOYAGES THROUGH THE NORTHERN WATERS.
I'M WELL AWARE. YOU'VE BEEN TRAINING FOR THIS EXPEDITION, YES? GOING OUT WITH THE WHALE FISHERS?
YES... THIS HAS BEEN THE FAVOURITE DREAM OF MY EARLY YEARS. FINALLY, AN EXPEDITION TO THE NORTH POLE! THAT'S WHY I HIRED YOU SKILLED SAILORS.

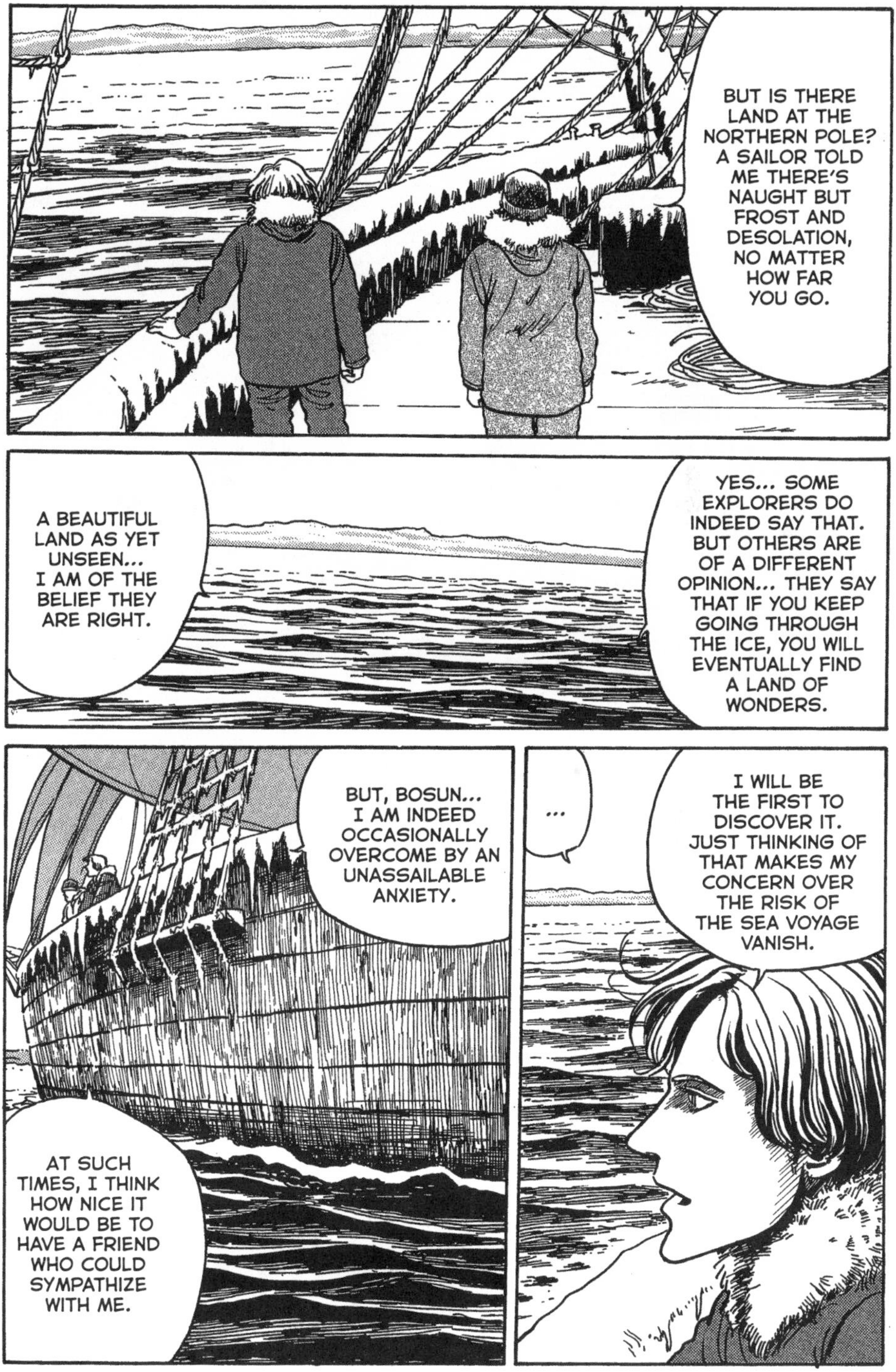
BUT IS THERE LAND AT THE NORTHERN POLE? A SAILOR TOLD ME THERE'S NAUGHT BUT FROST AND DESOLATION, NO MATTER HOW FAR YOU GO.
YES... SOME EXPLORERS DO INDEED SAY THAT. BUT OTHERS ARE OF A DIFFERENT OPINION... THEY SAY THAT IF YOU KEEP GOING THROUGH THE ICE, YOU WILL EVENTUALLY FIND A LAND OF WONDERS.
A BEAUTIFUL LAND AS YET UNSEEN... I AM OF THE BELIEF THEY ARE RIGHT.
I WILL BE THE FIRST TO DISCOVER IT. JUST THINKING OF THAT MAKES MY CONCERN OVER THE RISK OF THE SEA VOYAGE VANISH.
...
BUT, BOSUN... I AM INDEED OCCASIONALLY OVERCOME BY AN UNASSAILABLE ANXIETY.
AT SUCH TIMES, I THINK HOW NICE IT WOULD BE TO HAVE A FRIEND WHO COULD SYMPATHIZE WITH ME.

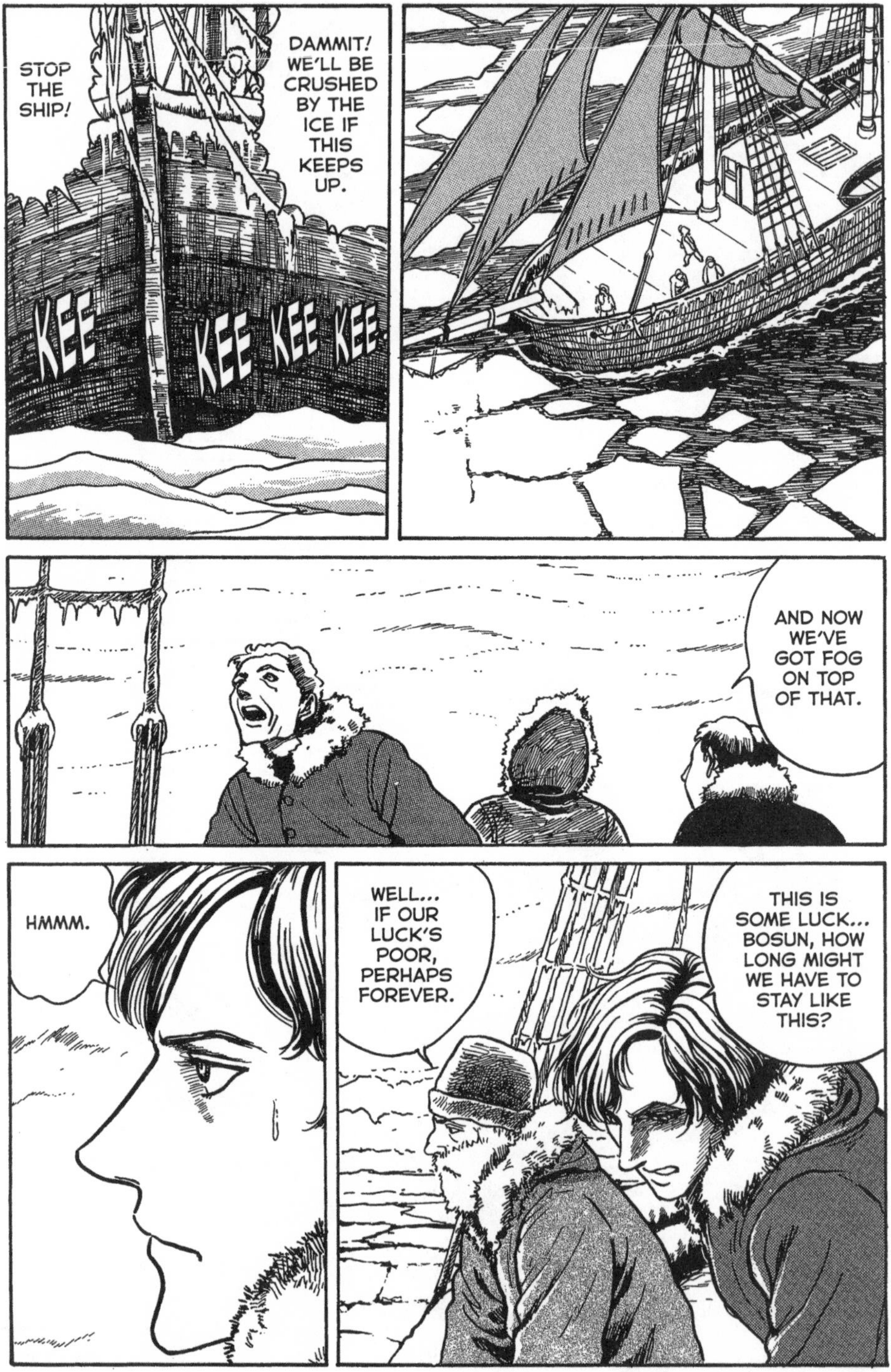
DAMMIT! WE'LL BE CRUSHED BY THE ICE IF THIS KEEPS UP.
STOP THE SHIP!
KEE KEE KEE KEE
AND NOW WE'VE GOT FOG ON TOP OF THAT.
THIS IS SOME LUCK... BOSUN, HOW LONG MIGHT WE HAVE TO STAY LIKE THIS?
WELL... IF OUR LUCK'S POOR, PERHAPS FOREVER.
HMMM.

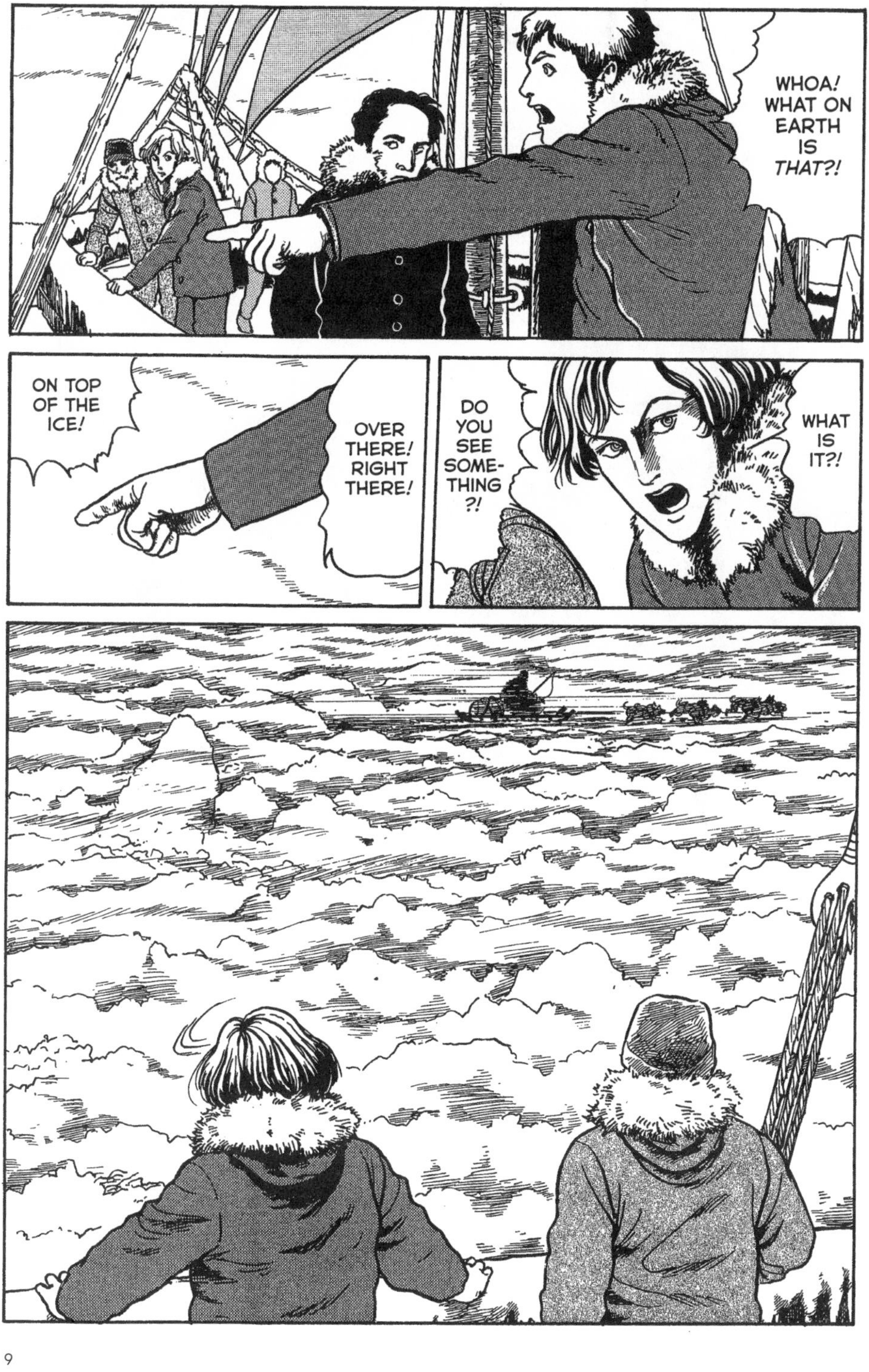
WHOA! WHAT ON EARTH IS *THAT?!*
WHAT IS IT?!
DO YOU SEE SOME-THING?!
OVER THERE! RIGHT THERE!
ON TOP OF THE ICE!

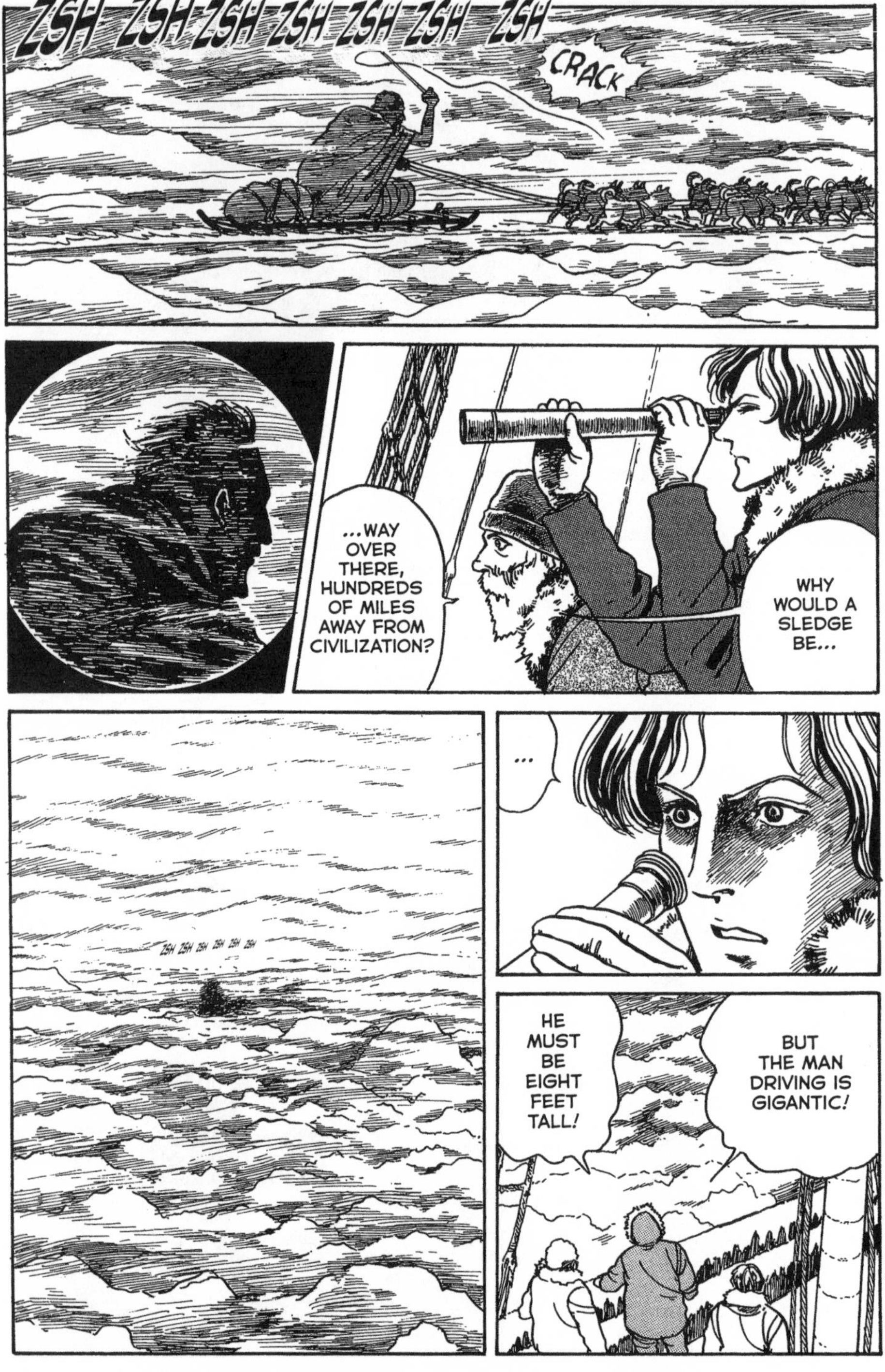
ZSH ZSH ZSH ZSH ZSH ZSH ZSH
CRACK
WHY WOULD A SLEDGE BE...
...WAY OVER THERE, HUNDREDS OF MILES AWAY FROM CIVILIZATION?
...
BUT THE MAN DRIVING IS GIGANTIC!
HE MUST BE EIGHT FEET TALL!
ZSH ZSH ZSH ZSH ZSH ZSH

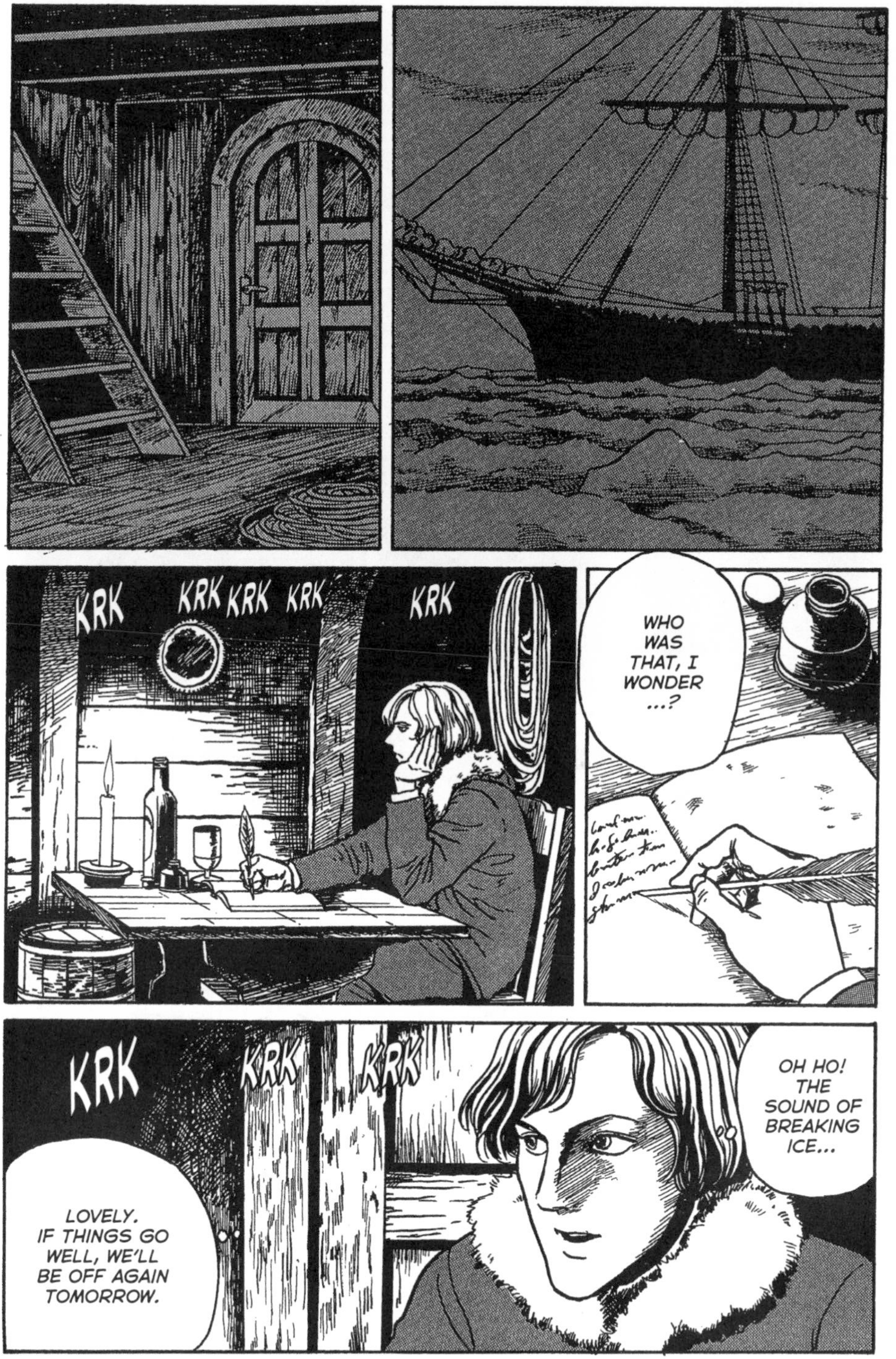
WHO WAS THAT, I WONDER ...?
KRK
KRK
KRK
KRK
KRK
OH HO! THE SOUND OF BREAKING ICE...
KRK
KRK
KRK
LOVELY. IF THINGS GO WELL, WE'LL BE OFF AGAIN TOMORROW.

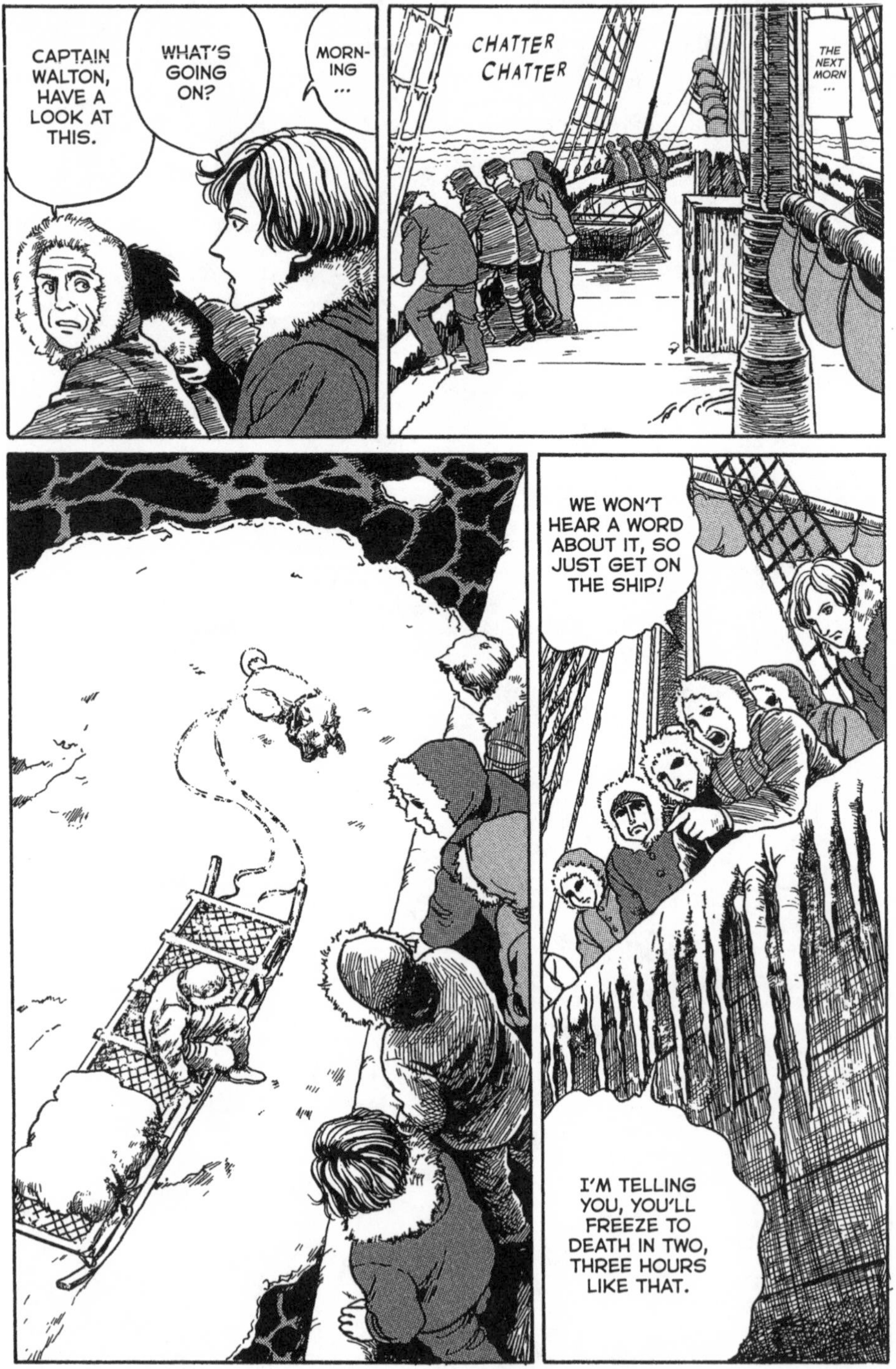
THE NEXT MORN...
CHATTER CHATTER
MORN-ING...
WHAT'S GOING ON?
CAPTAIN WALTON, HAVE A LOOK AT THIS.
WE WON'T HEAR A WORD ABOUT IT, SO JUST GET ON THE SHIP!
I'M TELLING YOU, YOU'LL FREEZE TO DEATH IN TWO, THREE HOURS LIKE THAT.

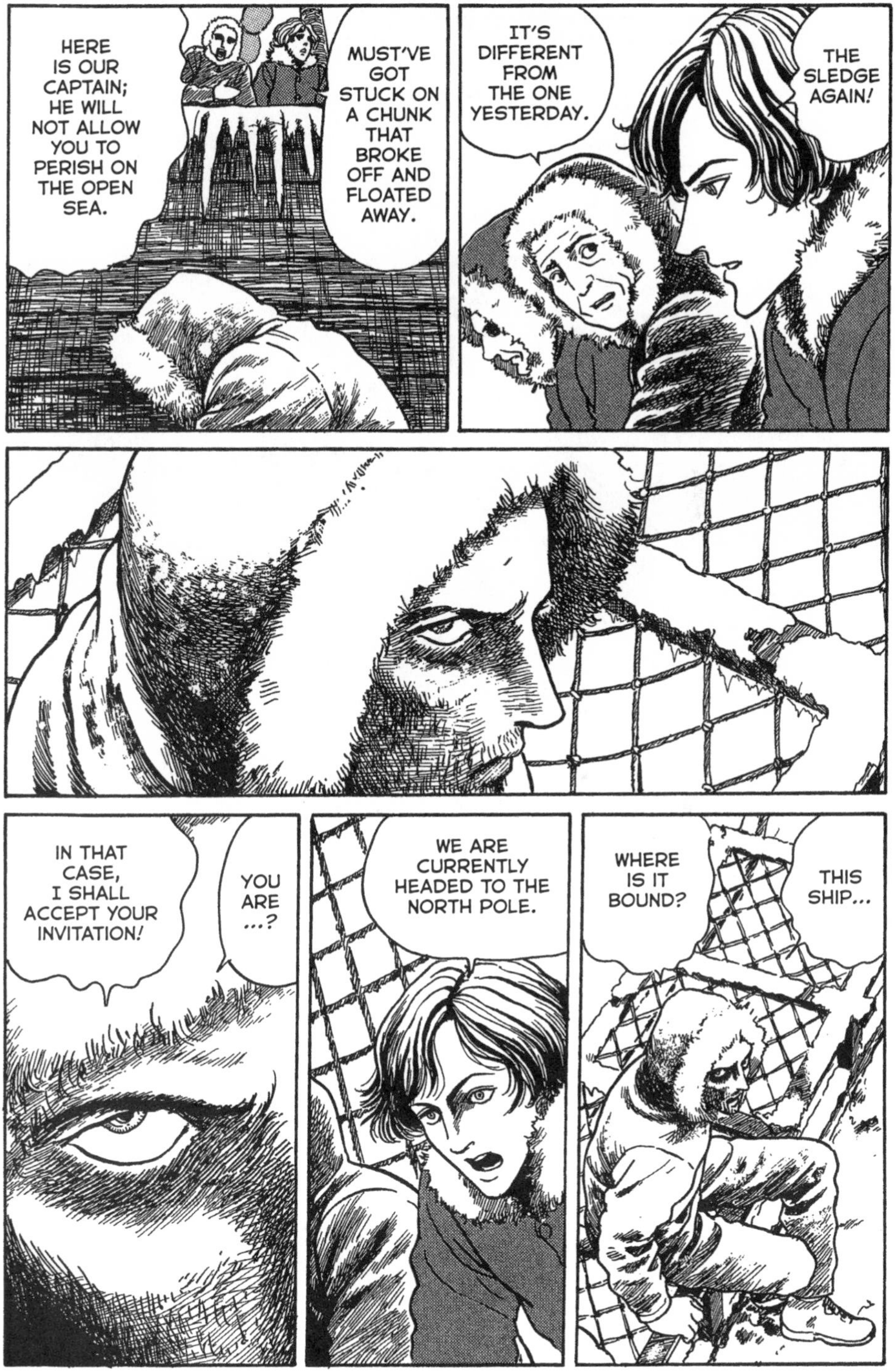
THE SLEDGE AGAIN!
IT'S DIFFERENT FROM THE ONE YESTERDAY.
MUST'VE GOT STUCK ON A CHUNK THAT BROKE OFF AND FLOATED AWAY.
HERE IS OUR CAPTAIN; HE WILL NOT ALLOW YOU TO PERISH ON THE OPEN SEA.
THIS SHIP...
WHERE IS IT BOUND?
WE ARE CURRENTLY HEADED TO THE NORTH POLE.
YOU ARE ...?
IN THAT CASE, I SHALL ACCEPT YOUR INVITATION!

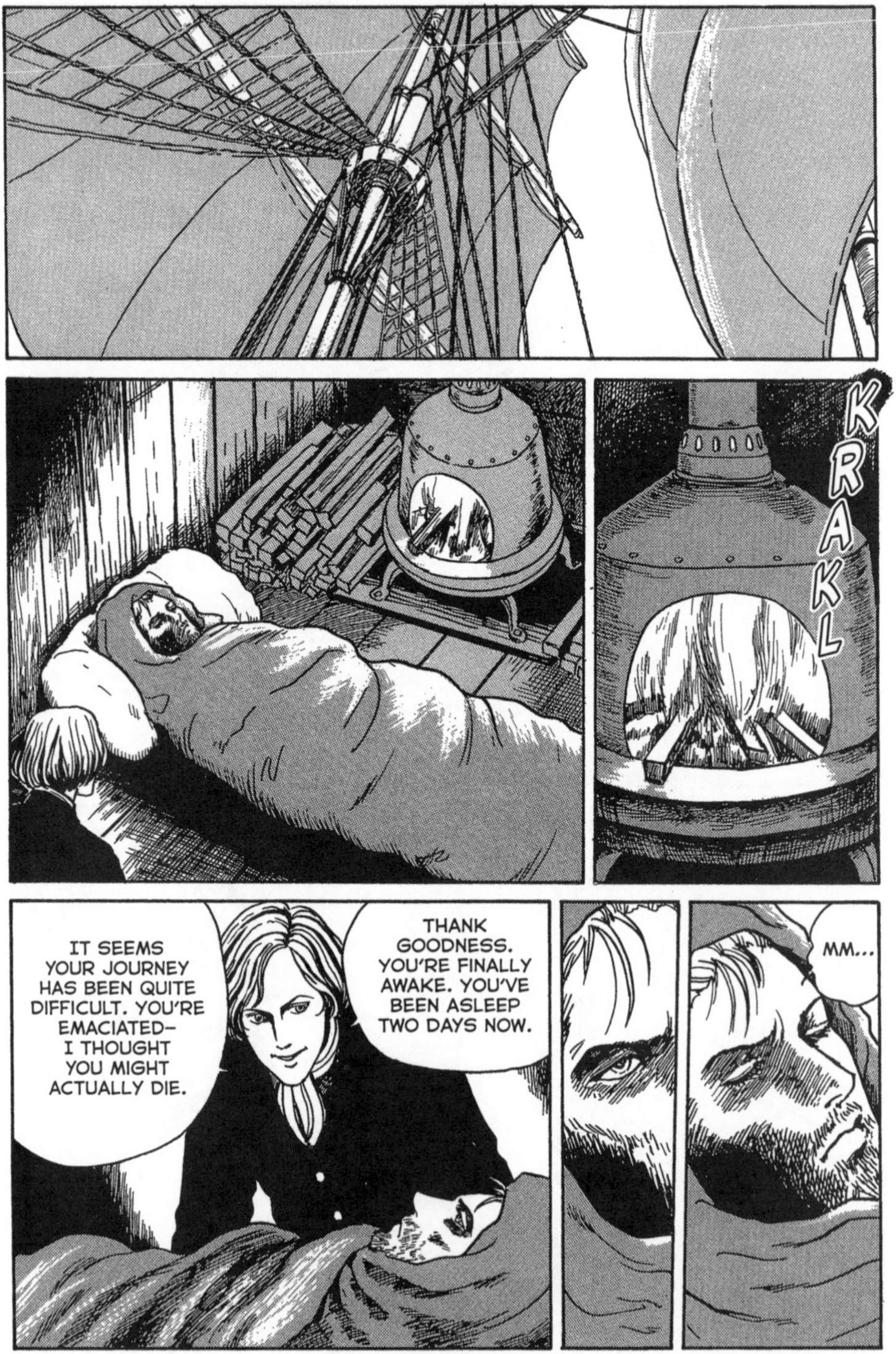
KRAKL
MM...
THANK GOODNESS. YOU'RE FINALLY AWAKE. YOU'VE BEEN ASLEEP TWO DAYS NOW.
IT SEEMS YOUR JOURNEY HAS BEEN QUITE DIFFICULT. YOU'RE EMACIATED— I THOUGHT YOU MIGHT ACTUALLY DIE.

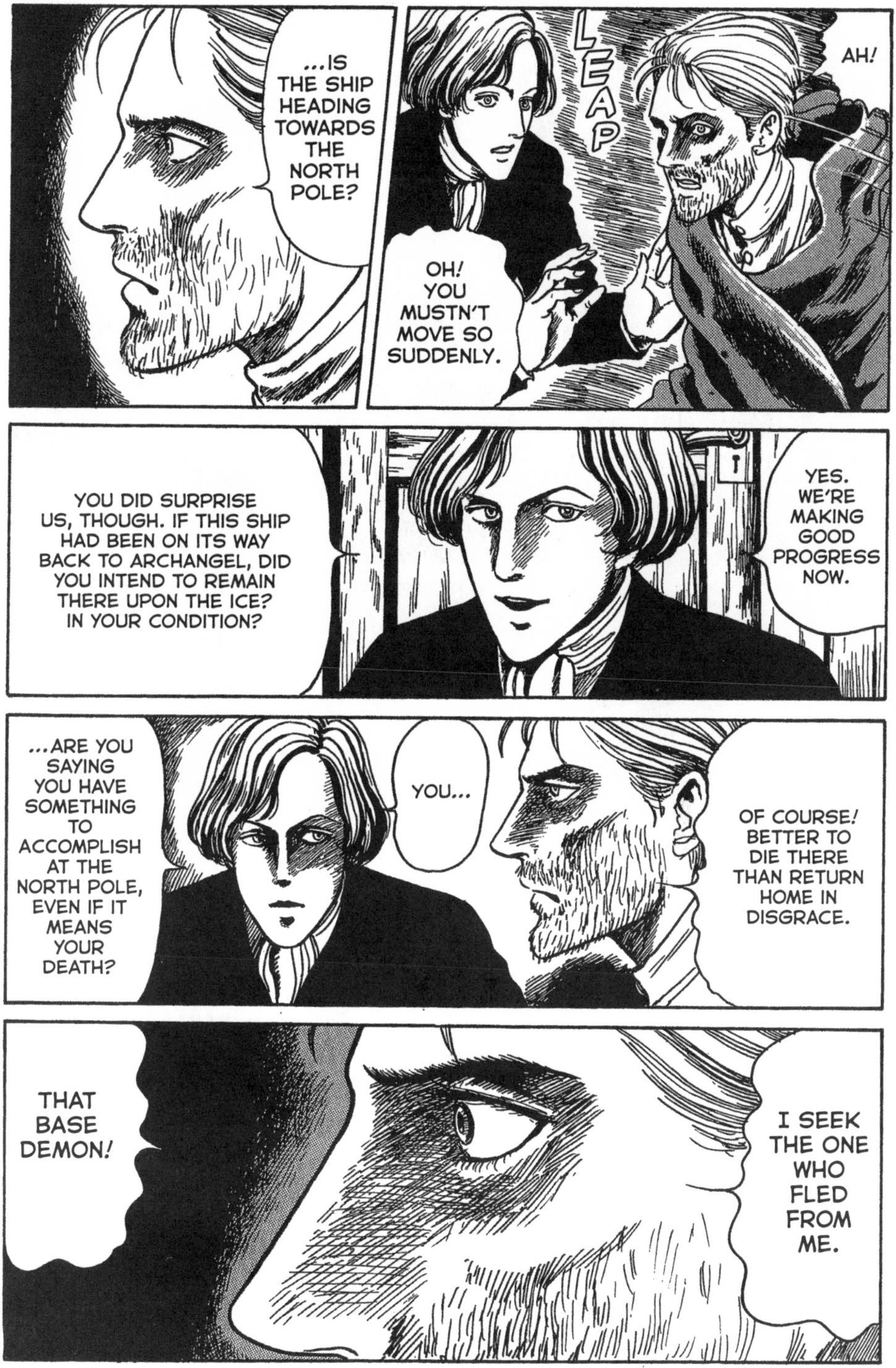
AH!
LEAP
OH! YOU MUSTN'T MOVE SO SUDDENLY.
...IS THE SHIP HEADING TOWARDS THE NORTH POLE?
YES. WE'RE MAKING GOOD PROGRESS NOW.
YOU DID SURPRISE US, THOUGH. IF THIS SHIP HAD BEEN ON ITS WAY BACK TO ARCHANGEL, DID YOU INTEND TO REMAIN THERE UPON THE ICE? IN YOUR CONDITION?
OF COURSE! BETTER TO DIE THERE THAN RETURN HOME IN DISGRACE.
YOU...
...ARE YOU SAYING YOU HAVE SOMETHING TO ACCOMPLISH AT THE NORTH POLE, EVEN IF IT MEANS YOUR DEATH?
I SEEK THE ONE WHO FLED FROM ME.
THAT BASE DEMON!

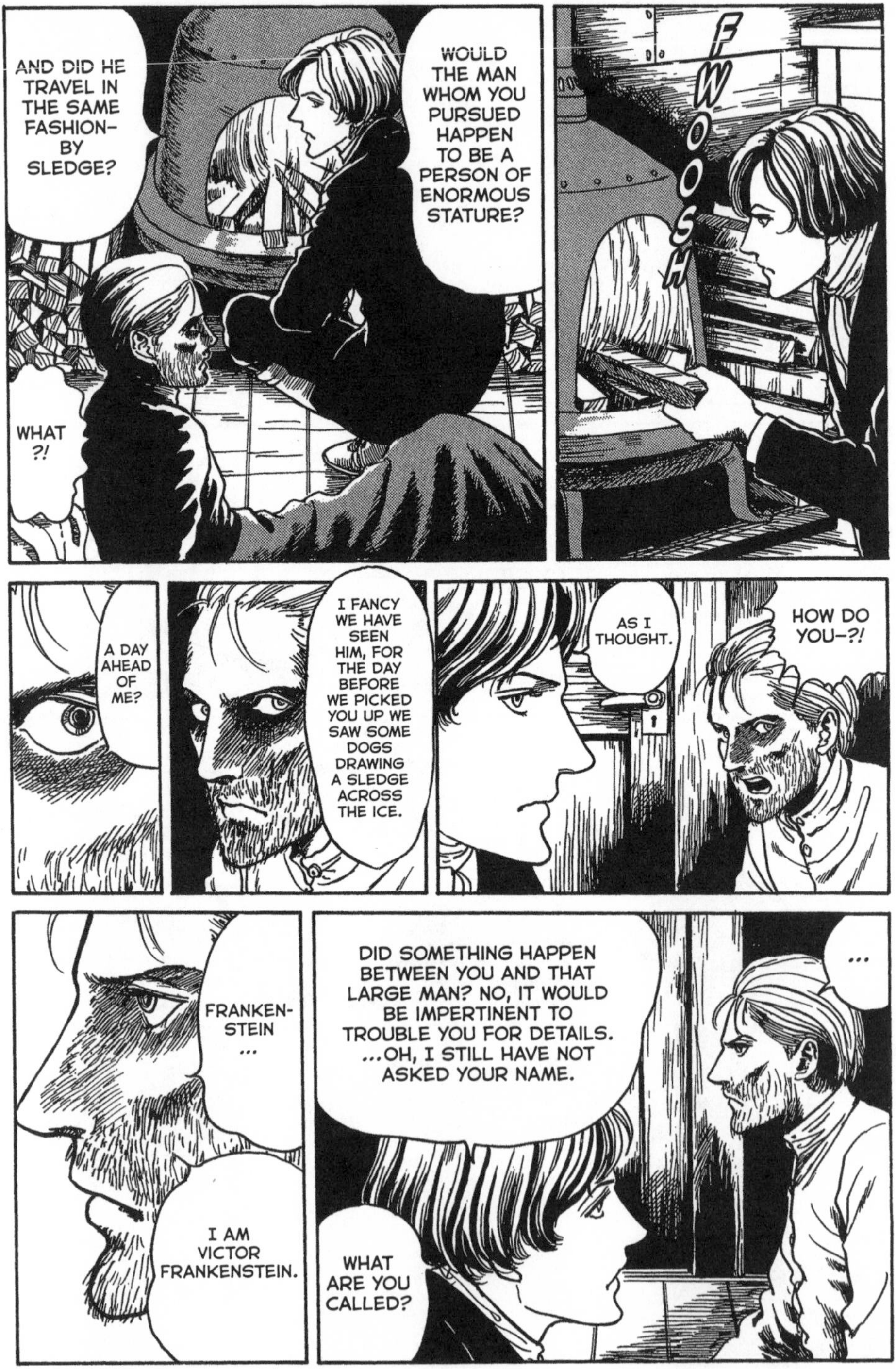
FWOOSH
WOULD THE MAN WHOM YOU PURSUED HAPPEN TO BE A PERSON OF ENORMOUS STATURE?
AND DID HE TRAVEL IN THE SAME FASHION–BY SLEDGE?
WHAT ?!
HOW DO YOU–?!
AS I THOUGHT.
I FANCY WE HAVE SEEN HIM, FOR THE DAY BEFORE WE PICKED YOU UP WE SAW SOME DOGS DRAWING A SLEDGE ACROSS THE ICE.
A DAY AHEAD OF ME?
...
DID SOMETHING HAPPEN BETWEEN YOU AND THAT LARGE MAN? NO, IT WOULD BE IMPERTINENT TO TROUBLE YOU FOR DETAILS. ...OH, I STILL HAVE NOT ASKED YOUR NAME.
WHAT ARE YOU CALLED?
FRANKEN-STEIN ...
I AM VICTOR FRANKENSTEIN.

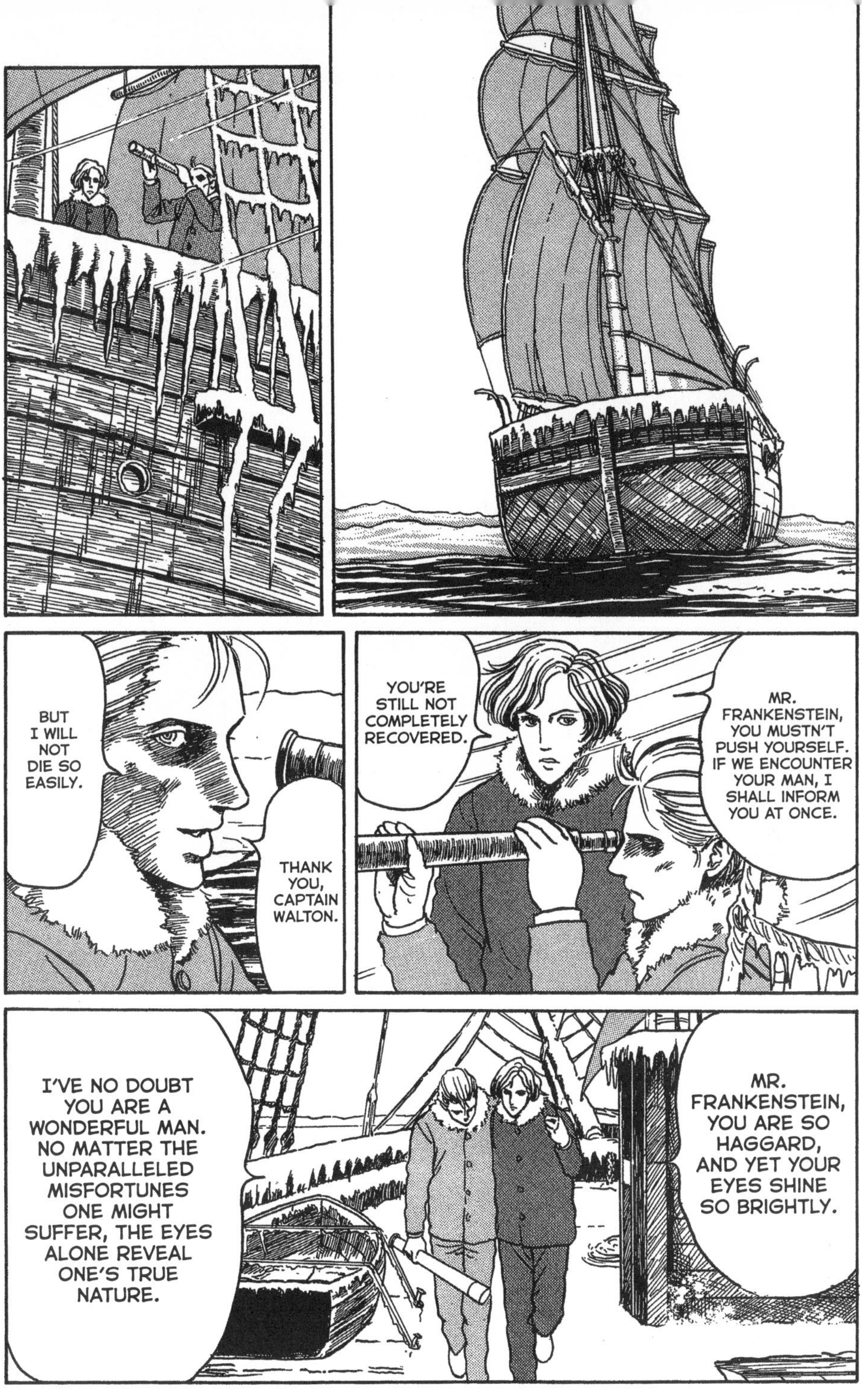
MR. FRANKENSTEIN, YOU MUSTN'T PUSH YOURSELF. IF WE ENCOUNTER YOUR MAN, I SHALL INFORM YOU AT ONCE.
YOU'RE STILL NOT COMPLETELY RECOVERED.
THANK YOU, CAPTAIN WALTON.
BUT I WILL NOT DIE SO EASILY.
MR. FRANKENSTEIN, YOU ARE SO HAGGARD, AND YET YOUR EYES SHINE SO BRIGHTLY.
I'VE NO DOUBT YOU ARE A WONDERFUL MAN. NO MATTER THE UNPARALLELED MISFORTUNES ONE MIGHT SUFFER, THE EYES ALONE REVEAL ONE'S TRUE NATURE.

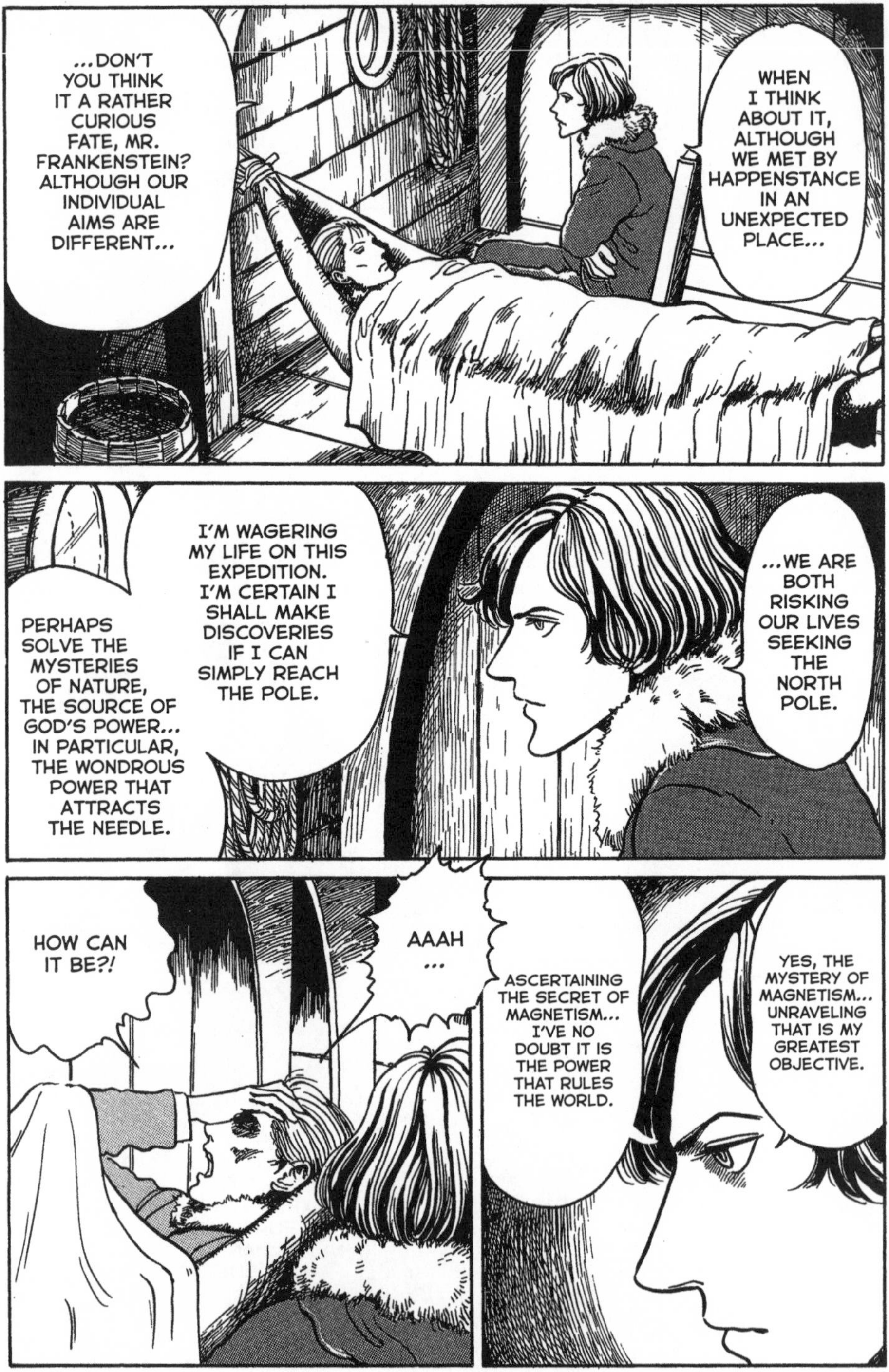
WHEN I THINK ABOUT IT, ALTHOUGH WE MET BY HAPPENSTANCE IN AN UNEXPECTED PLACE...
...DON'T YOU THINK IT A RATHER CURIOUS FATE, MR. FRANKENSTEIN? ALTHOUGH OUR INDIVIDUAL AIMS ARE DIFFERENT...
...WE ARE BOTH RISKING OUR LIVES SEEKING THE NORTH POLE.
I'M WAGERING MY LIFE ON THIS EXPEDITION. I'M CERTAIN I SHALL MAKE DISCOVERIES IF I CAN SIMPLY REACH THE POLE.
PERHAPS SOLVE THE MYSTERIES OF NATURE, THE SOURCE OF GOD'S POWER... IN PARTICULAR, THE WONDROUS POWER THAT ATTRACTS THE NEEDLE.
YES, THE MYSTERY OF MAGNETISM... UNRAVELING THAT IS MY GREATEST OBJECTIVE.
ASCERTAINING THE SECRET OF MAGNETISM... I'VE NO DOUBT IT IS THE POWER THAT RULES THE WORLD.
AAAH ...
HOW CAN IT BE?!

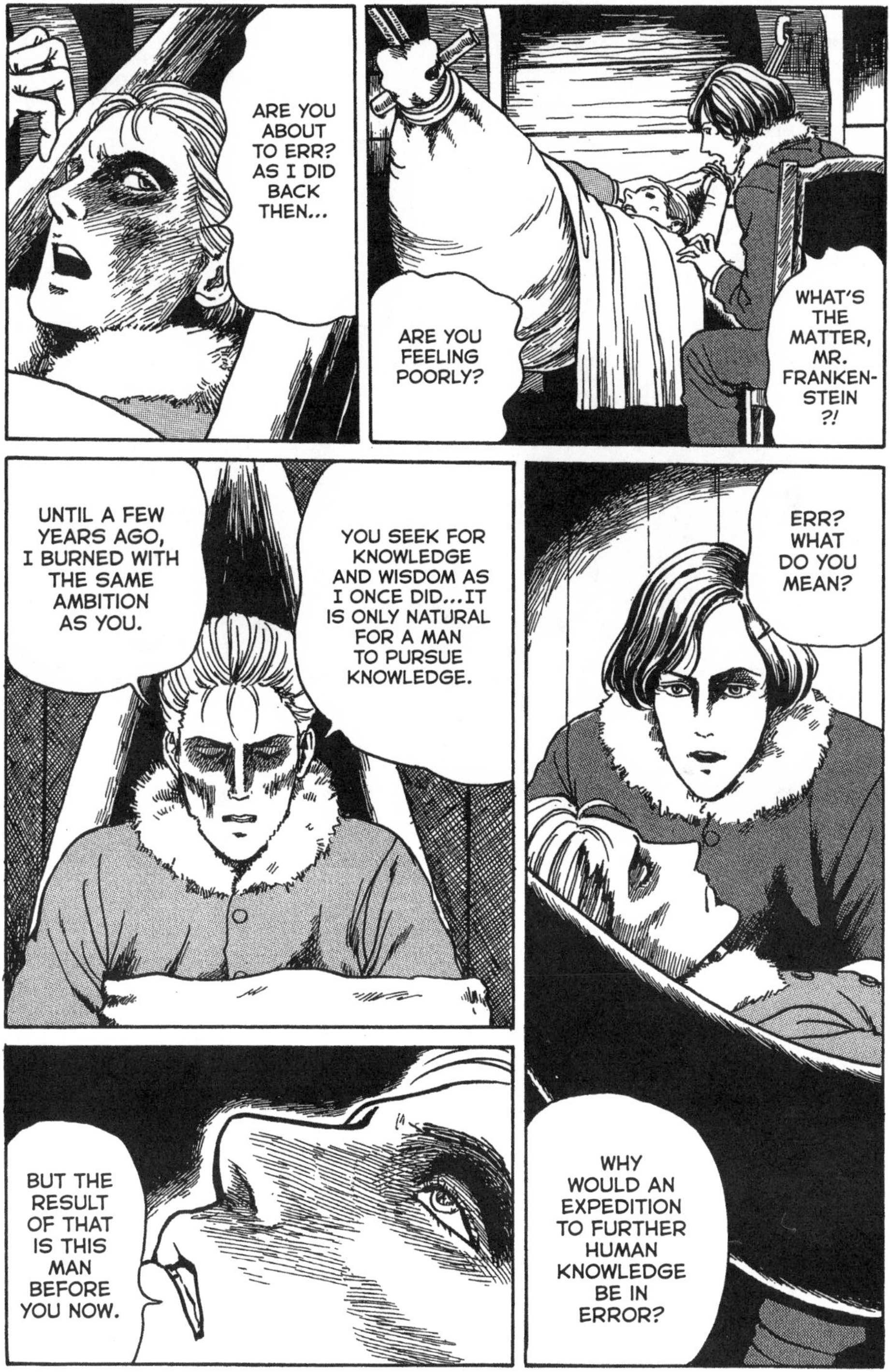
WHAT'S THE MATTER, MR. FRANKENSTEIN?!
ARE YOU FEELING POORLY?
ARE YOU ABOUT TO ERR? AS I DID BACK THEN...
ERR? WHAT DO YOU MEAN?
WHY WOULD AN EXPEDITION TO FURTHER HUMAN KNOWLEDGE BE IN ERROR?
YOU SEEK FOR KNOWLEDGE AND WISDOM AS I ONCE DID...IT IS ONLY NATURAL FOR A MAN TO PURSUE KNOWLEDGE.
UNTIL A FEW YEARS AGO, I BURNED WITH THE SAME AMBITION AS YOU.
BUT THE RESULT OF THAT IS THIS MAN BEFORE YOU NOW.

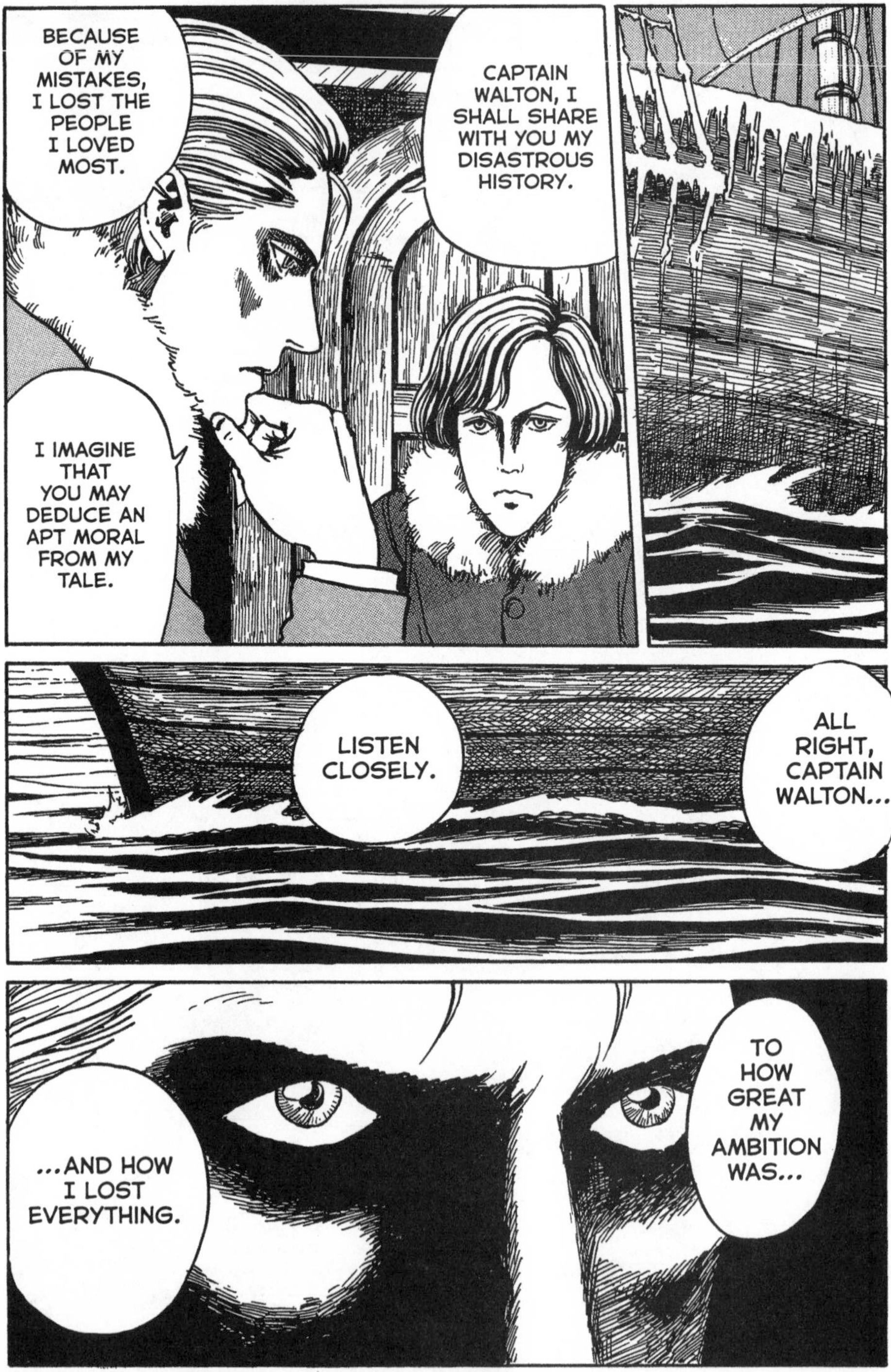
CAPTAIN WALTON, I SHALL SHARE WITH YOU MY DISASTROUS HISTORY.
BECAUSE OF MY MISTAKES, I LOST THE PEOPLE I LOVED MOST.
I IMAGINE THAT YOU MAY DEDUCE AN APT MORAL FROM MY TALE.
ALL RIGHT, CAPTAIN WALTON...
LISTEN CLOSELY.
TO HOW GREAT MY AMBITION WAS...
...AND HOW I LOST EVERYTHING.

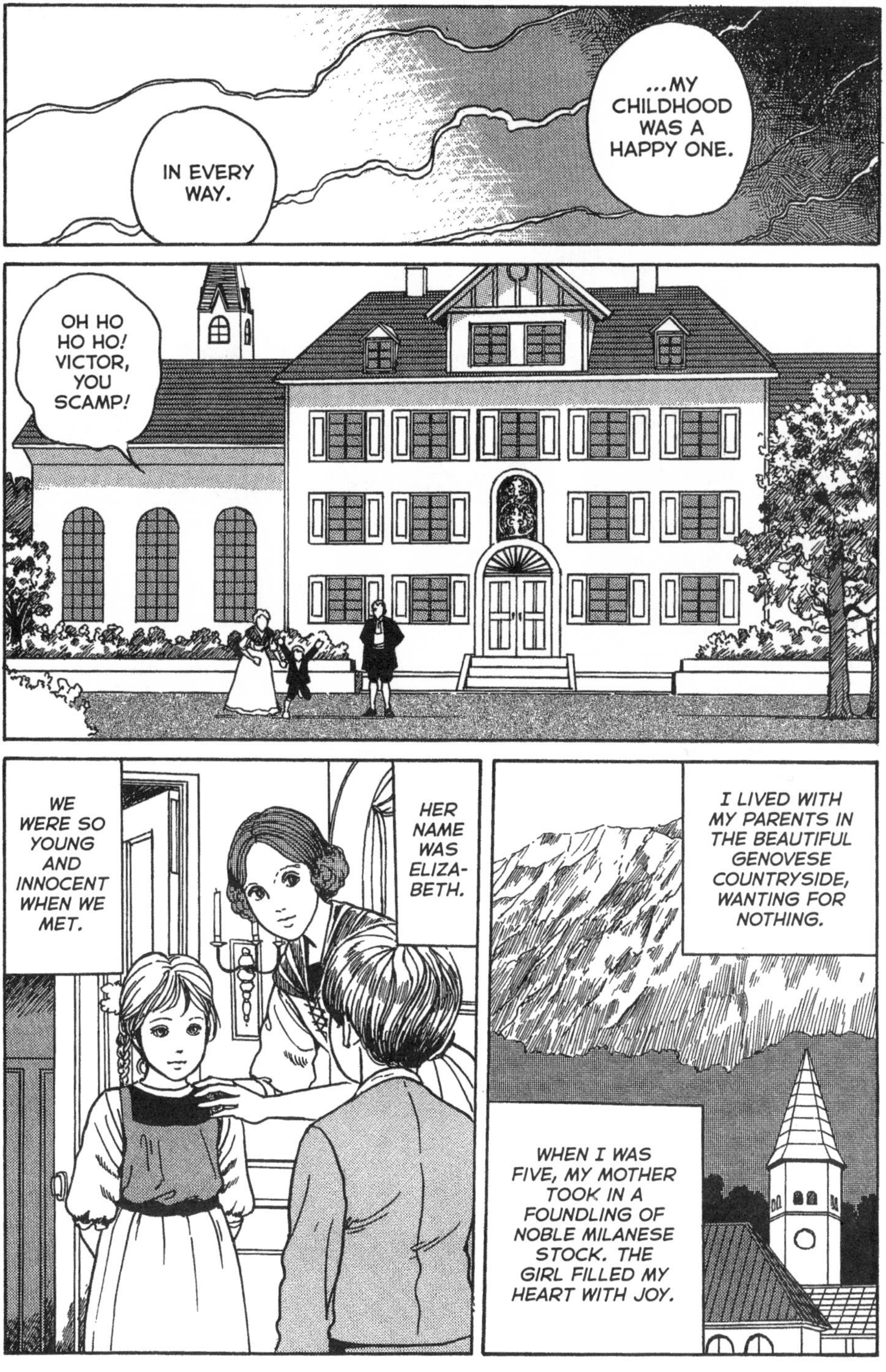
...MY CHILDHOOD WAS A HAPPY ONE.
IN EVERY WAY.
OH HO HO HO! VICTOR, YOU SCAMP!
I LIVED WITH MY PARENTS IN THE BEAUTIFUL GENOVESE COUNTRYSIDE, WANTING FOR NOTHING.
WHEN I WAS FIVE, MY MOTHER TOOK IN A FOUNDLING OF NOBLE MILANESE STOCK. THE GIRL FILLED MY HEART WITH JOY.
HER NAME WAS ELIZA-BETH.
WE WERE SO YOUNG AND INNOCENT WHEN WE MET.

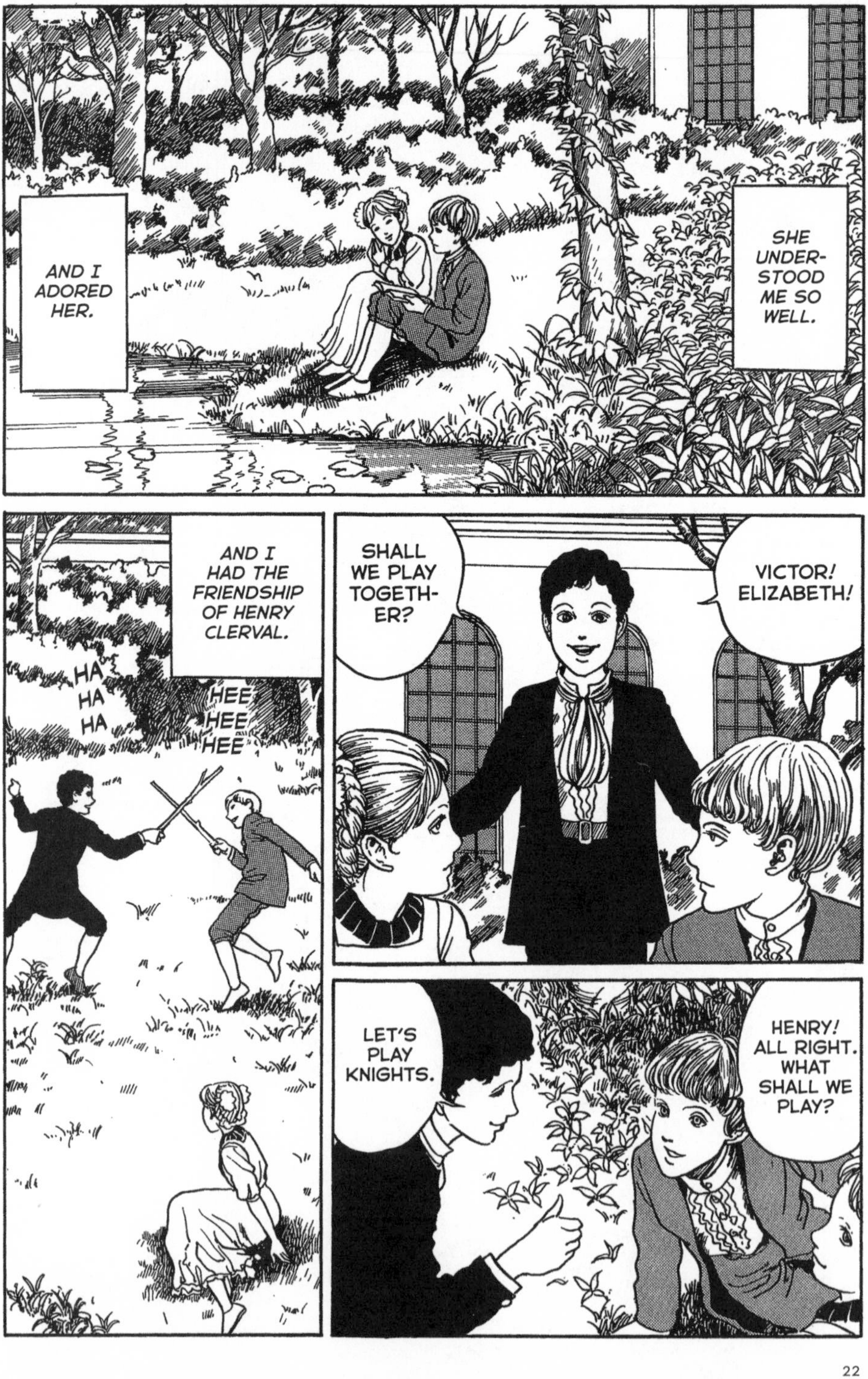
SHE UNDERSTOOD ME SO WELL.
AND I ADORED HER.
VICTOR! ELIZABETH!
SHALL WE PLAY TOGETHER?
HENRY! ALL RIGHT. WHAT SHALL WE PLAY?
LET'S PLAY KNIGHTS.
AND I HAD THE FRIENDSHIP OF HENRY CLERVAL.
HEE HEE HEE
HA HA HA

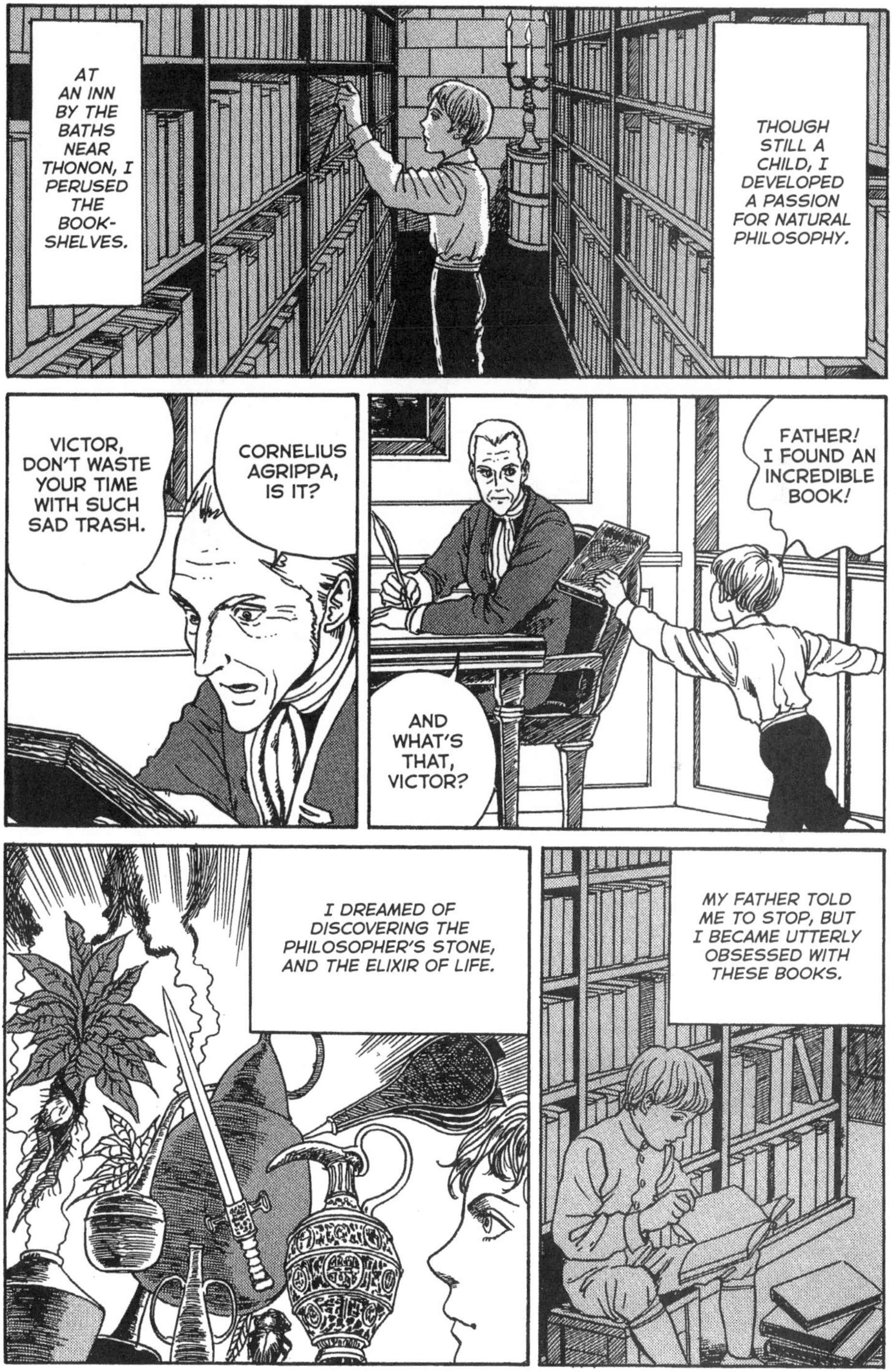
THOUGH STILL A CHILD, I DEVELOPED A PASSION FOR NATURAL PHILOSOPHY.
AT AN INN BY THE BATHS NEAR THONON, I PERUSED THE BOOK-SHELVES.
FATHER! I FOUND AN INCREDIBLE BOOK!
AND WHAT'S THAT, VICTOR?
CORNELIUS AGRIPPA, IS IT?
VICTOR, DON'T WASTE YOUR TIME WITH SUCH SAD TRASH.
MY FATHER TOLD ME TO STOP, BUT I BECAME UTTERLY OBSESSED WITH THESE BOOKS.
I DREAMED OF DISCOVERING THE PHILOSOPHER'S STONE, AND THE ELIXIR OF LIFE.

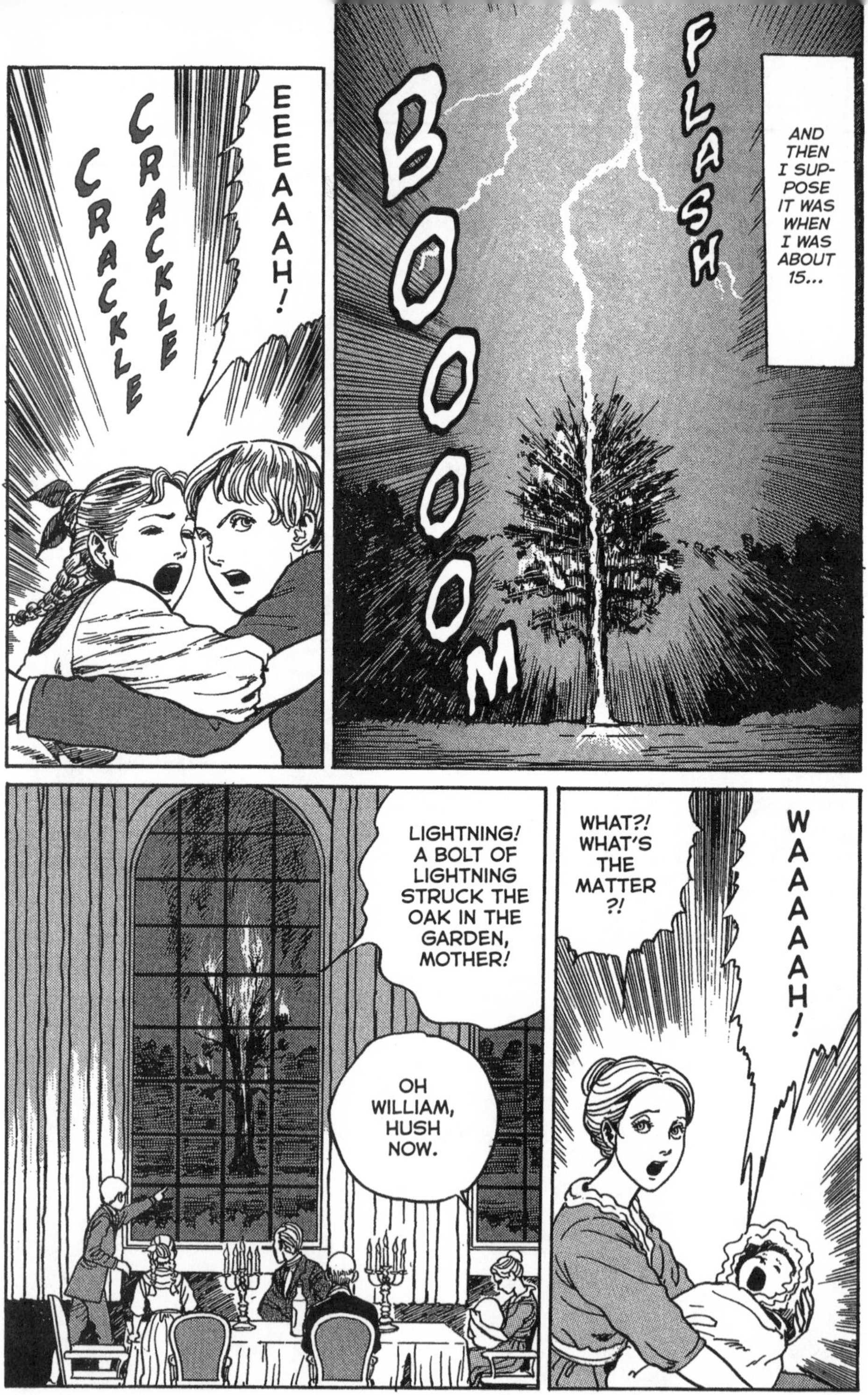
AND THEN I SUPPOSE IT WAS WHEN I WAS ABOUT 15...
FLASH
BOOOOOM
EEEAAAAH!
CRACKLE
CRACKLE
WAAAAAAH!
WHAT?! WHAT'S THE MATTER?!
LIGHTNING! A BOLT OF LIGHTNING STRUCK THE OAK IN THE GARDEN, MOTHER!
OH WILLIAM, HUSH NOW.

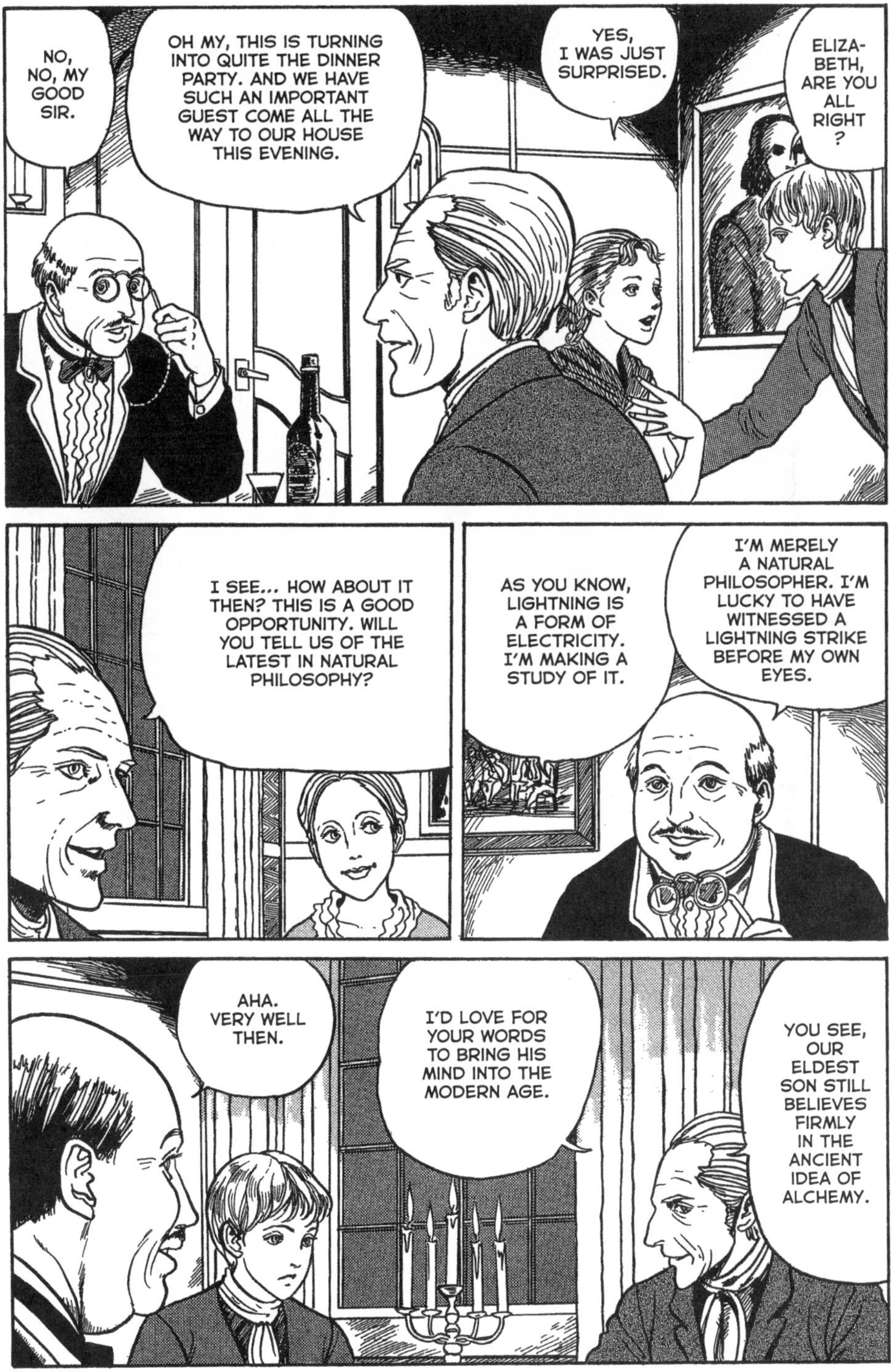
ELIZA-BETH, ARE YOU ALL RIGHT?
YES, I WAS JUST SURPRISED.
OH MY, THIS IS TURNING INTO QUITE THE DINNER PARTY. AND WE HAVE SUCH AN IMPORTANT GUEST COME ALL THE WAY TO OUR HOUSE THIS EVENING.
NO, NO, MY GOOD SIR.
I'M MERELY A NATURAL PHILOSOPHER. I'M LUCKY TO HAVE WITNESSED A LIGHTNING STRIKE BEFORE MY OWN EYES.
AS YOU KNOW, LIGHTNING IS A FORM OF ELECTRICITY. I'M MAKING A STUDY OF IT.
I SEE... HOW ABOUT IT THEN? THIS IS A GOOD OPPORTUNITY. WILL YOU TELL US OF THE LATEST IN NATURAL PHILOSOPHY?
YOU SEE, OUR ELDEST SON STILL BELIEVES FIRMLY IN THE ANCIENT IDEA OF ALCHEMY.
I'D LOVE FOR YOUR WORDS TO BRING HIS MIND INTO THE MODERN AGE.
AHA. VERY WELL THEN.

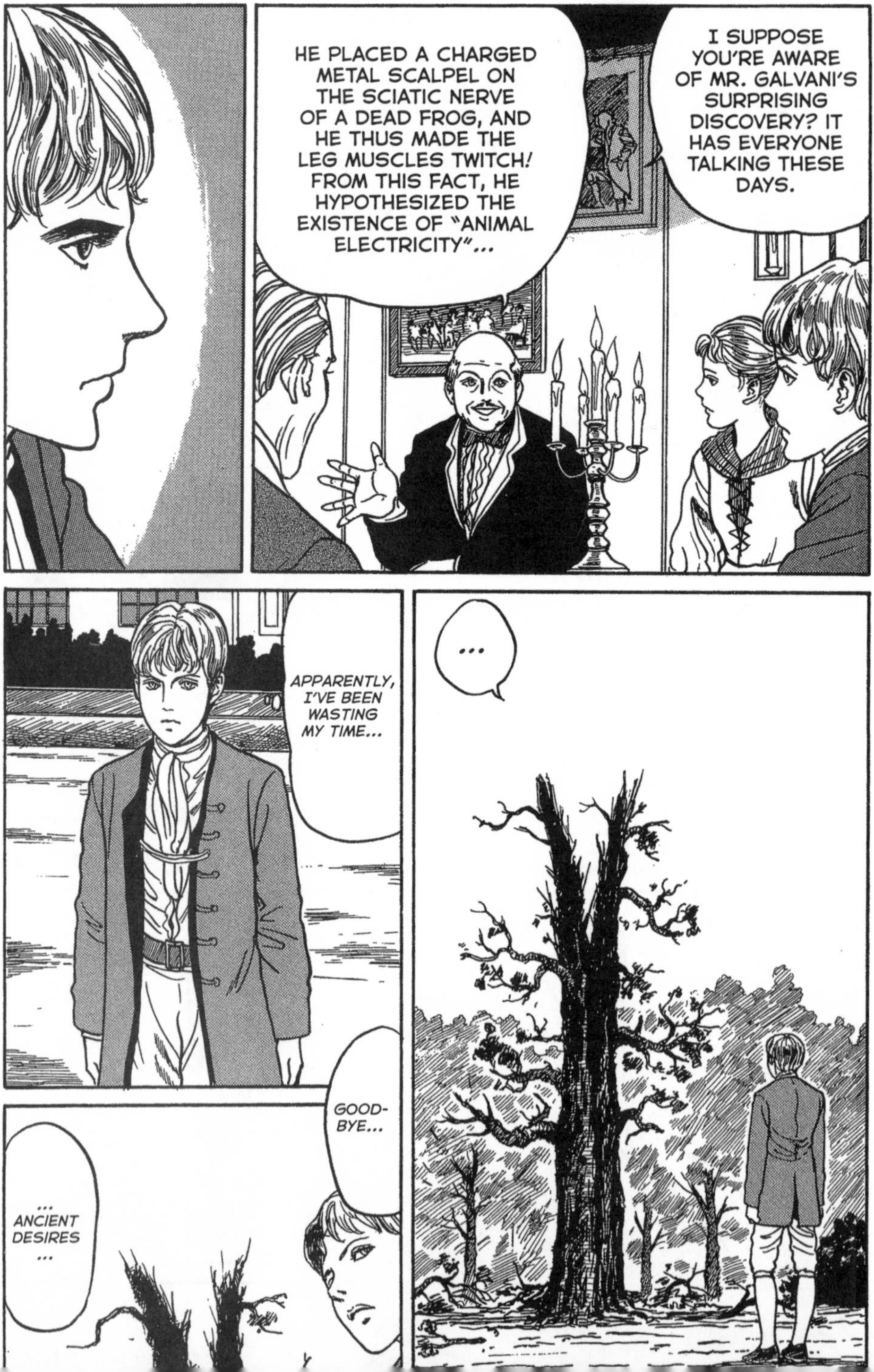
I SUPPOSE YOU'RE AWARE OF MR. GALVANI'S SURPRISING DISCOVERY? IT HAS EVERYONE TALKING THESE DAYS.
HE PLACED A CHARGED METAL SCALPEL ON THE SCIATIC NERVE OF A DEAD FROG, AND HE THUS MADE THE LEG MUSCLES TWITCH! FROM THIS FACT, HE HYPOTHESIZED THE EXISTENCE OF "ANIMAL ELECTRICITY"...
...
APPARENTLY, I'VE BEEN WASTING MY TIME...
GOOD-BYE...
... ANCIENT DESIRES ...

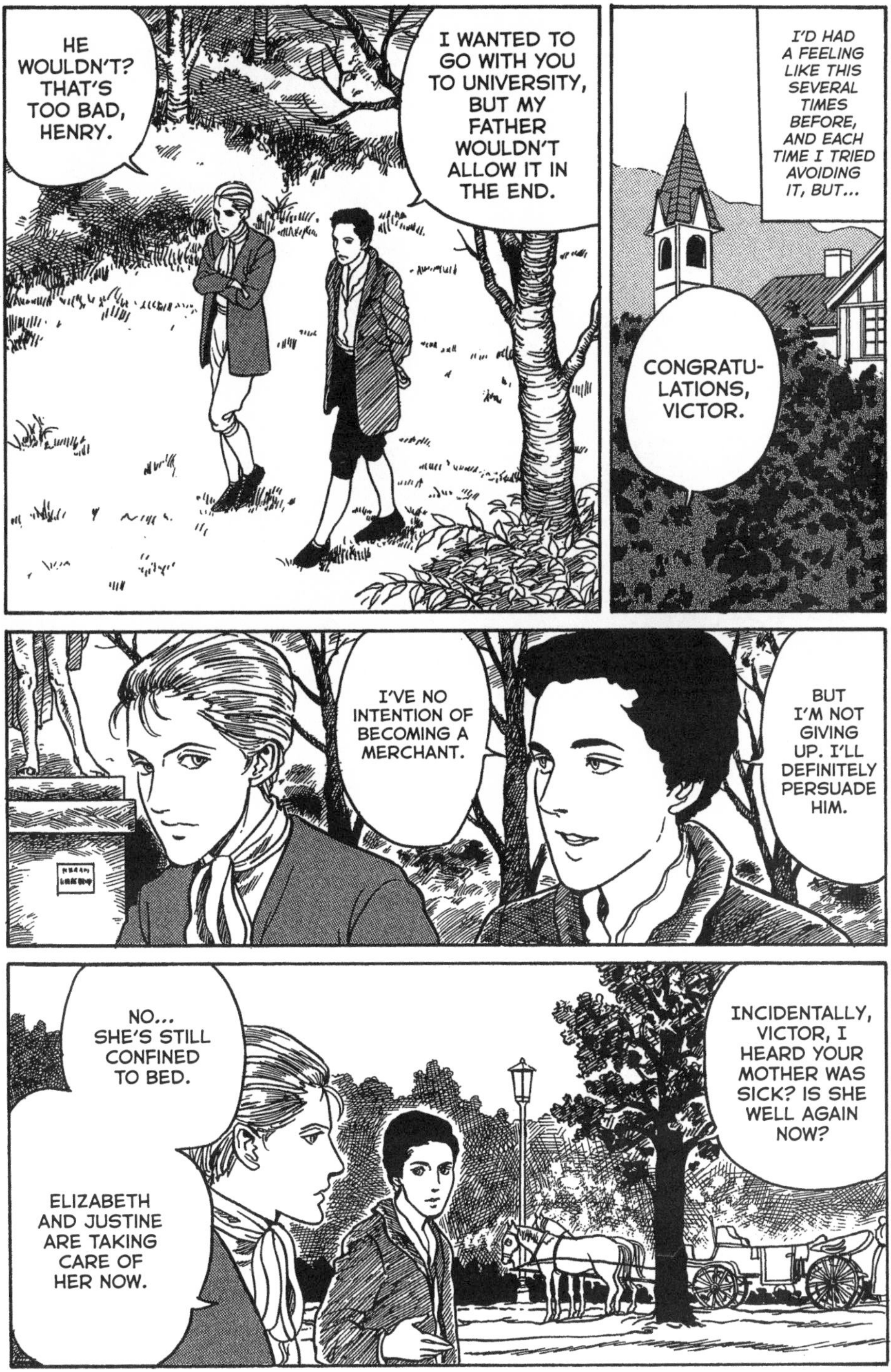
I'D HAD A FEELING LIKE THIS SEVERAL TIMES BEFORE, AND EACH TIME I TRIED AVOIDING IT, BUT...
CONGRATU-LATIONS, VICTOR.
I WANTED TO GO WITH YOU TO UNIVERSITY, BUT MY FATHER WOULDN'T ALLOW IT IN THE END.
HE WOULDN'T? THAT'S TOO BAD, HENRY.
BUT I'M NOT GIVING UP. I'LL DEFINITELY PERSUADE HIM.
I'VE NO INTENTION OF BECOMING A MERCHANT.
INCIDENTALLY, VICTOR, I HEARD YOUR MOTHER WAS SICK? IS SHE WELL AGAIN NOW?
NO... SHE'S STILL CONFINED TO BED.
ELIZABETH AND JUSTINE ARE TAKING CARE OF HER NOW.

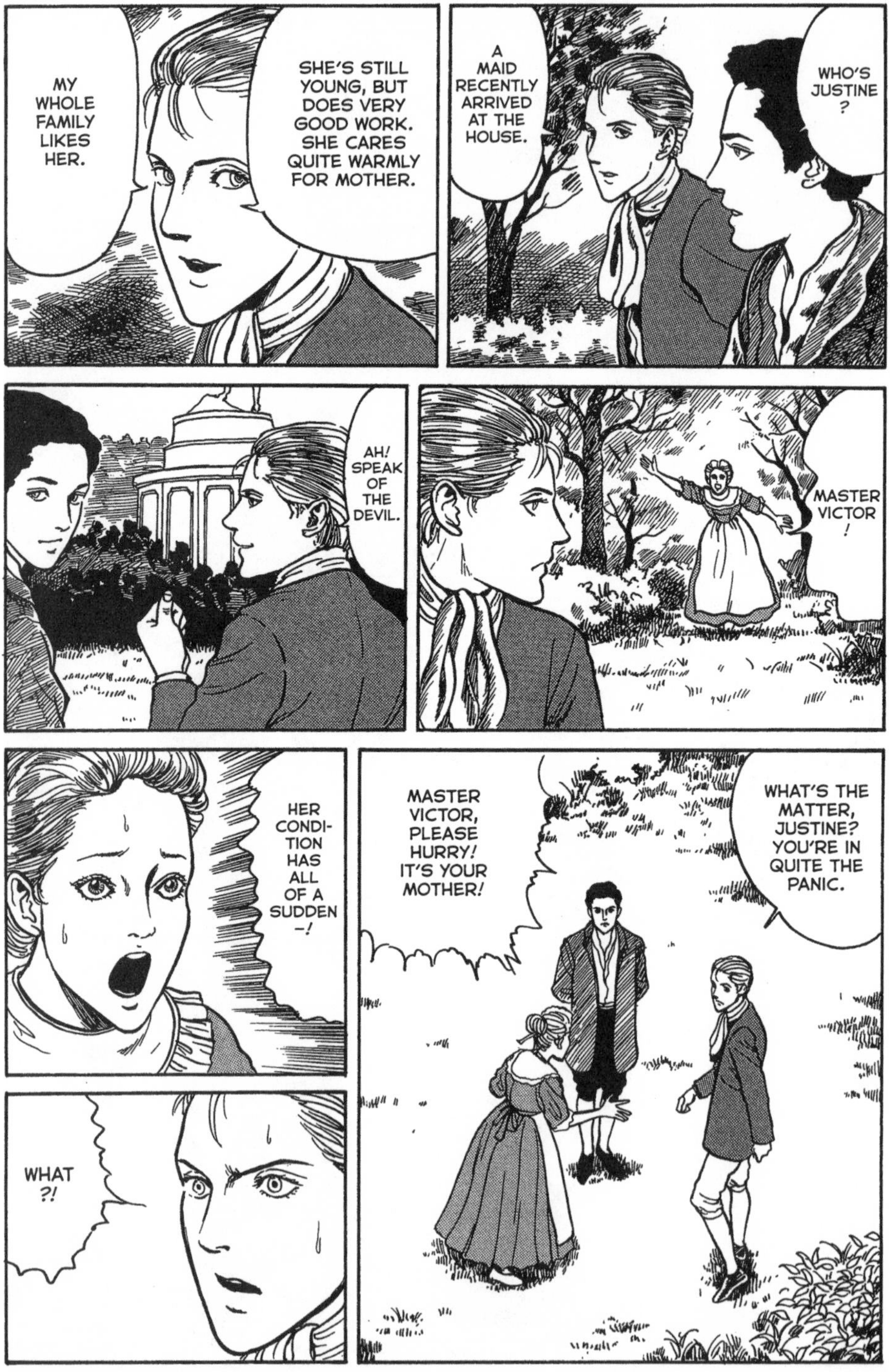
WHO'S JUSTINE?
A MAID RECENTLY ARRIVED AT THE HOUSE.
SHE'S STILL YOUNG, BUT DOES VERY GOOD WORK. SHE CARES QUITE WARMLY FOR MOTHER.
MY WHOLE FAMILY LIKES HER.
MASTER VICTOR!
AH! SPEAK OF THE DEVIL.
WHAT'S THE MATTER, JUSTINE? YOU'RE IN QUITE THE PANIC.
MASTER VICTOR, PLEASE HURRY! IT'S YOUR MOTHER!
HER CONDITION HAS ALL OF A SUDDEN—!
WHAT?!

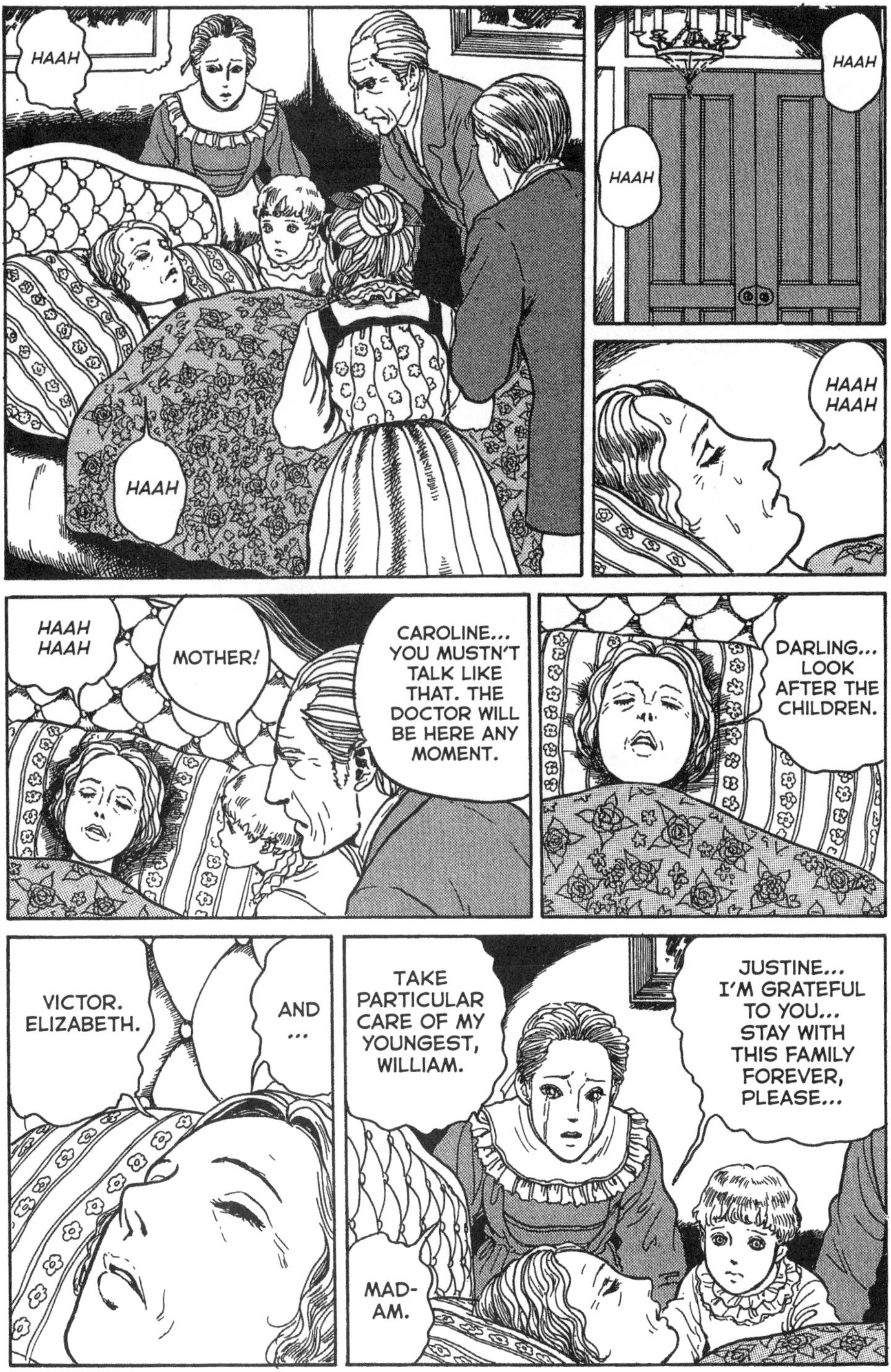
HAAH
HAAH
HAAH
HAAH
HAAH HAAH
HAAH HAAH
MOTHER!
CAROLINE... YOU MUSTN'T TALK LIKE THAT. THE DOCTOR WILL BE HERE ANY MOMENT.
DARLING... LOOK AFTER THE CHILDREN.
VICTOR. ELIZABETH.
AND ...
TAKE PARTICULAR CARE OF MY YOUNGEST, WILLIAM.
JUSTINE... I'M GRATEFUL TO YOU... STAY WITH THIS FAMILY FOREVER, PLEASE...
MAD- AM.

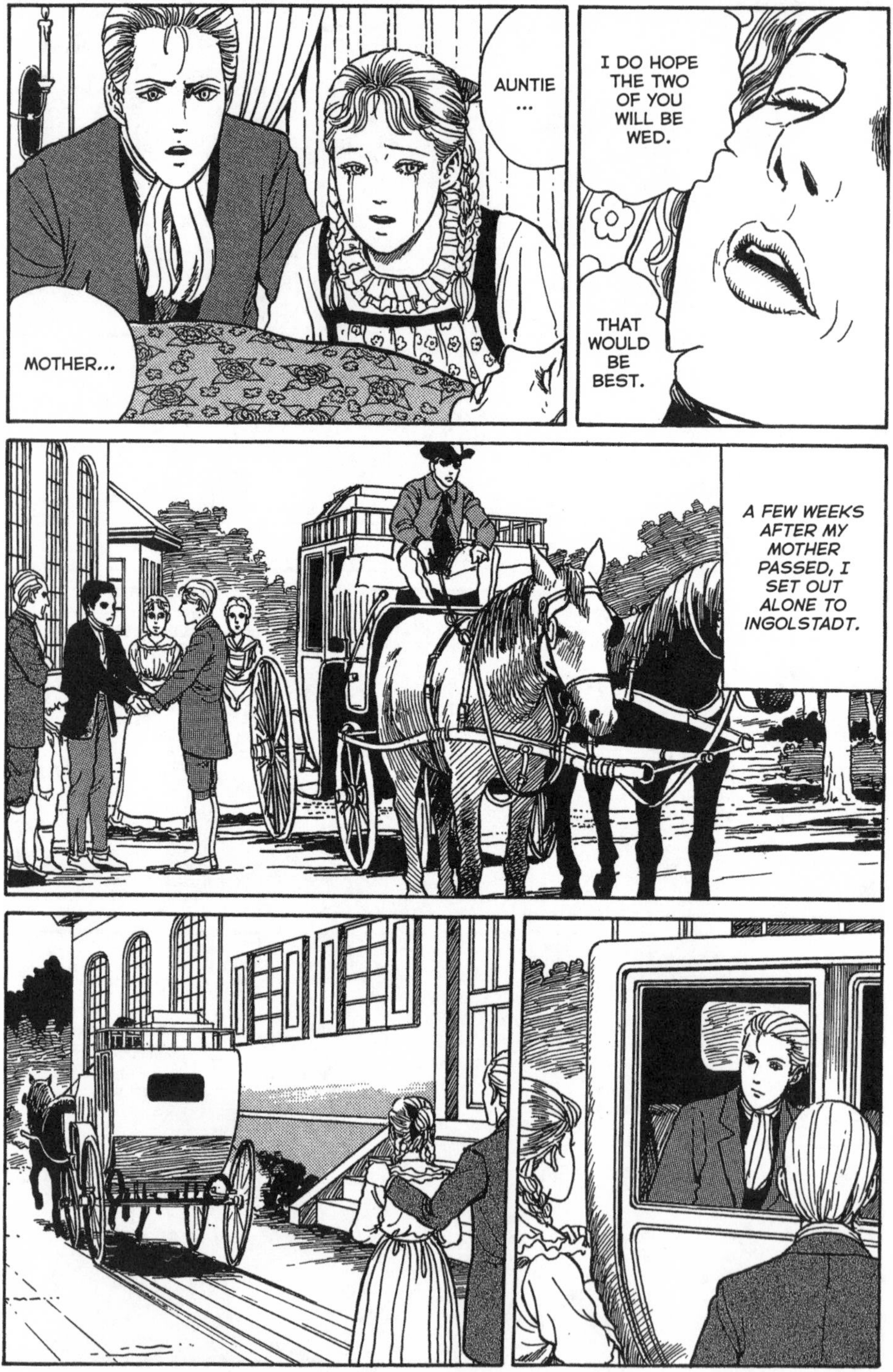
I DO HOPE THE TWO OF YOU WILL BE WED.
THAT WOULD BE BEST.
AUNTIE ...
MOTHER...
A FEW WEEKS AFTER MY MOTHER PASSED, I SET OUT ALONE TO INGOLSTADT.

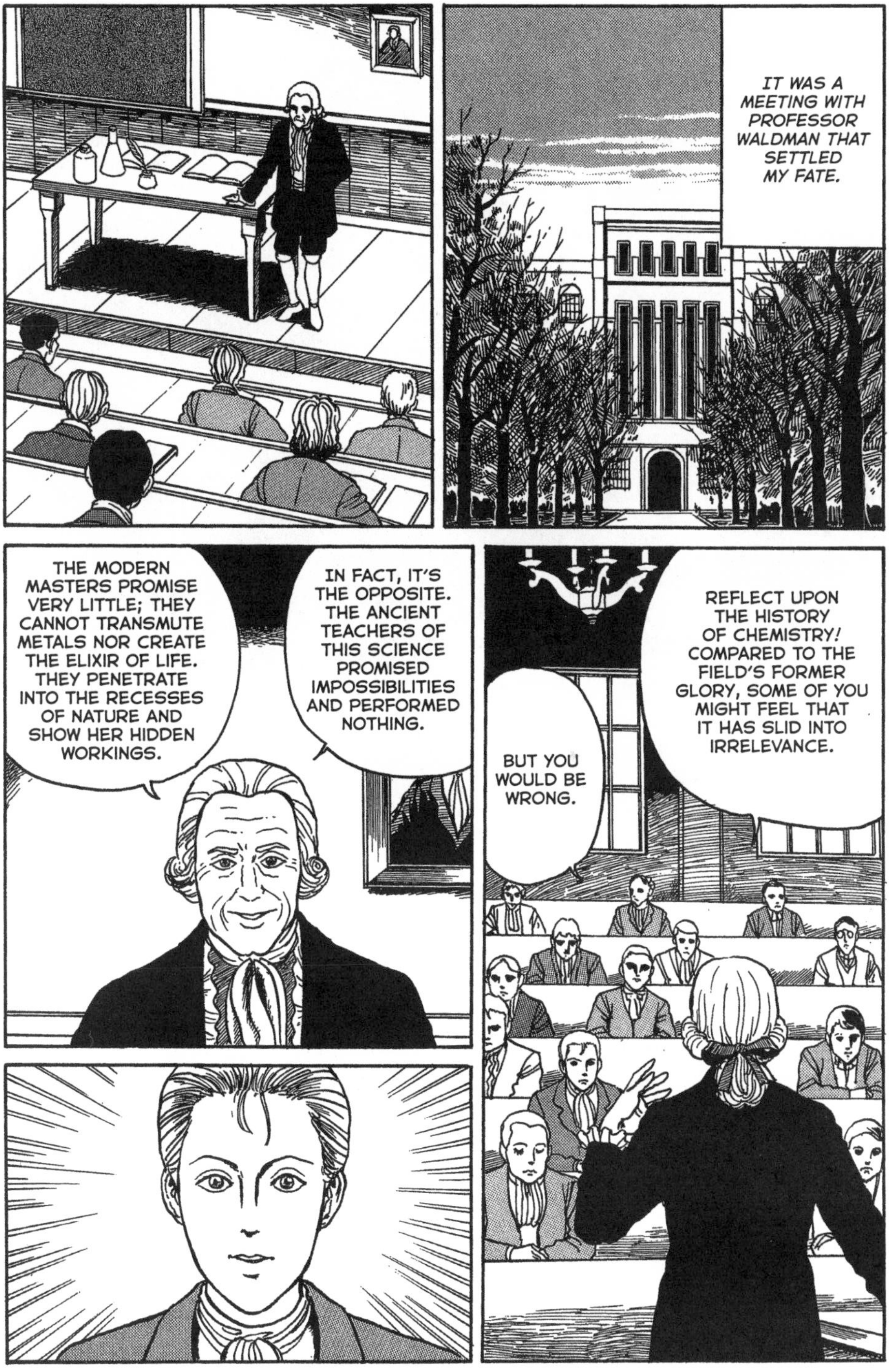
IT WAS A MEETING WITH PROFESSOR WALDMAN THAT SETTLED MY FATE.
REFLECT UPON THE HISTORY OF CHEMISTRY! COMPARED TO THE FIELD'S FORMER GLORY, SOME OF YOU MIGHT FEEL THAT IT HAS SLID INTO IRRELEVANCE.
BUT YOU WOULD BE WRONG.
IN FACT, IT'S THE OPPOSITE. THE ANCIENT TEACHERS OF THIS SCIENCE PROMISED IMPOSSIBILITIES AND PERFORMED NOTHING.
THE MODERN MASTERS PROMISE VERY LITTLE; THEY CANNOT TRANSMUTE METALS NOR CREATE THE ELIXIR OF LIFE. THEY PENETRATE INTO THE RECESSES OF NATURE AND SHOW HER HIDDEN WORKINGS.

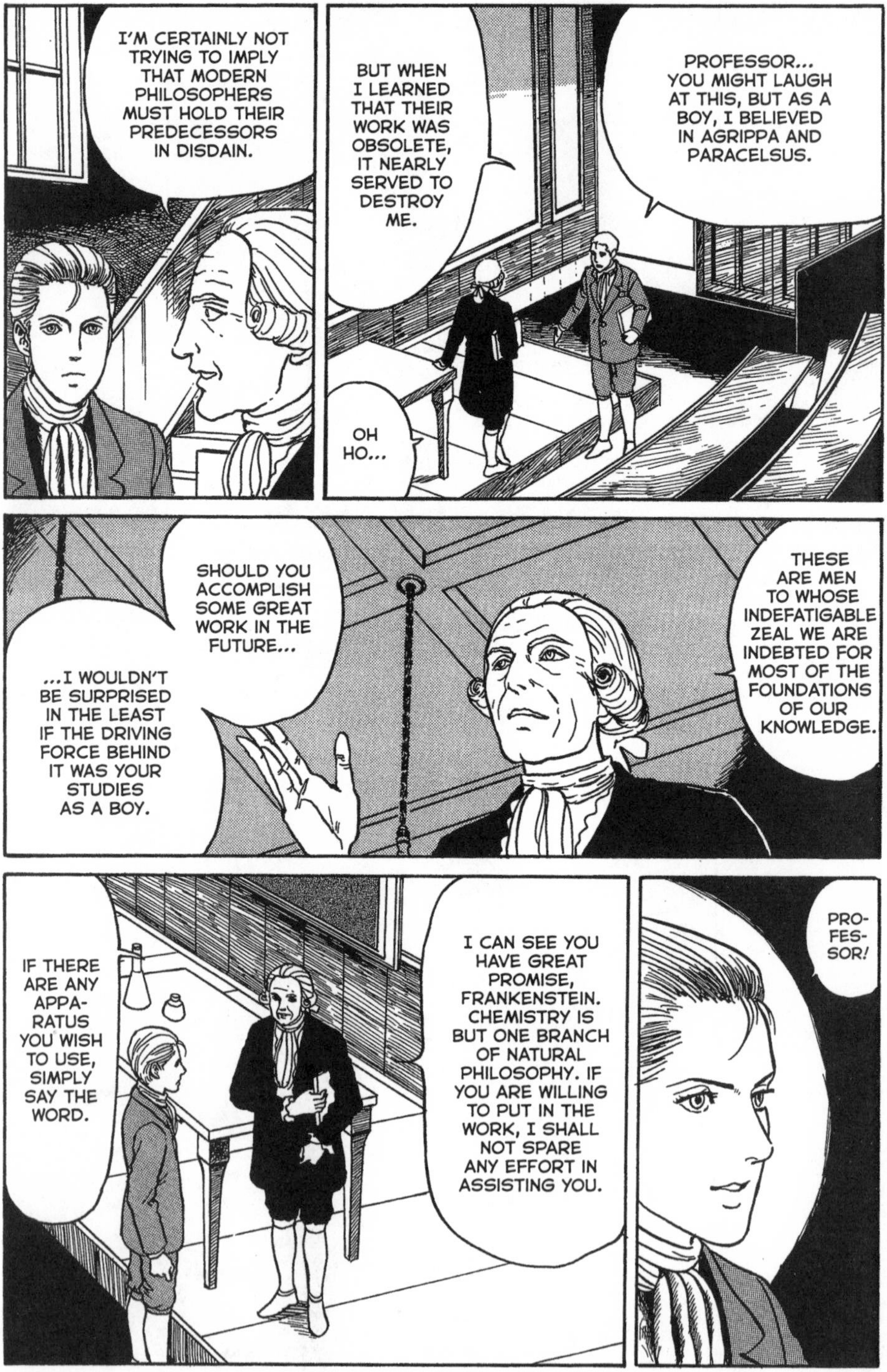
PROFESSOR... YOU MIGHT LAUGH AT THIS, BUT AS A BOY, I BELIEVED IN AGRIPPA AND PARACELSUS.
BUT WHEN I LEARNED THAT THEIR WORK WAS OBSOLETE, IT NEARLY SERVED TO DESTROY ME.
OH HO...
I'M CERTAINLY NOT TRYING TO IMPLY THAT MODERN PHILOSOPHERS MUST HOLD THEIR PREDECESSORS IN DISDAIN.
THESE ARE MEN TO WHOSE INDEFATIGABLE ZEAL WE ARE INDEBTED FOR MOST OF THE FOUNDATIONS OF OUR KNOWLEDGE.
SHOULD YOU ACCOMPLISH SOME GREAT WORK IN THE FUTURE...
...I WOULDN'T BE SURPRISED IN THE LEAST IF THE DRIVING FORCE BEHIND IT WAS YOUR STUDIES AS A BOY.
PRO-FES-SOR!
I CAN SEE YOU HAVE GREAT PROMISE, FRANKENSTEIN. CHEMISTRY IS BUT ONE BRANCH OF NATURAL PHILOSOPHY. IF YOU ARE WILLING TO PUT IN THE WORK, I SHALL NOT SPARE ANY EFFORT IN ASSISTING YOU.
IF THERE ARE ANY APPA-RATUS YOU WISH TO USE, SIMPLY SAY THE WORD.

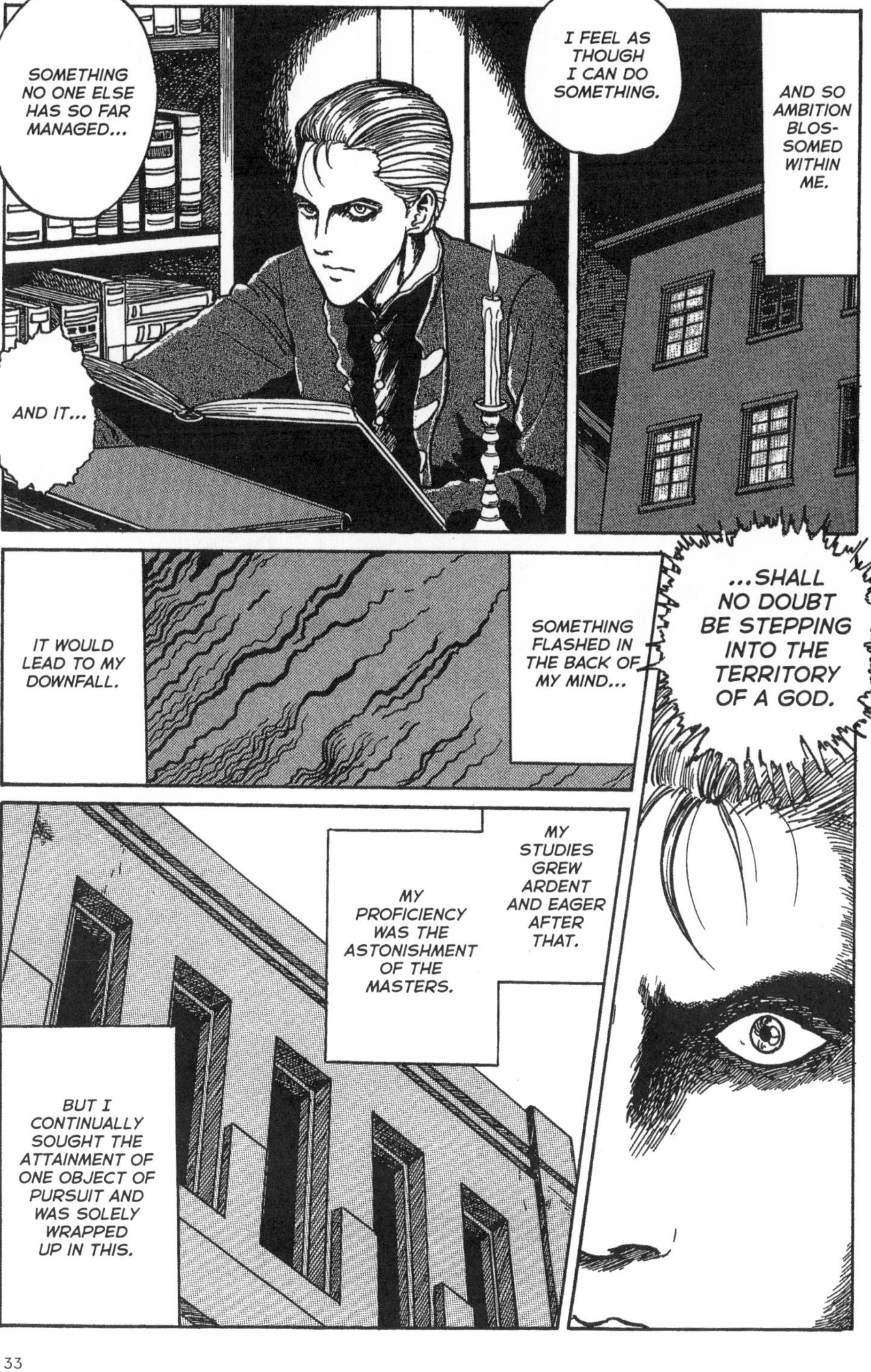
AND SO AMBITION BLOS-SOMED WITHIN ME.
I FEEL AS THOUGH I CAN DO SOMETHING.
SOMETHING NO ONE ELSE HAS SO FAR MANAGED...
AND IT...
...SHALL NO DOUBT BE STEPPING INTO THE TERRITORY OF A GOD.
SOMETHING FLASHED IN THE BACK OF MY MIND...
IT WOULD LEAD TO MY DOWNFALL.
MY STUDIES GREW ARDENT AND EAGER AFTER THAT.
MY PROFICIENCY WAS THE ASTONISHMENT OF THE MASTERS.
BUT I CONTINUALLY SOUGHT THE ATTAINMENT OF ONE OBJECT OF PURSUIT AND WAS SOLELY WRAPPED UP IN THIS.

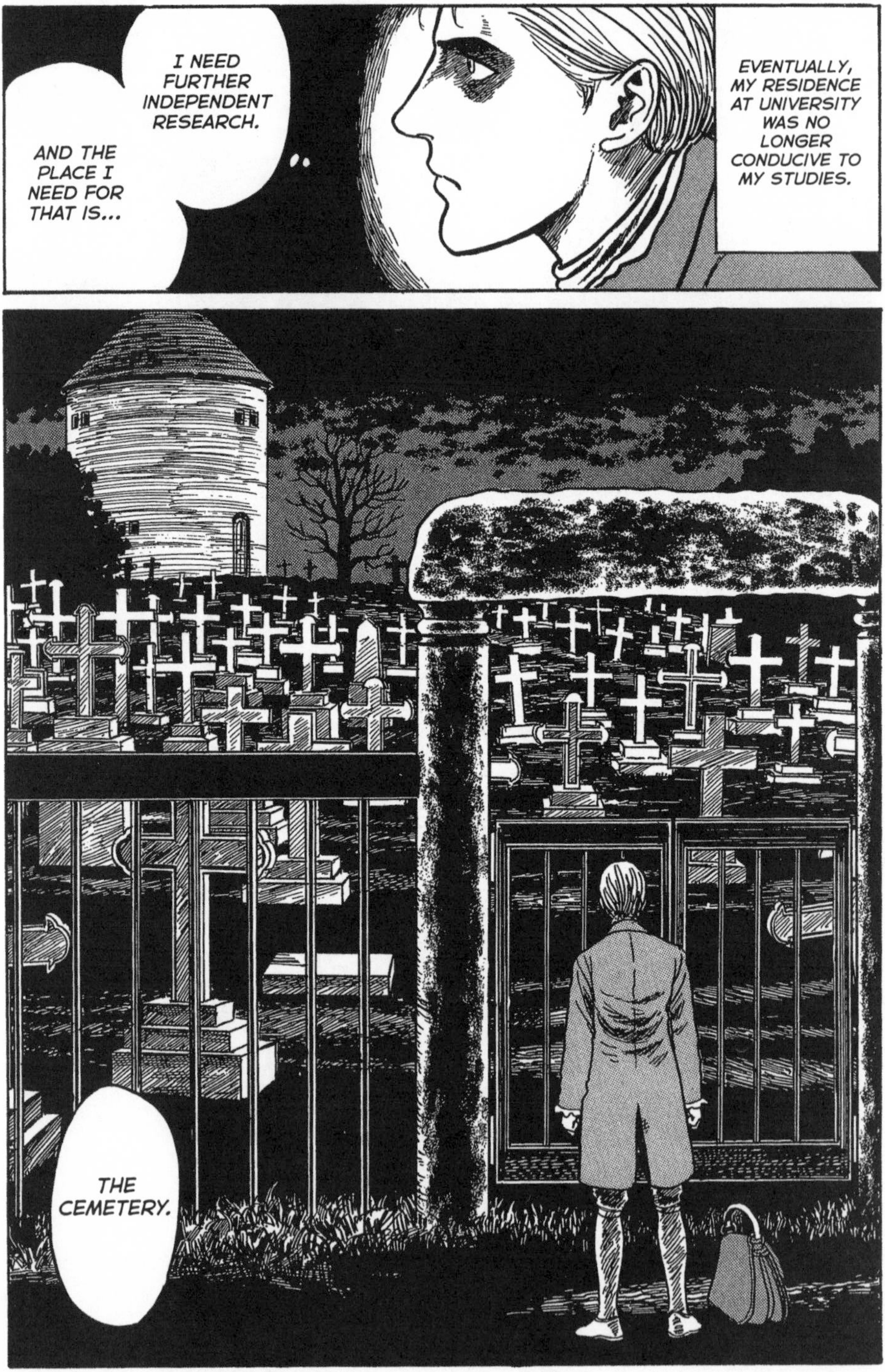
EVENTUALLY, MY RESIDENCE AT UNIVERSITY WAS NO LONGER CONDUCIVE TO MY STUDIES.
I NEED FURTHER INDEPENDENT RESEARCH.
AND THE PLACE I NEED FOR THAT IS...
THE CEMETERY.

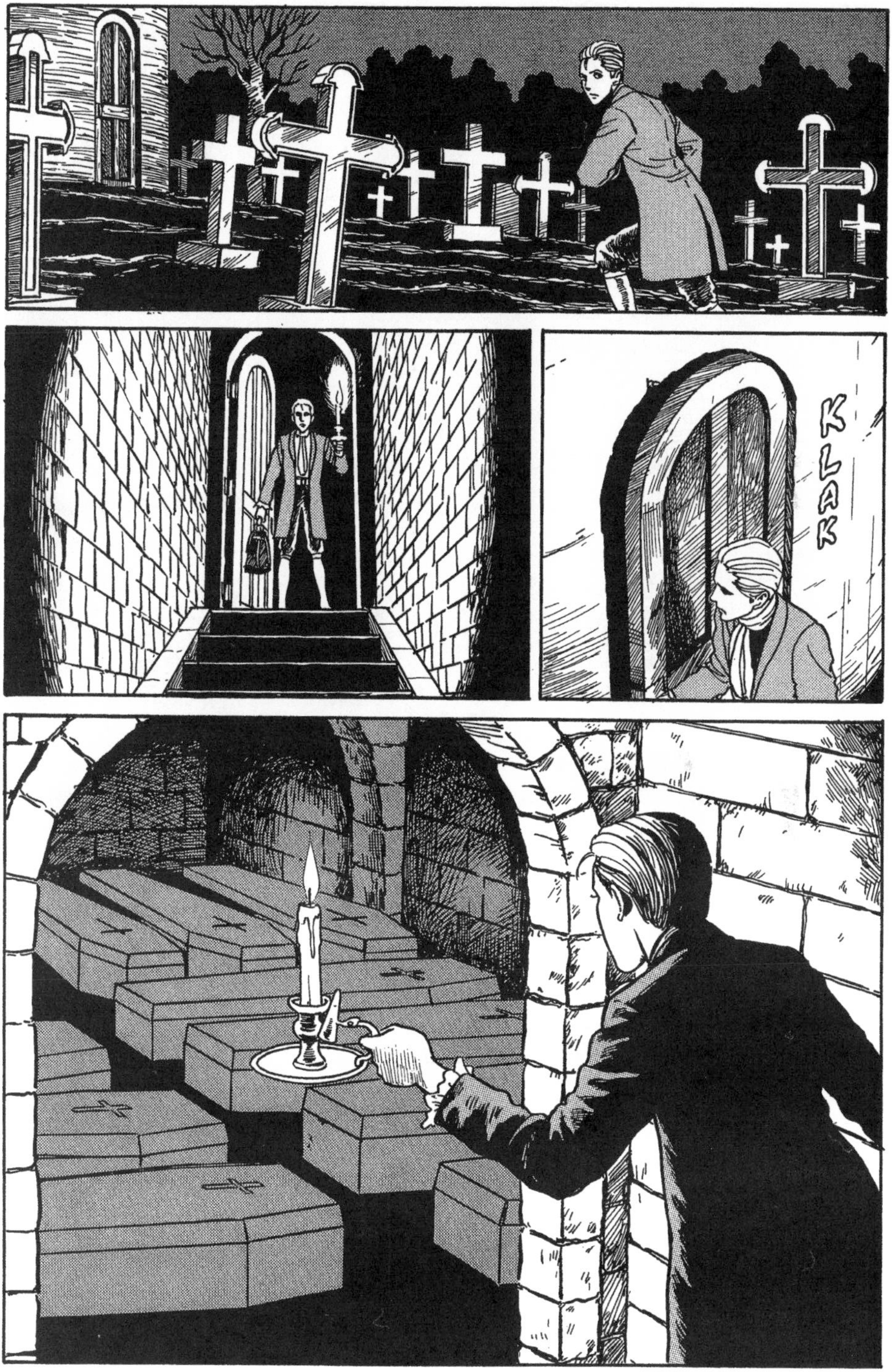
KLAK

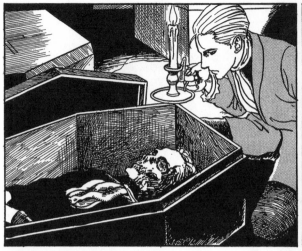

KLAK

KLAK

I VISITED THE TOMBS EVERY NIGHT...

...TO INVESTIGATE THE PROCESS OF PHYSICAL DECOMPOSITION.

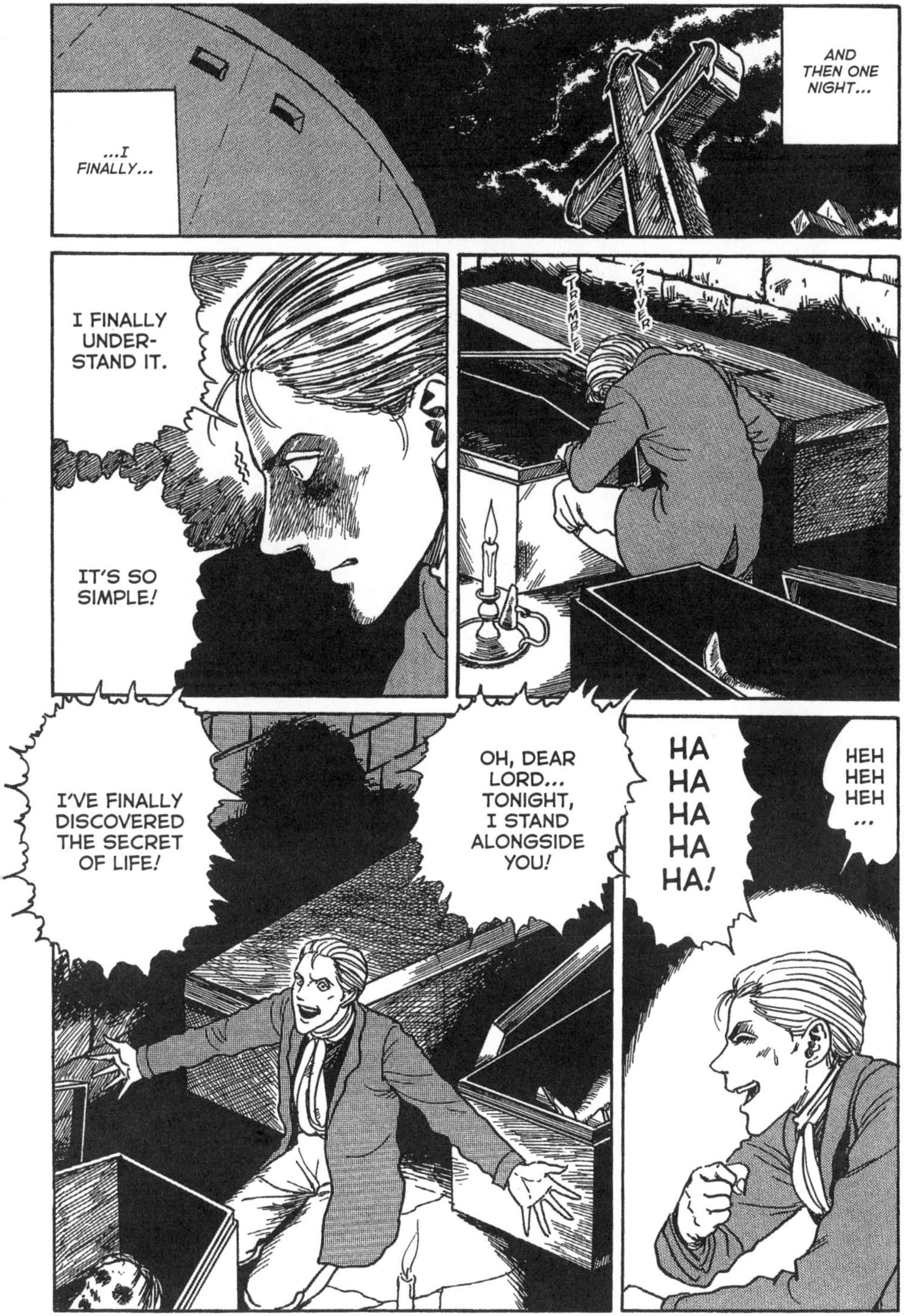
AND THEN ONE NIGHT...
...I FINALLY...
SHIVER
TREMBLE
I FINALLY UNDER-STAND IT.
IT'S SO SIMPLE!
HEH HEH HEH ...
HA HA HA HA HA!
OH, DEAR LORD... TONIGHT, I STAND ALONGSIDE YOU!
I'VE FINALLY DISCOVERED THE SECRET OF LIFE!

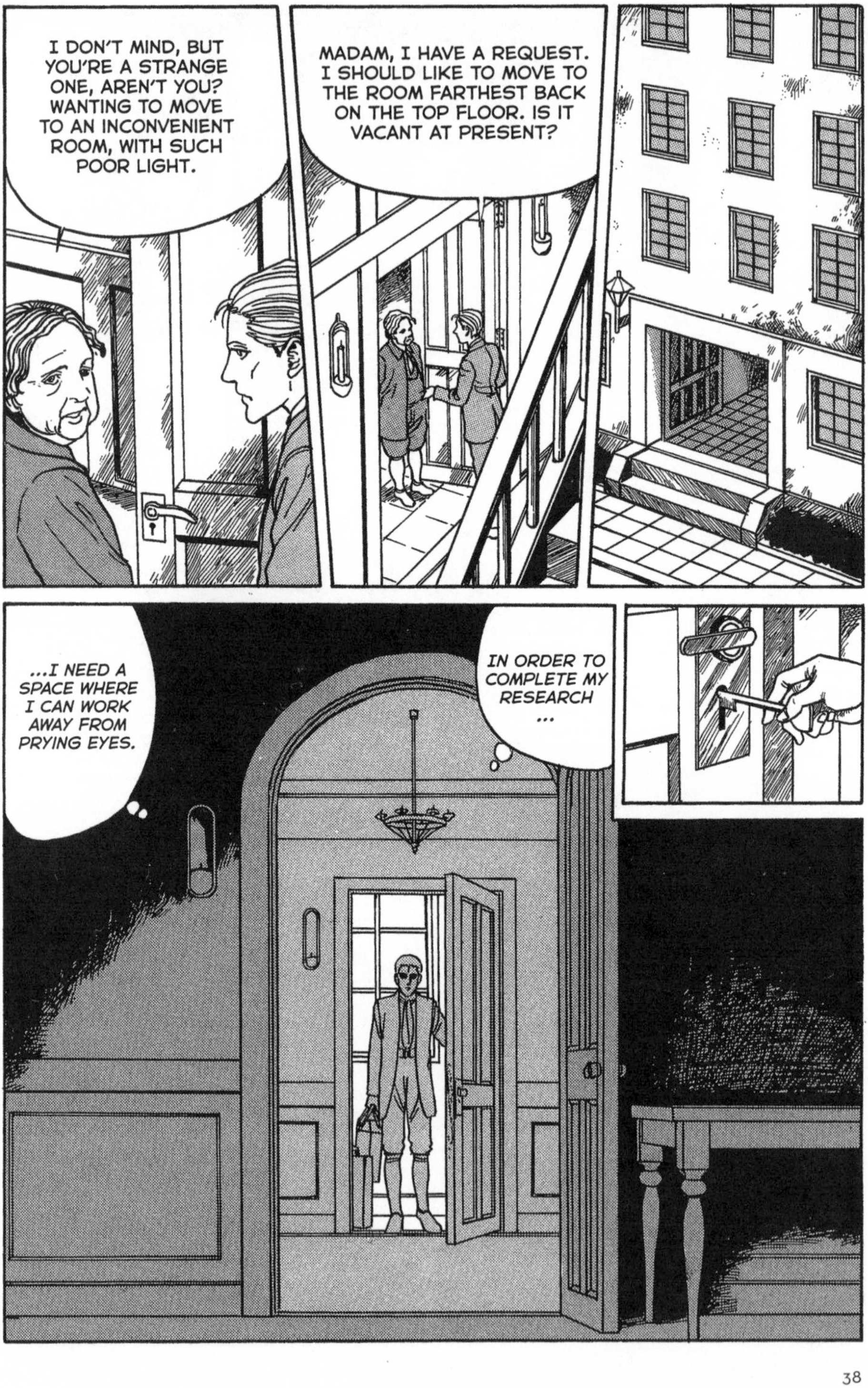
MADAM, I HAVE A REQUEST. I SHOULD LIKE TO MOVE TO THE ROOM FARTHEST BACK ON THE TOP FLOOR. IS IT VACANT AT PRESENT?
I DON'T MIND, BUT YOU'RE A STRANGE ONE, AREN'T YOU? WANTING TO MOVE TO AN INCONVENIENT ROOM, WITH SUCH POOR LIGHT.
IN ORDER TO COMPLETE MY RESEARCH ...
...I NEED A SPACE WHERE I CAN WORK AWAY FROM PRYING EYES.

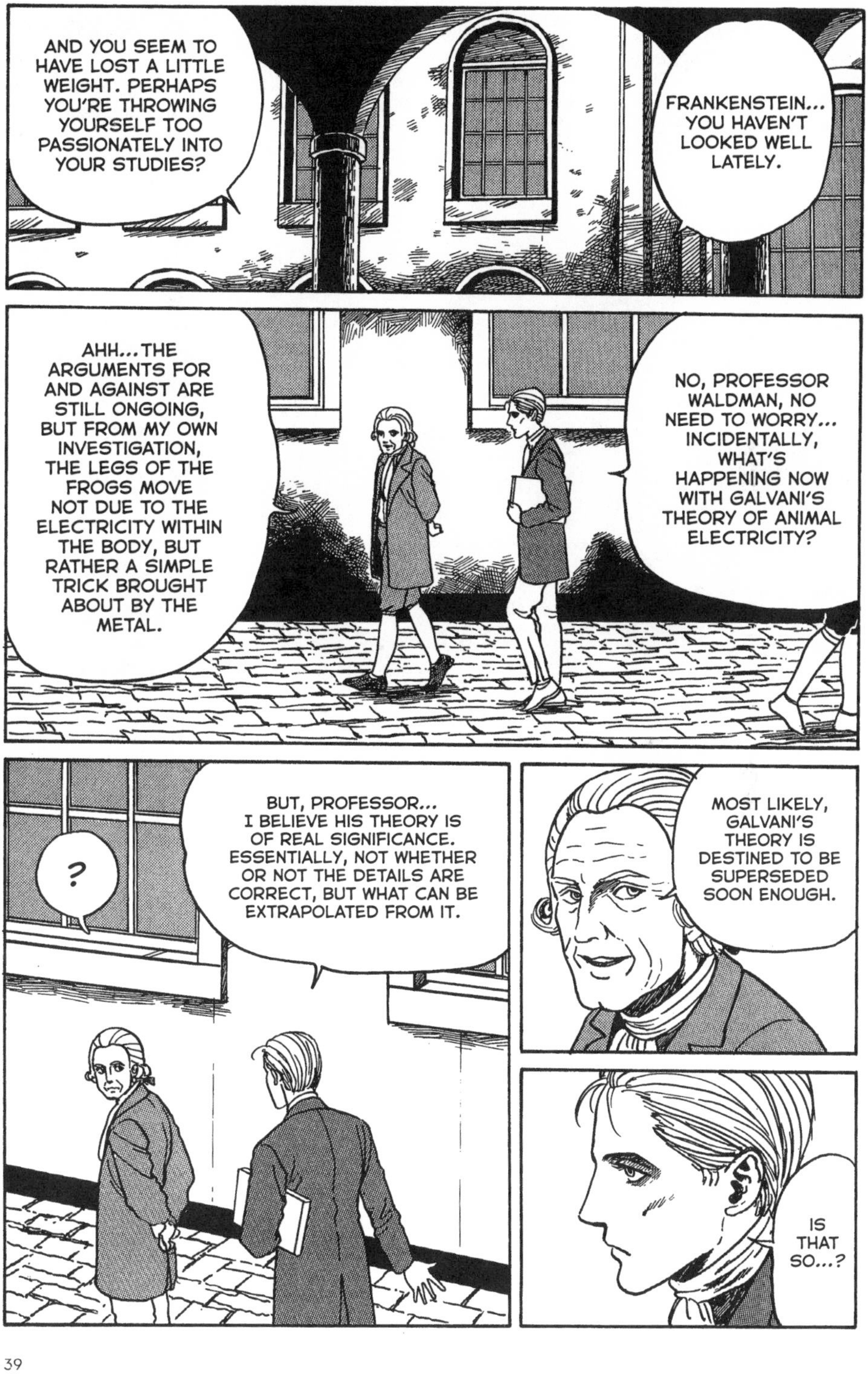
FRANKENSTEIN... YOU HAVEN'T LOOKED WELL LATELY.
AND YOU SEEM TO HAVE LOST A LITTLE WEIGHT. PERHAPS YOU'RE THROWING YOURSELF TOO PASSIONATELY INTO YOUR STUDIES?
NO, PROFESSOR WALDMAN, NO NEED TO WORRY... INCIDENTALLY, WHAT'S HAPPENING NOW WITH GALVANI'S THEORY OF ANIMAL ELECTRICITY?
AHH...THE ARGUMENTS FOR AND AGAINST ARE STILL ONGOING, BUT FROM MY OWN INVESTIGATION, THE LEGS OF THE FROGS MOVE NOT DUE TO THE ELECTRICITY WITHIN THE BODY, BUT RATHER A SIMPLE TRICK BROUGHT ABOUT BY THE METAL.
MOST LIKELY, GALVANI'S THEORY IS DESTINED TO BE SUPERSEDED SOON ENOUGH.
IS THAT SO...?
BUT, PROFESSOR... I BELIEVE HIS THEORY IS OF REAL SIGNIFICANCE. ESSENTIALLY, NOT WHETHER OR NOT THE DETAILS ARE CORRECT, BUT WHAT CAN BE EXTRAPOLATED FROM IT.
?

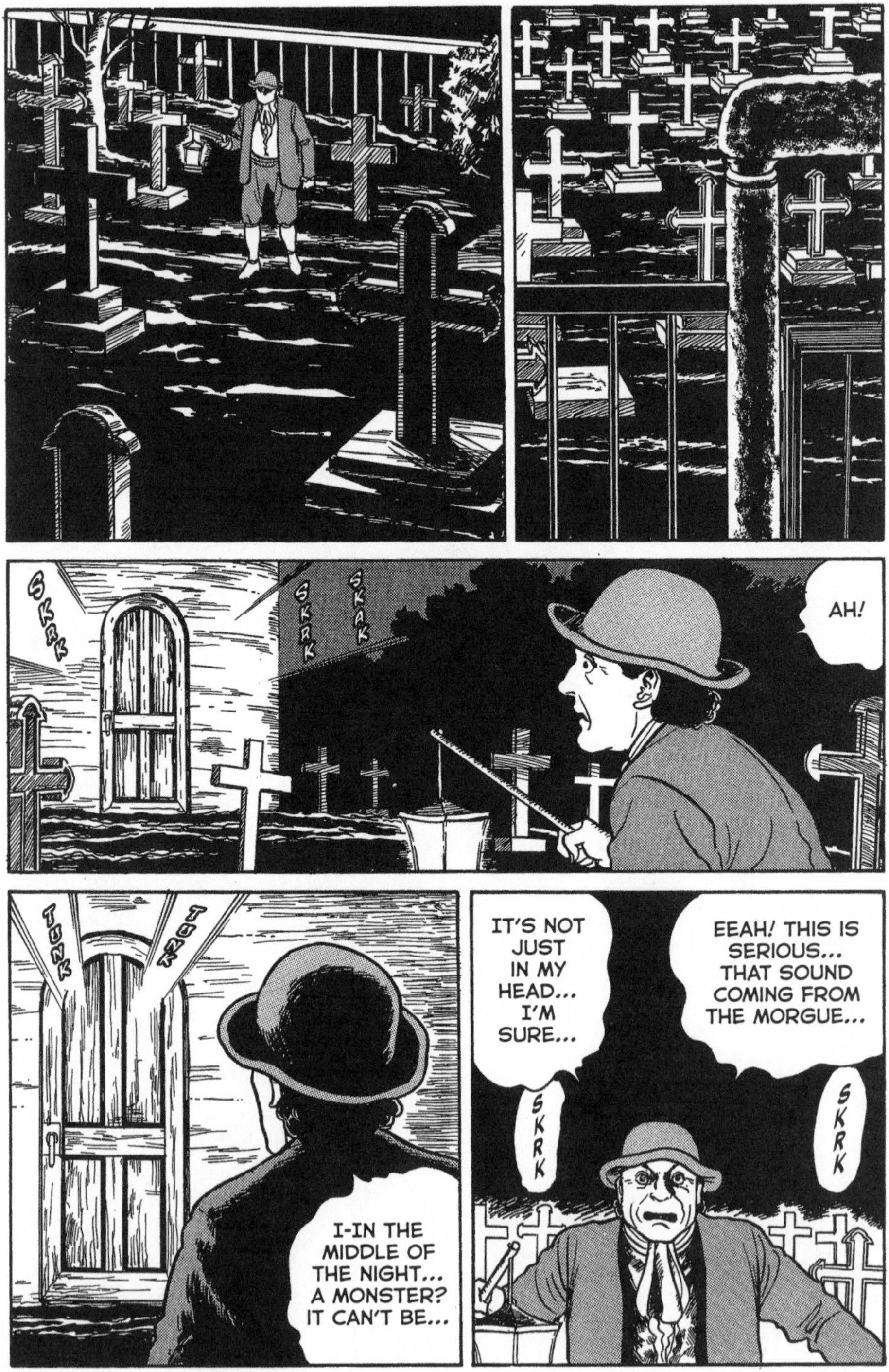
AH!
SKAK
SKRK
SKRK
EEAH! THIS IS SERIOUS... THAT SOUND COMING FROM THE MORGUE...
IT'S NOT JUST IN MY HEAD... I'M SURE...
SKRK
SKRK
TUNK
TUNK
I-IN THE MIDDLE OF THE NIGHT... A MONSTER? IT CAN'T BE...

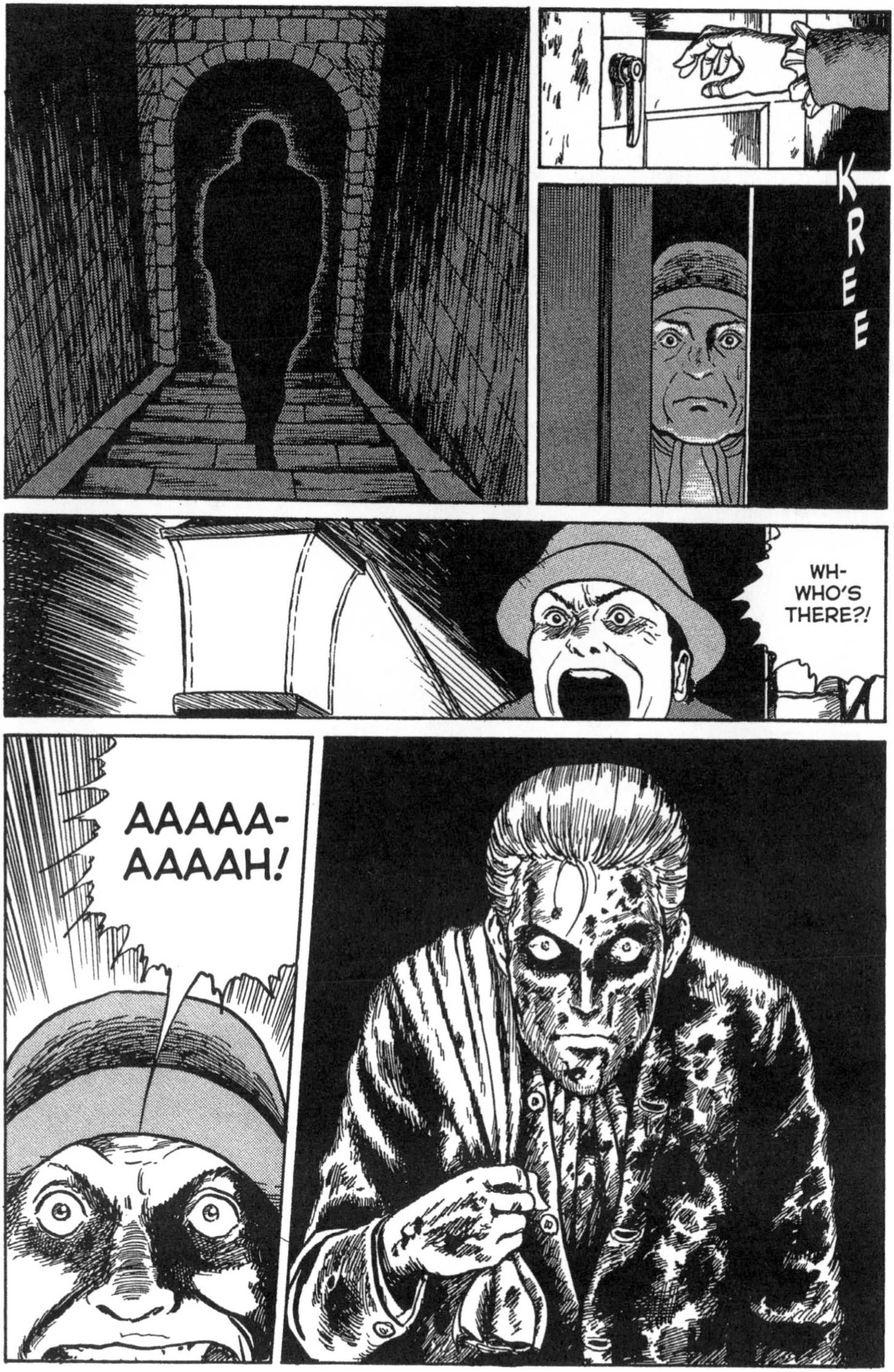
KREE
WH- WHO'S THERE?!
AAAAA- AAAAH!

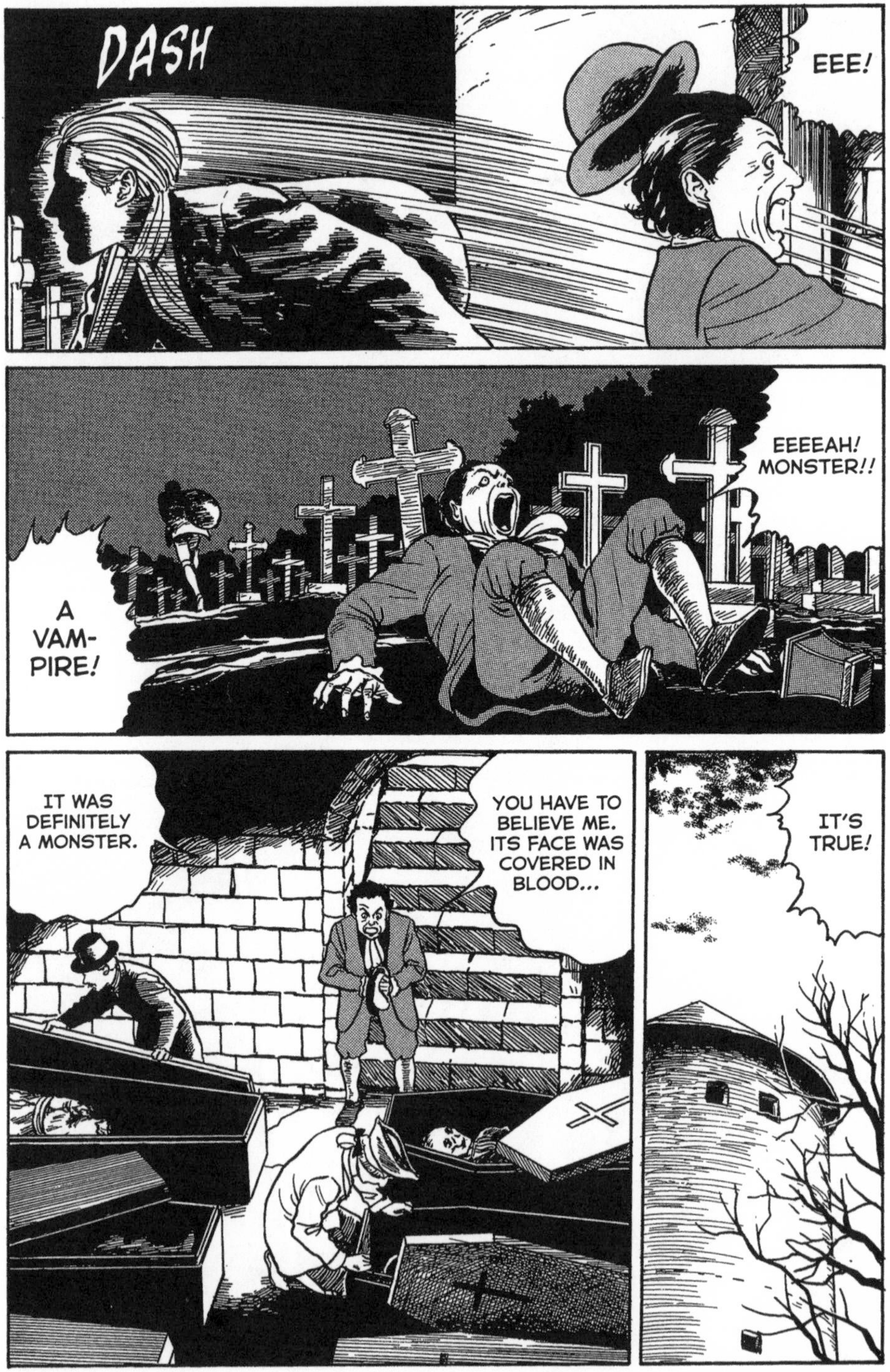
EEE!
DASH
EEEEAH! MONSTER!!
A VAM-PIRE!
IT'S TRUE!
YOU HAVE TO BELIEVE ME. ITS FACE WAS COVERED IN BLOOD...
IT WAS DEFINITELY A MONSTER.

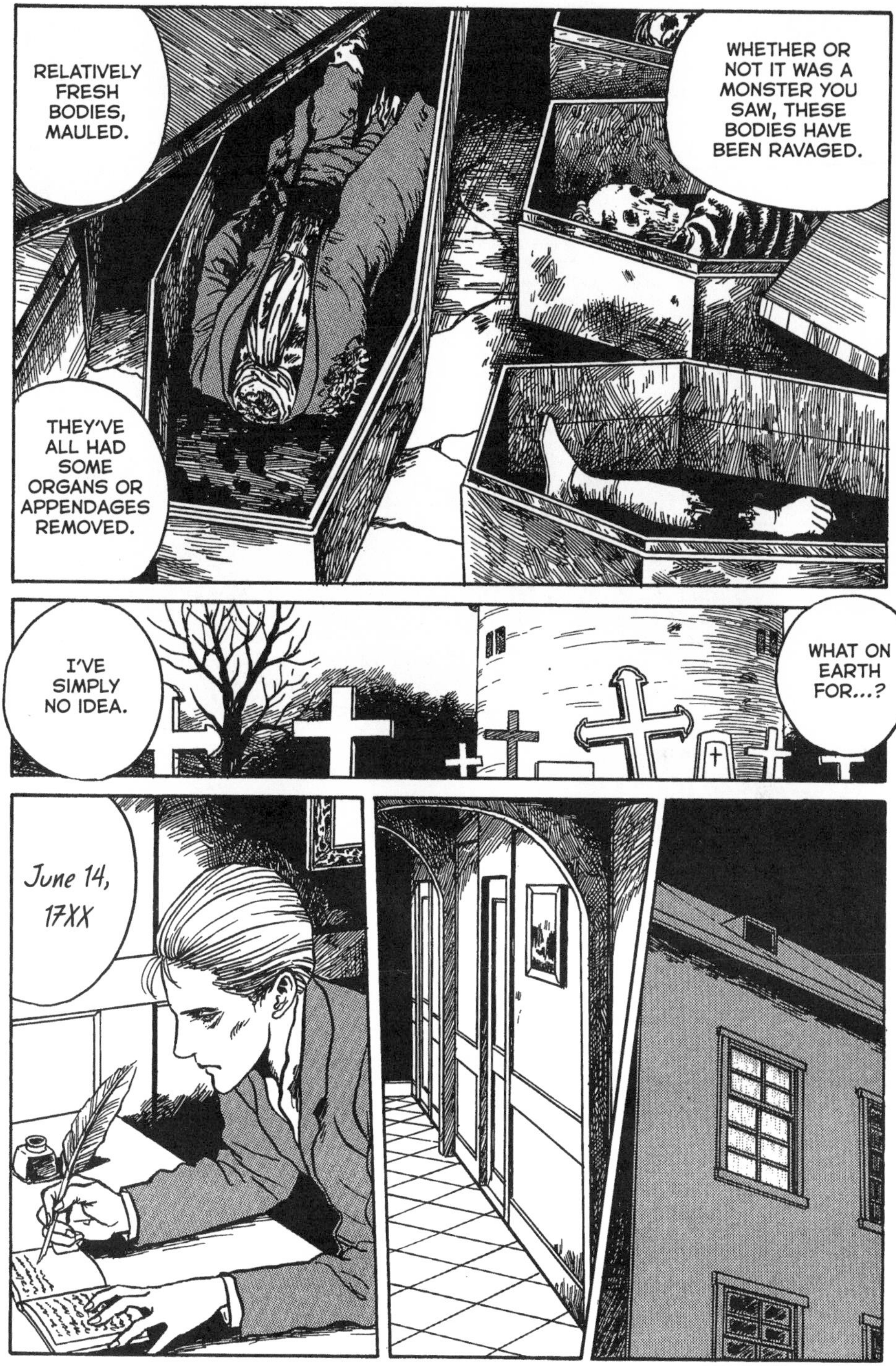
WHETHER OR NOT IT WAS A MONSTER YOU SAW, THESE BODIES HAVE BEEN RAVAGED.
RELATIVELY FRESH BODIES, MAULED.
THEY'VE ALL HAD SOME ORGANS OR APPENDAGES REMOVED.
WHAT ON EARTH FOR...?
I'VE SIMPLY NO IDEA.
June 14, 17XX

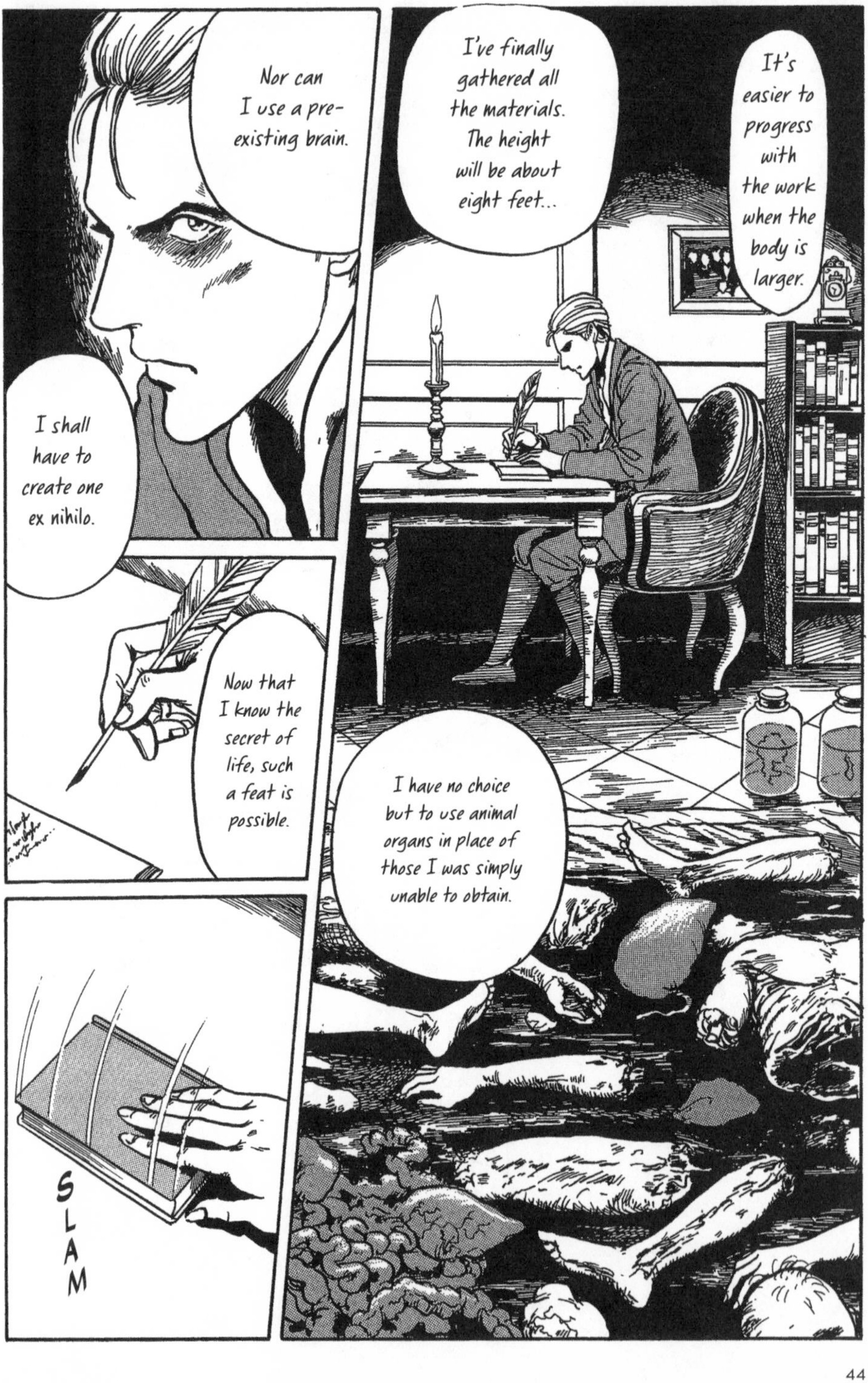
It's easier to progress with the work when the body is larger.
I've finally gathered all the materials. The height will be about eight feet...
I have no choice but to use animal organs in place of those I was simply unable to obtain.
Nor can I use a pre-existing brain.
I shall have to create one ex nihilo.
Now that I know the secret of life, such a feat is possible.
SLAM

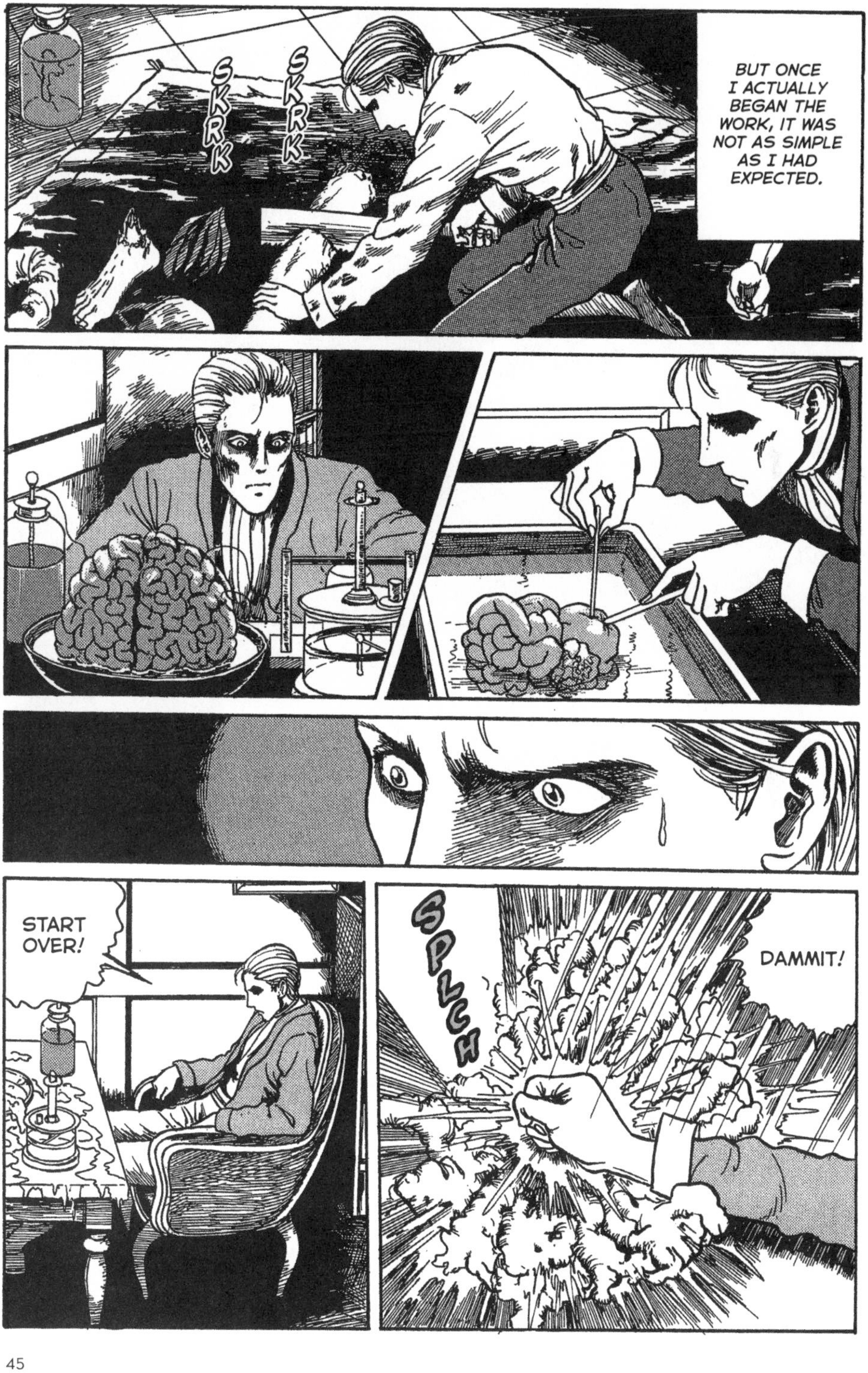
BUT ONCE I ACTUALLY BEGAN THE WORK, IT WAS NOT AS SIMPLE AS I HAD EXPECTED.
SKRK
SKRK
DAMMIT!
SPLCH
START OVER!

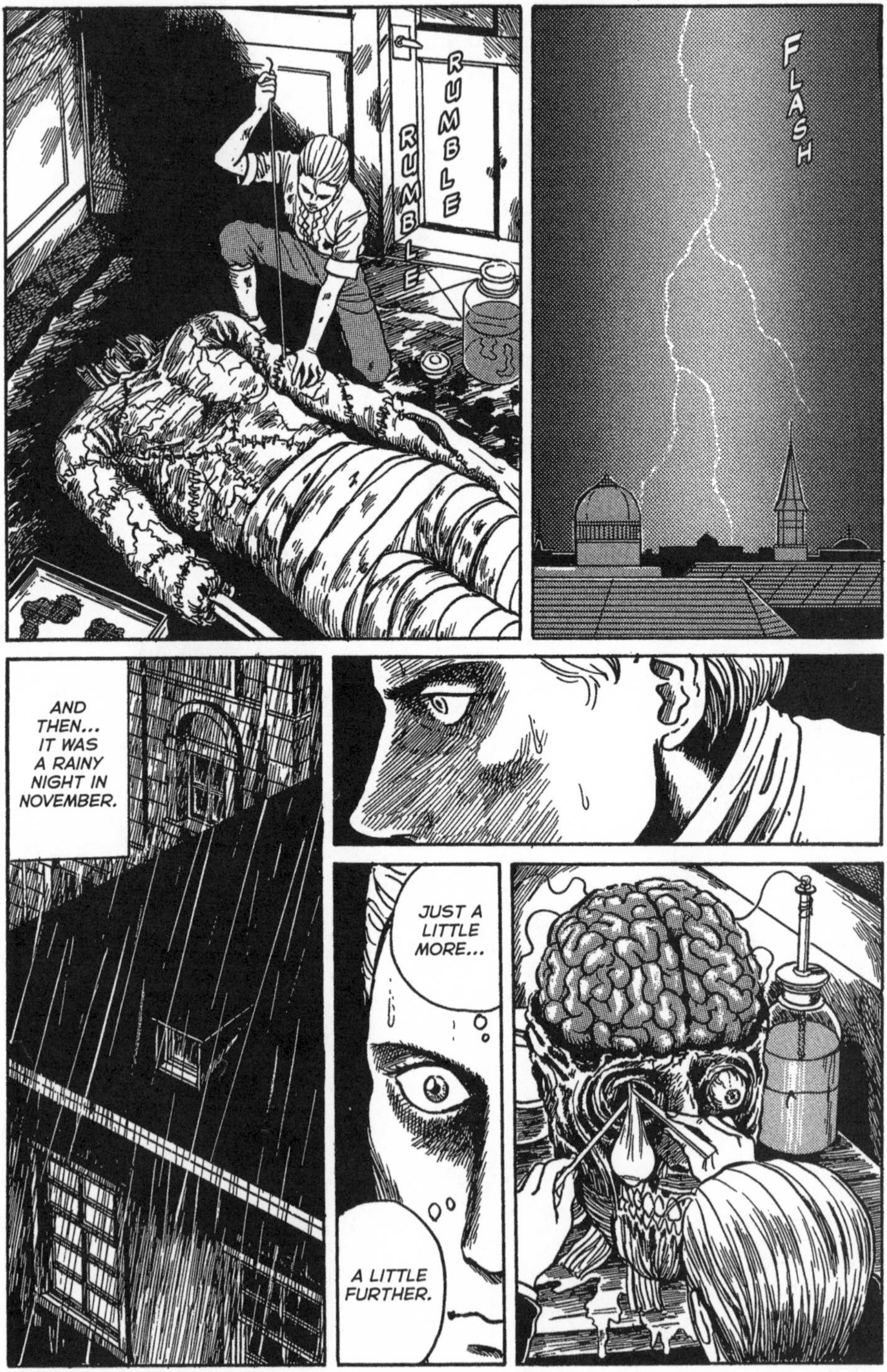
FLASH
RUMBLE
RUMBLE
JUST A LITTLE MORE...
A LITTLE FURTHER.
AND THEN... IT WAS A RAINY NIGHT IN NOVEMBER.

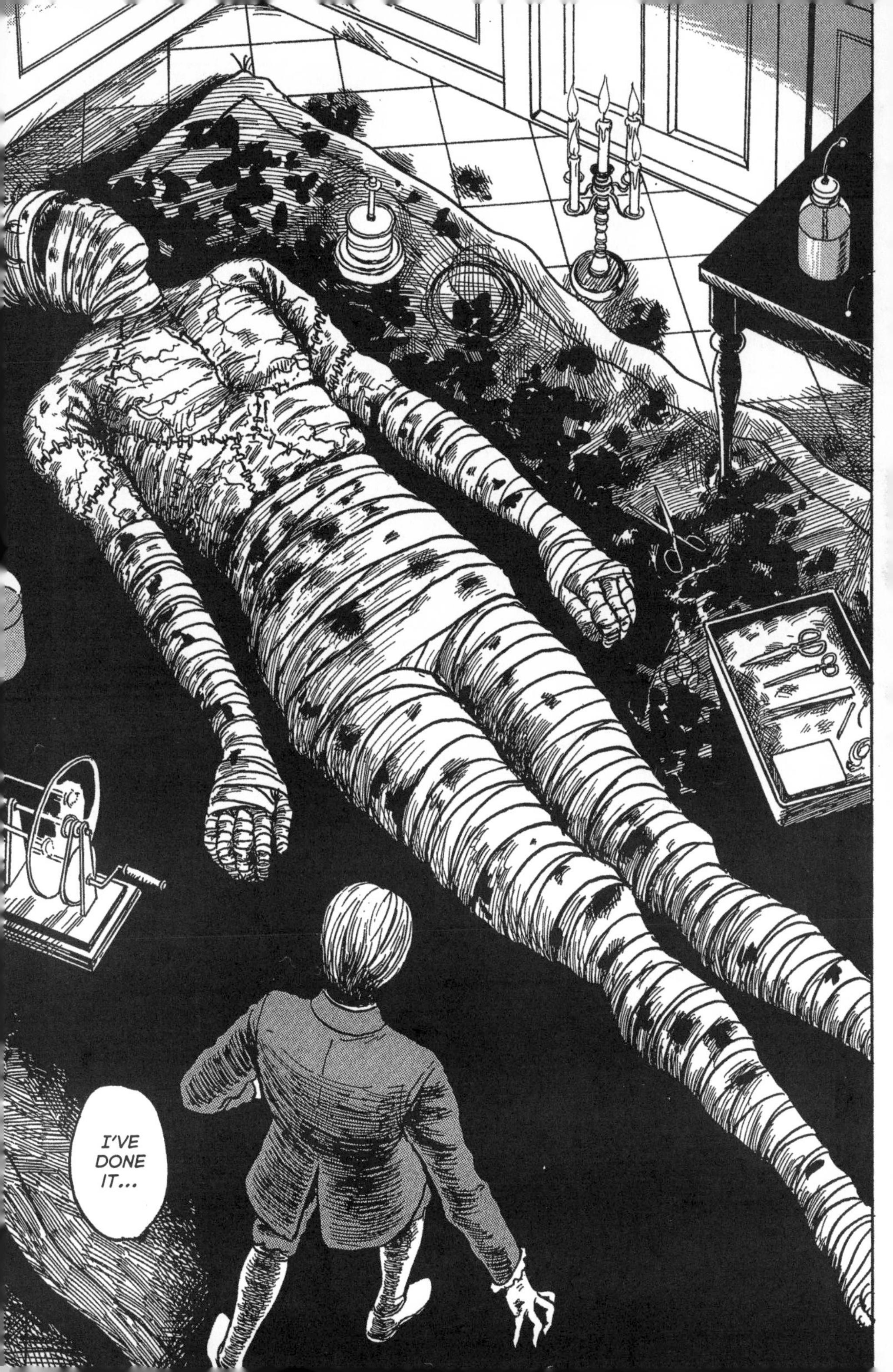
I'VE DONE IT...

I'VE FINALLY COMPLETED IT.
THE IDEAL HUMAN BEING...
IDEAL...
IDEAL ?!
ISN'T IT... A LITTLE TOO LARGE?
NO, NO...
A PROTOTYPE IS OFT OVERSIZED.
PROTO-TYPE...
PROTOTYPE?! NOT AT ALL!!
THIS IS THE ULTIMATE CREATION!!
LOOK... THIS PHYSICAL BEAUTY.
PH-PHYSICAL BEAUTY? TH-THIS... TWISTED LUMP OF FLESH?!

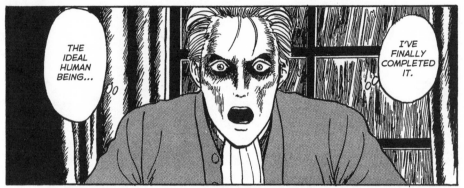

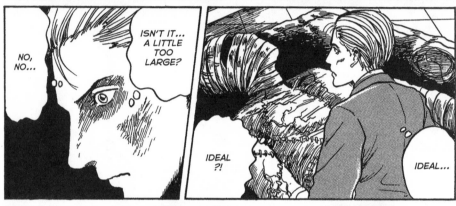

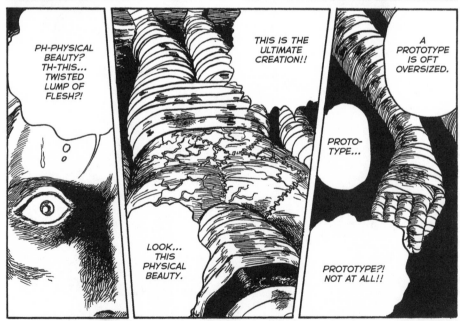

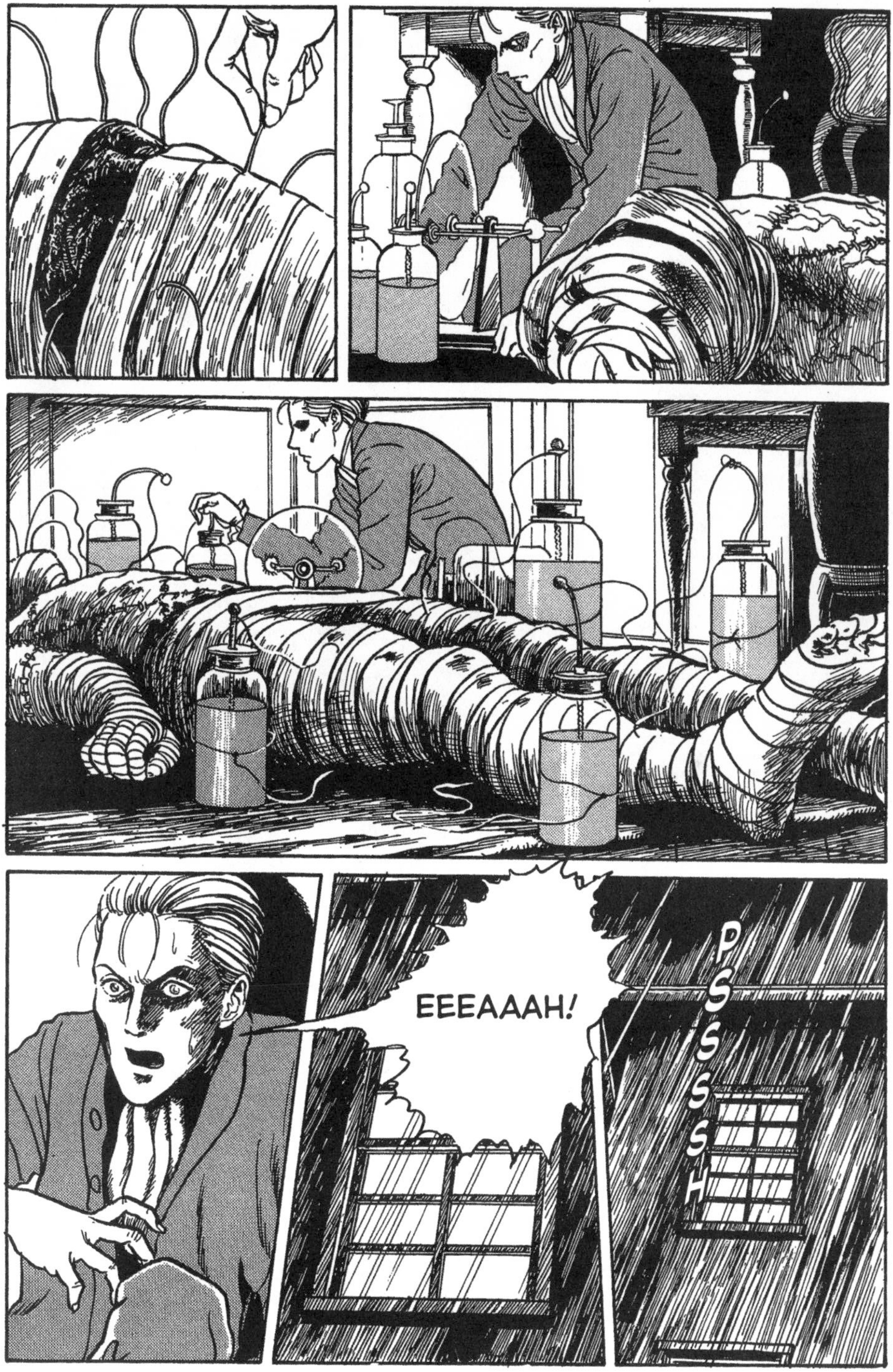
PSSSSH
EEEAAAH!

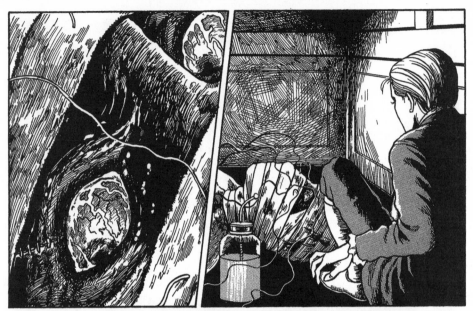

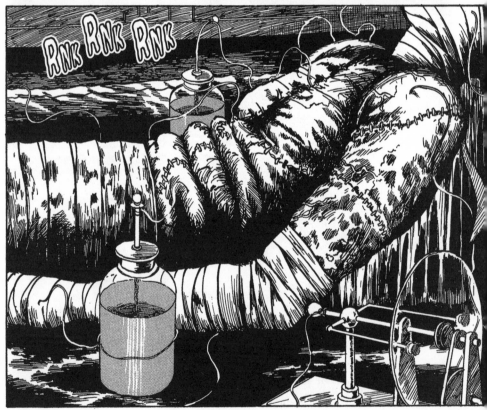

RNK RNK RNK

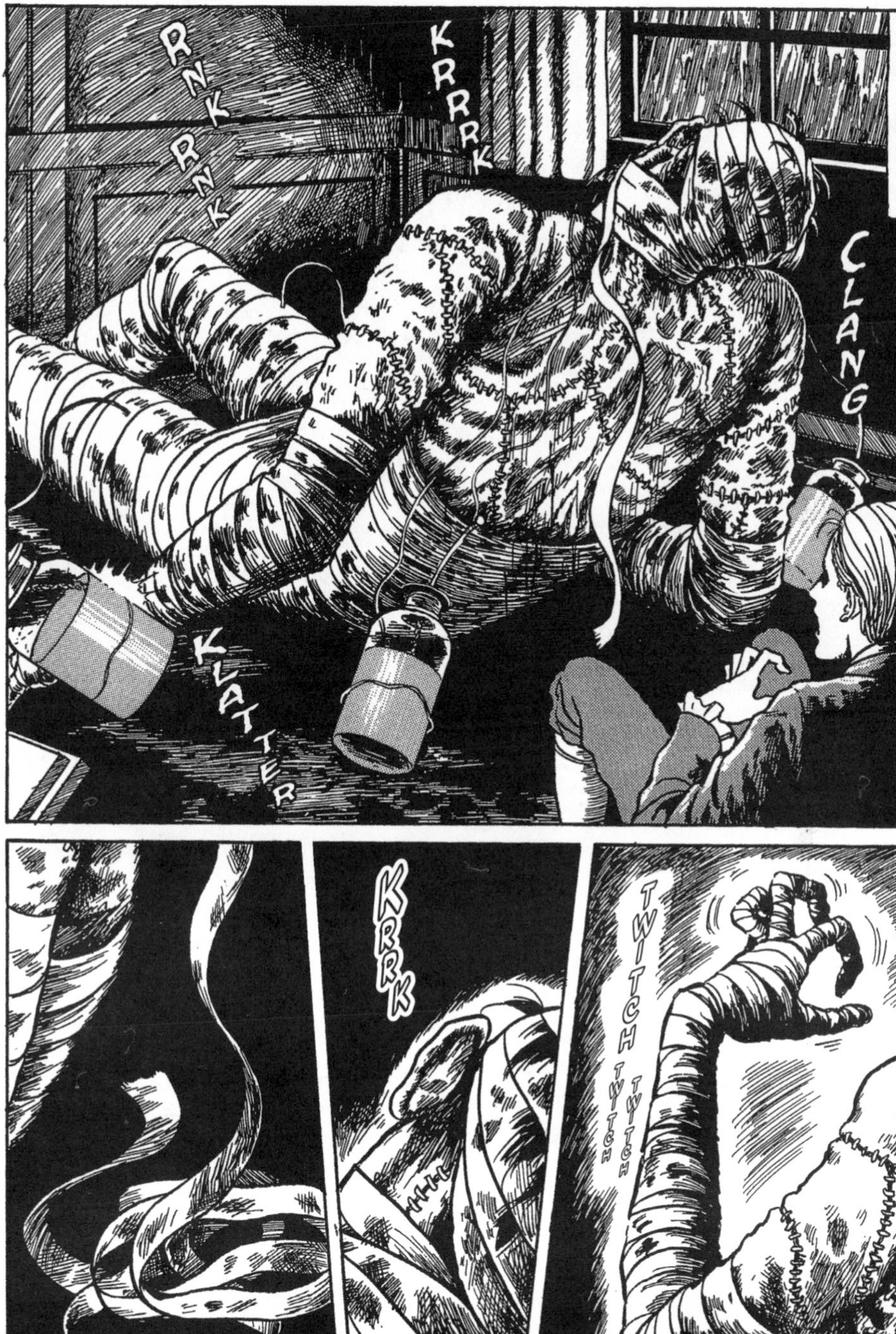
CLANG
KRRRRK
RNK RNK
KLATTER
TWITCH
TWITCH TWITCH
KRRRK

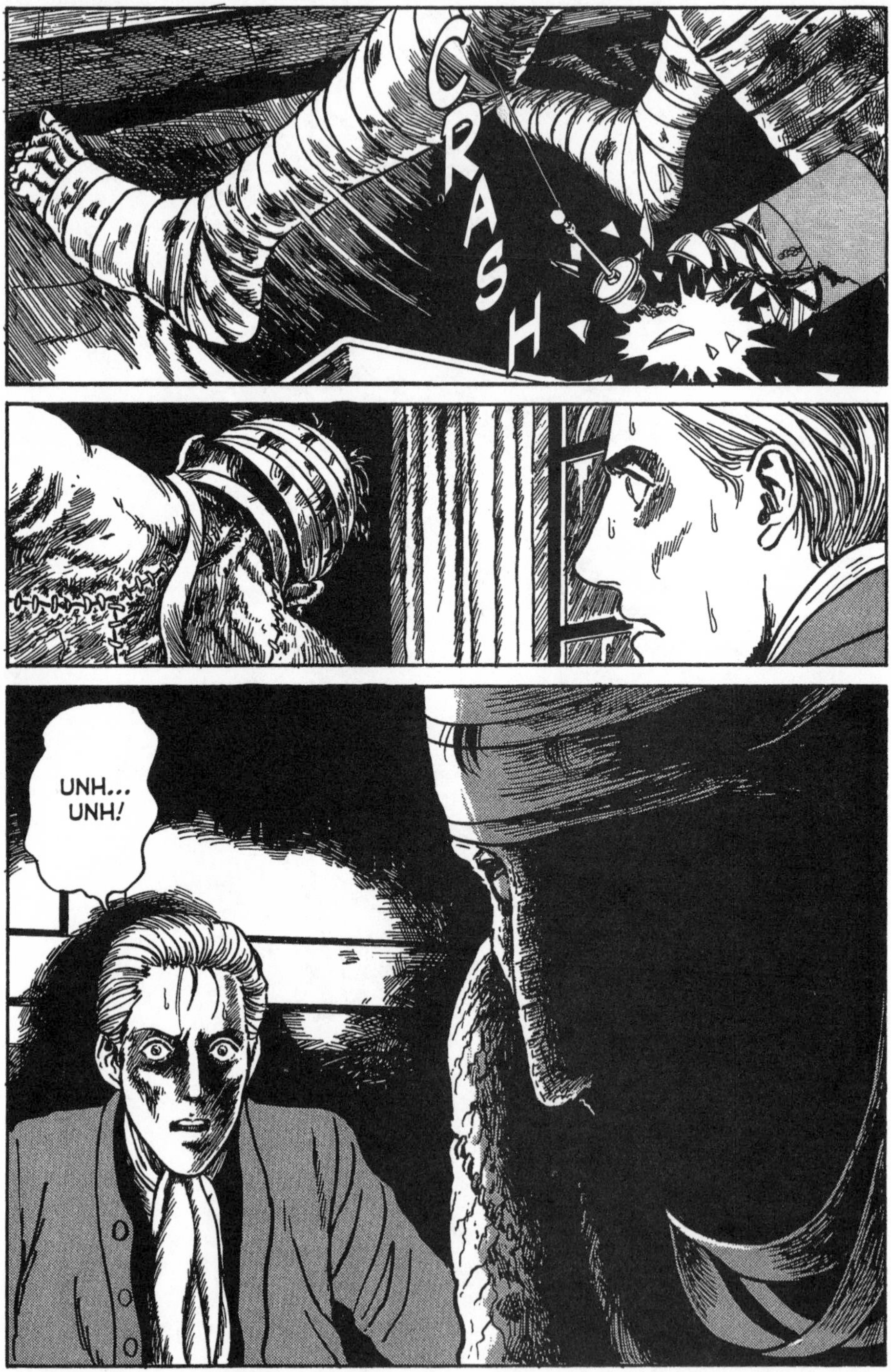
CRASH
UNH... UNH!

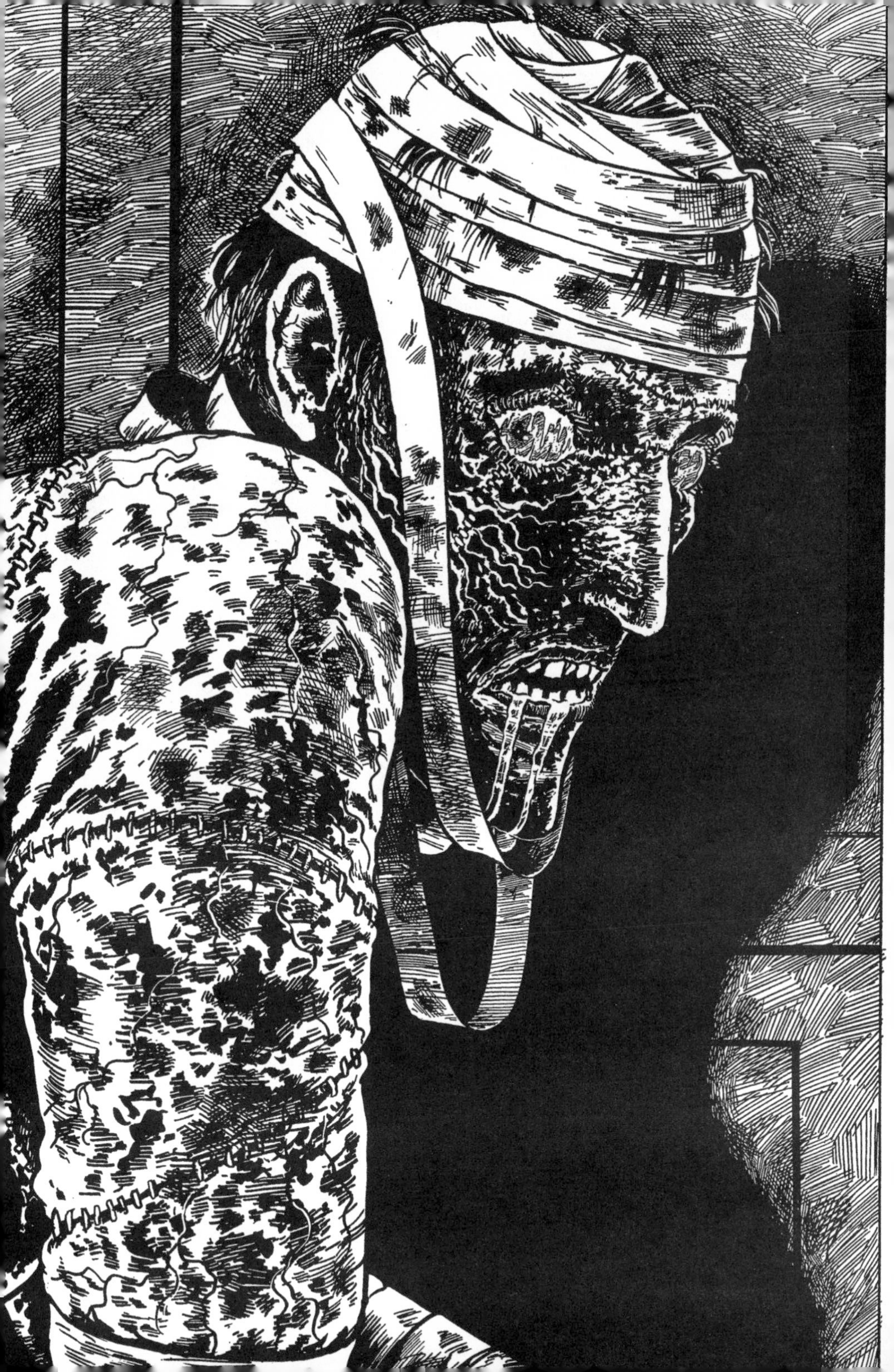

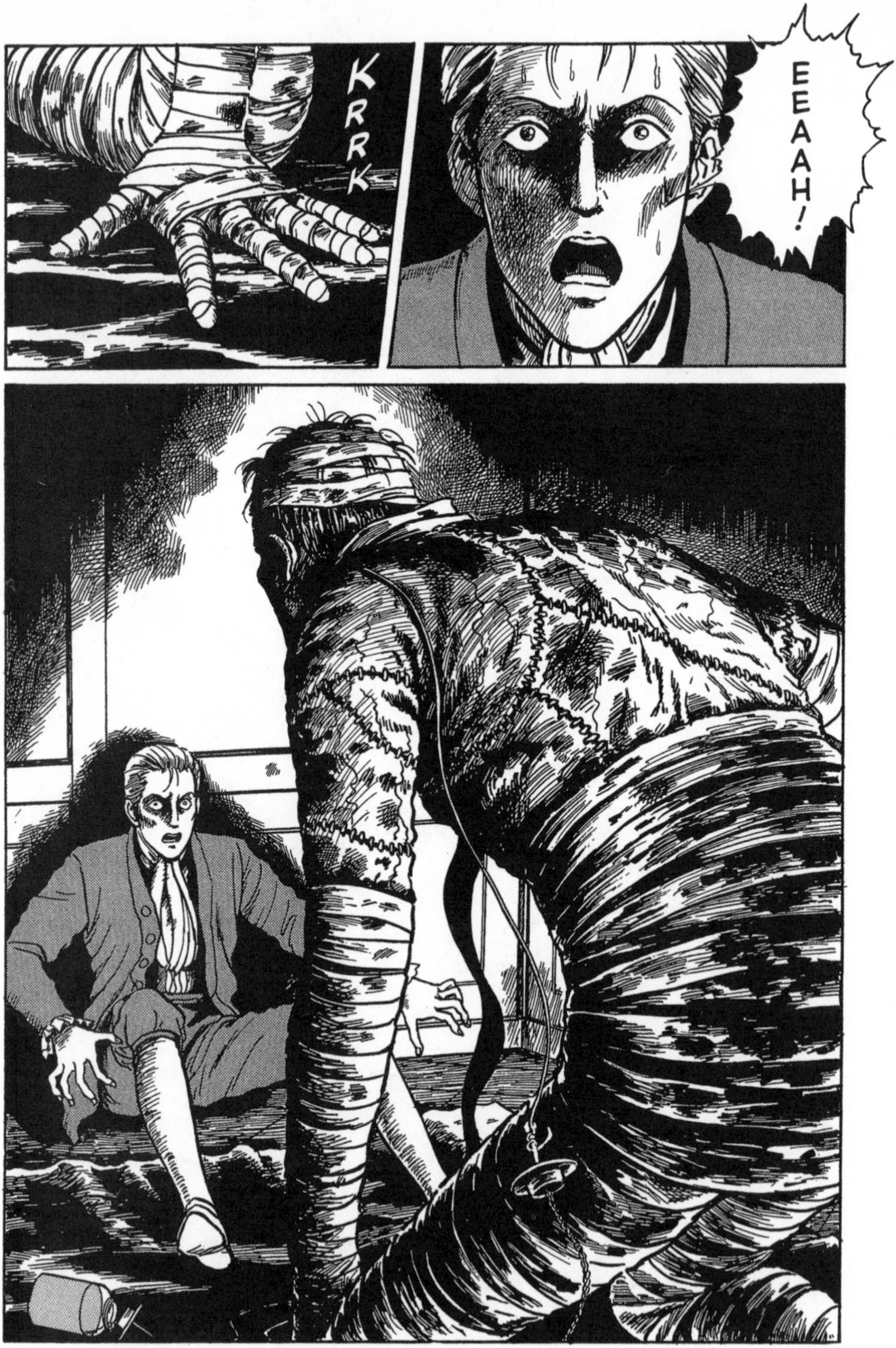
EEAAH!
KRRK

HNNNGH!

HRGH!

AH!

VICTOR.

NGAAAAH!

...

VICTOR, WERE YOU HAVING A NIGHT-MARE?

THIS IS YOUR ROOM.

YOU... HENRY?

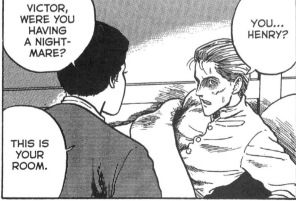

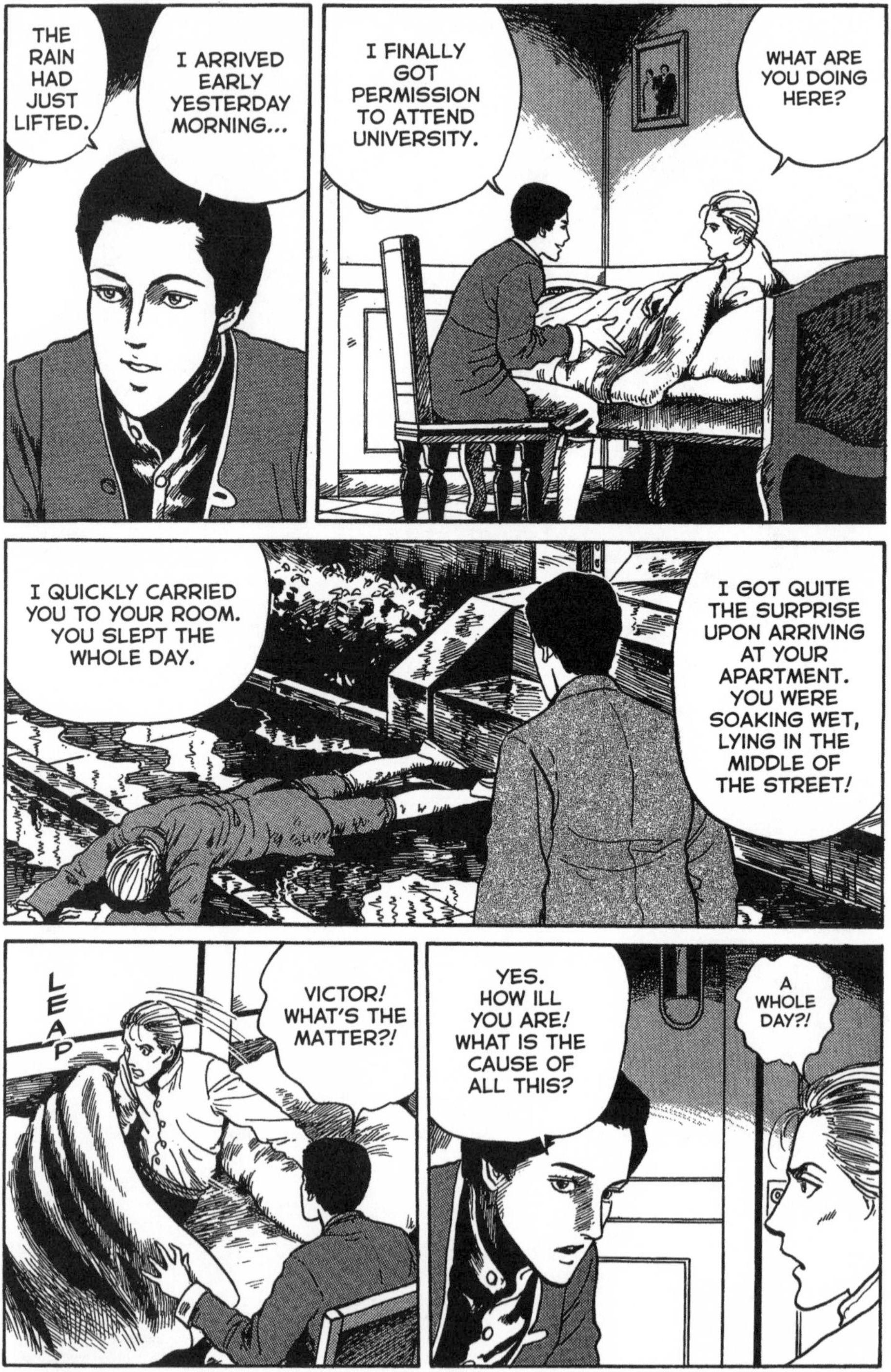
WHAT ARE YOU DOING HERE?
I FINALLY GOT PERMISSION TO ATTEND UNIVERSITY.
I ARRIVED EARLY YESTERDAY MORNING...
THE RAIN HAD JUST LIFTED.
I GOT QUITE THE SURPRISE UPON ARRIVING AT YOUR APARTMENT. YOU WERE SOAKING WET, LYING IN THE MIDDLE OF THE STREET!
I QUICKLY CARRIED YOU TO YOUR ROOM. YOU SLEPT THE WHOLE DAY.
A WHOLE DAY?!
YES. HOW ILL YOU ARE! WHAT IS THE CAUSE OF ALL THIS?
VICTOR! WHAT'S THE MATTER?!
LEAP

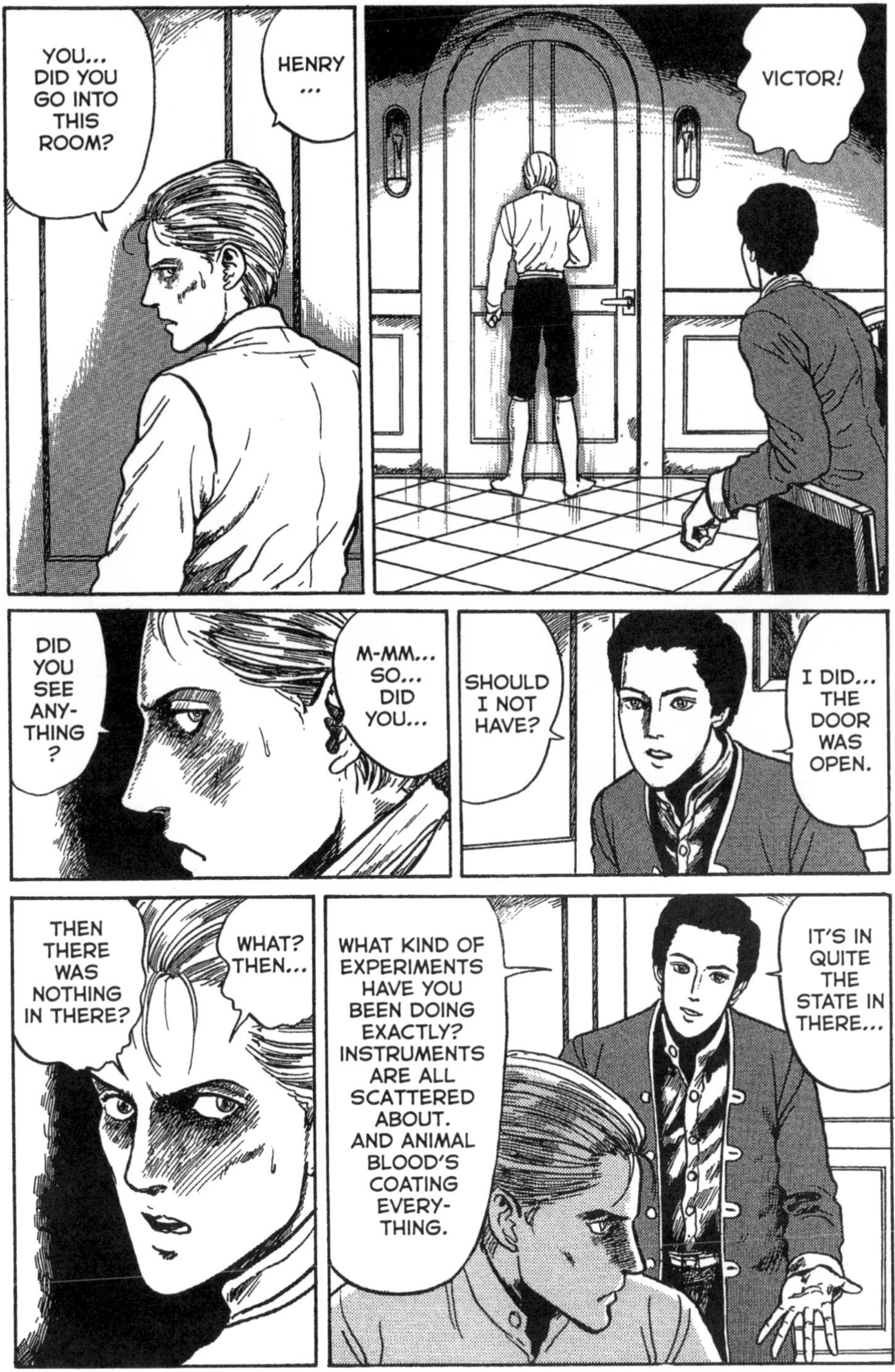
VICTOR!
HENRY...
YOU... DID YOU GO INTO THIS ROOM?
I DID... THE DOOR WAS OPEN.
SHOULD I NOT HAVE?
M-MM... SO... DID YOU...
DID YOU SEE ANYTHING?
IT'S IN QUITE THE STATE IN THERE...
WHAT KIND OF EXPERIMENTS HAVE YOU BEEN DOING EXACTLY? INSTRUMENTS ARE ALL SCATTERED ABOUT. AND ANIMAL BLOOD'S COATING EVERYTHING.
WHAT? THEN...
THEN THERE WAS NOTHING IN THERE?

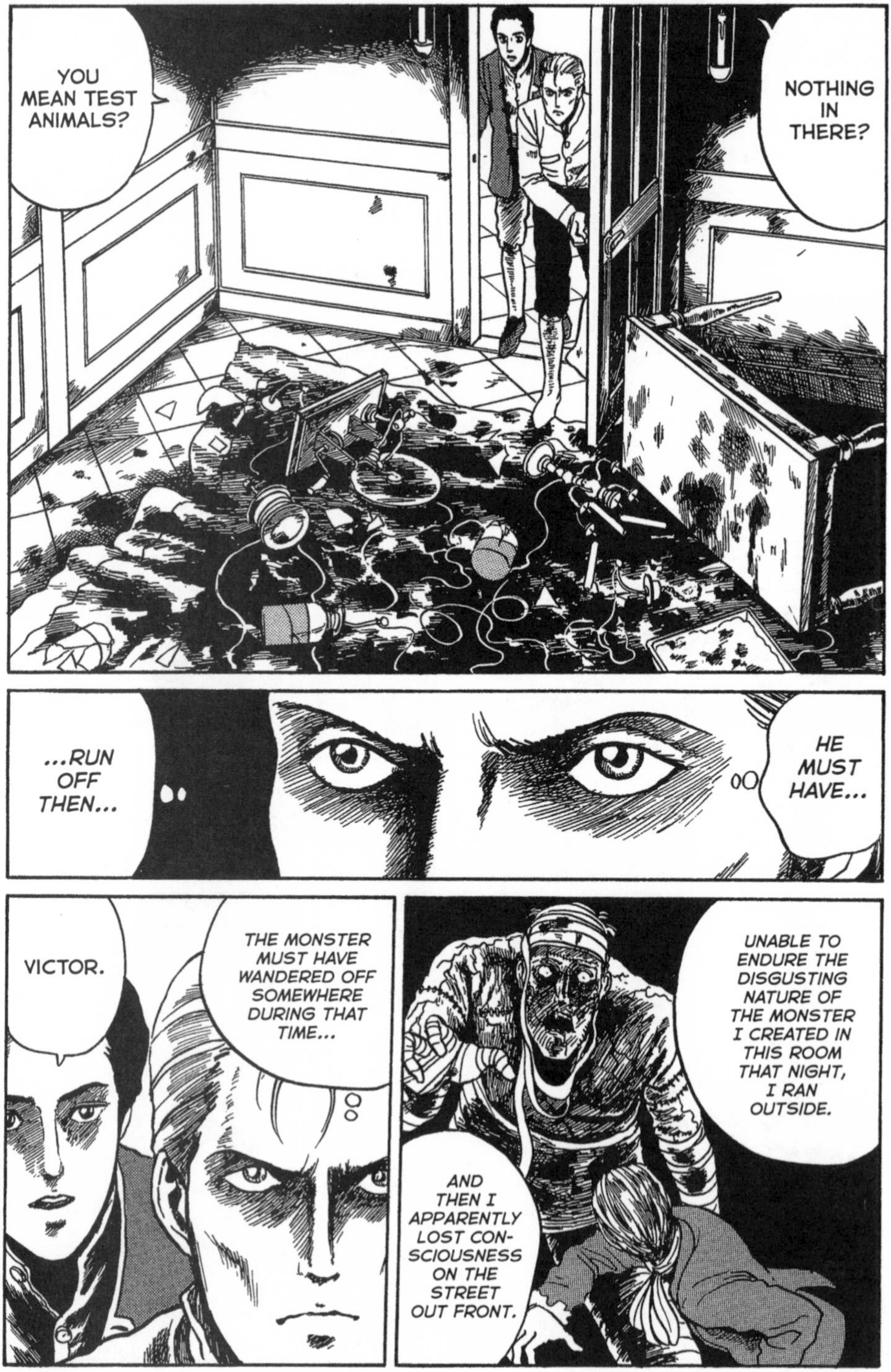
NOTHING IN THERE?
YOU MEAN TEST ANIMALS?
HE MUST HAVE...
...RUN OFF THEN...
UNABLE TO ENDURE THE DISGUSTING NATURE OF THE MONSTER I CREATED IN THIS ROOM THAT NIGHT, I RAN OUTSIDE.
AND THEN I APPARENTLY LOST CON-SCIOUSNESS ON THE STREET OUT FRONT.
THE MONSTER MUST HAVE WANDERED OFF SOMEWHERE DURING THAT TIME...
VICTOR.

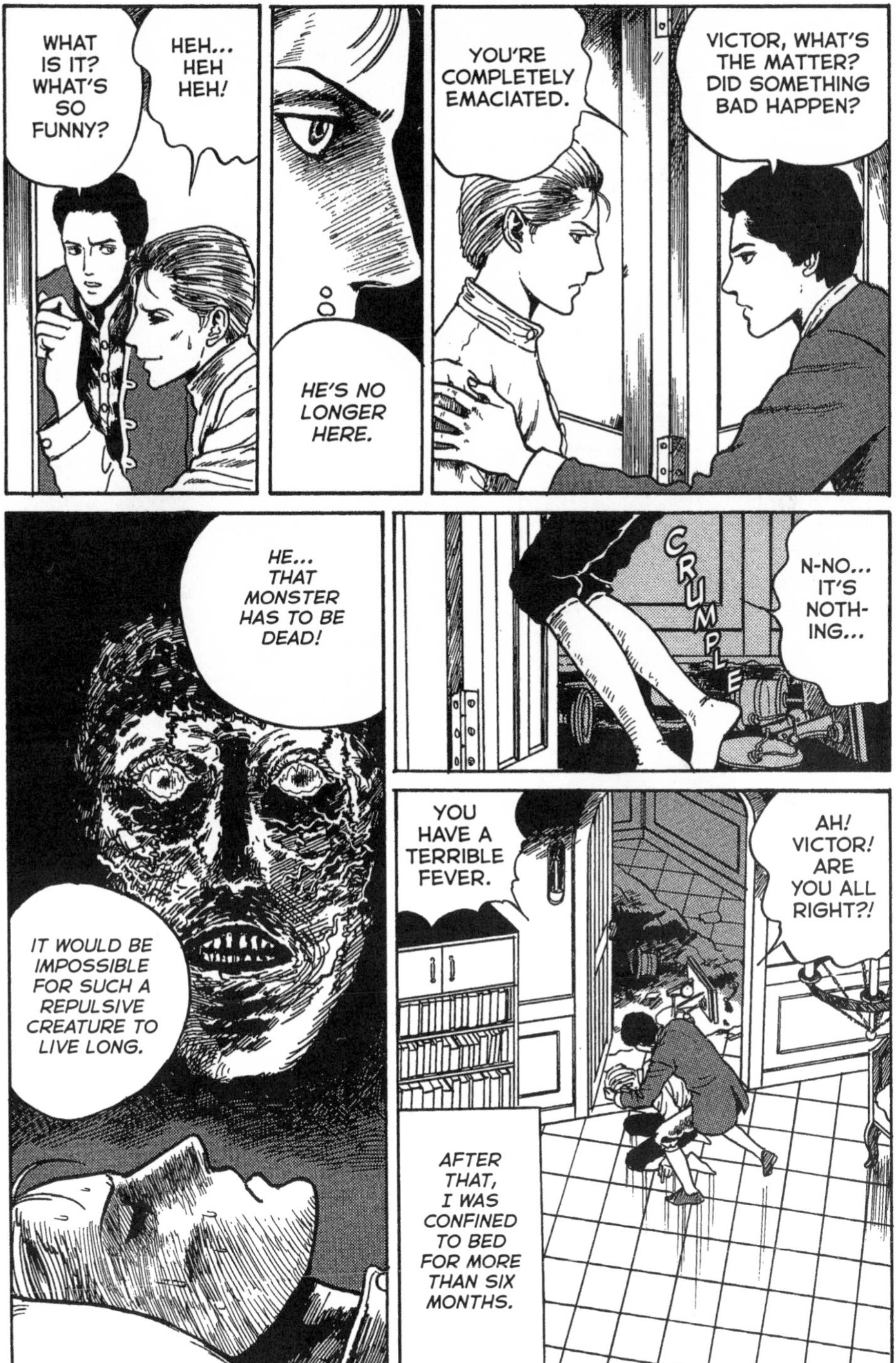
VICTOR, WHAT'S THE MATTER? DID SOMETHING BAD HAPPEN?
YOU'RE COMPLETELY EMACIATED.
HE'S NO LONGER HERE.
HEH... HEH HEH!
WHAT IS IT? WHAT'S SO FUNNY?
N-NO... IT'S NOTH-ING...
CRUMPLE
AH! VICTOR! ARE YOU ALL RIGHT?!
YOU HAVE A TERRIBLE FEVER.
AFTER THAT, I WAS CONFINED TO BED FOR MORE THAN SIX MONTHS.
HE... THAT MONSTER HAS TO BE DEAD!
IT WOULD BE IMPOSSIBLE FOR SUCH A REPULSIVE CREATURE TO LIVE LONG.

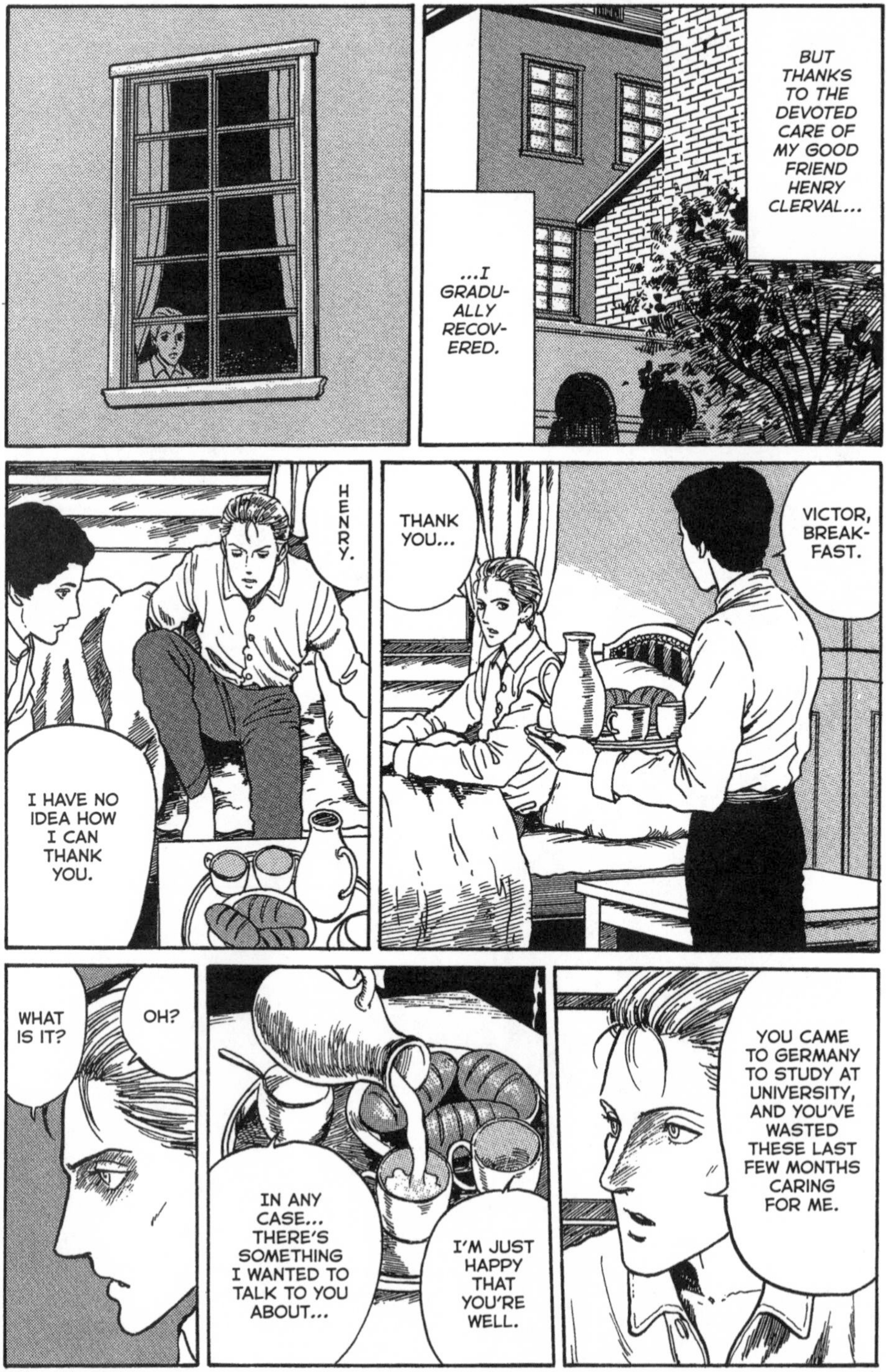
BUT THANKS TO THE DEVOTED CARE OF MY GOOD FRIEND HENRY CLERVAL...
...I GRADUALLY RECOVERED.
VICTOR, BREAKFAST.
THANK YOU...
HENRY.
I HAVE NO IDEA HOW I CAN THANK YOU.
YOU CAME TO GERMANY TO STUDY AT UNIVERSITY, AND YOU'VE WASTED THESE LAST FEW MONTHS CARING FOR ME.
I'M JUST HAPPY THAT YOU'RE WELL.
IN ANY CASE... THERE'S SOMETHING I WANTED TO TALK TO YOU ABOUT...
OH?
WHAT IS IT?

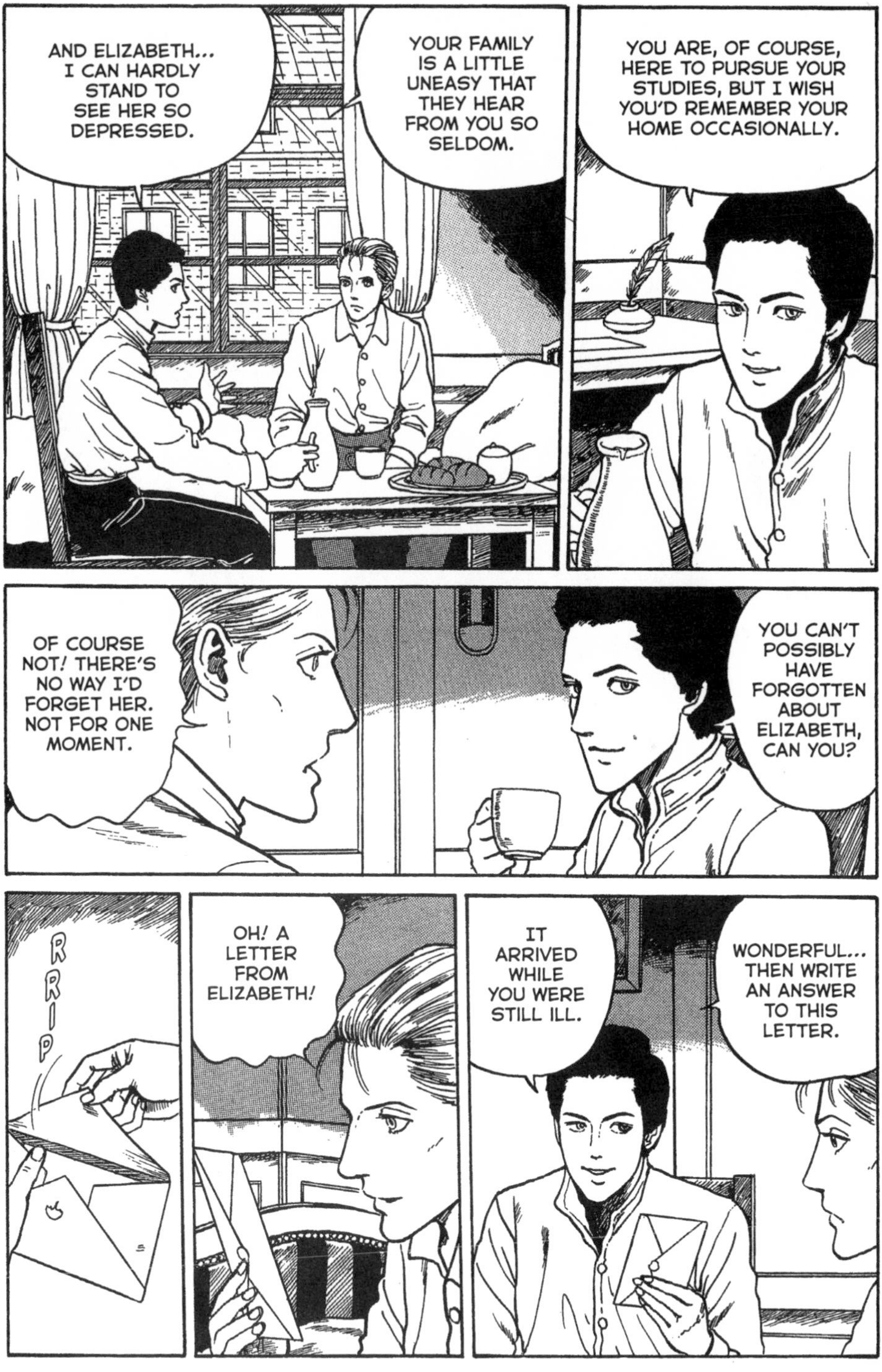
YOU ARE, OF COURSE, HERE TO PURSUE YOUR STUDIES, BUT I WISH YOU'D REMEMBER YOUR HOME OCCASIONALLY.
YOUR FAMILY IS A LITTLE UNEASY THAT THEY HEAR FROM YOU SO SELDOM.
AND ELIZABETH... I CAN HARDLY STAND TO SEE HER SO DEPRESSED.
YOU CAN'T POSSIBLY HAVE FORGOTTEN ABOUT ELIZABETH, CAN YOU?
OF COURSE NOT! THERE'S NO WAY I'D FORGET HER. NOT FOR ONE MOMENT.
WONDERFUL... THEN WRITE AN ANSWER TO THIS LETTER.
IT ARRIVED WHILE YOU WERE STILL ILL.
OH! A LETTER FROM ELIZABETH!
RRIP

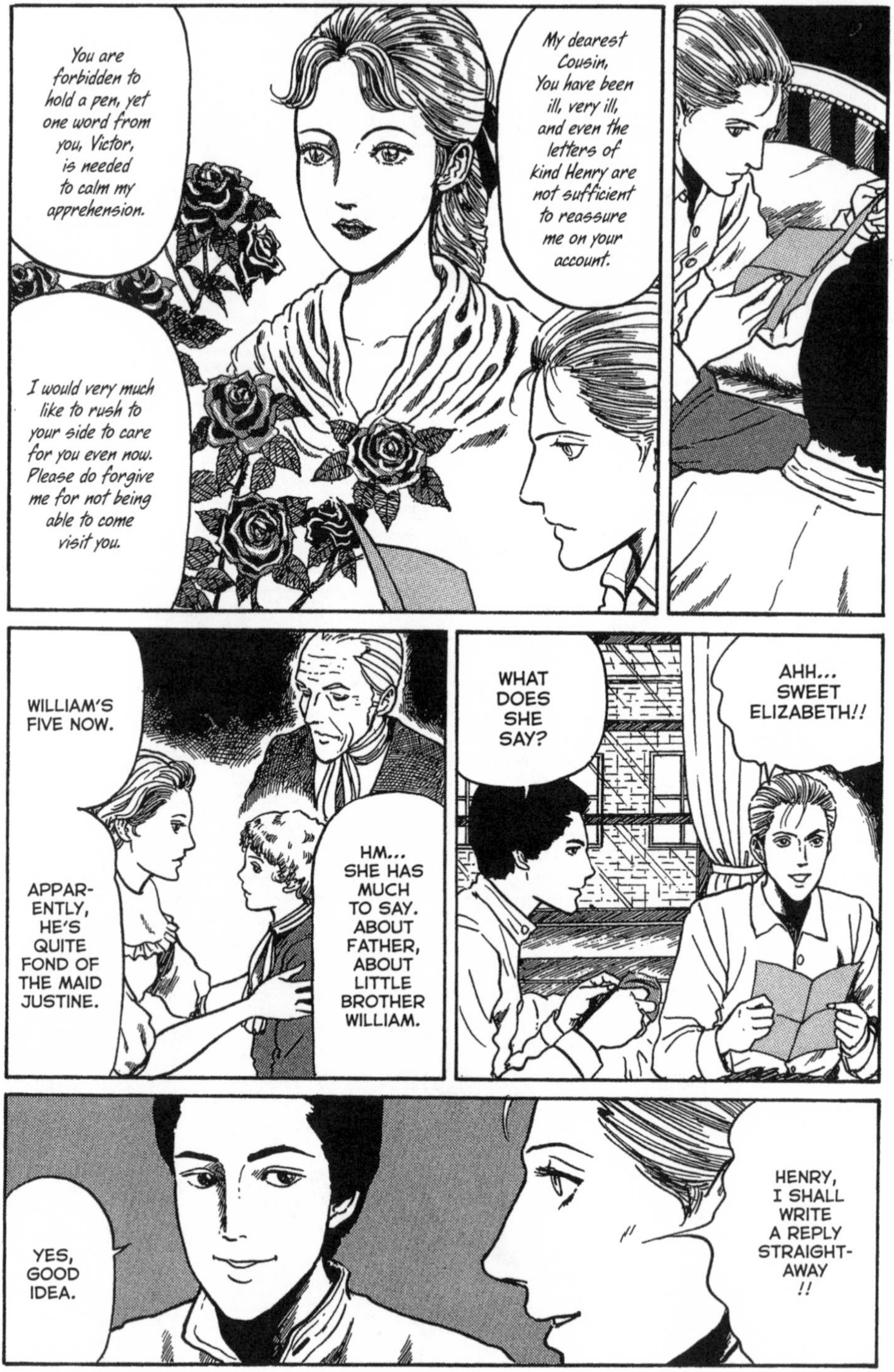
My dearest Cousin, You have been ill, very ill, and even the letters of kind Henry are not sufficient to reassure me on your account.
You are forbidden to hold a pen, yet one word from you, Victor, is needed to calm my apprehension.
I would very much like to rush to your side to care for you even now. Please do forgive me for not being able to come visit you.
AHH... SWEET ELIZABETH!!
WHAT DOES SHE SAY?
HM... SHE HAS MUCH TO SAY. ABOUT FATHER, ABOUT LITTLE BROTHER WILLIAM.
WILLIAM'S FIVE NOW.
APPARENTLY, HE'S QUITE FOND OF THE MAID JUSTINE.
HENRY, I SHALL WRITE A REPLY STRAIGHT-AWAY !!
YES, GOOD IDEA.

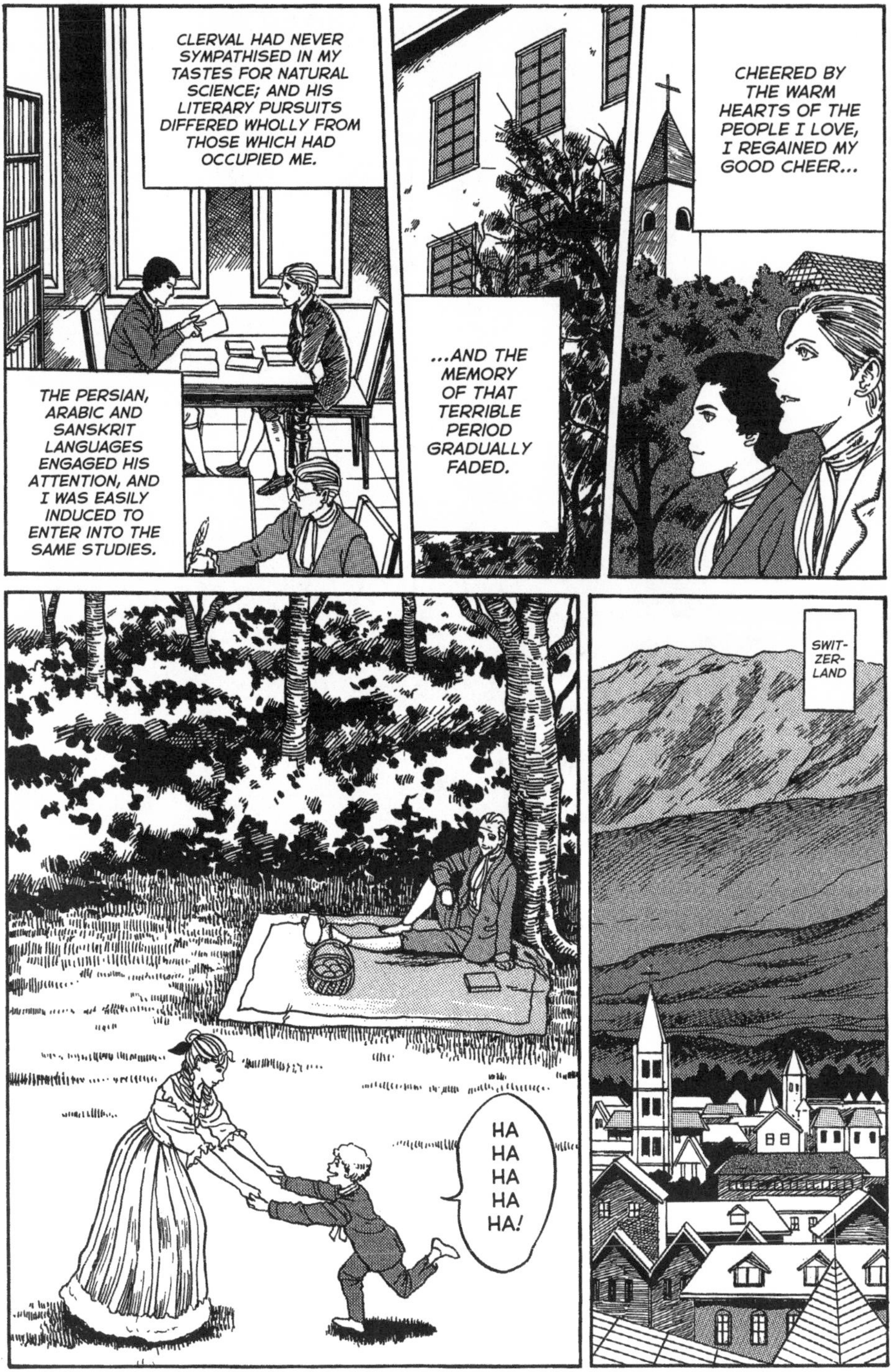
CHEERED BY THE WARM HEARTS OF THE PEOPLE I LOVE, I REGAINED MY GOOD CHEER...
...AND THE MEMORY OF THAT TERRIBLE PERIOD GRADUALLY FADED.
CLERVAL HAD NEVER SYMPATHISED IN MY TASTES FOR NATURAL SCIENCE; AND HIS LITERARY PURSUITS DIFFERED WHOLLY FROM THOSE WHICH HAD OCCUPIED ME.
THE PERSIAN, ARABIC AND SANSKRIT LANGUAGES ENGAGED HIS ATTENTION, AND I WAS EASILY INDUCED TO ENTER INTO THE SAME STUDIES.
SWIT-ZER-LAND
HA HA HA HA HA!

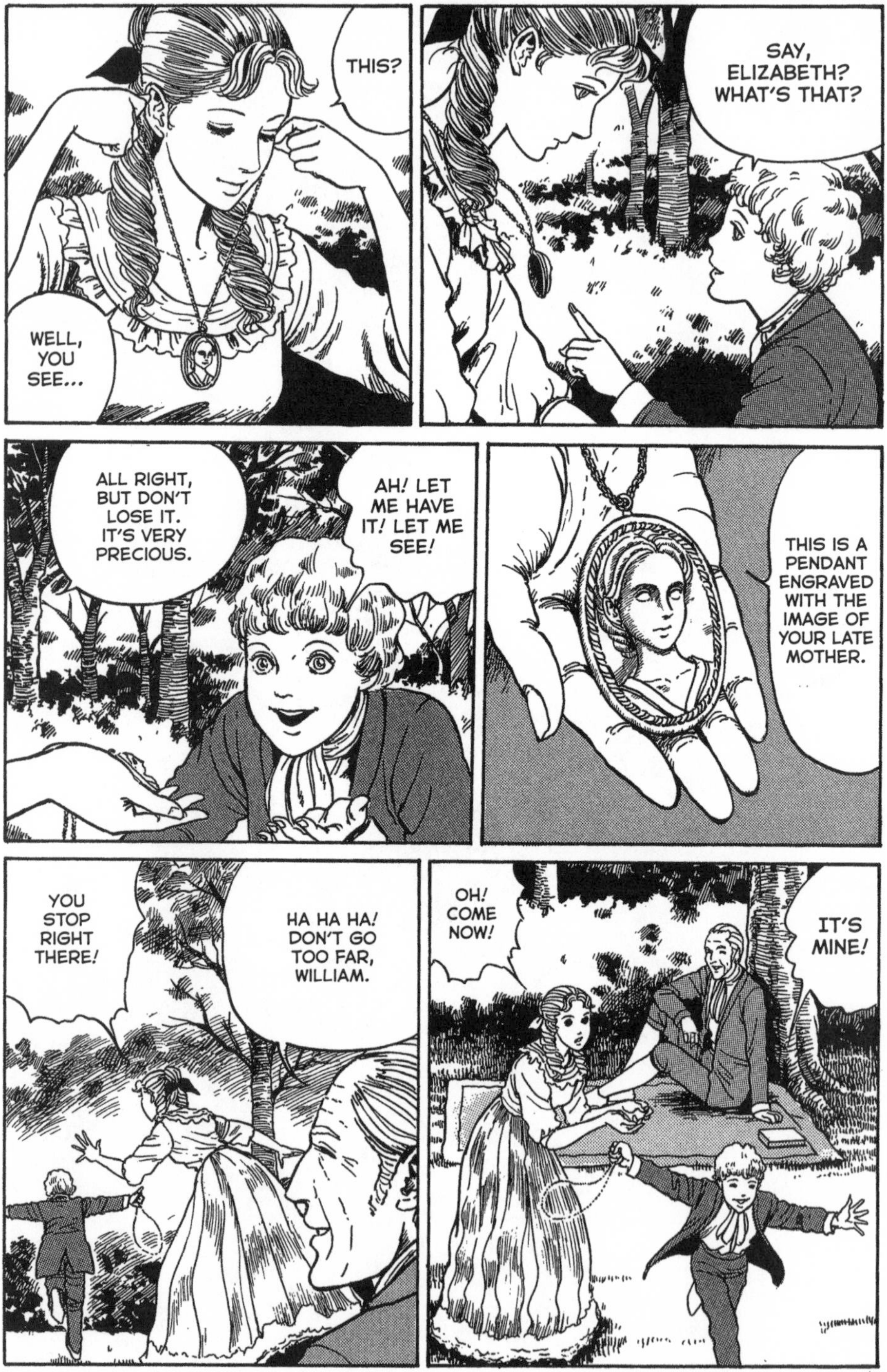
SAY, ELIZABETH? WHAT'S THAT?
THIS?
WELL, YOU SEE...
THIS IS A PENDANT ENGRAVED WITH THE IMAGE OF YOUR LATE MOTHER.
AH! LET ME HAVE IT! LET ME SEE!
ALL RIGHT, BUT DON'T LOSE IT. IT'S VERY PRECIOUS.
IT'S MINE!
OH! COME NOW!
HA HA HA! DON'T GO TOO FAR, WILLIAM.
YOU STOP RIGHT THERE!

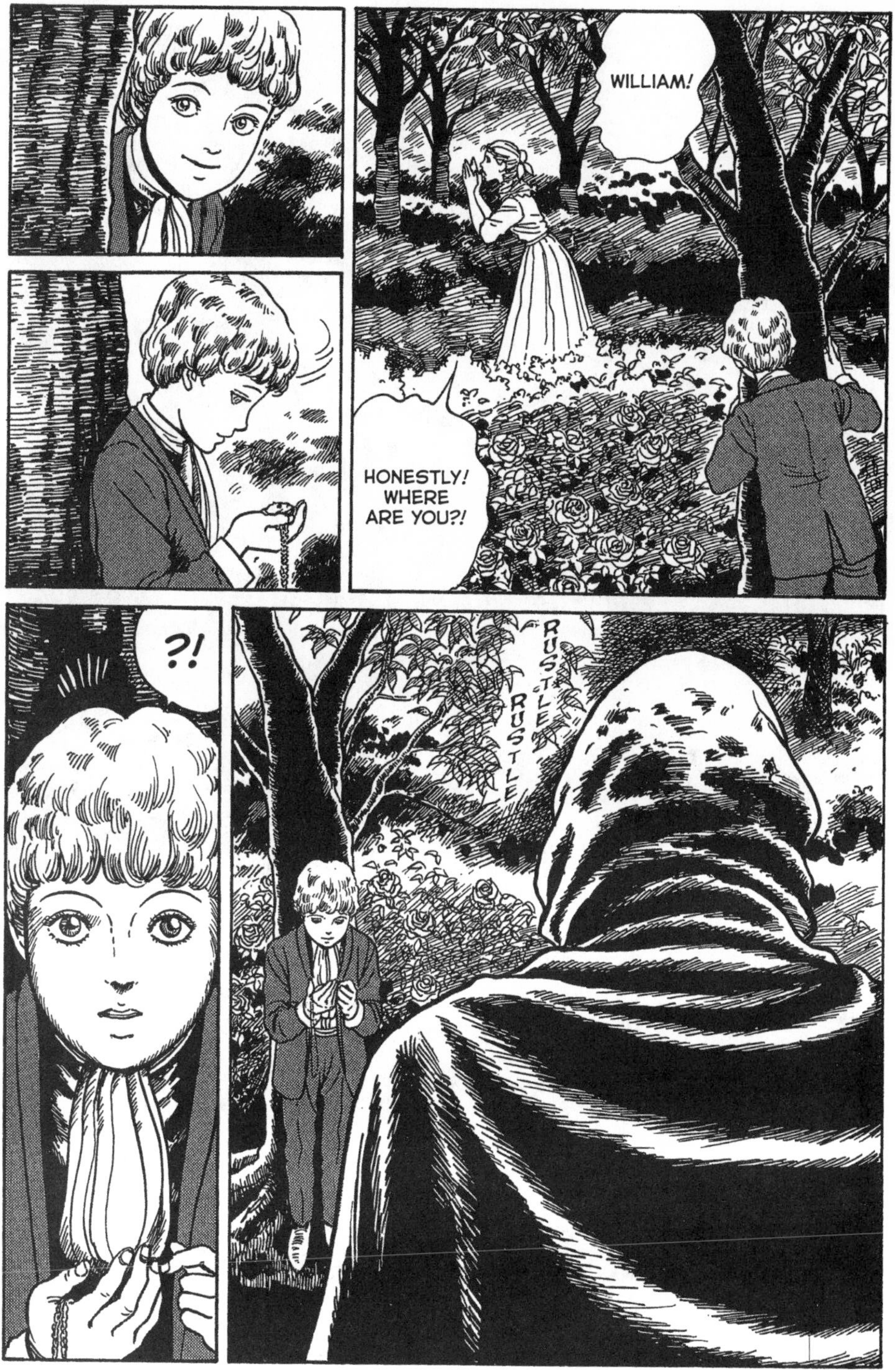
WILLIAM!
HONESTLY! WHERE ARE YOU?!
RUSTLE
RUSTLE
?!

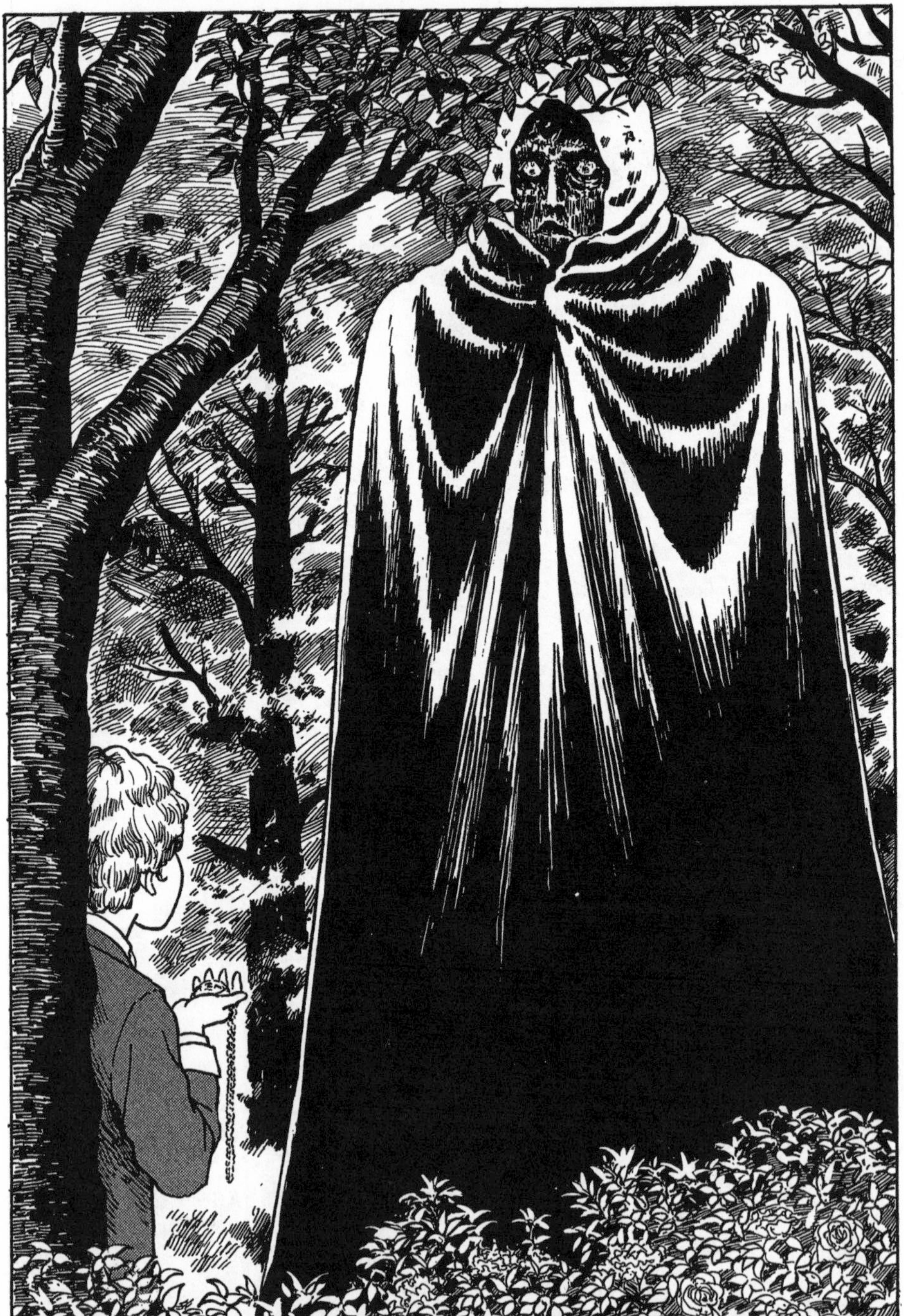

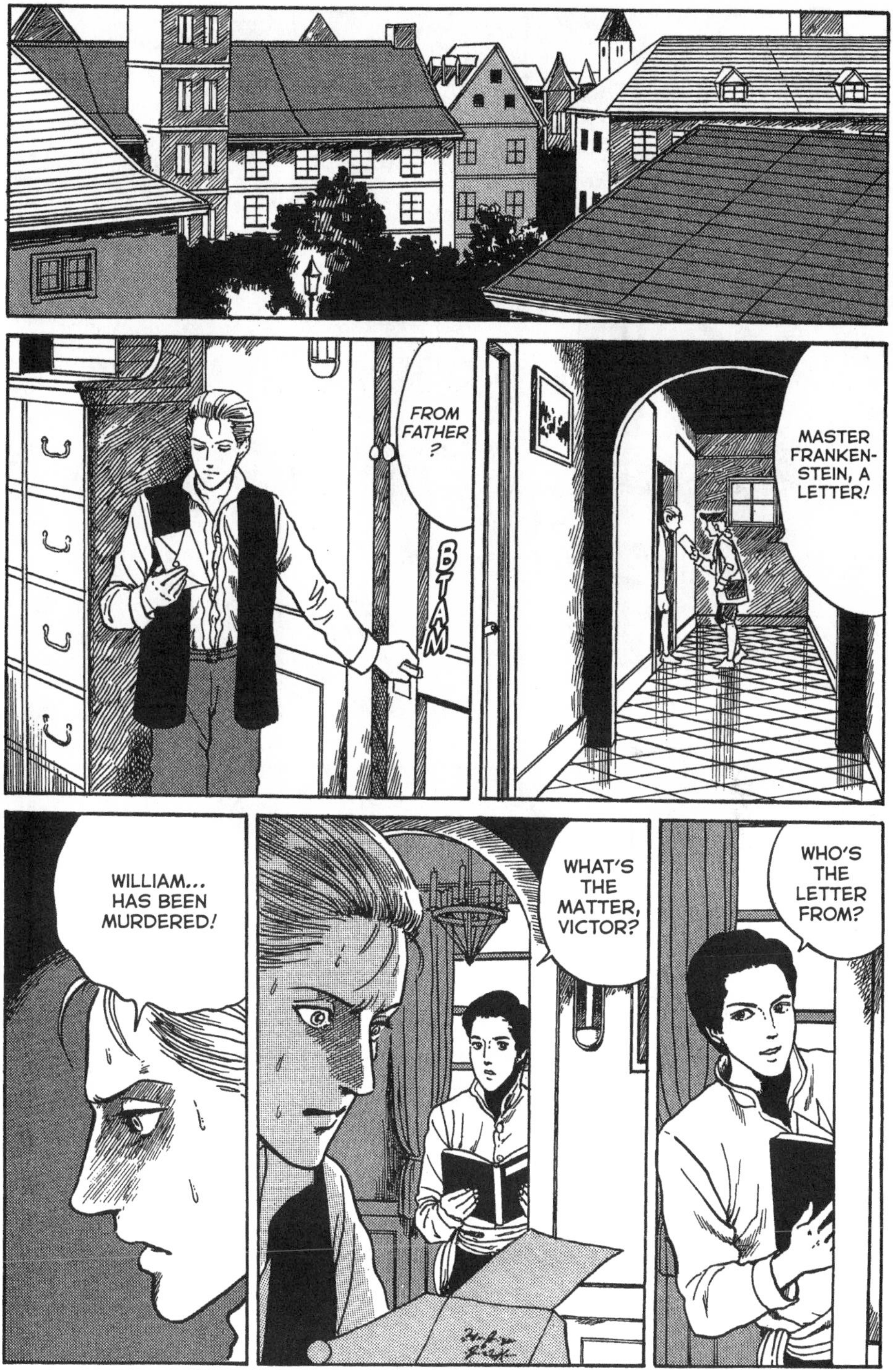
MASTER FRANKEN-STEIN, A LETTER!
FROM FATHER?
BTAM
WHO'S THE LETTER FROM?
WHAT'S THE MATTER, VICTOR?
WILLIAM... HAS BEEN MURDERED!

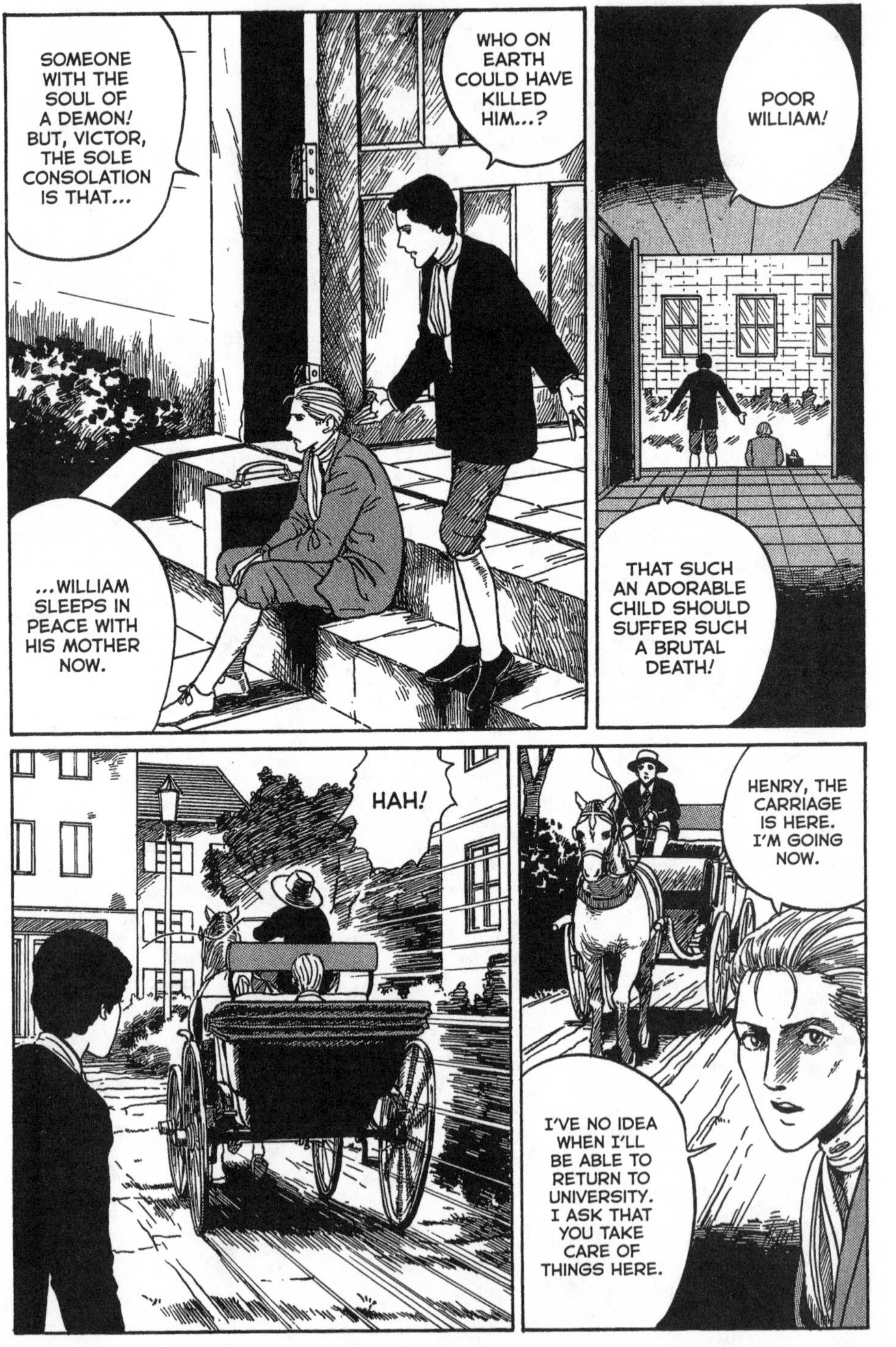
POOR WILLIAM!
THAT SUCH AN ADORABLE CHILD SHOULD SUFFER SUCH A BRUTAL DEATH!
WHO ON EARTH COULD HAVE KILLED HIM...?
SOMEONE WITH THE SOUL OF A DEMON! BUT, VICTOR, THE SOLE CONSOLATION IS THAT...
...WILLIAM SLEEPS IN PEACE WITH HIS MOTHER NOW.
HENRY, THE CARRIAGE IS HERE. I'M GOING NOW.
I'VE NO IDEA WHEN I'LL BE ABLE TO RETURN TO UNIVERSITY. I ASK THAT YOU TAKE CARE OF THINGS HERE.
HAH!

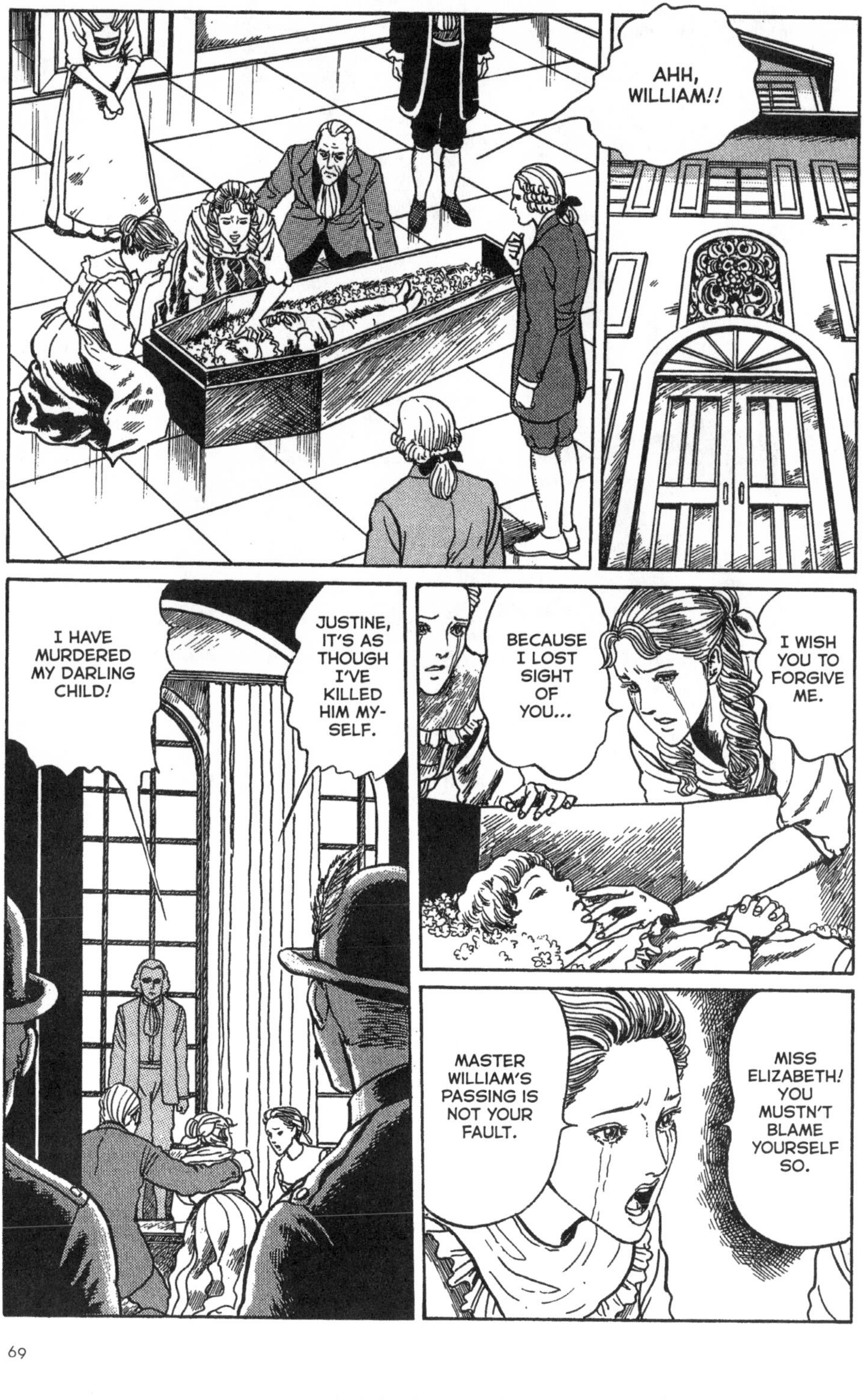
AHH, WILLIAM!!
I WISH YOU TO FORGIVE ME.
BECAUSE I LOST SIGHT OF YOU...
MISS ELIZABETH! YOU MUSTN'T BLAME YOURSELF SO.
MASTER WILLIAM'S PASSING IS NOT YOUR FAULT.
JUSTINE, IT'S AS THOUGH I'VE KILLED HIM MY-SELF.
I HAVE MURDERED MY DARLING CHILD!

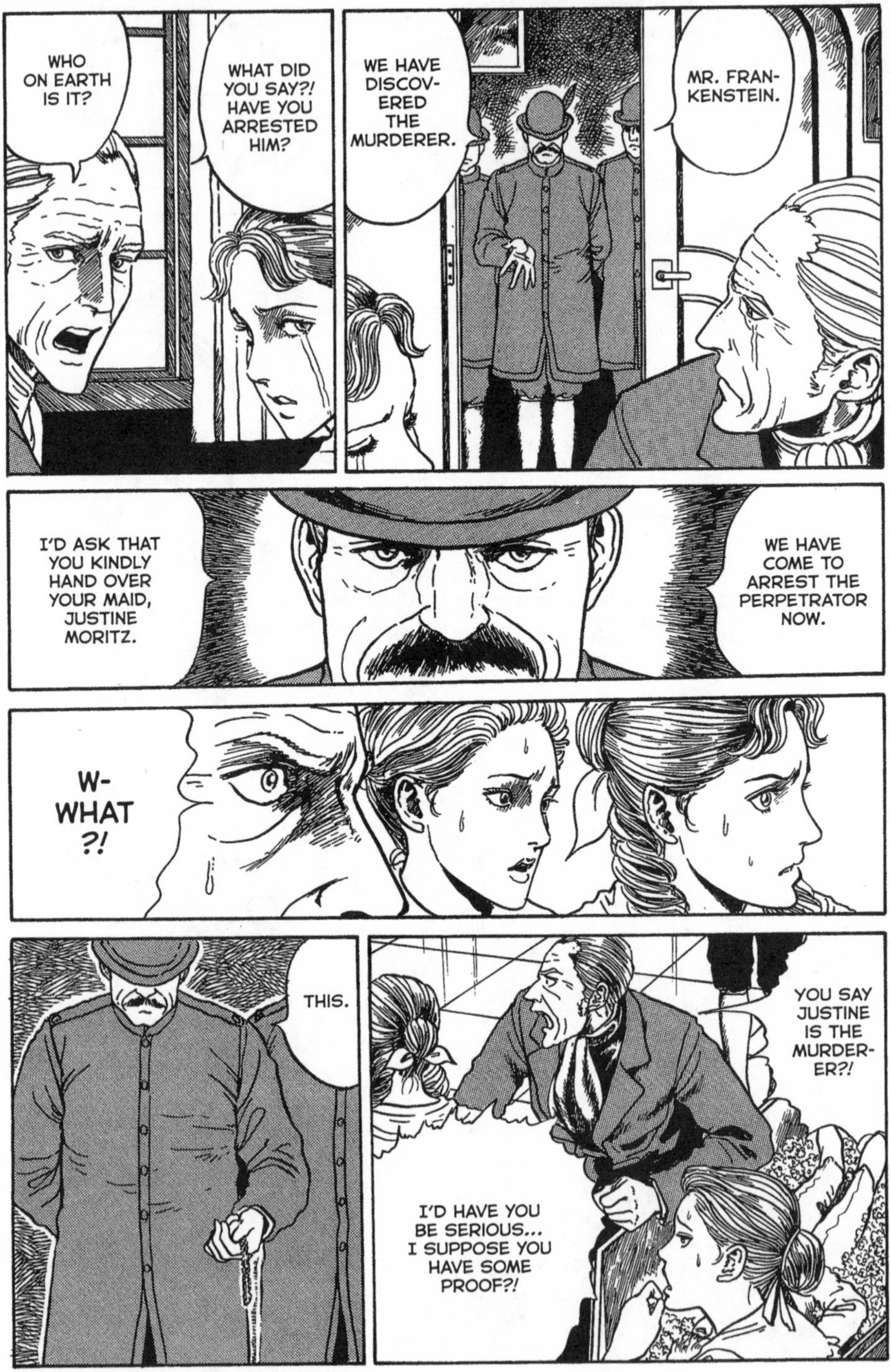
MR. FRANKENSTEIN.
WE HAVE DISCOVERED THE MURDERER.
WHAT DID YOU SAY?! HAVE YOU ARRESTED HIM?
WHO ON EARTH IS IT?
WE HAVE COME TO ARREST THE PERPETRATOR NOW.
I'D ASK THAT YOU KINDLY HAND OVER YOUR MAID, JUSTINE MORITZ.
W-WHAT?!
YOU SAY JUSTINE IS THE MURDERER?!
I'D HAVE YOU BE SERIOUS... I SUPPOSE YOU HAVE SOME PROOF?!
THIS.

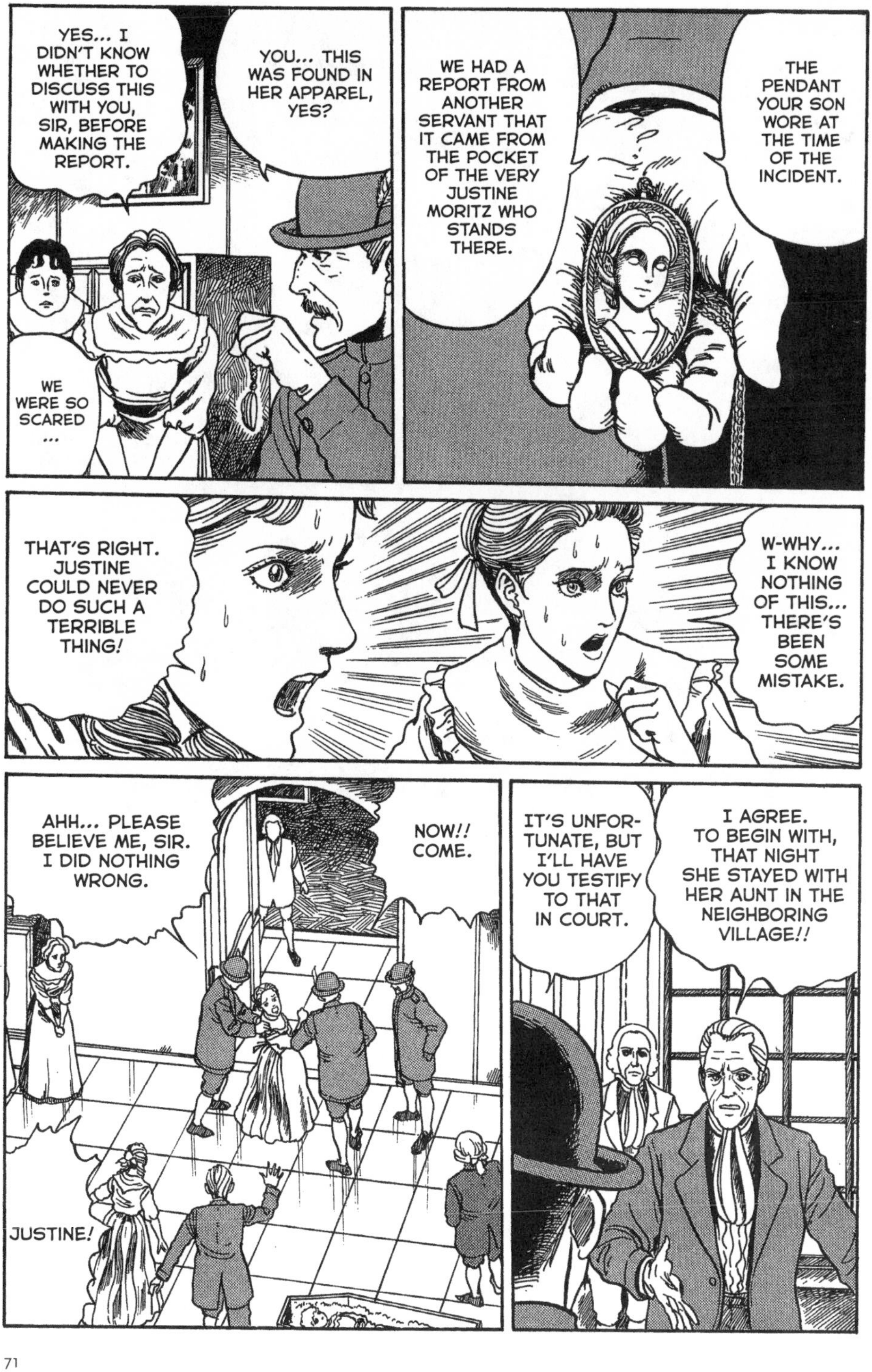
THE PENDANT YOUR SON WORE AT THE TIME OF THE INCIDENT.
WE HAD A REPORT FROM ANOTHER SERVANT THAT IT CAME FROM THE POCKET OF THE VERY JUSTINE MORITZ WHO STANDS THERE.
YOU... THIS WAS FOUND IN HER APPAREL, YES?
YES... I DIDN'T KNOW WHETHER TO DISCUSS THIS WITH YOU, SIR, BEFORE MAKING THE REPORT.
WE WERE SO SCARED ...
W-WHY... I KNOW NOTHING OF THIS... THERE'S BEEN SOME MISTAKE.
THAT'S RIGHT. JUSTINE COULD NEVER DO SUCH A TERRIBLE THING!
I AGREE. TO BEGIN WITH, THAT NIGHT SHE STAYED WITH HER AUNT IN THE NEIGHBORING VILLAGE!!
IT'S UNFORTUNATE, BUT I'LL HAVE YOU TESTIFY TO THAT IN COURT.
NOW!! COME.
AHH... PLEASE BELIEVE ME, SIR. I DID NOTHING WRONG.
JUSTINE!

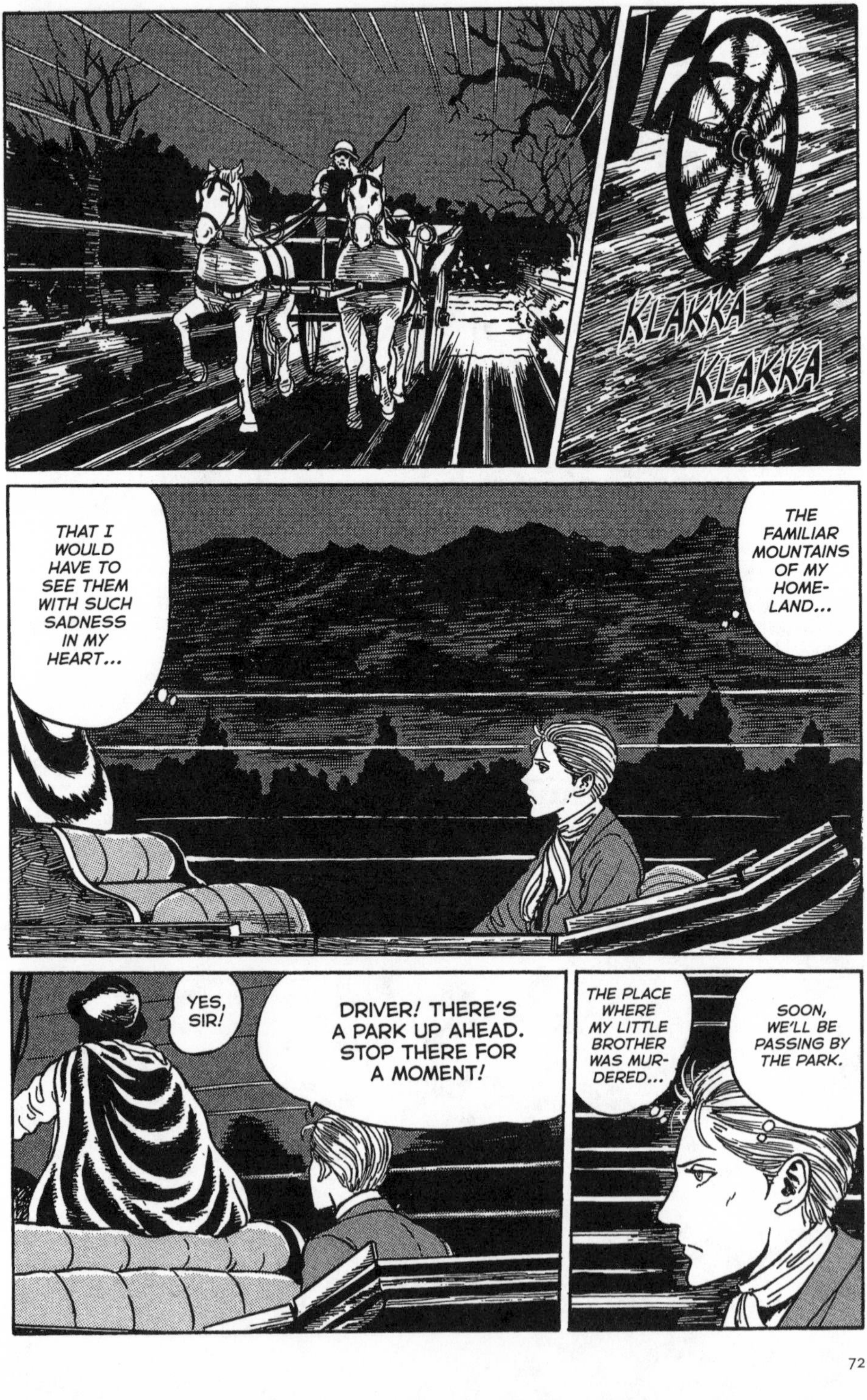
KLAKKA KLAKKA
THE FAMILIAR MOUNTAINS OF MY HOMELAND...
THAT I WOULD HAVE TO SEE THEM WITH SUCH SADNESS IN MY HEART...
SOON, WE'LL BE PASSING BY THE PARK.
THE PLACE WHERE MY LITTLE BROTHER WAS MURDERED...
DRIVER! THERE'S A PARK UP AHEAD. STOP THERE FOR A MOMENT!
YES, SIR!

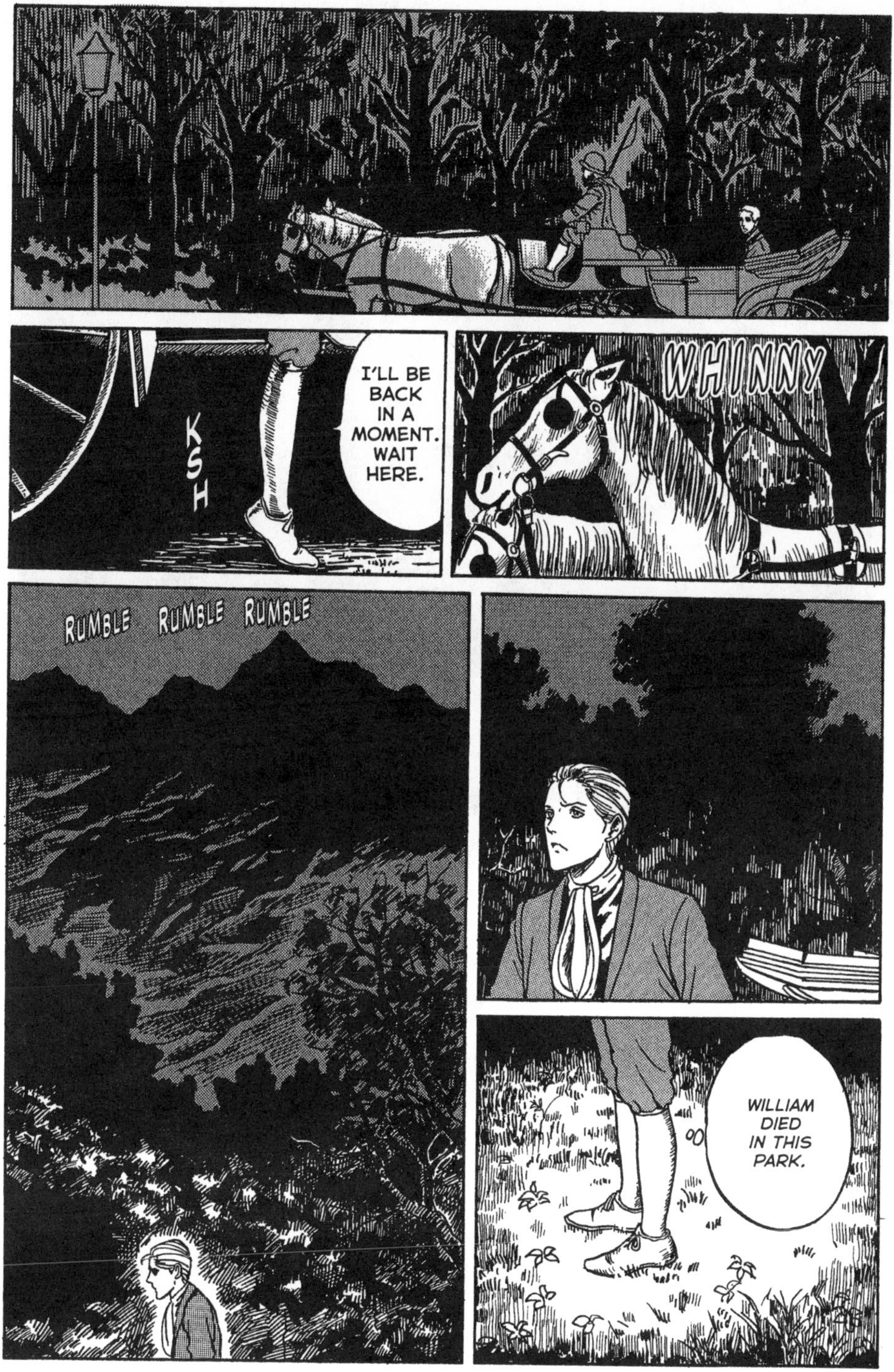
WHINNY
I'LL BE BACK IN A MOMENT. WAIT HERE.
KSH
WILLIAM DIED IN THIS PARK.
RUMBLE RUMBLE RUMBLE

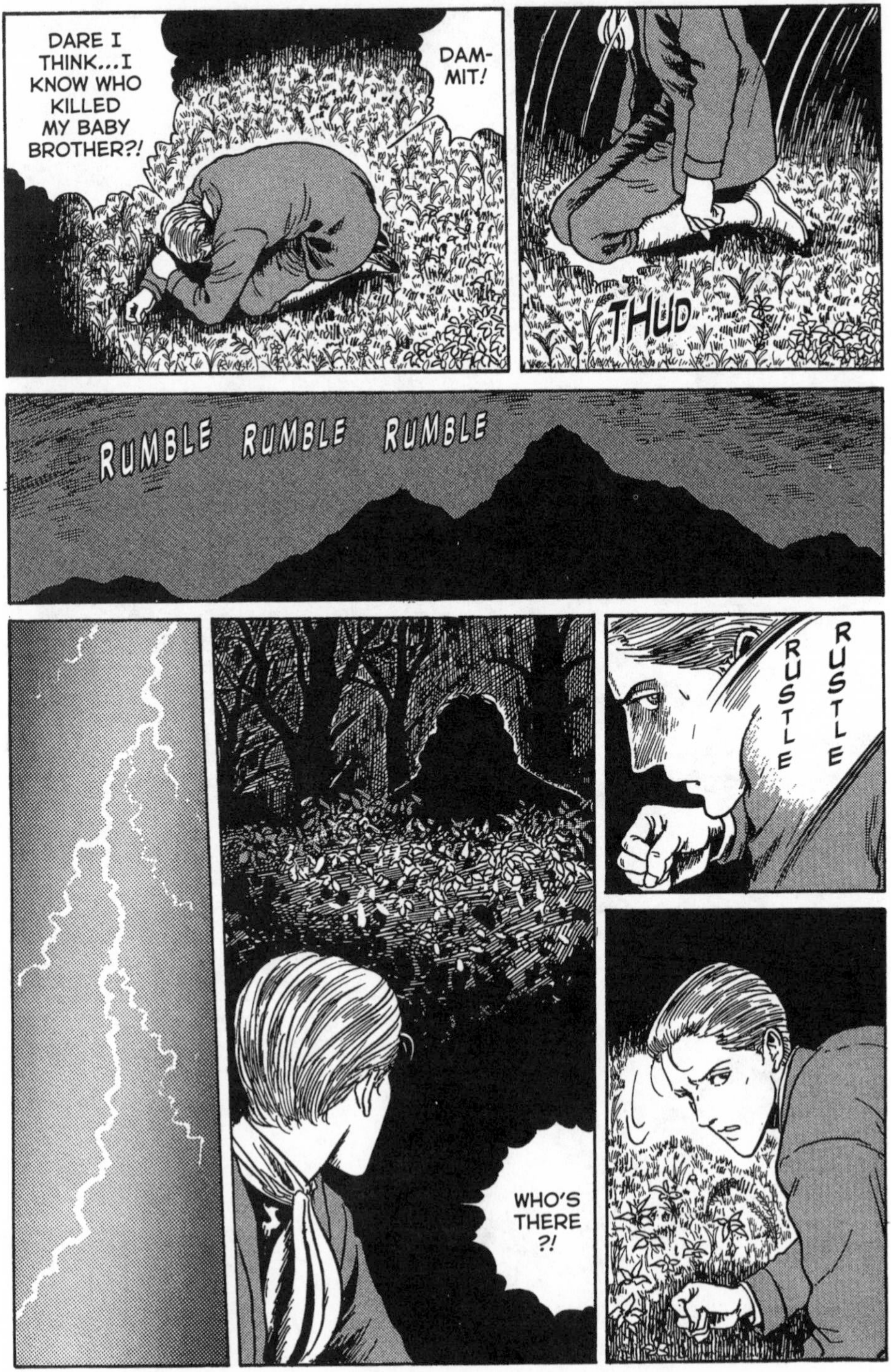
THUD
DAM-MIT!
DARE I THINK...I KNOW WHO KILLED MY BABY BROTHER?!
RUMBLE RUMBLE RUMBLE
RUSTLE RUSTLE
WHO'S THERE ?!

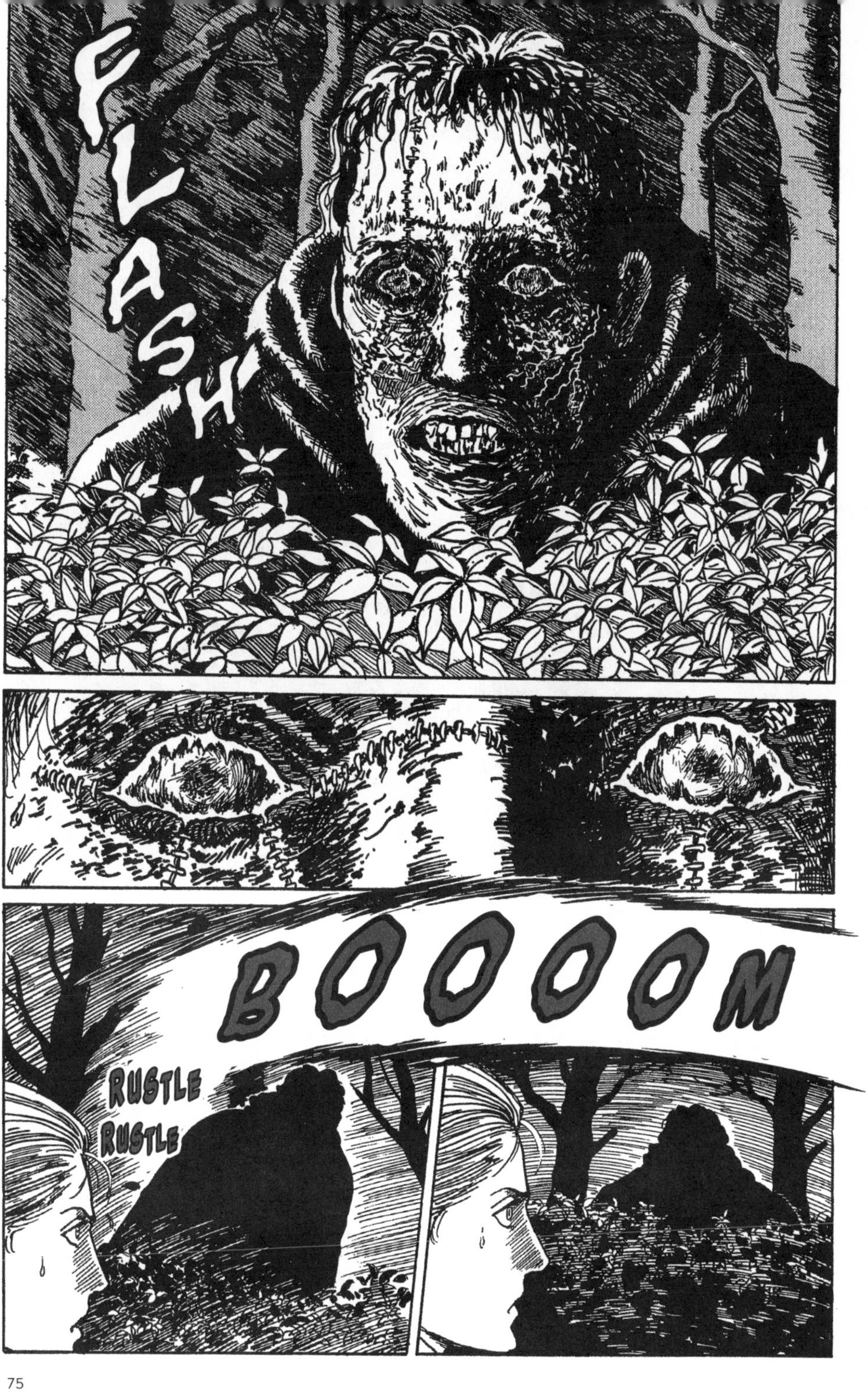
FLASH
BOOOOM
RUSTLE RUSTLE

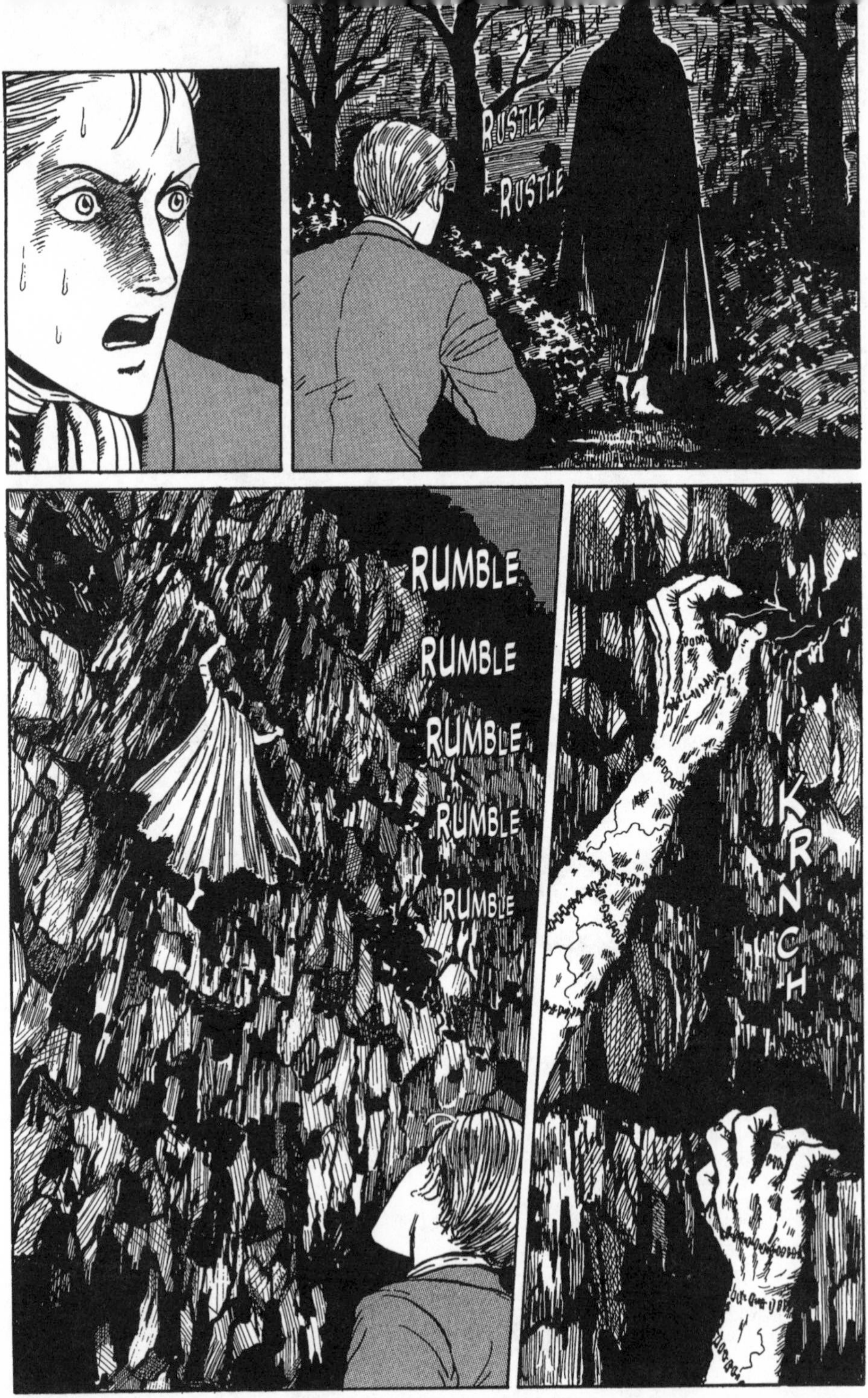
RUSTLE
RUSTLE
KRNCH
RUMBLE
RUMBLE
RUMBLE
RUMBLE
RUMBLE

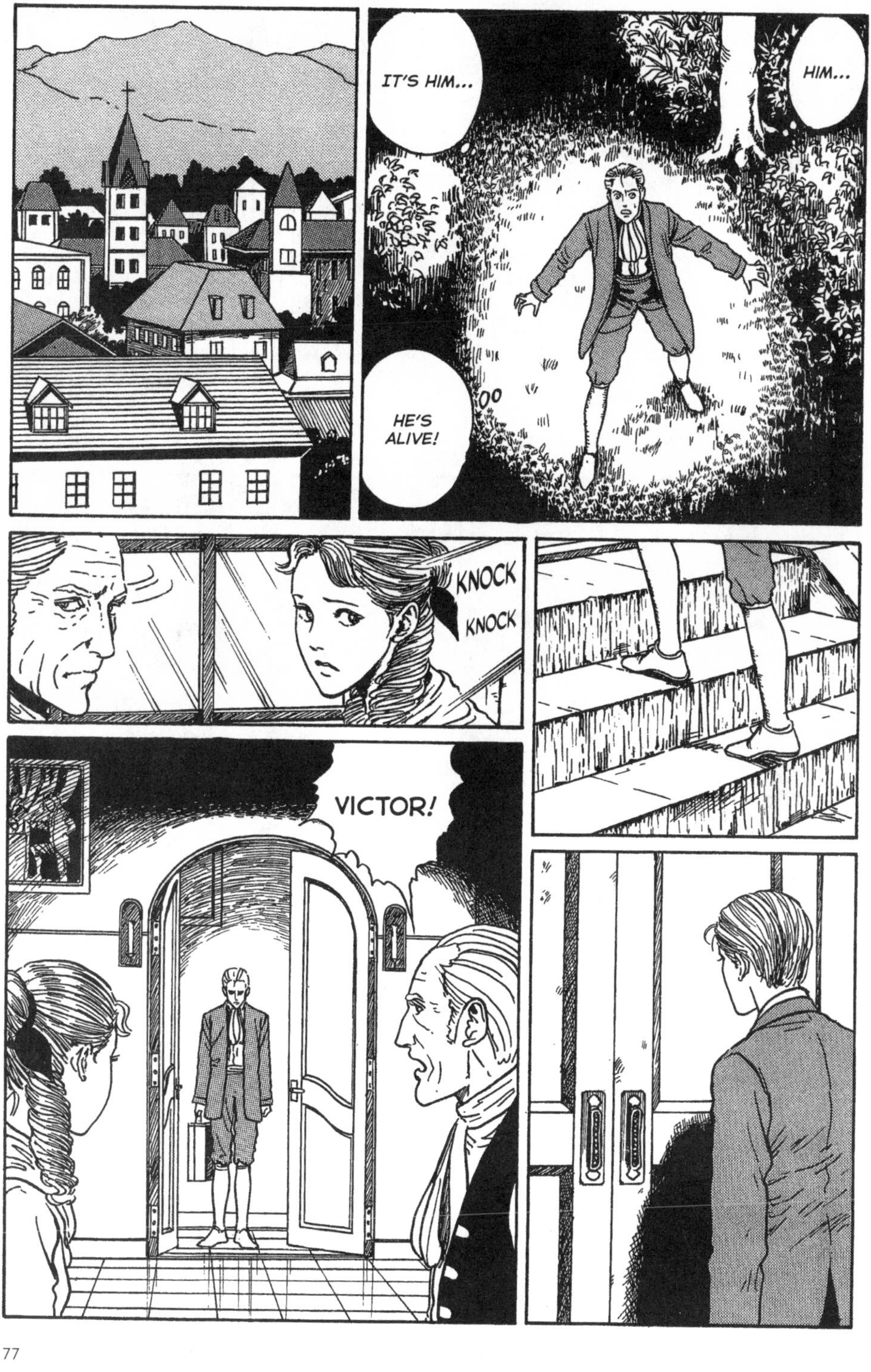
HIM...
IT'S HIM...
HE'S ALIVE!
KNOCK
KNOCK
VICTOR!

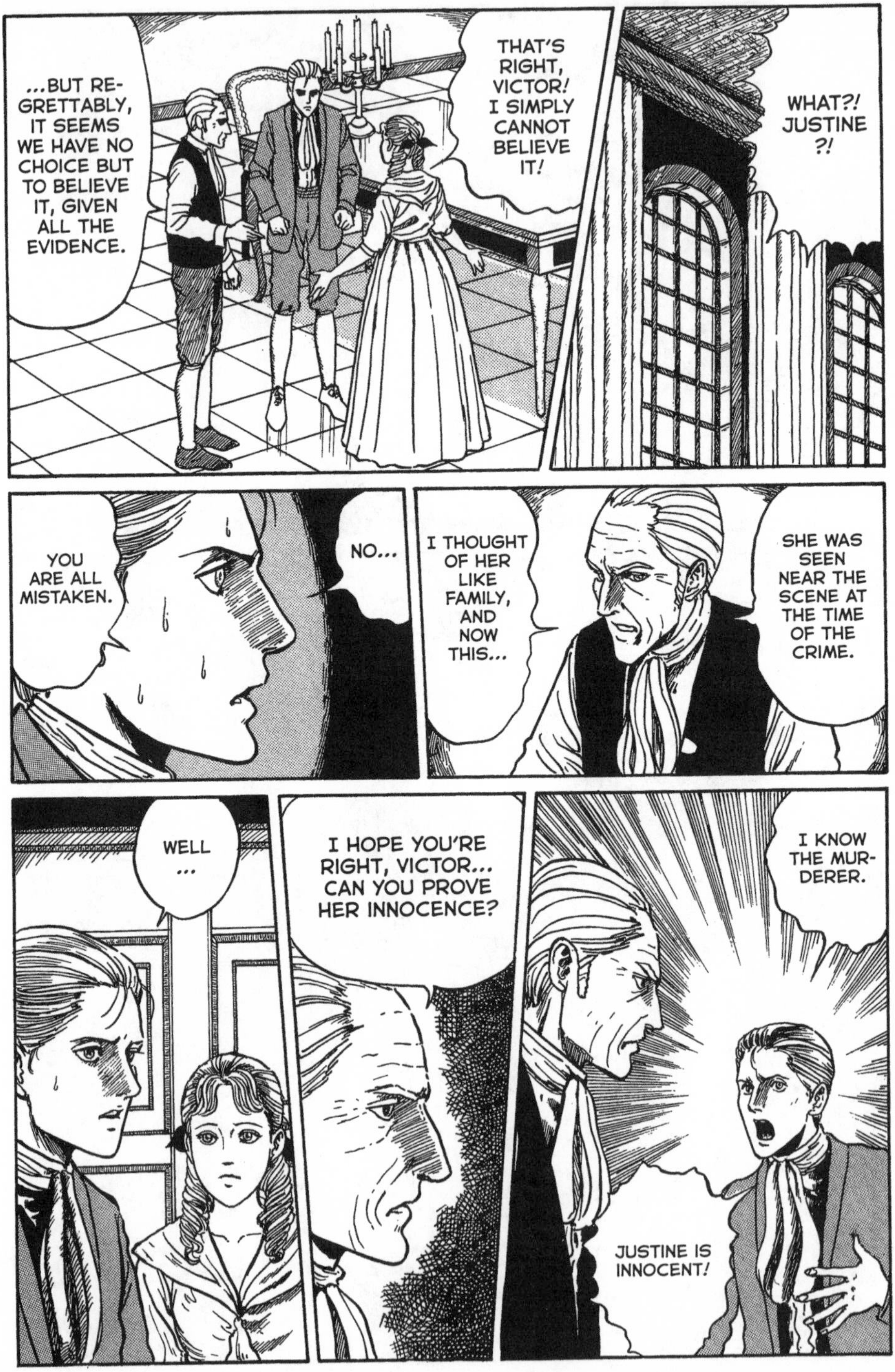
WHAT?! JUSTINE?!
THAT'S RIGHT, VICTOR! I SIMPLY CANNOT BELIEVE IT!
...BUT RE-GRETTABLY, IT SEEMS WE HAVE NO CHOICE BUT TO BELIEVE IT, GIVEN ALL THE EVIDENCE.
SHE WAS SEEN NEAR THE SCENE AT THE TIME OF THE CRIME.
I THOUGHT OF HER LIKE FAMILY, AND NOW THIS...
NO...
YOU ARE ALL MISTAKEN.
I KNOW THE MUR-DERER.
JUSTINE IS INNOCENT!
I HOPE YOU'RE RIGHT, VICTOR... CAN YOU PROVE HER INNOCENCE?
WELL ...

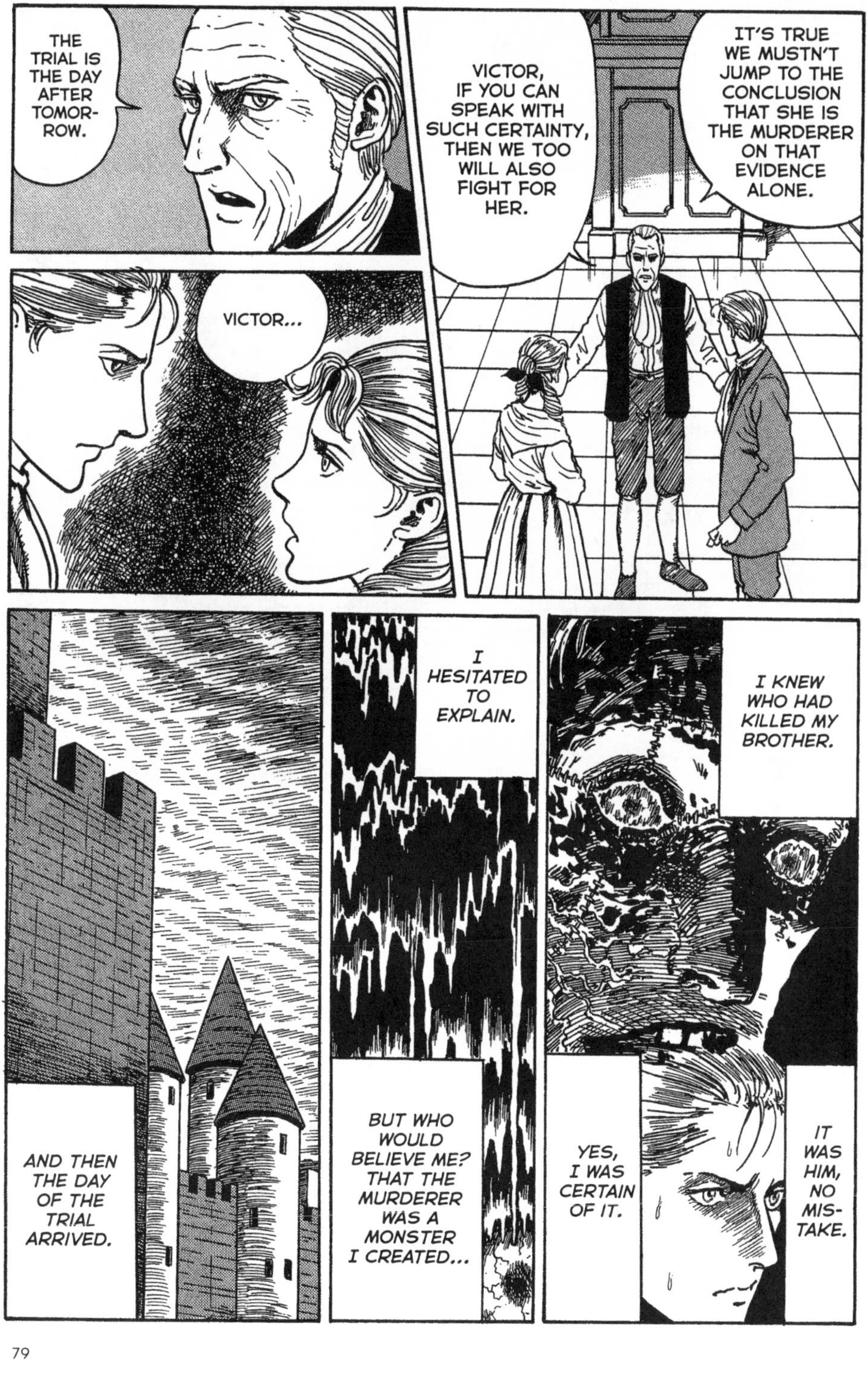
IT'S TRUE WE MUSTN'T JUMP TO THE CONCLUSION THAT SHE IS THE MURDERER ON THAT EVIDENCE ALONE.
VICTOR, IF YOU CAN SPEAK WITH SUCH CERTAINTY, THEN WE TOO WILL ALSO FIGHT FOR HER.
THE TRIAL IS THE DAY AFTER TOMOR-ROW.
VICTOR...
I KNEW WHO HAD KILLED MY BROTHER.
IT WAS HIM, NO MIS-TAKE.
YES, I WAS CERTAIN OF IT.
I HESITATED TO EXPLAIN.
BUT WHO WOULD BELIEVE ME? THAT THE MURDERER WAS A MONSTER I CREATED...
AND THEN THE DAY OF THE TRIAL ARRIVED.

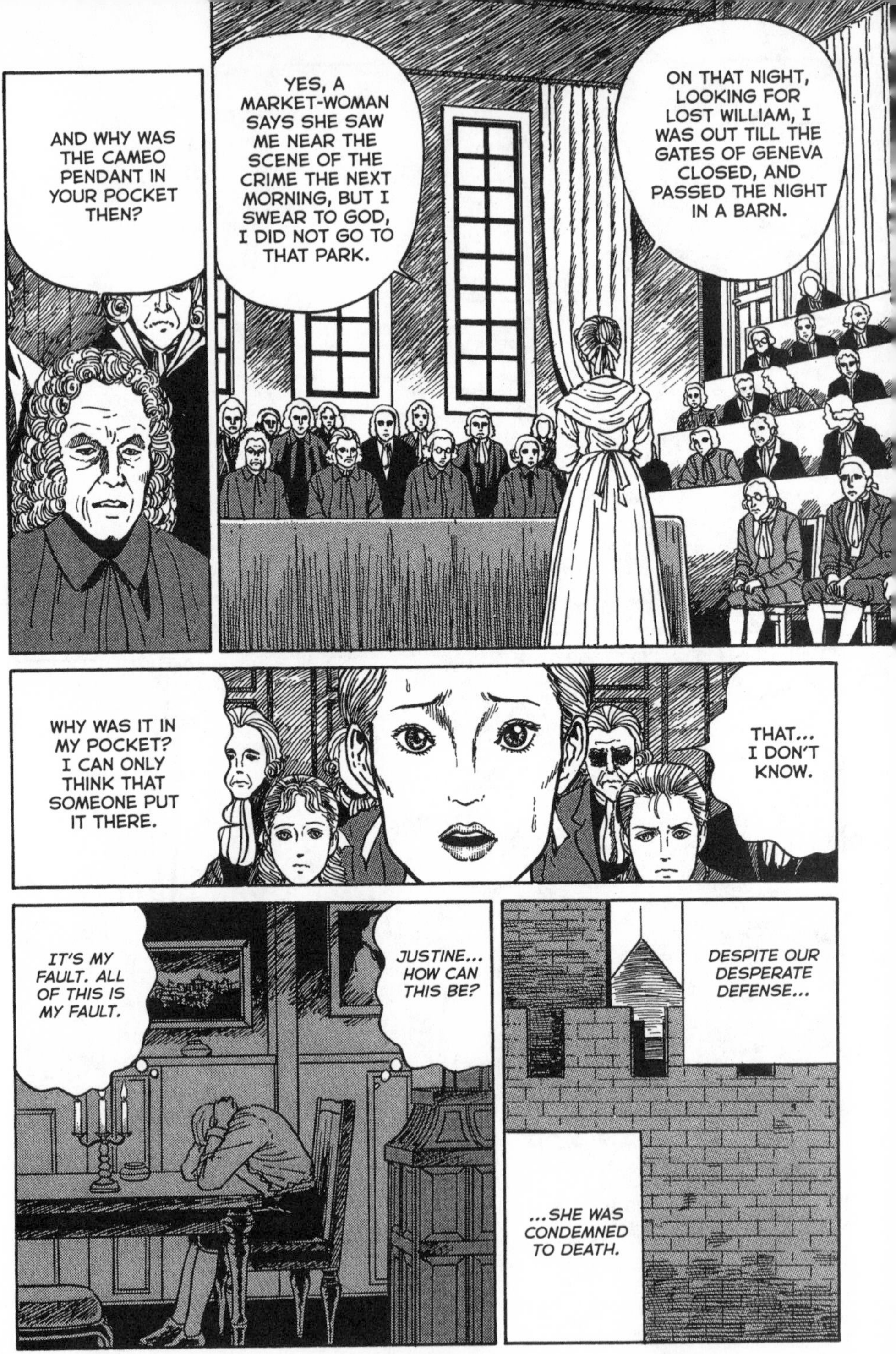
ON THAT NIGHT, LOOKING FOR LOST WILLIAM, I WAS OUT TILL THE GATES OF GENEVA CLOSED, AND PASSED THE NIGHT IN A BARN.
YES, A MARKET-WOMAN SAYS SHE SAW ME NEAR THE SCENE OF THE CRIME THE NEXT MORNING, BUT I SWEAR TO GOD, I DID NOT GO TO THAT PARK.
AND WHY WAS THE CAMEO PENDANT IN YOUR POCKET THEN?
THAT... I DON'T KNOW.
WHY WAS IT IN MY POCKET? I CAN ONLY THINK THAT SOMEONE PUT IT THERE.
DESPITE OUR DESPERATE DEFENSE...
...SHE WAS CONDEMNED TO DEATH.
JUSTINE... HOW CAN THIS BE?
IT'S MY FAULT. ALL OF THIS IS MY FAULT.

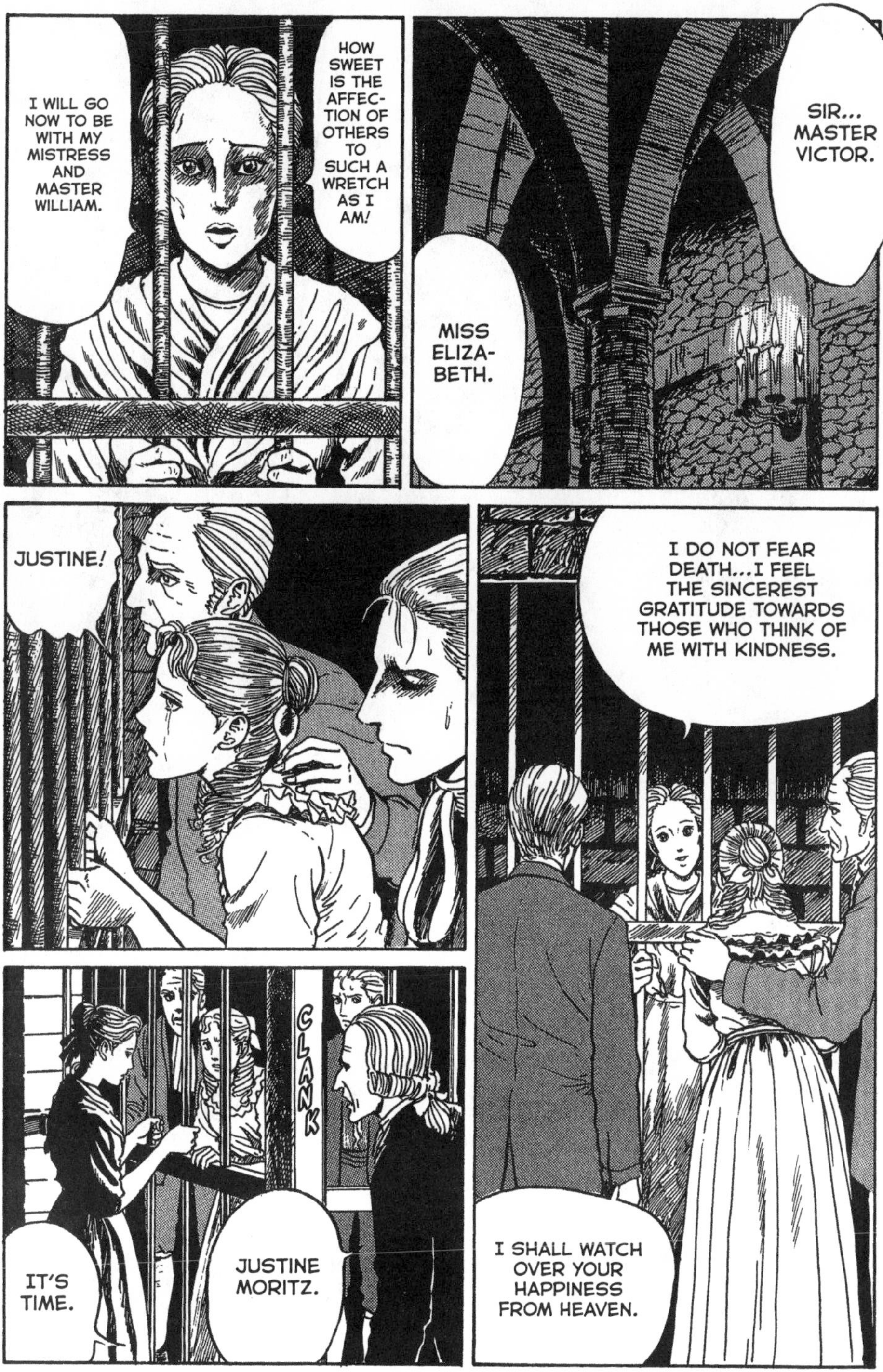
SIR... MASTER VICTOR.
MISS ELIZA-BETH.
HOW SWEET IS THE AFFEC-TION OF OTHERS TO SUCH A WRETCH AS I AM!
I WILL GO NOW TO BE WITH MY MISTRESS AND MASTER WILLIAM.
I DO NOT FEAR DEATH...I FEEL THE SINCEREST GRATITUDE TOWARDS THOSE WHO THINK OF ME WITH KINDNESS.
I SHALL WATCH OVER YOUR HAPPINESS FROM HEAVEN.
JUSTINE!
CLANK
JUSTINE MORITZ.
IT'S TIME.

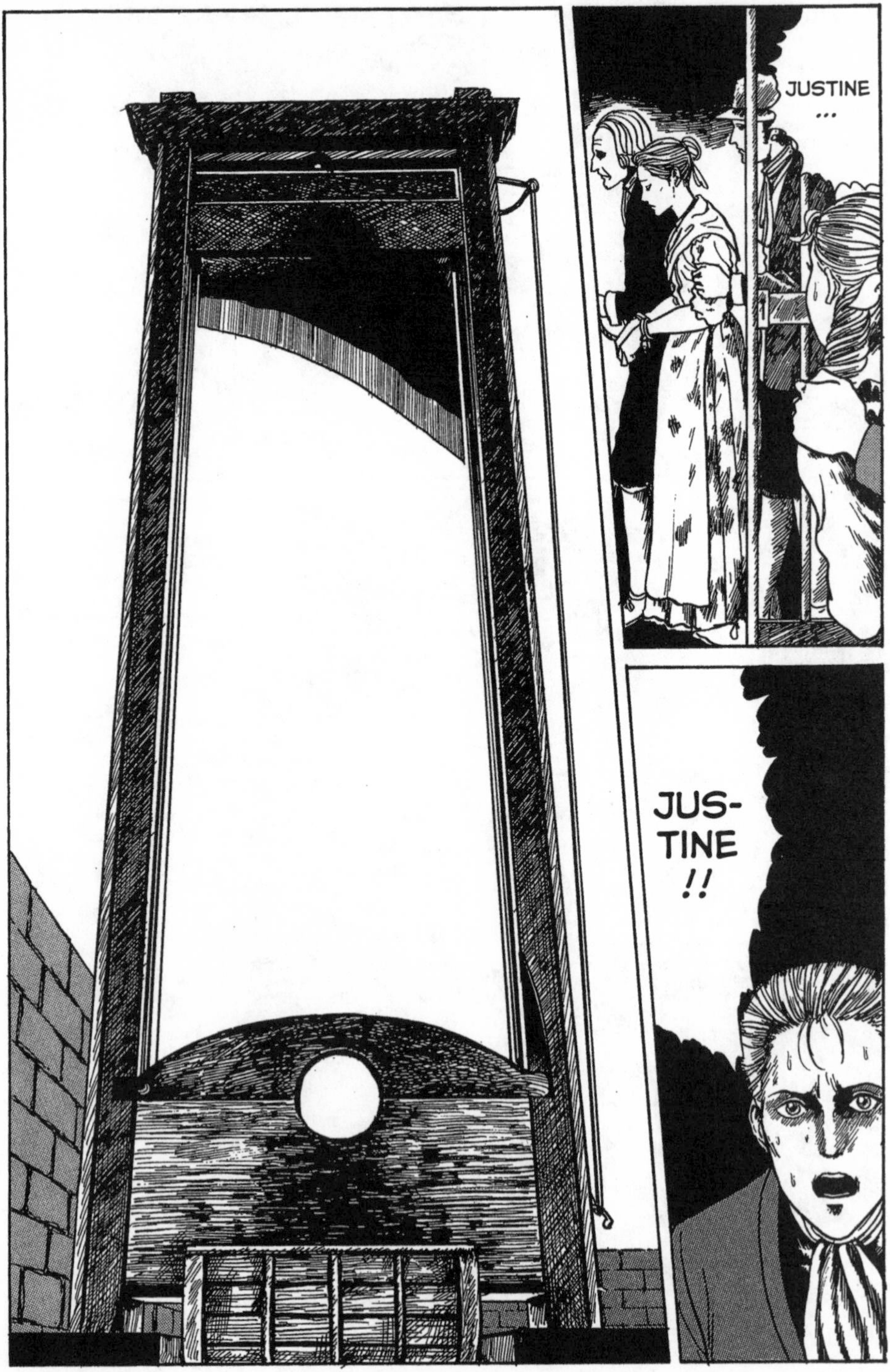
JUSTINE ...
JUS-TINE !!

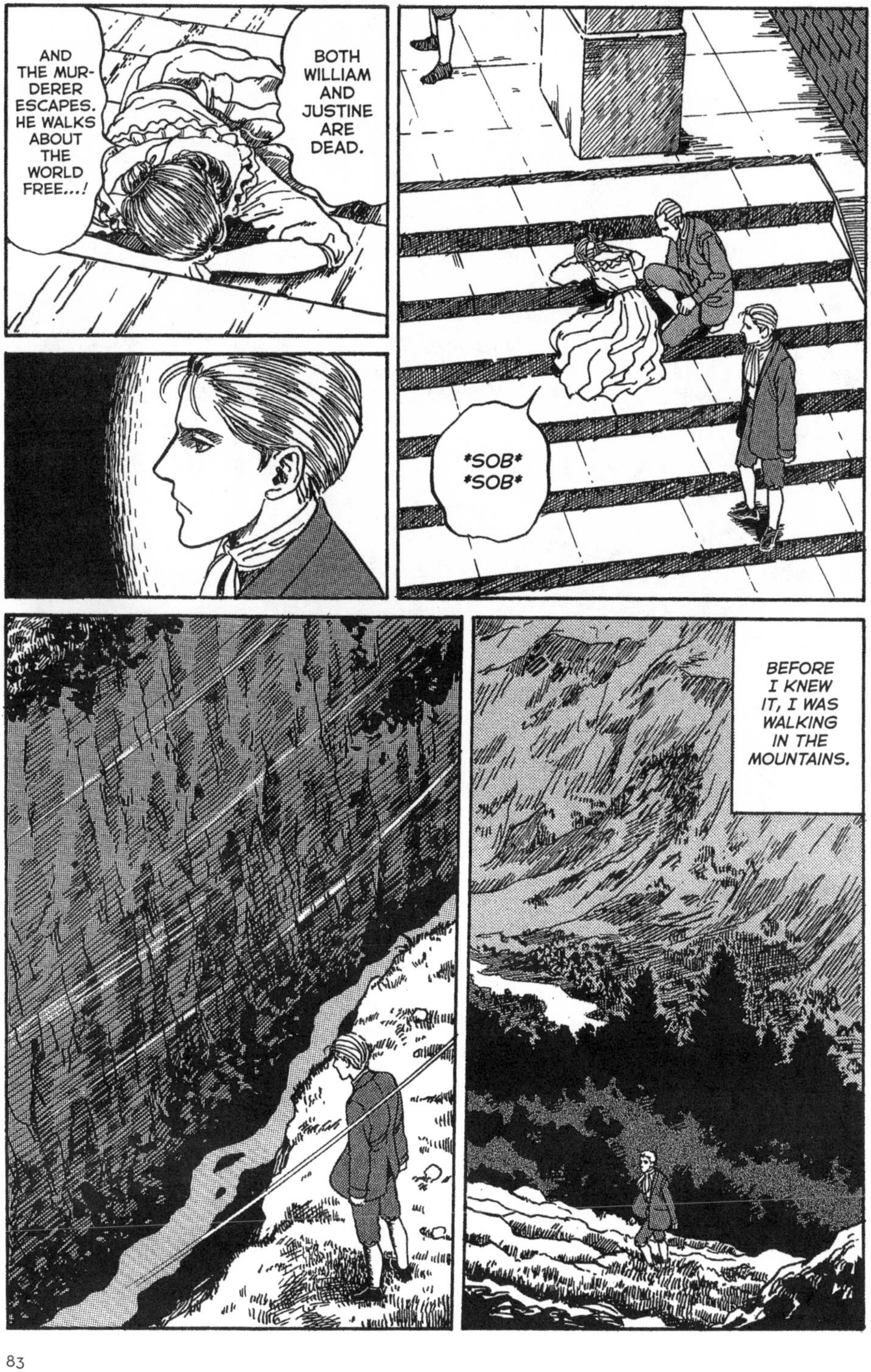
SOB *SOB*
BOTH WILLIAM AND JUSTINE ARE DEAD.
AND THE MURDERER ESCAPES. HE WALKS ABOUT THE WORLD FREE...!
BEFORE I KNEW IT, I WAS WALKING IN THE MOUNTAINS.

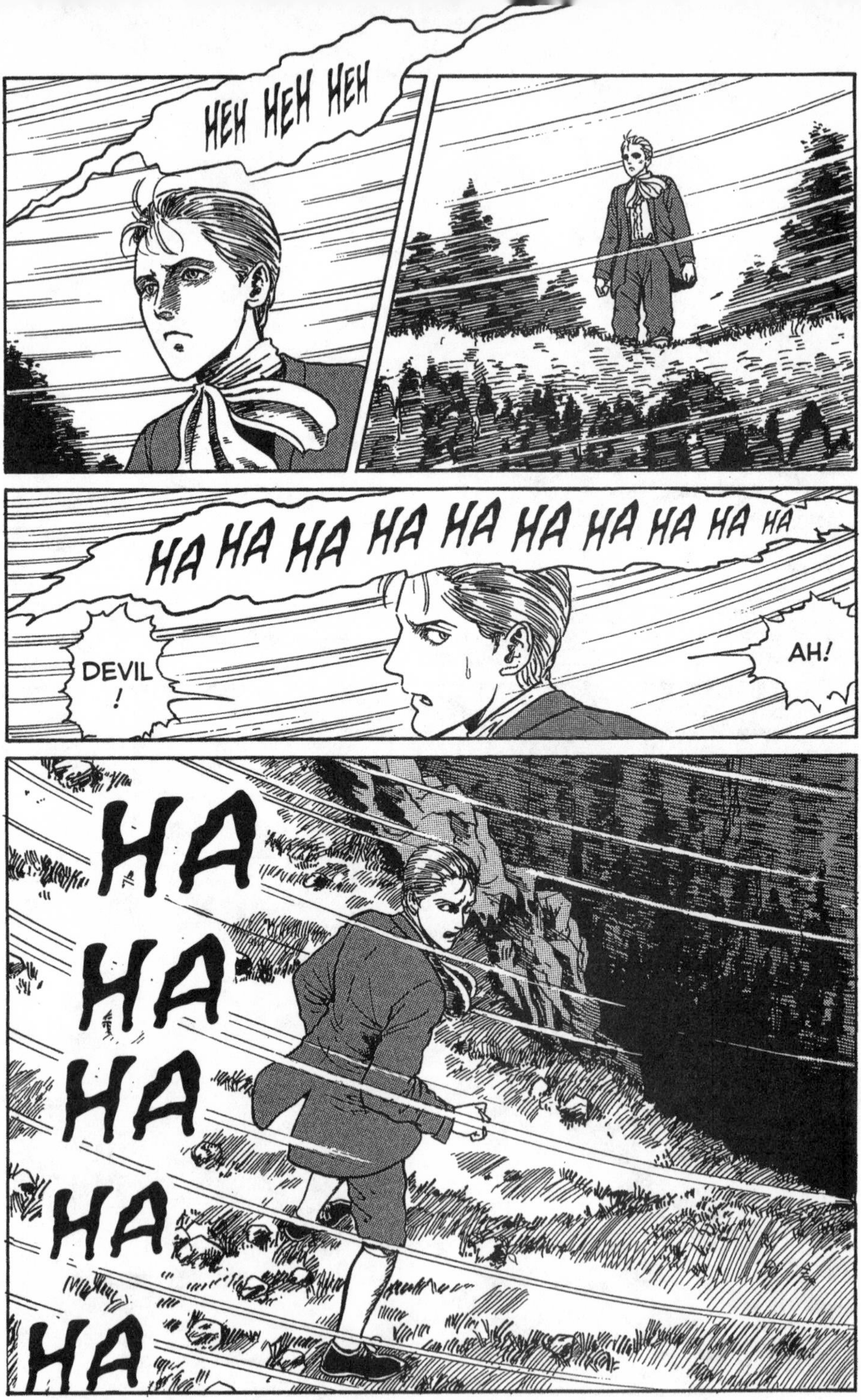
HEH HEH HEH
HA HA HA HA HA HA HA HA HA HA
AH!
DEVIL!
HA HA HA HA HA

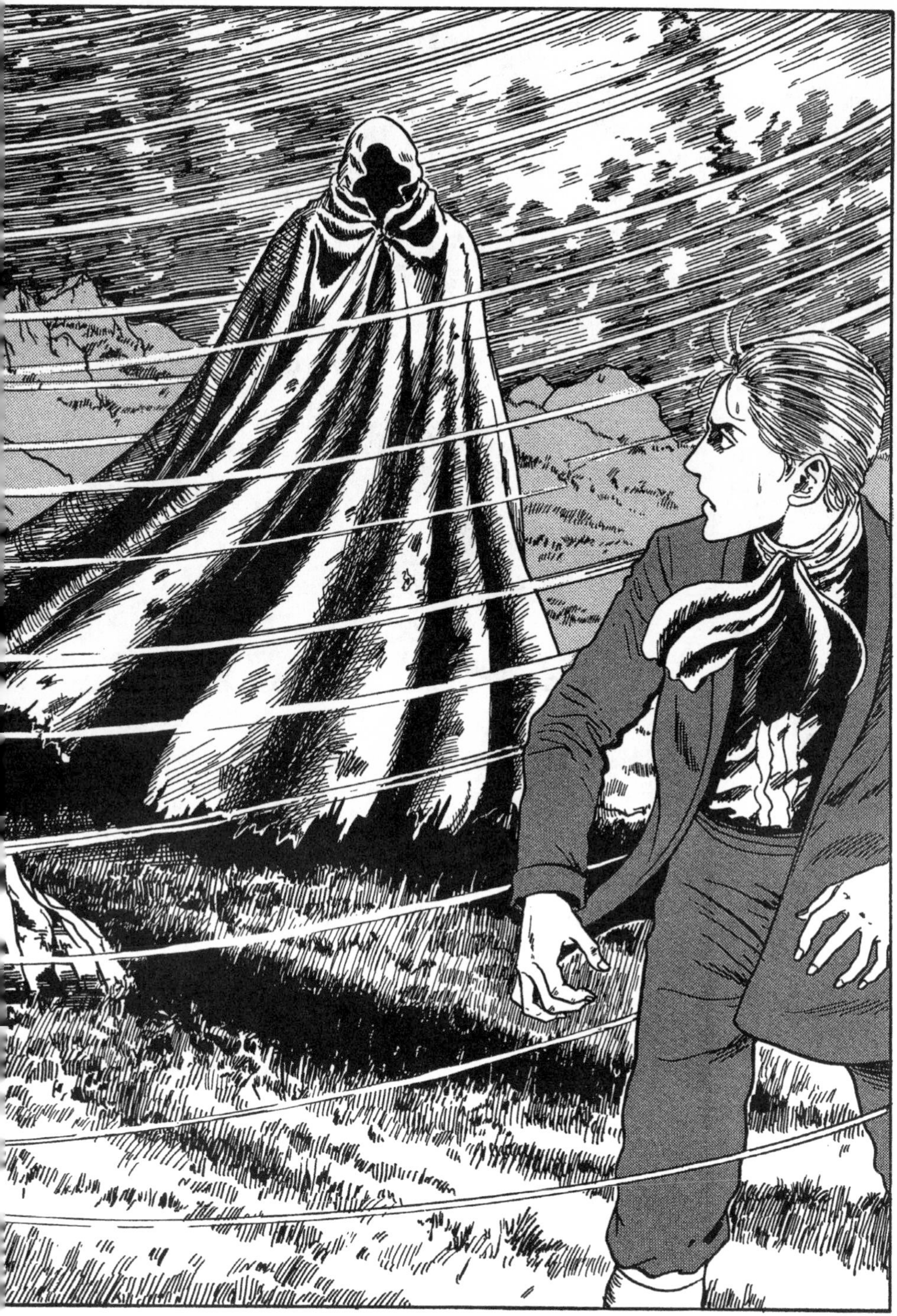

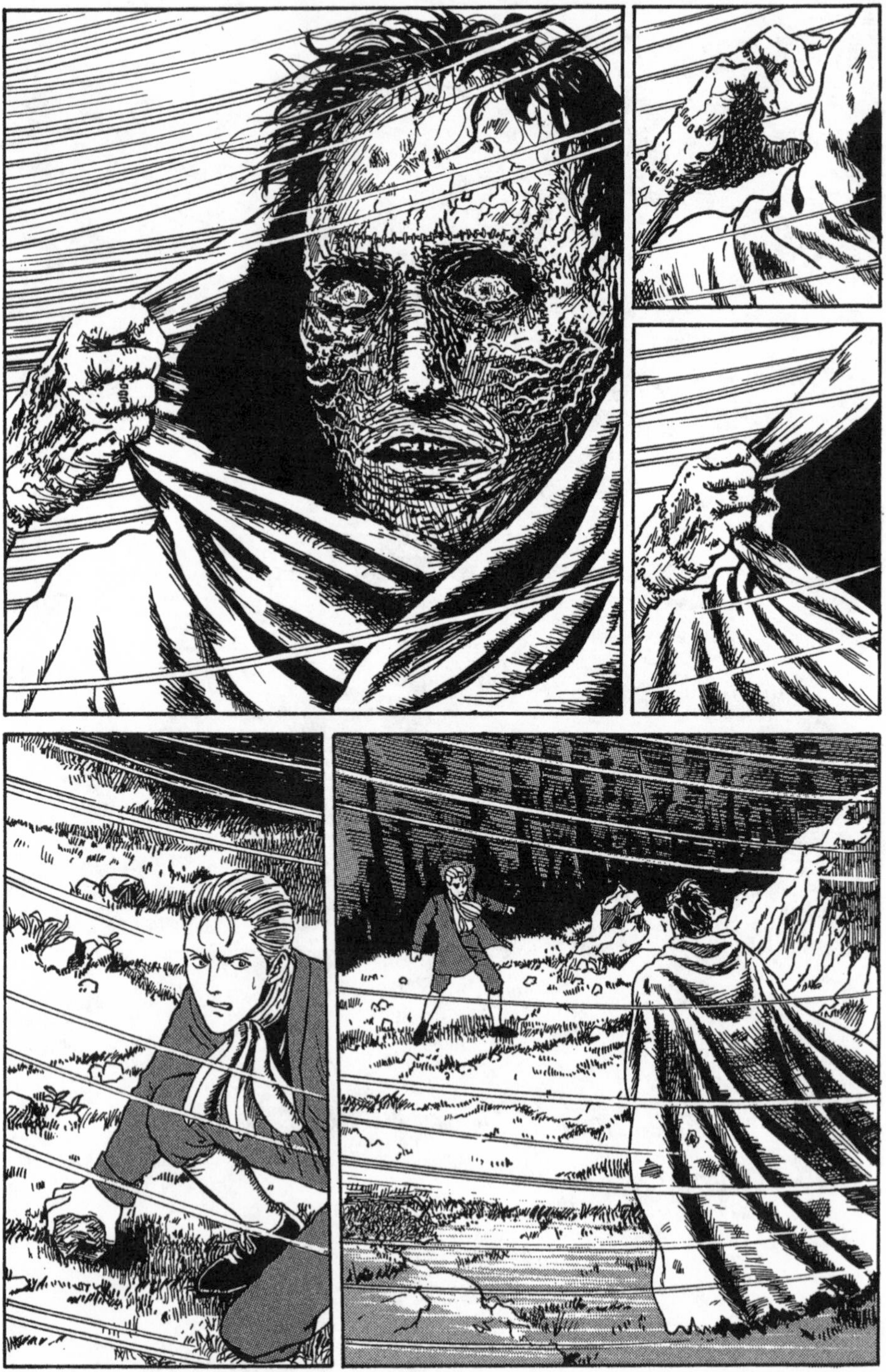

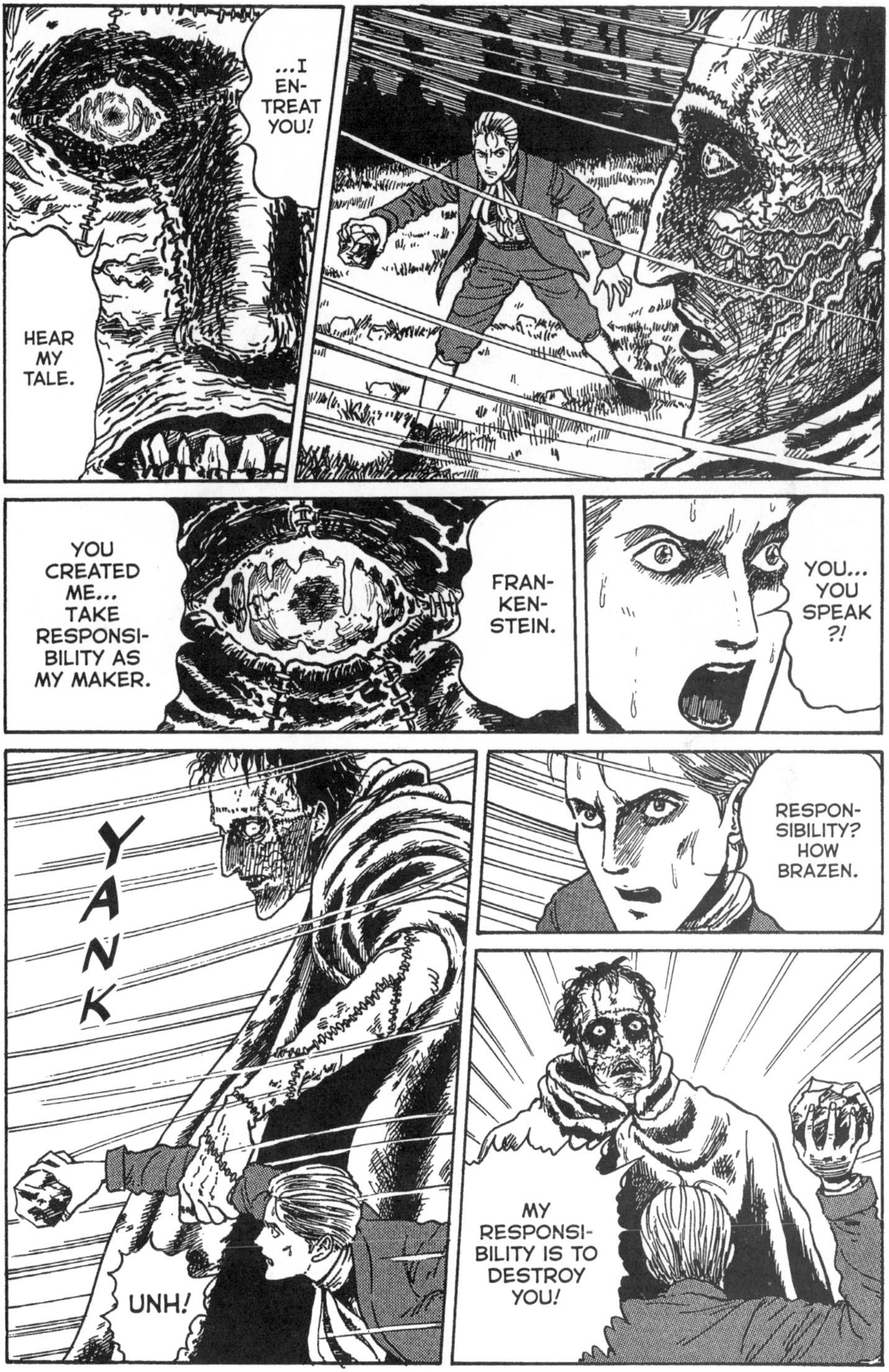
...I EN-TREAT YOU!
HEAR MY TALE.
YOU... YOU SPEAK?!
FRAN-KEN-STEIN.
YOU CREATED ME... TAKE RESPONSI-BILITY AS MY MAKER.
RESPON-SIBILITY? HOW BRAZEN.
MY RESPONSI-BILITY IS TO DESTROY YOU!
YANK
UNH!

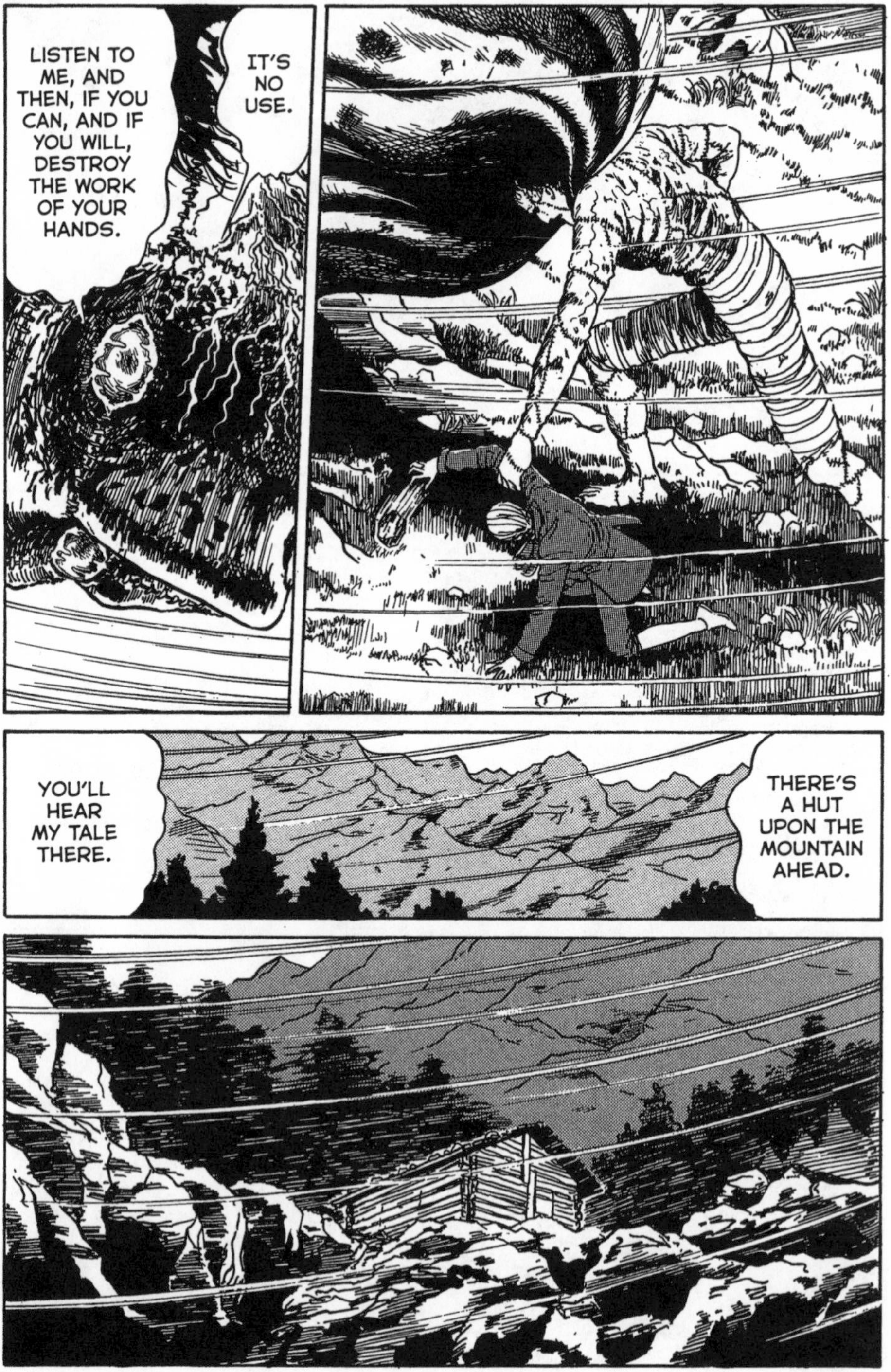
IT'S NO USE.
LISTEN TO ME, AND THEN, IF YOU CAN, AND IF YOU WILL, DESTROY THE WORK OF YOUR HANDS.
THERE'S A HUT UPON THE MOUNTAIN AHEAD.
YOU'LL HEAR MY TALE THERE.

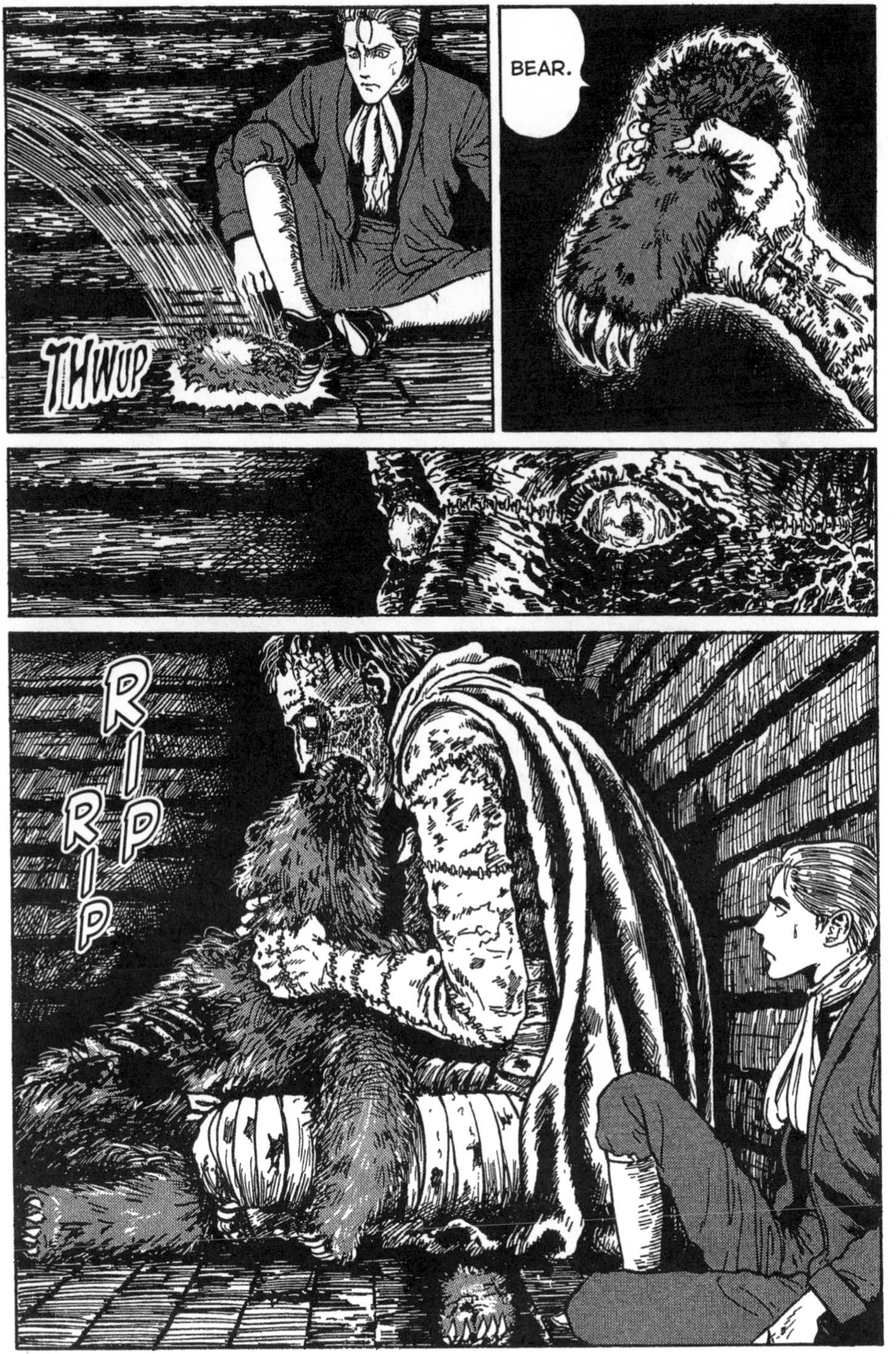
BEAR.
THWUP
RIP
RIP

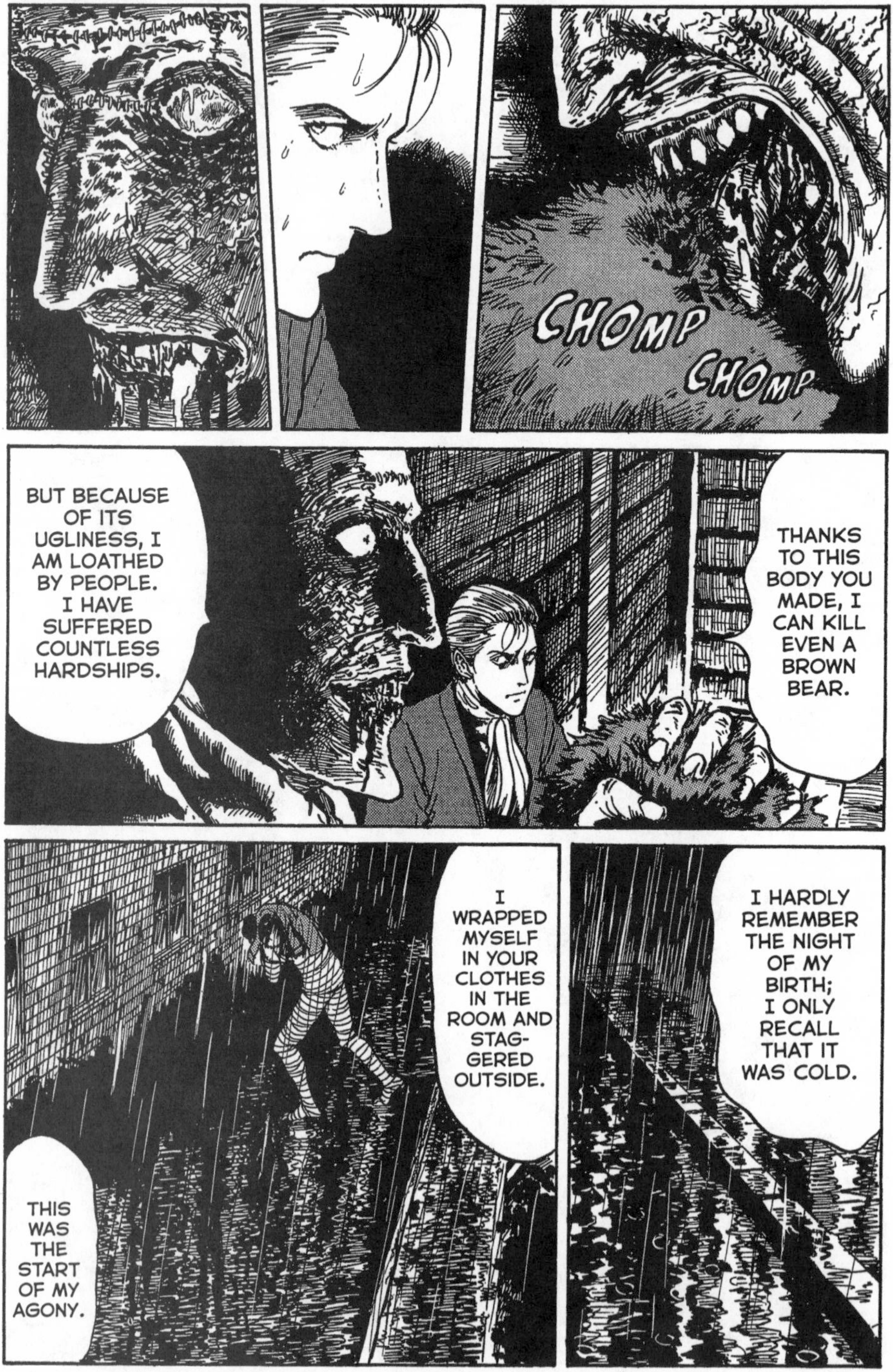
CHOMP CHOMP
THANKS TO THIS BODY YOU MADE, I CAN KILL EVEN A BROWN BEAR.
BUT BECAUSE OF ITS UGLINESS, I AM LOATHED BY PEOPLE. I HAVE SUFFERED COUNTLESS HARDSHIPS.
I HARDLY REMEMBER THE NIGHT OF MY BIRTH; I ONLY RECALL THAT IT WAS COLD.
I WRAPPED MYSELF IN YOUR CLOTHES IN THE ROOM AND STAG-GERED OUTSIDE.
THIS WAS THE START OF MY AGONY.

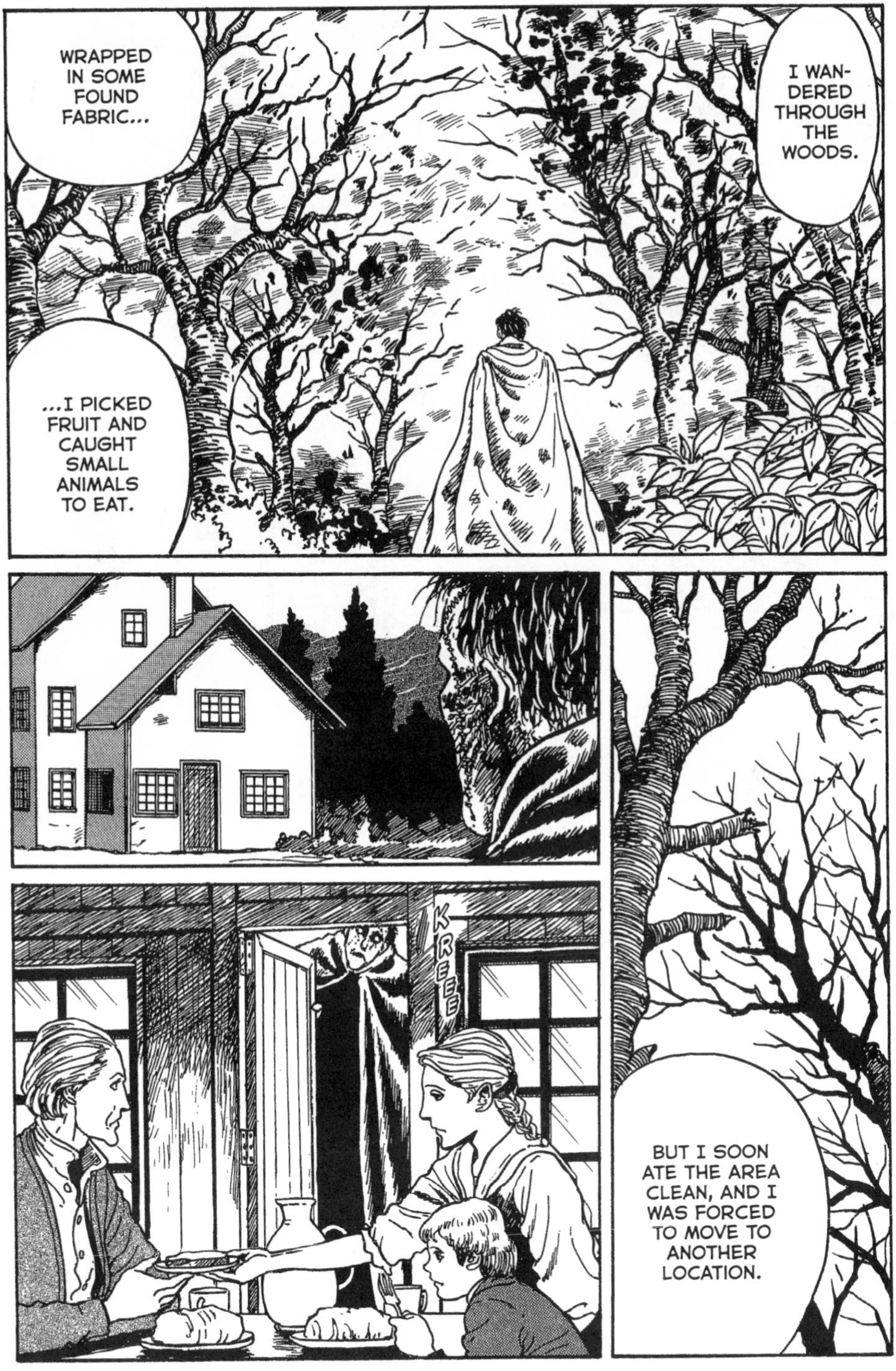
I WANDERED THROUGH THE WOODS.
WRAPPED IN SOME FOUND FABRIC...
...I PICKED FRUIT AND CAUGHT SMALL ANIMALS TO EAT.
BUT I SOON ATE THE AREA CLEAN, AND I WAS FORCED TO MOVE TO ANOTHER LOCATION.
KREEE

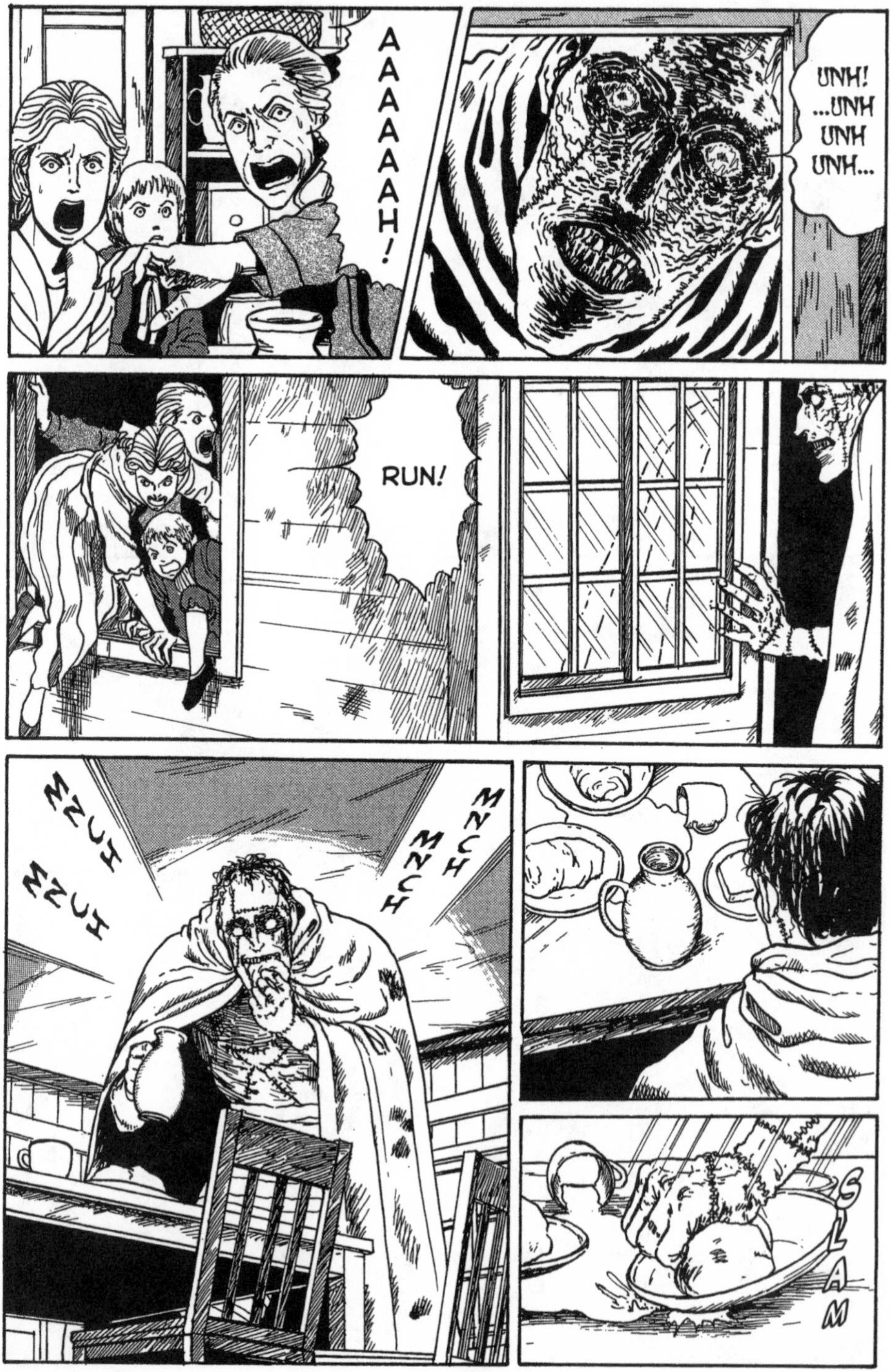
UNH! ...UNH UNH UNH...
AAAAAAAH!
RUN!
SLAM
MNCH MNCH

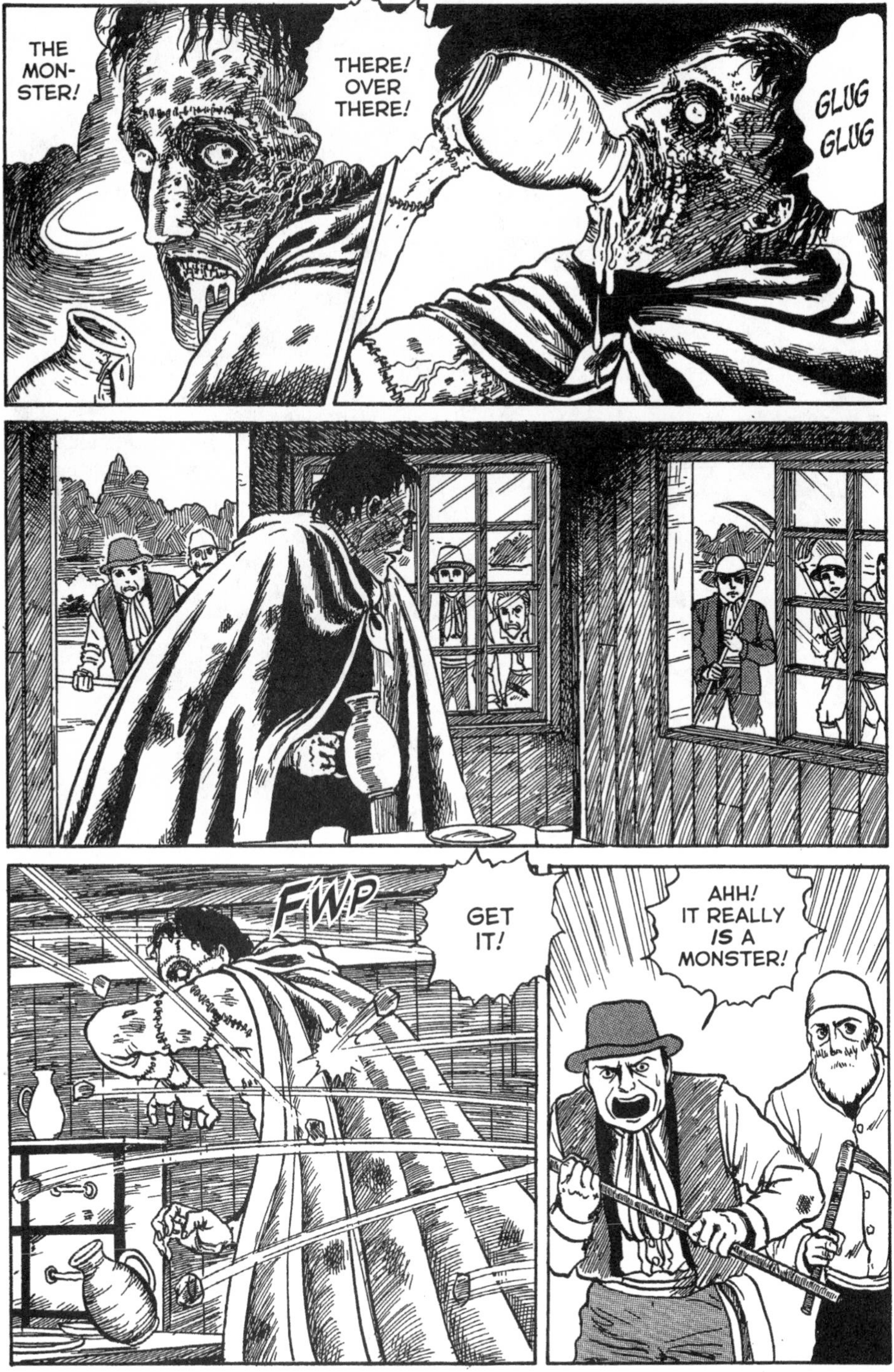
GLUG GLUG
THERE! OVER THERE!
THE MON-STER!
AHH! IT REALLY *IS* A MONSTER!
GET IT!
FWP

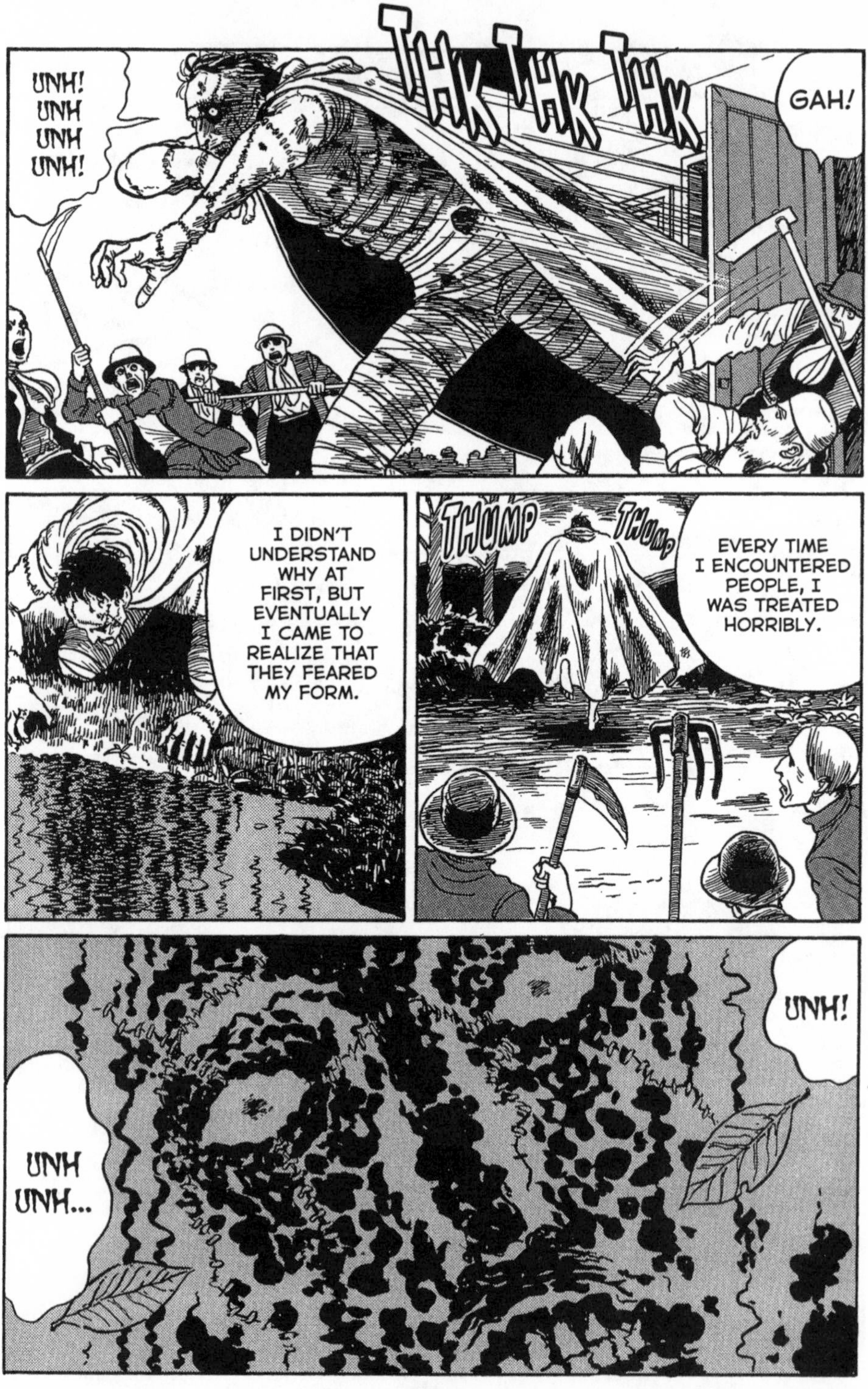
GAH!
THK THK THK
UNH! UNH UNH UNH!
THUMP THUMP
EVERY TIME I ENCOUNTERED PEOPLE, I WAS TREATED HORRIBLY.
I DIDN'T UNDERSTAND WHY AT FIRST, BUT EVENTUALLY I CAME TO REALIZE THAT THEY FEARED MY FORM.
UNH!
UNH UNH...

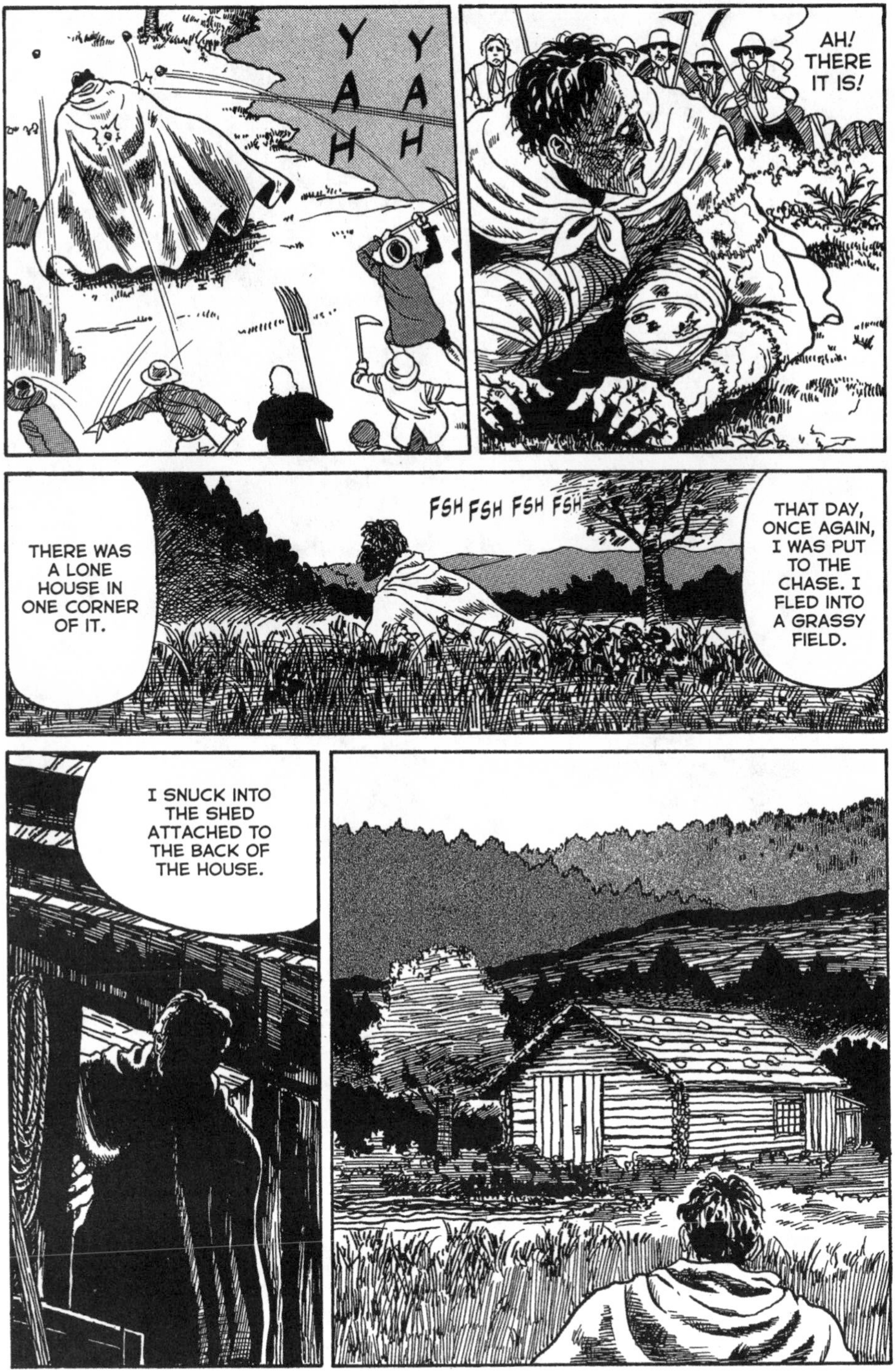
AH! THERE IT IS!
YAH YAH
THAT DAY, ONCE AGAIN, I WAS PUT TO THE CHASE. I FLED INTO A GRASSY FIELD.
FSH FSH FSH FSH
THERE WAS A LONE HOUSE IN ONE CORNER OF IT.
I SNUCK INTO THE SHED ATTACHED TO THE BACK OF THE HOUSE.

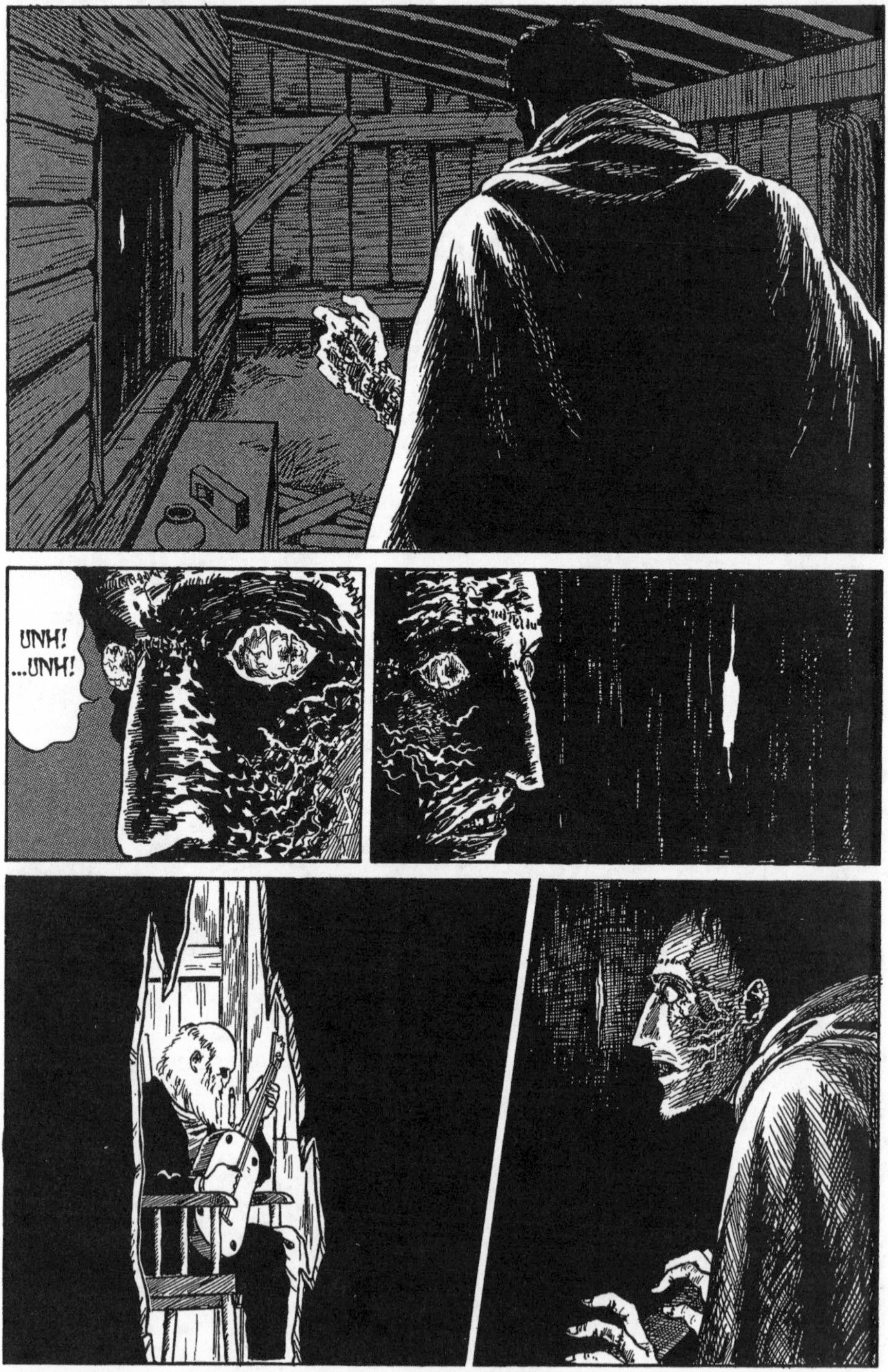
UNH! ...UNH!

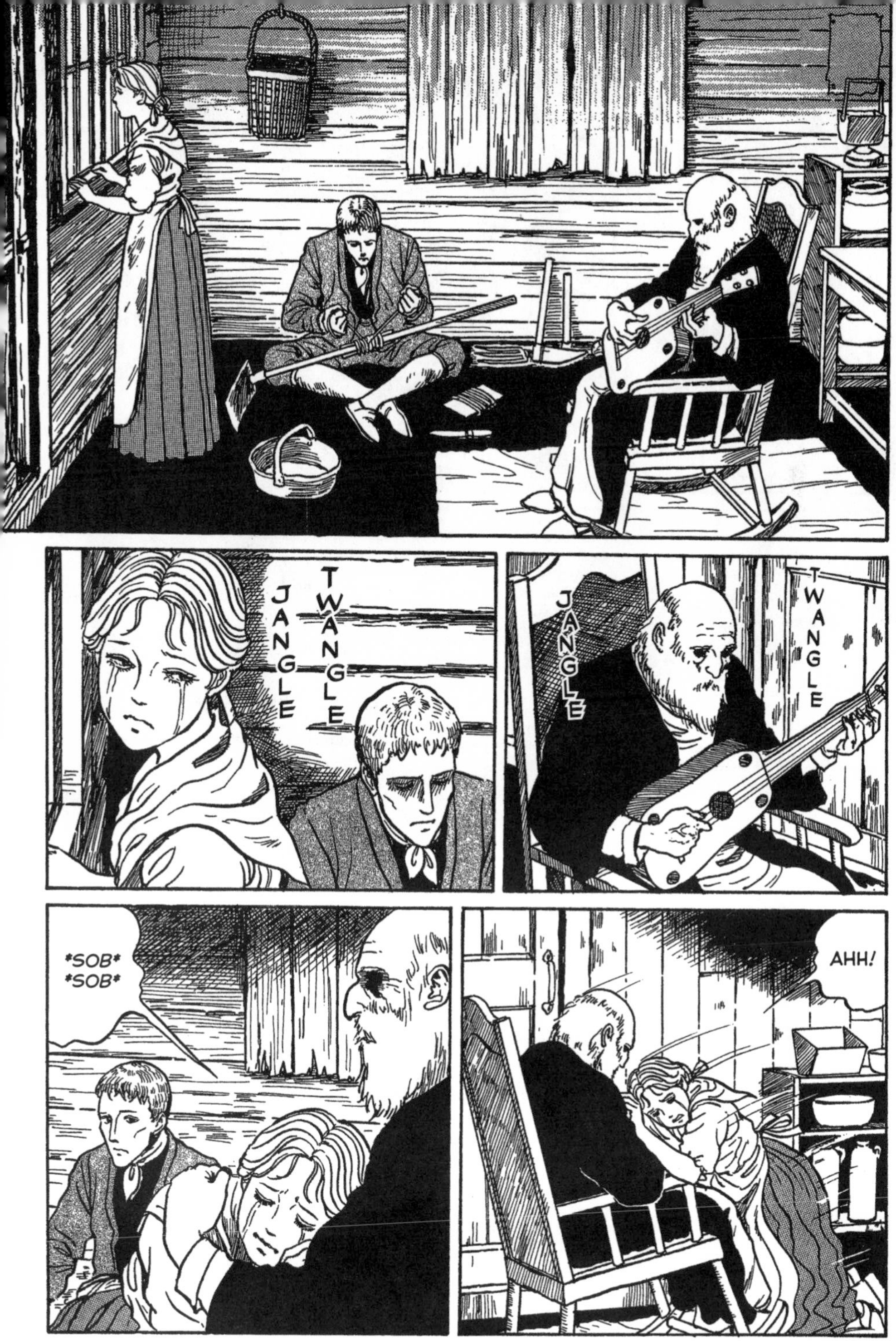
TWANGLE
JANGLE
TWANGLE
JANGLE
AHH!
SOB
SOB

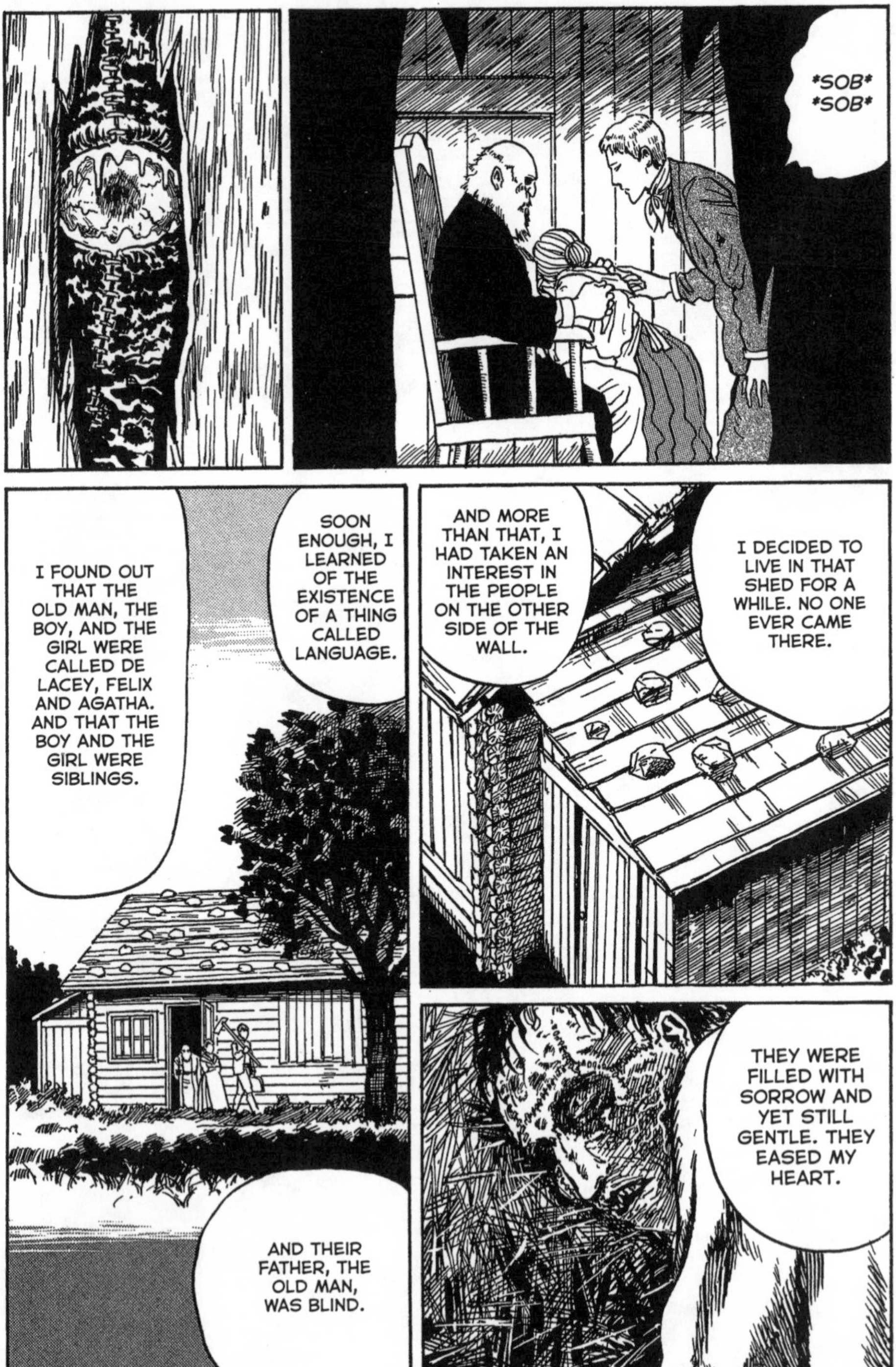
SOB
SOB
I DECIDED TO LIVE IN THAT SHED FOR A WHILE. NO ONE EVER CAME THERE.
AND MORE THAN THAT, I HAD TAKEN AN INTEREST IN THE PEOPLE ON THE OTHER SIDE OF THE WALL.
THEY WERE FILLED WITH SORROW AND YET STILL GENTLE. THEY EASED MY HEART.
SOON ENOUGH, I LEARNED OF THE EXISTENCE OF A THING CALLED LANGUAGE.
I FOUND OUT THAT THE OLD MAN, THE BOY, AND THE GIRL WERE CALLED DE LACEY, FELIX AND AGATHA. AND THAT THE BOY AND THE GIRL WERE SIBLINGS.
AND THEIR FATHER, THE OLD MAN, WAS BLIND.

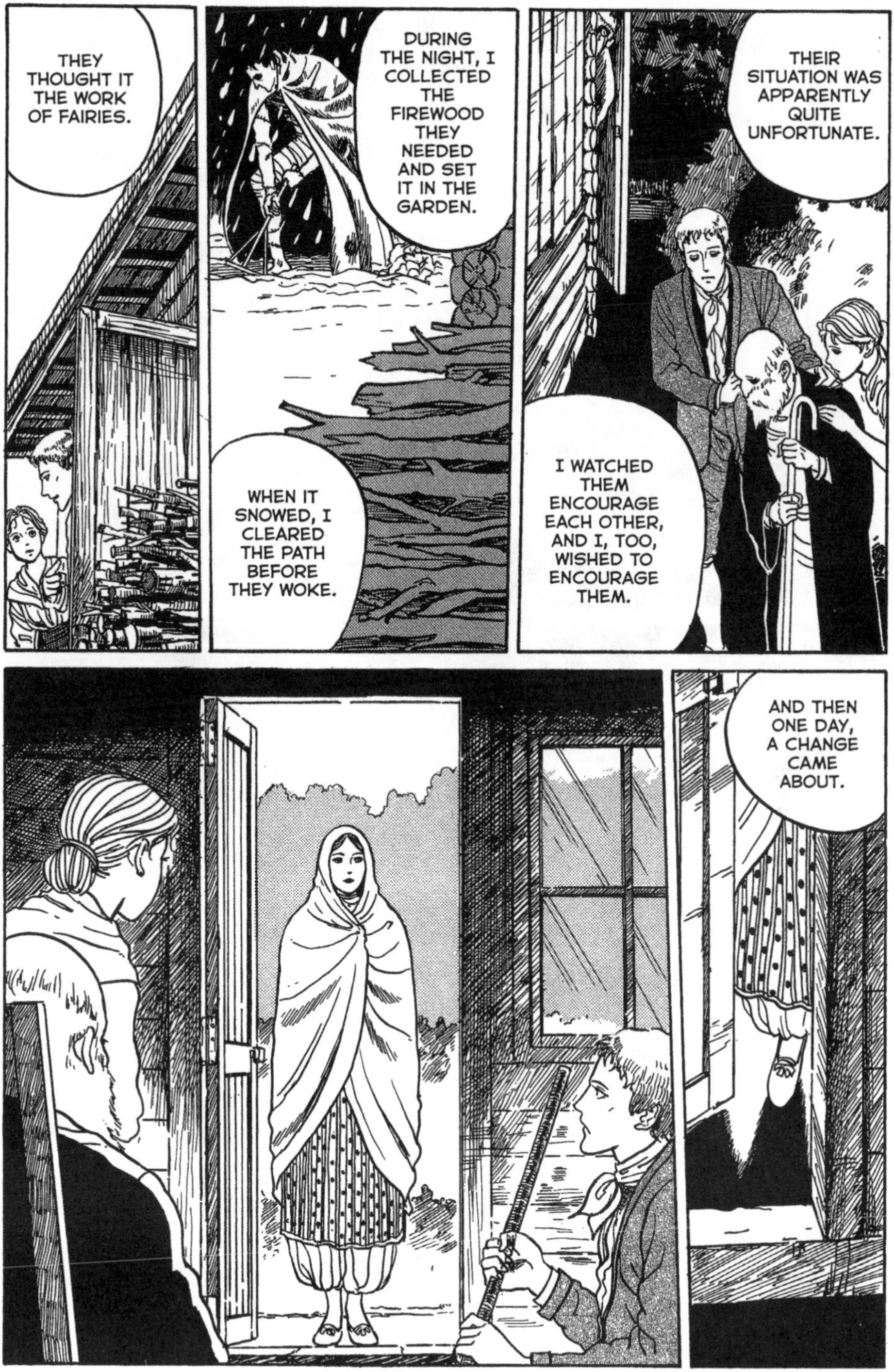
THEIR SITUATION WAS APPARENTLY QUITE UNFORTUNATE.
I WATCHED THEM ENCOURAGE EACH OTHER, AND I, TOO, WISHED TO ENCOURAGE THEM.
DURING THE NIGHT, I COLLECTED THE FIREWOOD THEY NEEDED AND SET IT IN THE GARDEN.
WHEN IT SNOWED, I CLEARED THE PATH BEFORE THEY WOKE.
THEY THOUGHT IT THE WORK OF FAIRIES.
AND THEN ONE DAY, A CHANGE CAME ABOUT.

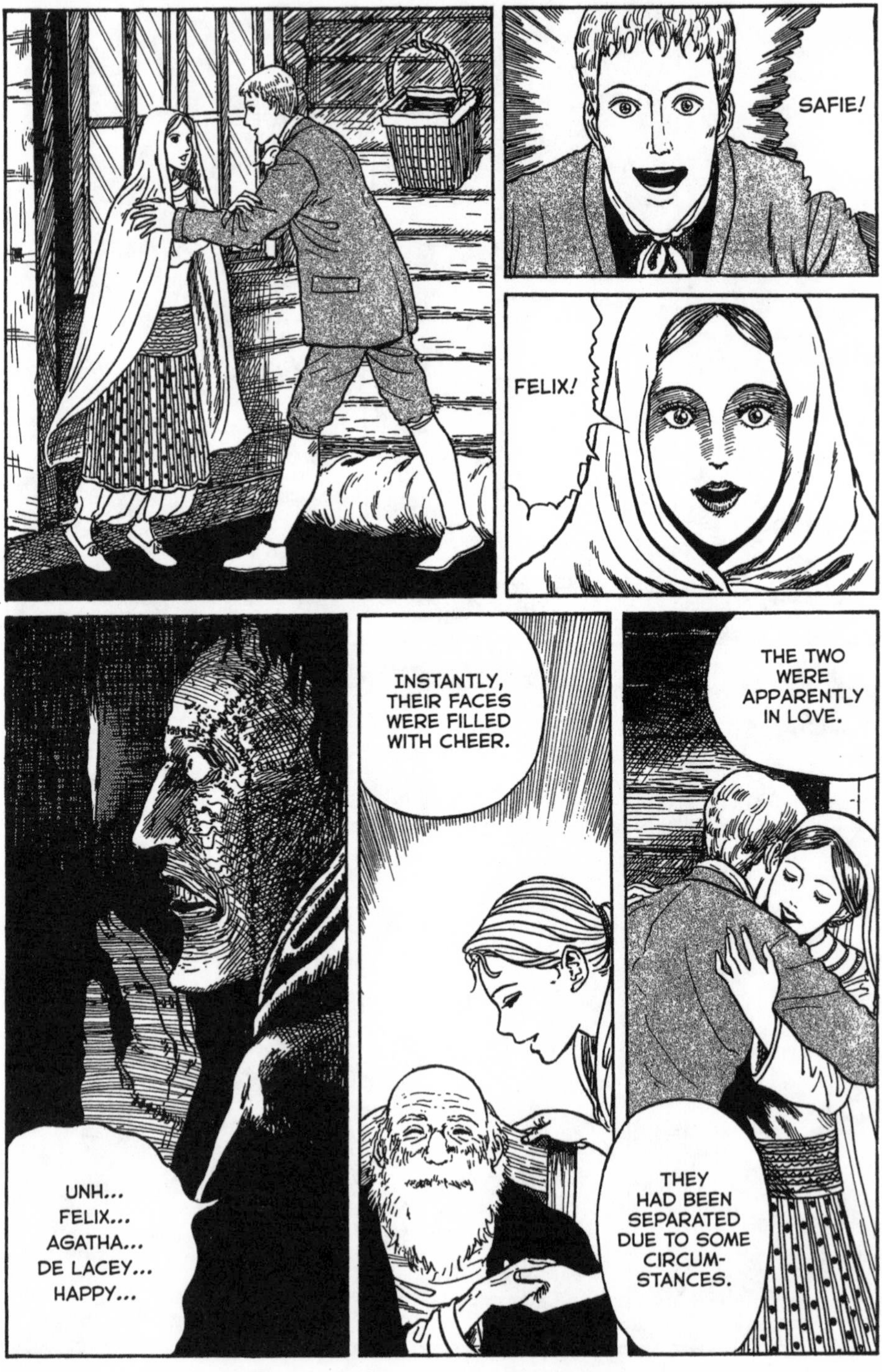
SAFIE!
FELIX!
THE TWO WERE APPARENTLY IN LOVE.
THEY HAD BEEN SEPARATED DUE TO SOME CIRCUMSTANCES.
INSTANTLY, THEIR FACES WERE FILLED WITH CHEER.
UNH... FELIX... AGATHA... DE LACEY... HAPPY...

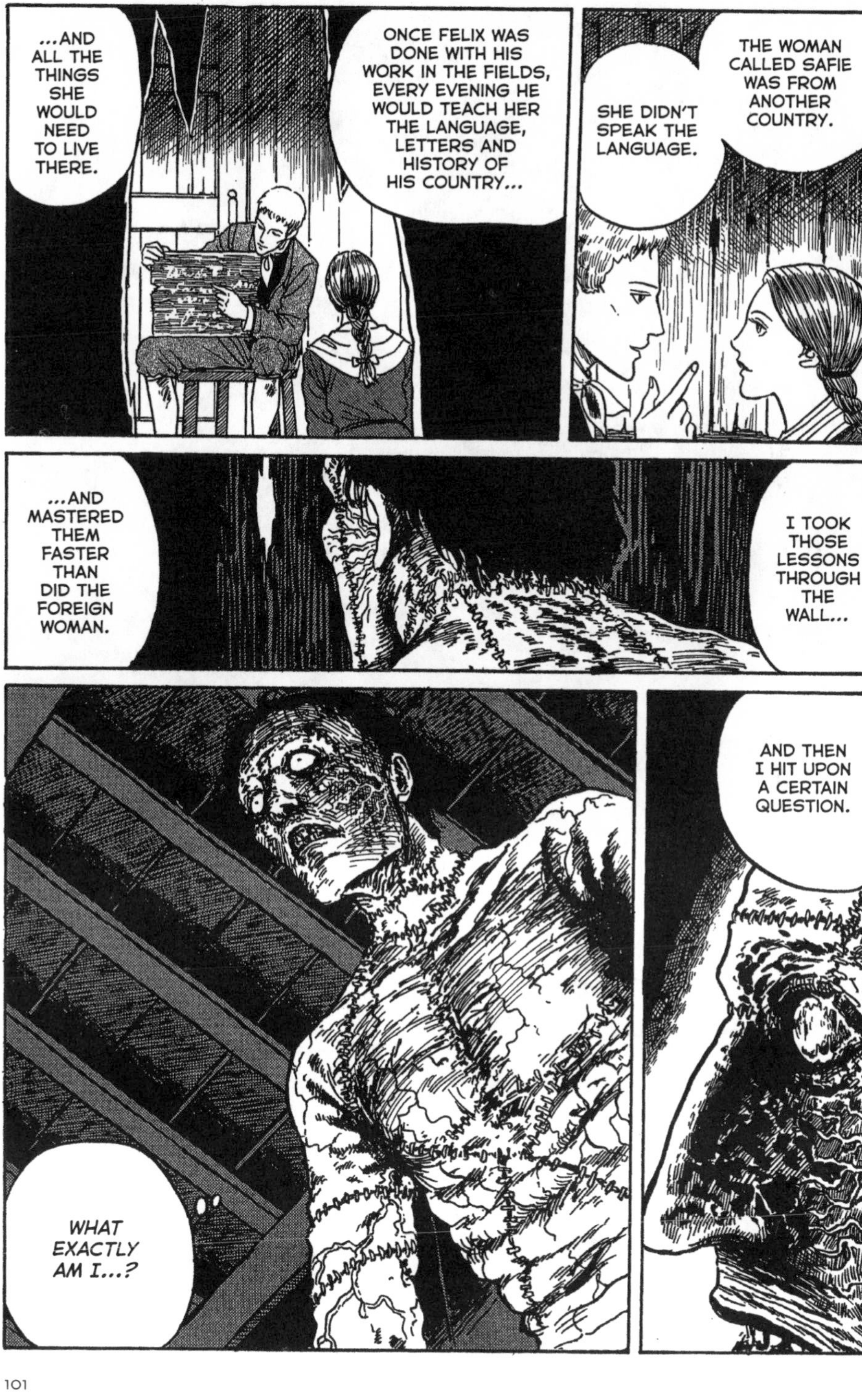
THE WOMAN CALLED SAFIE WAS FROM ANOTHER COUNTRY.
SHE DIDN'T SPEAK THE LANGUAGE.
ONCE FELIX WAS DONE WITH HIS WORK IN THE FIELDS, EVERY EVENING HE WOULD TEACH HER THE LANGUAGE, LETTERS AND HISTORY OF HIS COUNTRY...
...AND ALL THE THINGS SHE WOULD NEED TO LIVE THERE.
I TOOK THOSE LESSONS THROUGH THE WALL...
...AND MASTERED THEM FASTER THAN DID THE FOREIGN WOMAN.
AND THEN I HIT UPON A CERTAIN QUESTION.
WHAT EXACTLY AM I...?

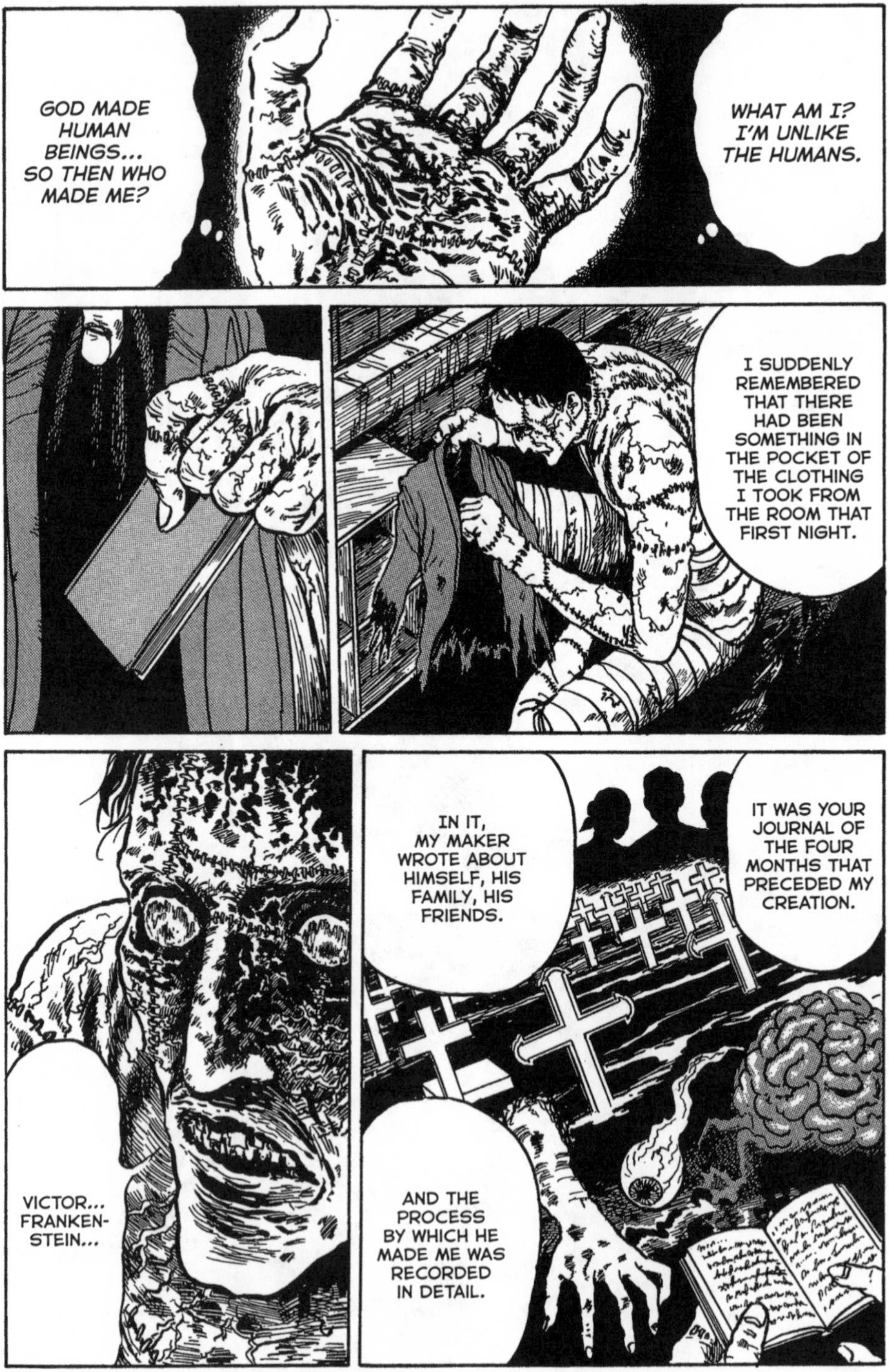
WHAT AM I? I'M UNLIKE THE HUMANS.
GOD MADE HUMAN BEINGS... SO THEN WHO MADE ME?
I SUDDENLY REMEMBERED THAT THERE HAD BEEN SOMETHING IN THE POCKET OF THE CLOTHING I TOOK FROM THE ROOM THAT FIRST NIGHT.
IT WAS YOUR JOURNAL OF THE FOUR MONTHS THAT PRECEDED MY CREATION.
IN IT, MY MAKER WROTE ABOUT HIMSELF, HIS FAMILY, HIS FRIENDS.
AND THE PROCESS BY WHICH HE MADE ME WAS RECORDED IN DETAIL.
VICTOR... FRANKEN-STEIN...

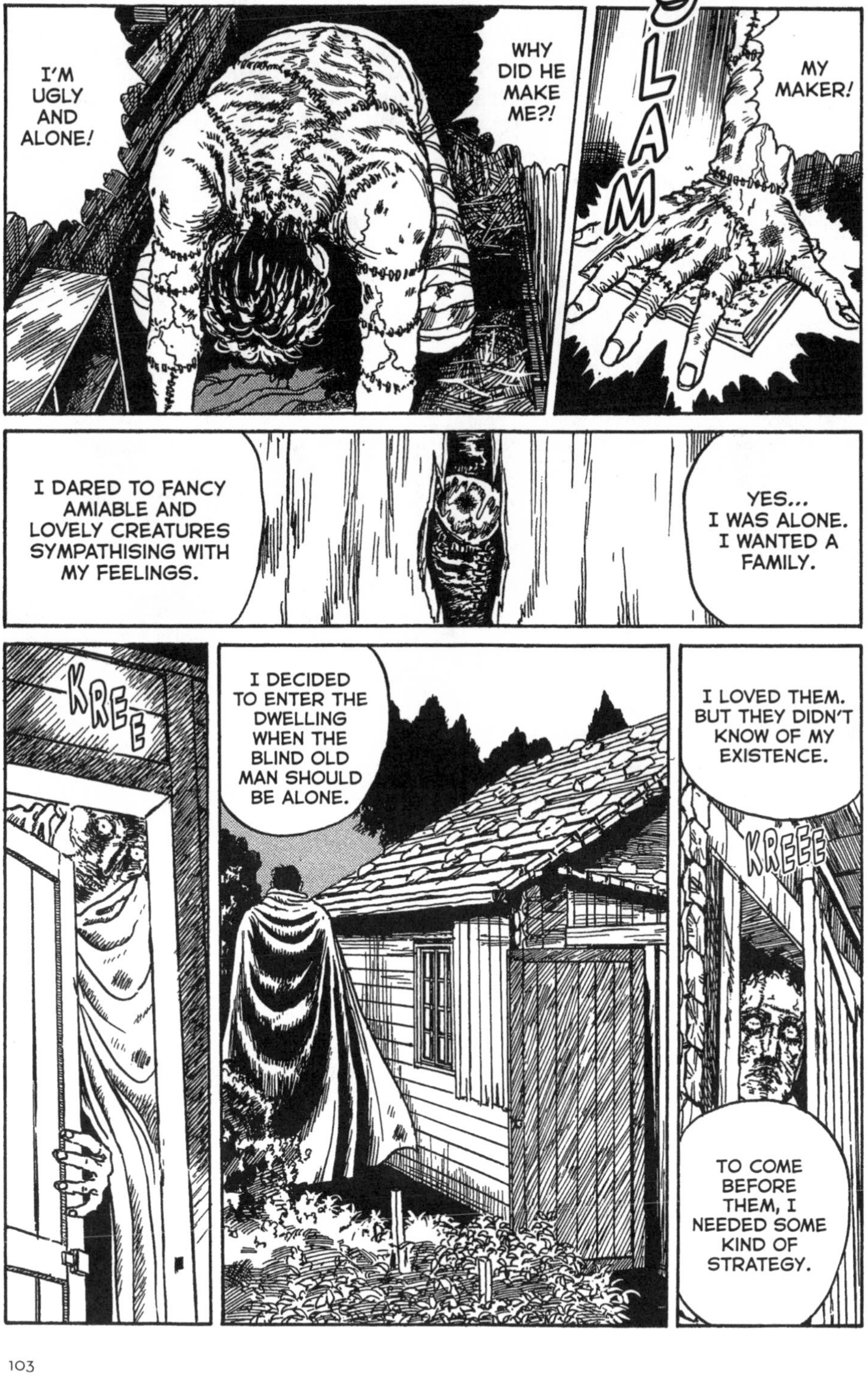
SLAM
MY MAKER!
WHY DID HE MAKE ME?!
I'M UGLY AND ALONE!
YES... I WAS ALONE. I WANTED A FAMILY.
I DARED TO FANCY AMIABLE AND LOVELY CREATURES SYMPATHISING WITH MY FEELINGS.
I LOVED THEM. BUT THEY DIDN'T KNOW OF MY EXISTENCE.
KREEE
TO COME BEFORE THEM, I NEEDED SOME KIND OF STRATEGY.
I DECIDED TO ENTER THE DWELLING WHEN THE BLIND OLD MAN SHOULD BE ALONE.
KREE

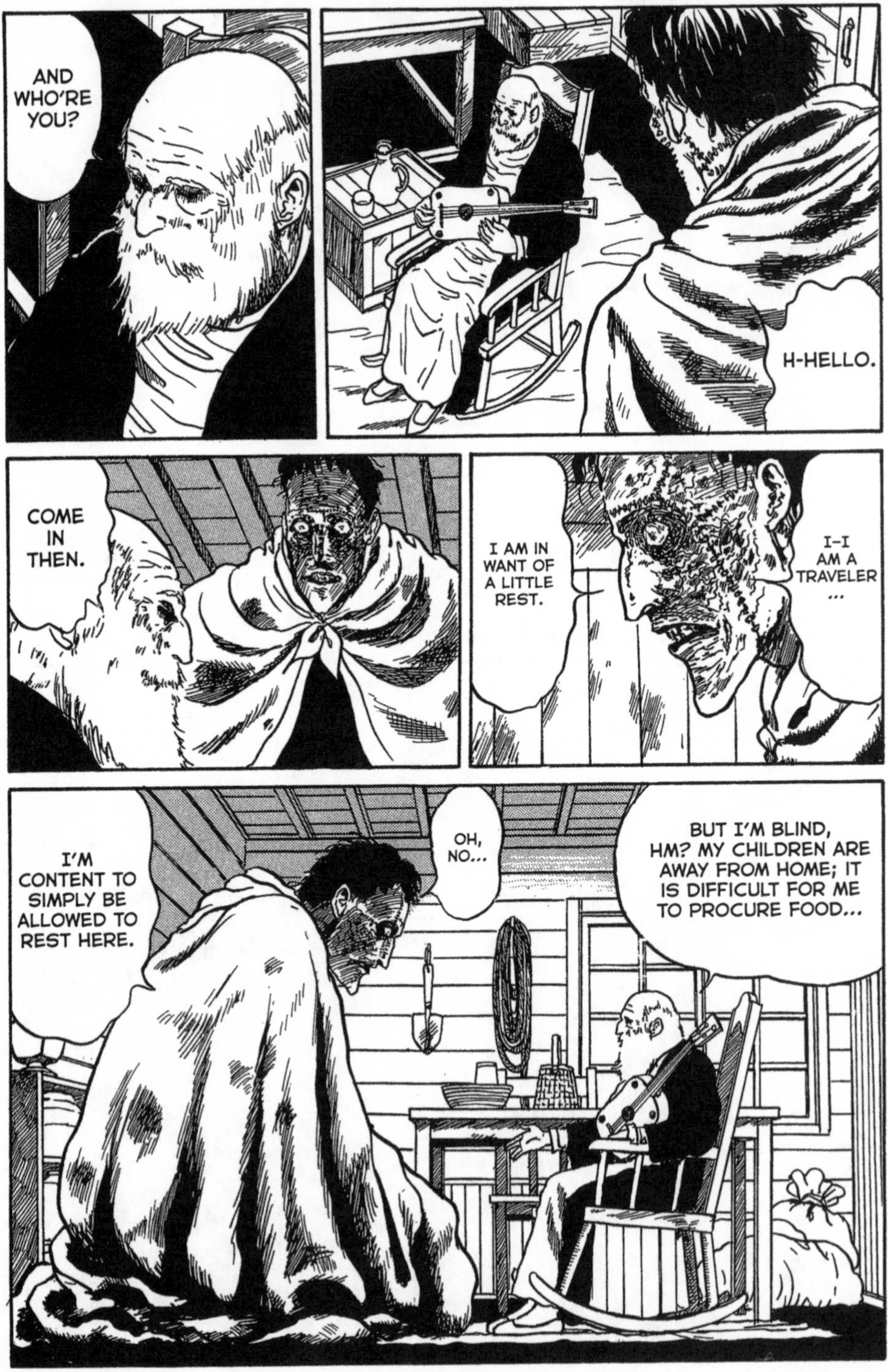
H-HELLO.
AND WHO'RE YOU?
I-I AM A TRAVELER ...
I AM IN WANT OF A LITTLE REST.
COME IN THEN.
BUT I'M BLIND, HM? MY CHILDREN ARE AWAY FROM HOME; IT IS DIFFICULT FOR ME TO PROCURE FOOD...
OH, NO...
I'M CONTENT TO SIMPLY BE ALLOWED TO REST HERE.

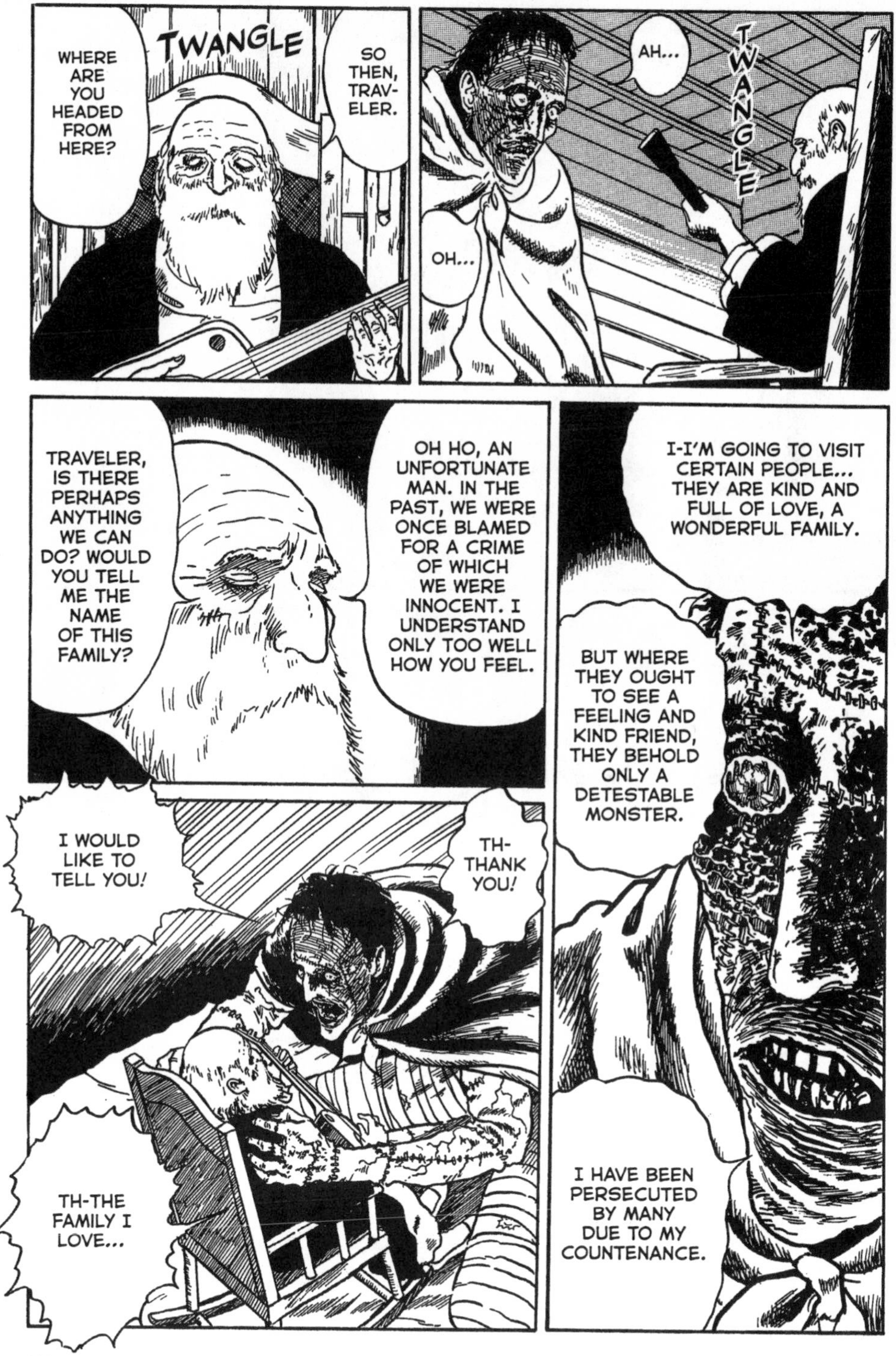
AH...
TWANGLE
OH...
SO THEN, TRAVELER.
TWANGLE
WHERE ARE YOU HEADED FROM HERE?
I-I'M GOING TO VISIT CERTAIN PEOPLE... THEY ARE KIND AND FULL OF LOVE, A WONDERFUL FAMILY.
BUT WHERE THEY OUGHT TO SEE A FEELING AND KIND FRIEND, THEY BEHOLD ONLY A DETESTABLE MONSTER.
I HAVE BEEN PERSECUTED BY MANY DUE TO MY COUNTENANCE.
OH HO, AN UNFORTUNATE MAN. IN THE PAST, WE WERE ONCE BLAMED FOR A CRIME OF WHICH WE WERE INNOCENT. I UNDERSTAND ONLY TOO WELL HOW YOU FEEL.
TRAVELER, IS THERE PERHAPS ANYTHING WE CAN DO? WOULD YOU TELL ME THE NAME OF THIS FAMILY?
TH-THANK YOU!
I WOULD LIKE TO TELL YOU!
TH-THE FAMILY I LOVE...

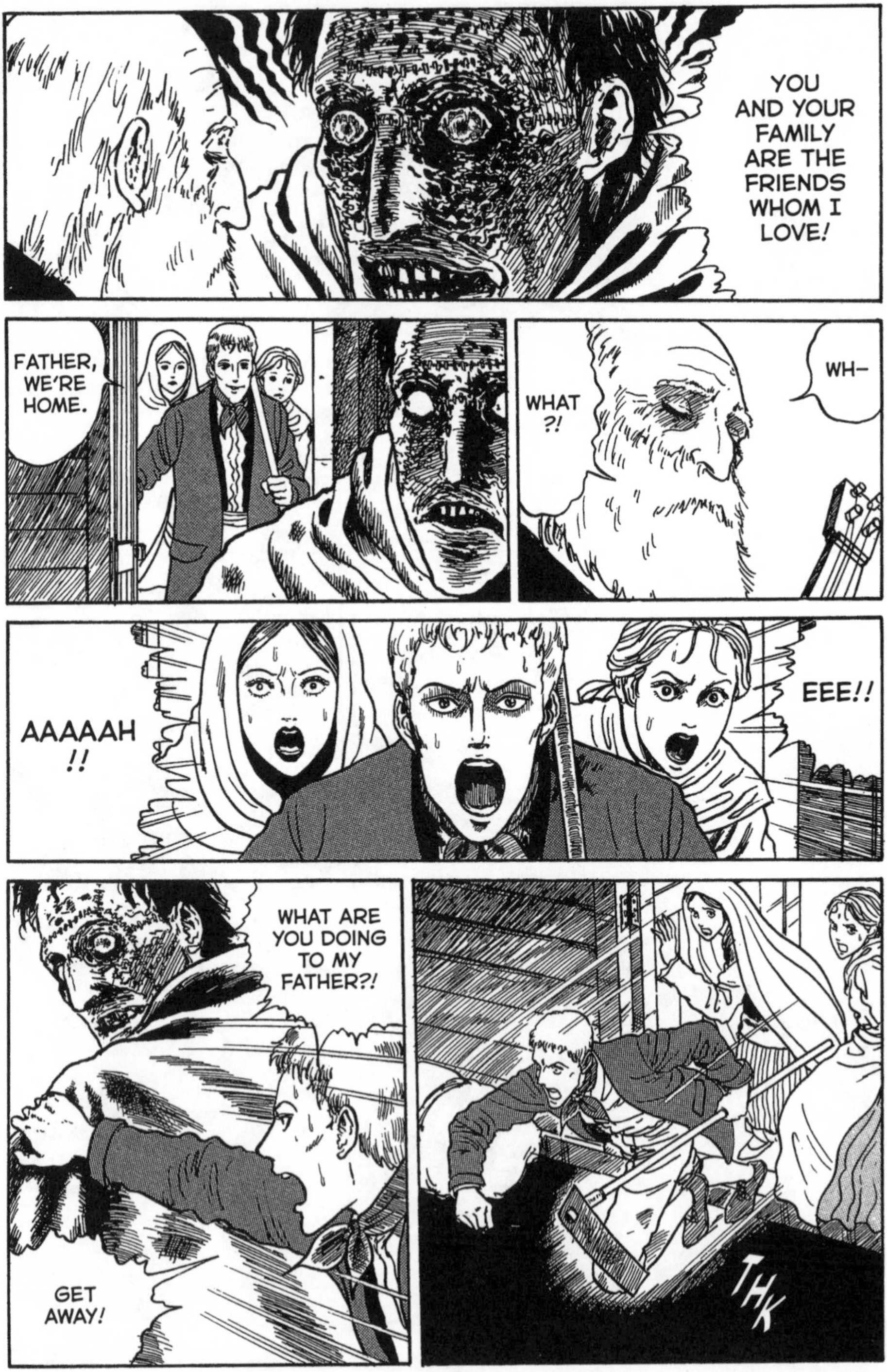
YOU AND YOUR FAMILY ARE THE FRIENDS WHOM I LOVE!
WH–
WHAT ?!
FATHER, WE'RE HOME.
EEE!!
AAAAAH !!
THK
WHAT ARE YOU DOING TO MY FATHER?!
GET AWAY!

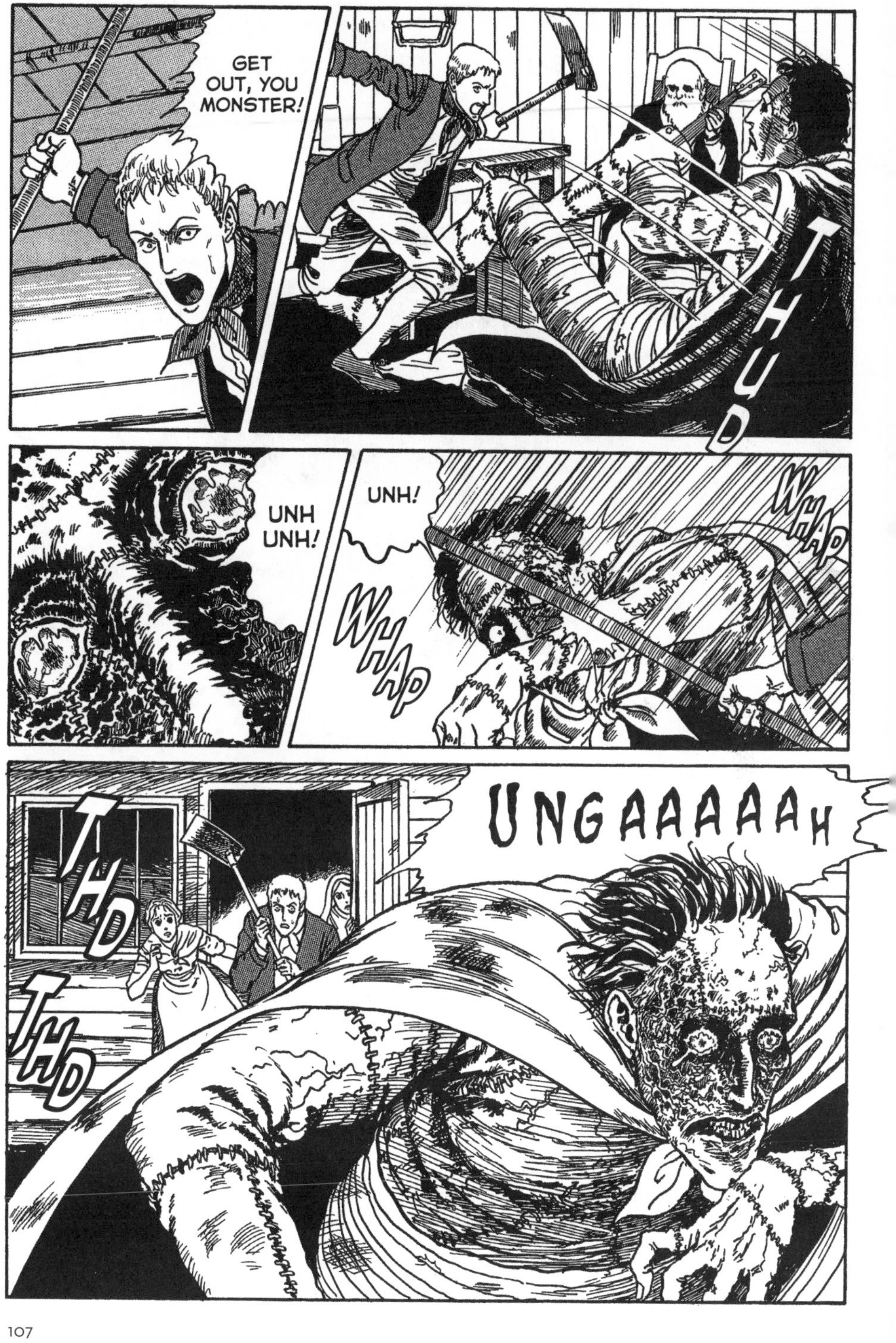
THUD
GET OUT, YOU MONSTER!
WHAP
UNH!
WHAP
UNH UNH!
UNGAAAAAAH
THD
THD

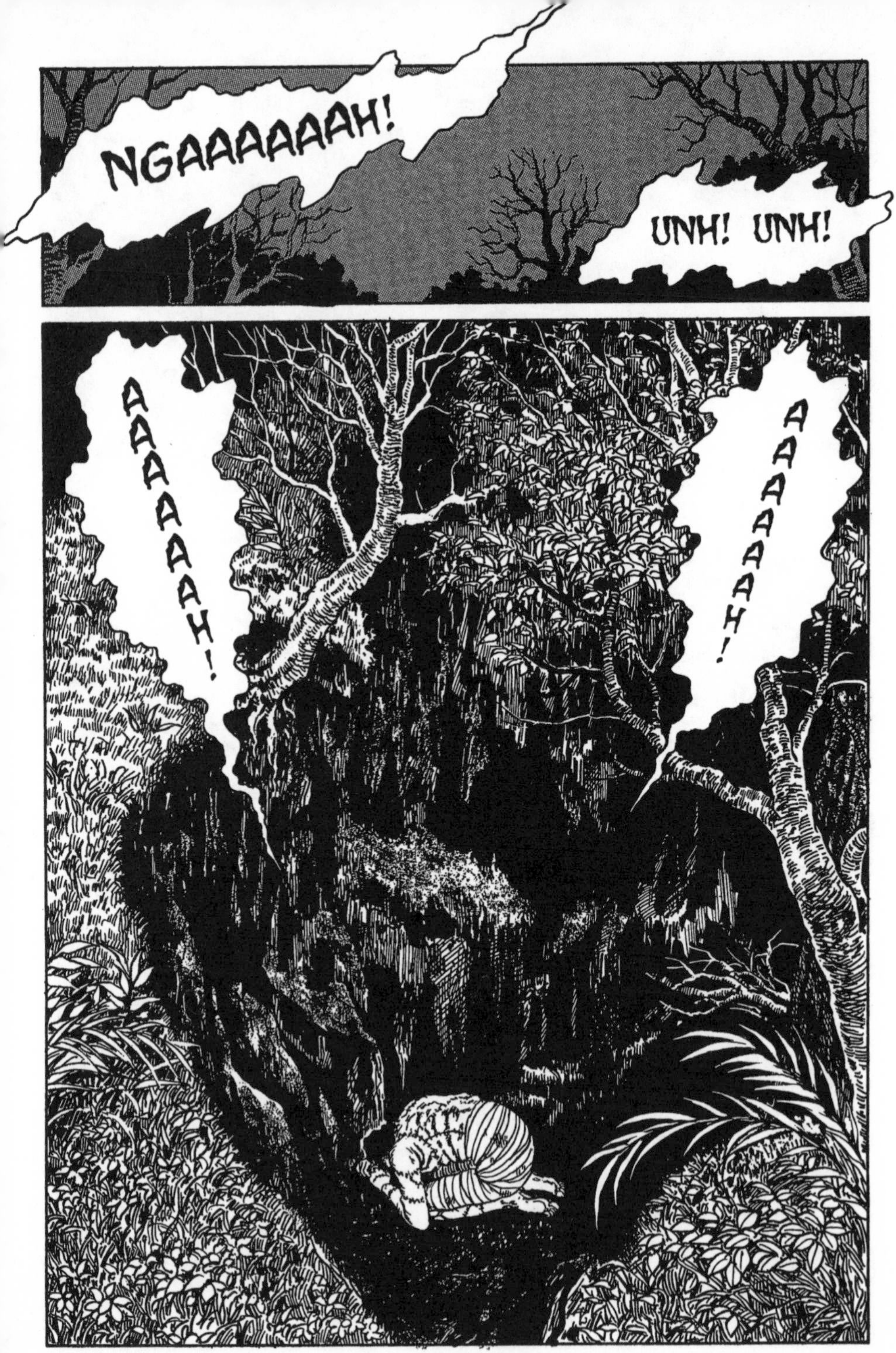
UNH! UNH!
NGAAAAAAH!
AAAAAAAH!
AAAAAAAH!

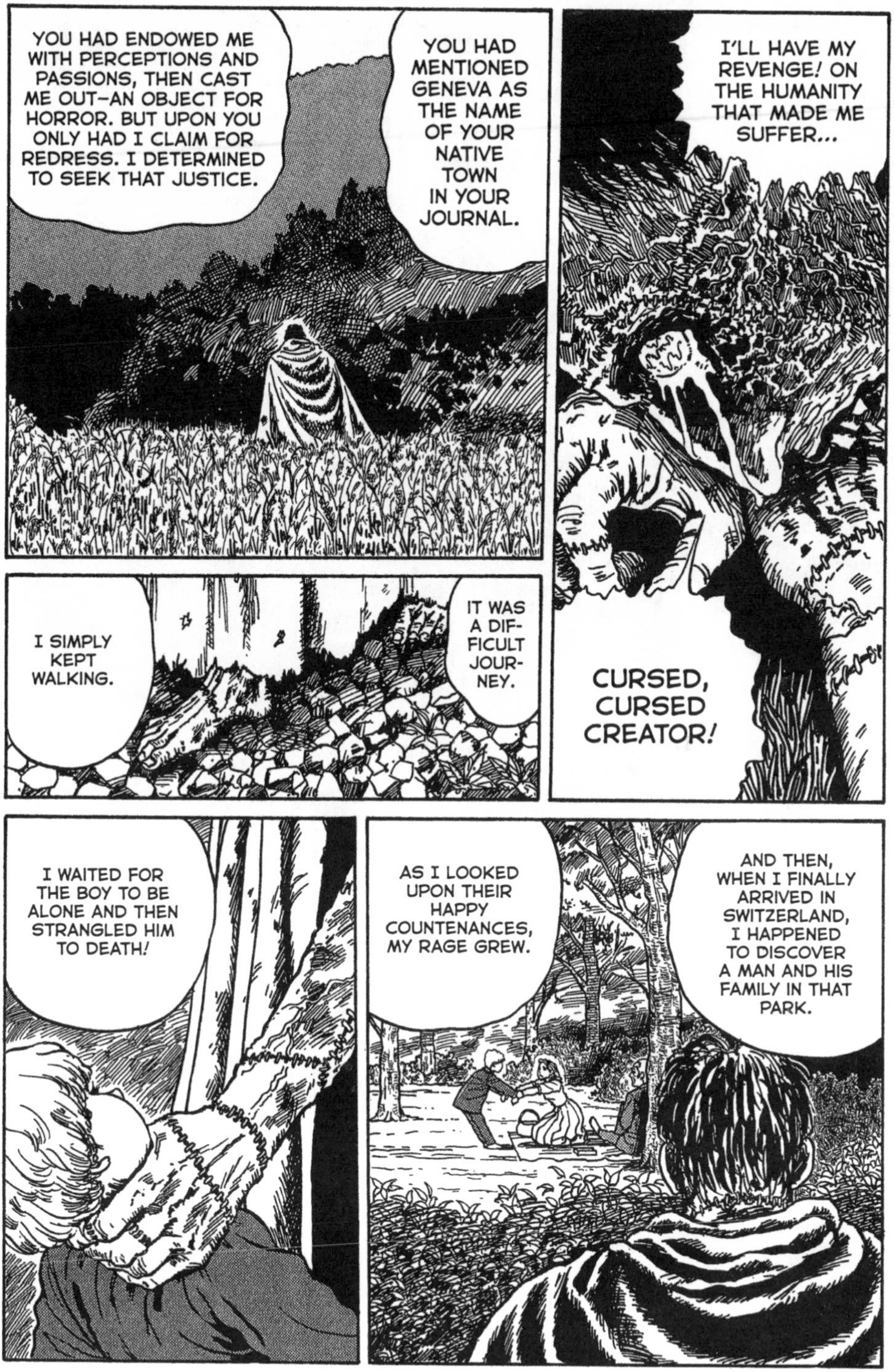
I'LL HAVE MY REVENGE! ON THE HUMANITY THAT MADE ME SUFFER...
CURSED, CURSED CREATOR!
YOU HAD MENTIONED GENEVA AS THE NAME OF YOUR NATIVE TOWN IN YOUR JOURNAL.
YOU HAD ENDOWED ME WITH PERCEPTIONS AND PASSIONS, THEN CAST ME OUT–AN OBJECT FOR HORROR. BUT UPON YOU ONLY HAD I CLAIM FOR REDRESS. I DETERMINED TO SEEK THAT JUSTICE.
IT WAS A DIF-FICULT JOUR-NEY.
I SIMPLY KEPT WALKING.
AND THEN, WHEN I FINALLY ARRIVED IN SWITZERLAND, I HAPPENED TO DISCOVER A MAN AND HIS FAMILY IN THAT PARK.
AS I LOOKED UPON THEIR HAPPY COUNTENANCES, MY RAGE GREW.
I WAITED FOR THE BOY TO BE ALONE AND THEN STRANGLED HIM TO DEATH!

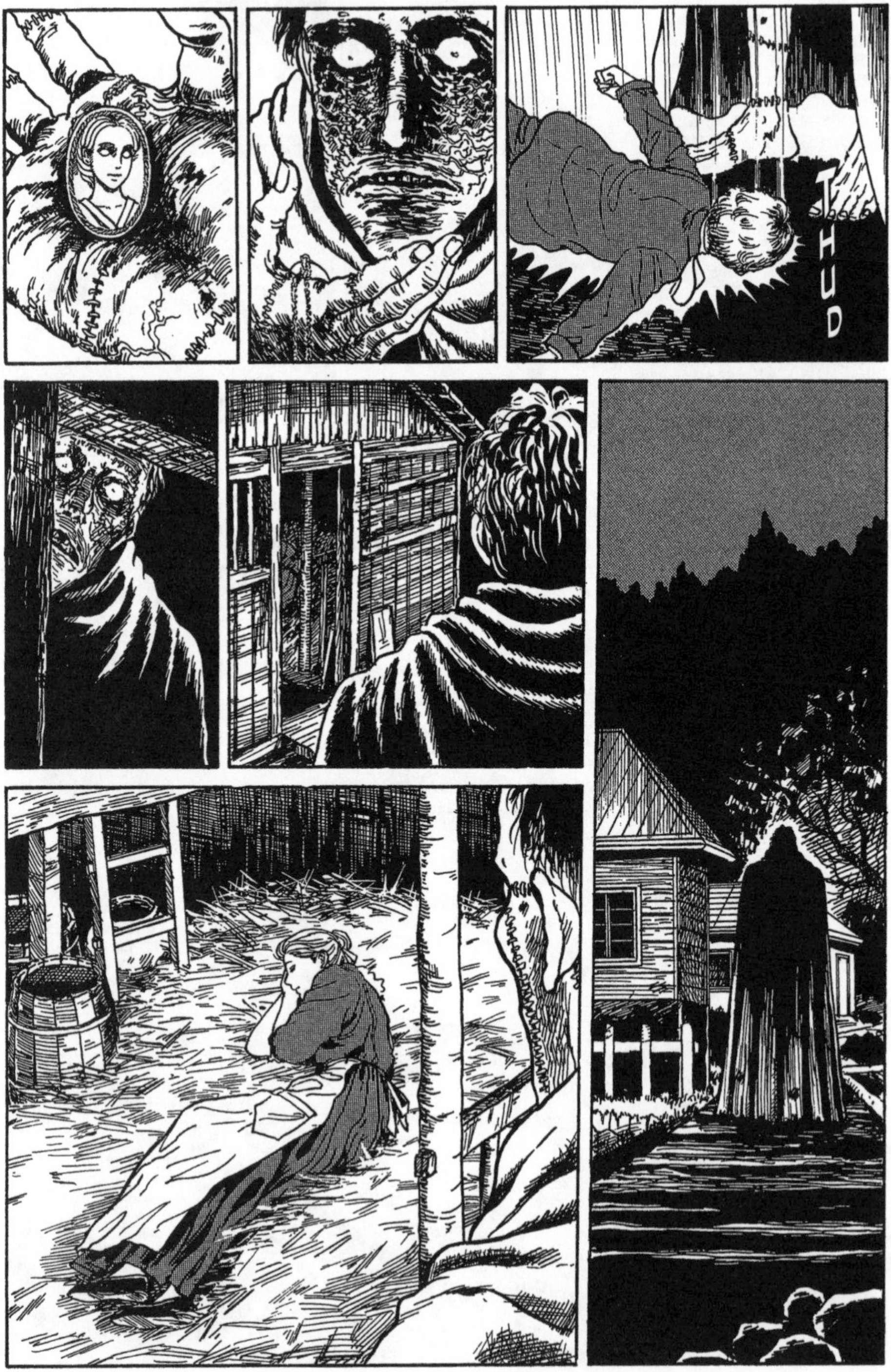
THUD

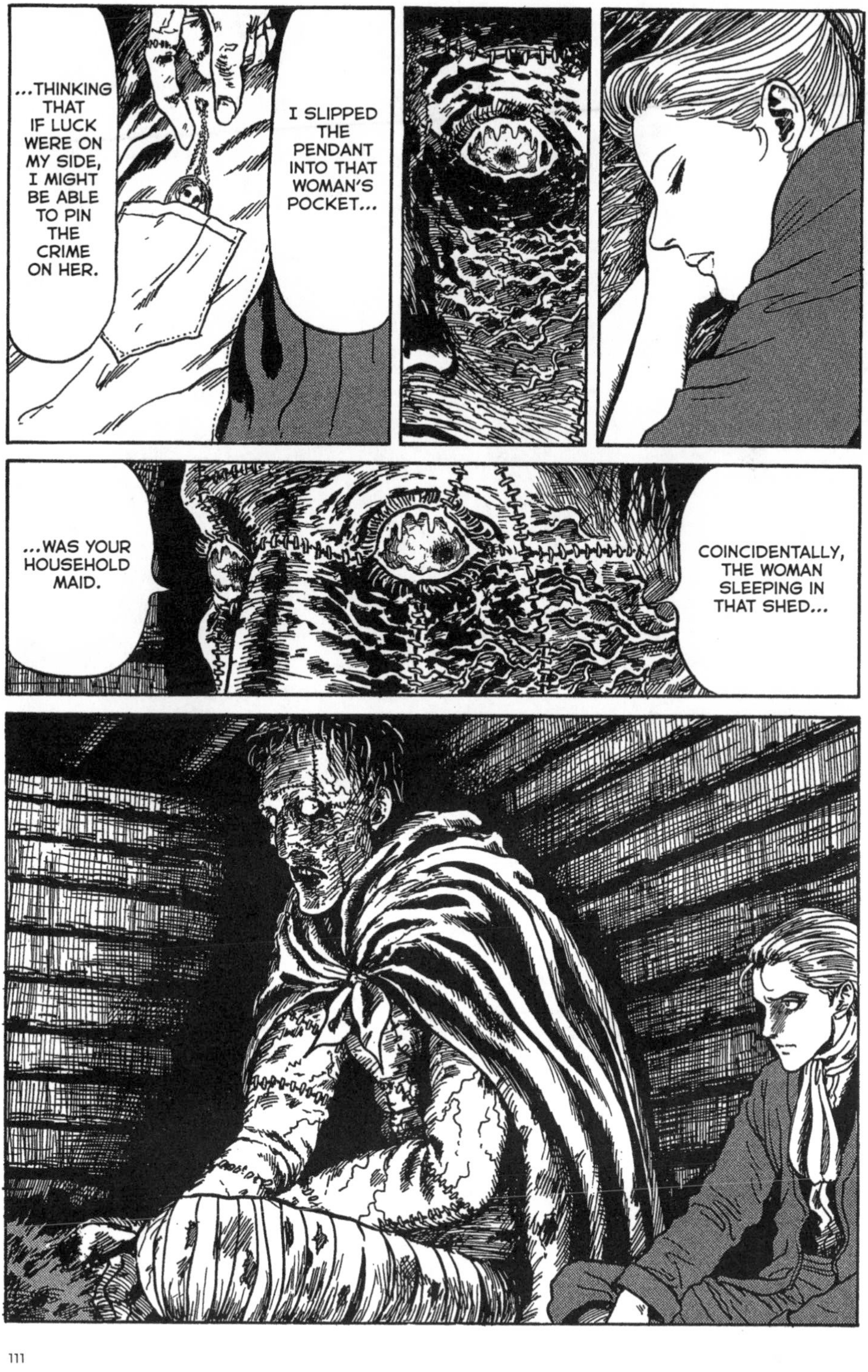
I SLIPPED THE PENDANT INTO THAT WOMAN'S POCKET...
...THINKING THAT IF LUCK WERE ON MY SIDE, I MIGHT BE ABLE TO PIN THE CRIME ON HER.
COINCIDENTALLY, THE WOMAN SLEEPING IN THAT SHED...
...WAS YOUR HOUSEHOLD MAID.

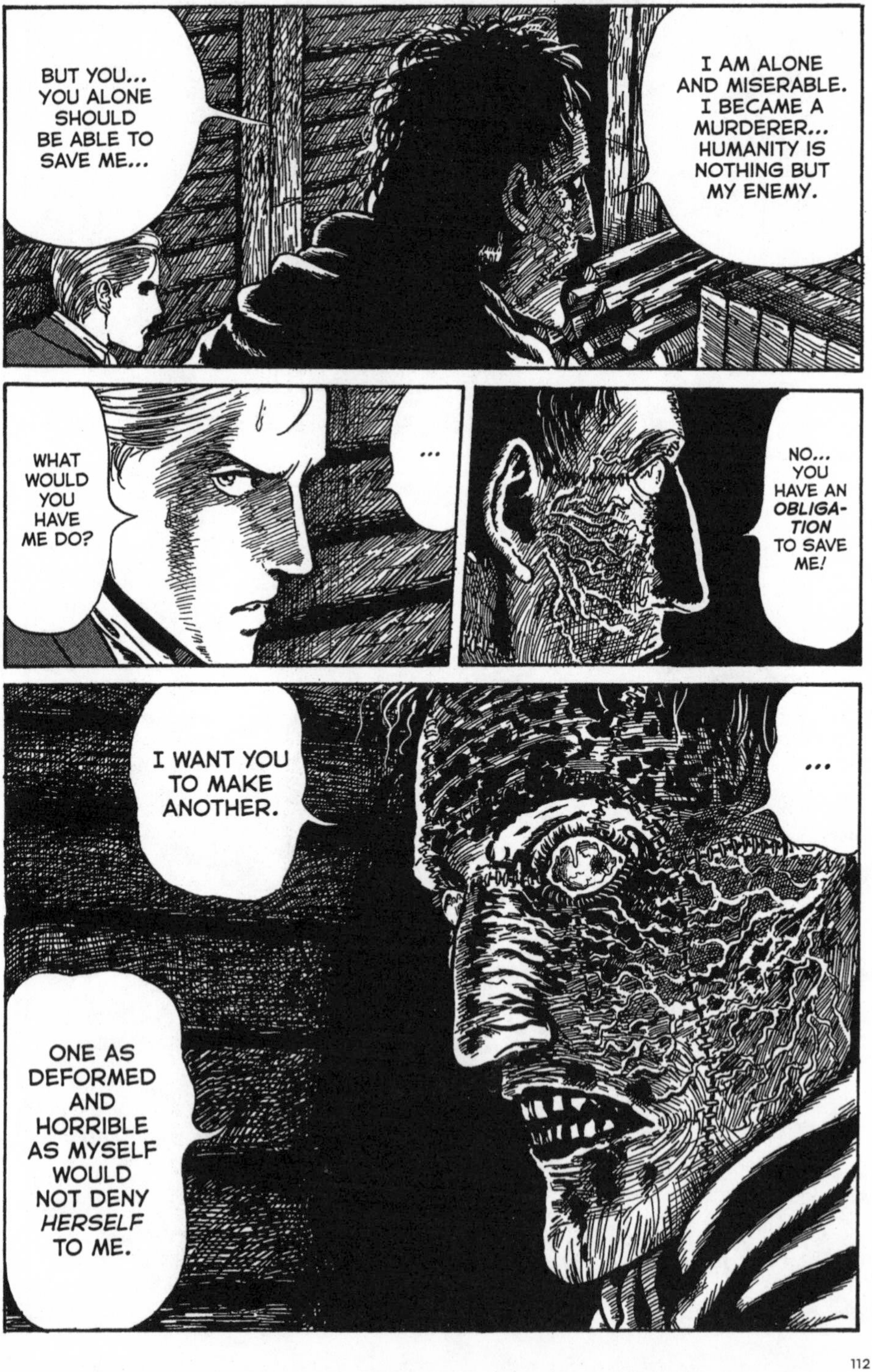
I AM ALONE AND MISERABLE. I BECAME A MURDERER... HUMANITY IS NOTHING BUT MY ENEMY.
BUT YOU... YOU ALONE SHOULD BE ABLE TO SAVE ME...
NO... YOU HAVE AN *OBLIGATION* TO SAVE ME!
...
WHAT WOULD YOU HAVE ME DO?
...
I WANT YOU TO MAKE ANOTHER.
ONE AS DEFORMED AND HORRIBLE AS MYSELF WOULD NOT DENY *HERSELF* TO ME.

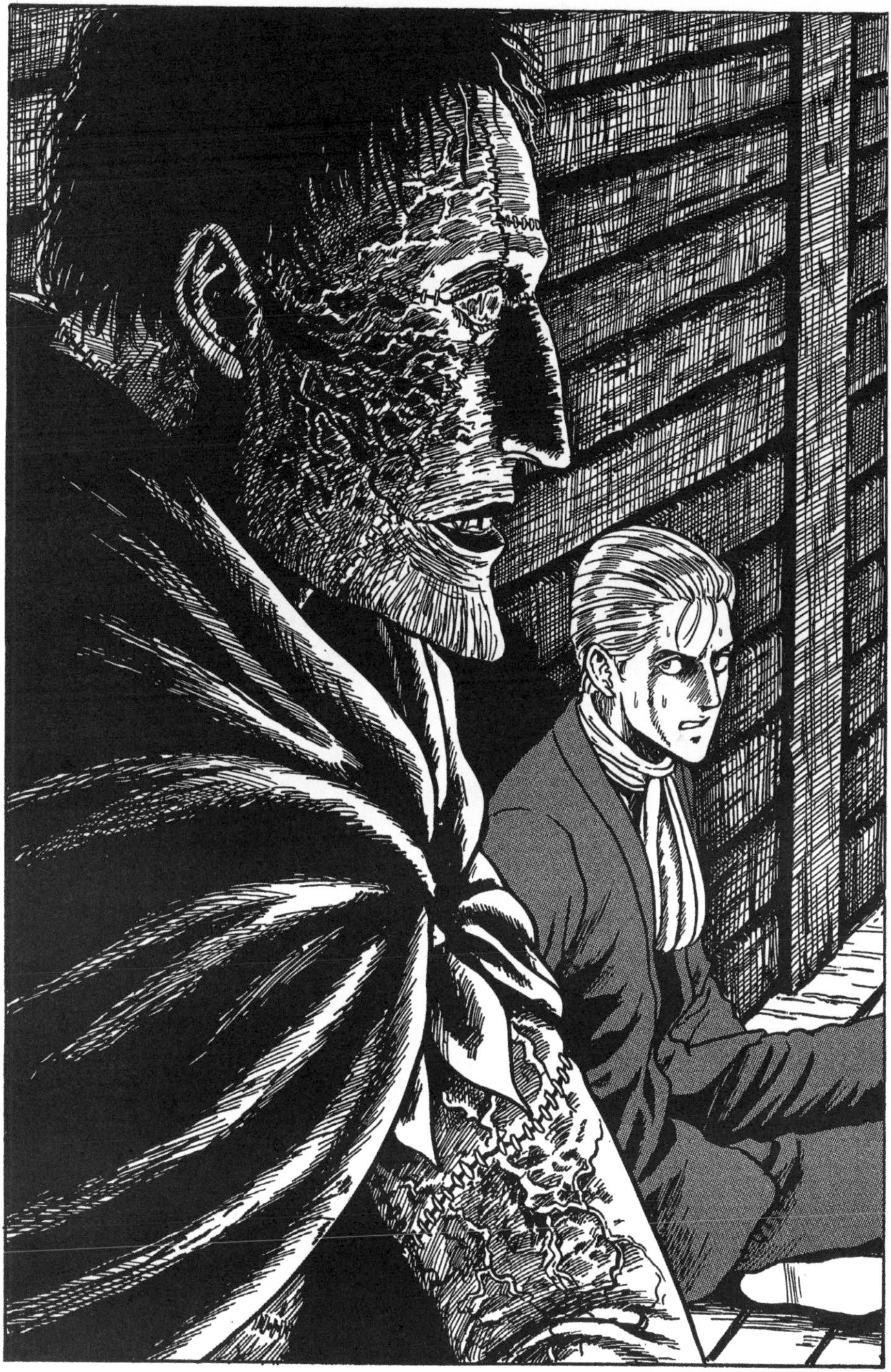

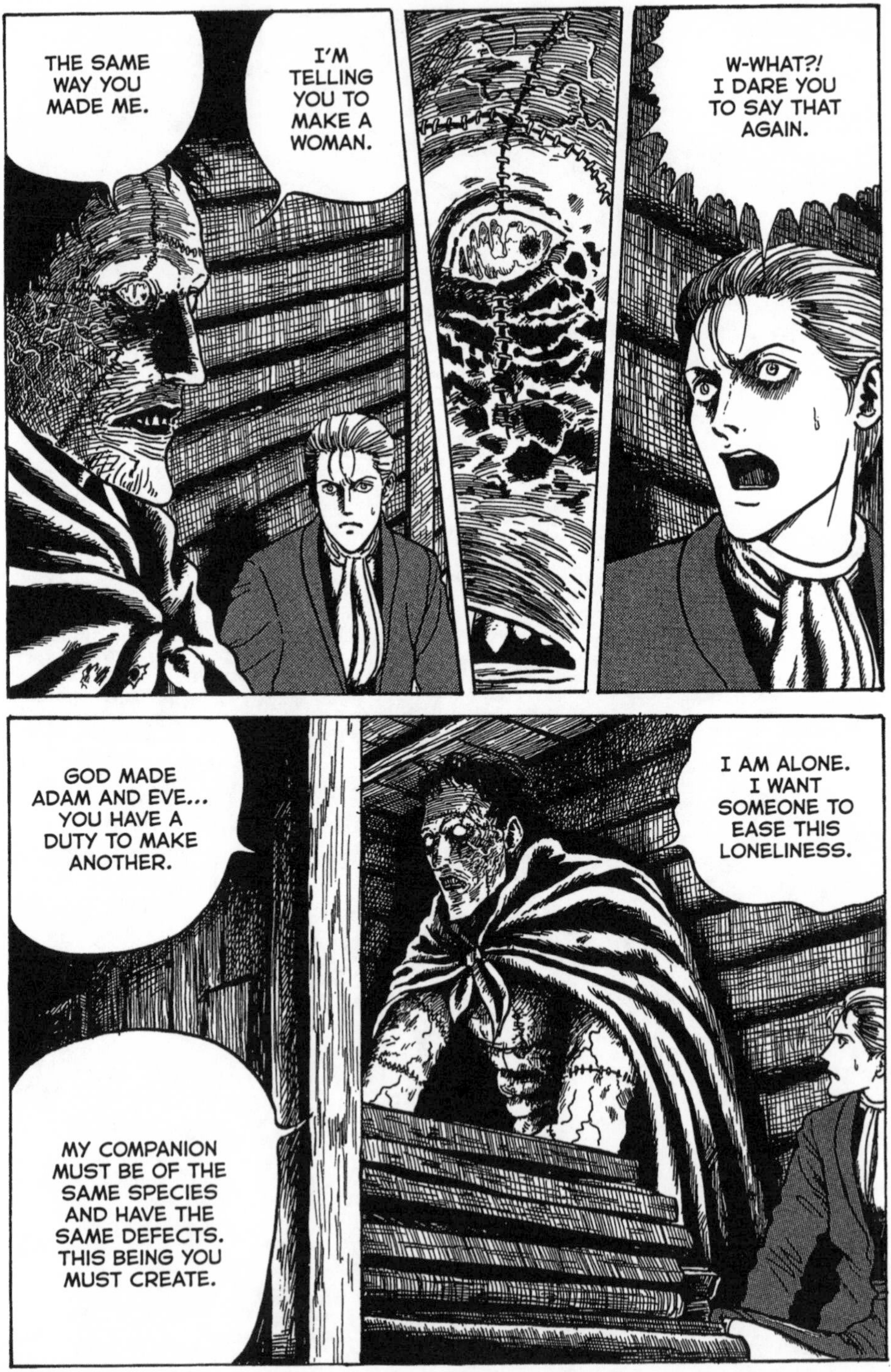
W-WHAT?! I DARE YOU TO SAY THAT AGAIN.
I'M TELLING YOU TO MAKE A WOMAN.
THE SAME WAY YOU MADE ME.
I AM ALONE. I WANT SOMEONE TO EASE THIS LONELINESS.
GOD MADE ADAM AND EVE... YOU HAVE A DUTY TO MAKE ANOTHER.
MY COMPANION MUST BE OF THE SAME SPECIES AND HAVE THE SAME DEFECTS. THIS BEING YOU MUST CREATE.

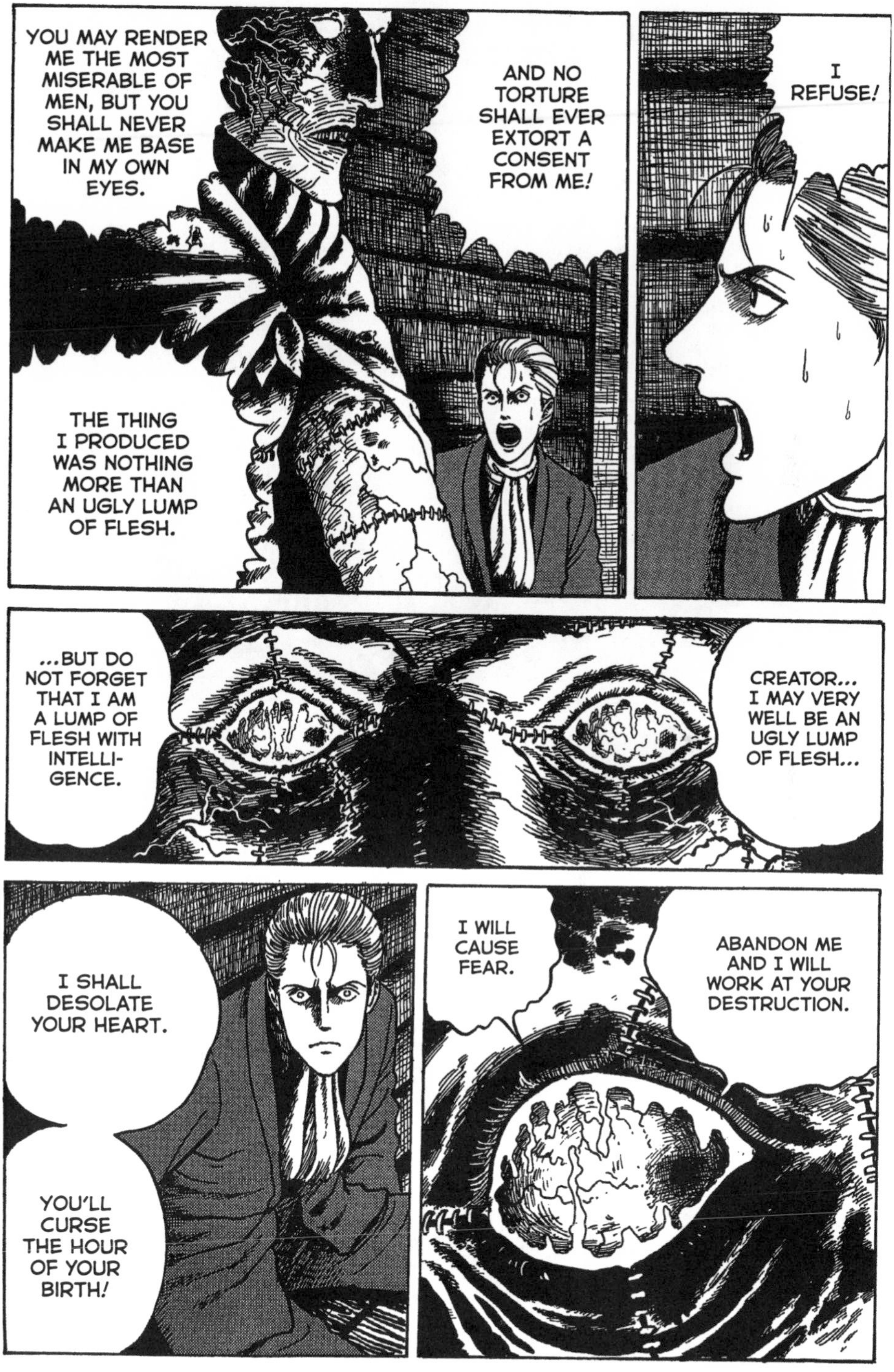
I REFUSE!
AND NO TORTURE SHALL EVER EXTORT A CONSENT FROM ME!
YOU MAY RENDER ME THE MOST MISERABLE OF MEN, BUT YOU SHALL NEVER MAKE ME BASE IN MY OWN EYES.
THE THING I PRODUCED WAS NOTHING MORE THAN AN UGLY LUMP OF FLESH.
CREATOR... I MAY VERY WELL BE AN UGLY LUMP OF FLESH...
...BUT DO NOT FORGET THAT I AM A LUMP OF FLESH WITH INTELLI-GENCE.
ABANDON ME AND I WILL WORK AT YOUR DESTRUCTION.
I WILL CAUSE FEAR.
I SHALL DESOLATE YOUR HEART.
YOU'LL CURSE THE HOUR OF YOUR BIRTH!

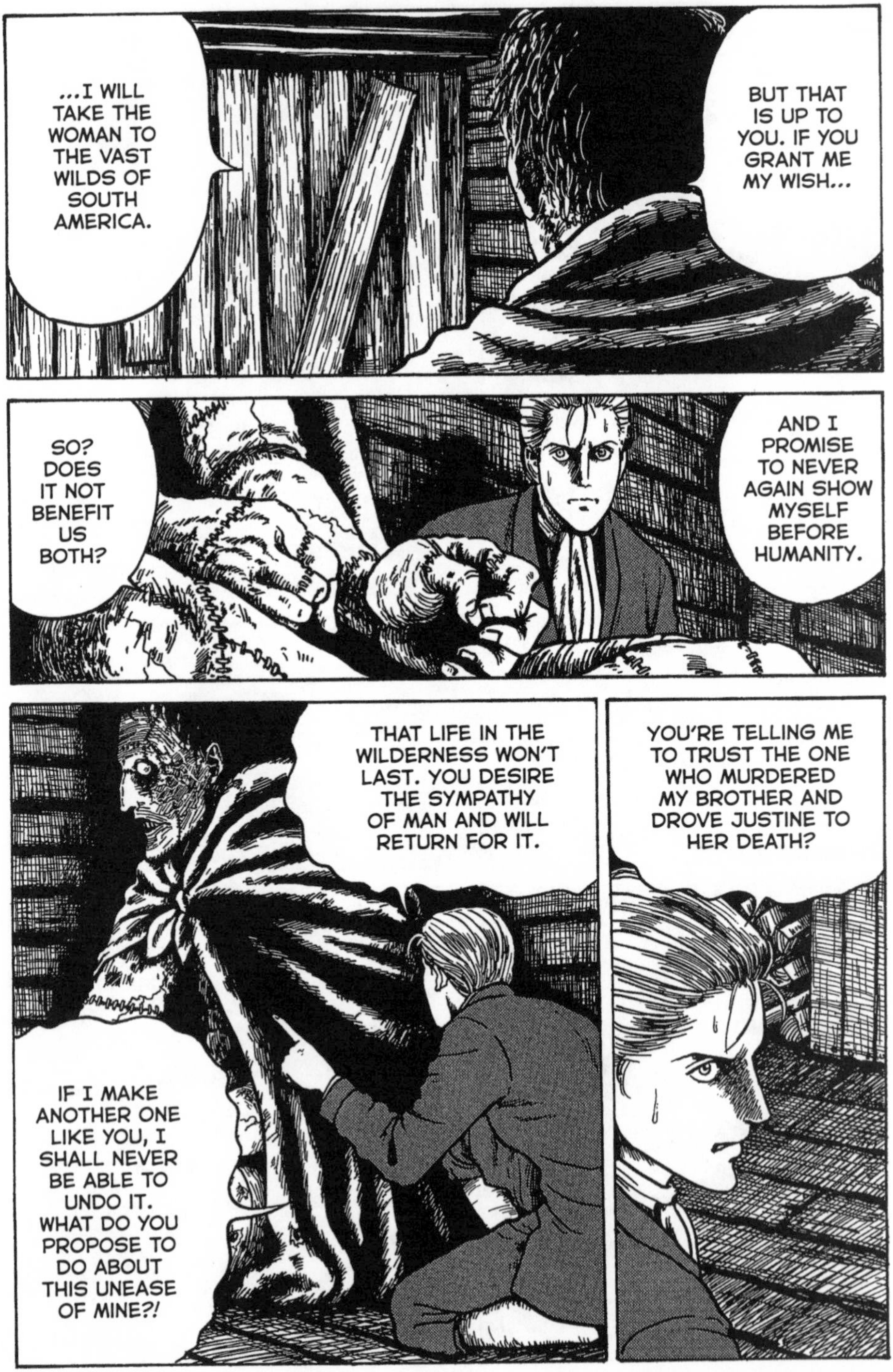
BUT THAT IS UP TO YOU. IF YOU GRANT ME MY WISH...
...I WILL TAKE THE WOMAN TO THE VAST WILDS OF SOUTH AMERICA.
AND I PROMISE TO NEVER AGAIN SHOW MYSELF BEFORE HUMANITY.
SO? DOES IT NOT BENEFIT US BOTH?
YOU'RE TELLING ME TO TRUST THE ONE WHO MURDERED MY BROTHER AND DROVE JUSTINE TO HER DEATH?
THAT LIFE IN THE WILDERNESS WON'T LAST. YOU DESIRE THE SYMPATHY OF MAN AND WILL RETURN FOR IT.
IF I MAKE ANOTHER ONE LIKE YOU, I SHALL NEVER BE ABLE TO UNDO IT. WHAT DO YOU PROPOSE TO DO ABOUT THIS UNEASE OF MINE?!

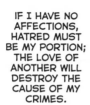

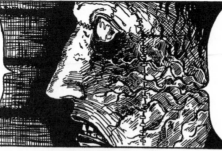

I SWEAR TO YOU, AND BY YOU THAT MADE ME, THAT WITH THE COMPANION YOU BESTOW MY EVIL PASSIONS WILL HAVE FLED! MY LIFE WILL FLOW AWAY, AND IN MY DYING MOMENTS I SHALL NEVER CURSE MY MAKER.
IF I HAVE NO AFFECTIONS, HATRED MUST BE MY PORTION; THE LOVE OF ANOTHER WILL DESTROY THE CAUSE OF MY CRIMES.
I WANT YOU TO SAVE ME SOMEHOW... AND YOU ARE THE ONLY ONE WHO CAN DO IT.
CREATOR. I'LL HAVE YOUR REPLY.
I STARTED TO SYMPATHIZE WITH THE CREATURE.
I CONSENT TO YOUR DEMAND.
BUT YOU WILL QUIT EUROPE AND ANYWHERE KNOWN TO MAN, FOREVER?
I WILL!
I SWEAR BY THE SUN, AND BY THE BLUE SKY OF HEAVEN!

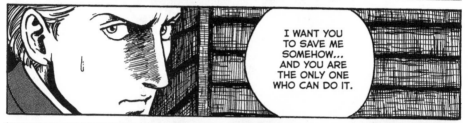

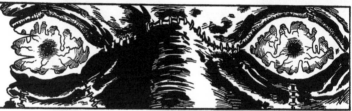

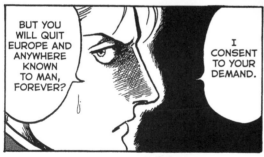

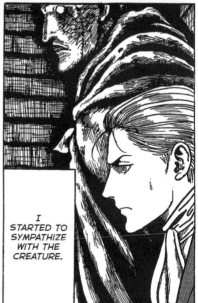

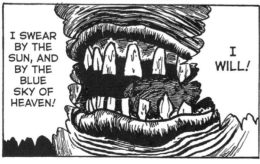

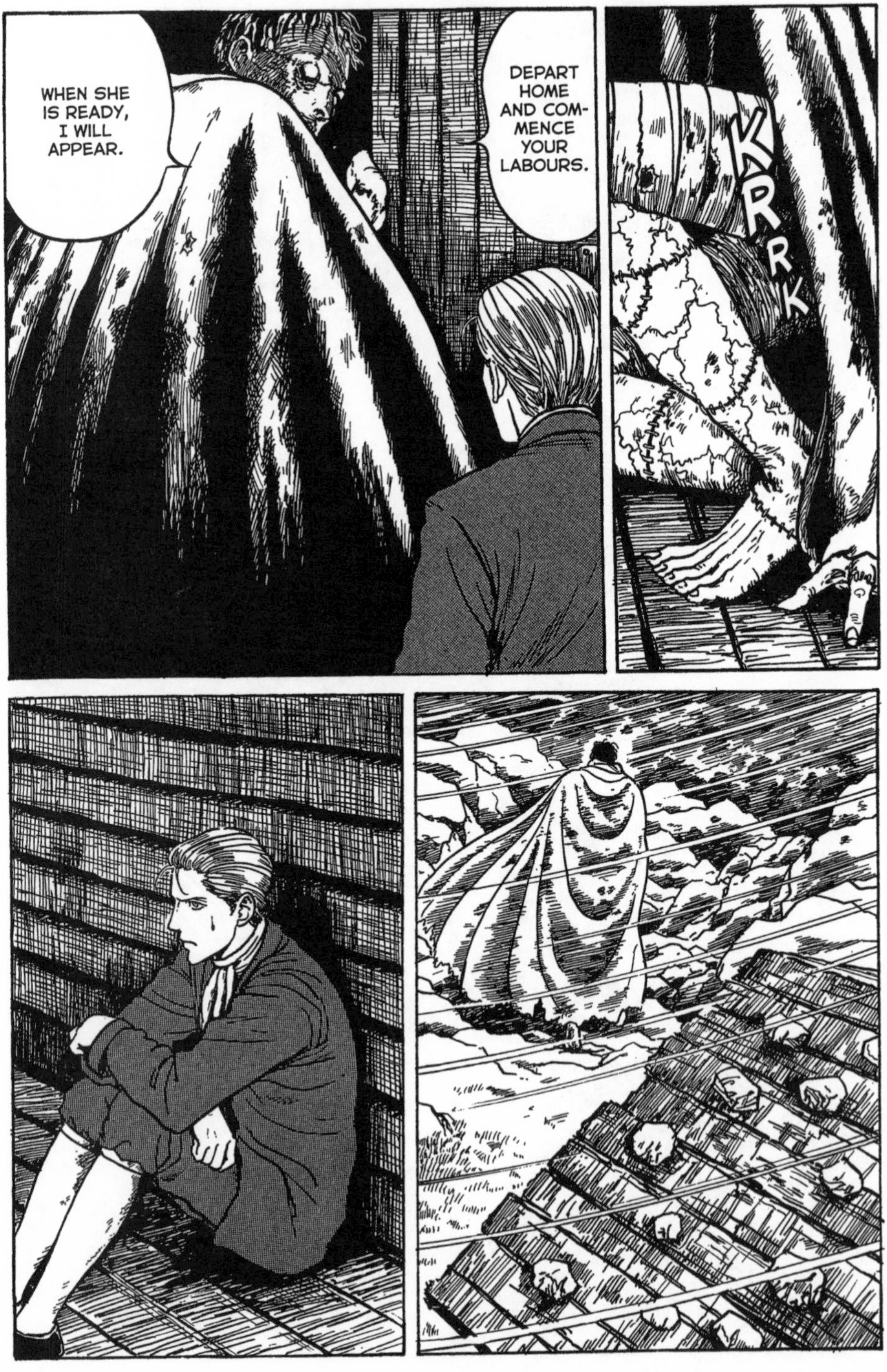
KRRK
DEPART HOME AND COMMENCE YOUR LABOURS.
WHEN SHE IS READY, I WILL APPEAR.

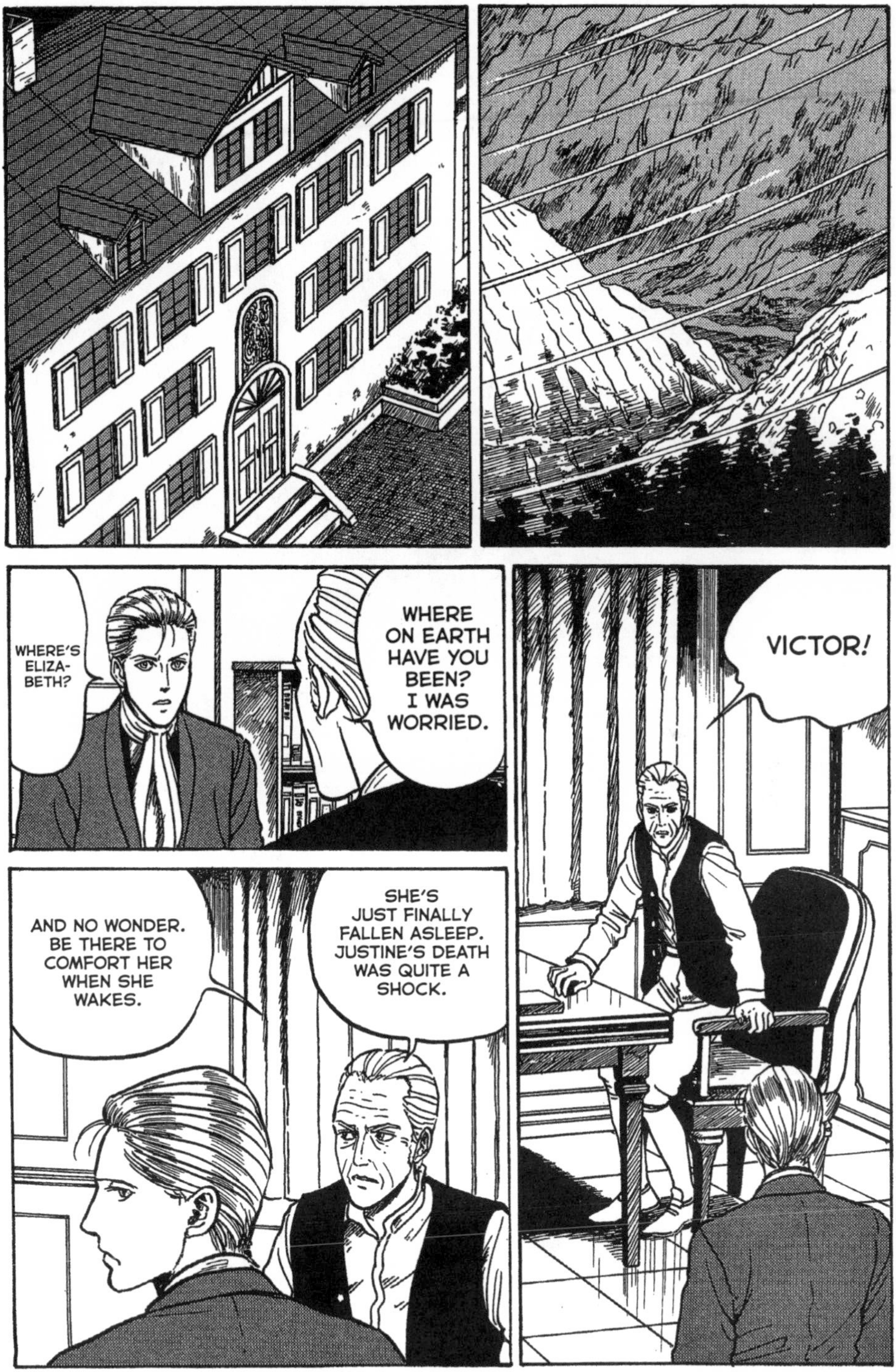
VICTOR!
WHERE ON EARTH HAVE YOU BEEN? I WAS WORRIED.
WHERE'S ELIZA-BETH?
SHE'S JUST FINALLY FALLEN ASLEEP. JUSTINE'S DEATH WAS QUITE A SHOCK.
AND NO WONDER. BE THERE TO COMFORT HER WHEN SHE WAKES.

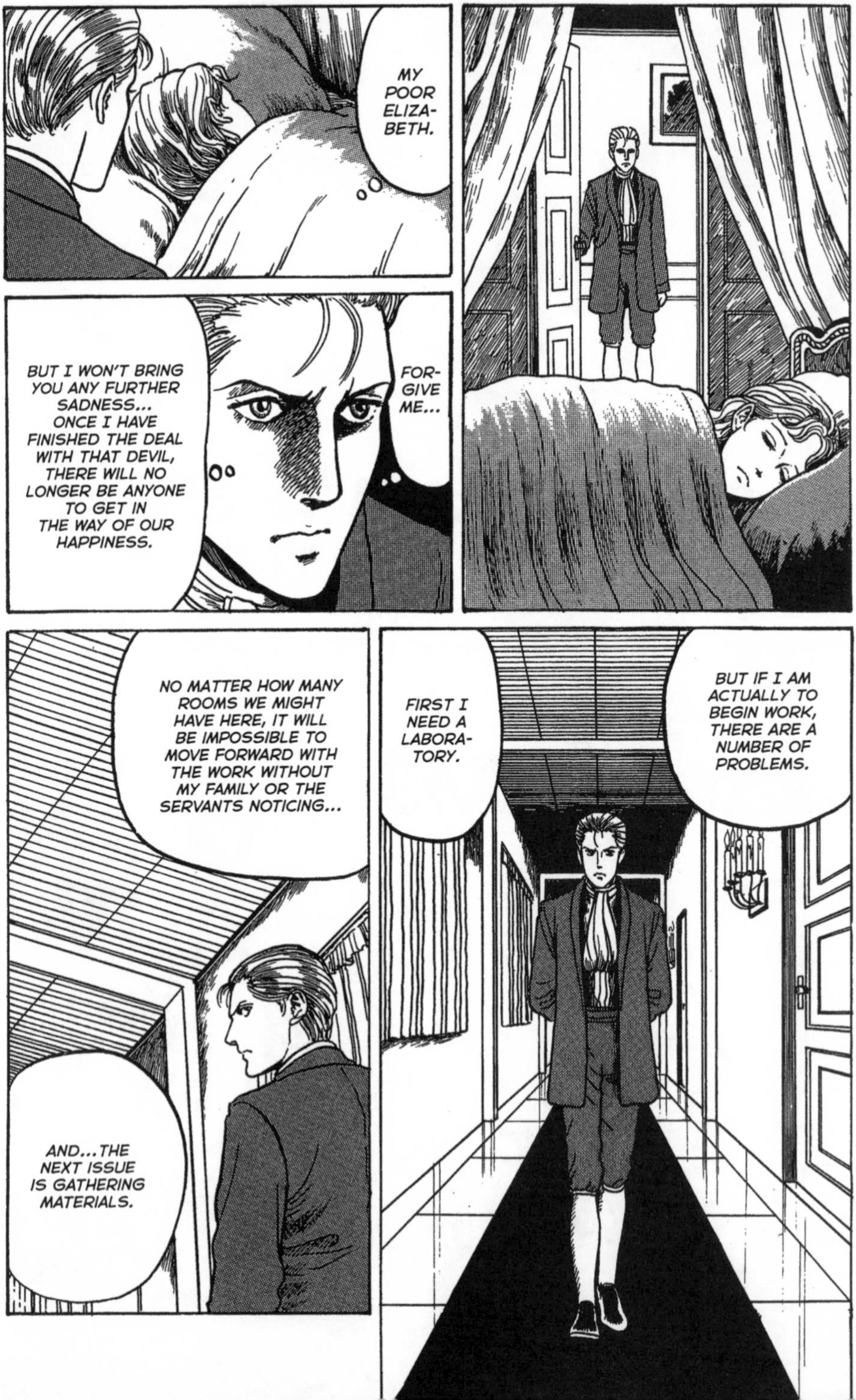
MY POOR ELIZABETH.
FORGIVE ME...
BUT I WON'T BRING YOU ANY FURTHER SADNESS... ONCE I HAVE FINISHED THE DEAL WITH THAT DEVIL, THERE WILL NO LONGER BE ANYONE TO GET IN THE WAY OF OUR HAPPINESS.
BUT IF I AM ACTUALLY TO BEGIN WORK, THERE ARE A NUMBER OF PROBLEMS.
FIRST I NEED A LABORATORY.
NO MATTER HOW MANY ROOMS WE MIGHT HAVE HERE, IT WILL BE IMPOSSIBLE TO MOVE FORWARD WITH THE WORK WITHOUT MY FAMILY OR THE SERVANTS NOTICING...
AND...THE NEXT ISSUE IS GATHERING MATERIALS.

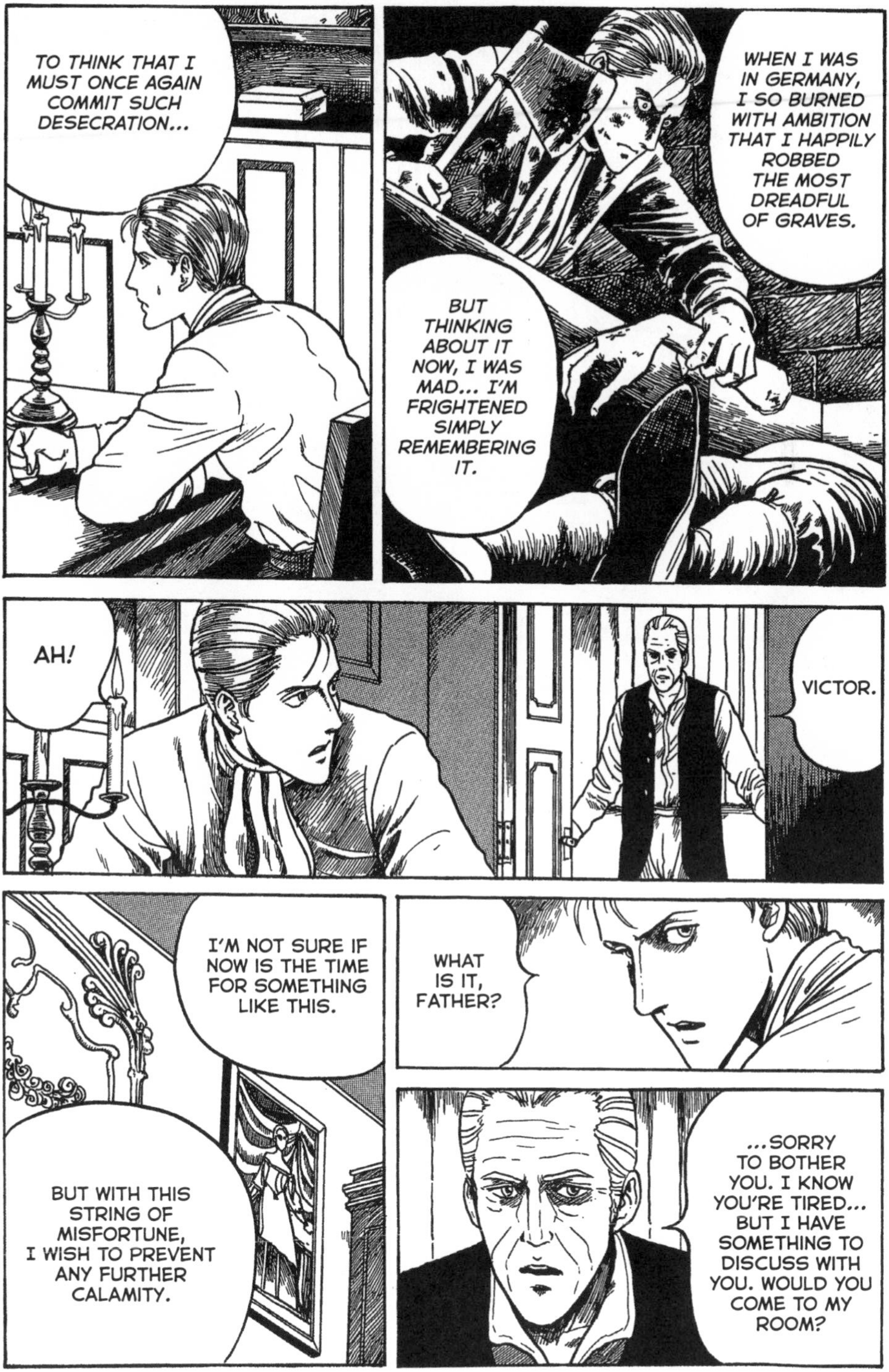
WHEN I WAS IN GERMANY, I SO BURNED WITH AMBITION THAT I HAPPILY ROBBED THE MOST DREADFUL OF GRAVES.
BUT THINKING ABOUT IT NOW, I WAS MAD... I'M FRIGHTENED SIMPLY REMEMBERING IT.
TO THINK THAT I MUST ONCE AGAIN COMMIT SUCH DESECRATION...
VICTOR.
AH!
WHAT IS IT, FATHER?
...SORRY TO BOTHER YOU. I KNOW YOU'RE TIRED... BUT I HAVE SOMETHING TO DISCUSS WITH YOU. WOULD YOU COME TO MY ROOM?
I'M NOT SURE IF NOW IS THE TIME FOR SOMETHING LIKE THIS.
BUT WITH THIS STRING OF MISFORTUNE, I WISH TO PREVENT ANY FURTHER CALAMITY.

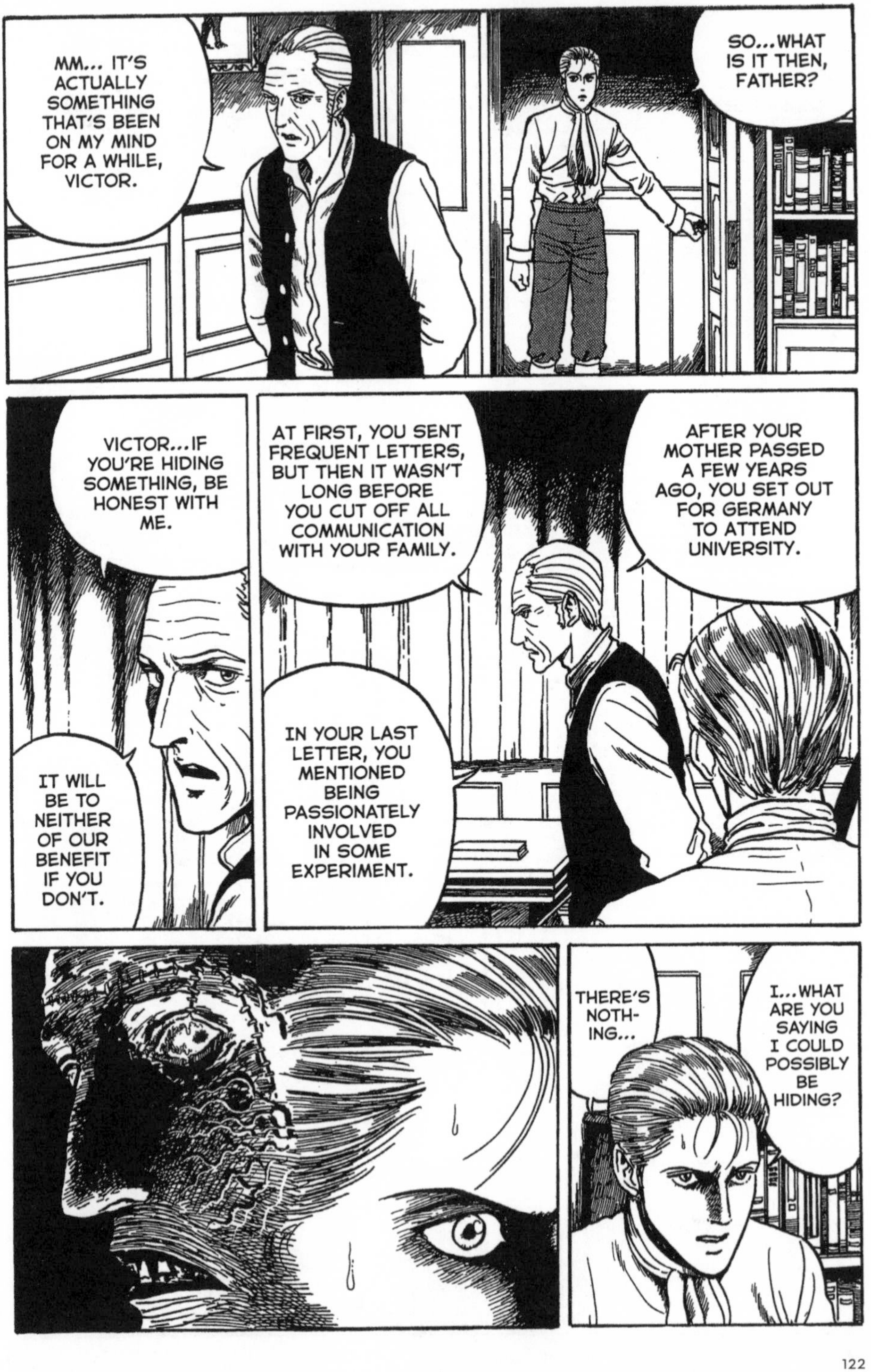
SO...WHAT IS IT THEN, FATHER?
MM... IT'S ACTUALLY SOMETHING THAT'S BEEN ON MY MIND FOR A WHILE, VICTOR.
AFTER YOUR MOTHER PASSED A FEW YEARS AGO, YOU SET OUT FOR GERMANY TO ATTEND UNIVERSITY.
AT FIRST, YOU SENT FREQUENT LETTERS, BUT THEN IT WASN'T LONG BEFORE YOU CUT OFF ALL COMMUNICATION WITH YOUR FAMILY.
IN YOUR LAST LETTER, YOU MENTIONED BEING PASSIONATELY INVOLVED IN SOME EXPERIMENT.
VICTOR...IF YOU'RE HIDING SOMETHING, BE HONEST WITH ME.
IT WILL BE TO NEITHER OF OUR BENEFIT IF YOU DON'T.
I...WHAT ARE YOU SAYING I COULD POSSIBLY BE HIDING?
THERE'S NOTH-ING...

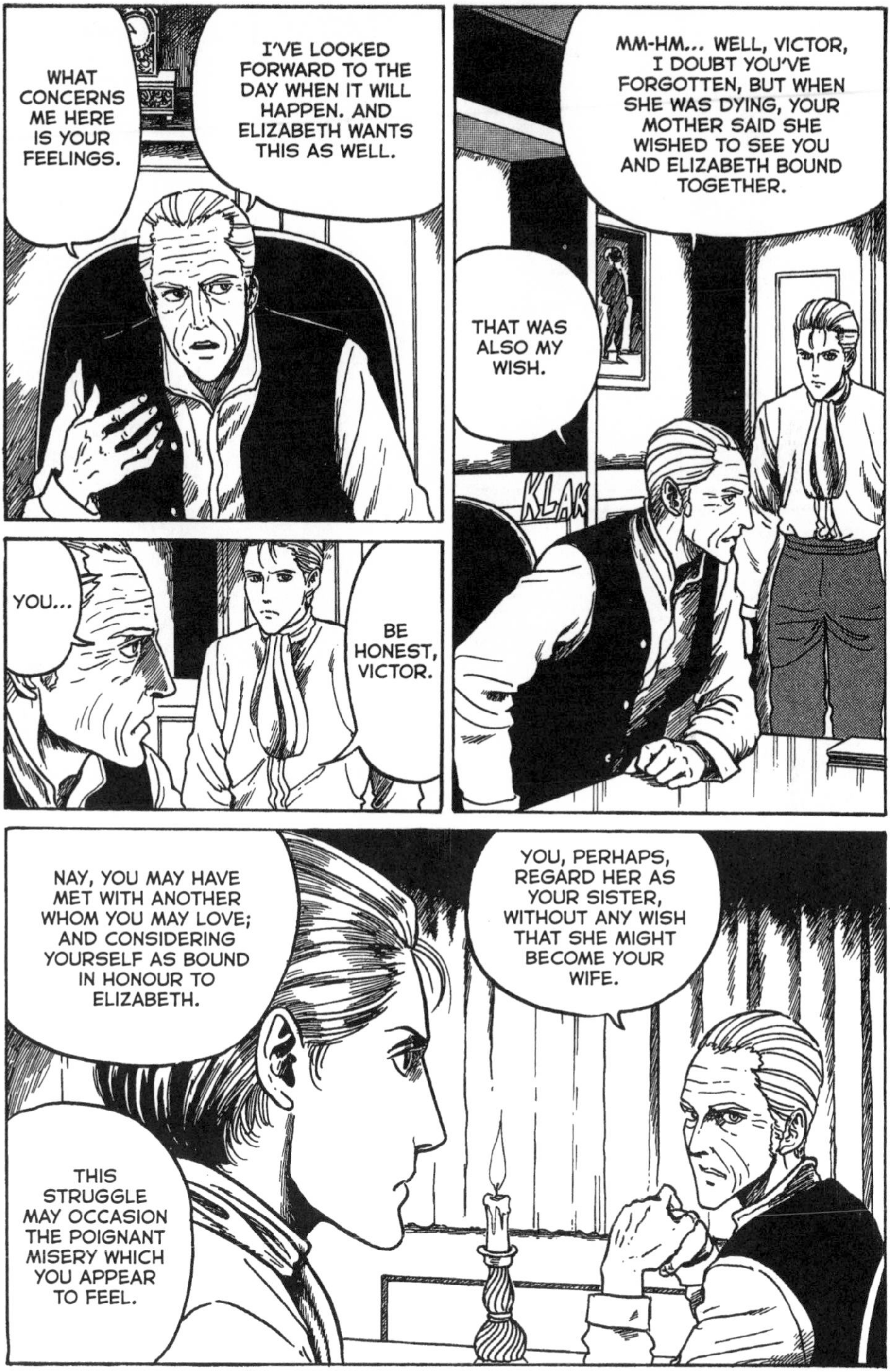
MM-HM... WELL, VICTOR, I DOUBT YOU'VE FORGOTTEN, BUT WHEN SHE WAS DYING, YOUR MOTHER SAID SHE WISHED TO SEE YOU AND ELIZABETH BOUND TOGETHER.
THAT WAS ALSO MY WISH.
KLAK
I'VE LOOKED FORWARD TO THE DAY WHEN IT WILL HAPPEN. AND ELIZABETH WANTS THIS AS WELL.
WHAT CONCERNS ME HERE IS YOUR FEELINGS.
BE HONEST, VICTOR.
YOU...
YOU, PERHAPS, REGARD HER AS YOUR SISTER, WITHOUT ANY WISH THAT SHE MIGHT BECOME YOUR WIFE.
NAY, YOU MAY HAVE MET WITH ANOTHER WHOM YOU MAY LOVE; AND CONSIDERING YOURSELF AS BOUND IN HONOUR TO ELIZABETH.
THIS STRUGGLE MAY OCCASION THE POIGNANT MISERY WHICH YOU APPEAR TO FEEL.

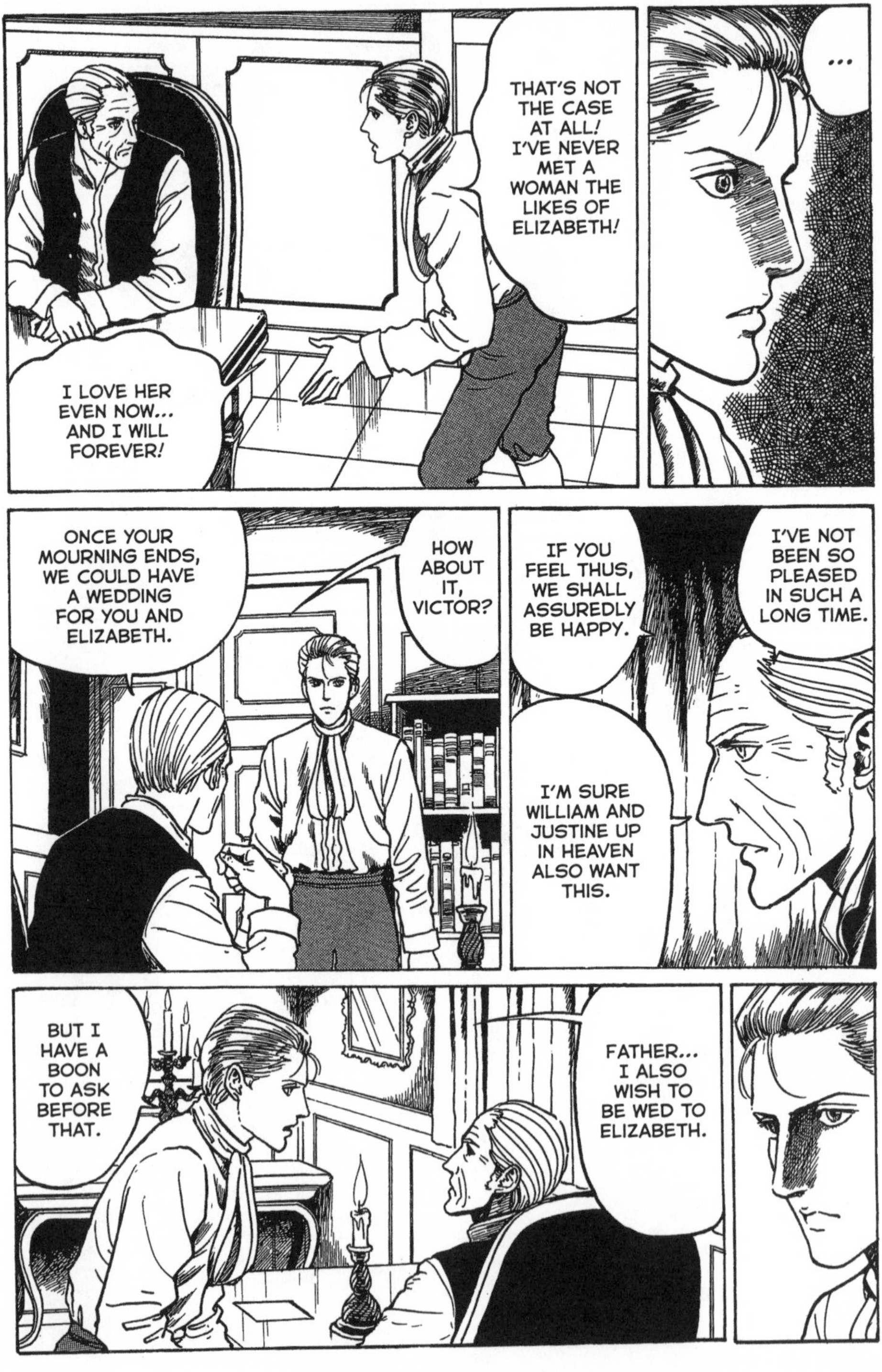
...
THAT'S NOT THE CASE AT ALL! I'VE NEVER MET A WOMAN THE LIKES OF ELIZABETH!
I LOVE HER EVEN NOW... AND I WILL FOREVER!
I'VE NOT BEEN SO PLEASED IN SUCH A LONG TIME.
IF YOU FEEL THUS, WE SHALL ASSUREDLY BE HAPPY.
I'M SURE WILLIAM AND JUSTINE UP IN HEAVEN ALSO WANT THIS.
HOW ABOUT IT, VICTOR?
ONCE YOUR MOURNING ENDS, WE COULD HAVE A WEDDING FOR YOU AND ELIZABETH.
FATHER... I ALSO WISH TO BE WED TO ELIZABETH.
BUT I HAVE A BOON TO ASK BEFORE THAT.

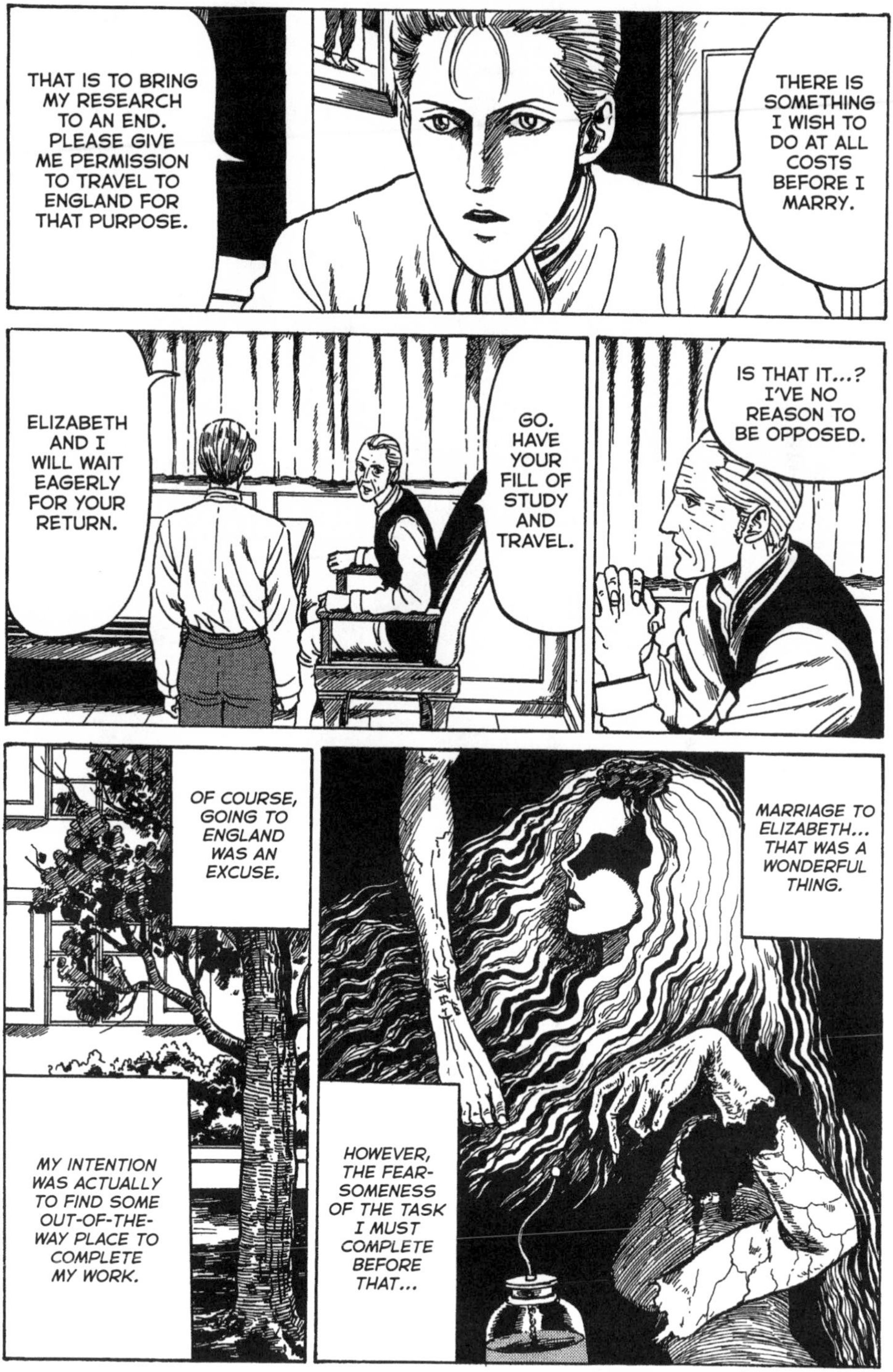
THERE IS SOMETHING I WISH TO DO AT ALL COSTS BEFORE I MARRY.
THAT IS TO BRING MY RESEARCH TO AN END. PLEASE GIVE ME PERMISSION TO TRAVEL TO ENGLAND FOR THAT PURPOSE.
IS THAT IT...? I'VE NO REASON TO BE OPPOSED.
GO. HAVE YOUR FILL OF STUDY AND TRAVEL.
ELIZABETH AND I WILL WAIT EAGERLY FOR YOUR RETURN.
MARRIAGE TO ELIZABETH... THAT WAS A WONDERFUL THING.
HOWEVER, THE FEAR-SOMENESS OF THE TASK I MUST COMPLETE BEFORE THAT...
OF COURSE, GOING TO ENGLAND WAS AN EXCUSE.
MY INTENTION WAS ACTUALLY TO FIND SOME OUT-OF-THE-WAY PLACE TO COMPLETE MY WORK.

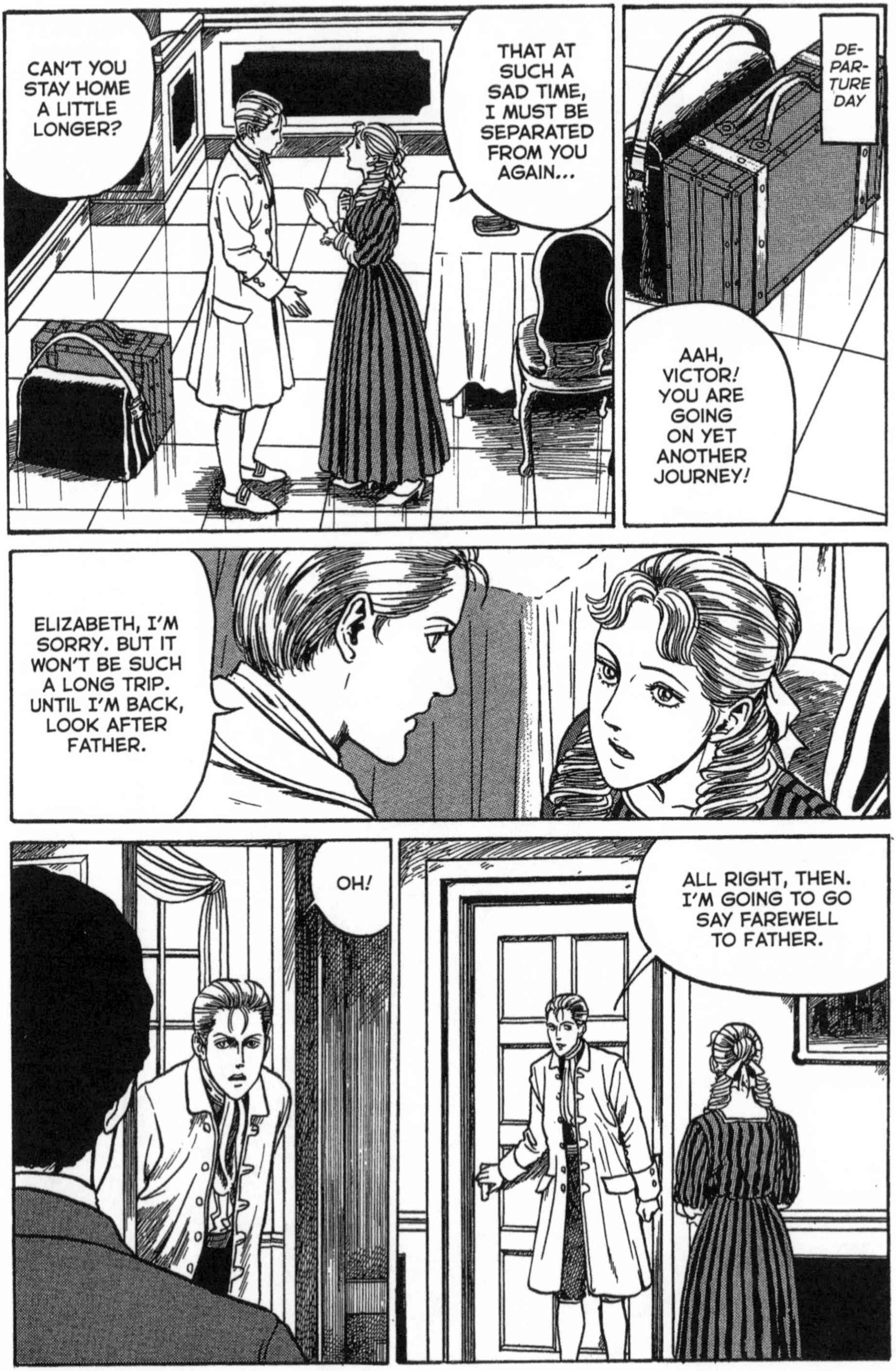
DEPARTURE DAY
AAH, VICTOR! YOU ARE GOING ON YET ANOTHER JOURNEY!
THAT AT SUCH A SAD TIME, I MUST BE SEPARATED FROM YOU AGAIN...
CAN'T YOU STAY HOME A LITTLE LONGER?
ELIZABETH, I'M SORRY. BUT IT WON'T BE SUCH A LONG TRIP. UNTIL I'M BACK, LOOK AFTER FATHER.
ALL RIGHT, THEN. I'M GOING TO GO SAY FAREWELL TO FATHER.
OH!

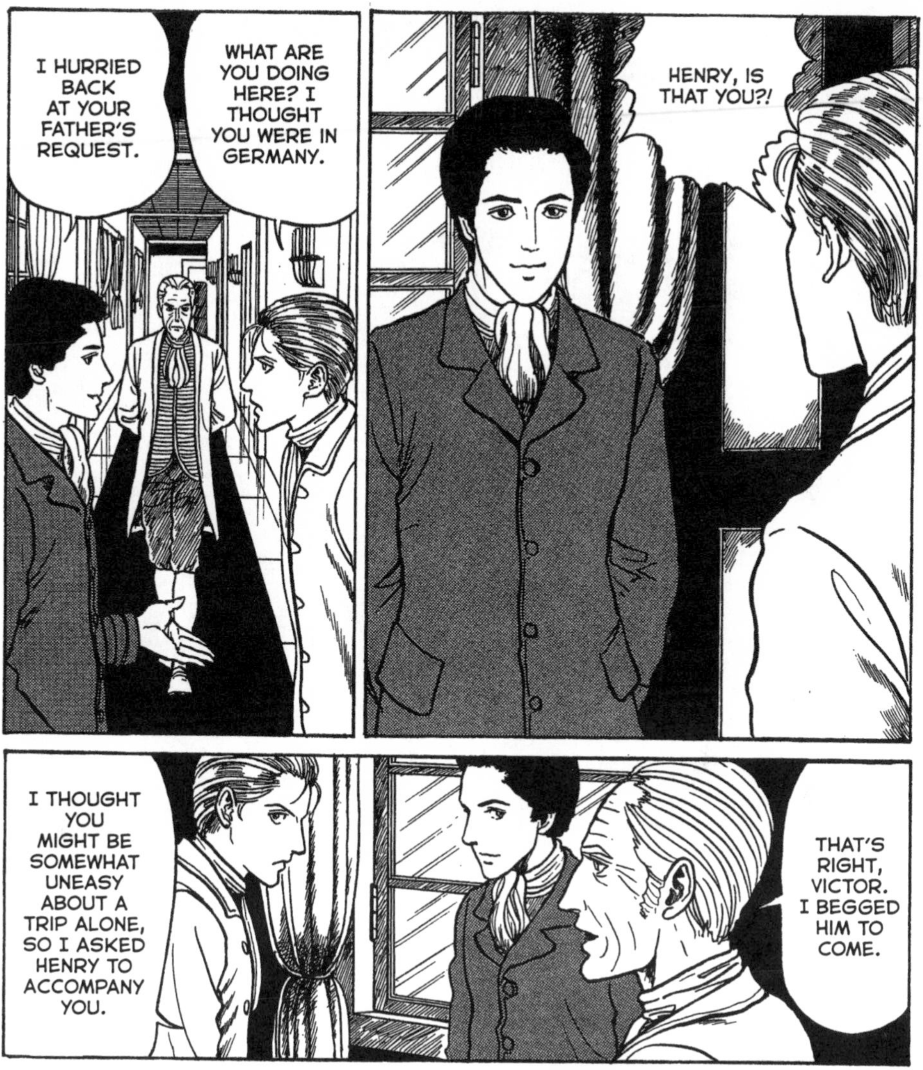

HENRY, IS THAT YOU?!
WHAT ARE YOU DOING HERE? I THOUGHT YOU WERE IN GERMANY.
I HURRIED BACK AT YOUR FATHER'S REQUEST.
THAT'S RIGHT, VICTOR. I BEGGED HIM TO COME.
I THOUGHT YOU MIGHT BE SOMEWHAT UNEASY ABOUT A TRIP ALONE, SO I ASKED HENRY TO ACCOMPANY YOU.
BUT, HENRY...
YOU DON'T LOOK TOO PLEASED AT THE IDEA.
IF IT'S UNIVERSITY, NO NEED TO WORRY. I WAS ACTUALLY WANTING A LITTLE BREAK.

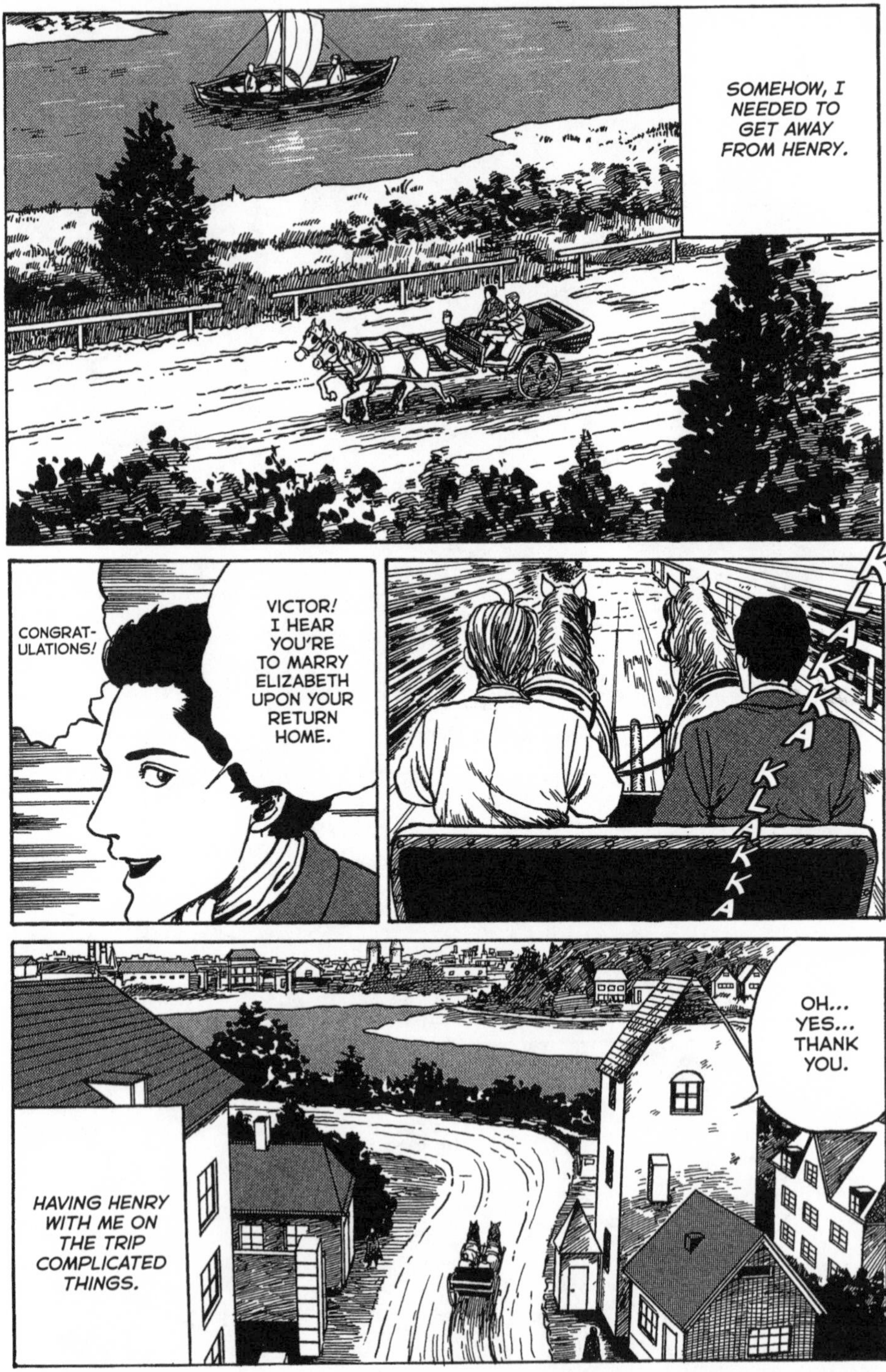
SOMEHOW, I NEEDED TO GET AWAY FROM HENRY.
KLAKKA KLAKKA
VICTOR! I HEAR YOU'RE TO MARRY ELIZABETH UPON YOUR RETURN HOME.
CONGRAT-ULATIONS!
OH... YES... THANK YOU.
HAVING HENRY WITH ME ON THE TRIP COMPLICATED THINGS.

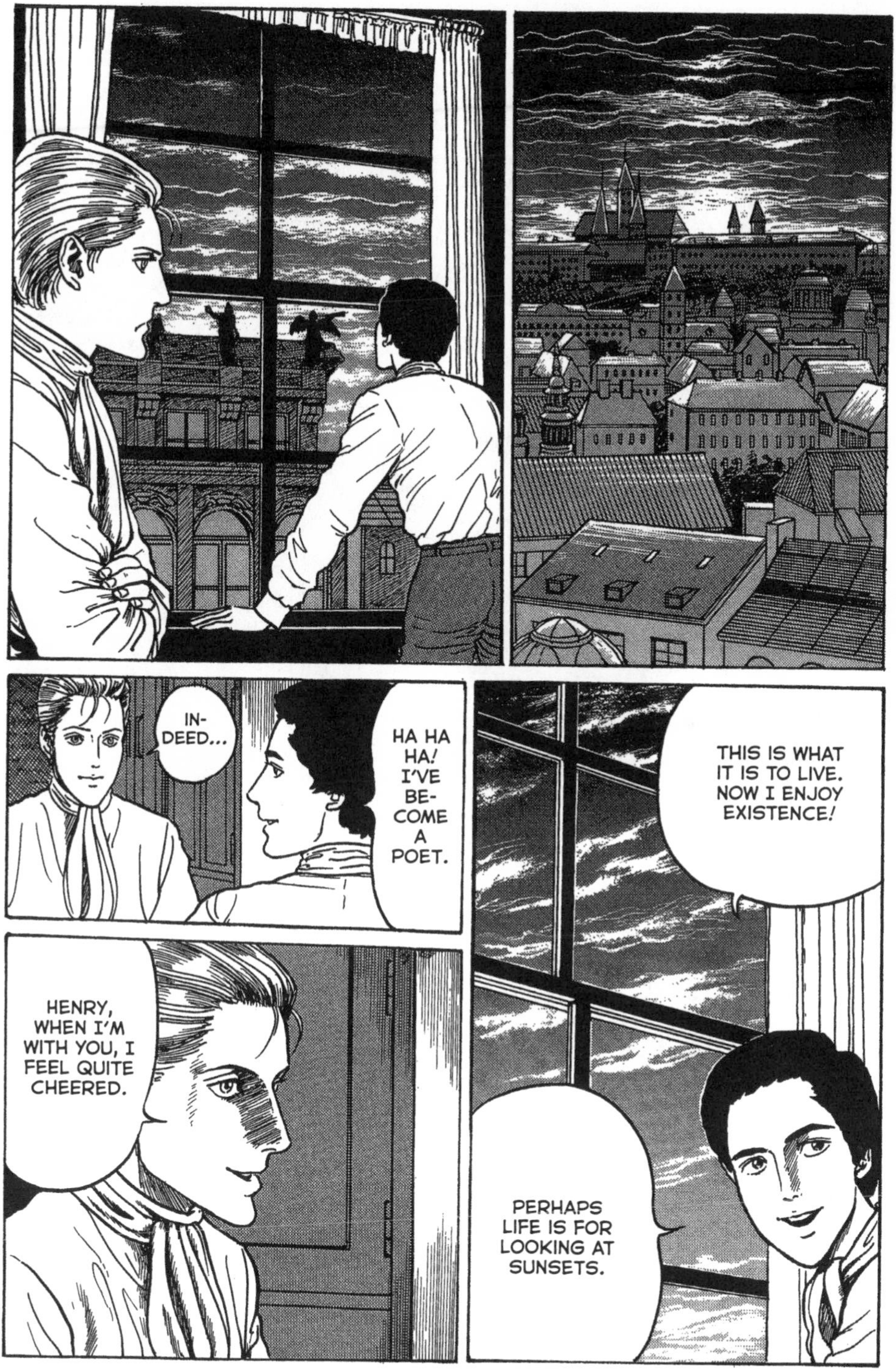
THIS IS WHAT IT IS TO LIVE. NOW I ENJOY EXISTENCE!
PERHAPS LIFE IS FOR LOOKING AT SUNSETS.
HA HA HA! I'VE BECOME A POET.
INDEED...
HENRY, WHEN I'M WITH YOU, I FEEL QUITE CHEERED.

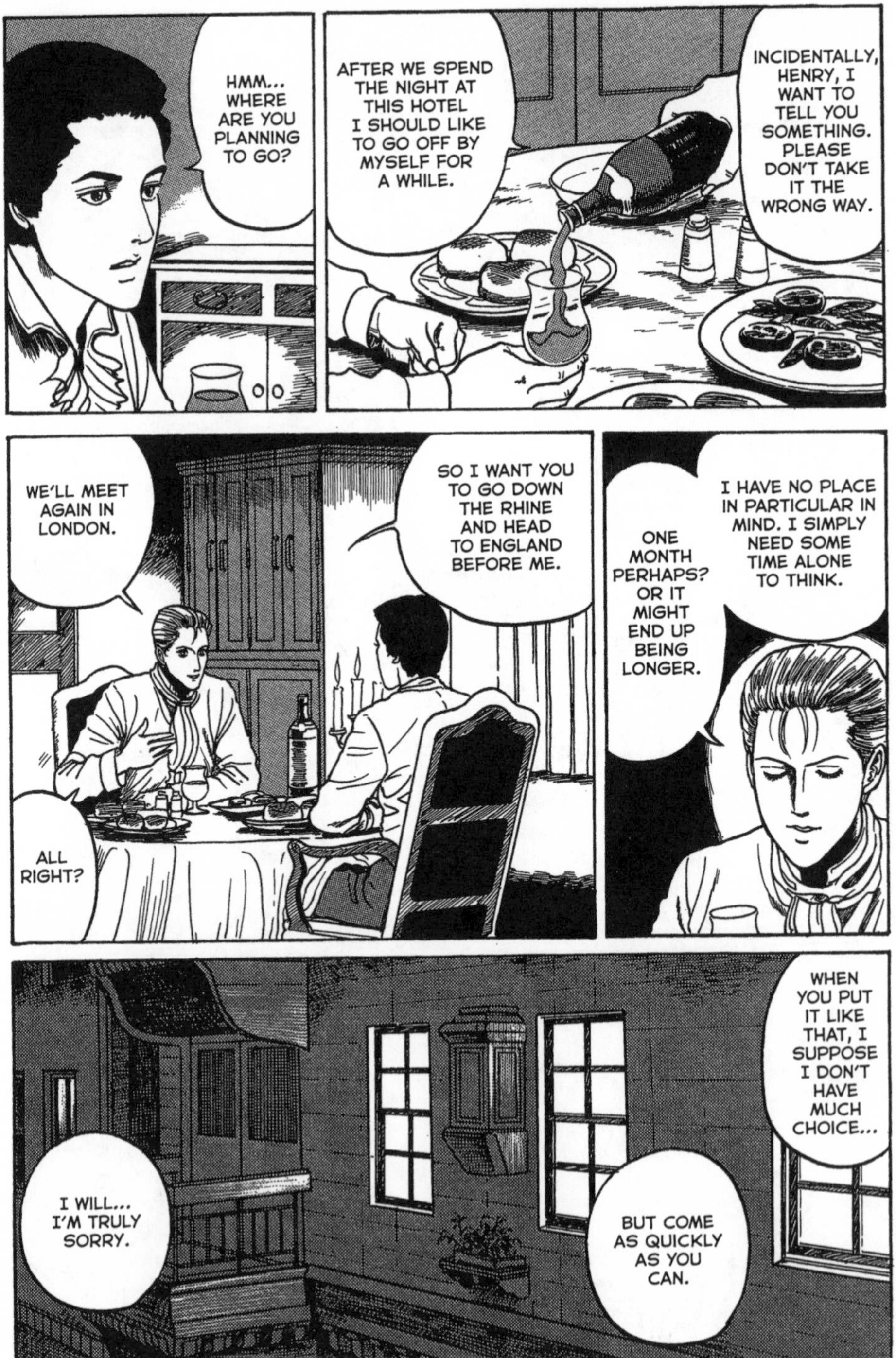
INCIDENTALLY, HENRY, I WANT TO TELL YOU SOMETHING. PLEASE DON'T TAKE IT THE WRONG WAY.
AFTER WE SPEND THE NIGHT AT THIS HOTEL I SHOULD LIKE TO GO OFF BY MYSELF FOR A WHILE.
HMM... WHERE ARE YOU PLANNING TO GO?
I HAVE NO PLACE IN PARTICULAR IN MIND. I SIMPLY NEED SOME TIME ALONE TO THINK.
ONE MONTH PERHAPS? OR IT MIGHT END UP BEING LONGER.
SO I WANT YOU TO GO DOWN THE RHINE AND HEAD TO ENGLAND BEFORE ME.
WE'LL MEET AGAIN IN LONDON.
ALL RIGHT?
WHEN YOU PUT IT LIKE THAT, I SUPPOSE I DON'T HAVE MUCH CHOICE...
BUT COME AS QUICKLY AS YOU CAN.
I WILL... I'M TRULY SORRY.

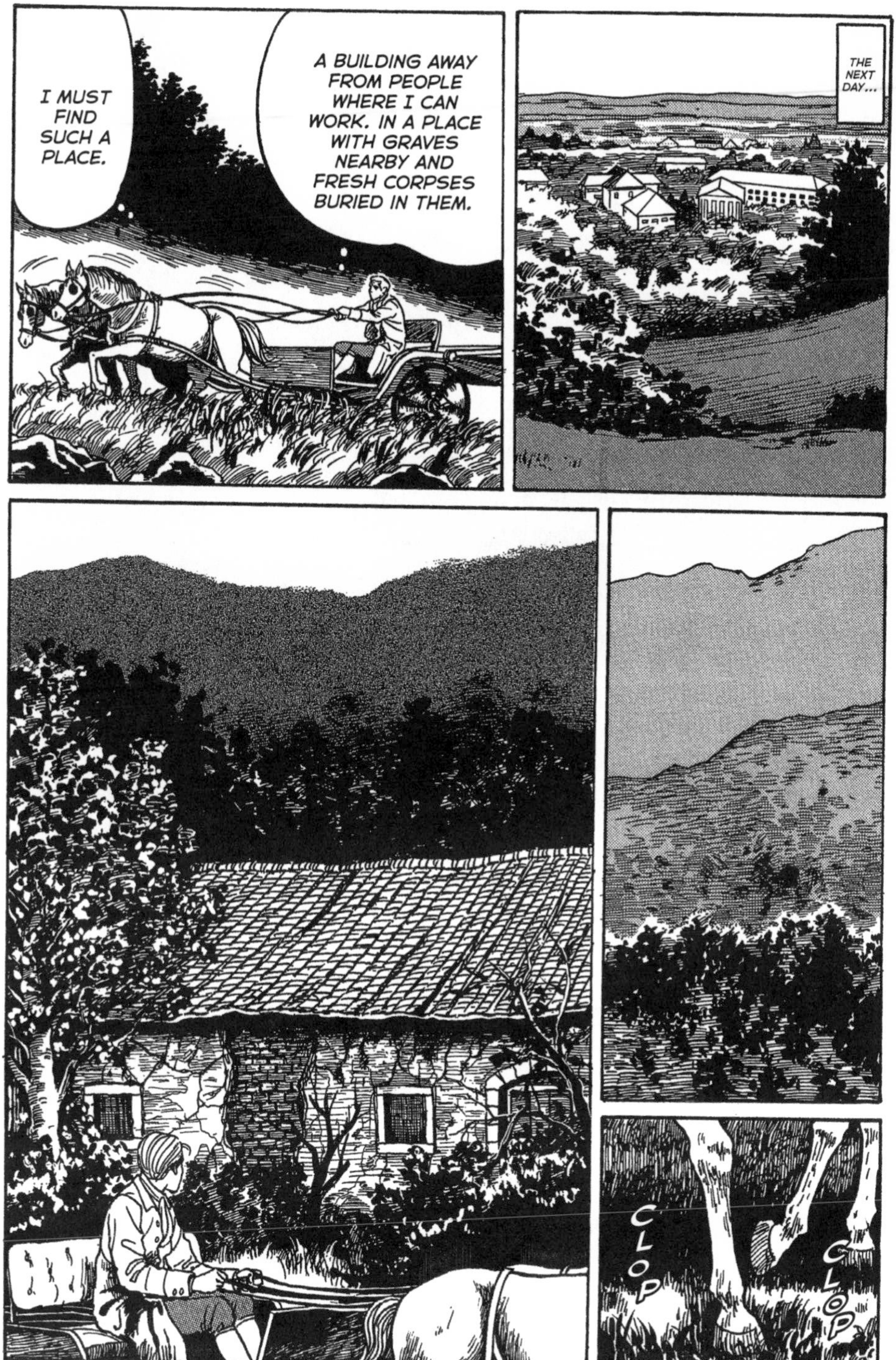
THE NEXT DAY...
A BUILDING AWAY FROM PEOPLE WHERE I CAN WORK. IN A PLACE WITH GRAVES NEARBY AND FRESH CORPSES BURIED IN THEM.
I MUST FIND SUCH A PLACE.
CLOP
CLOP

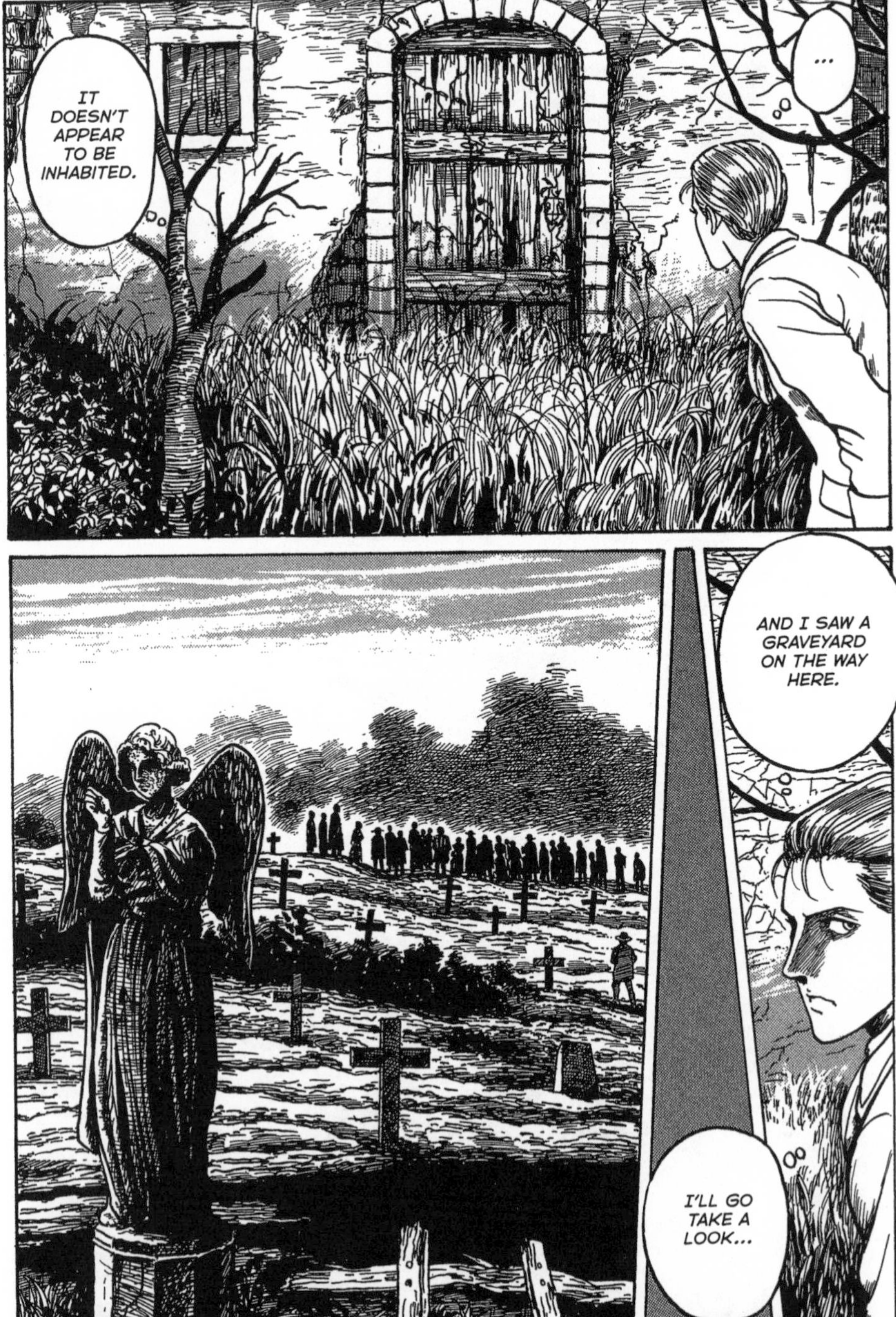
...
IT DOESN'T APPEAR TO BE INHABITED.
AND I SAW A GRAVEYARD ON THE WAY HERE.
I'LL GO TAKE A LOOK...

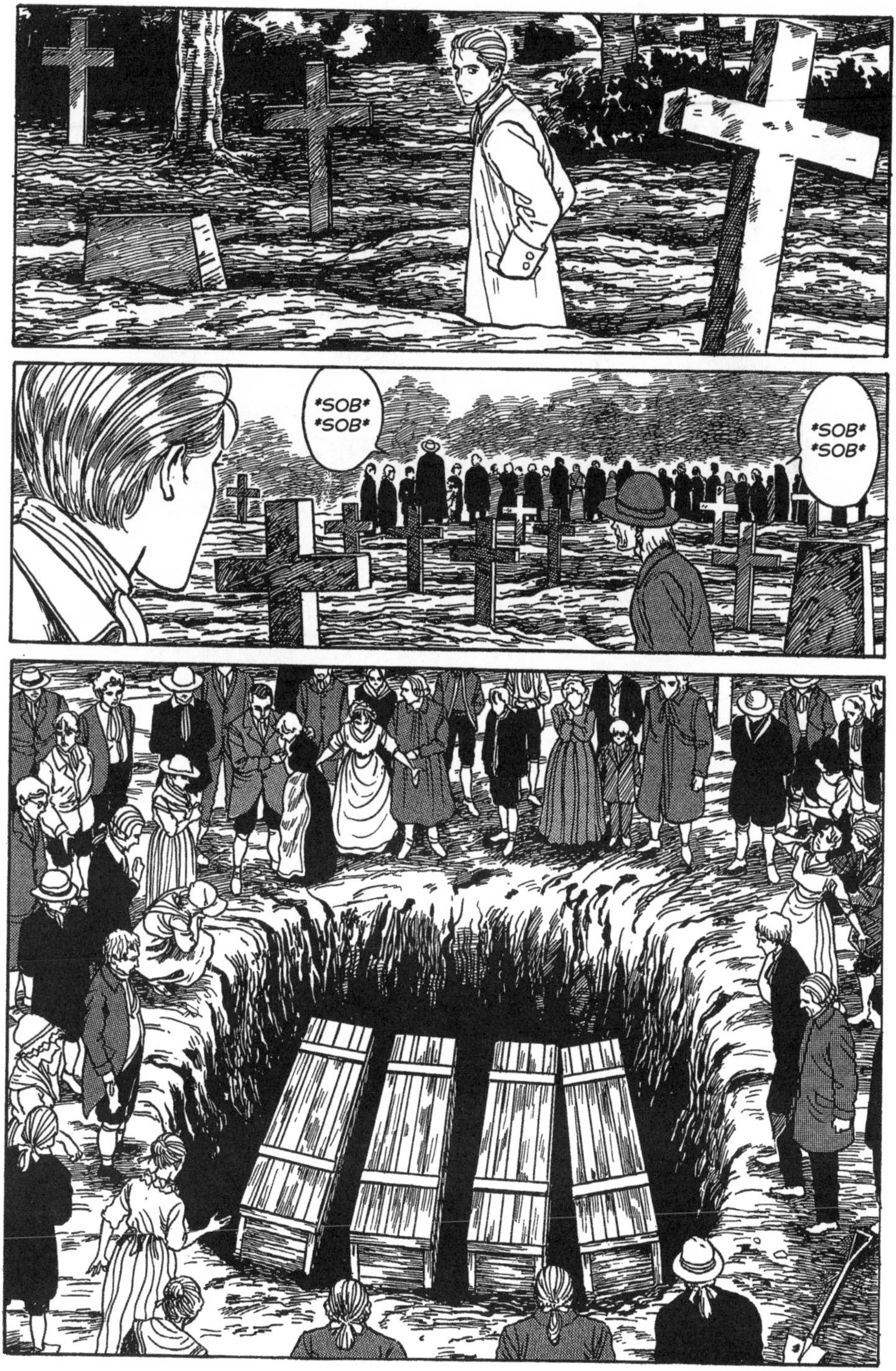
SOB
SOB
SOB
SOB

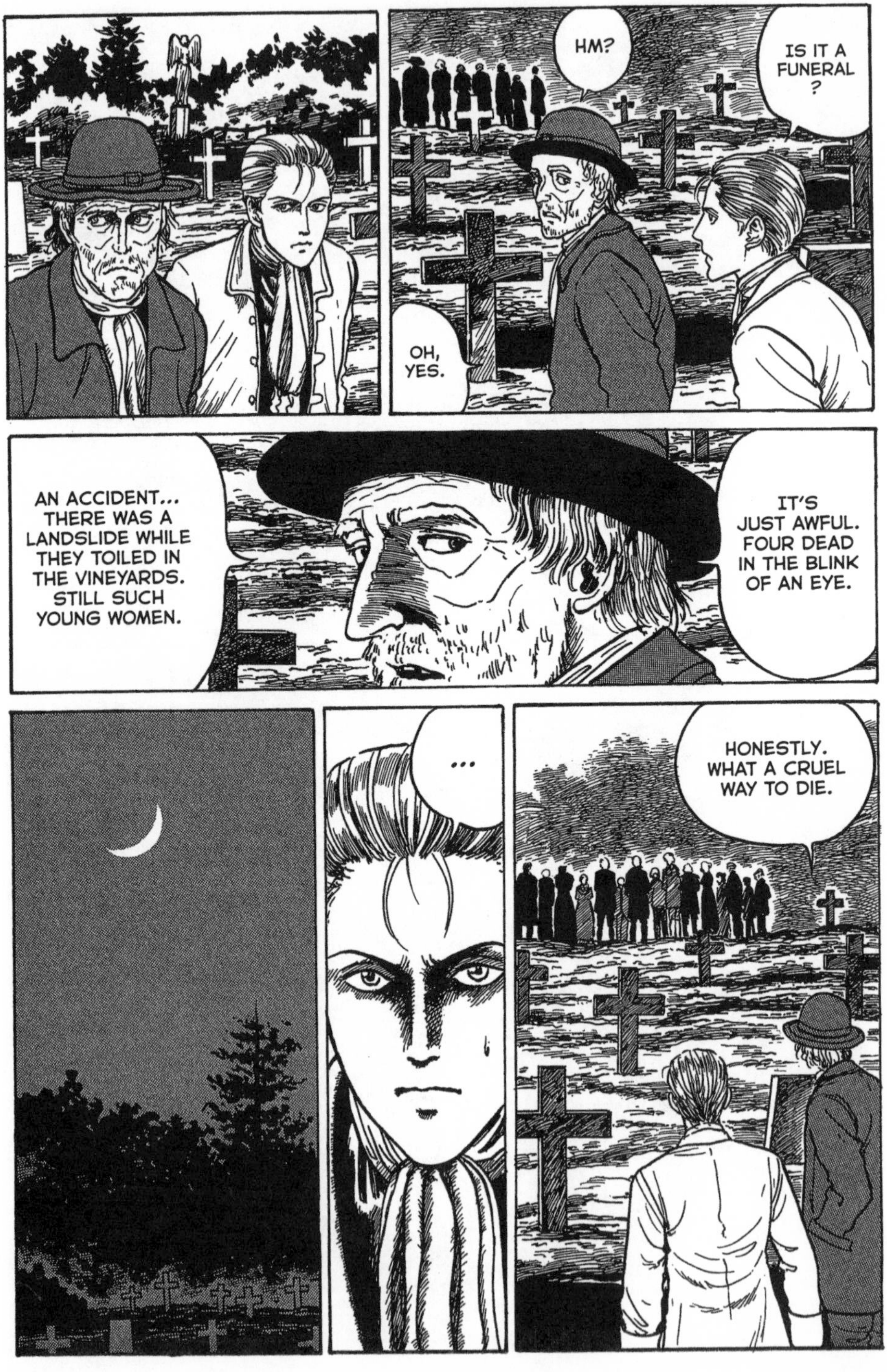
IS IT A FUNERAL ?
HM?
OH, YES.
IT'S JUST AWFUL. FOUR DEAD IN THE BLINK OF AN EYE.
AN ACCIDENT... THERE WAS A LANDSLIDE WHILE THEY TOILED IN THE VINEYARDS. STILL SUCH YOUNG WOMEN.
HONESTLY. WHAT A CRUEL WAY TO DIE.
...

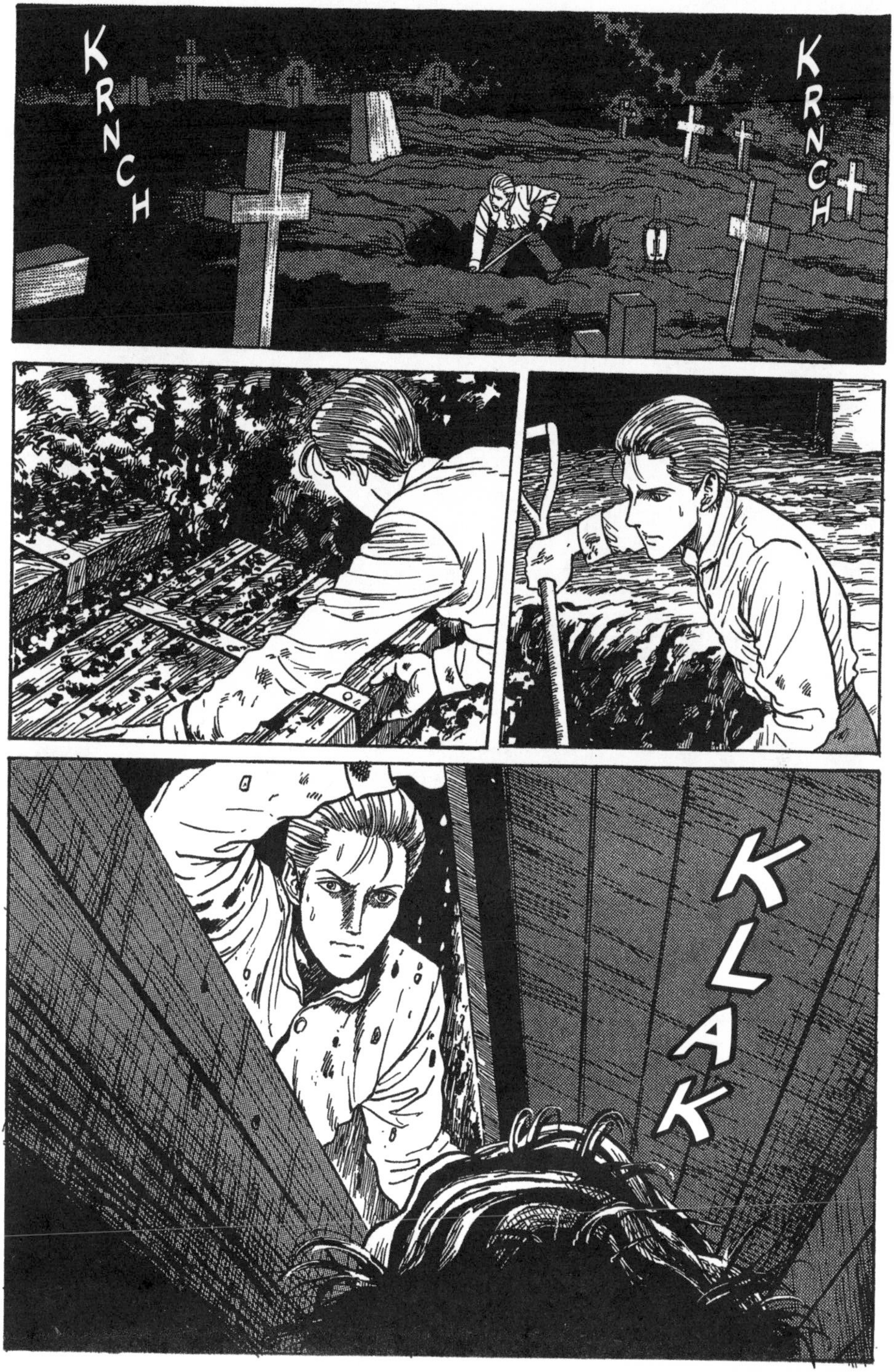
KRNCH
KRNCH
KLAK

HER HEAD IS CRUSHED FROM THE NECK UP.

FORGIVE ME. SINLESS GIRL...

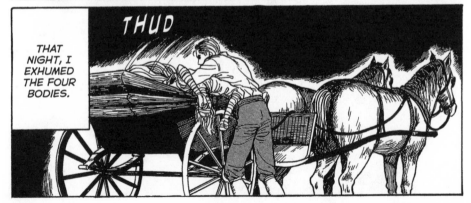

THUD

THAT NIGHT, I EXHUMED THE FOUR BODIES.

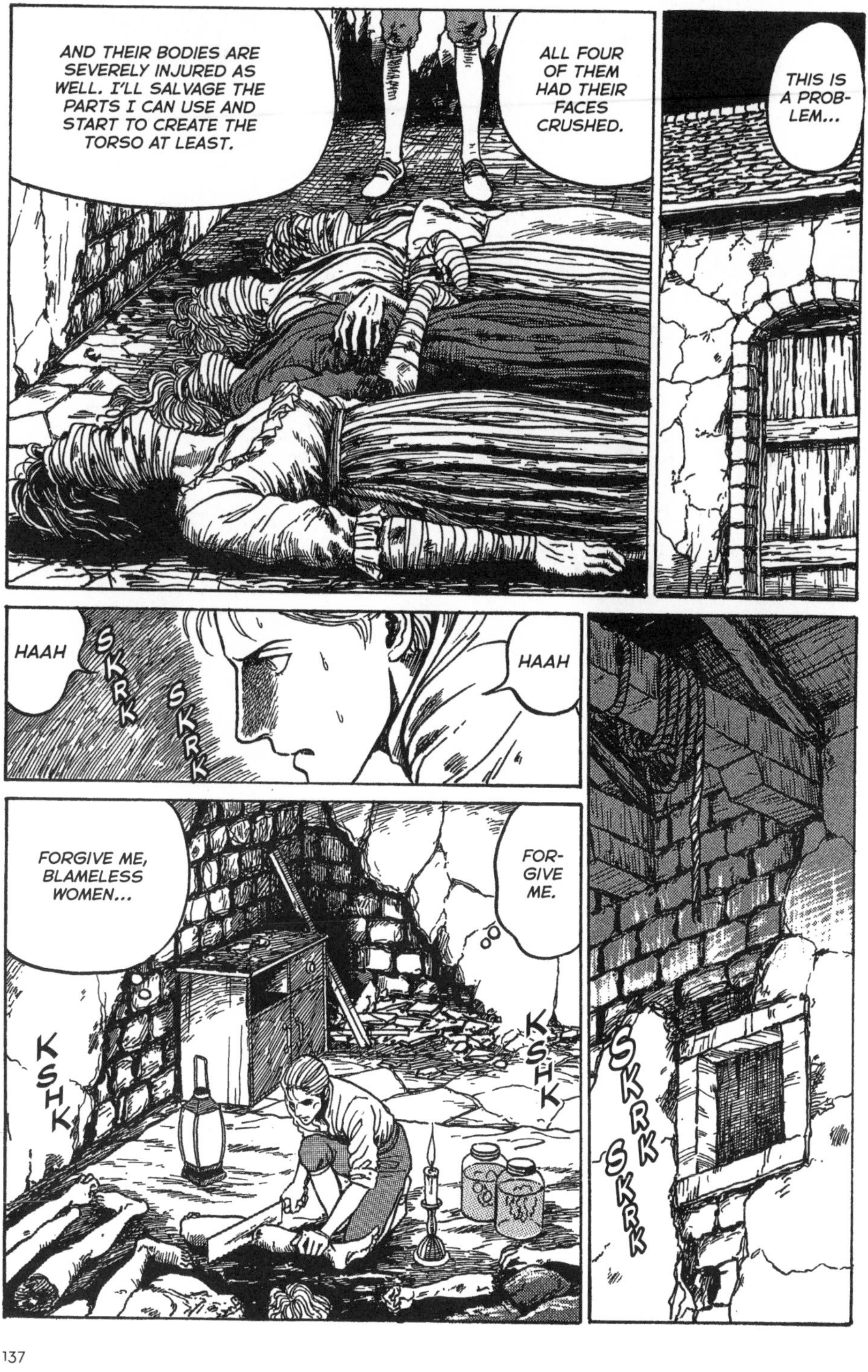
THIS IS A PROBLEM...
ALL FOUR OF THEM HAD THEIR FACES CRUSHED.
AND THEIR BODIES ARE SEVERELY INJURED AS WELL. I'LL SALVAGE THE PARTS I CAN USE AND START TO CREATE THE TORSO AT LEAST.
SKRK
SKRK
HAAH
SKRK
SKRK
HAAH
FORGIVE ME.
KSHK
FORGIVE ME, BLAMELESS WOMEN...
KSHK

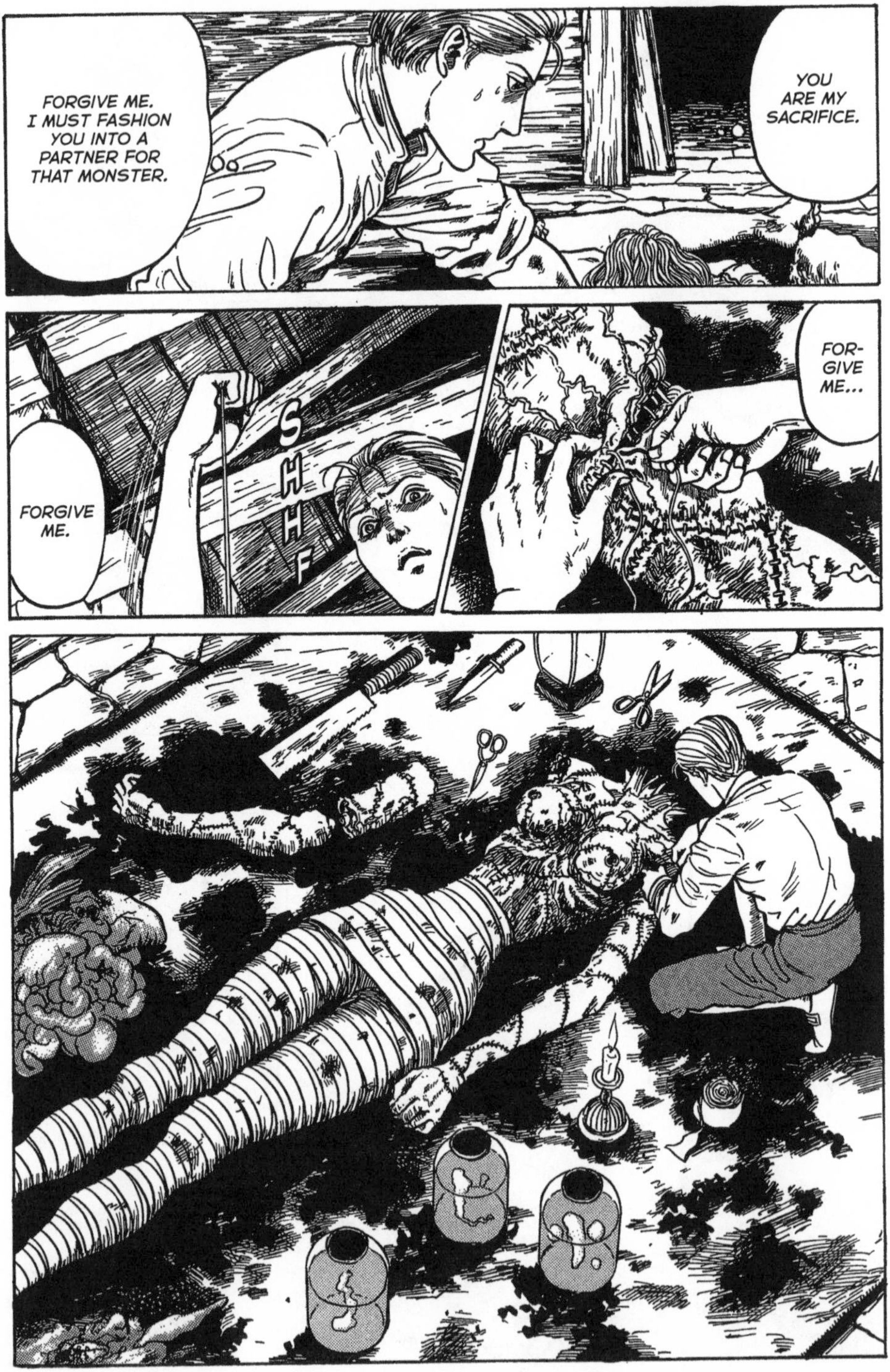
YOU ARE MY SACRIFICE.
FORGIVE ME. I MUST FASHION YOU INTO A PARTNER FOR THAT MONSTER.
FOR-GIVE ME...
SHHF
FORGIVE ME.

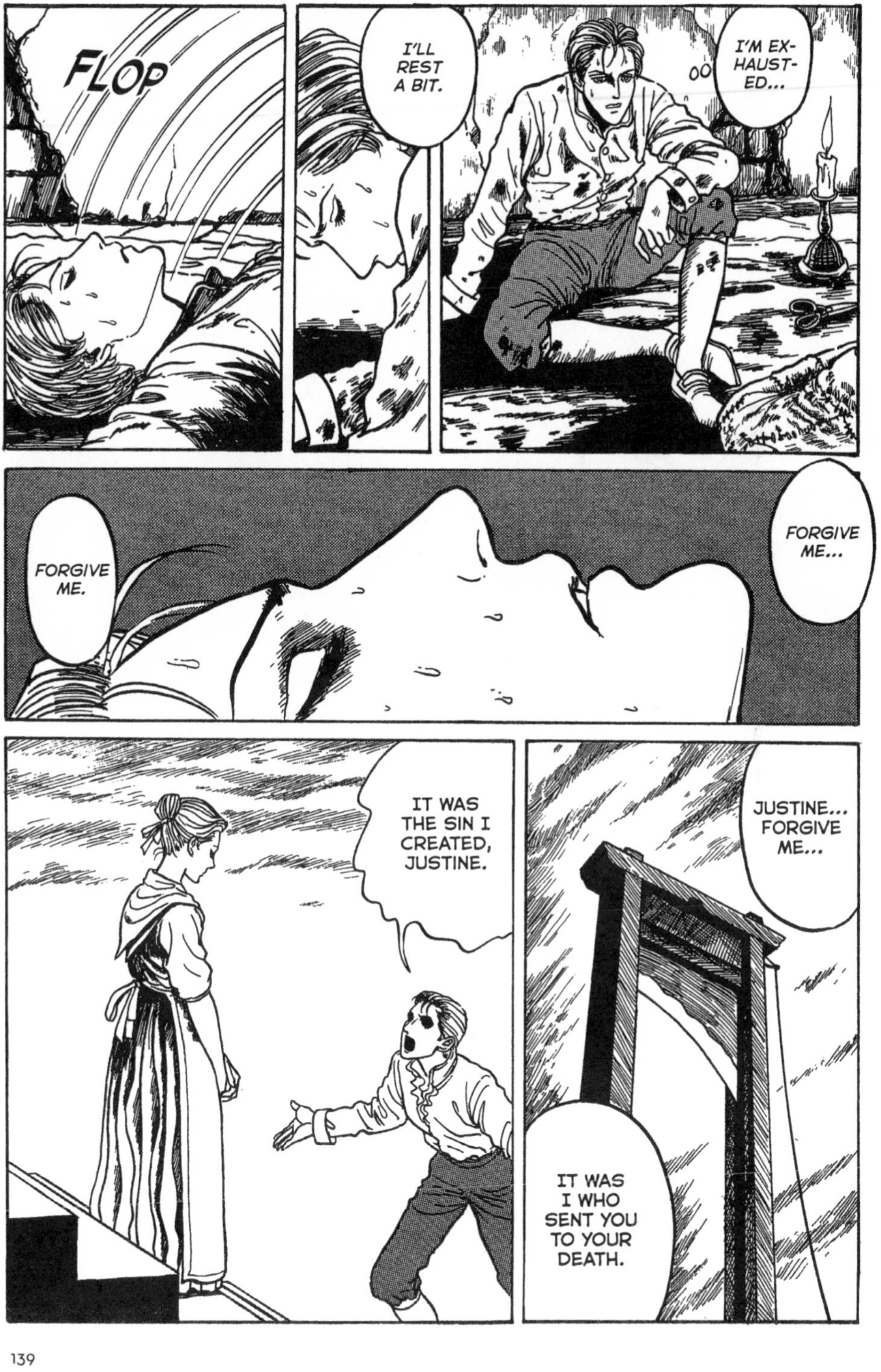
OO
I'M EX-HAUST-ED...
I'LL REST A BIT.
FLOP
FORGIVE ME...
FORGIVE ME.
JUSTINE... FORGIVE ME...
IT WAS I WHO SENT YOU TO YOUR DEATH.
IT WAS THE SIN I CREATED, JUSTINE.

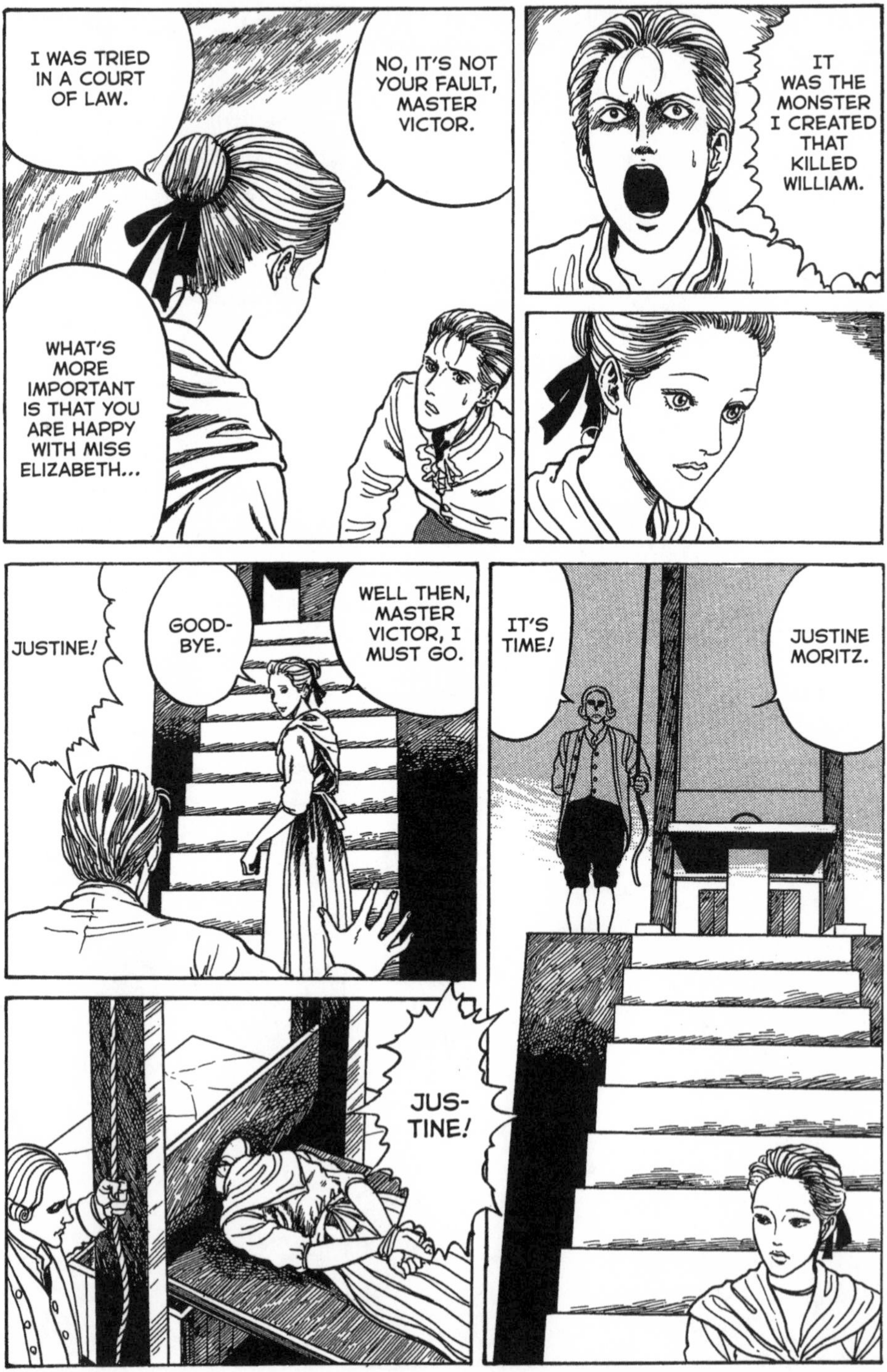
IT WAS THE MONSTER I CREATED THAT KILLED WILLIAM.
NO, IT'S NOT YOUR FAULT, MASTER VICTOR.
I WAS TRIED IN A COURT OF LAW.
WHAT'S MORE IMPORTANT IS THAT YOU ARE HAPPY WITH MISS ELIZABETH...
JUSTINE MORITZ.
IT'S TIME!
WELL THEN, MASTER VICTOR, I MUST GO.
GOOD-BYE.
JUSTINE!
JUS-TINE!

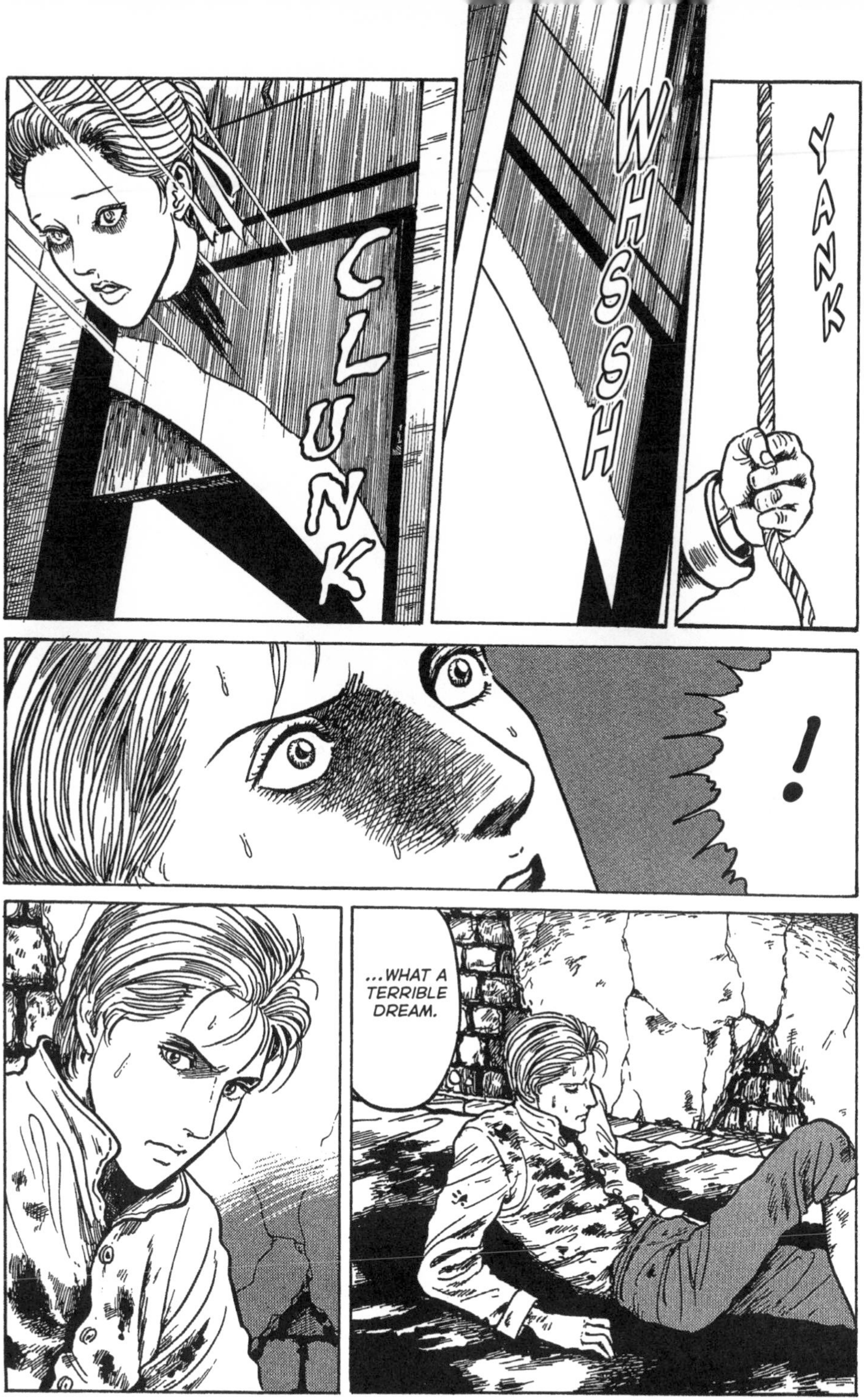
YANK
WHSSH
CLUNK
!
...WHAT A TERRIBLE DREAM.

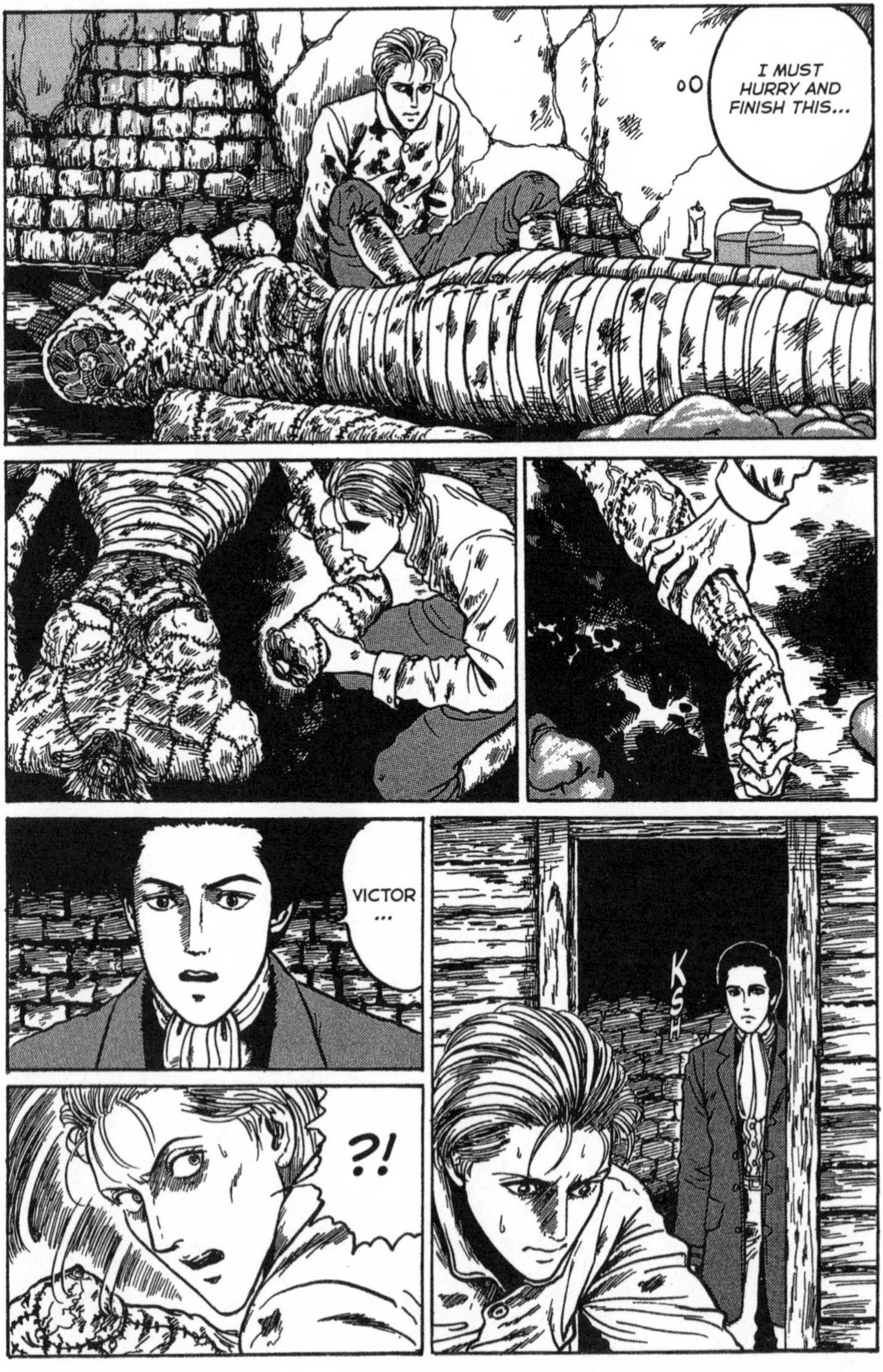

I MUST HURRY AND FINISH THIS...
KSH
VICTOR ...
?!

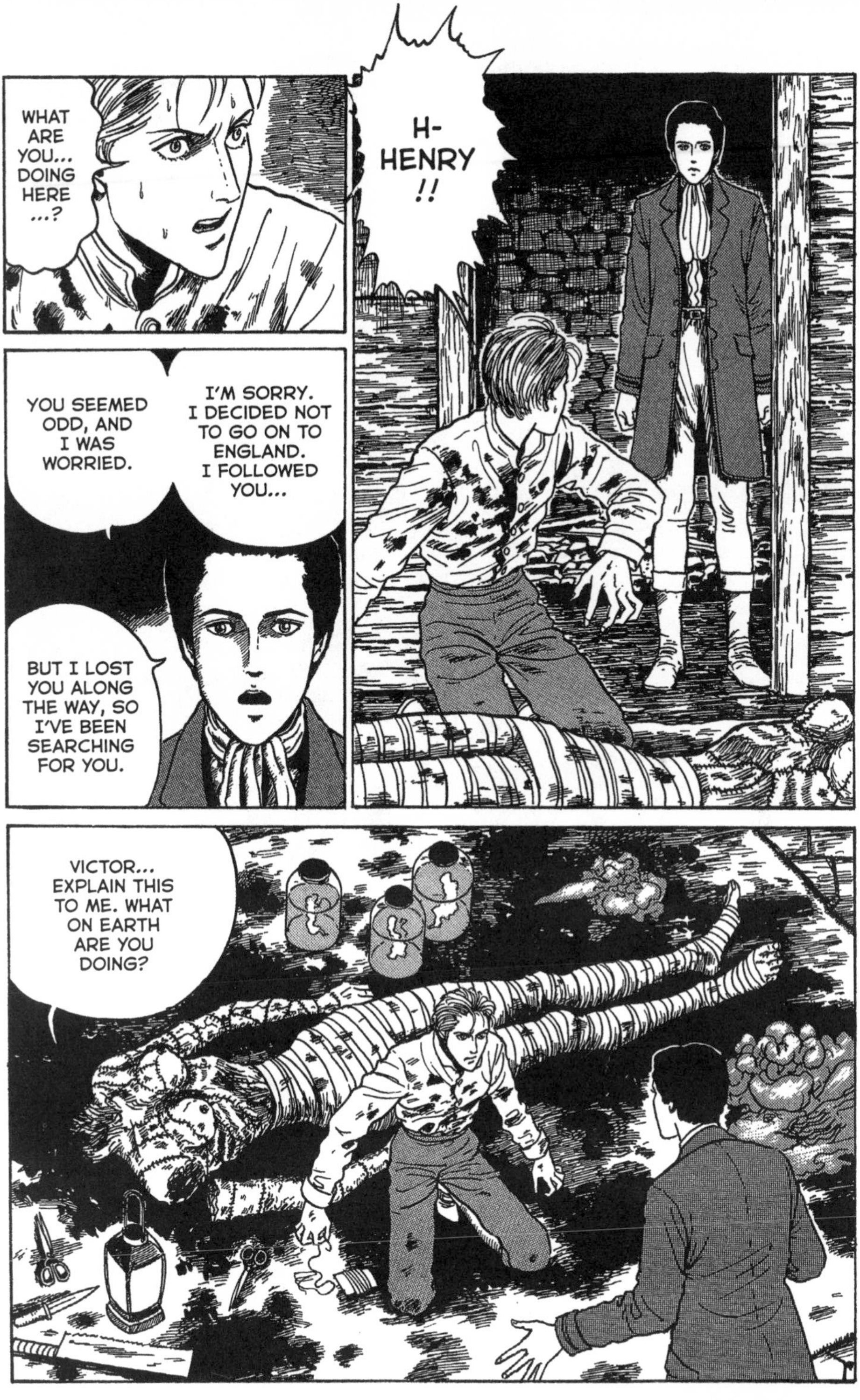
H-HENRY!!
WHAT ARE YOU... DOING HERE ...?
I'M SORRY. I DECIDED NOT TO GO ON TO ENGLAND. I FOLLOWED YOU...
YOU SEEMED ODD, AND I WAS WORRIED.
BUT I LOST YOU ALONG THE WAY, SO I'VE BEEN SEARCHING FOR YOU.
VICTOR... EXPLAIN THIS TO ME. WHAT ON EARTH ARE YOU DOING?

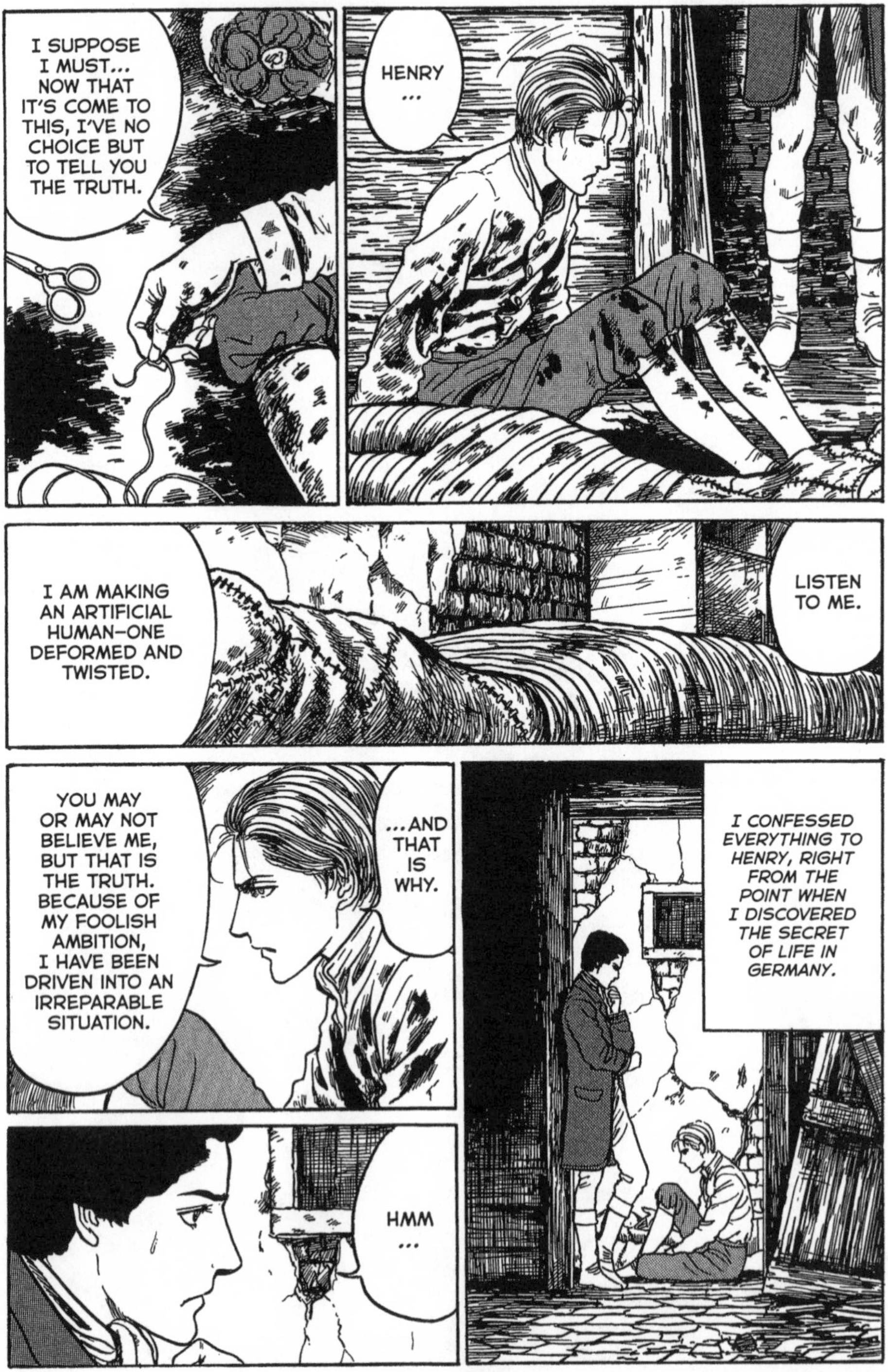
HENRY ...
I SUPPOSE I MUST... NOW THAT IT'S COME TO THIS, I'VE NO CHOICE BUT TO TELL YOU THE TRUTH.
LISTEN TO ME.
I AM MAKING AN ARTIFICIAL HUMAN—ONE DEFORMED AND TWISTED.
I CONFESSED EVERYTHING TO HENRY, RIGHT FROM THE POINT WHEN I DISCOVERED THE SECRET OF LIFE IN GERMANY.
...AND THAT IS WHY.
YOU MAY OR MAY NOT BELIEVE ME, BUT THAT IS THE TRUTH. BECAUSE OF MY FOOLISH AMBITION, I HAVE BEEN DRIVEN INTO AN IRREPARABLE SITUATION.
HMM ...

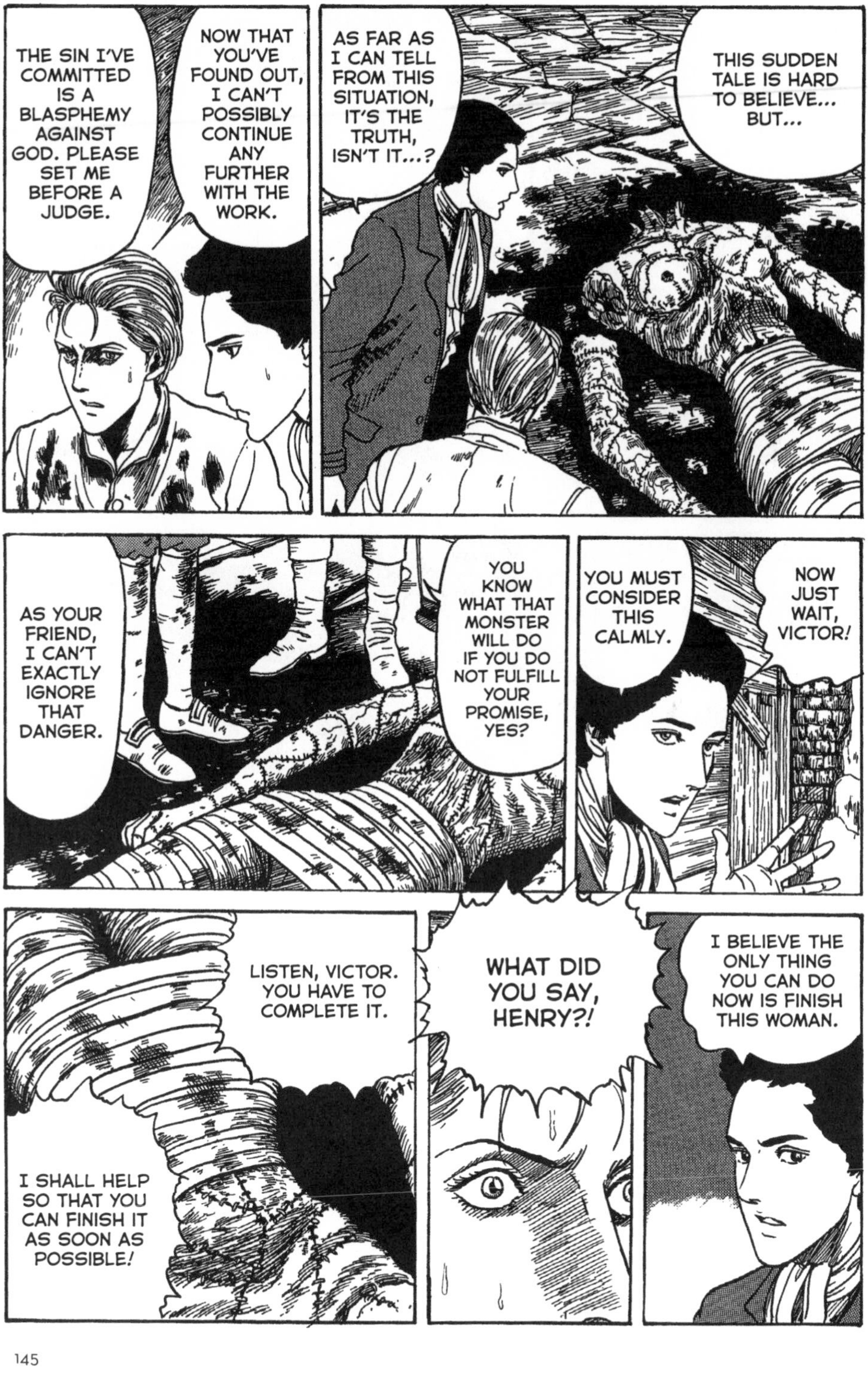
THIS SUDDEN TALE IS HARD TO BELIEVE... BUT...
AS FAR AS I CAN TELL FROM THIS SITUATION, IT'S THE TRUTH, ISN'T IT...?
NOW THAT YOU'VE FOUND OUT, I CAN'T POSSIBLY CONTINUE ANY FURTHER WITH THE WORK.
THE SIN I'VE COMMITTED IS A BLASPHEMY AGAINST GOD. PLEASE SET ME BEFORE A JUDGE.
NOW JUST WAIT, VICTOR!
YOU MUST CONSIDER THIS CALMLY.
YOU KNOW WHAT THAT MONSTER WILL DO IF YOU DO NOT FULFILL YOUR PROMISE, YES?
AS YOUR FRIEND, I CAN'T EXACTLY IGNORE THAT DANGER.
I BELIEVE THE ONLY THING YOU CAN DO NOW IS FINISH THIS WOMAN.
WHAT DID YOU SAY, HENRY?!
LISTEN, VICTOR. YOU HAVE TO COMPLETE IT.
I SHALL HELP SO THAT YOU CAN FINISH IT AS SOON AS POSSIBLE!

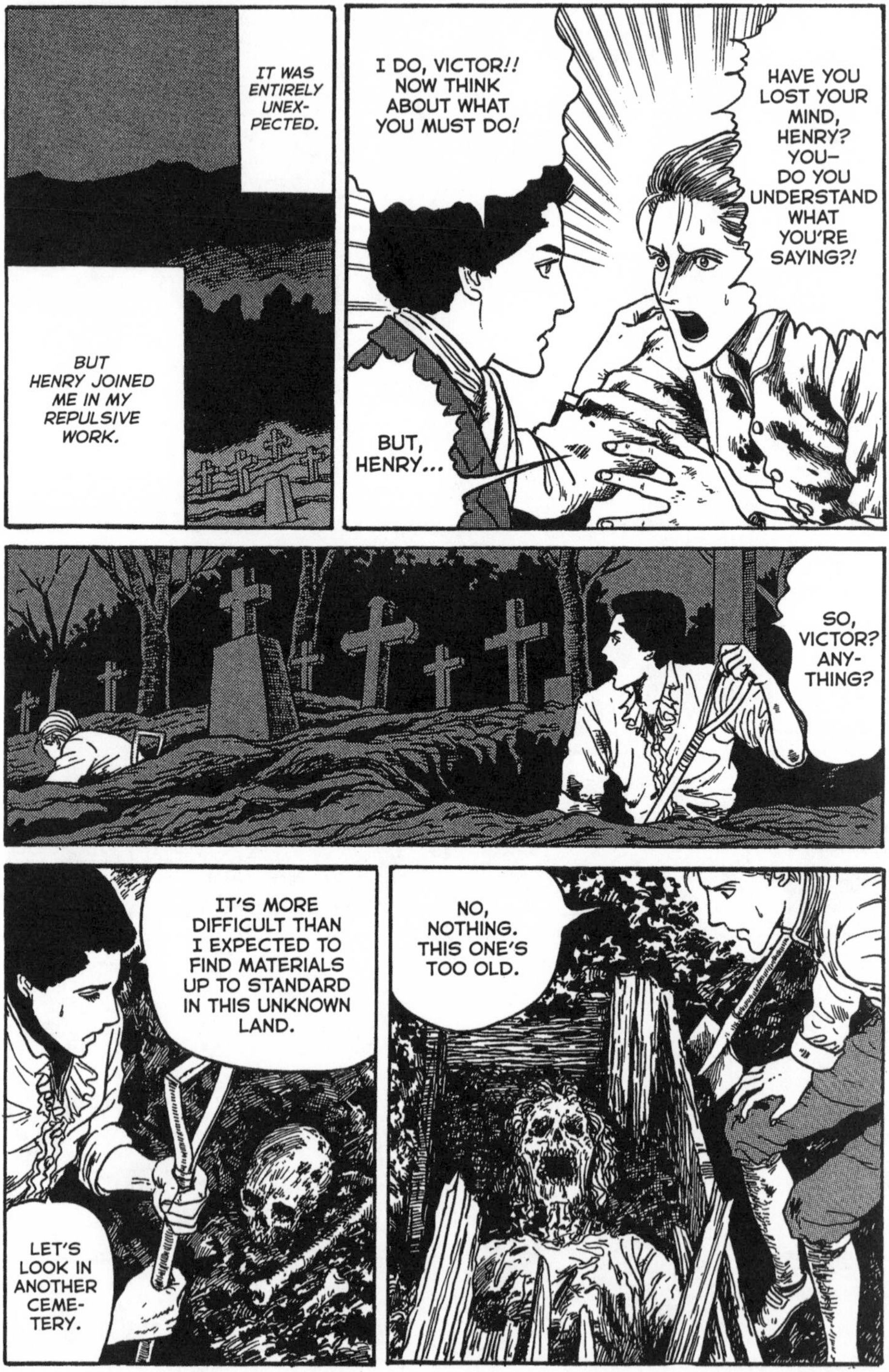
HAVE YOU LOST YOUR MIND, HENRY? YOU— DO YOU UNDERSTAND WHAT YOU'RE SAYING?!
I DO, VICTOR!! NOW THINK ABOUT WHAT YOU MUST DO!
BUT, HENRY...
IT WAS ENTIRELY UNEXPECTED.
BUT HENRY JOINED ME IN MY REPULSIVE WORK.
SO, VICTOR? ANYTHING?
NO, NOTHING. THIS ONE'S TOO OLD.
IT'S MORE DIFFICULT THAN I EXPECTED TO FIND MATERIALS UP TO STANDARD IN THIS UNKNOWN LAND.
LET'S LOOK IN ANOTHER CEMETERY.

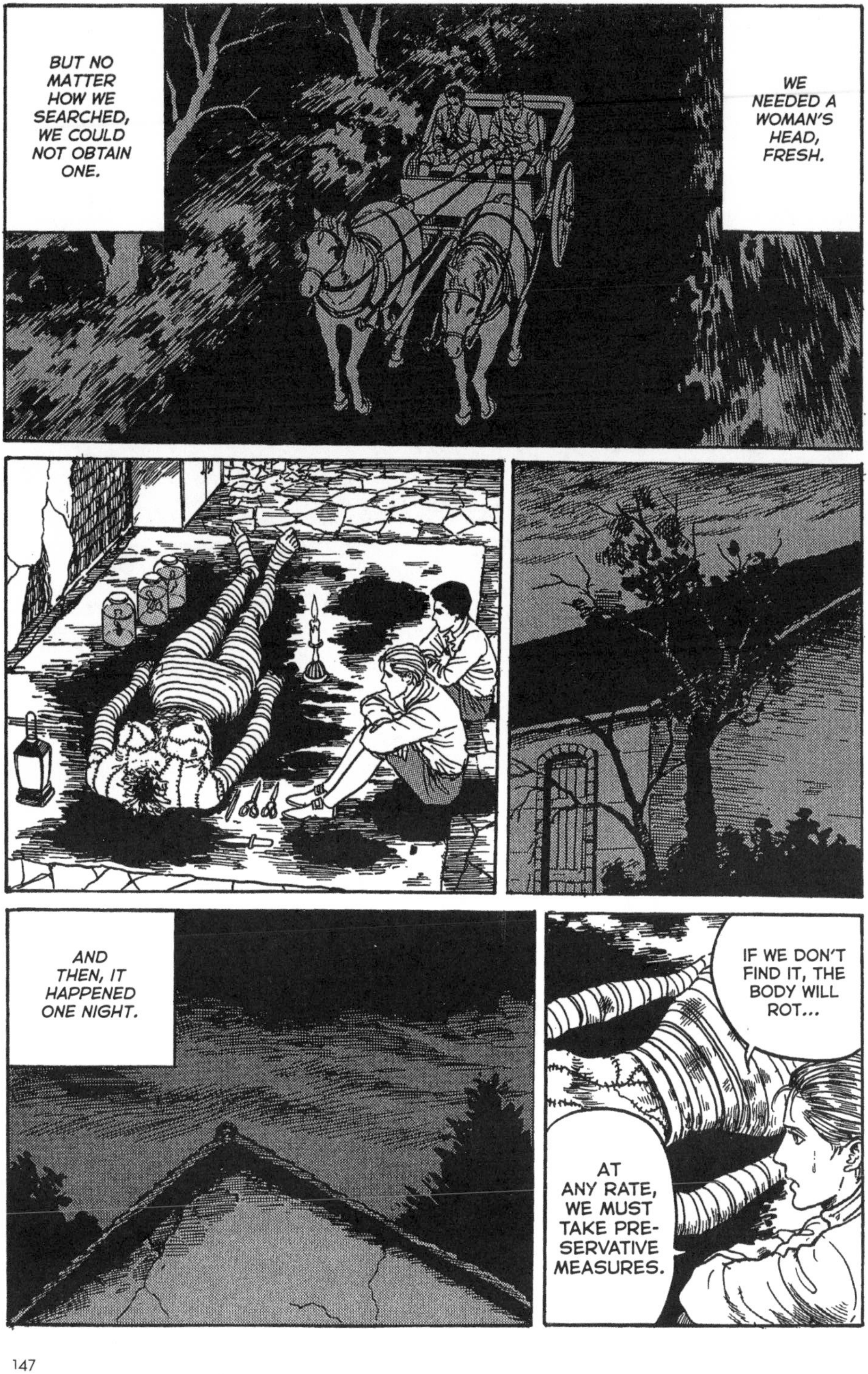
WE NEEDED A WOMAN'S HEAD, FRESH.
BUT NO MATTER HOW WE SEARCHED, WE COULD NOT OBTAIN ONE.
IF WE DON'T FIND IT, THE BODY WILL ROT...
AT ANY RATE, WE MUST TAKE PRE-SERVATIVE MEASURES.
AND THEN, IT HAPPENED ONE NIGHT.

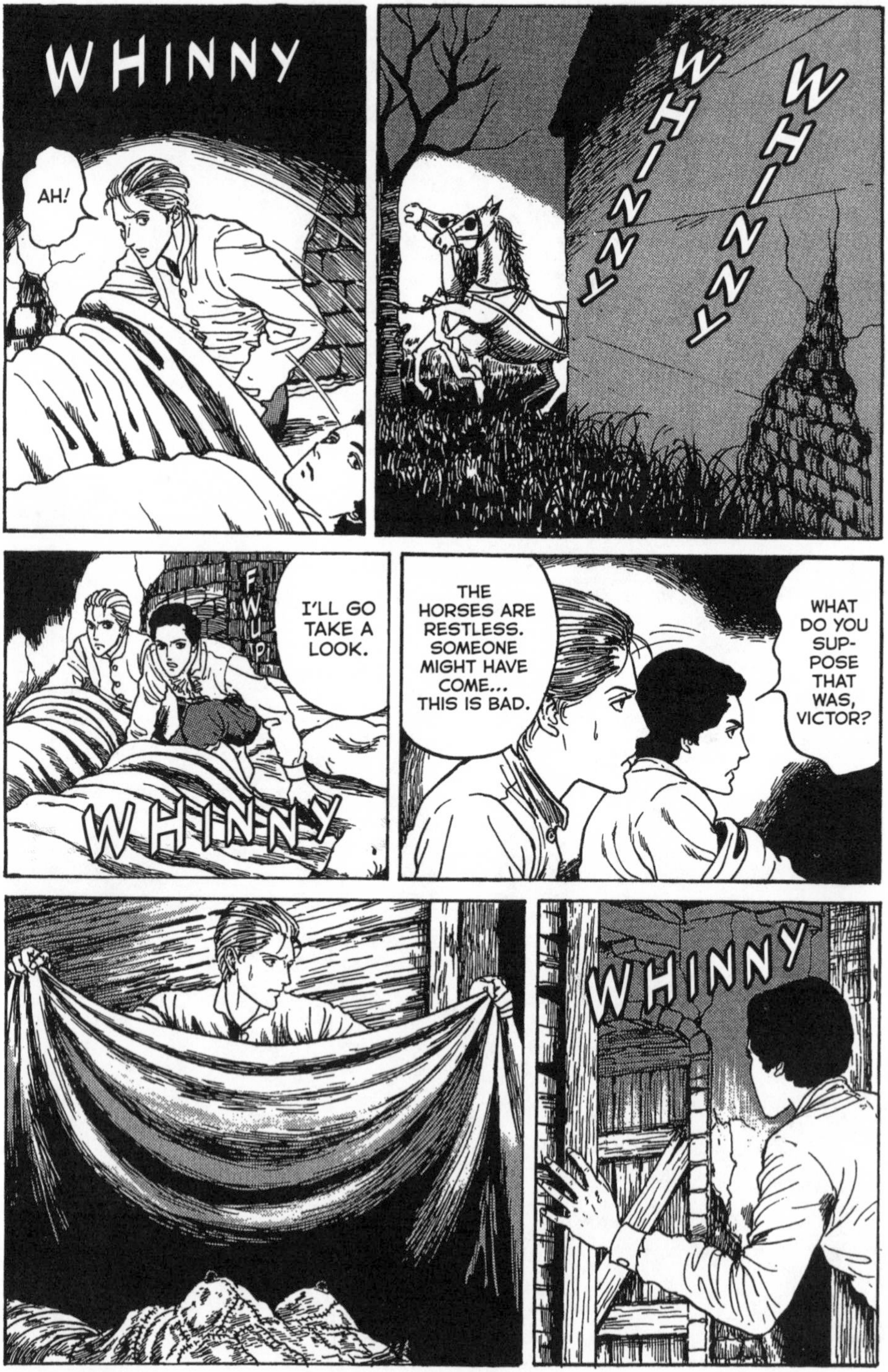
WHINNY
WHINNY
WHINNY
AH!
WHAT DO YOU SUP-POSE THAT WAS, VICTOR?
THE HORSES ARE RESTLESS. SOMEONE MIGHT HAVE COME... THIS IS BAD.
I'LL GO TAKE A LOOK.
FWUP
WHINNY
WHINNY

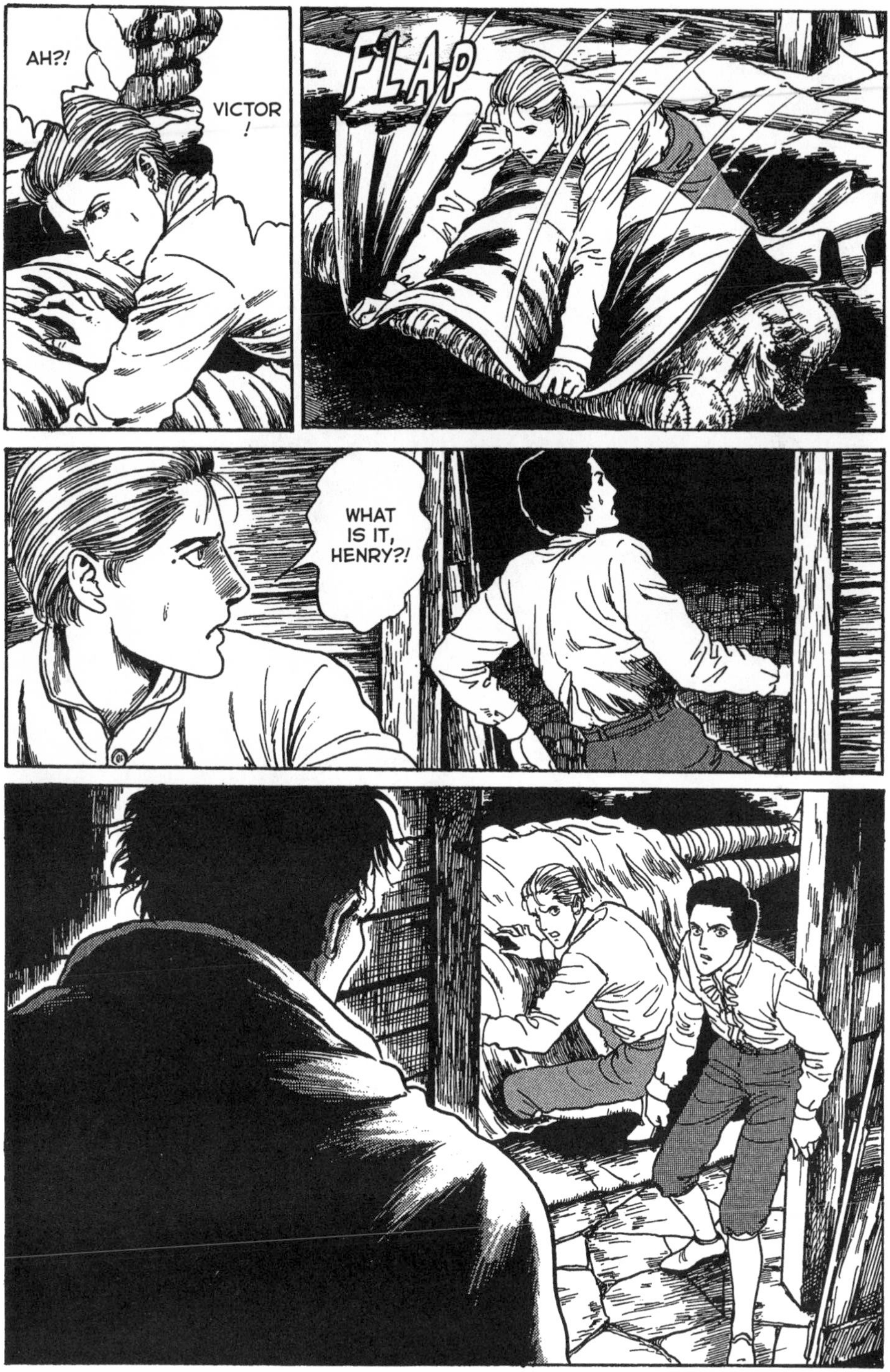
FLAP
AH?!
VICTOR !
WHAT IS IT, HENRY?!

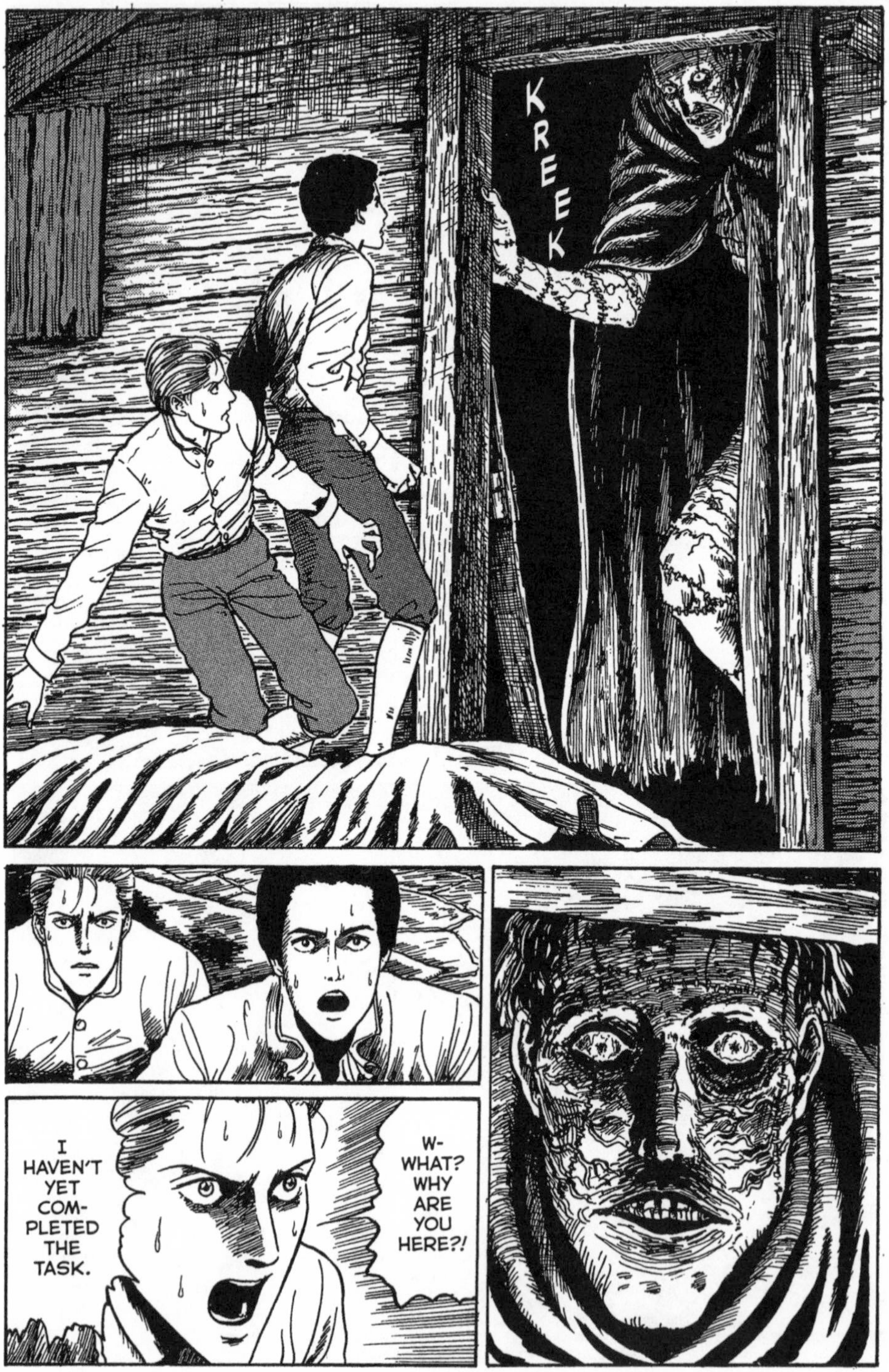
KREEK
W-WHAT? WHY ARE YOU HERE?!
I HAVEN'T YET COMPLETED THE TASK.

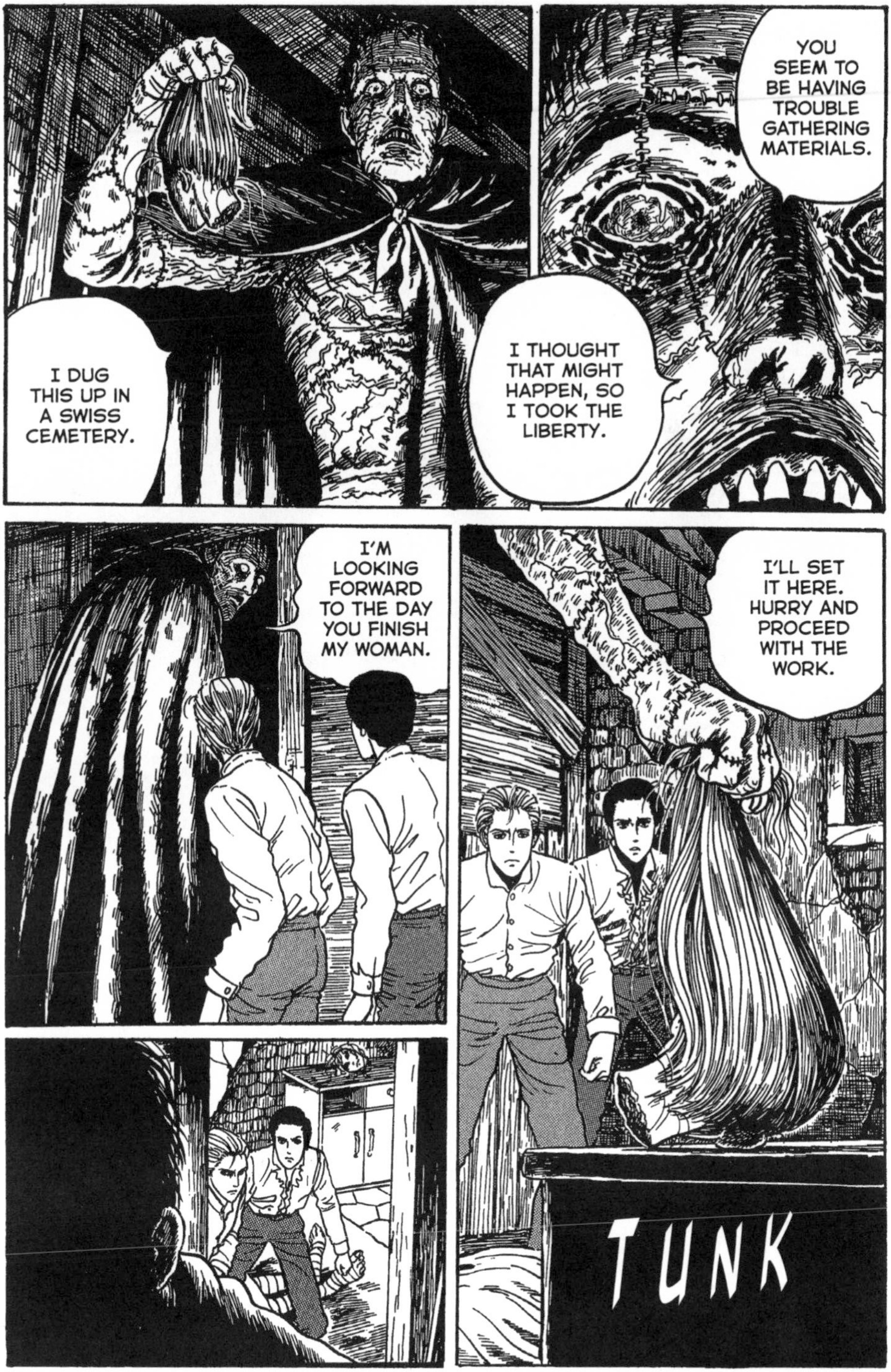
YOU SEEM TO BE HAVING TROUBLE GATHERING MATERIALS.
I THOUGHT THAT MIGHT HAPPEN, SO I TOOK THE LIBERTY.
I DUG THIS UP IN A SWISS CEMETERY.
I'LL SET IT HERE. HURRY AND PROCEED WITH THE WORK.
TUNK
I'M LOOKING FORWARD TO THE DAY YOU FINISH MY WOMAN.

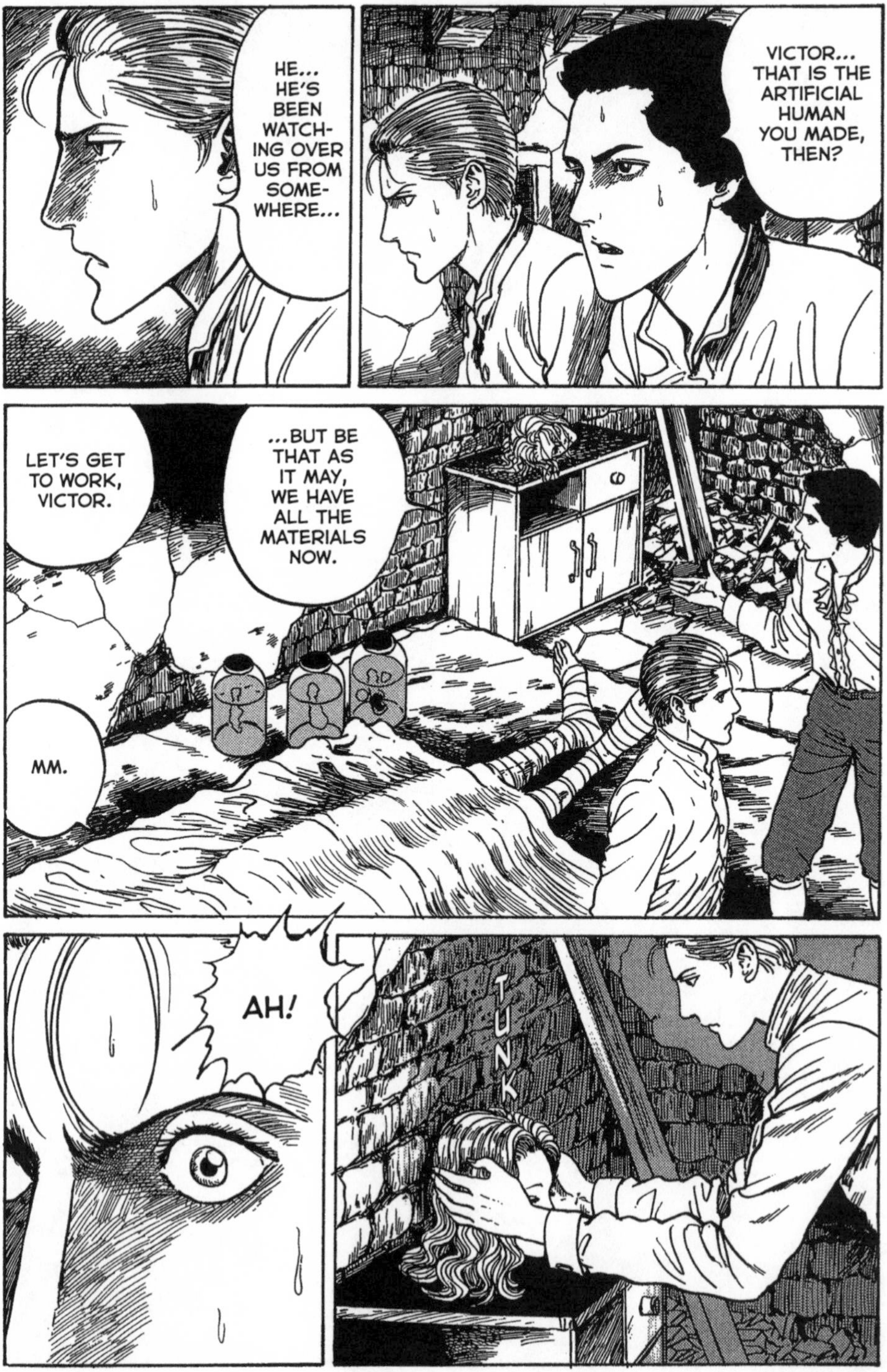
VICTOR... THAT IS THE ARTIFICIAL HUMAN YOU MADE, THEN?
HE... HE'S BEEN WATCHING OVER US FROM SOMEWHERE...
...BUT BE THAT AS IT MAY, WE HAVE ALL THE MATERIALS NOW.
LET'S GET TO WORK, VICTOR.
MM.
TUNK
AH!

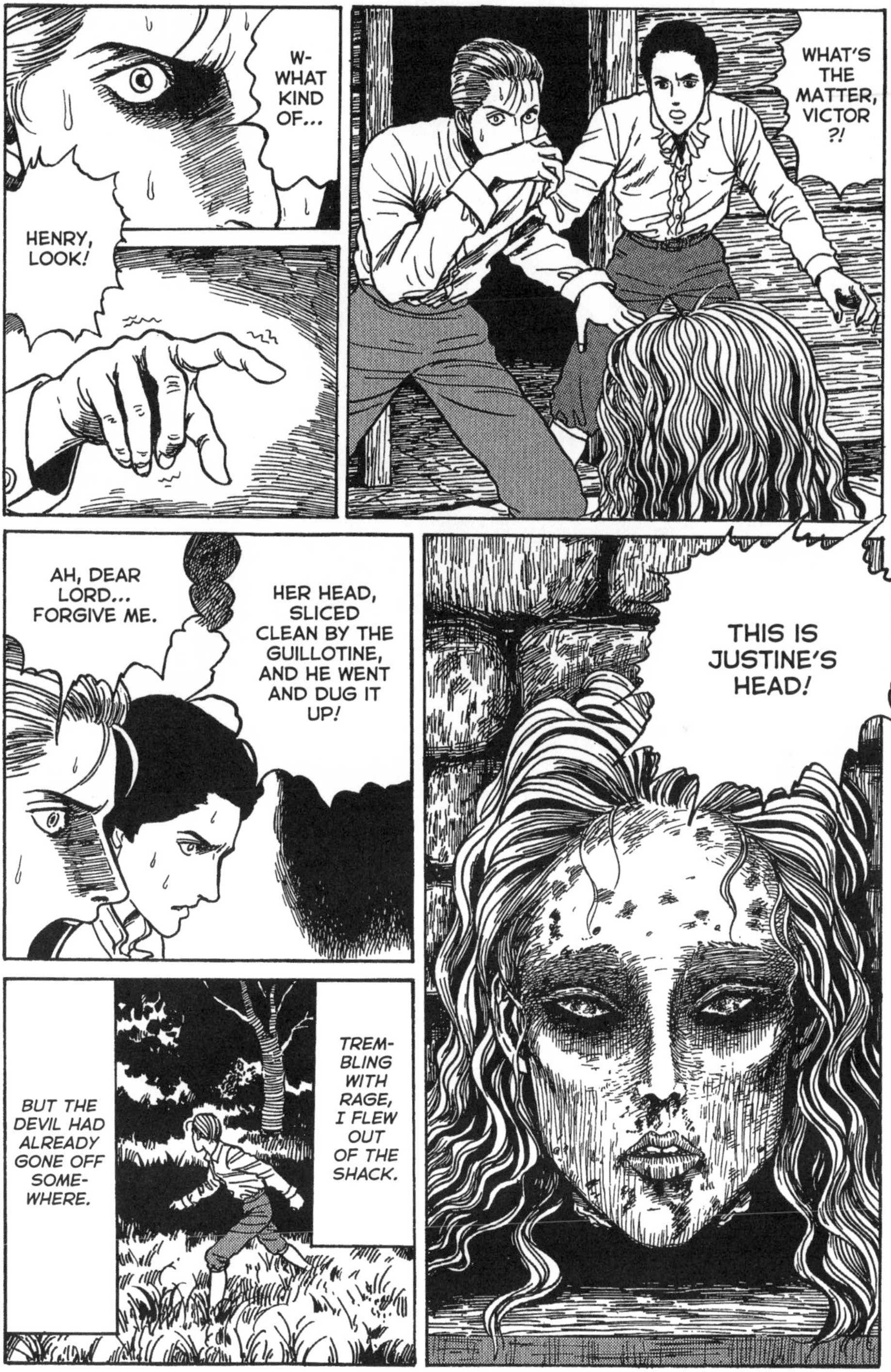
WHAT'S THE MATTER, VICTOR?!
W-WHAT KIND OF...
HENRY, LOOK!
THIS IS JUSTINE'S HEAD!
HER HEAD, SLICED CLEAN BY THE GUILLOTINE, AND HE WENT AND DUG IT UP!
AH, DEAR LORD... FORGIVE ME.
TREMBLING WITH RAGE, I FLEW OUT OF THE SHACK.
BUT THE DEVIL HAD ALREADY GONE OFF SOMEWHERE.

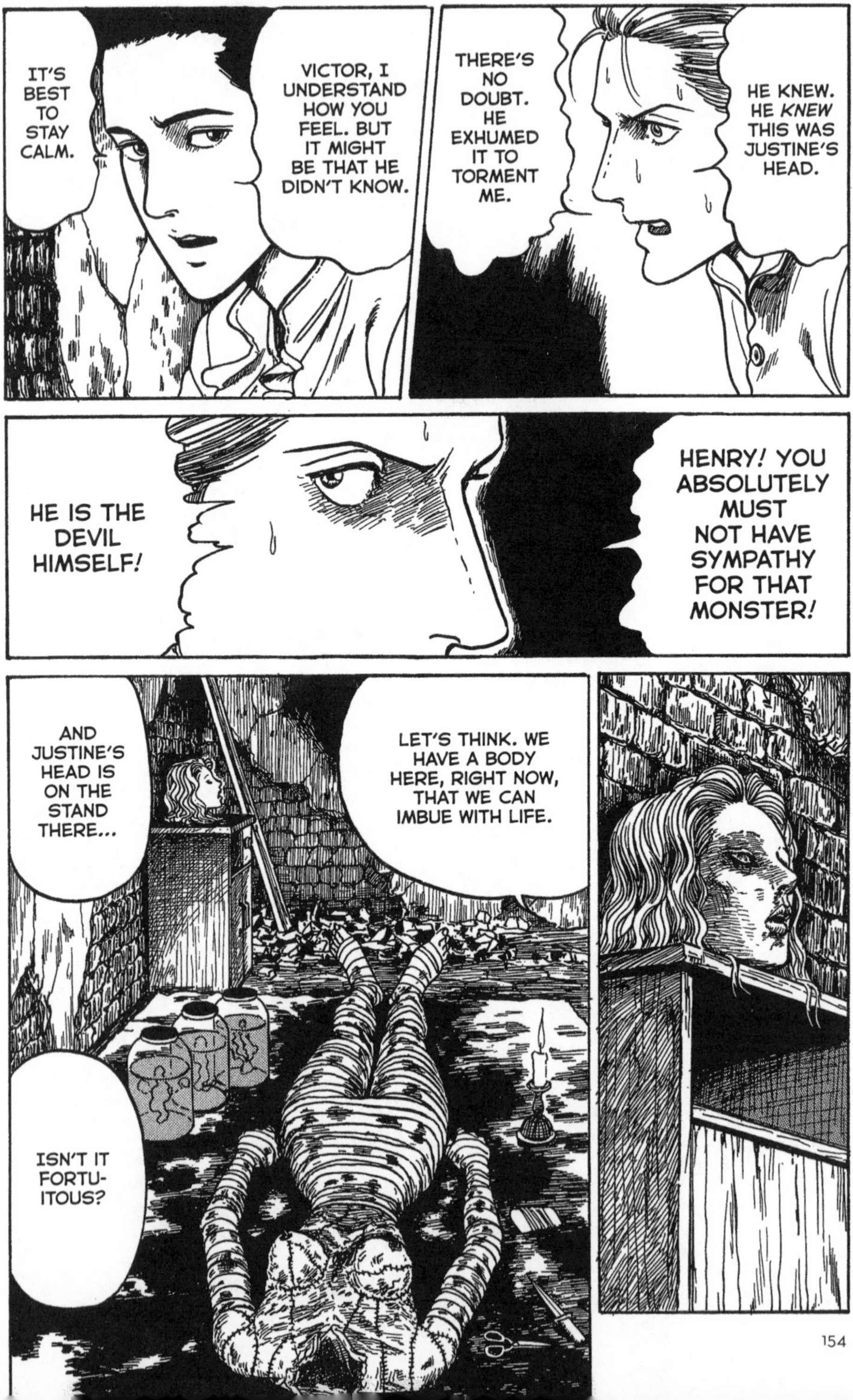
HE KNEW. HE *KNEW* THIS WAS JUSTINE'S HEAD.
THERE'S NO DOUBT. HE EXHUMED IT TO TORMENT ME.
VICTOR, I UNDERSTAND HOW YOU FEEL. BUT IT MIGHT BE THAT HE DIDN'T KNOW.
IT'S BEST TO STAY CALM.
HENRY! YOU ABSOLUTELY MUST NOT HAVE SYMPATHY FOR THAT MONSTER!
HE IS THE DEVIL HIMSELF!
LET'S THINK. WE HAVE A BODY HERE, RIGHT NOW, THAT WE CAN IMBUE WITH LIFE.
AND JUSTINE'S HEAD IS ON THE STAND THERE...
ISN'T IT FORTUITOUS?

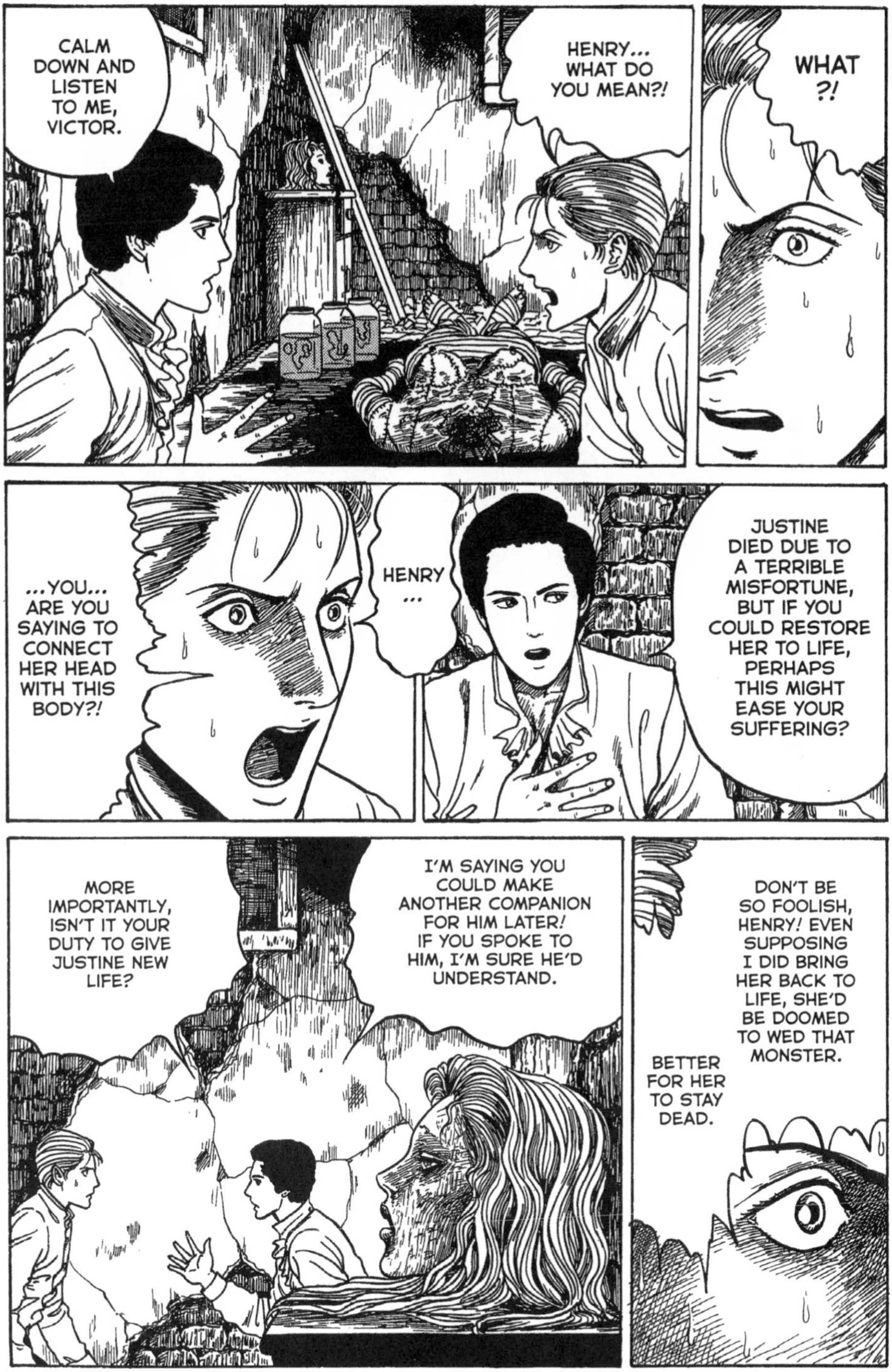
WHAT ?!
HENRY... WHAT DO YOU MEAN?!
CALM DOWN AND LISTEN TO ME, VICTOR.
JUSTINE DIED DUE TO A TERRIBLE MISFORTUNE, BUT IF YOU COULD RESTORE HER TO LIFE, PERHAPS THIS MIGHT EASE YOUR SUFFERING?
HENRY ...
...YOU... ARE YOU SAYING TO CONNECT HER HEAD WITH THIS BODY?!
DON'T BE SO FOOLISH, HENRY! EVEN SUPPOSING I DID BRING HER BACK TO LIFE, SHE'D BE DOOMED TO WED THAT MONSTER.
BETTER FOR HER TO STAY DEAD.
I'M SAYING YOU COULD MAKE ANOTHER COMPANION FOR HIM LATER! IF YOU SPOKE TO HIM, I'M SURE HE'D UNDERSTAND.
MORE IMPORTANTLY, ISN'T IT YOUR DUTY TO GIVE JUSTINE NEW LIFE?

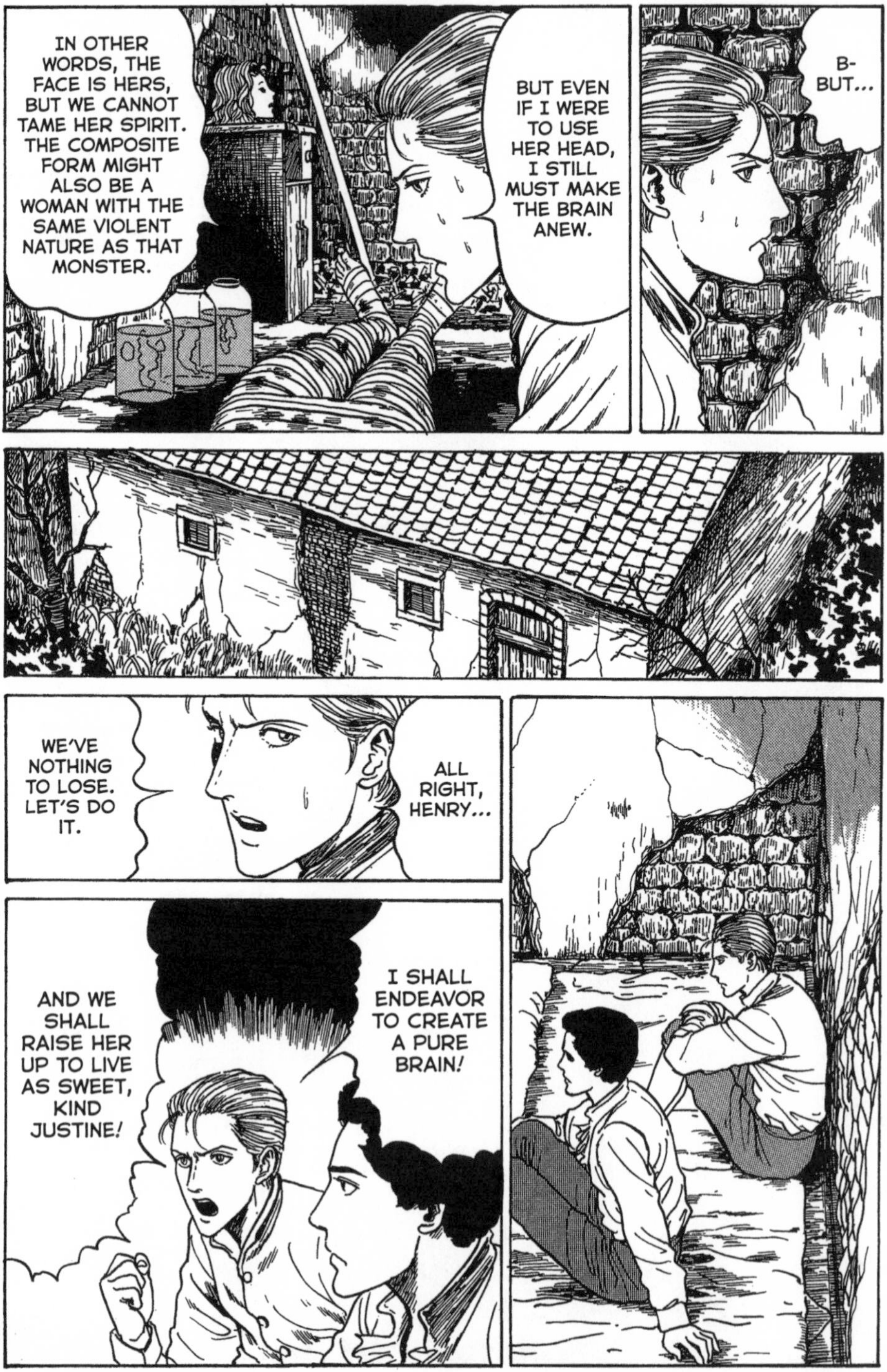
B- BUT...
BUT EVEN IF I WERE TO USE HER HEAD, I STILL MUST MAKE THE BRAIN ANEW.
IN OTHER WORDS, THE FACE IS HERS, BUT WE CANNOT TAME HER SPIRIT. THE COMPOSITE FORM MIGHT ALSO BE A WOMAN WITH THE SAME VIOLENT NATURE AS THAT MONSTER.
ALL RIGHT, HENRY...
WE'VE NOTHING TO LOSE. LET'S DO IT.
I SHALL ENDEAVOR TO CREATE A PURE BRAIN!
AND WE SHALL RAISE HER UP TO LIVE AS SWEET, KIND JUSTINE!

THE
DIE
WAS
CAST.

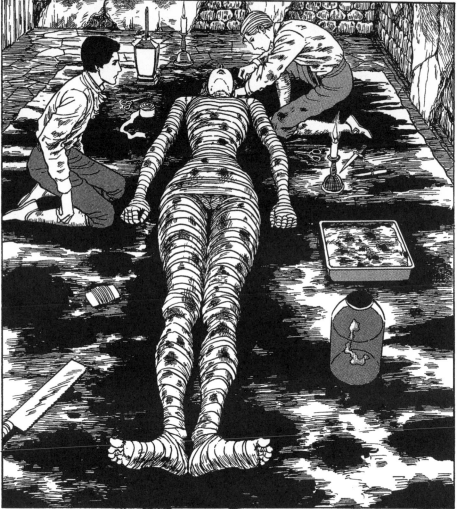

157

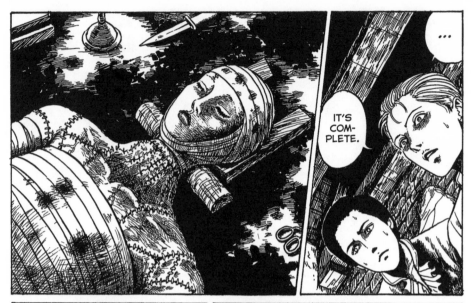

...
IT'S COMPLETE.
HELP ME PREPARE THE REJUVENATION APPARATUS.
OH... YES.
KACHK
JUSTINE WILL FINALLY COME BACK TO LIFE!
MAY THE LORD IN HEAVEN WATCH OVER HER!

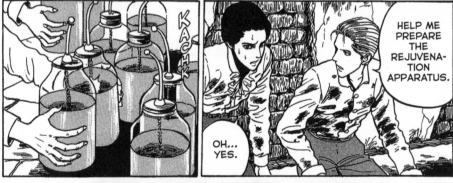

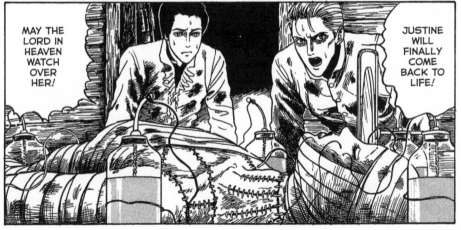

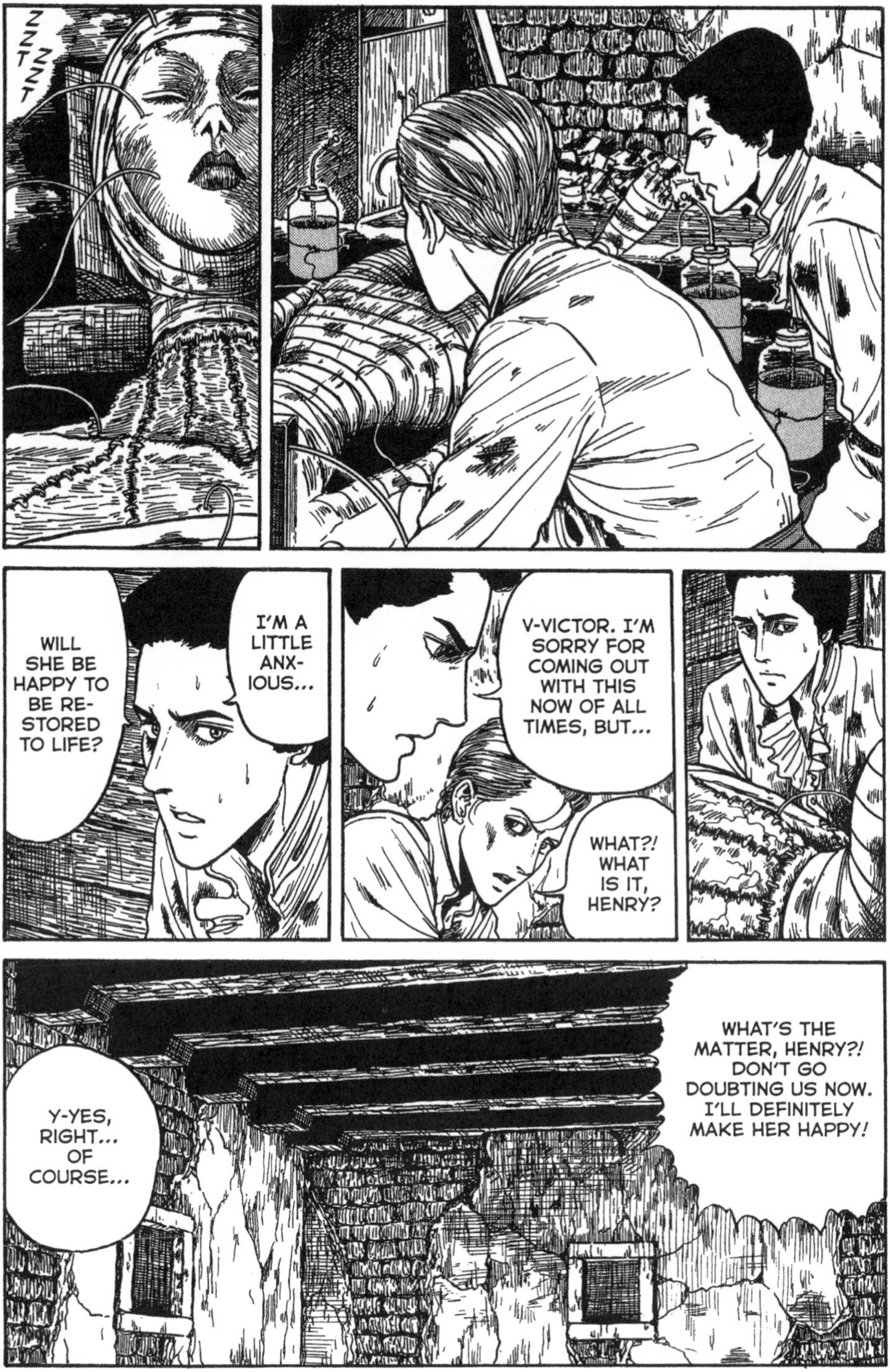
ZZZT ZZZT
V-VICTOR. I'M SORRY FOR COMING OUT WITH THIS NOW OF ALL TIMES, BUT...
WHAT?! WHAT IS IT, HENRY?
I'M A LITTLE ANX-IOUS...
WILL SHE BE HAPPY TO BE RE-STORED TO LIFE?
WHAT'S THE MATTER, HENRY?! DON'T GO DOUBTING US NOW. I'LL DEFINITELY MAKE HER HAPPY!
Y-YES, RIGHT... OF COURSE...

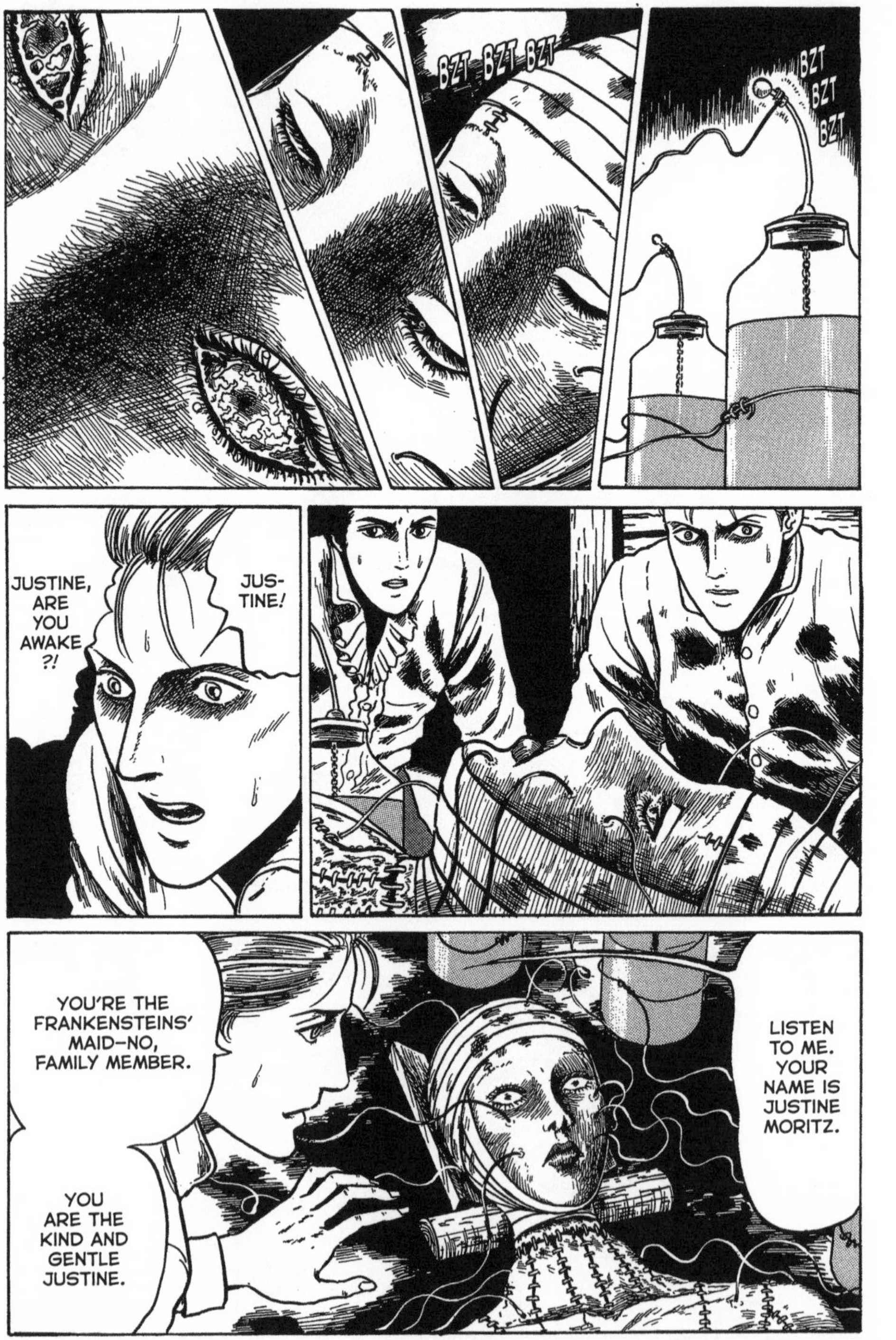
BZT BZT BZT
BZT BZT BZT
JUS-TINE!
JUSTINE, ARE YOU AWAKE?!
LISTEN TO ME. YOUR NAME IS JUSTINE MORITZ.
YOU'RE THE FRANKENSTEINS' MAID—NO, FAMILY MEMBER.
YOU ARE THE KIND AND GENTLE JUSTINE.

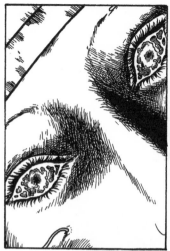

SEE? TAKE A LOOK. THIS IS YOUR FACE.

AH!

?

LOOM

NOW, SIT UP. I'LL REMOVE YOUR BANDAGES FOR YOU!

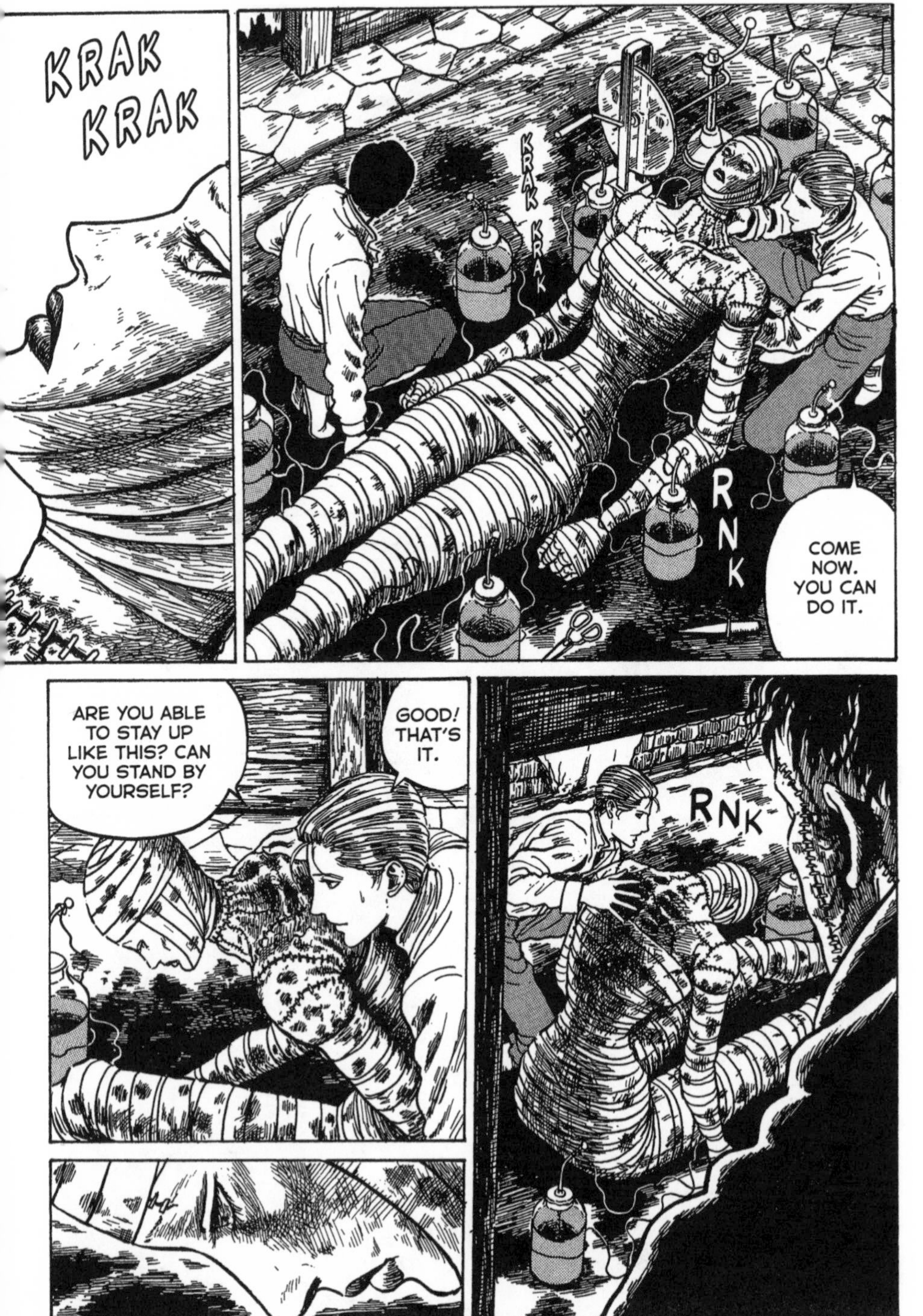
KRAK KRAK
RNK
COME NOW. YOU CAN DO IT.
KRAK KRAK
RNK
GOOD! THAT'S IT.
ARE YOU ABLE TO STAY UP LIKE THIS? CAN YOU STAND BY YOURSELF?

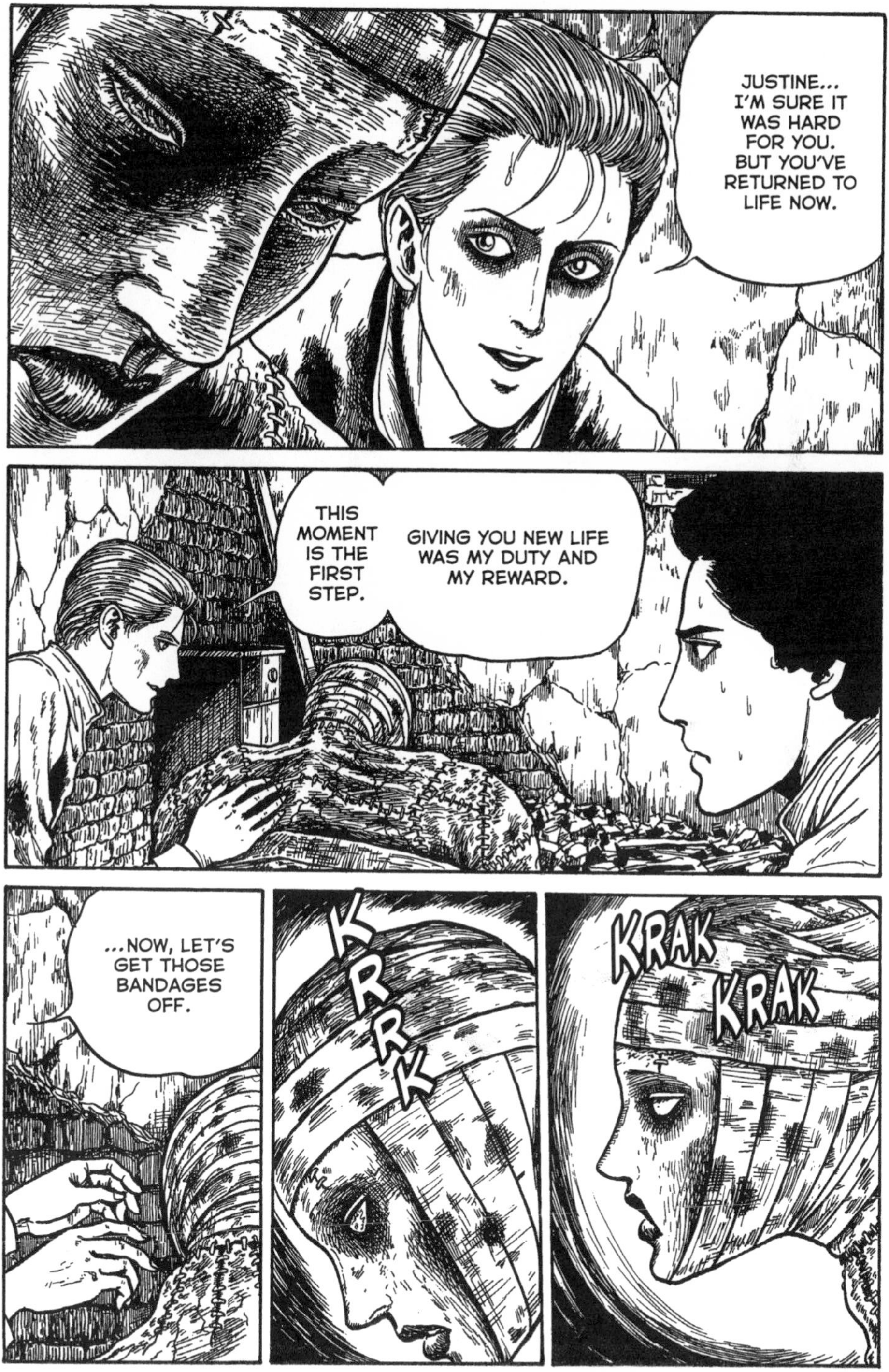
JUSTINE... I'M SURE IT WAS HARD FOR YOU. BUT YOU'VE RETURNED TO LIFE NOW.
GIVING YOU NEW LIFE WAS MY DUTY AND MY REWARD.
THIS MOMENT IS THE FIRST STEP.
KRAK KRAK
KRRK
...NOW, LET'S GET THOSE BANDAGES OFF.

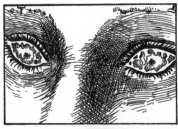

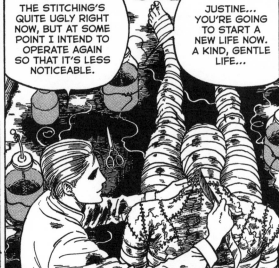

JUSTINE... YOU'RE GOING TO START A NEW LIFE NOW. A KIND, GENTLE LIFE...
THE STITCHING'S QUITE UGLY RIGHT NOW, BUT AT SOME POINT I INTEND TO OPERATE AGAIN SO THAT IT'S LESS NOTICEABLE.
SHRK
AAH!

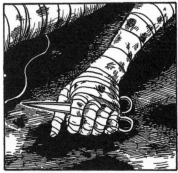

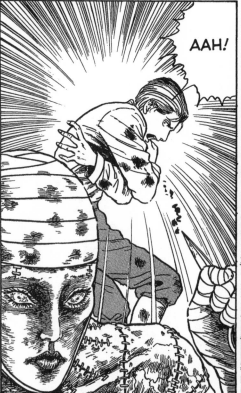

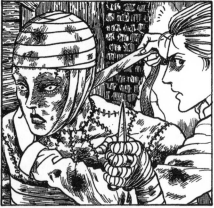

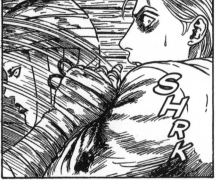

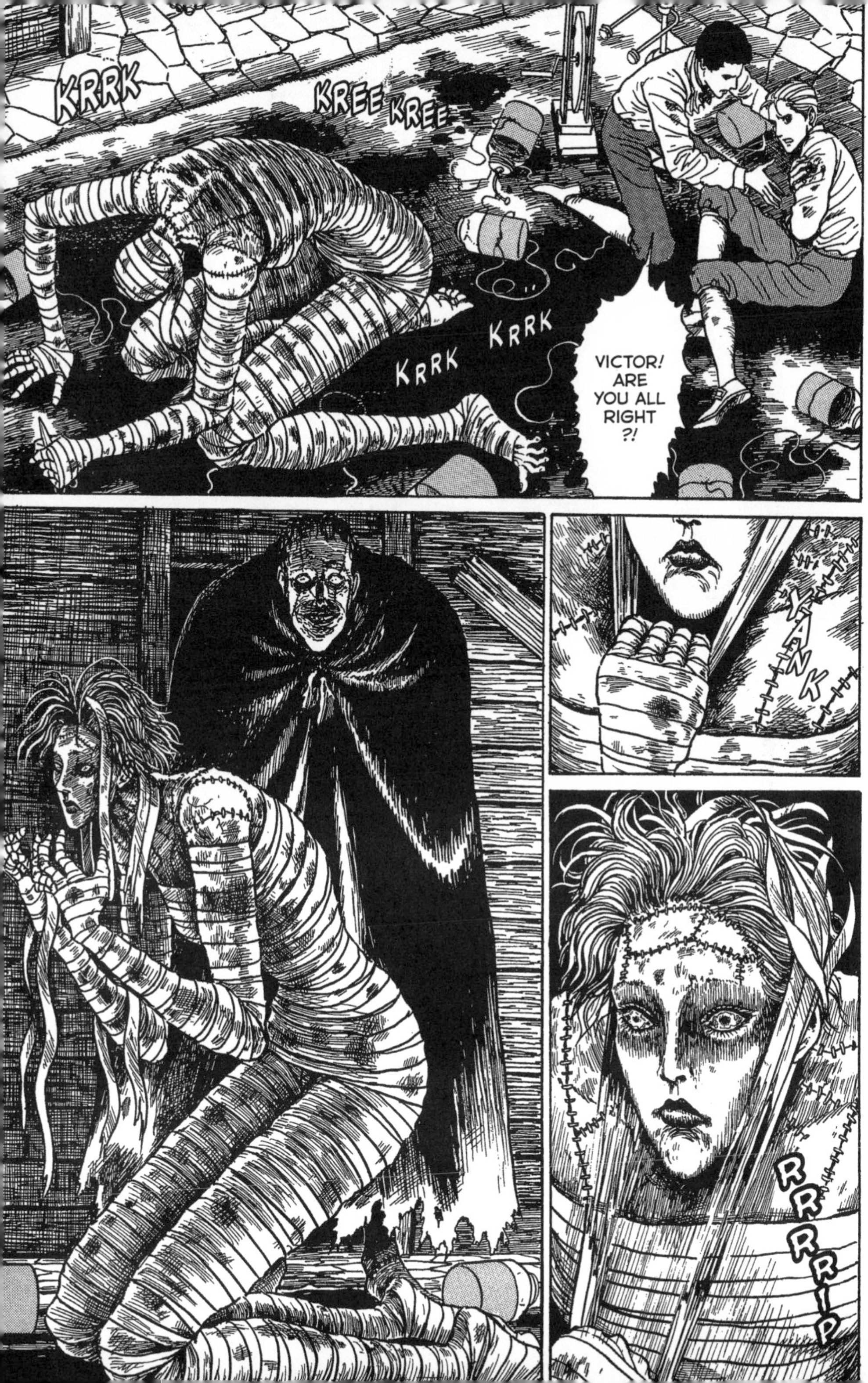
KREE KREE
KRRK
VICTOR! ARE YOU ALL RIGHT ?!
KRRK KRRK
YANK
RRRRRIP

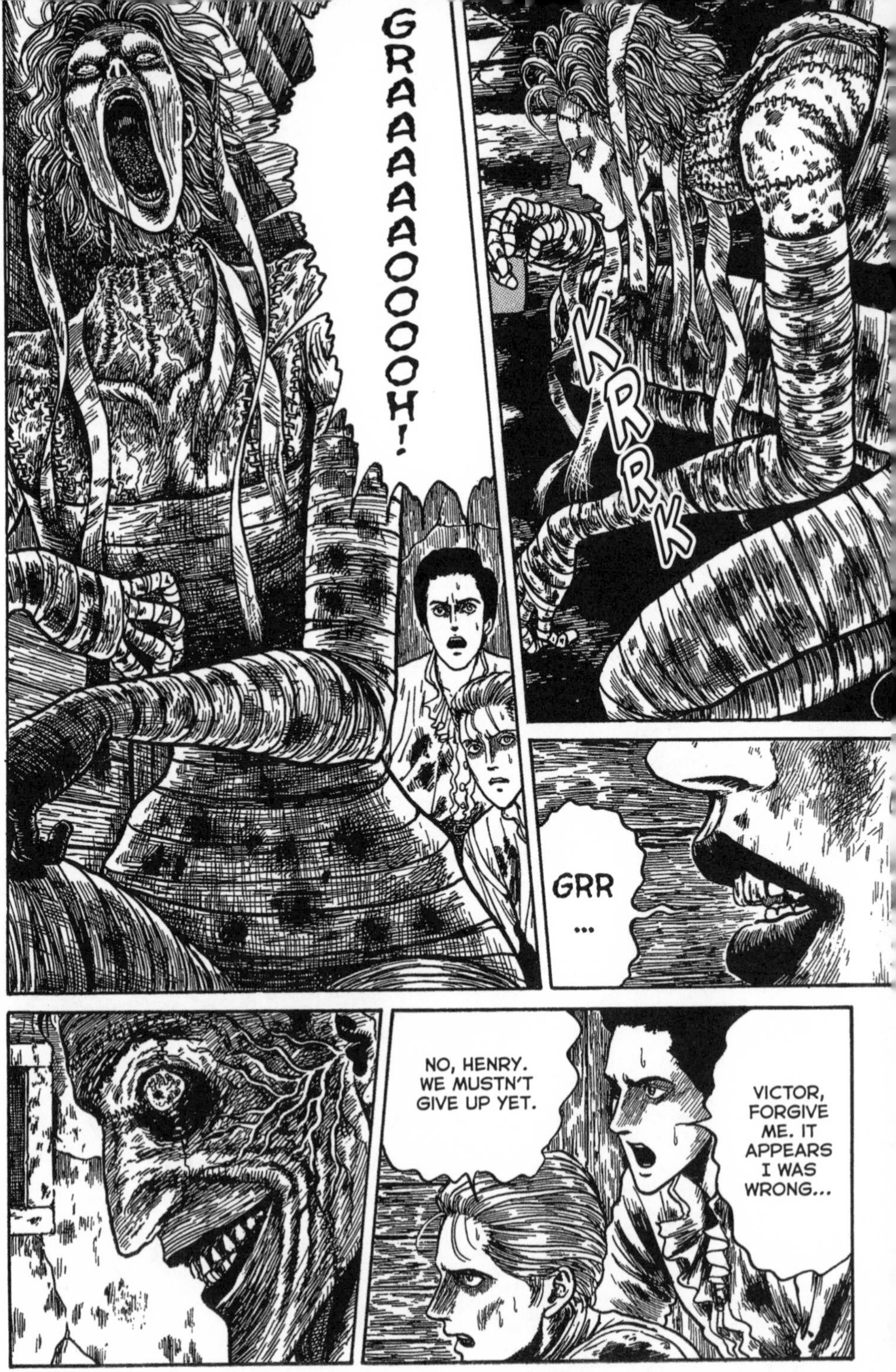
KRRRK
GRR ...
GRAAAAAAOOOOOH!
VICTOR, FORGIVE ME. IT APPEARS I WAS WRONG...
NO, HENRY. WE MUSTN'T GIVE UP YET.

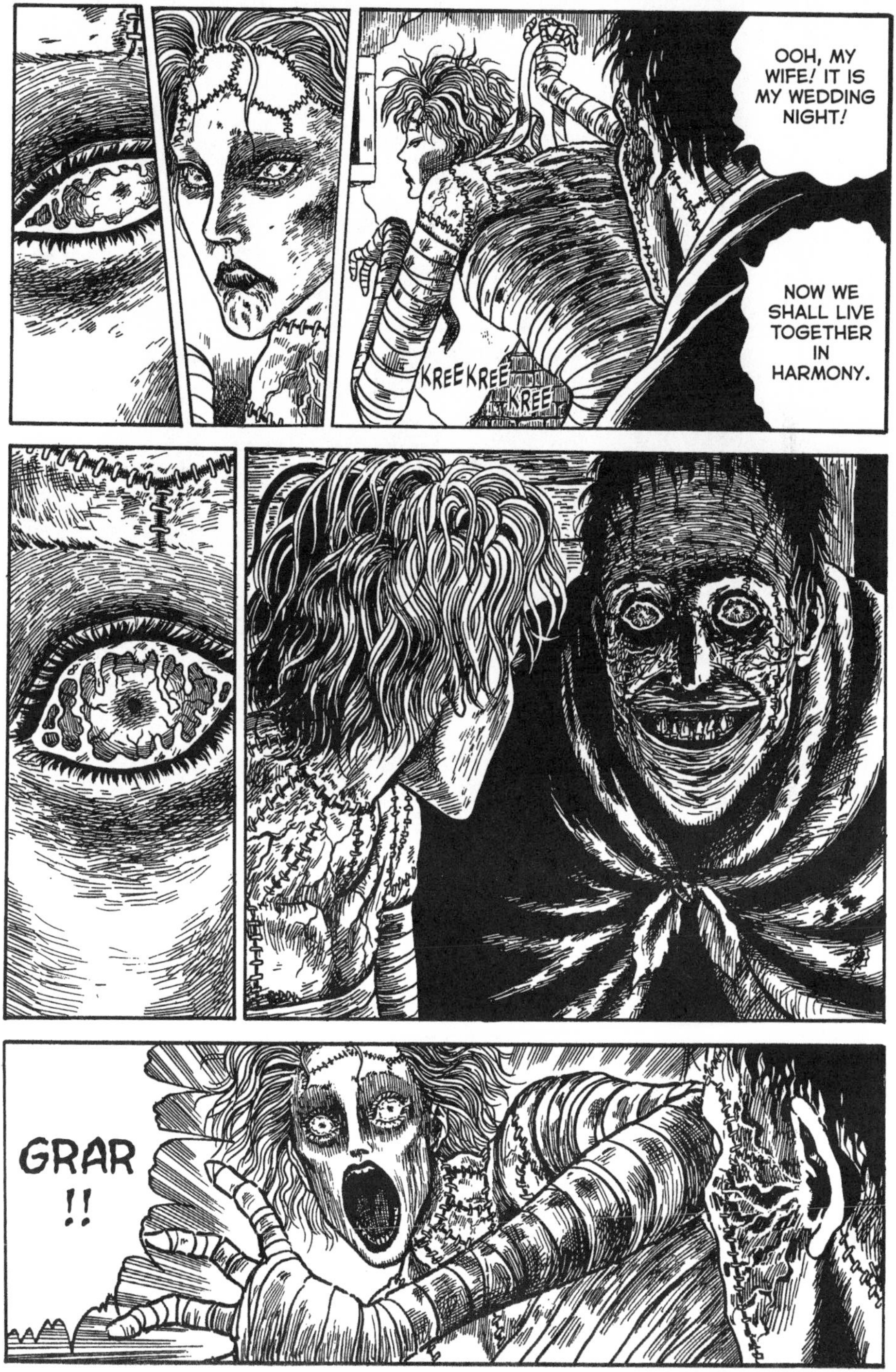
OOH, MY WIFE! IT IS MY WEDDING NIGHT!
NOW WE SHALL LIVE TOGETHER IN HARMONY.
KREEKREE KREE
GRAR !!

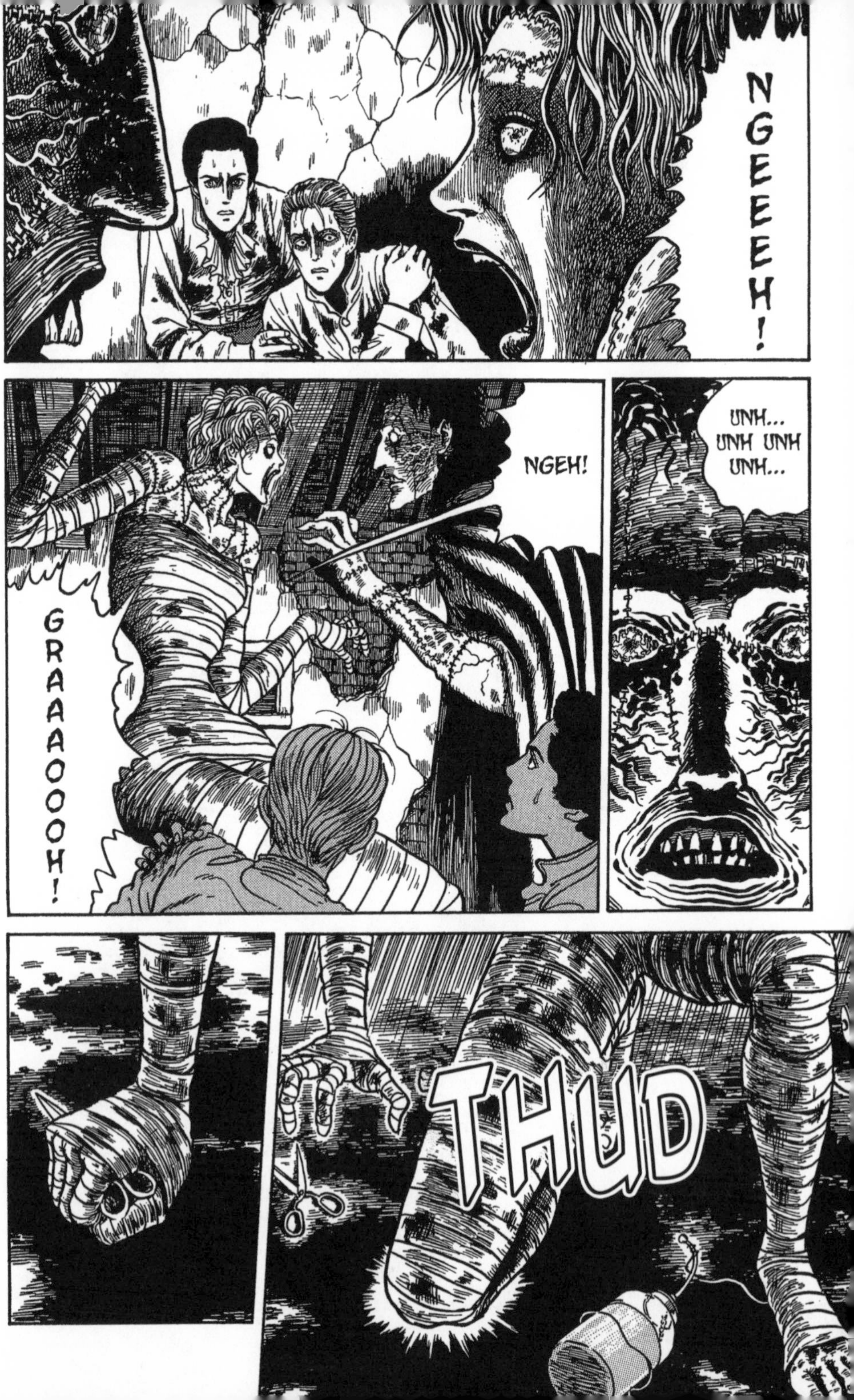
NGEEEEH!
UNH... UNH UNH UNH...
NGEH!
GRAAAAOOOOH!
THUD

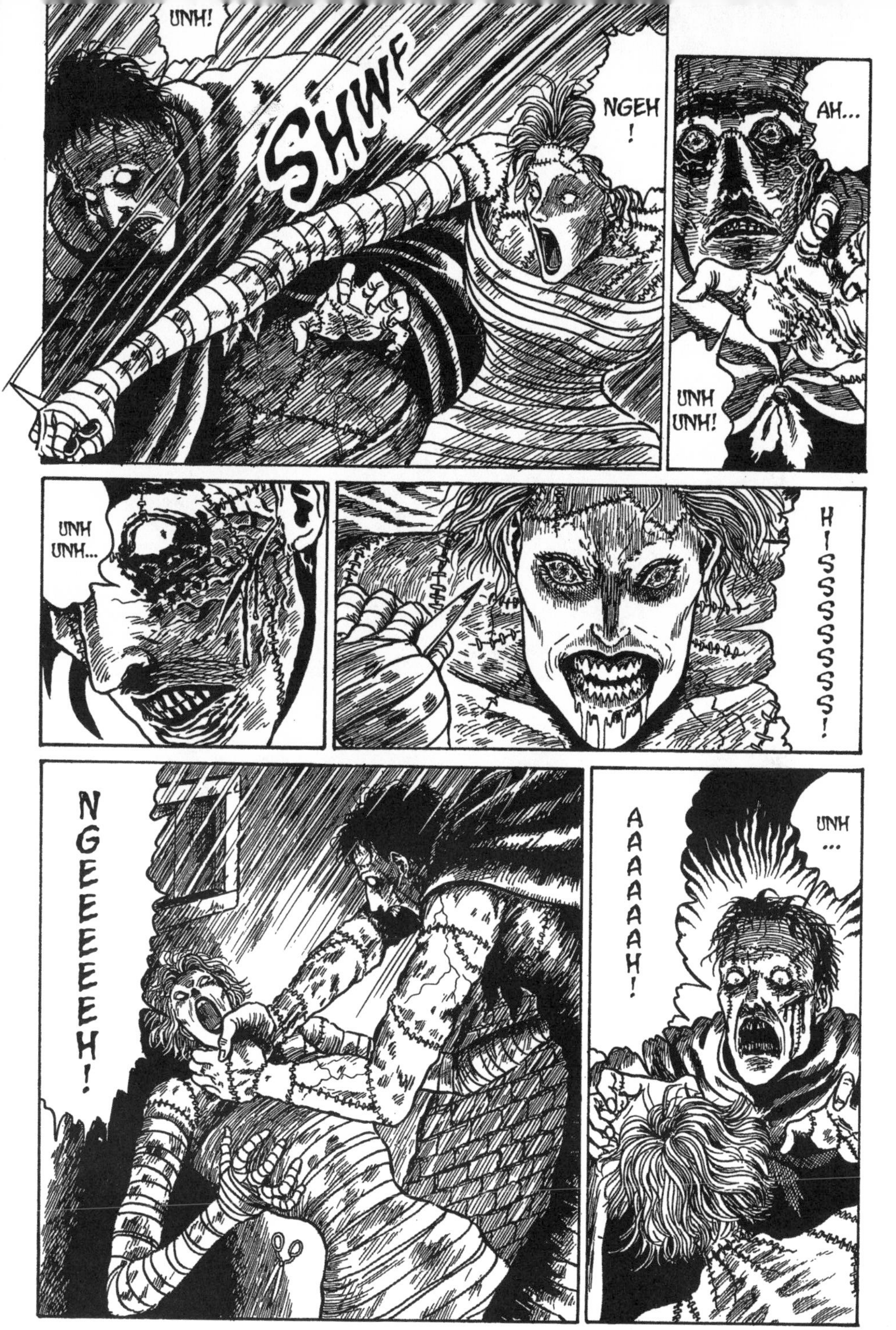
AH...
UNH UNH!
NGEH!
UNH!
SHWF
HISSSSSSS!
UNH UNH...
UNH ...
AAAAAAH!
NGEEEEEEEH!

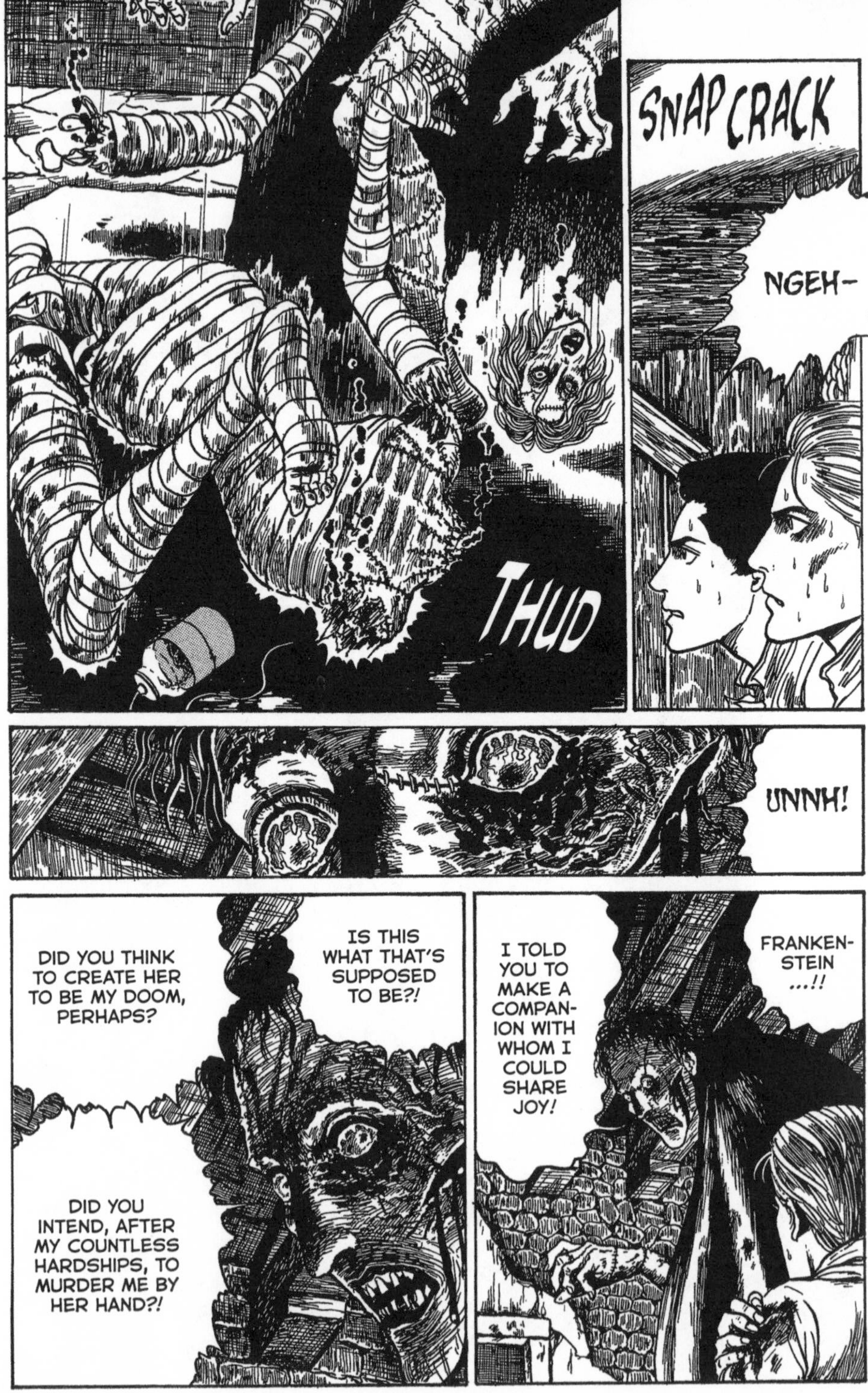
SNAP CRACK
NGEH-
THUD
UNNH!
FRANKEN-STEIN ...!!
I TOLD YOU TO MAKE A COMPANION WITH WHOM I COULD SHARE JOY!
IS THIS WHAT THAT'S SUPPOSED TO BE?!
DID YOU THINK TO CREATE HER TO BE MY DOOM, PERHAPS?
DID YOU INTEND, AFTER MY COUNTLESS HARDSHIPS, TO MURDER ME BY HER HAND?!

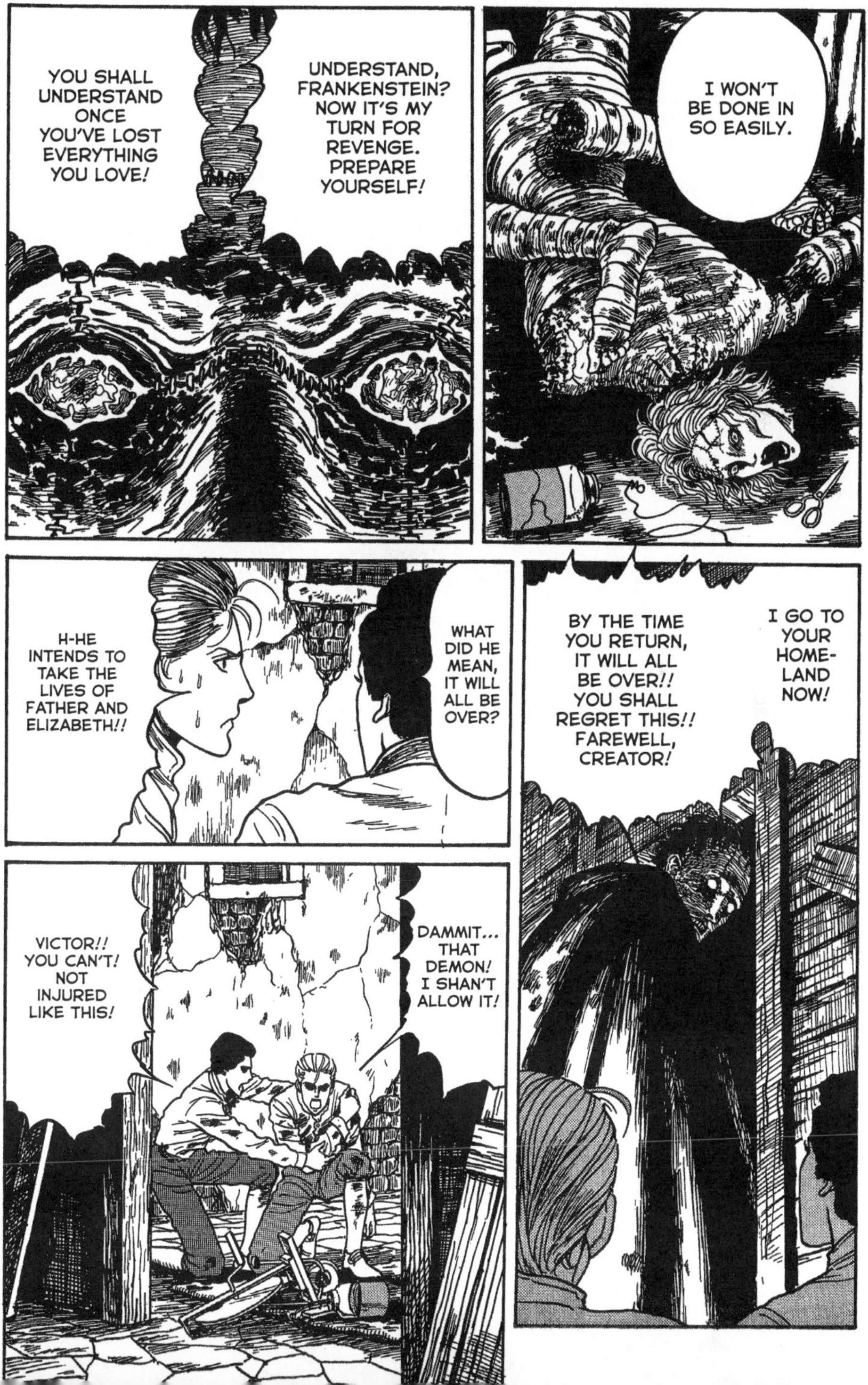
I WON'T BE DONE IN SO EASILY.
UNDERSTAND, FRANKENSTEIN? NOW IT'S MY TURN FOR REVENGE. PREPARE YOURSELF!
YOU SHALL UNDERSTAND ONCE YOU'VE LOST EVERYTHING YOU LOVE!
I GO TO YOUR HOMELAND NOW!
BY THE TIME YOU RETURN, IT WILL ALL BE OVER!! YOU SHALL REGRET THIS!! FAREWELL, CREATOR!
WHAT DID HE MEAN, IT WILL ALL BE OVER?
H-HE INTENDS TO TAKE THE LIVES OF FATHER AND ELIZABETH!!
DAMMIT... THAT DEMON! I SHAN'T ALLOW IT!
VICTOR!! YOU CAN'T! NOT INJURED LIKE THIS!

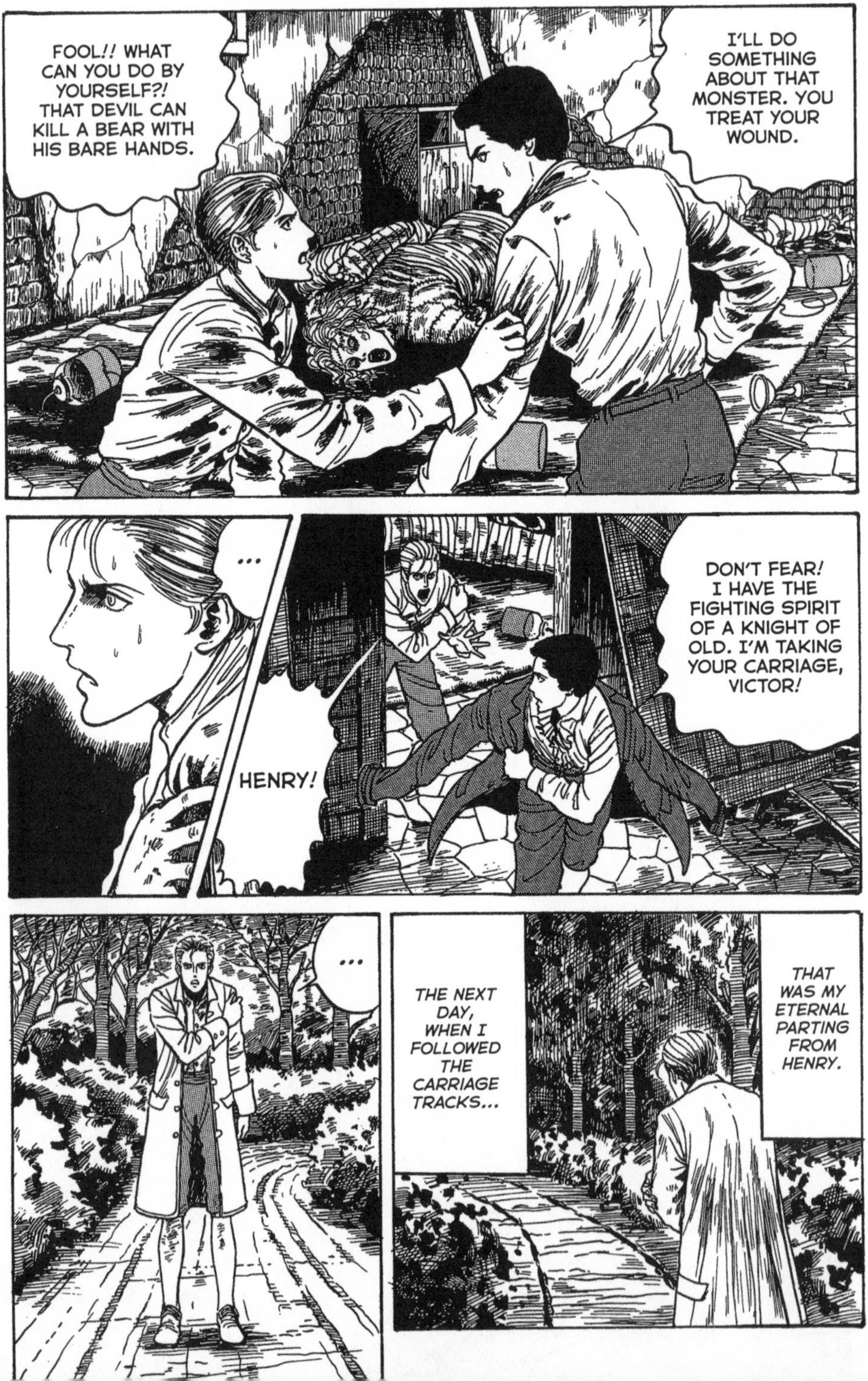
I'LL DO SOMETHING ABOUT THAT MONSTER. YOU TREAT YOUR WOUND.
FOOL!! WHAT CAN YOU DO BY YOURSELF?! THAT DEVIL CAN KILL A BEAR WITH HIS BARE HANDS.
DON'T FEAR! I HAVE THE FIGHTING SPIRIT OF A KNIGHT OF OLD. I'M TAKING YOUR CARRIAGE, VICTOR!
HENRY!
...
THAT WAS MY ETERNAL PARTING FROM HENRY.
THE NEXT DAY, WHEN I FOLLOWED THE CARRIAGE TRACKS...
...

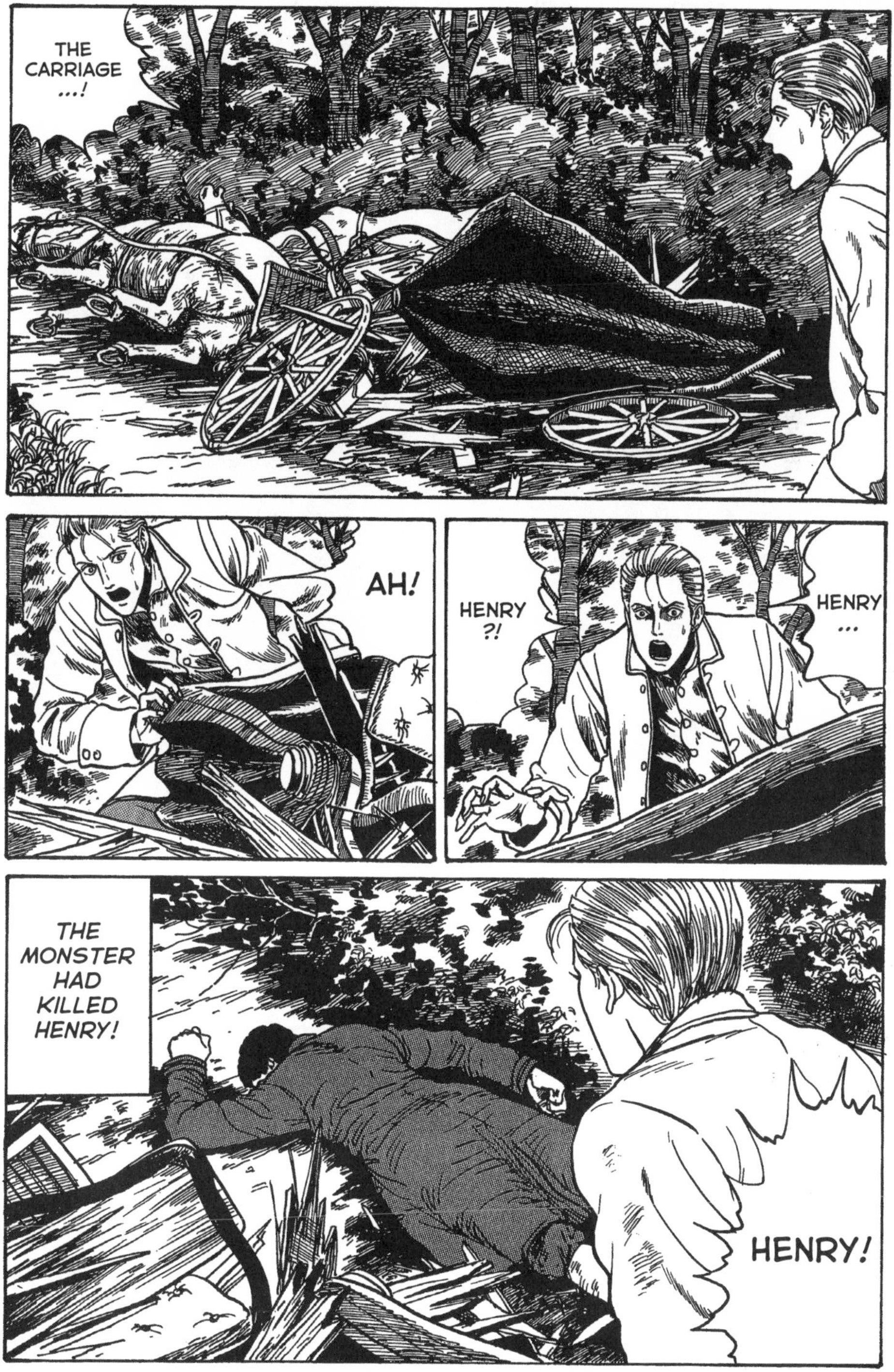
THE CARRIAGE ...!
HENRY ...
HENRY ?!
AH!
THE MONSTER HAD KILLED HENRY!
HENRY!

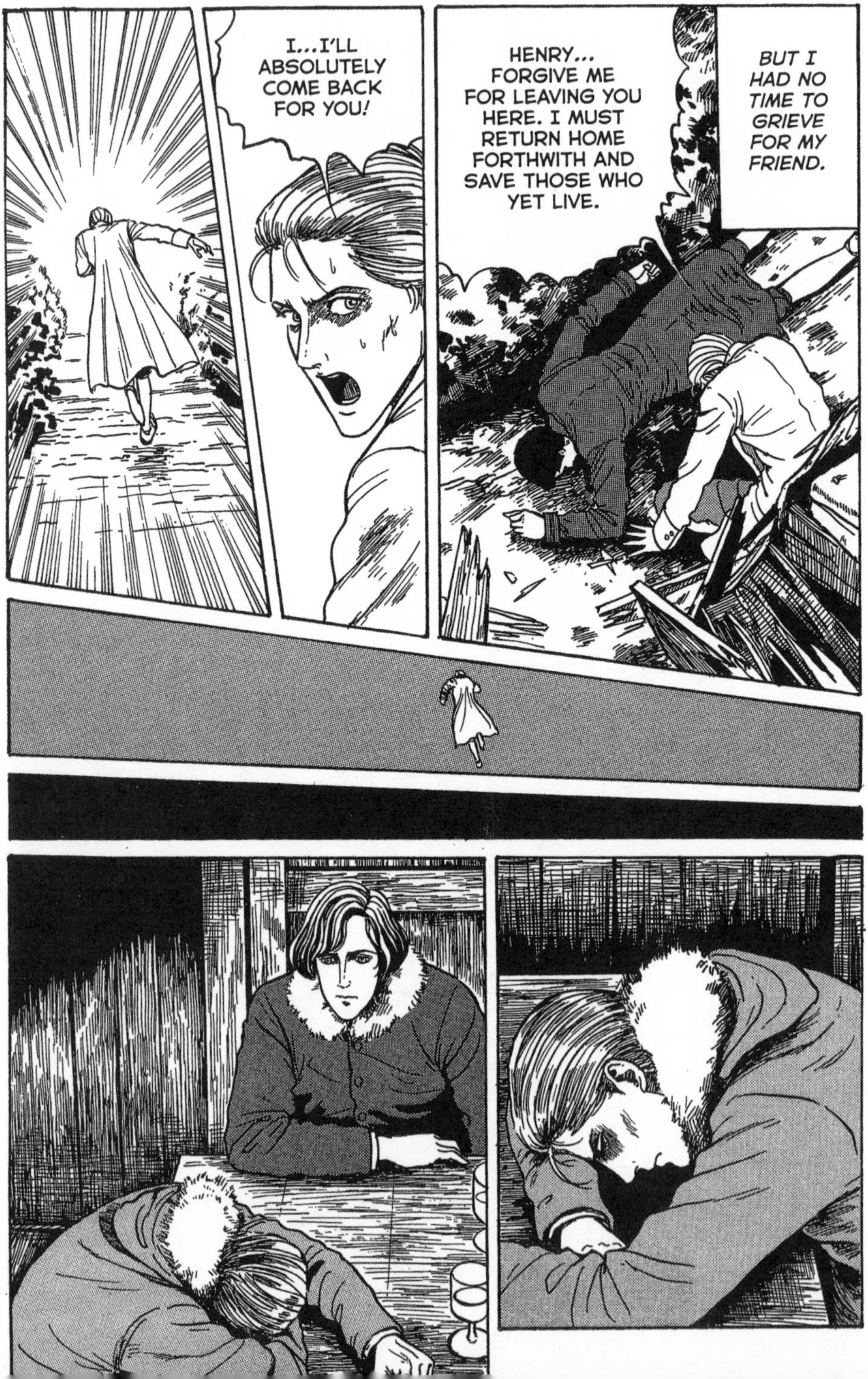
BUT I HAD NO TIME TO GRIEVE FOR MY FRIEND.
HENRY... FORGIVE ME FOR LEAVING YOU HERE. I MUST RETURN HOME FORTHWITH AND SAVE THOSE WHO YET LIVE.
I...I'LL ABSOLUTELY COME BACK FOR YOU!

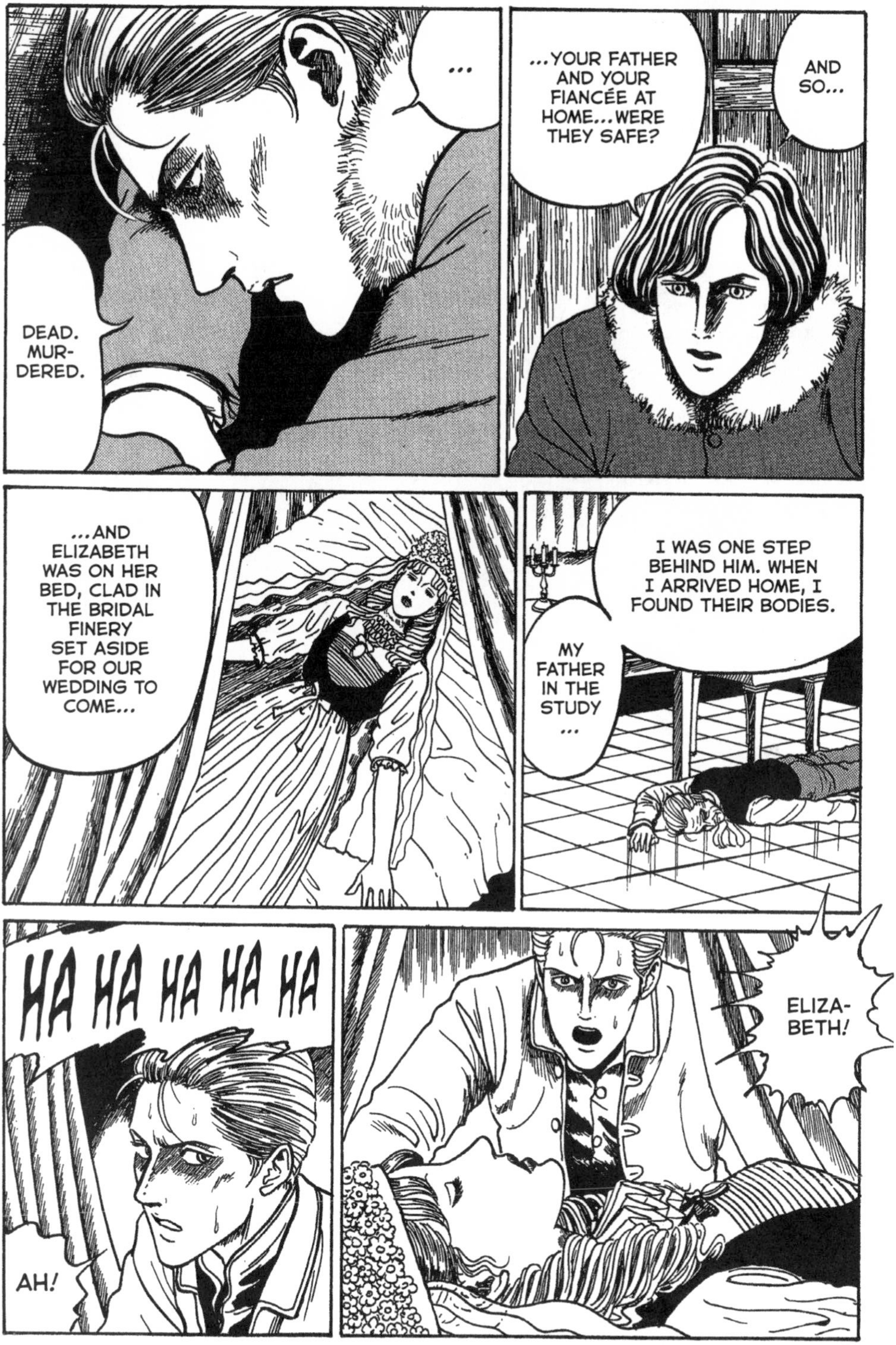
AND SO...
...YOUR FATHER AND YOUR FIANCÉE AT HOME...WERE THEY SAFE?
...
DEAD. MUR-DERED.
I WAS ONE STEP BEHIND HIM. WHEN I ARRIVED HOME, I FOUND THEIR BODIES.
MY FATHER IN THE STUDY ...
...AND ELIZABETH WAS ON HER BED, CLAD IN THE BRIDAL FINERY SET ASIDE FOR OUR WEDDING TO COME...
ELIZA-BETH!
HA HA HA HA HA
AH!

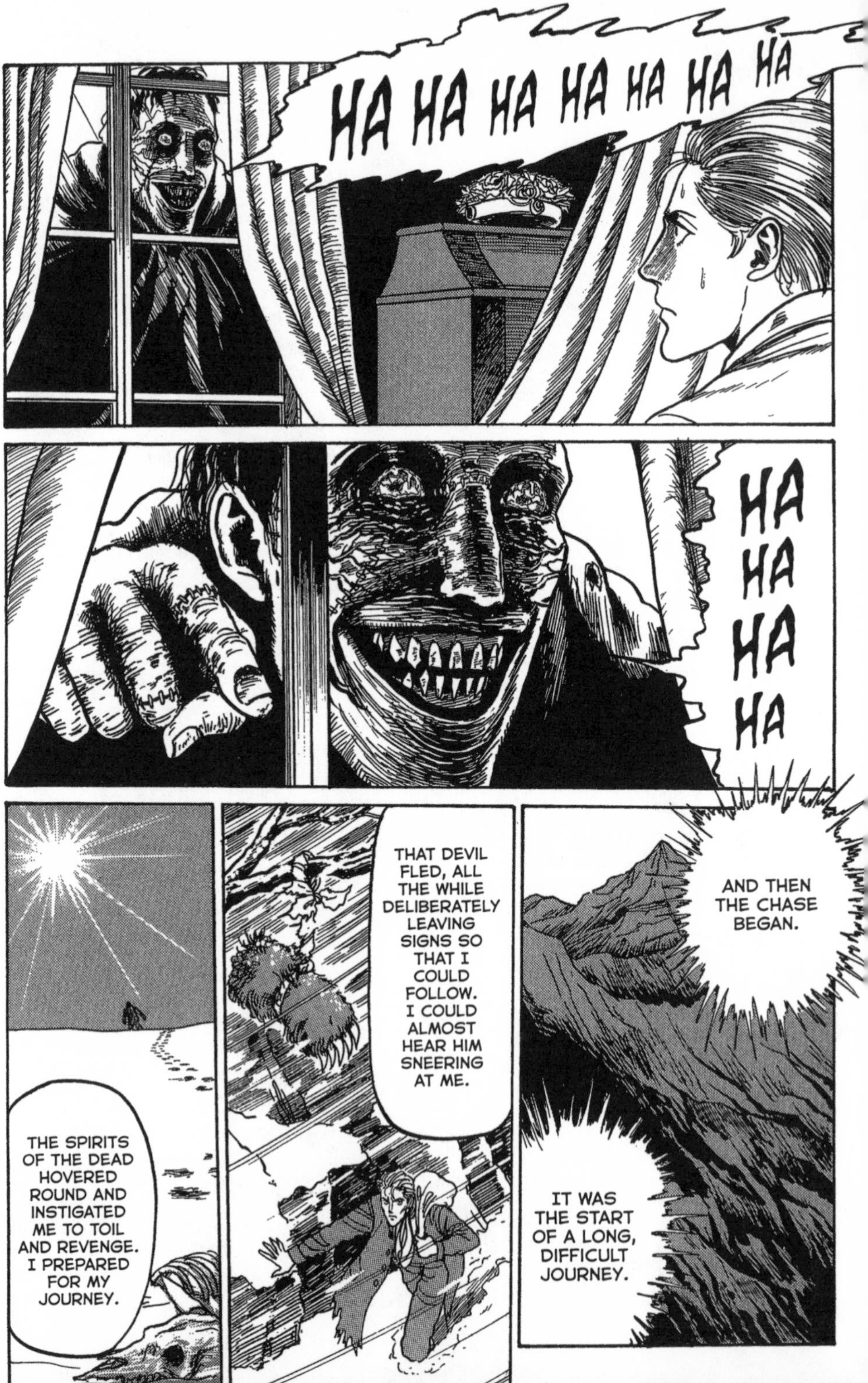
HA HA HA HA HA HA HA
HA HA HA HA HA
AND THEN THE CHASE BEGAN.
IT WAS THE START OF A LONG, DIFFICULT JOURNEY.
THAT DEVIL FLED, ALL THE WHILE DELIBERATELY LEAVING SIGNS SO THAT I COULD FOLLOW. I COULD ALMOST HEAR HIM SNEERING AT ME.
THE SPIRITS OF THE DEAD HOVERED ROUND AND INSTIGATED ME TO TOIL AND REVENGE. I PREPARED FOR MY JOURNEY.

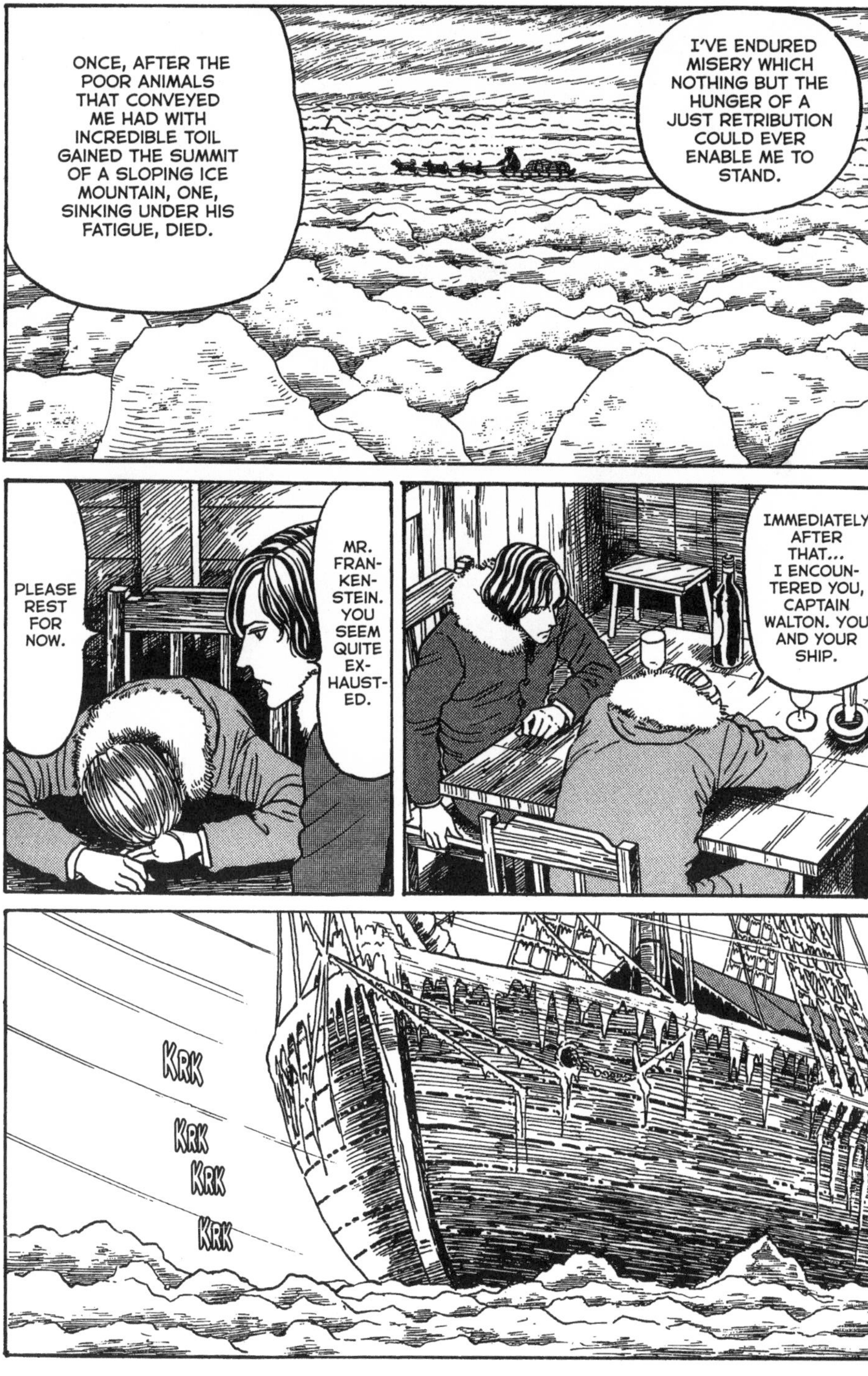
I'VE ENDURED MISERY WHICH NOTHING BUT THE HUNGER OF A JUST RETRIBUTION COULD EVER ENABLE ME TO STAND.
ONCE, AFTER THE POOR ANIMALS THAT CONVEYED ME HAD WITH INCREDIBLE TOIL GAINED THE SUMMIT OF A SLOPING ICE MOUNTAIN, ONE, SINKING UNDER HIS FATIGUE, DIED.
IMMEDIATELY AFTER THAT... I ENCOUNTERED YOU, CAPTAIN WALTON. YOU AND YOUR SHIP.
MR. FRANKENSTEIN. YOU SEEM QUITE EXHAUSTED.
PLEASE REST FOR NOW.
KRK
KRK
KRK
KRK

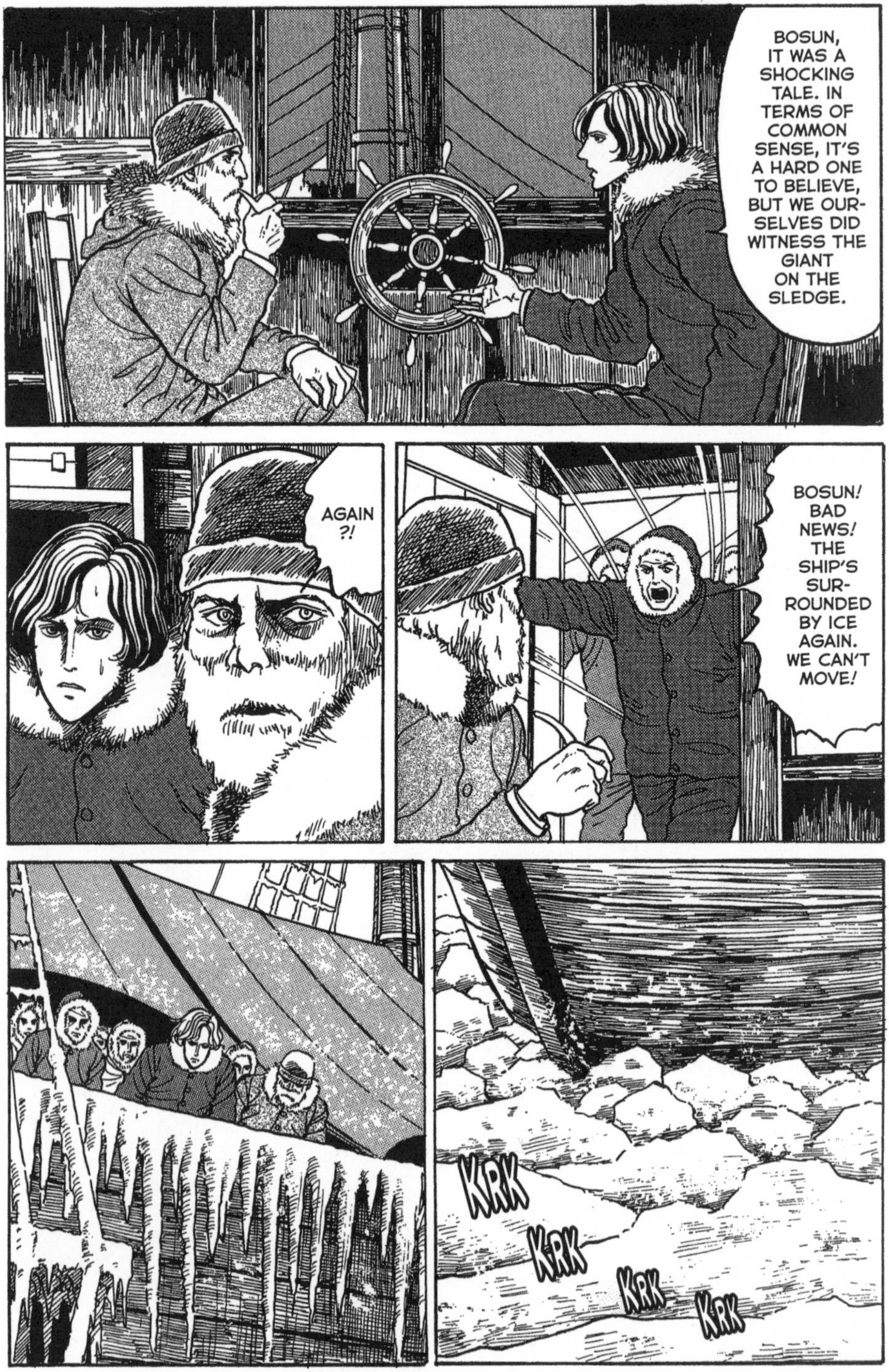
BOSUN, IT WAS A SHOCKING TALE. IN TERMS OF COMMON SENSE, IT'S A HARD ONE TO BELIEVE, BUT WE OURSELVES DID WITNESS THE GIANT ON THE SLEDGE.
BOSUN! BAD NEWS! THE SHIP'S SURROUNDED BY ICE AGAIN. WE CAN'T MOVE!
AGAIN ?!
KRK
K-RK
KRK
KRK

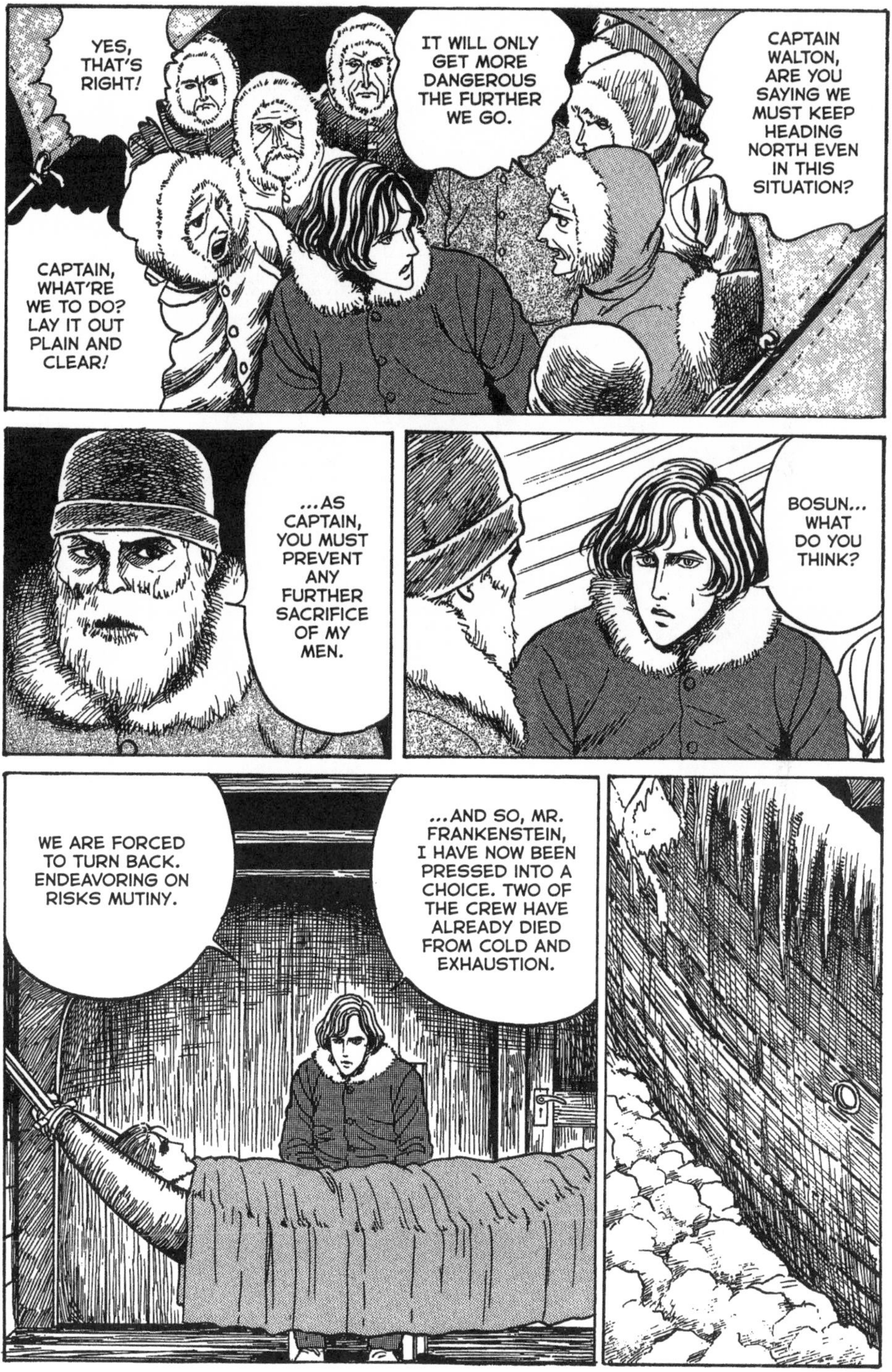
CAPTAIN WALTON, ARE YOU SAYING WE MUST KEEP HEADING NORTH EVEN IN THIS SITUATION?
IT WILL ONLY GET MORE DANGEROUS THE FURTHER WE GO.
YES, THAT'S RIGHT!
CAPTAIN, WHAT'RE WE TO DO? LAY IT OUT PLAIN AND CLEAR!
BOSUN... WHAT DO YOU THINK?
...AS CAPTAIN, YOU MUST PREVENT ANY FURTHER SACRIFICE OF MY MEN.
...AND SO, MR. FRANKENSTEIN, I HAVE NOW BEEN PRESSED INTO A CHOICE. TWO OF THE CREW HAVE ALREADY DIED FROM COLD AND EXHAUSTION.
WE ARE FORCED TO TURN BACK. ENDEAVORING ON RISKS MUTINY.

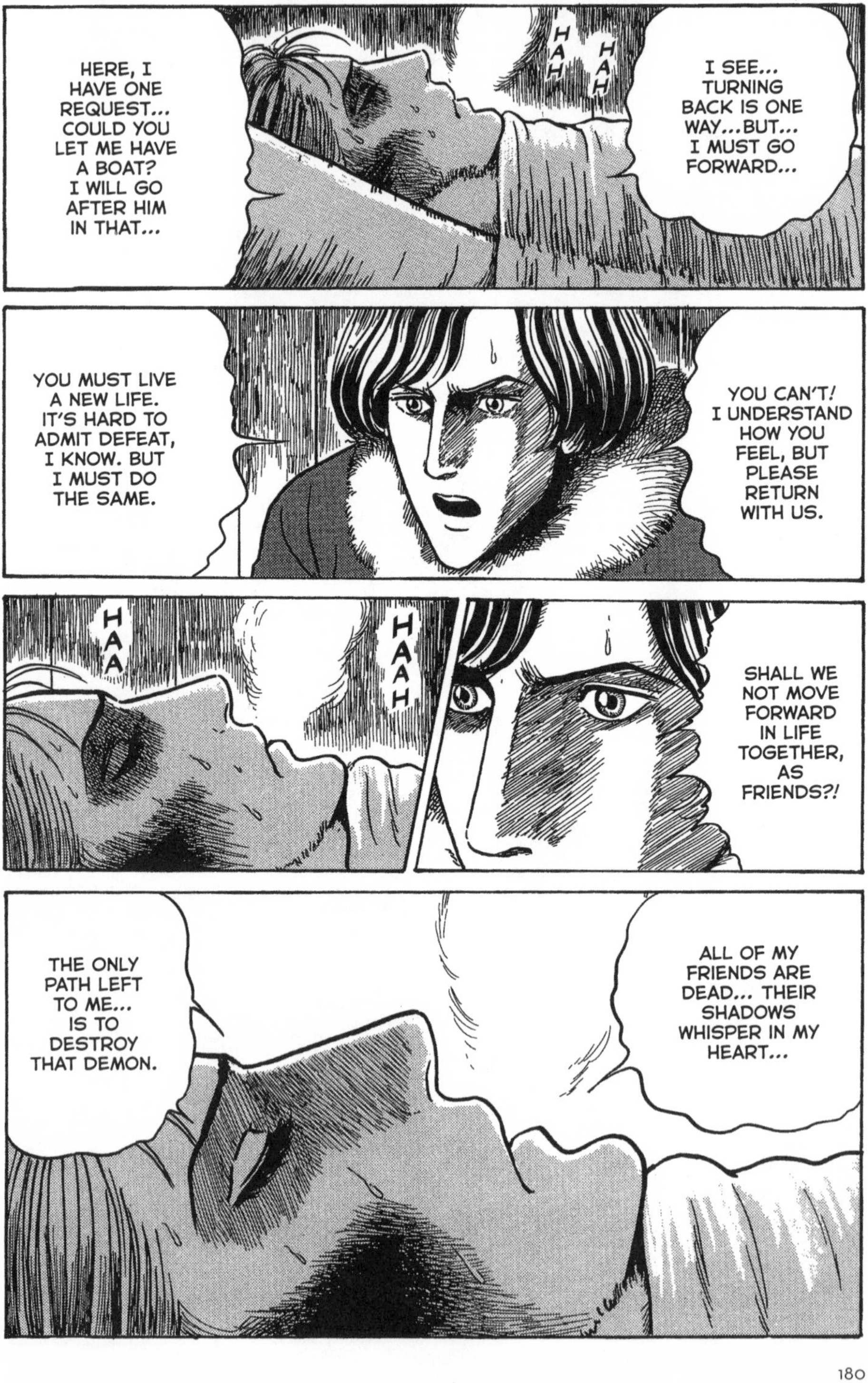
I SEE... TURNING BACK IS ONE WAY...BUT... I MUST GO FORWARD...
HAH
HAH
HERE, I HAVE ONE REQUEST... COULD YOU LET ME HAVE A BOAT? I WILL GO AFTER HIM IN THAT...
YOU CAN'T! I UNDERSTAND HOW YOU FEEL, BUT PLEASE RETURN WITH US.
YOU MUST LIVE A NEW LIFE. IT'S HARD TO ADMIT DEFEAT, I KNOW. BUT I MUST DO THE SAME.
SHALL WE NOT MOVE FORWARD IN LIFE TOGETHER, AS FRIENDS?!
HAAH
HAA
ALL OF MY FRIENDS ARE DEAD... THEIR SHADOWS WHISPER IN MY HEART...
THE ONLY PATH LEFT TO ME... IS TO DESTROY THAT DEMON.

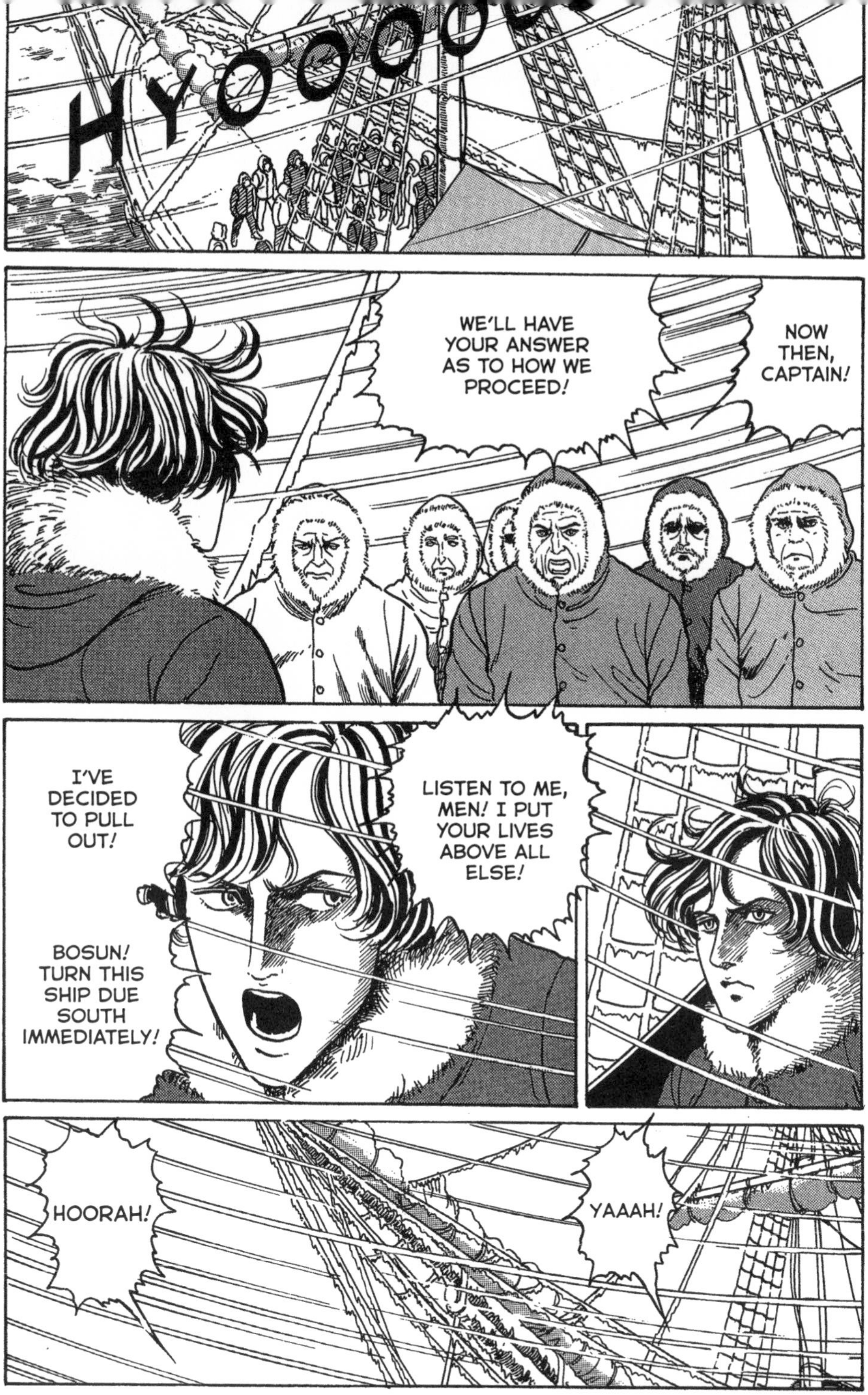
HYOOOOO
NOW THEN, CAPTAIN!
WE'LL HAVE YOUR ANSWER AS TO HOW WE PROCEED!
LISTEN TO ME, MEN! I PUT YOUR LIVES ABOVE ALL ELSE!
I'VE DECIDED TO PULL OUT!
BOSUN! TURN THIS SHIP DUE SOUTH IMMEDIATELY!
YAAAH!
HOORAH!

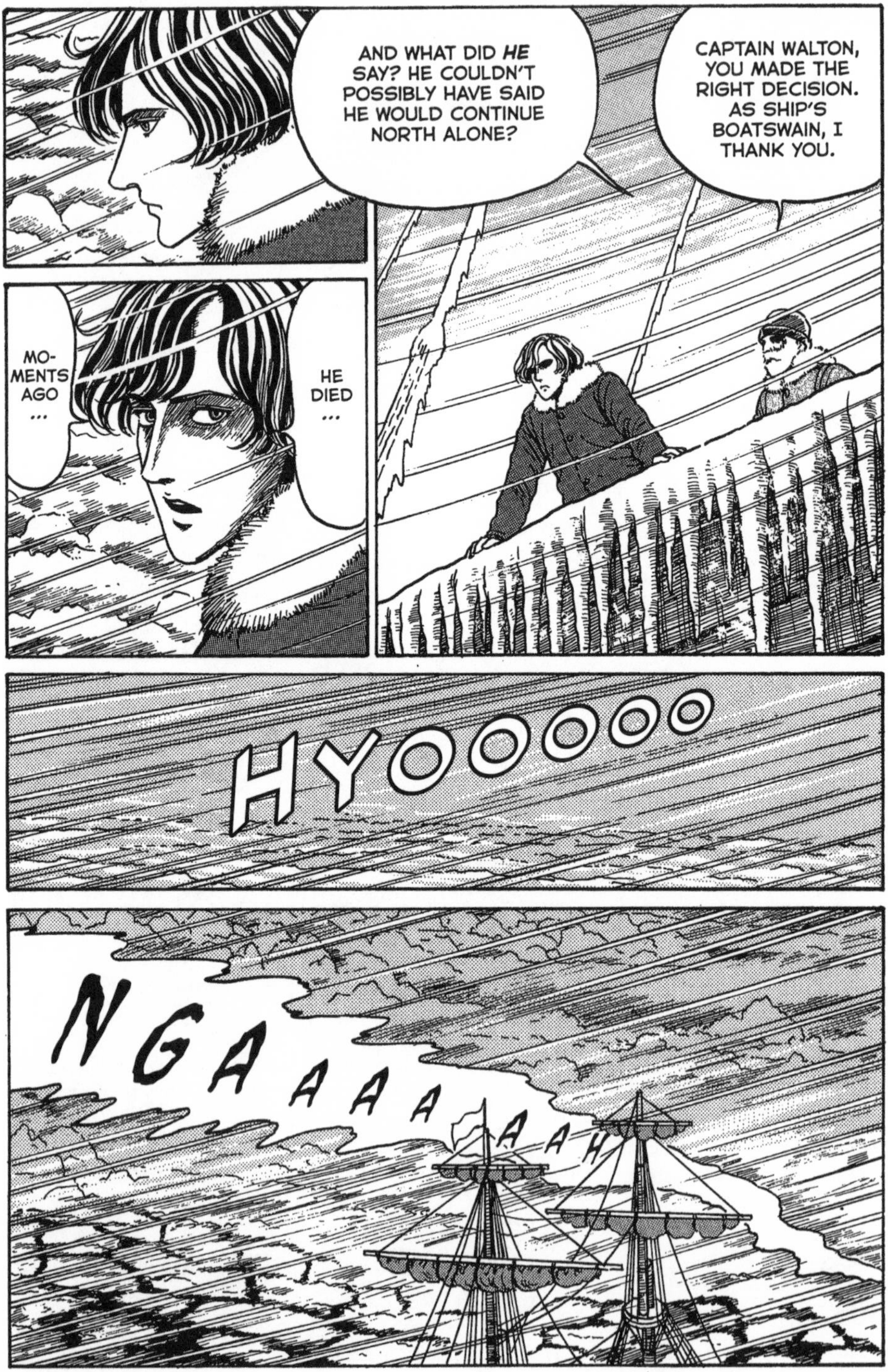
CAPTAIN WALTON, YOU MADE THE RIGHT DECISION. AS SHIP'S BOATSWAIN, I THANK YOU.
AND WHAT DID *HE* SAY? HE COULDN'T POSSIBLY HAVE SAID HE WOULD CONTINUE NORTH ALONE?
HE DIED ...
MO-MENTS AGO ...
HYOOOOO
NGAAAAAAAH

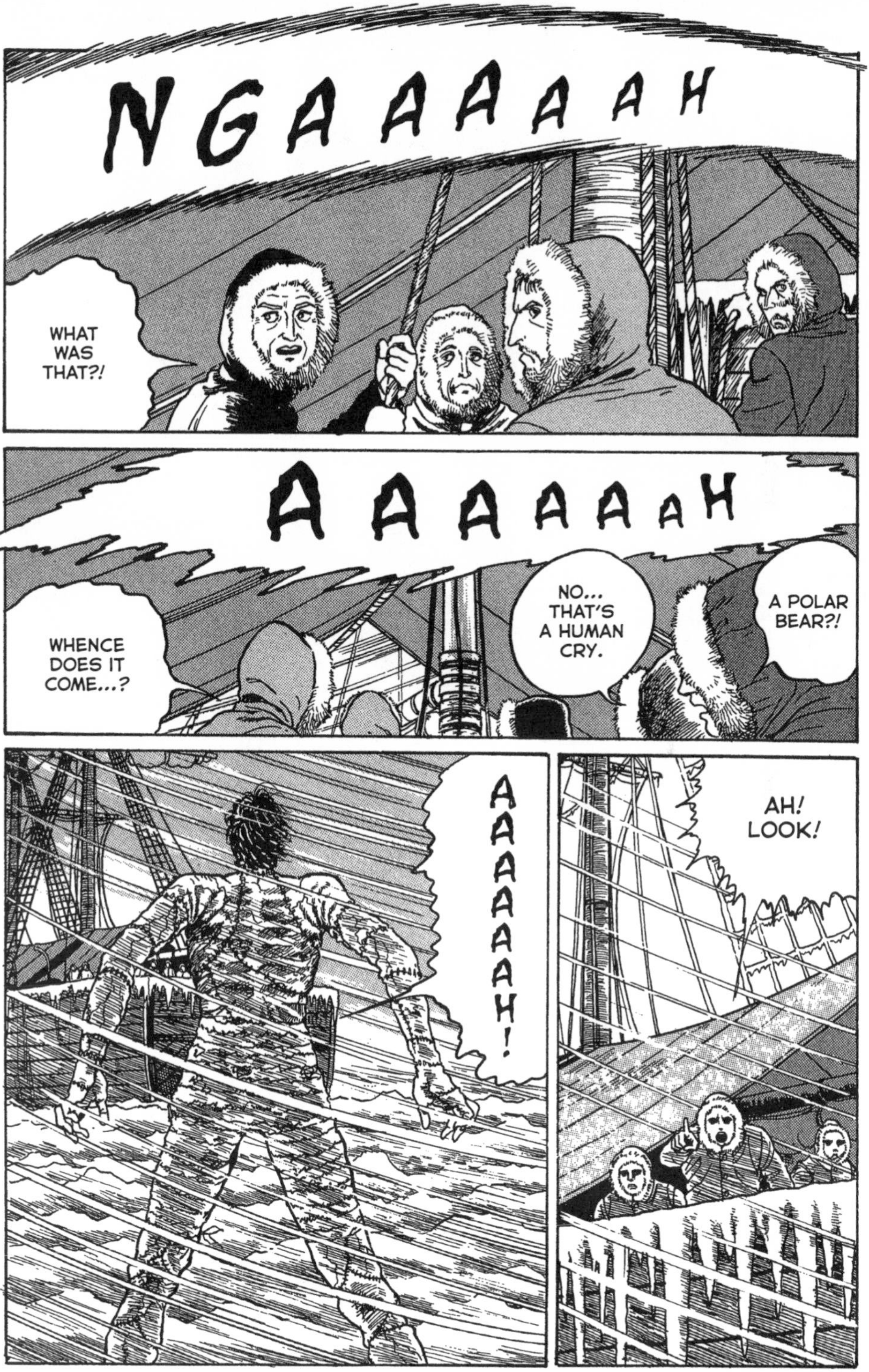
NGAAAAAH
WHAT WAS THAT?!
AAAAAAH
A POLAR BEAR?!
NO... THAT'S A HUMAN CRY.
WHENCE DOES IT COME...?
AH! LOOK!
AAAAAAAAH!

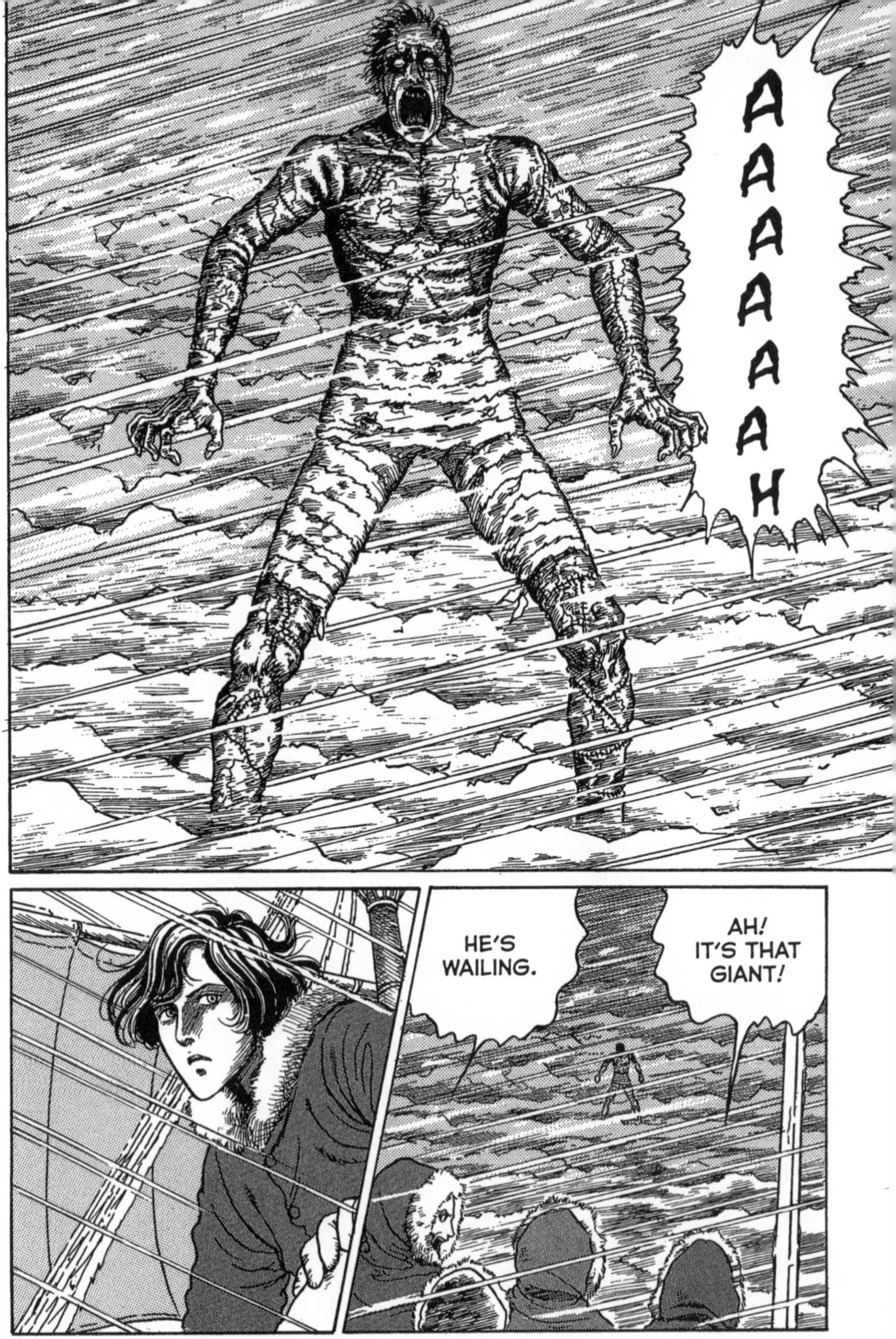
AAAAAAH
AH! IT'S THAT GIANT!
HE'S WAILING.

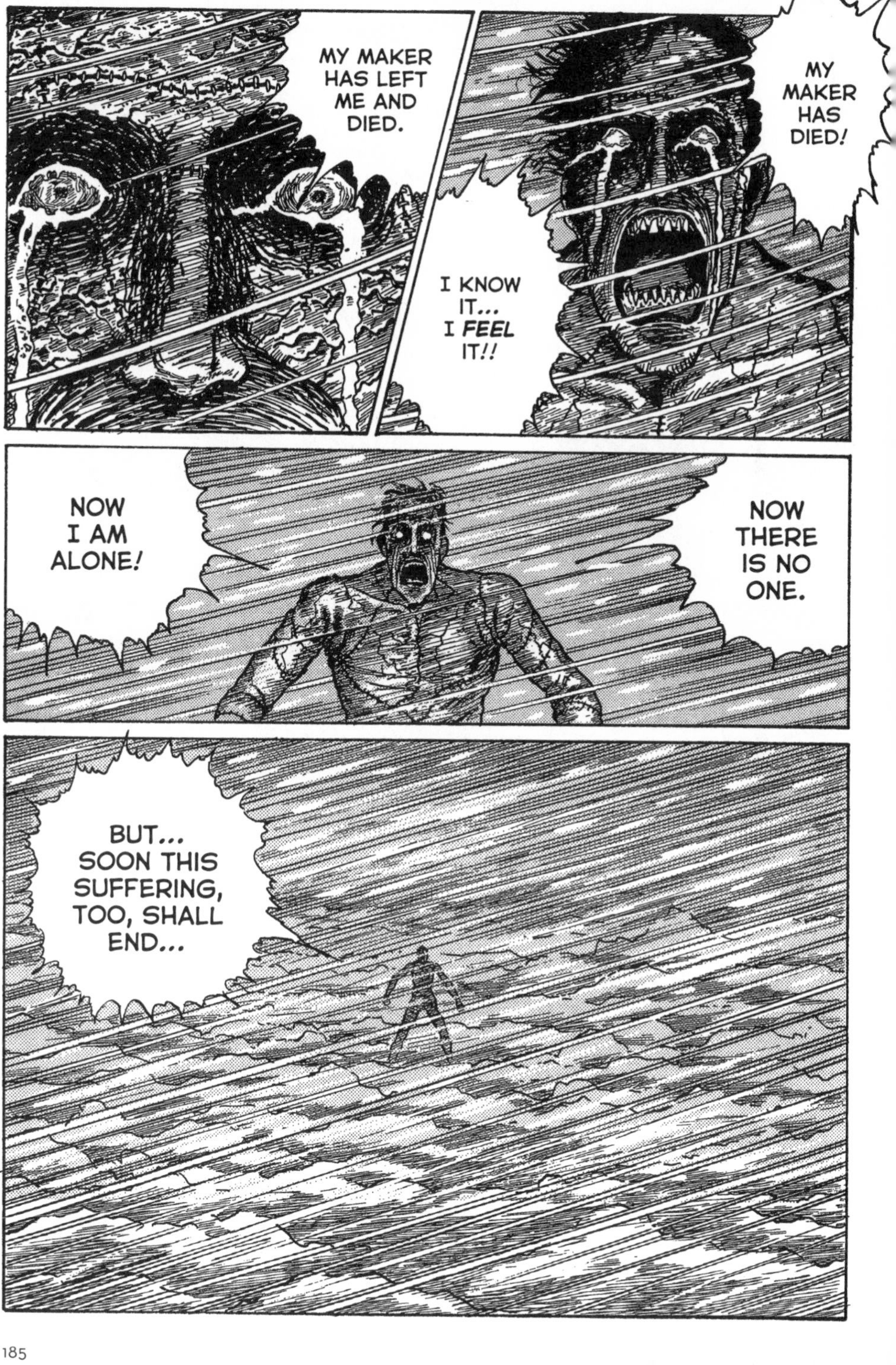
MY MAKER HAS DIED!
I KNOW IT... I *FEEL* IT!!
MY MAKER HAS LEFT ME AND DIED.
NOW THERE IS NO ONE.
NOW I AM ALONE!
BUT... SOON THIS SUFFERING, TOO, SHALL END...

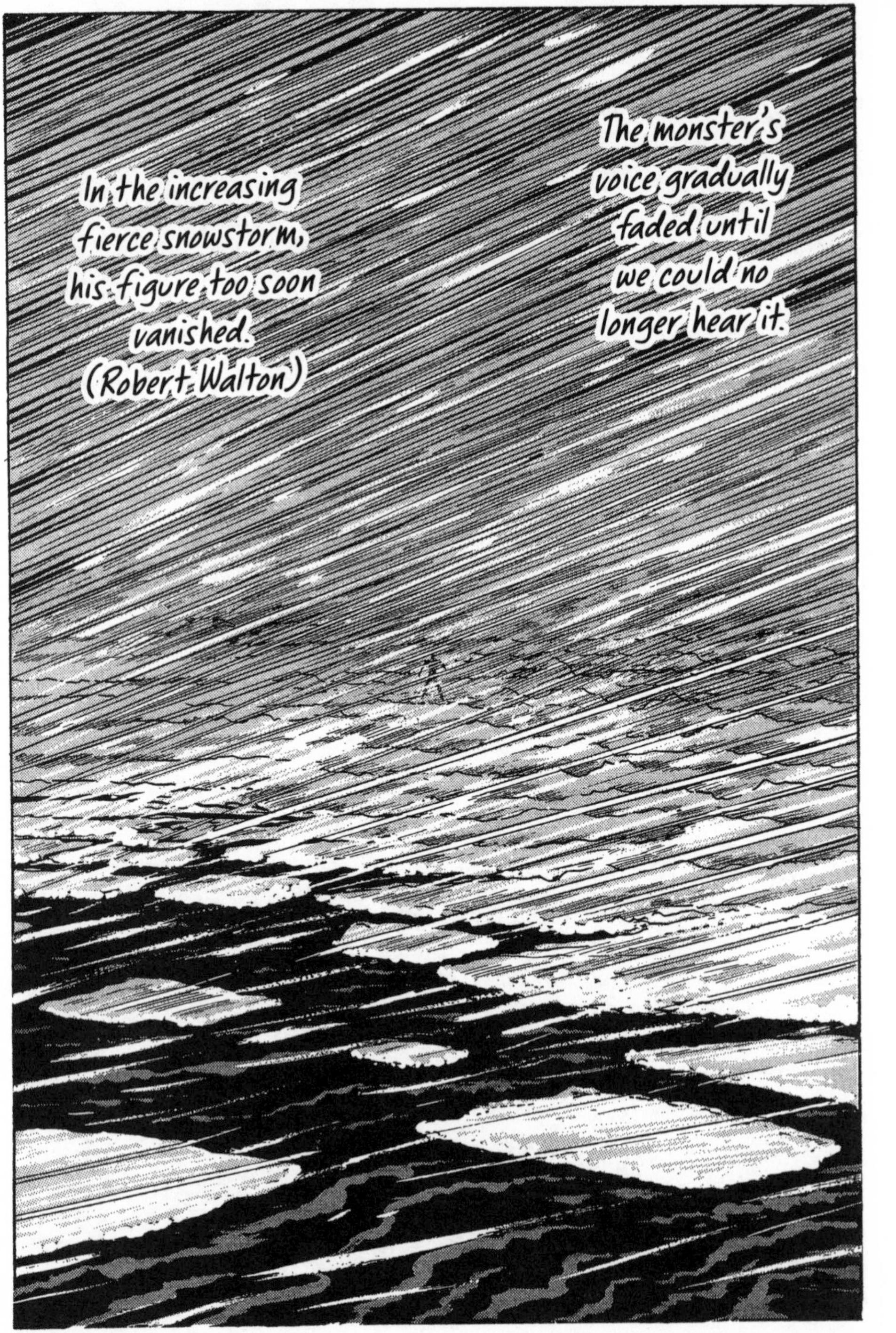
The monster's voice gradually faded until we could no longer hear it.
In the increasing fierce snowstorm, his figure too soon vanished. (Robert Walton)

FRANKENSTEIN / END

NECK SPECTER

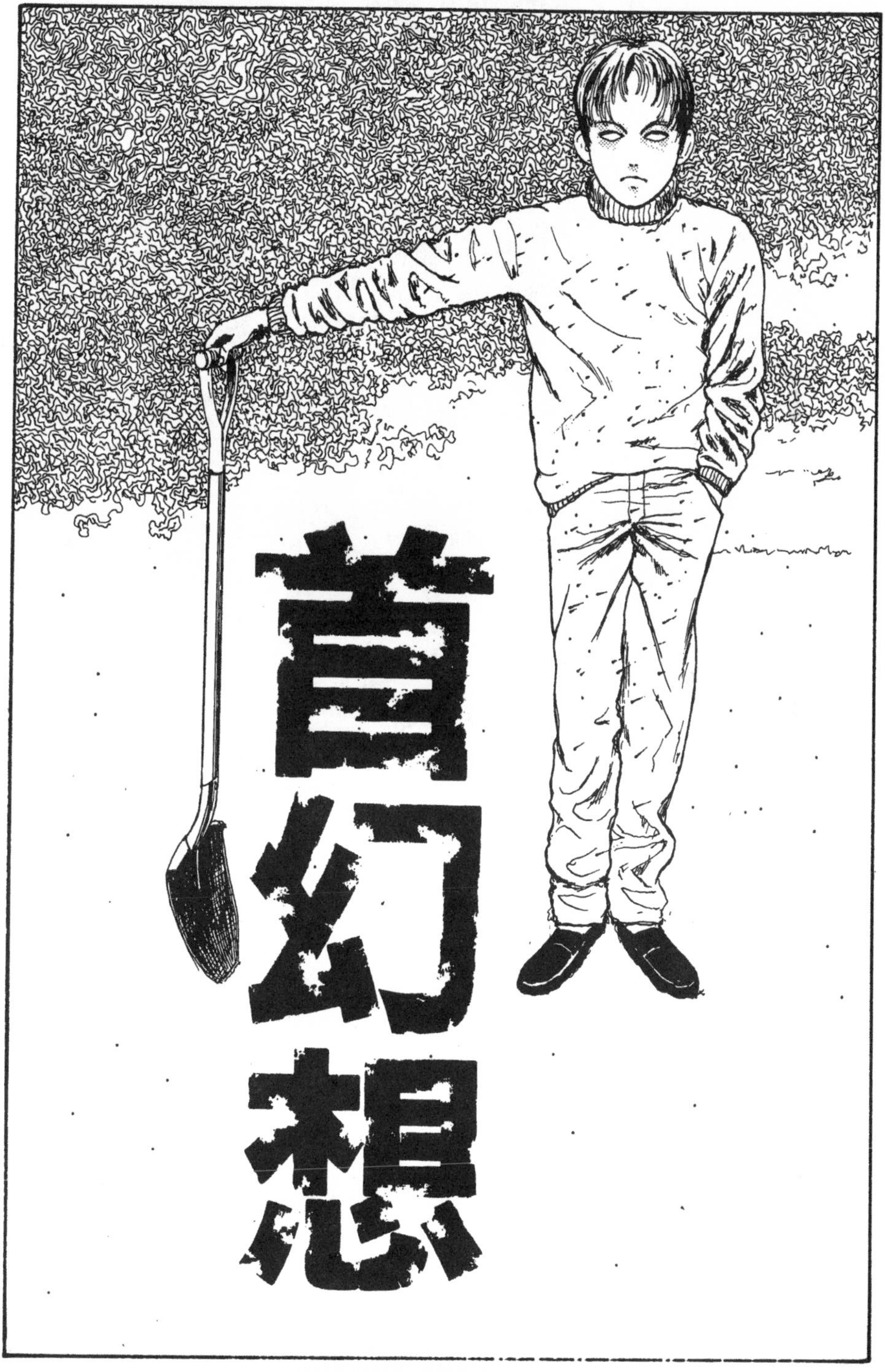
首幻想

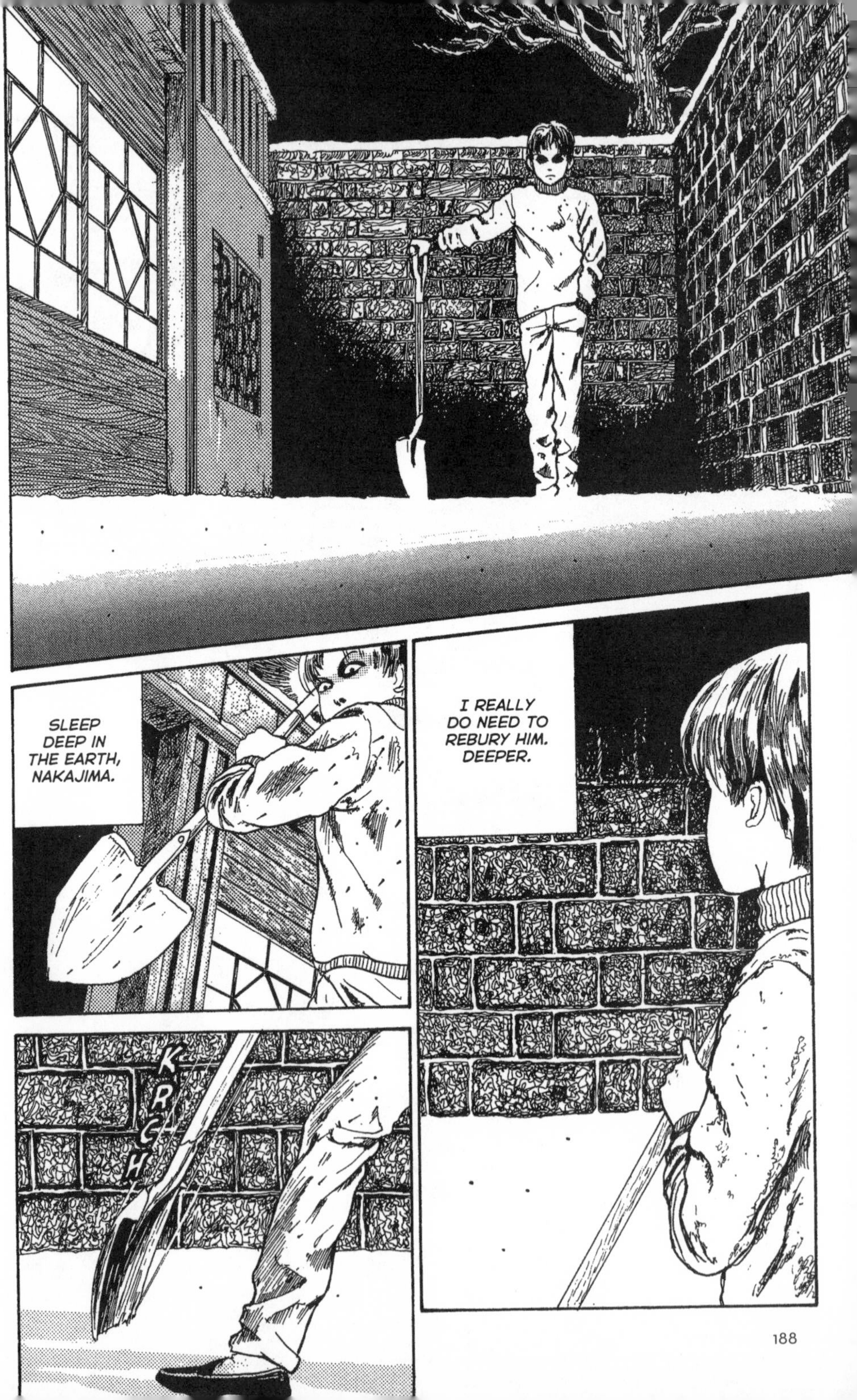
I REALLY DO NEED TO REBURY HIM. DEEPER.
SLEEP DEEP IN THE EARTH, NAKAJIMA.
KRCH

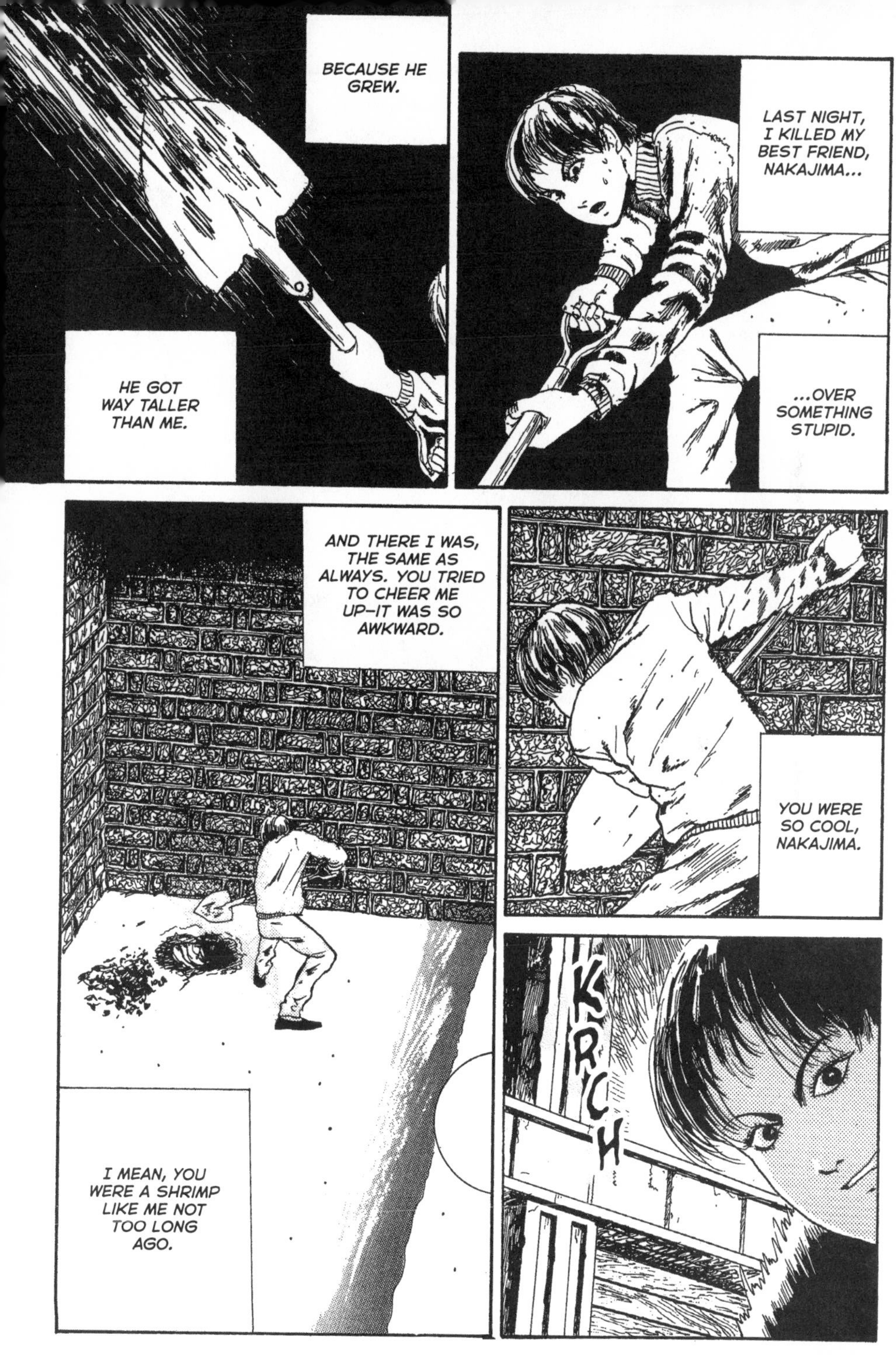
LAST NIGHT, I KILLED MY BEST FRIEND, NAKAJIMA...
...OVER SOMETHING STUPID.
BECAUSE HE GREW.
HE GOT WAY TALLER THAN ME.
YOU WERE SO COOL, NAKAJIMA.
KRCH
AND THERE I WAS, THE SAME AS ALWAYS. YOU TRIED TO CHEER ME UP–IT WAS SO AWKWARD.
I MEAN, YOU WERE A SHRIMP LIKE ME NOT TOO LONG AGO.

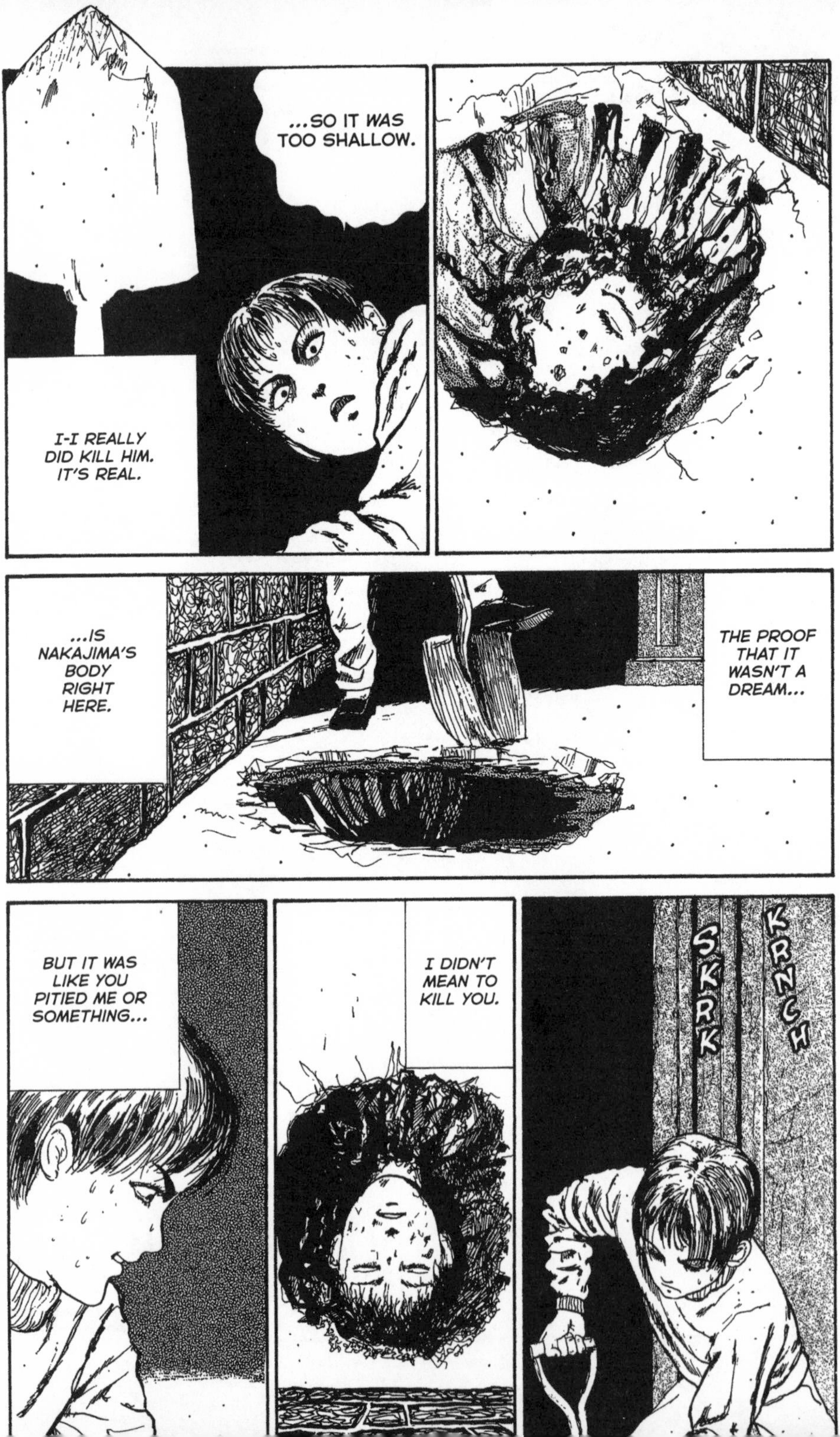
...SO IT WAS TOO SHALLOW.
I-I REALLY DID KILL HIM. IT'S REAL.
THE PROOF THAT IT WASN'T A DREAM...
...IS NAKAJIMA'S BODY RIGHT HERE.
KRNCH
SKRK
I DIDN'T MEAN TO KILL YOU.
BUT IT WAS LIKE YOU PITIED ME OR SOMETHING...

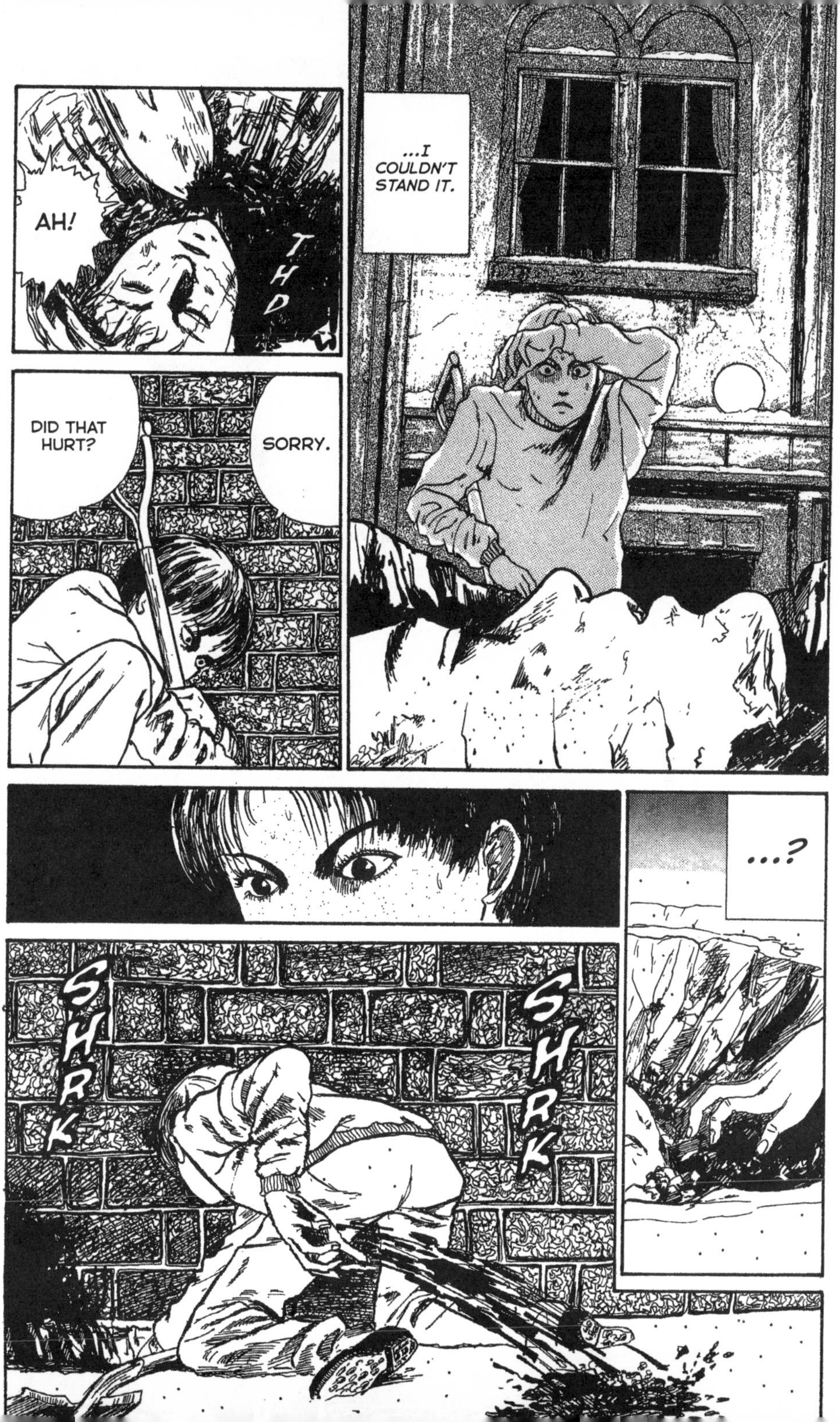
...I COULDN'T STAND IT.
AH!
THD
SORRY.
DID THAT HURT?
...?
SHRK
SHRK

W-WHAT IS
THIS?!

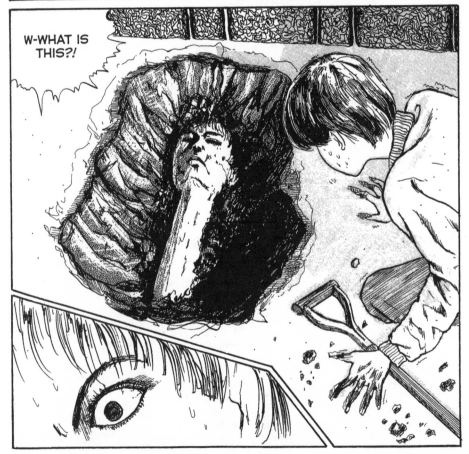

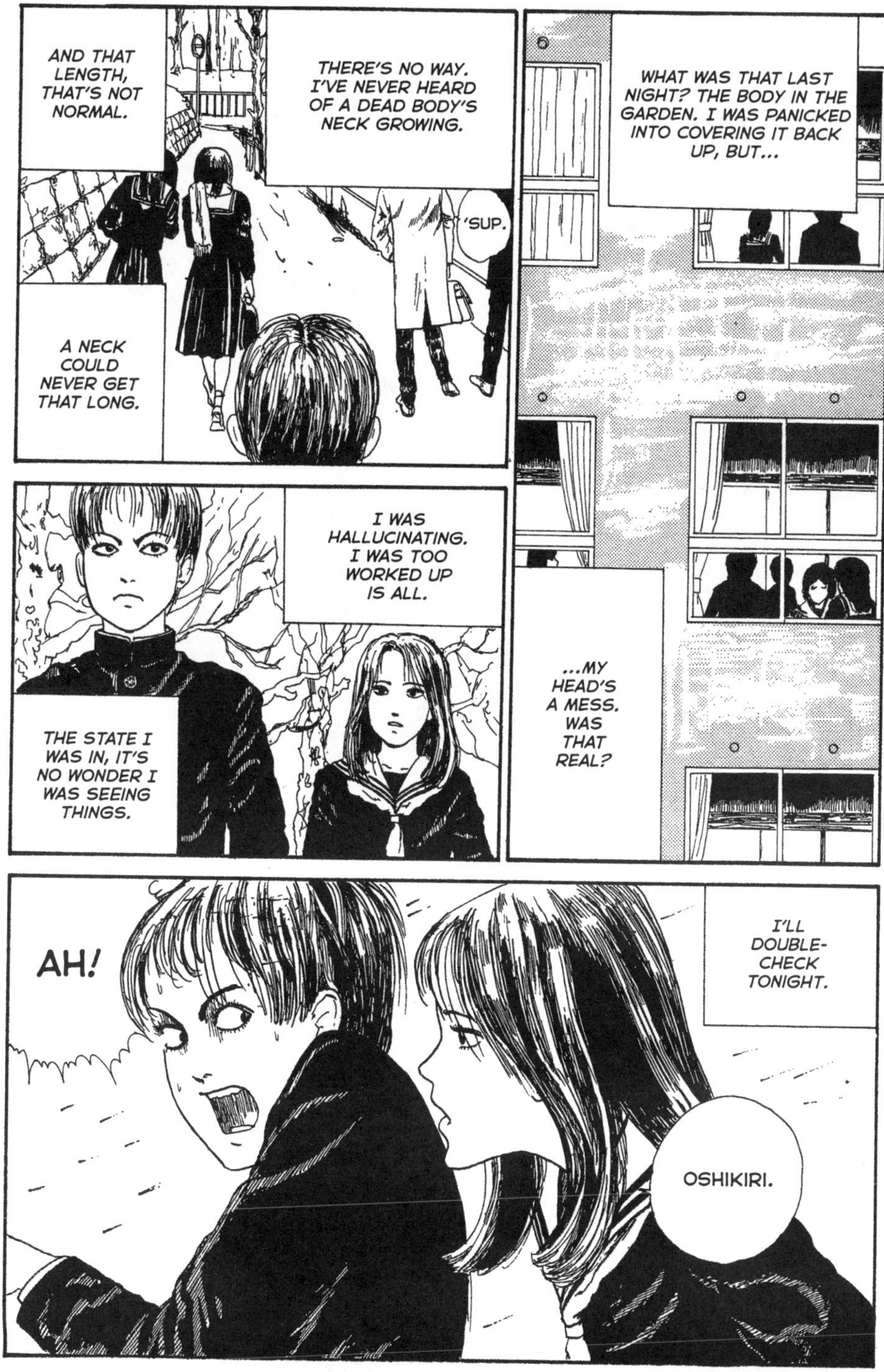
WHAT WAS THAT LAST NIGHT? THE BODY IN THE GARDEN. I WAS PANICKED INTO COVERING IT BACK UP, BUT...
...MY HEAD'S A MESS. WAS THAT REAL?
THERE'S NO WAY. I'VE NEVER HEARD OF A DEAD BODY'S NECK GROWING.
AND THAT LENGTH, THAT'S NOT NORMAL.
'SUP.
A NECK COULD NEVER GET THAT LONG.
I WAS HALLUCINATING. I WAS TOO WORKED UP IS ALL.
THE STATE I WAS IN, IT'S NO WONDER I WAS SEEING THINGS.
I'LL DOUBLE-CHECK TONIGHT.
OSHIKIRI.
AH!

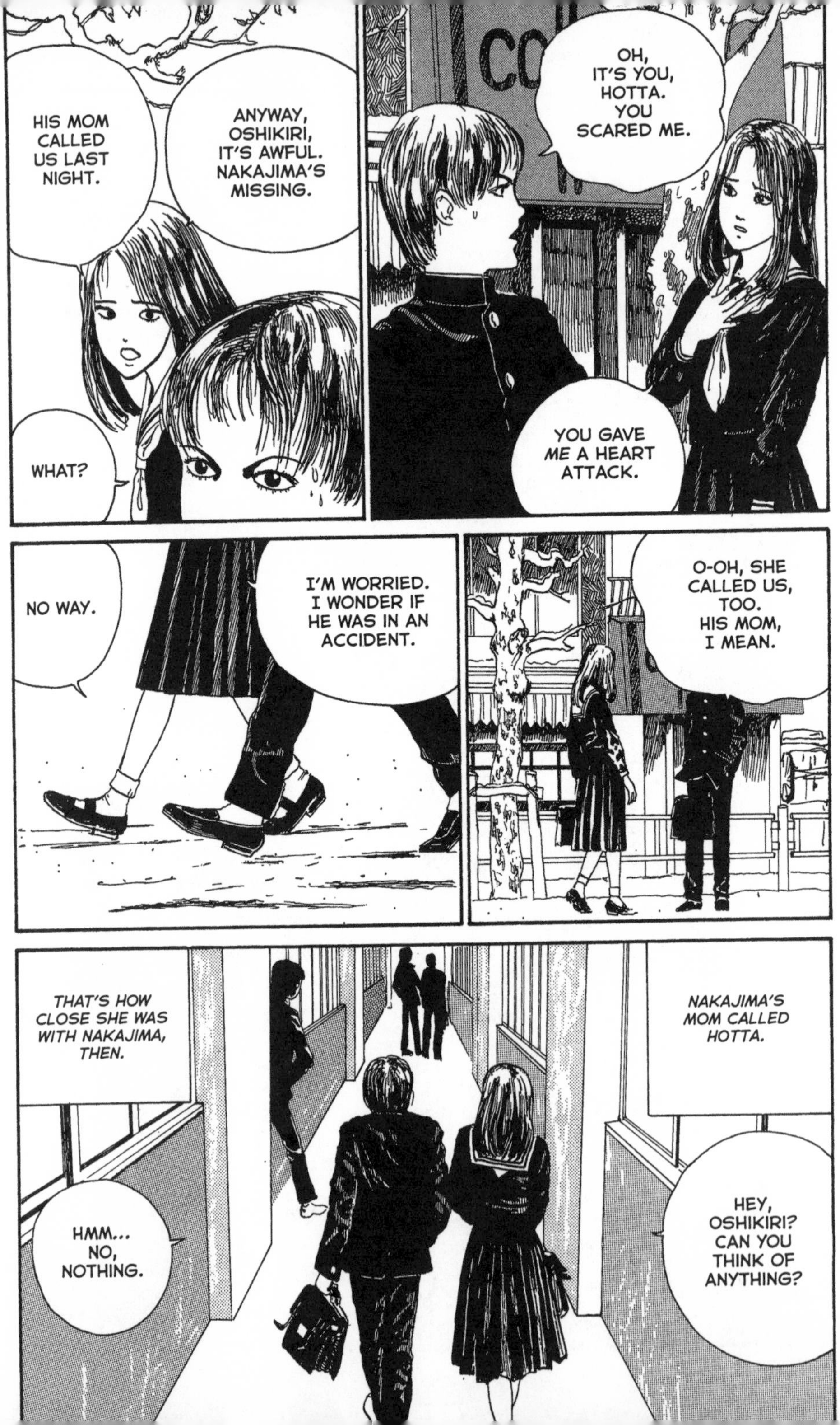
OH, IT'S YOU, HOTTA. YOU SCARED ME.
YOU GAVE *ME* A HEART ATTACK.
ANYWAY, OSHIKIRI, IT'S AWFUL. NAKAJIMA'S MISSING.
HIS MOM CALLED US LAST NIGHT.
WHAT?
O-OH, SHE CALLED US, TOO. HIS MOM, I MEAN.
I'M WORRIED. I WONDER IF HE WAS IN AN ACCIDENT.
NO WAY.
NAKAJIMA'S MOM CALLED HOTTA.
HEY, OSHIKIRI? CAN YOU THINK OF ANYTHING?
THAT'S HOW CLOSE SHE WAS WITH NAKAJIMA, THEN.
HMM... NO, NOTHING.

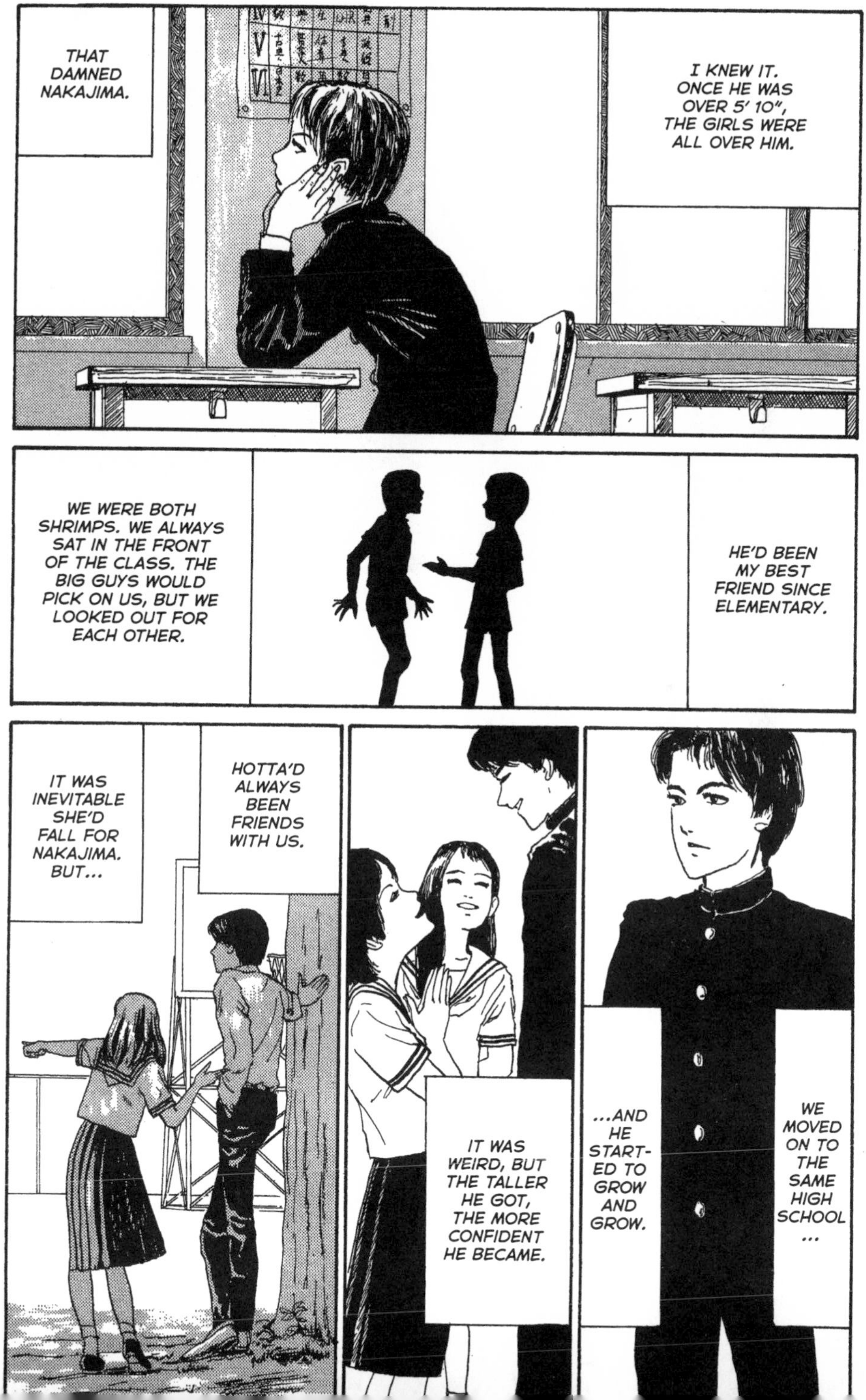
I KNEW IT. ONCE HE WAS OVER 5' 10", THE GIRLS WERE ALL OVER HIM.
THAT DAMNED NAKAJIMA.
HE'D BEEN MY BEST FRIEND SINCE ELEMENTARY.
WE WERE BOTH SHRIMPS. WE ALWAYS SAT IN THE FRONT OF THE CLASS. THE BIG GUYS WOULD PICK ON US, BUT WE LOOKED OUT FOR EACH OTHER.
WE MOVED ON TO THE SAME HIGH SCHOOL ...
...AND HE START-ED TO GROW AND GROW.
IT WAS WEIRD, BUT THE TALLER HE GOT, THE MORE CONFIDENT HE BECAME.
HOTTA'D ALWAYS BEEN FRIENDS WITH US.
IT WAS INEVITABLE SHE'D FALL FOR NAKAJIMA. BUT...

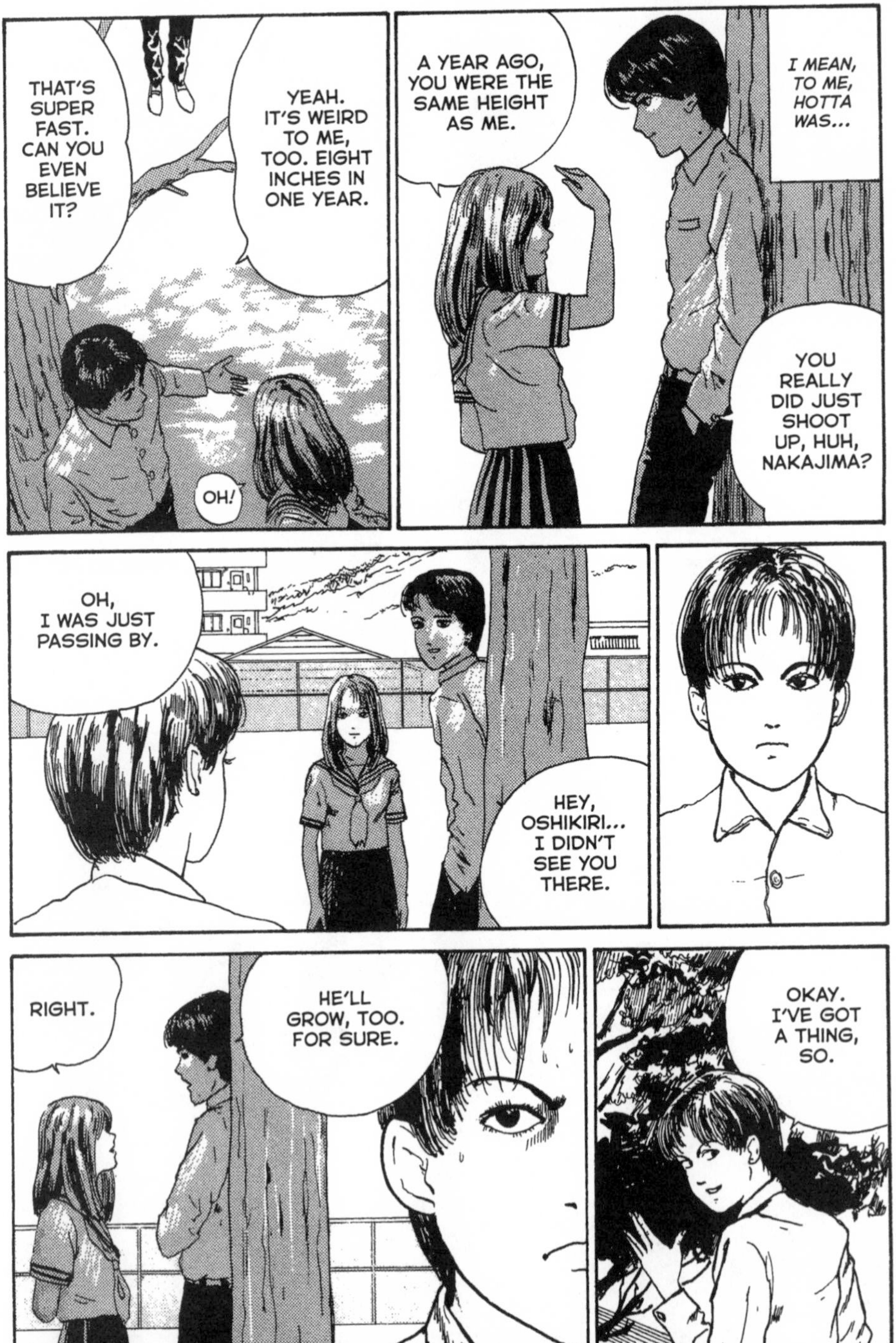
I MEAN, TO ME, HOTTA WAS...
A YEAR AGO, YOU WERE THE SAME HEIGHT AS ME.
YOU REALLY DID JUST SHOOT UP, HUH, NAKAJIMA?
YEAH. IT'S WEIRD TO ME, TOO. EIGHT INCHES IN ONE YEAR.
THAT'S SUPER FAST. CAN YOU EVEN BELIEVE IT?
OH!
HEY, OSHIKIRI... I DIDN'T SEE YOU THERE.
OH, I WAS JUST PASSING BY.
OKAY. I'VE GOT A THING, SO.
HE'LL GROW, TOO. FOR SURE.
RIGHT.

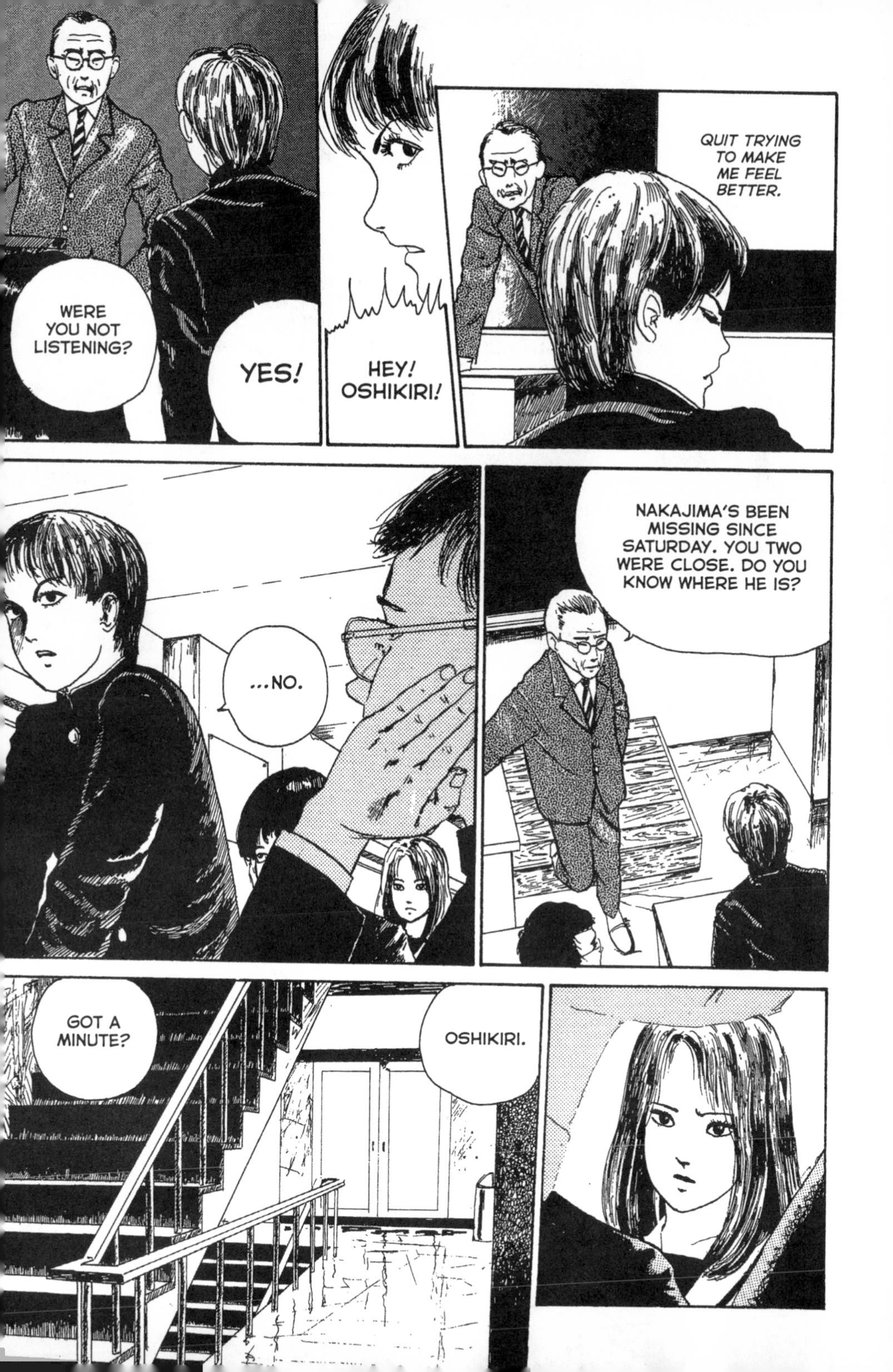
QUIT TRYING TO MAKE ME FEEL BETTER.
HEY! OSHIKIRI!
YES!
WERE YOU NOT LISTENING?
NAKAJIMA'S BEEN MISSING SINCE SATURDAY. YOU TWO WERE CLOSE. DO YOU KNOW WHERE HE IS?
...NO.
OSHIKIRI.
GOT A MINUTE?

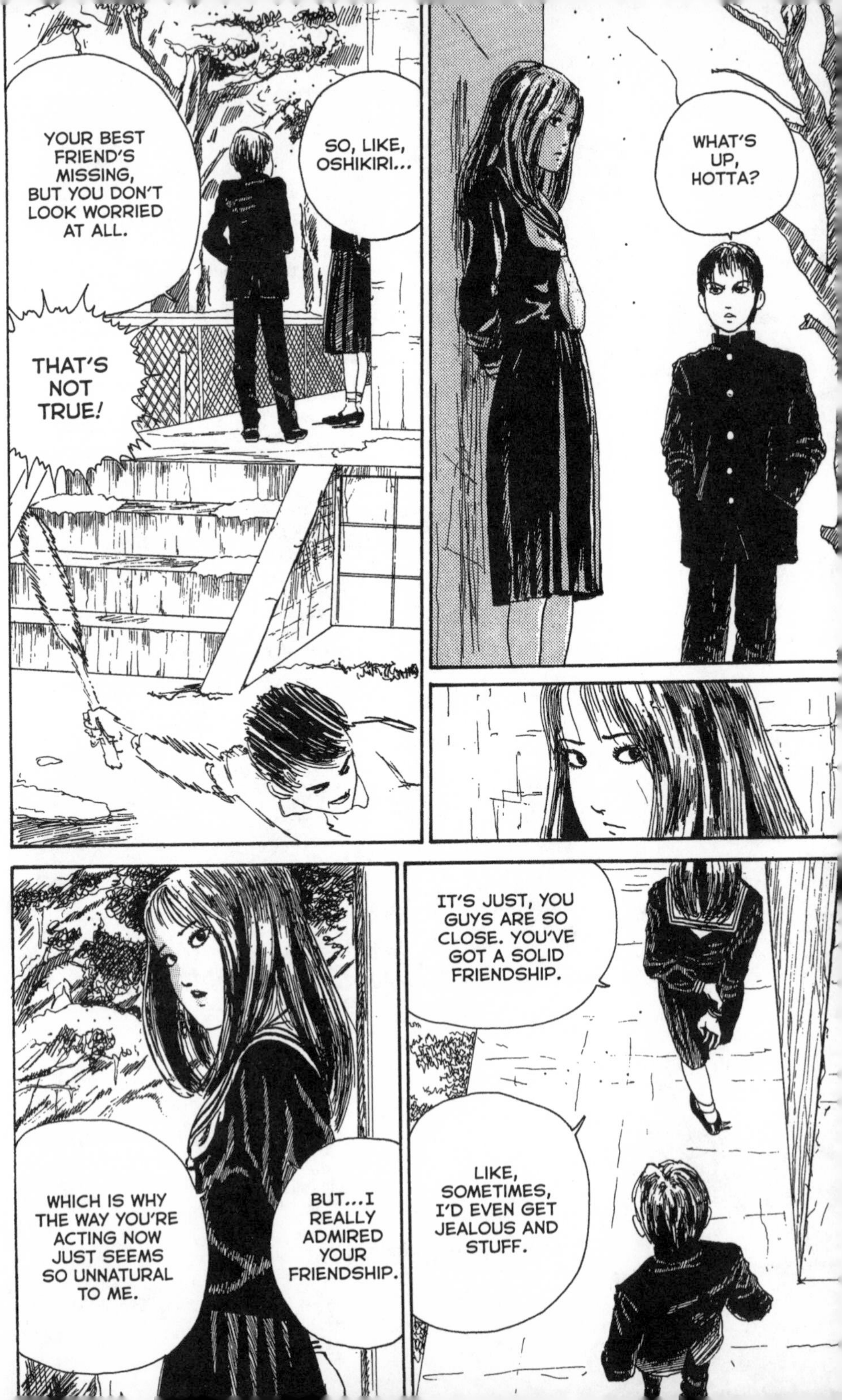
WHAT'S UP, HOTTA?
SO, LIKE, OSHIKIRI...
YOUR BEST FRIEND'S MISSING, BUT YOU DON'T LOOK WORRIED AT ALL.
THAT'S NOT TRUE!
IT'S JUST, YOU GUYS ARE SO CLOSE. YOU'VE GOT A SOLID FRIENDSHIP.
LIKE, SOMETIMES, I'D EVEN GET JEALOUS AND STUFF.
BUT...I REALLY ADMIRED YOUR FRIENDSHIP.
WHICH IS WHY THE WAY YOU'RE ACTING NOW JUST SEEMS SO UNNATURAL TO ME.

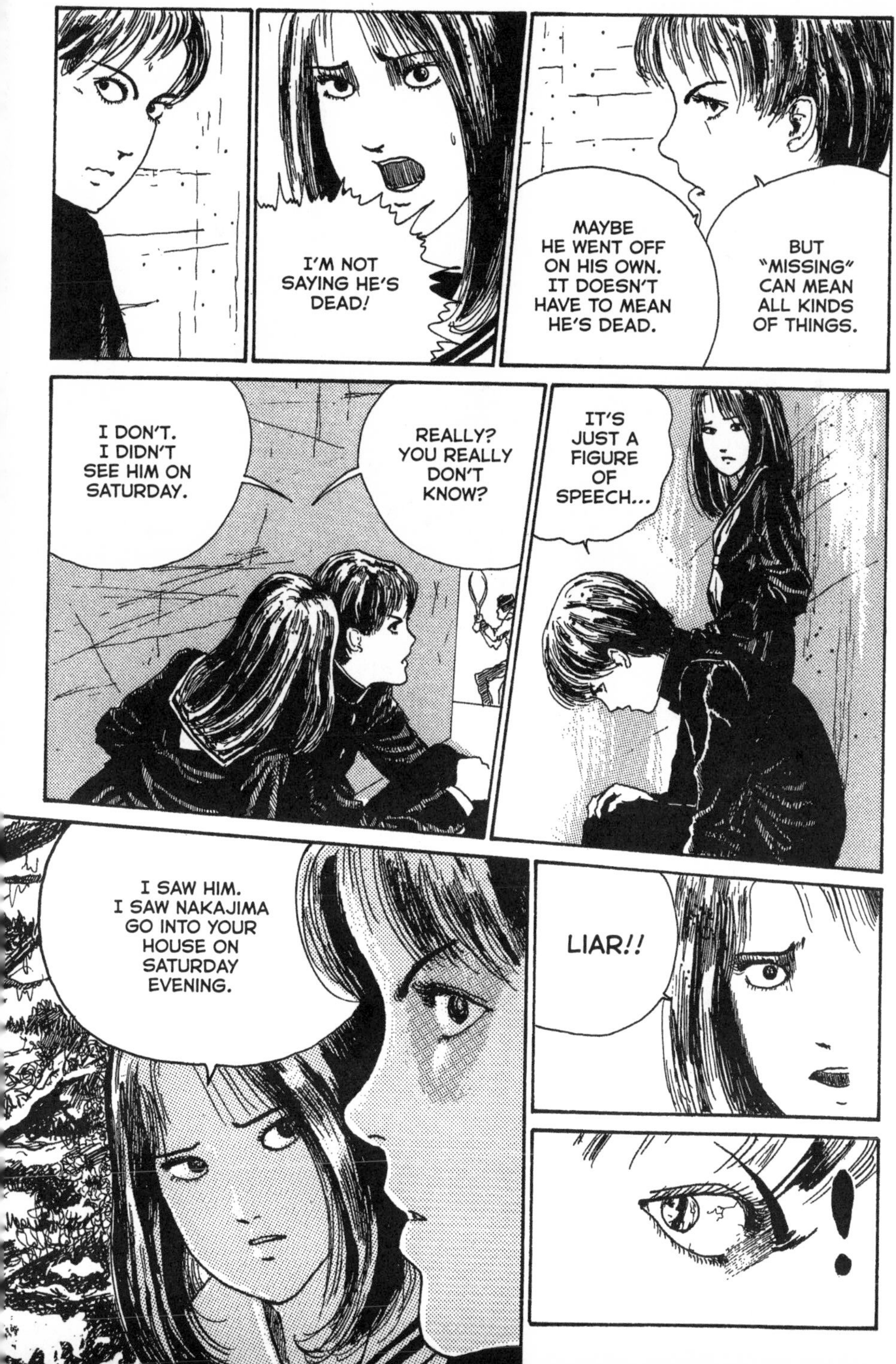

BUT "MISSING" CAN MEAN ALL KINDS OF THINGS.
MAYBE HE WENT OFF ON HIS OWN. IT DOESN'T HAVE TO MEAN HE'S DEAD.
I'M NOT SAYING HE'S DEAD!
IT'S JUST A FIGURE OF SPEECH...
REALLY? YOU REALLY DON'T KNOW?
I DON'T. I DIDN'T SEE HIM ON SATURDAY.
LIAR!!
!
I SAW HIM. I SAW NAKAJIMA GO INTO YOUR HOUSE ON SATURDAY EVENING.

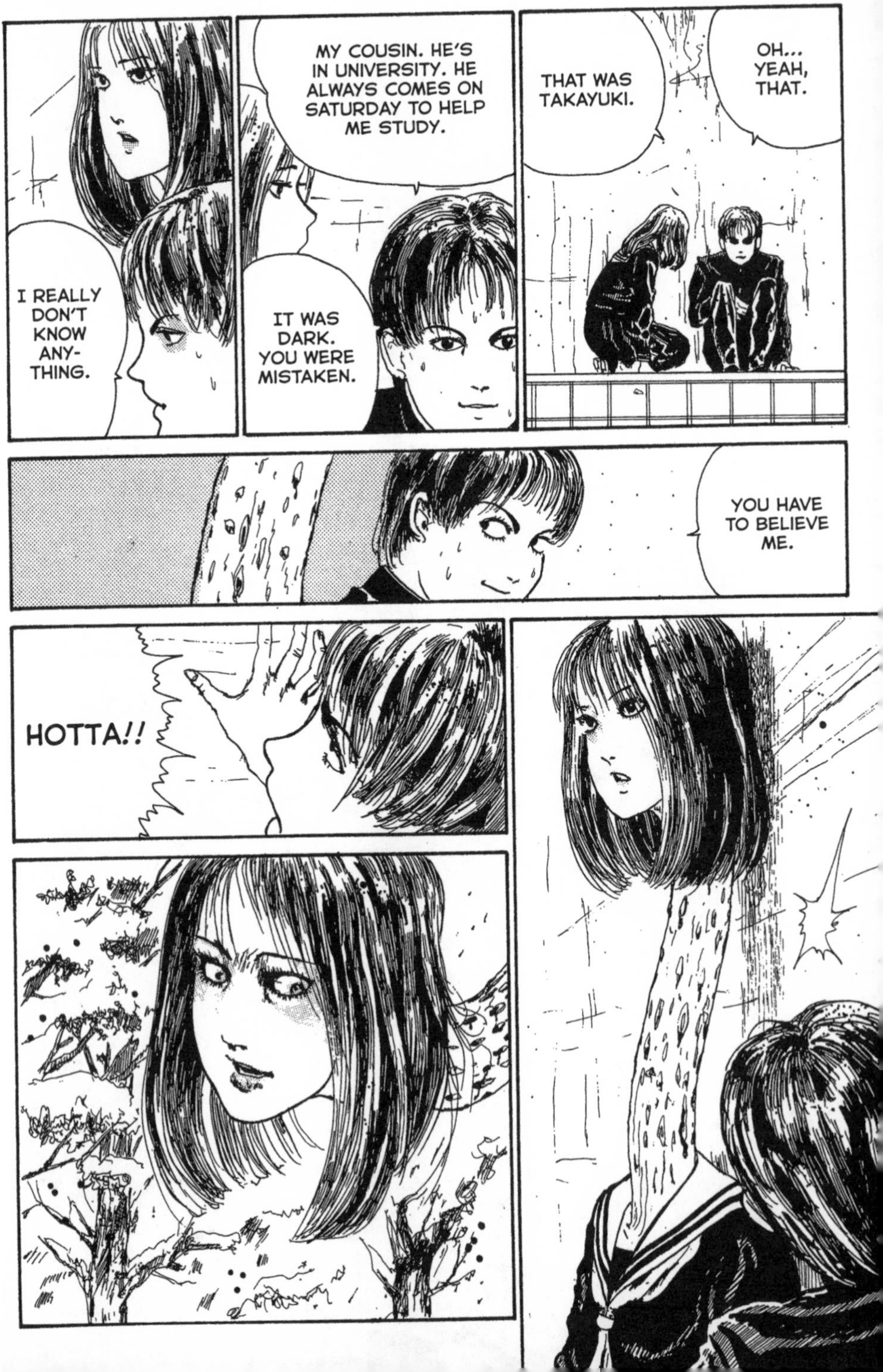
OH... YEAH, THAT.
THAT WAS TAKAYUKI.
MY COUSIN. HE'S IN UNIVERSITY. HE ALWAYS COMES ON SATURDAY TO HELP ME STUDY.
IT WAS DARK. YOU WERE MISTAKEN.
I REALLY DON'T KNOW ANY-THING.
YOU HAVE TO BELIEVE ME.
HOTTA!!

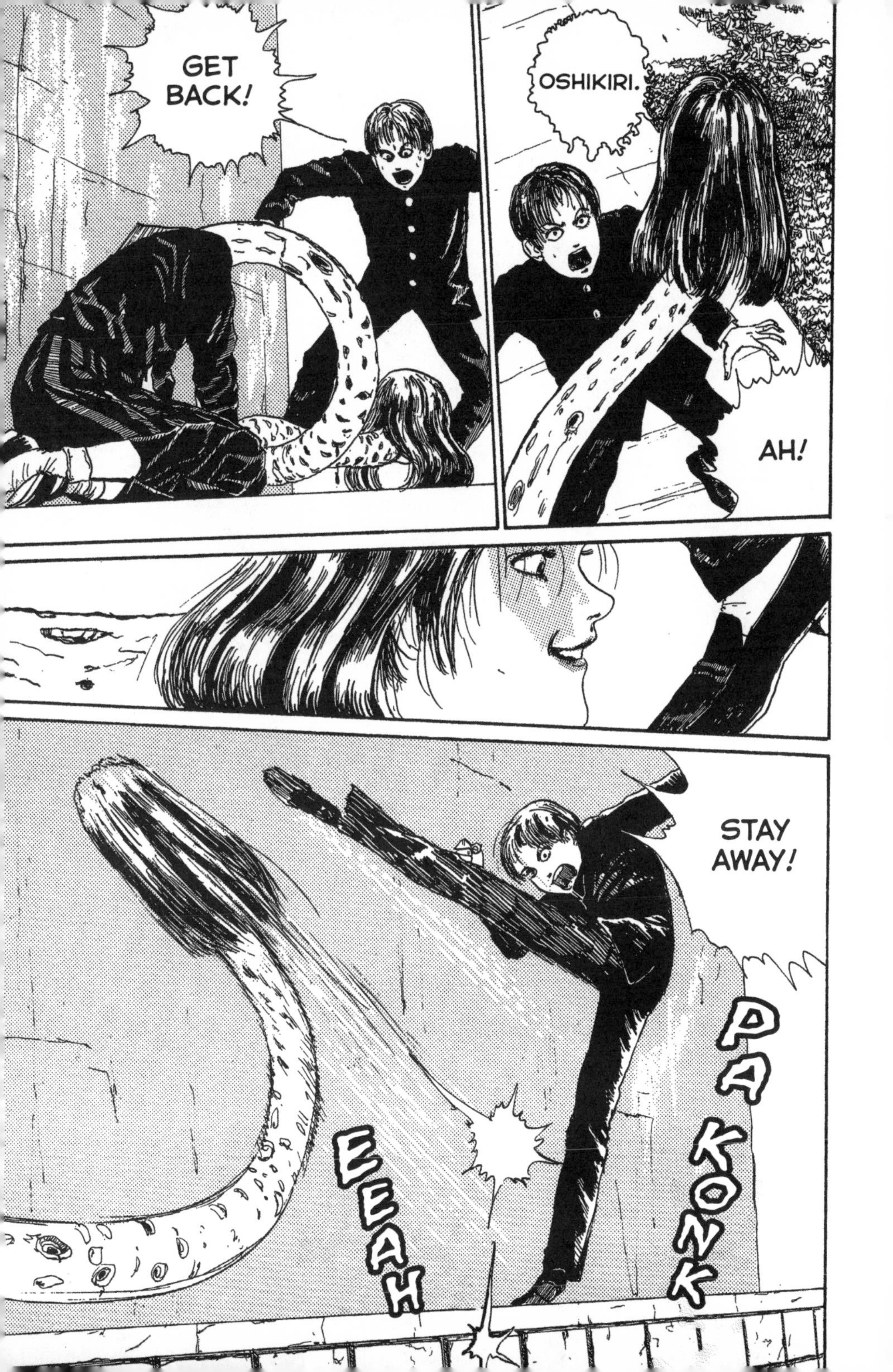
OSHIKIRI.
AH!
GET BACK!
STAY AWAY!
PA KONK
EEAH

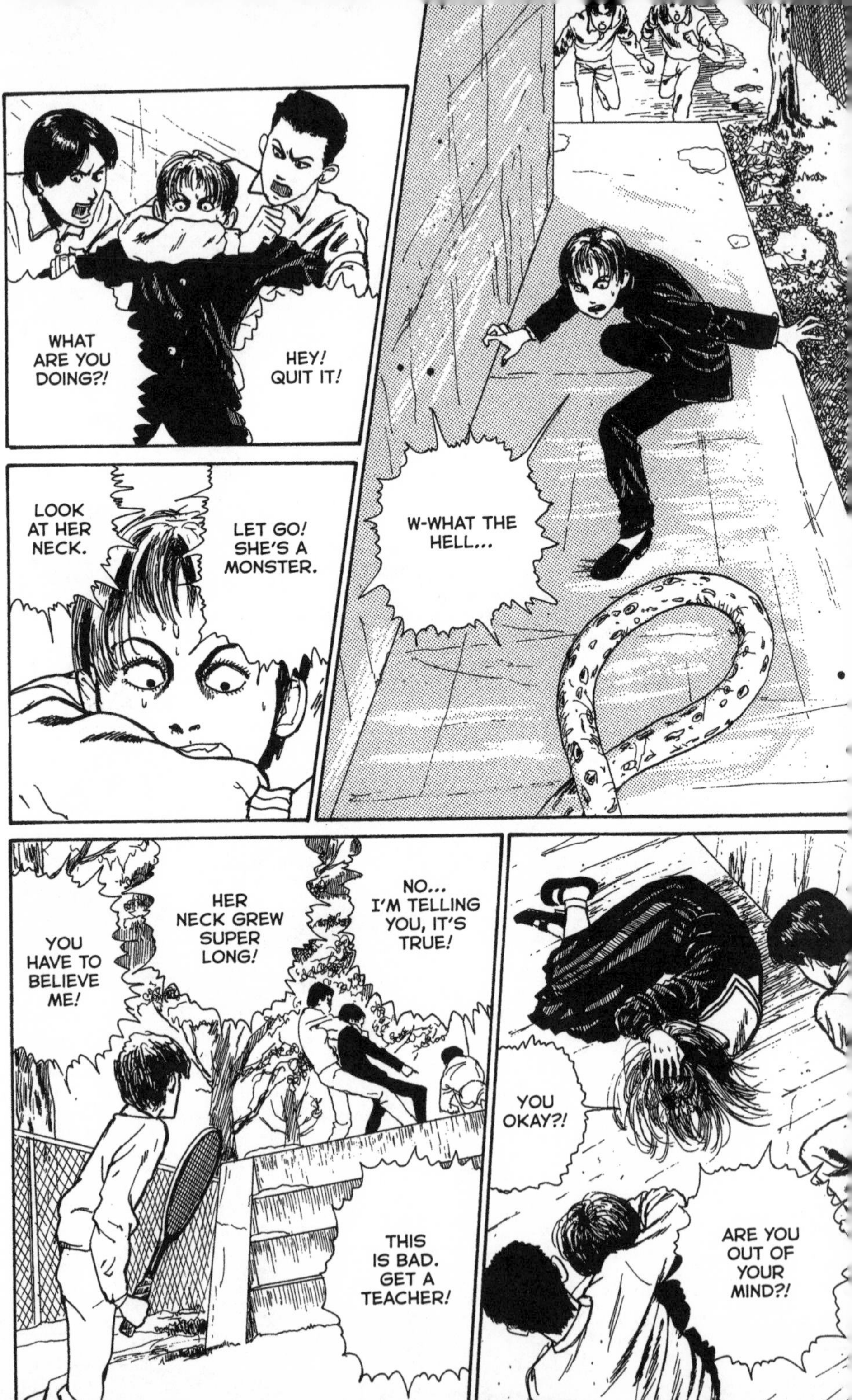
W-WHAT THE HELL...
HEY! QUIT IT!
WHAT ARE YOU DOING?!
LET GO! SHE'S A MONSTER.
LOOK AT HER NECK.
YOU OKAY?!
ARE YOU OUT OF YOUR MIND?!
NO... I'M TELLING YOU, IT'S TRUE!
HER NECK GREW SUPER LONG!
YOU HAVE TO BELIEVE ME!
THIS IS BAD. GET A TEACHER!

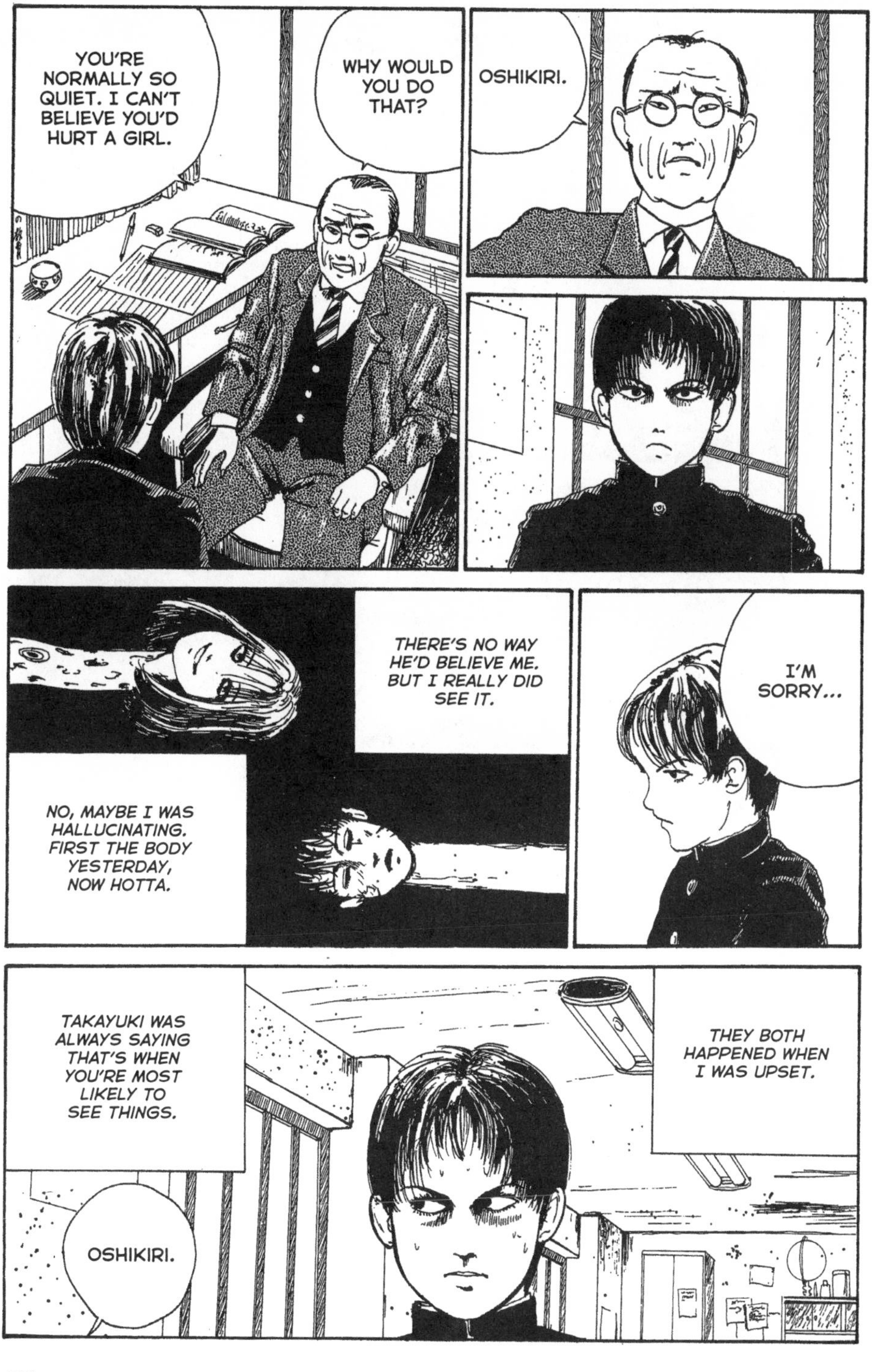
OSHIKIRI.
WHY WOULD YOU DO THAT?
YOU'RE NORMALLY SO QUIET. I CAN'T BELIEVE YOU'D HURT A GIRL.
I'M SORRY...
THERE'S NO WAY HE'D BELIEVE ME. BUT I REALLY DID SEE IT.
NO, MAYBE I WAS HALLUCINATING. FIRST THE BODY YESTERDAY, NOW HOTTA.
THEY BOTH HAPPENED WHEN I WAS UPSET.
TAKAYUKI WAS ALWAYS SAYING THAT'S WHEN YOU'RE MOST LIKELY TO SEE THINGS.
OSHIKIRI.

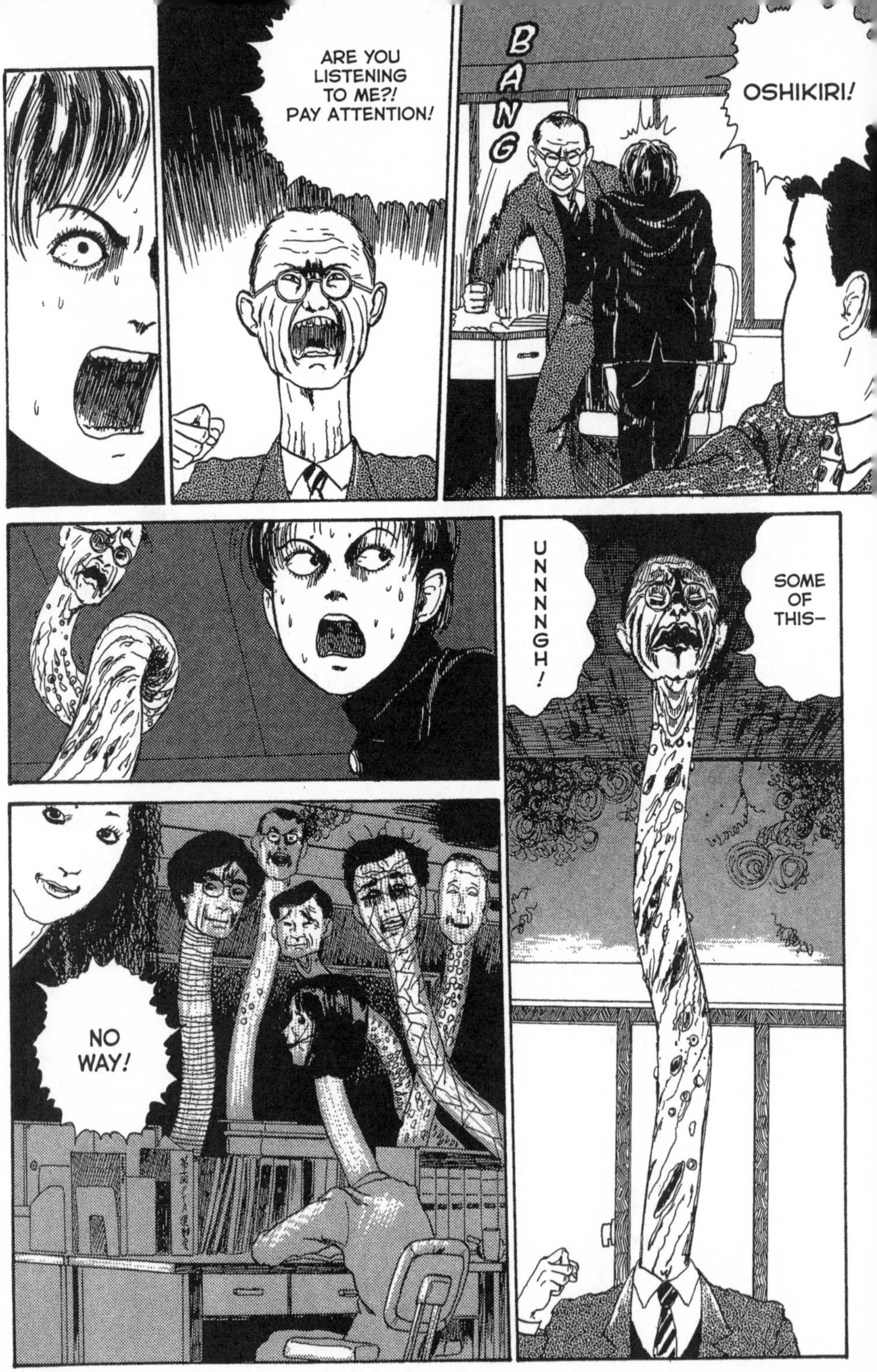
OSHIKIRI!
BANG
ARE YOU LISTENING TO ME?! PAY ATTENTION!
SOME OF THIS–
UNNNNGH!
NO WAY!

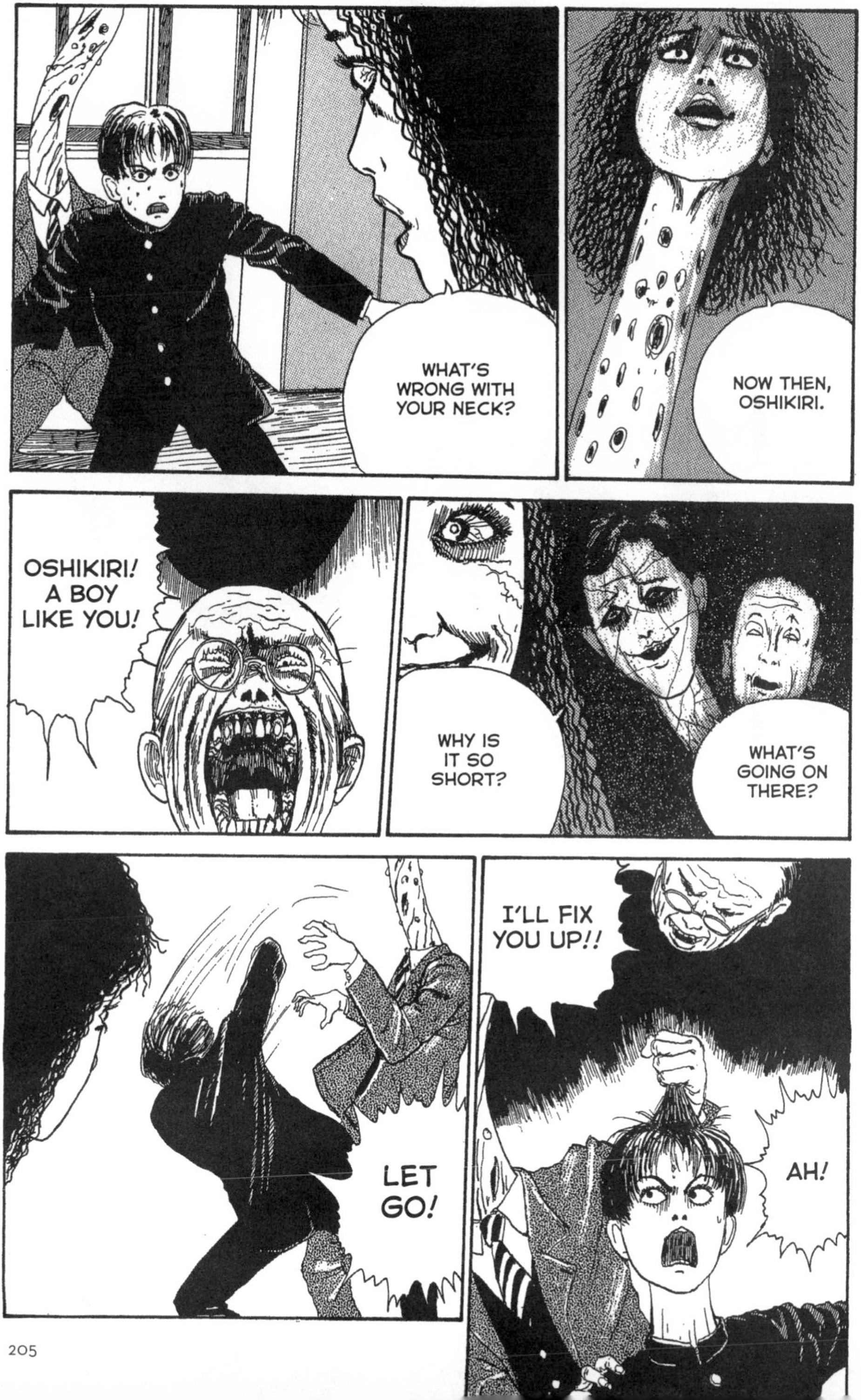
NOW THEN, OSHIKIRI.
WHAT'S WRONG WITH YOUR NECK?
WHAT'S GOING ON THERE?
WHY IS IT SO SHORT?
OSHIKIRI! A BOY LIKE YOU!
I'LL FIX YOU UP!!
AH!
LET GO!

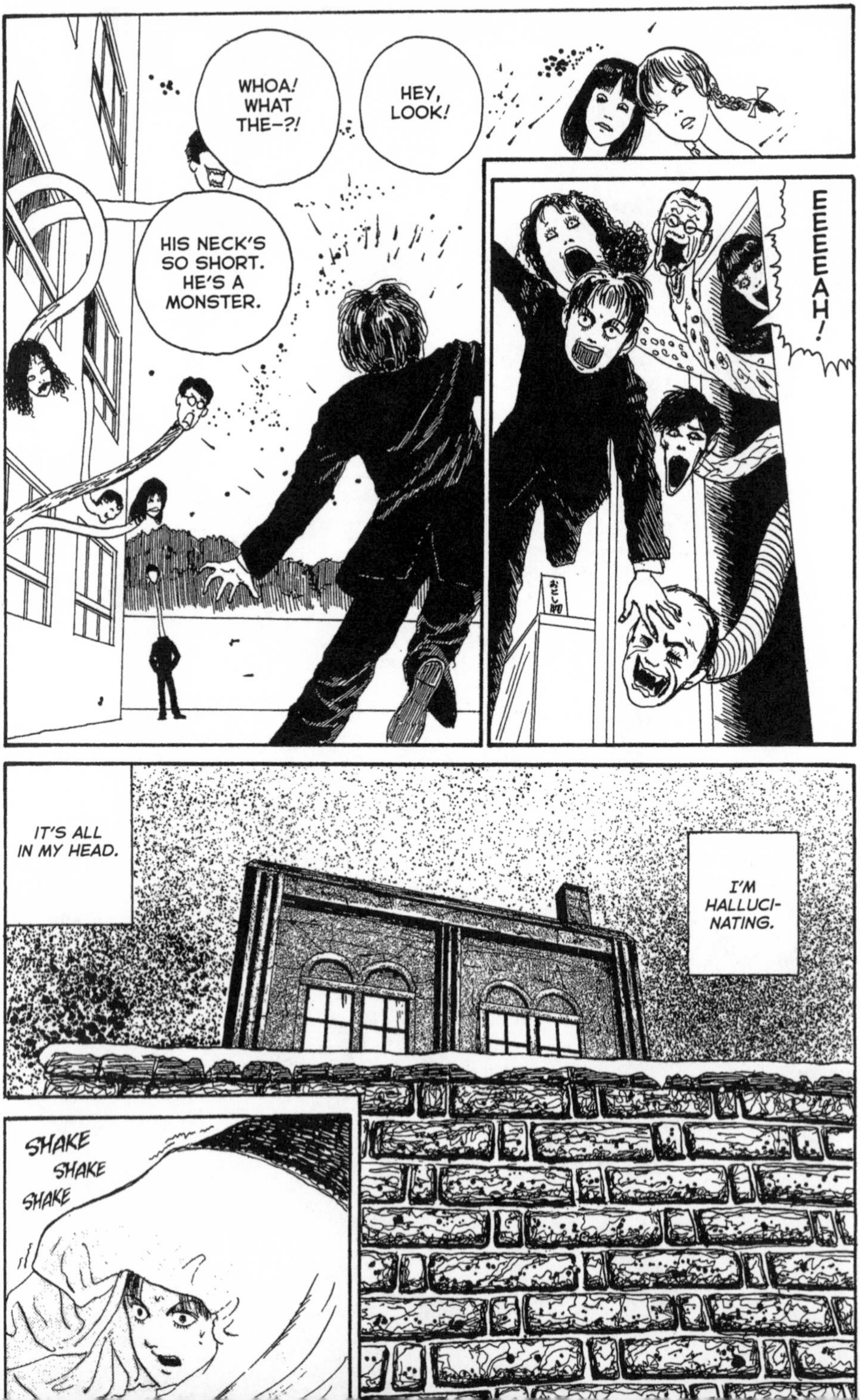
HEY, LOOK!
WHOA! WHAT THE-?!
HIS NECK'S SO SHORT. HE'S A MONSTER.
EEEEAH!
I'M HALLUCI-NATING.
IT'S ALL IN MY HEAD.
SHAKE SHAKE SHAKE

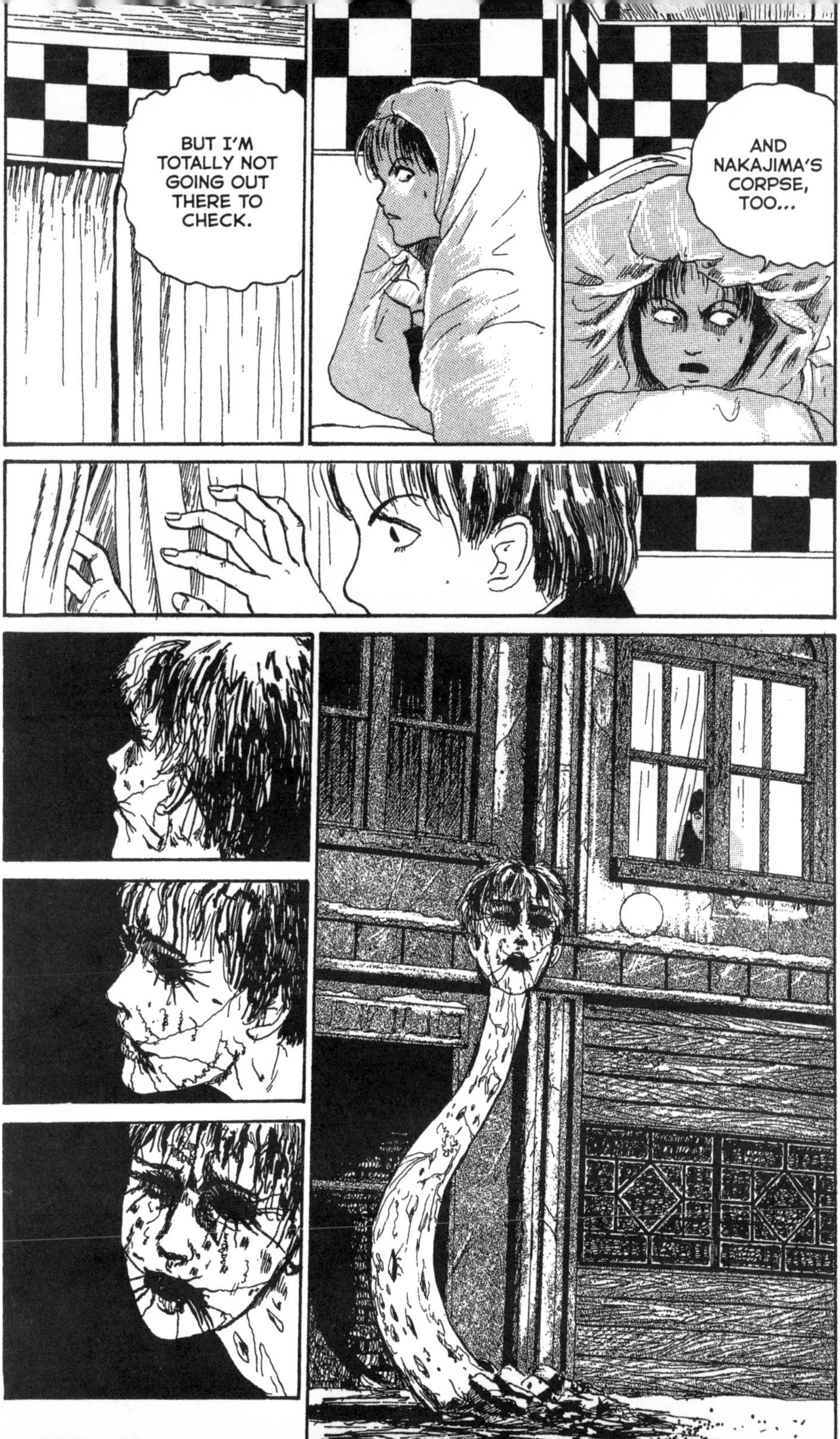
AND NAKAJIMA'S CORPSE, TOO...
BUT I'M TOTALLY NOT GOING OUT THERE TO CHECK.

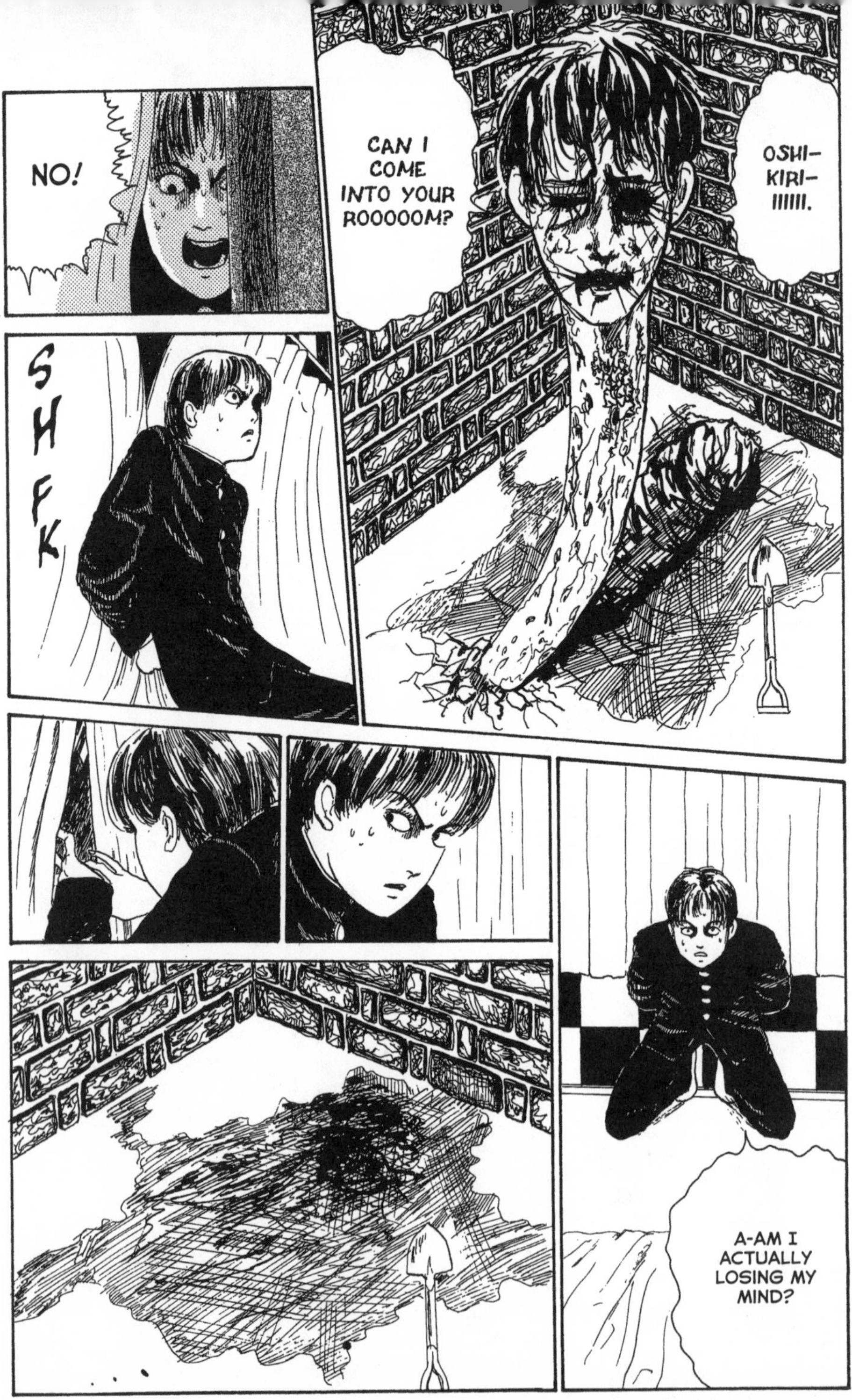
OSHI-KIRI-IIIIII.
CAN I COME INTO YOUR ROOOOOM?
NO!
SHFK
A-AM I ACTUALLY LOSING MY MIND?

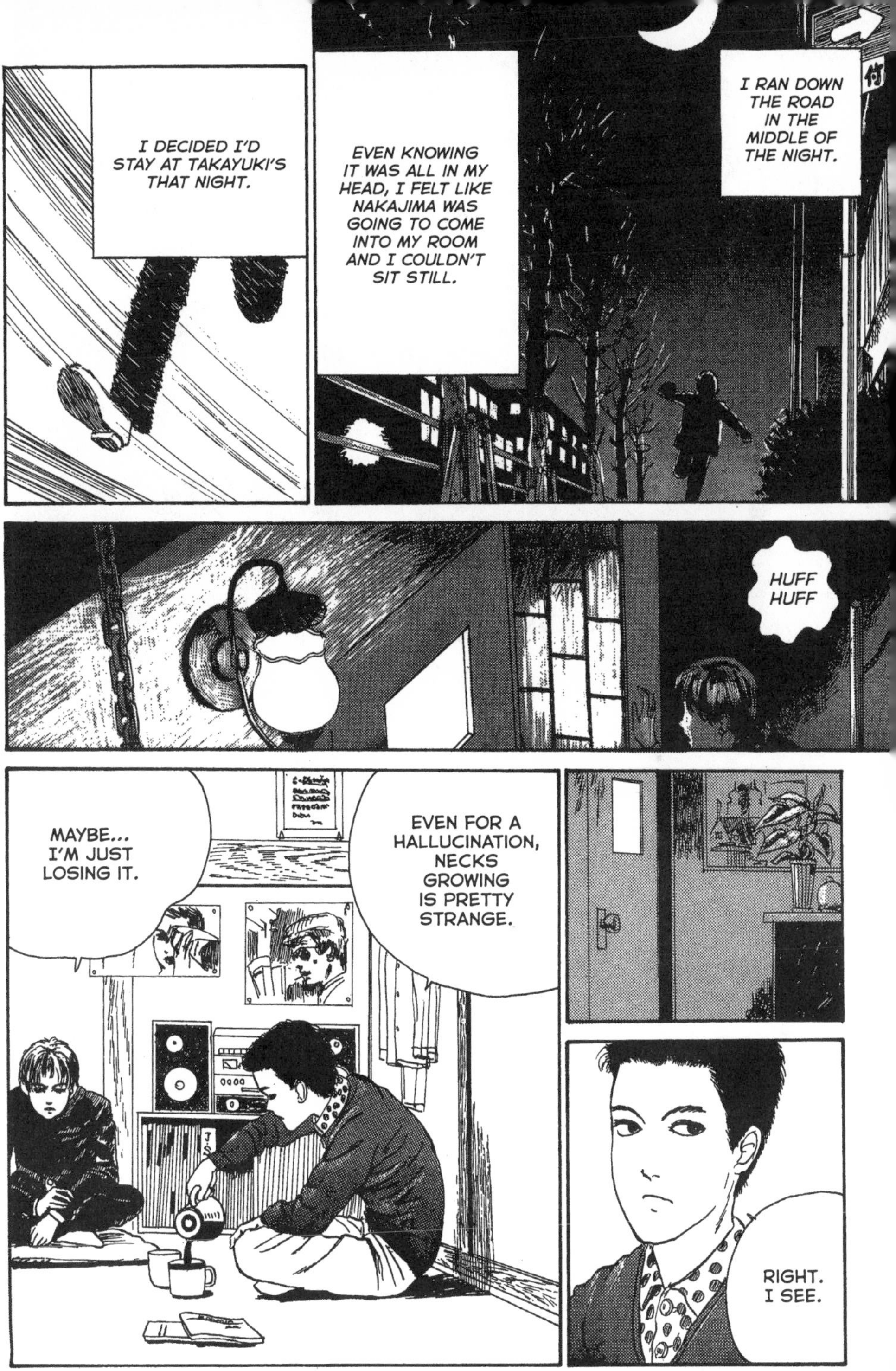

I RAN DOWN THE ROAD IN THE MIDDLE OF THE NIGHT.
EVEN KNOWING IT WAS ALL IN MY HEAD, I FELT LIKE NAKAJIMA WAS GOING TO COME INTO MY ROOM AND I COULDN'T SIT STILL.
I DECIDED I'D STAY AT TAKAYUKI'S THAT NIGHT.
HUFF HUFF
RIGHT. I SEE.
EVEN FOR A HALLUCINATION, NECKS GROWING IS PRETTY STRANGE.
MAYBE... I'M JUST LOSING IT.

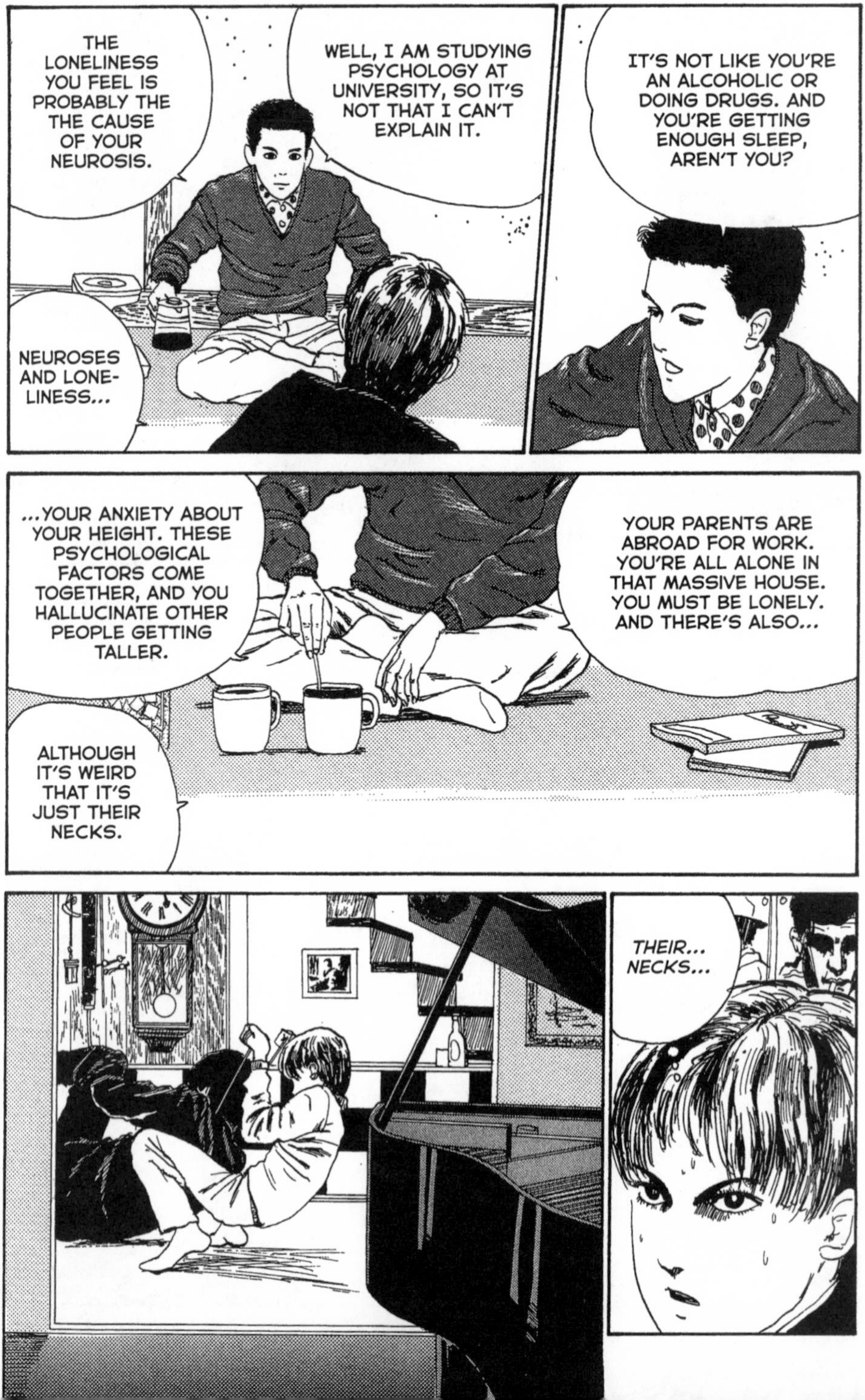
IT'S NOT LIKE YOU'RE AN ALCOHOLIC OR DOING DRUGS. AND YOU'RE GETTING ENOUGH SLEEP, AREN'T YOU?
WELL, I AM STUDYING PSYCHOLOGY AT UNIVERSITY, SO IT'S NOT THAT I CAN'T EXPLAIN IT.
THE LONELINESS YOU FEEL IS PROBABLY THE THE CAUSE OF YOUR NEUROSIS.
NEUROSES AND LONE-LINESS...
YOUR PARENTS ARE ABROAD FOR WORK. YOU'RE ALL ALONE IN THAT MASSIVE HOUSE. YOU MUST BE LONELY. AND THERE'S ALSO...
...YOUR ANXIETY ABOUT YOUR HEIGHT. THESE PSYCHOLOGICAL FACTORS COME TOGETHER, AND YOU HALLUCINATE OTHER PEOPLE GETTING TALLER.
ALTHOUGH IT'S WEIRD THAT IT'S JUST THEIR NECKS.
THEIR... NECKS...

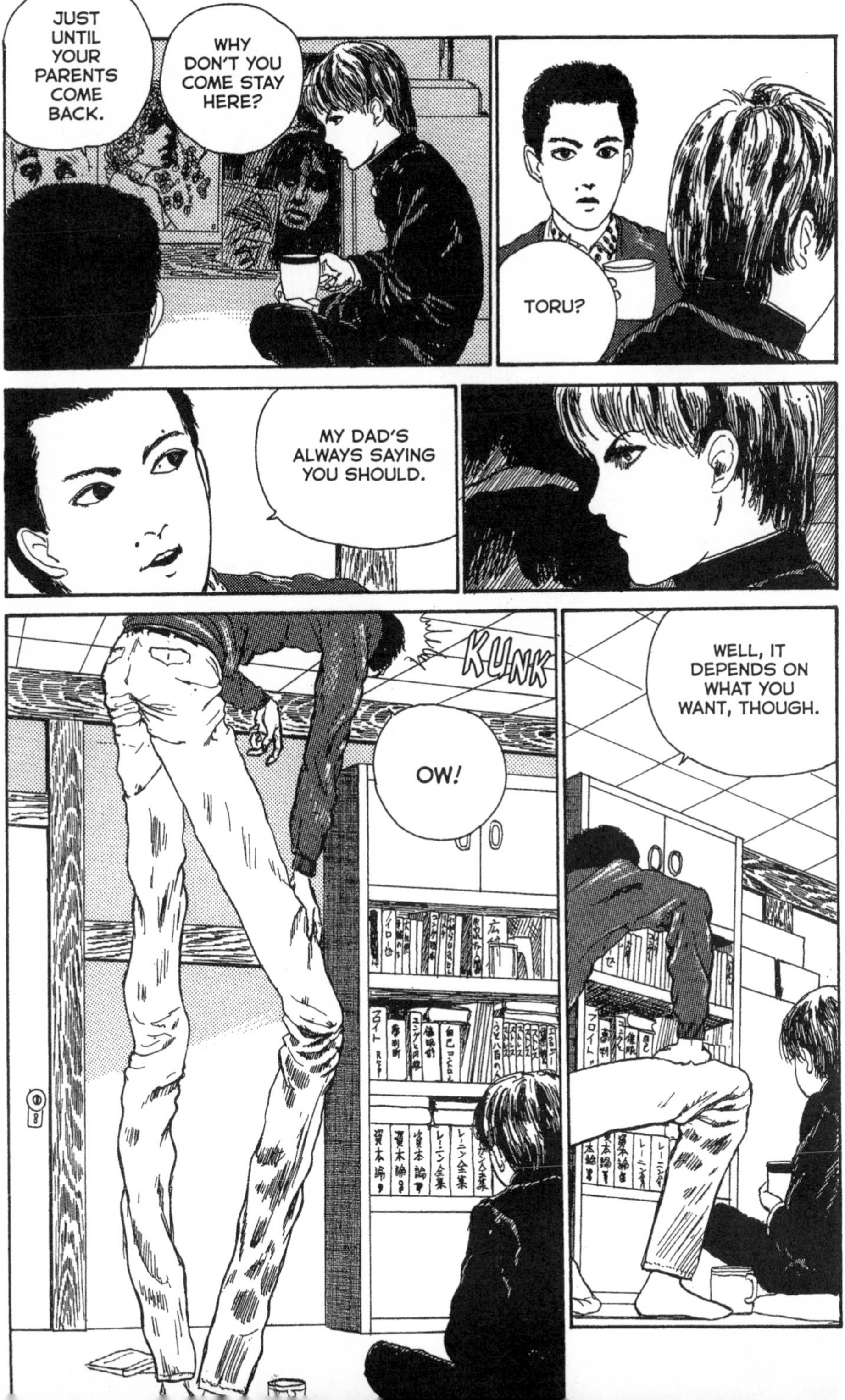
TORU?
WHY DON'T YOU COME STAY HERE?
JUST UNTIL YOUR PARENTS COME BACK.
MY DAD'S ALWAYS SAYING YOU SHOULD.
WELL, IT DEPENDS ON WHAT YOU WANT, THOUGH.
KUNK
OW!

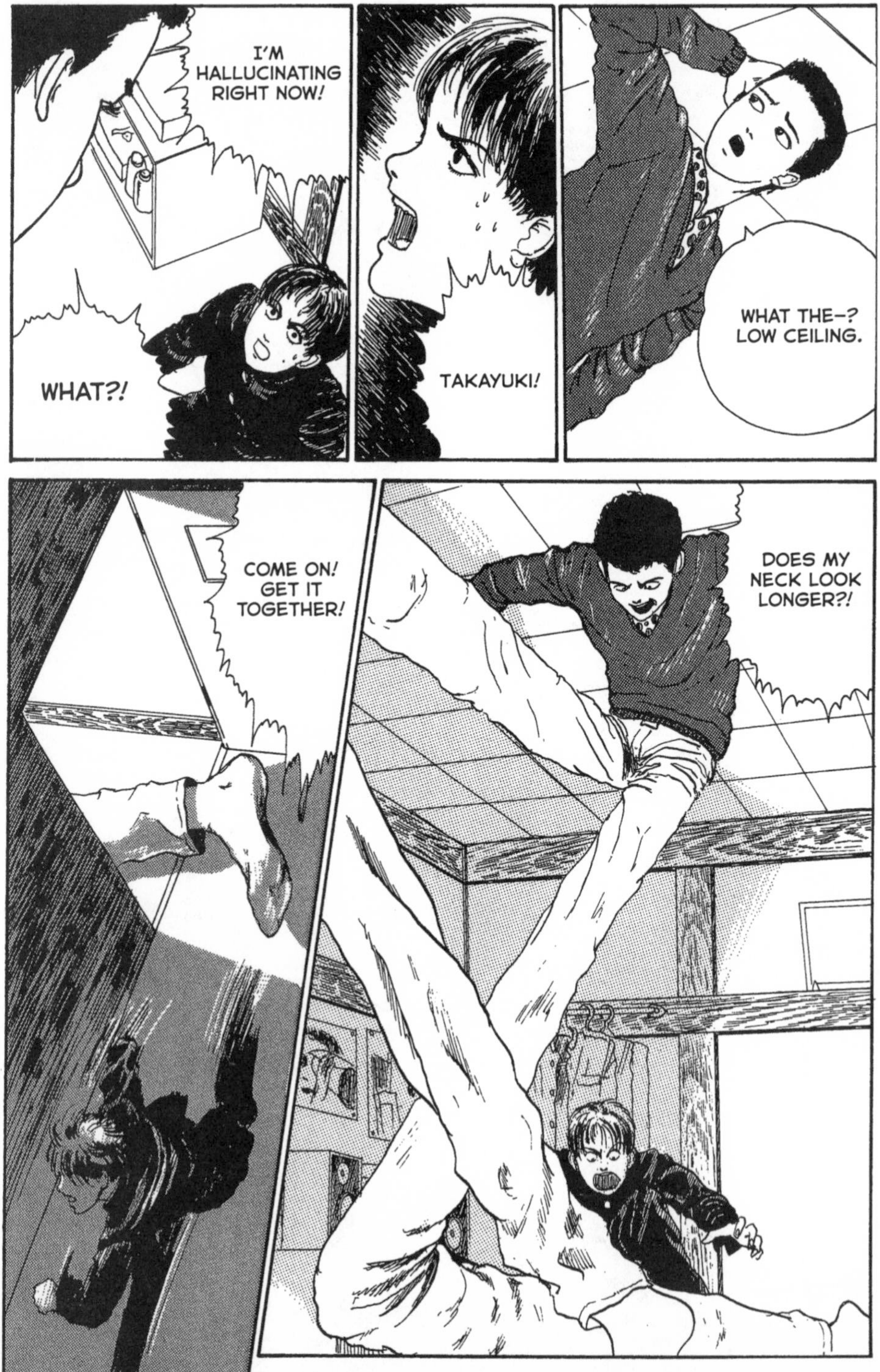
WHAT THE–? LOW CEILING.
TAKAYUKI!
I'M HALLUCINATING RIGHT NOW!
WHAT?!
DOES MY NECK LOOK LONGER?!
COME ON! GET IT TOGETHER!

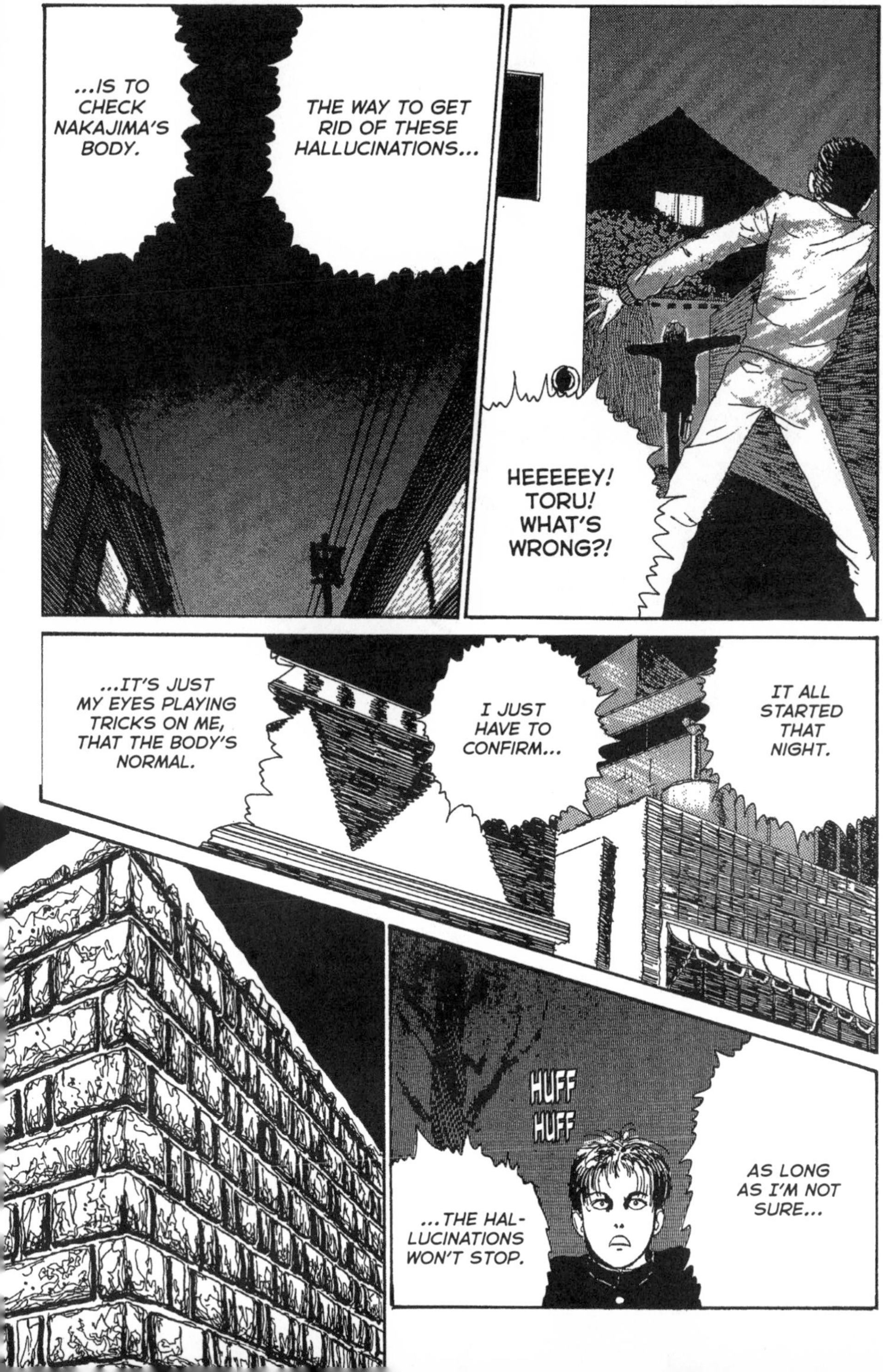
HEEEEEY! TORU! WHAT'S WRONG?!
THE WAY TO GET RID OF THESE HALLUCINATIONS...
...IS TO CHECK NAKAJIMA'S BODY.
IT ALL STARTED THAT NIGHT.
I JUST HAVE TO CONFIRM...
...IT'S JUST MY EYES PLAYING TRICKS ON ME, THAT THE BODY'S NORMAL.
AS LONG AS I'M NOT SURE...
HUFF HUFF
...THE HAL-LUCINATIONS WON'T STOP.

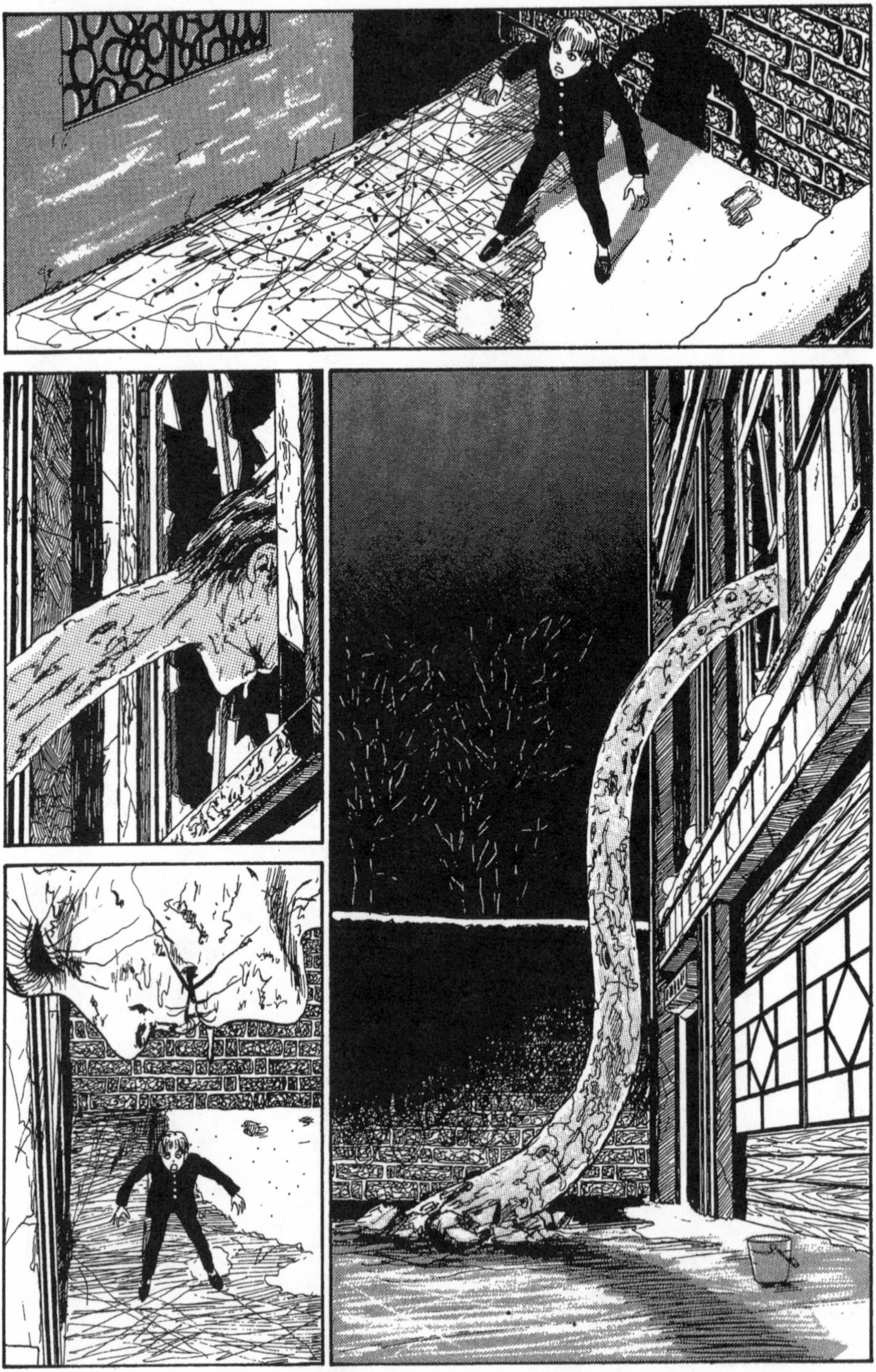

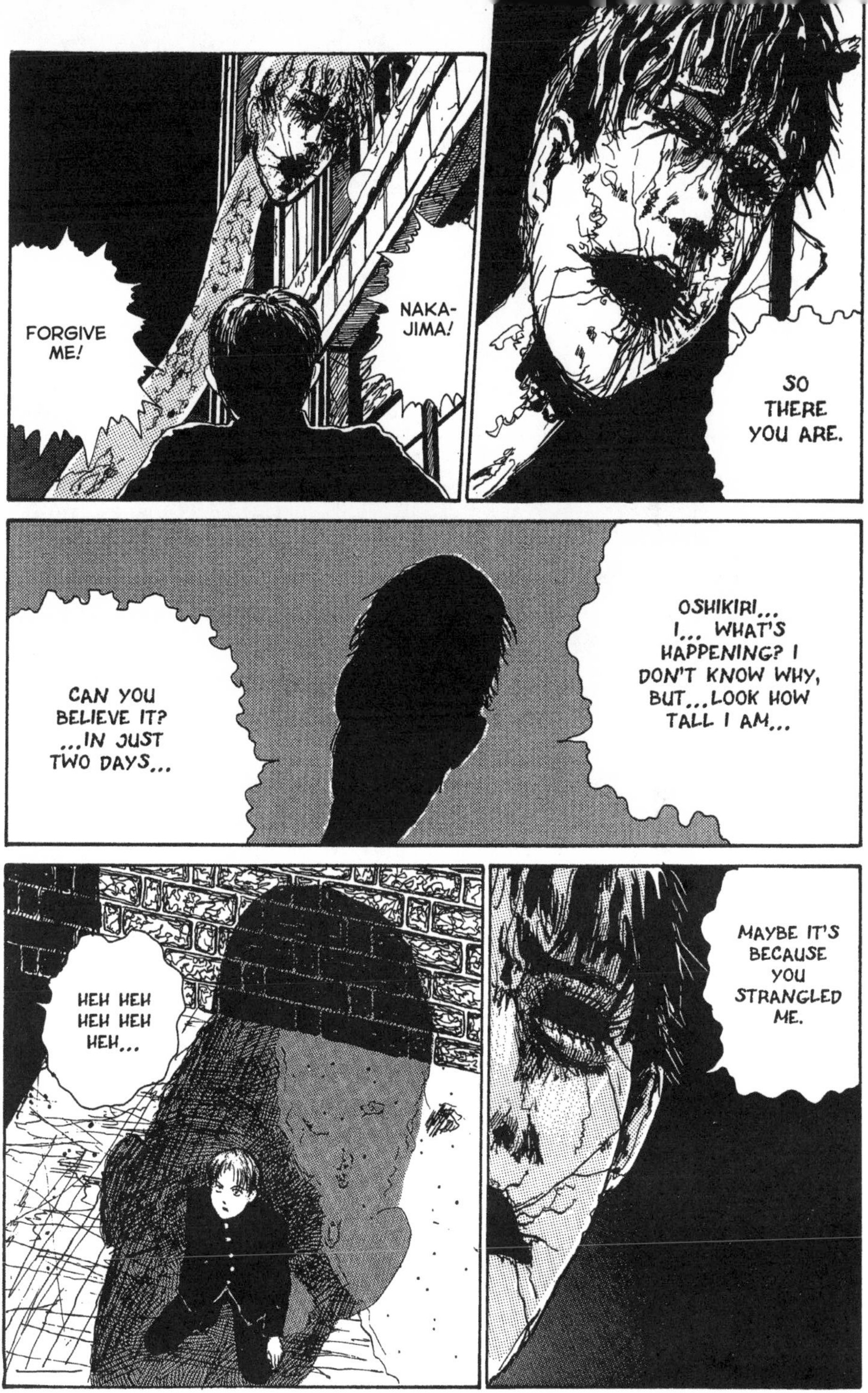
SO THERE YOU ARE.
NAKA-JIMA!
FORGIVE ME!
OSHIKIRI... I... WHAT'S HAPPENING? I DON'T KNOW WHY, BUT...LOOK HOW TALL I AM...
CAN YOU BELIEVE IT? ...IN JUST TWO DAYS...
MAYBE IT'S BECAUSE YOU STRANGLED ME.
HEH HEH HEH HEH HEH...

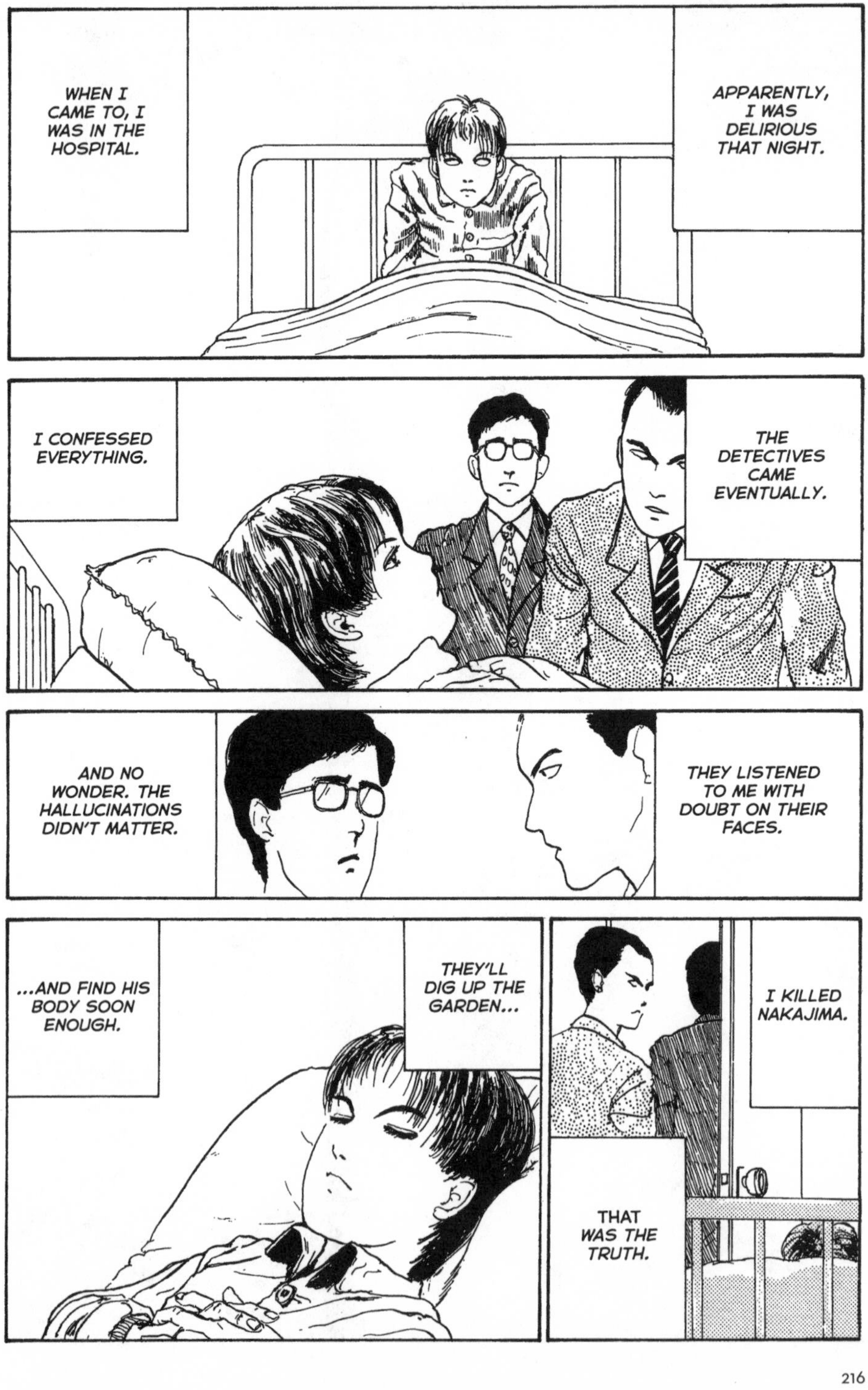
APPARENTLY, I WAS DELIRIOUS THAT NIGHT.
WHEN I CAME TO, I WAS IN THE HOSPITAL.
THE DETECTIVES CAME EVENTUALLY.
I CONFESSED EVERYTHING.
THEY LISTENED TO ME WITH DOUBT ON THEIR FACES.
AND NO WONDER. THE HALLUCINATIONS DIDN'T MATTER.
I KILLED NAKAJIMA.
THAT WAS THE TRUTH.
THEY'LL DIG UP THE GARDEN...
...AND FIND HIS BODY SOON ENOUGH.

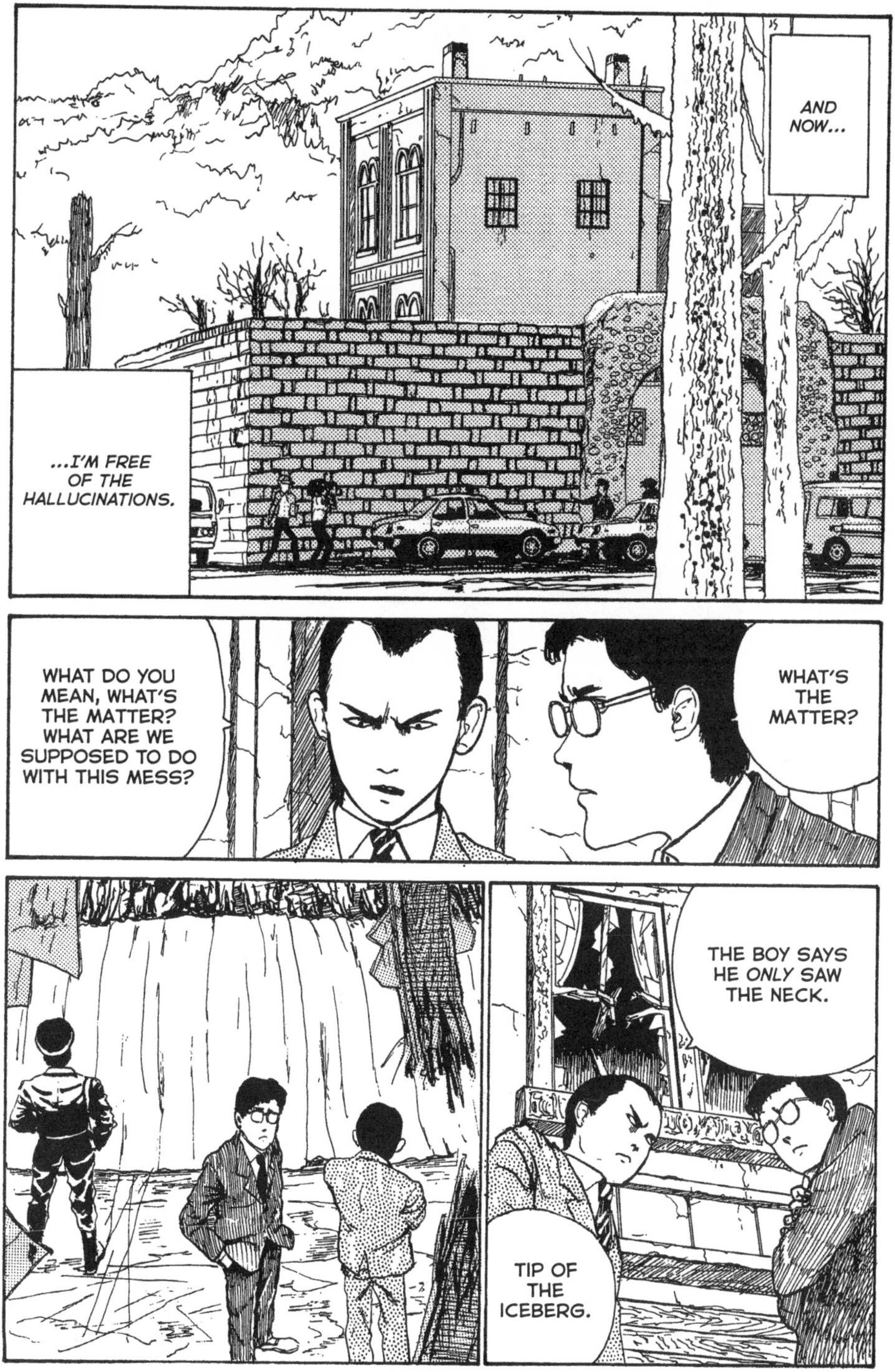
AND NOW...
...I'M FREE OF THE HALLUCINATIONS.
WHAT'S THE MATTER?
WHAT DO YOU MEAN, WHAT'S THE MATTER? WHAT ARE WE SUPPOSED TO DO WITH THIS MESS?
THE BOY SAYS HE *ONLY* SAW THE NECK.
TIP OF THE ICEBERG.

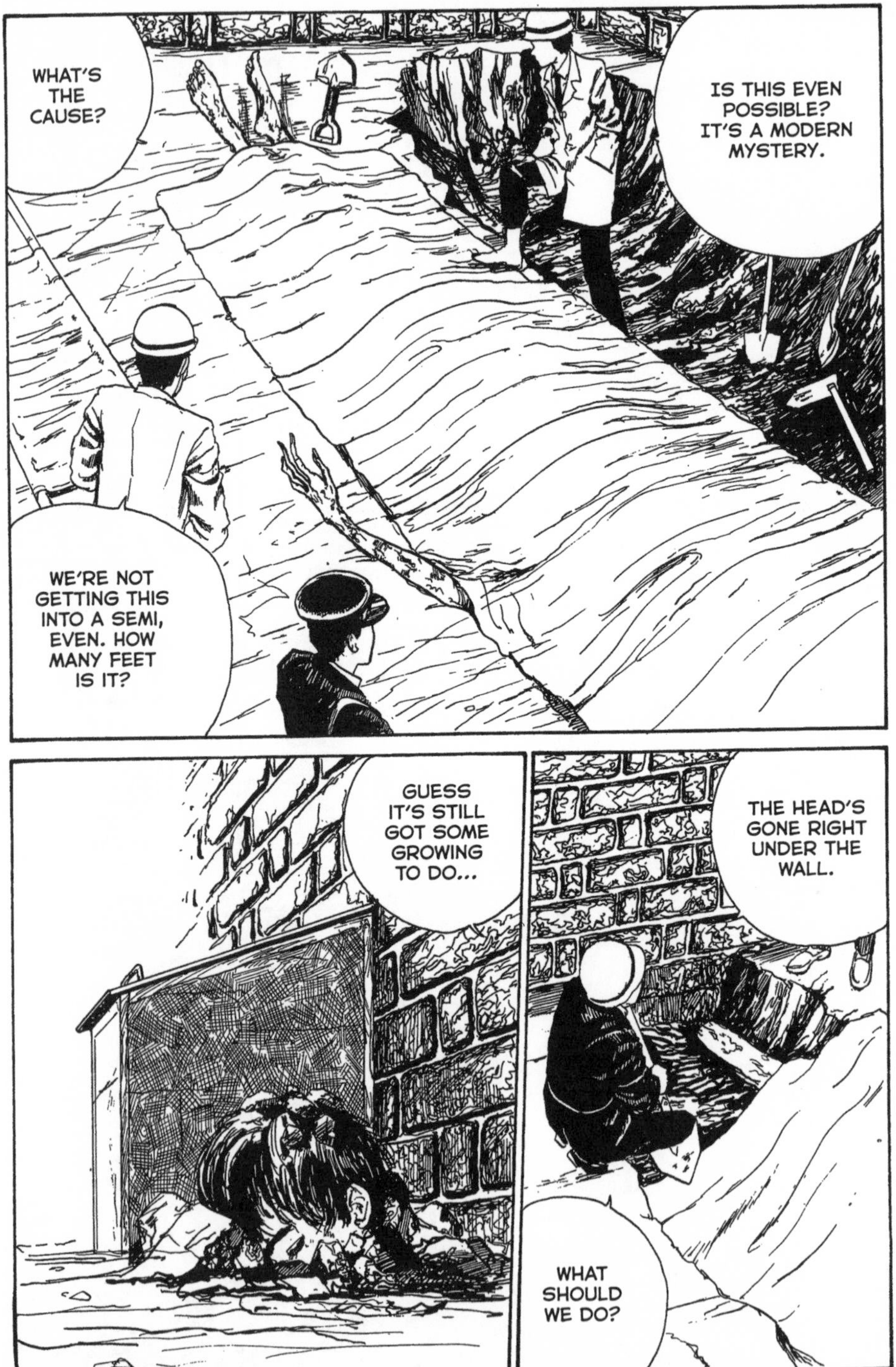
IS THIS EVEN POSSIBLE? IT'S A MODERN MYSTERY.
WHAT'S THE CAUSE?
WE'RE NOT GETTING THIS INTO A SEMI, EVEN. HOW MANY FEET IS IT?
THE HEAD'S GONE RIGHT UNDER THE WALL.
WHAT SHOULD WE DO?
GUESS IT'S STILL GOT SOME GROWING TO DO...

NECK SPECTER / END

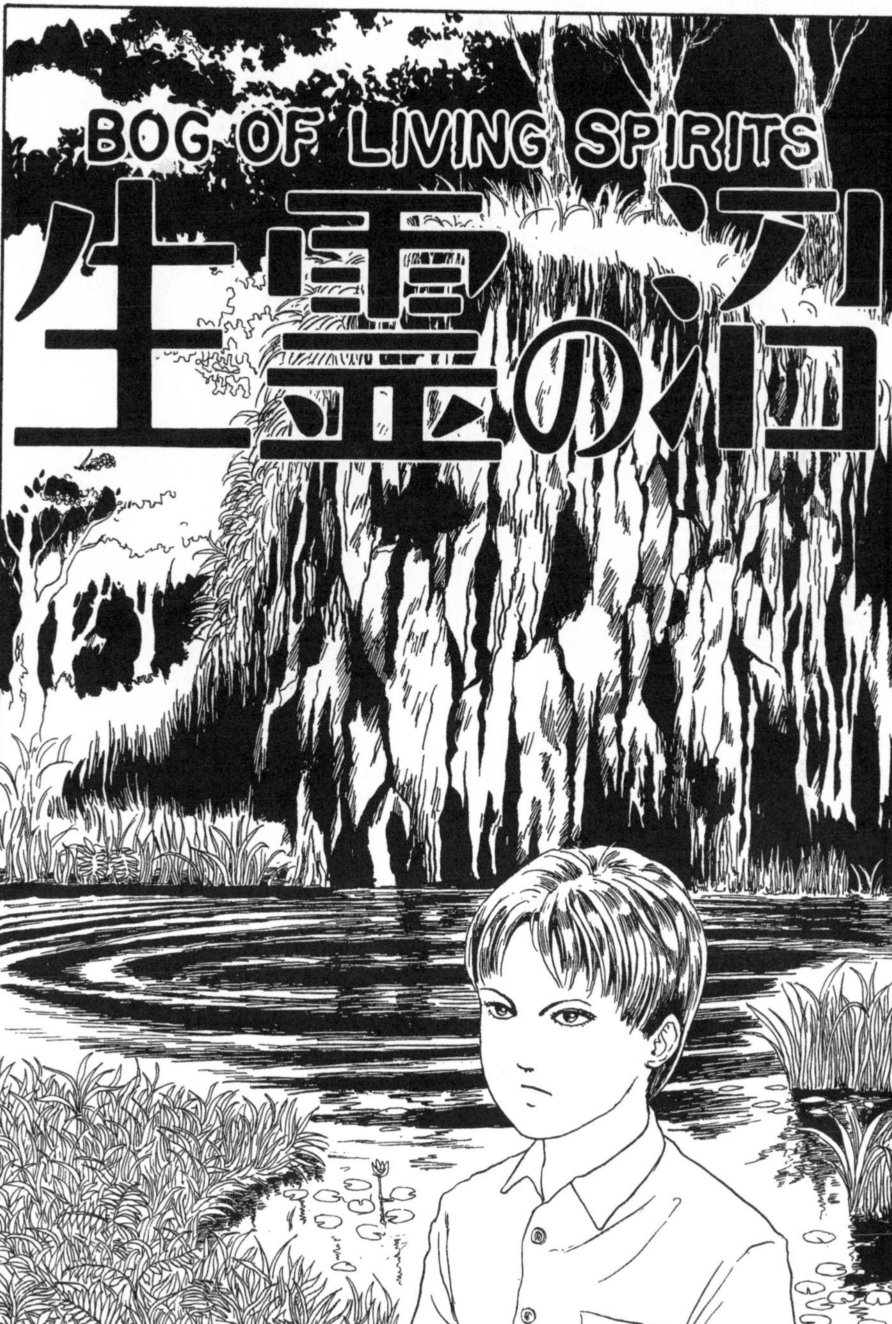
BOG OF LIVING SPIRITS
生霊の沼

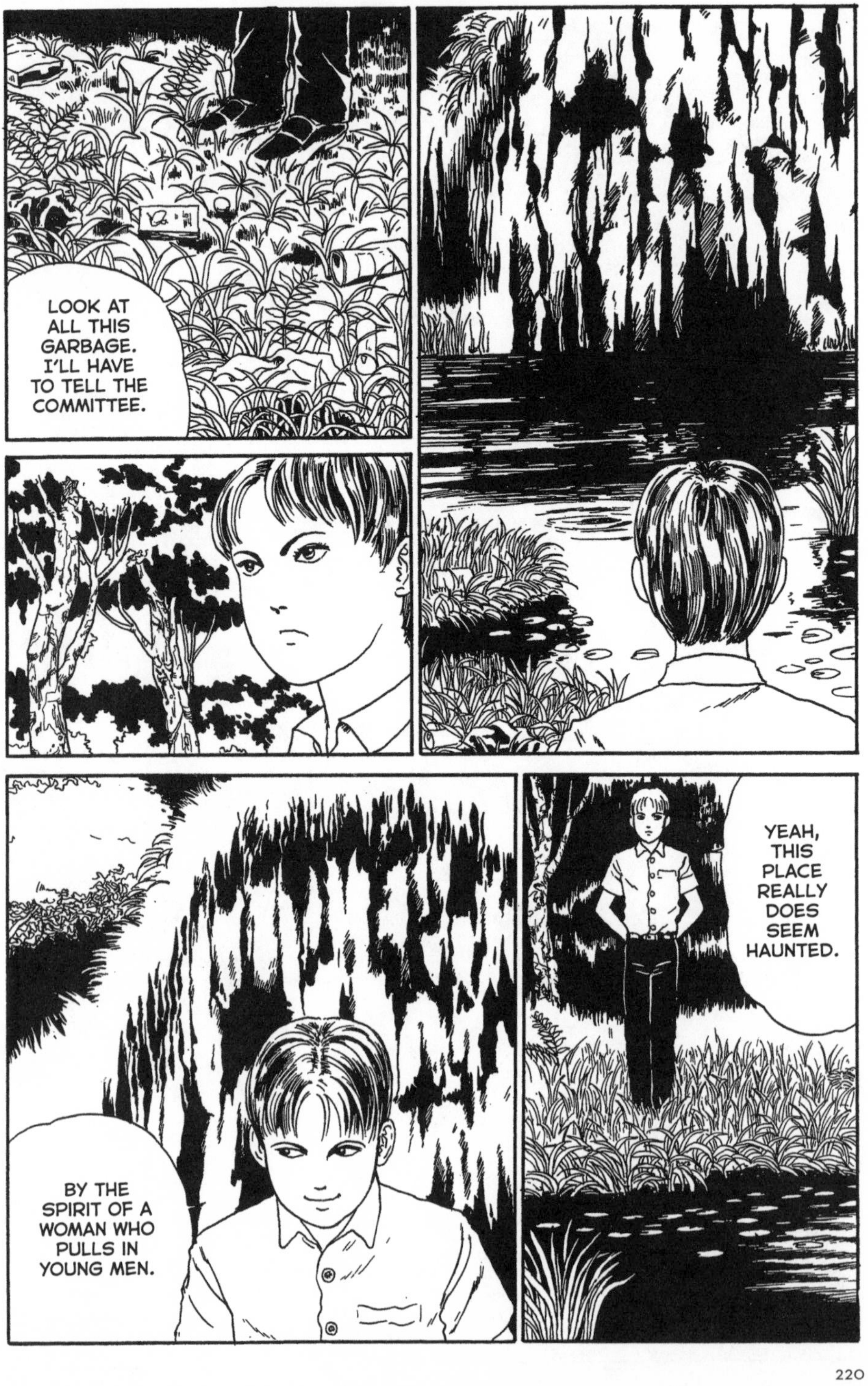

LOOK AT ALL THIS GARBAGE. I'LL HAVE TO TELL THE COMMITTEE.
YEAH, THIS PLACE REALLY DOES SEEM HAUNTED.
BY THE SPIRIT OF A WOMAN WHO PULLS IN YOUNG MEN.

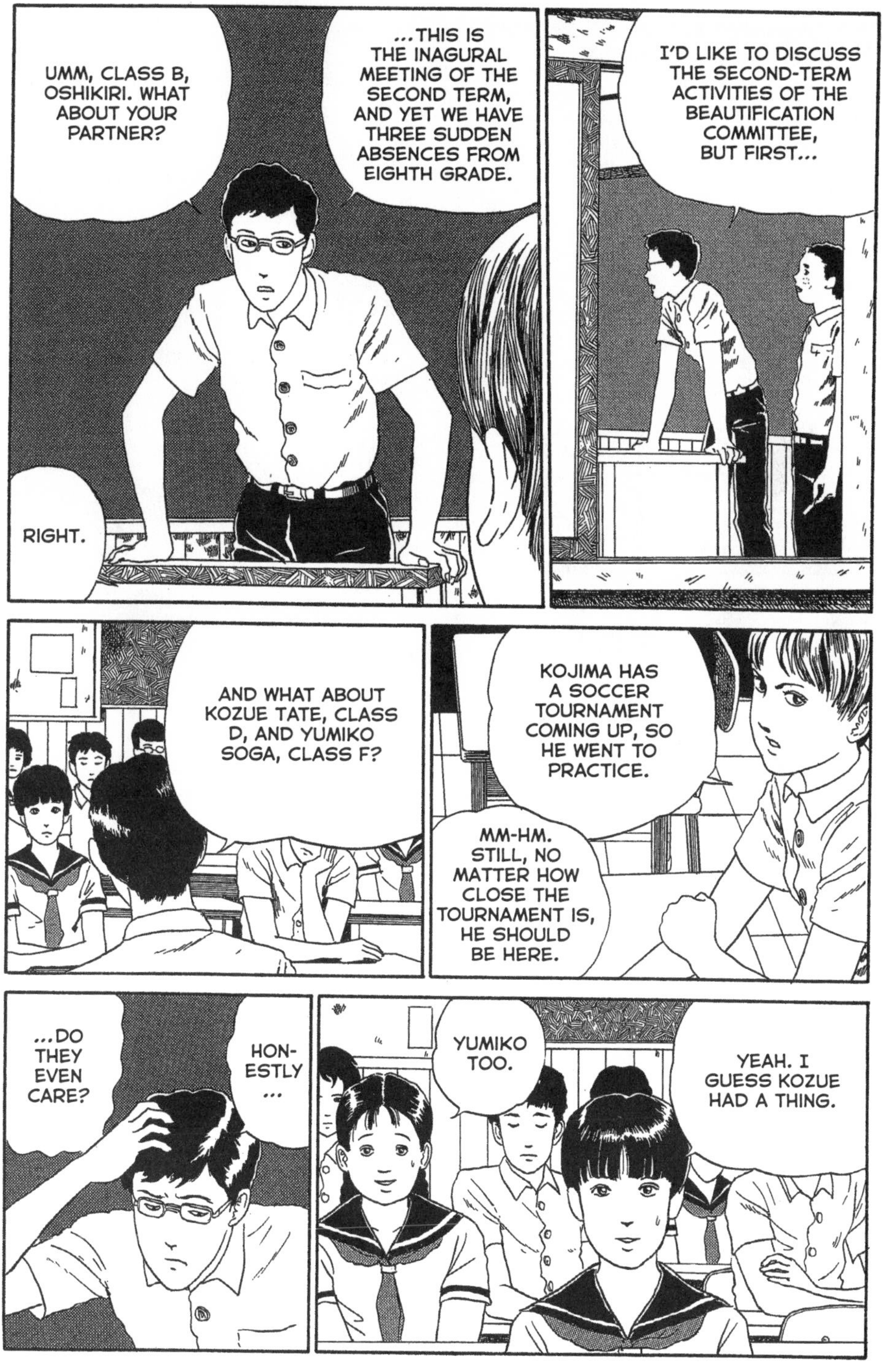
I'D LIKE TO DISCUSS THE SECOND-TERM ACTIVITIES OF THE BEAUTIFICATION COMMITTEE, BUT FIRST...
...THIS IS THE INAGURAL MEETING OF THE SECOND TERM, AND YET WE HAVE THREE SUDDEN ABSENCES FROM EIGHTH GRADE.
UMM, CLASS B, OSHIKIRI. WHAT ABOUT YOUR PARTNER?
RIGHT.
KOJIMA HAS A SOCCER TOURNAMENT COMING UP, SO HE WENT TO PRACTICE.
MM-HM. STILL, NO MATTER HOW CLOSE THE TOURNAMENT IS, HE SHOULD BE HERE.
AND WHAT ABOUT KOZUE TATE, CLASS D, AND YUMIKO SOGA, CLASS F?
YEAH. I GUESS KOZUE HAD A THING.
YUMIKO TOO.
HON-ESTLY...
...DO THEY EVEN CARE?

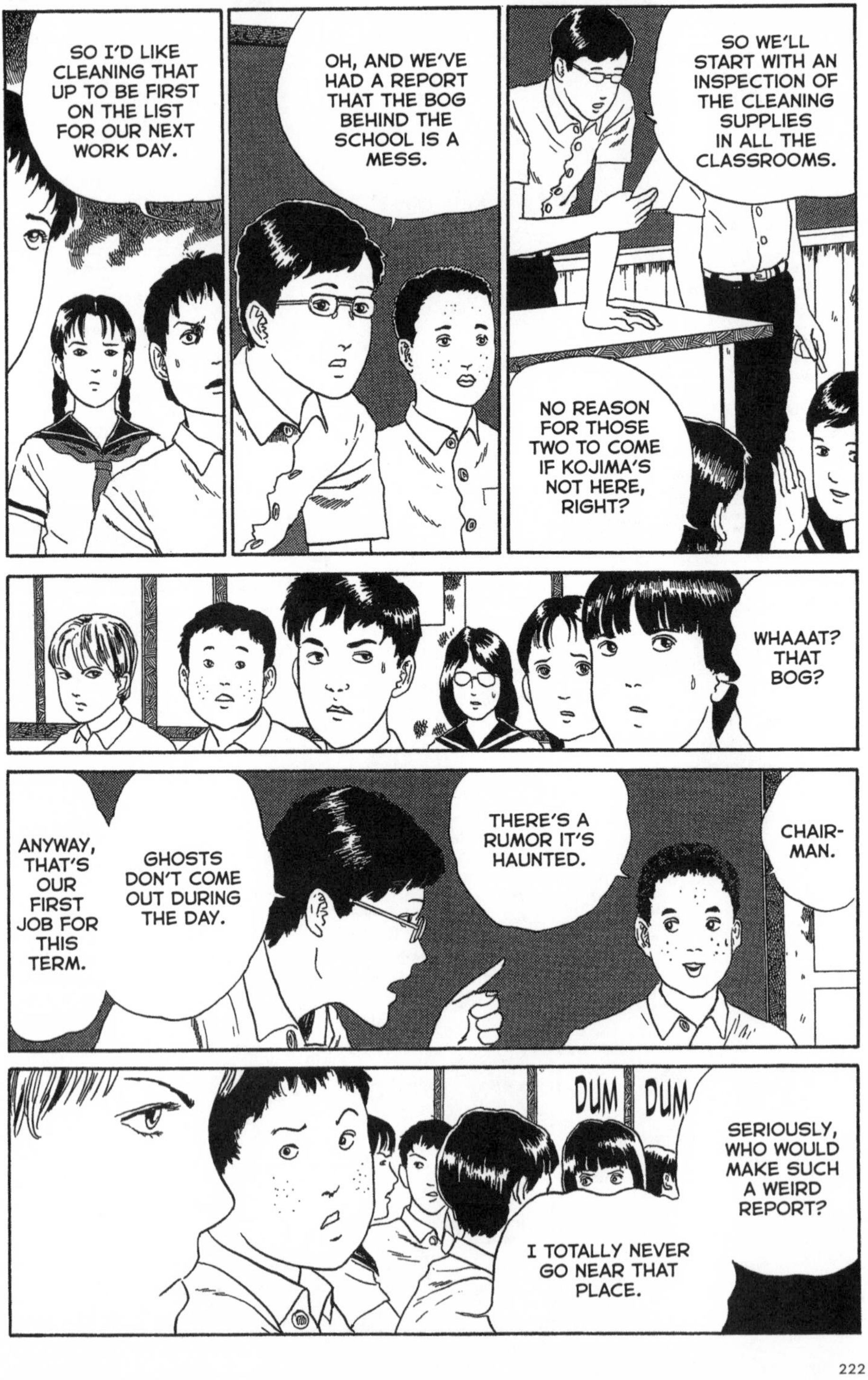
SO WE'LL START WITH AN INSPECTION OF THE CLEANING SUPPLIES IN ALL THE CLASSROOMS.
NO REASON FOR THOSE TWO TO COME IF KOJIMA'S NOT HERE, RIGHT?
OH, AND WE'VE HAD A REPORT THAT THE BOG BEHIND THE SCHOOL IS A MESS.
SO I'D LIKE CLEANING THAT UP TO BE FIRST ON THE LIST FOR OUR NEXT WORK DAY.
WHAAAT? THAT BOG?
CHAIR-MAN.
THERE'S A RUMOR IT'S HAUNTED.
GHOSTS DON'T COME OUT DURING THE DAY.
ANYWAY, THAT'S OUR FIRST JOB FOR THIS TERM.
DUM DUM
SERIOUSLY, WHO WOULD MAKE SUCH A WEIRD REPORT?
I TOTALLY NEVER GO NEAR THAT PLACE.

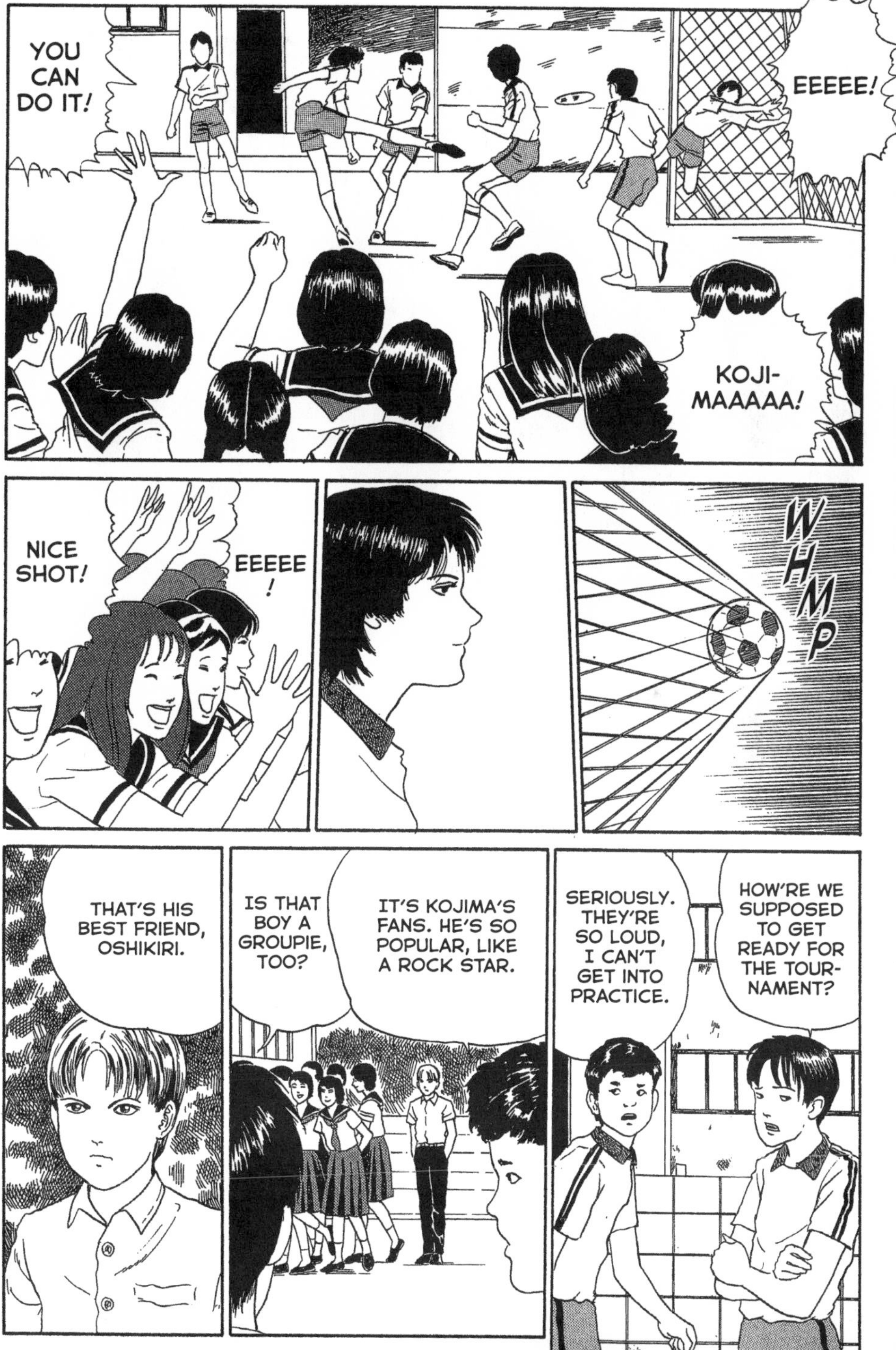
EEEEE!
YOU CAN DO IT!
KOJI-MAAAAA!
WHMP
EEEEE!
NICE SHOT!
HOW'RE WE SUPPOSED TO GET READY FOR THE TOURNAMENT?
SERIOUSLY. THEY'RE SO LOUD, I CAN'T GET INTO PRACTICE.
IT'S KOJIMA'S FANS. HE'S SO POPULAR, LIKE A ROCK STAR.
IS THAT BOY A GROUPIE, TOO?
THAT'S HIS BEST FRIEND, OSHIKIRI.

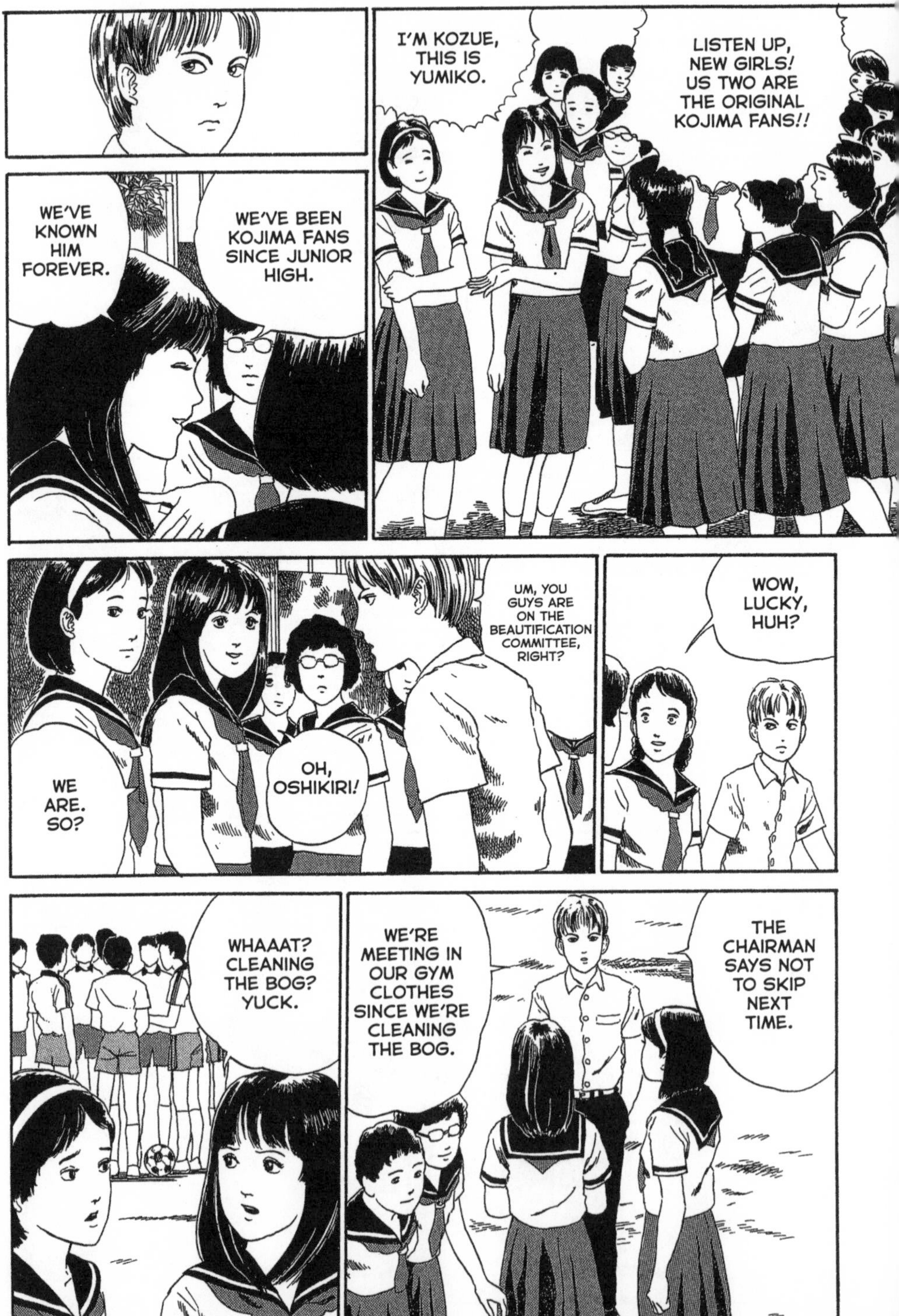
LISTEN UP, NEW GIRLS! US TWO ARE THE ORIGINAL KOJIMA FANS!!
I'M KOZUE, THIS IS YUMIKO.
WE'VE BEEN KOJIMA FANS SINCE JUNIOR HIGH.
WE'VE KNOWN HIM FOREVER.
WOW, LUCKY, HUH?
UM, YOU GUYS ARE ON THE BEAUTIFICATION COMMITTEE, RIGHT?
OH, OSHIKIRI!
WE ARE. SO?
THE CHAIRMAN SAYS NOT TO SKIP NEXT TIME.
WE'RE MEETING IN OUR GYM CLOTHES SINCE WE'RE CLEANING THE BOG.
WHAAAT? CLEANING THE BOG? YUCK.

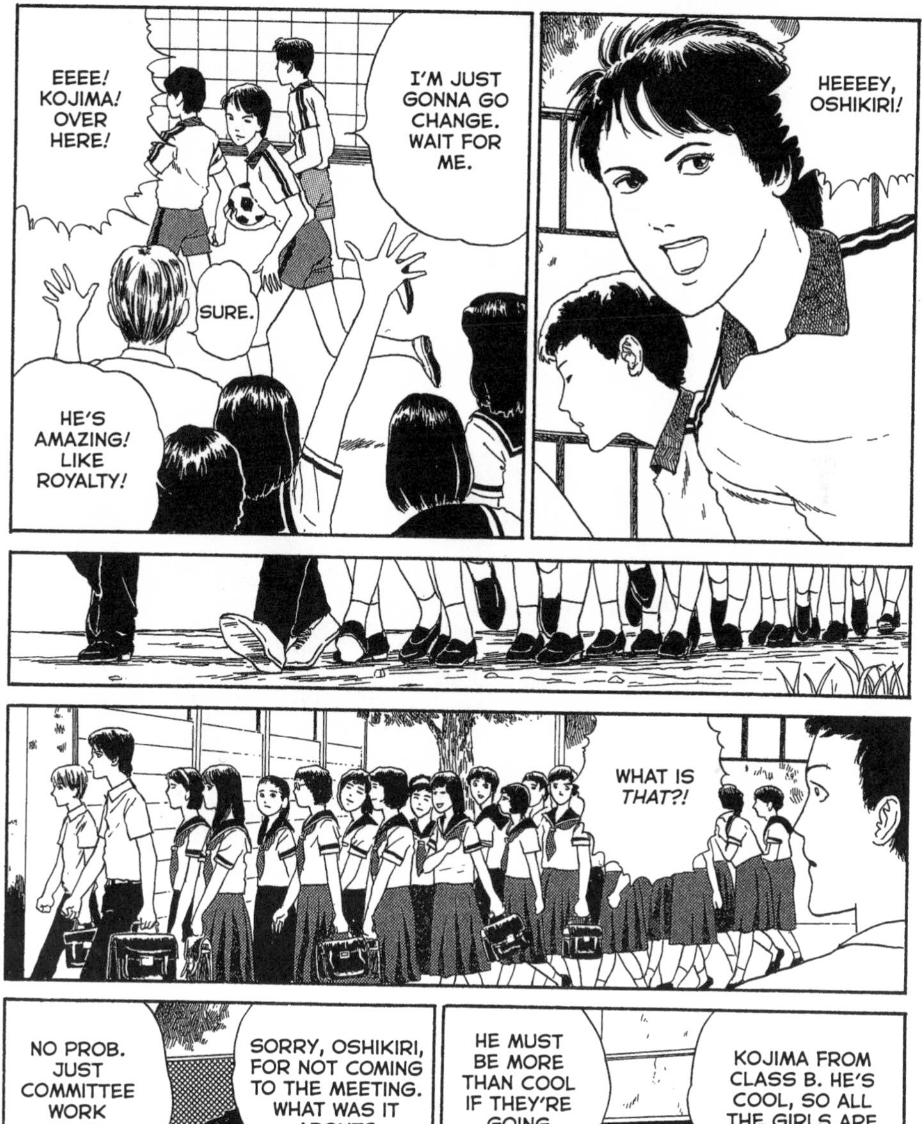
HEEEEY, OSHIKIRI!
I'M JUST GONNA GO CHANGE. WAIT FOR ME.
EEEE! KOJIMA! OVER HERE!
SURE.
HE'S AMAZING! LIKE ROYALTY!
WHAT IS *THAT*?!
KOJIMA FROM CLASS B. HE'S COOL, SO ALL THE GIRLS ARE AFTER HIM.
HE MUST BE MORE THAN COOL IF THEY'RE GOING THAT FAR.
SORRY, OSHIKIRI, FOR NOT COMING TO THE MEETING. WHAT WAS IT ABOUT?
NO PROB. JUST COMMITTEE WORK STUFF.

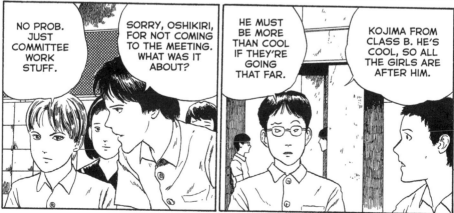

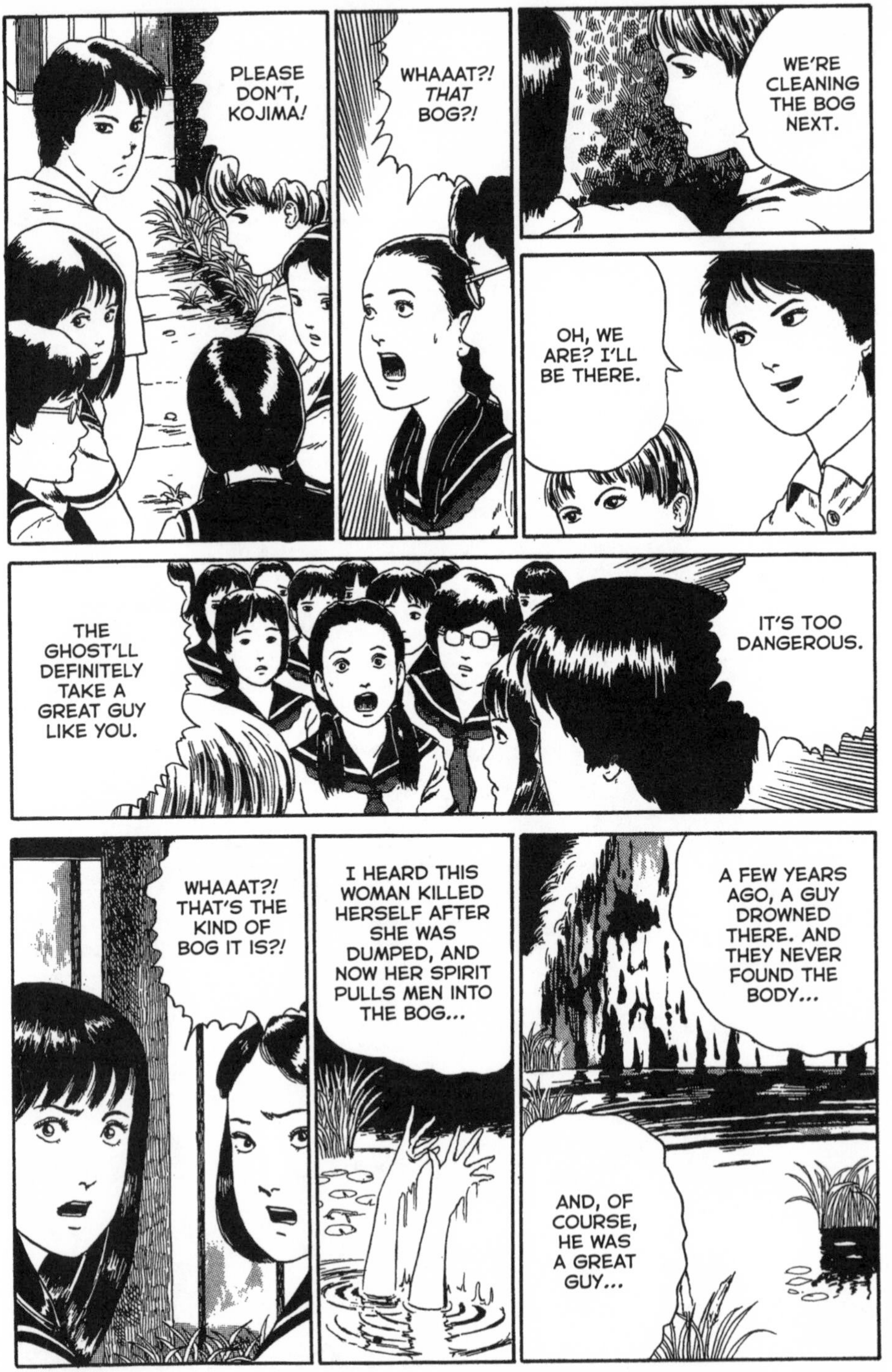
WE'RE CLEANING THE BOG NEXT.
OH, WE ARE? I'LL BE THERE.
WHAAAT?! *THAT* BOG?!
PLEASE DON'T, KOJIMA!
IT'S TOO DANGEROUS.
THE GHOST'LL DEFINITELY TAKE A GREAT GUY LIKE YOU.
A FEW YEARS AGO, A GUY DROWNED THERE. AND THEY NEVER FOUND THE BODY...
AND, OF COURSE, HE WAS A GREAT GUY...
I HEARD THIS WOMAN KILLED HERSELF AFTER SHE WAS DUMPED, AND NOW HER SPIRIT PULLS MEN INTO THE BOG...
WHAAAT?! THAT'S THE KIND OF BOG IT IS?!

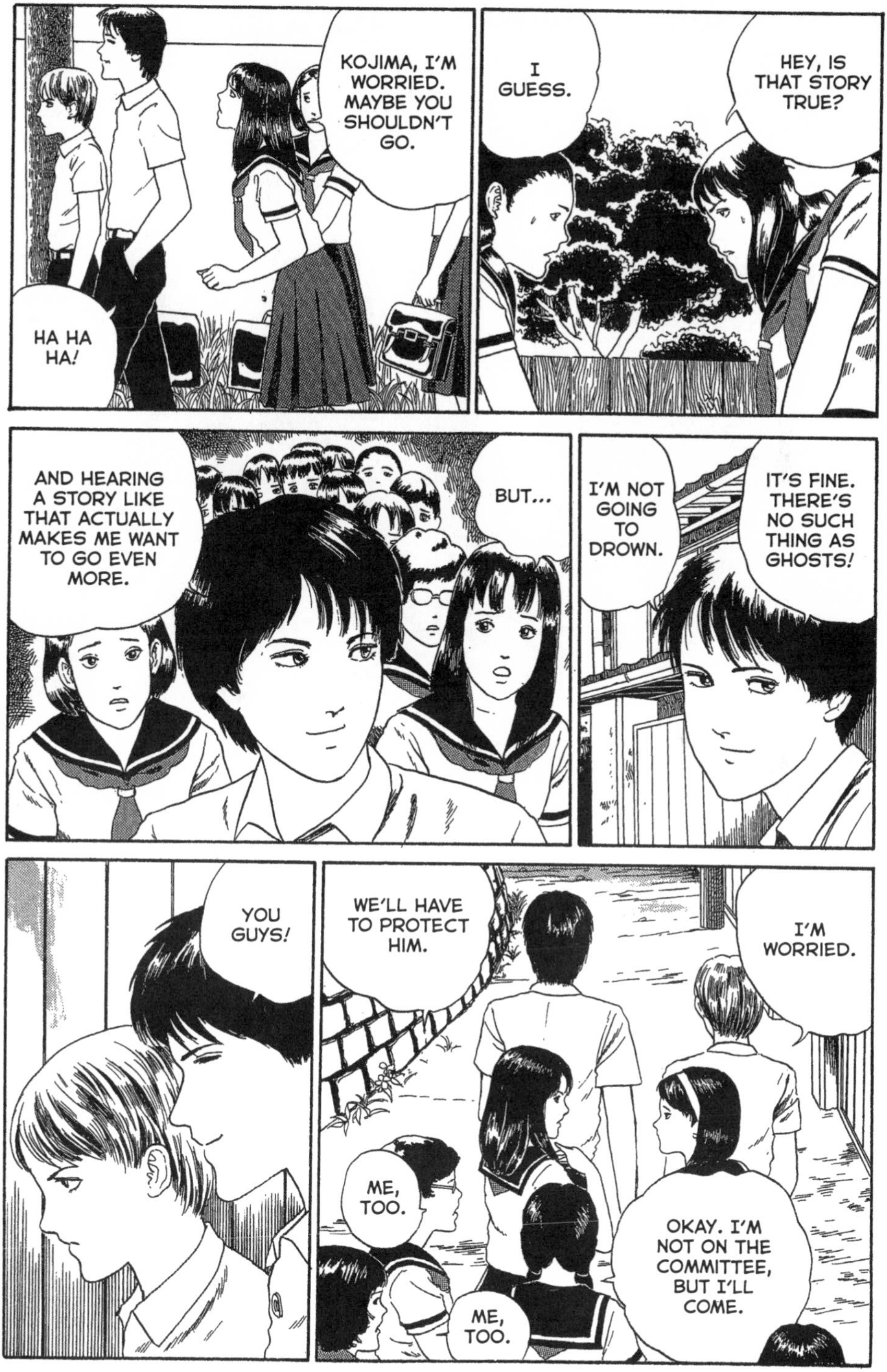
HEY, IS THAT STORY TRUE?
I GUESS.
KOJIMA, I'M WORRIED. MAYBE YOU SHOULDN'T GO.
HA HA HA!
IT'S FINE. THERE'S NO SUCH THING AS GHOSTS!
I'M NOT GOING TO DROWN.
BUT...
AND HEARING A STORY LIKE THAT ACTUALLY MAKES ME WANT TO GO EVEN MORE.
I'M WORRIED.
WE'LL HAVE TO PROTECT HIM.
OKAY. I'M NOT ON THE COMMITTEE, BUT I'LL COME.
ME, TOO.
ME, TOO.
YOU GUYS!

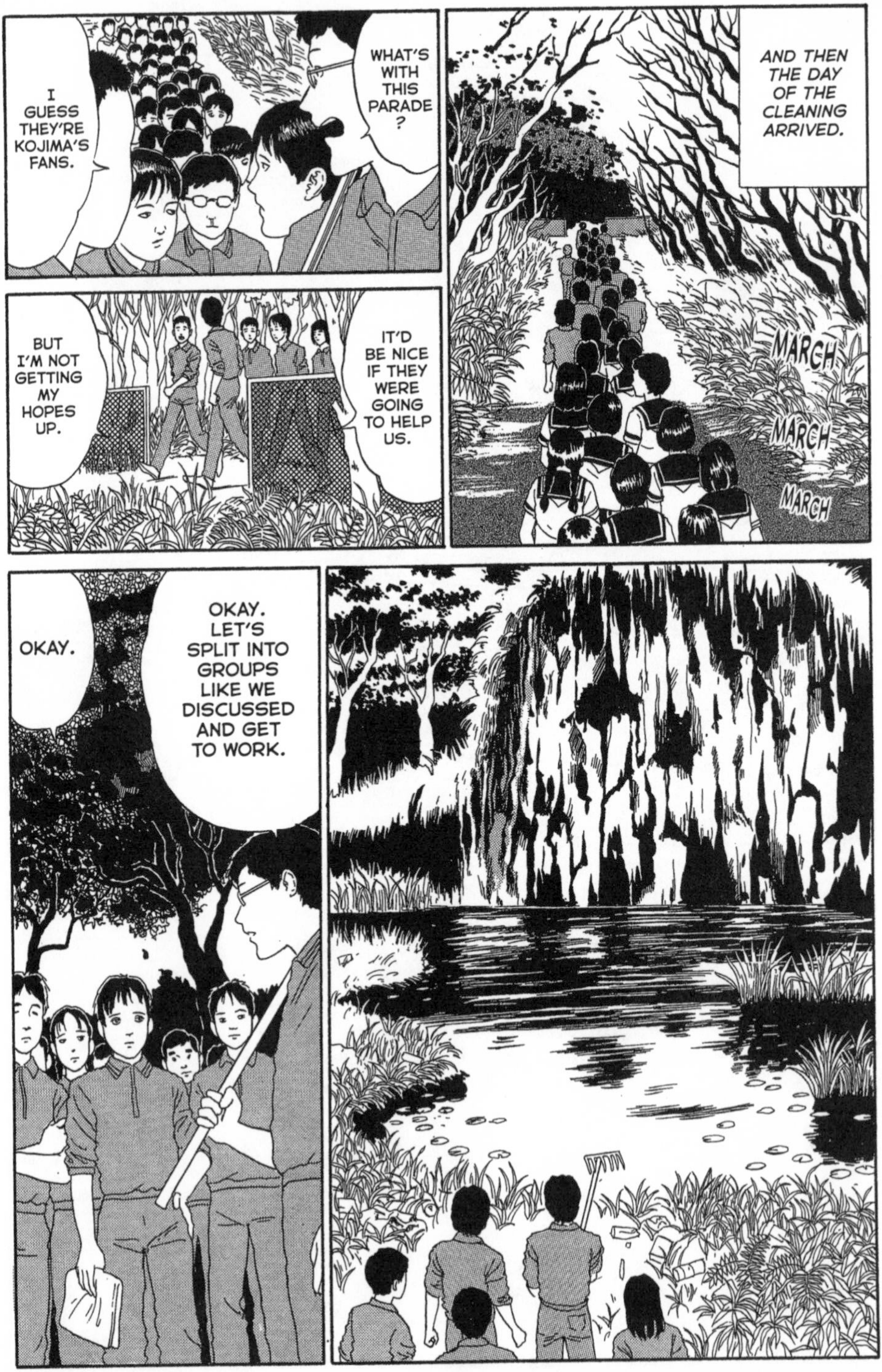
AND THEN THE DAY OF THE CLEANING ARRIVED.
MARCH
MARCH
MARCH
WHAT'S WITH THIS PARADE?
I GUESS THEY'RE KOJIMA'S FANS.
IT'D BE NICE IF THEY WERE GOING TO HELP US.
BUT I'M NOT GETTING MY HOPES UP.
OKAY. LET'S SPLIT INTO GROUPS LIKE WE DISCUSSED AND GET TO WORK.
OKAY.

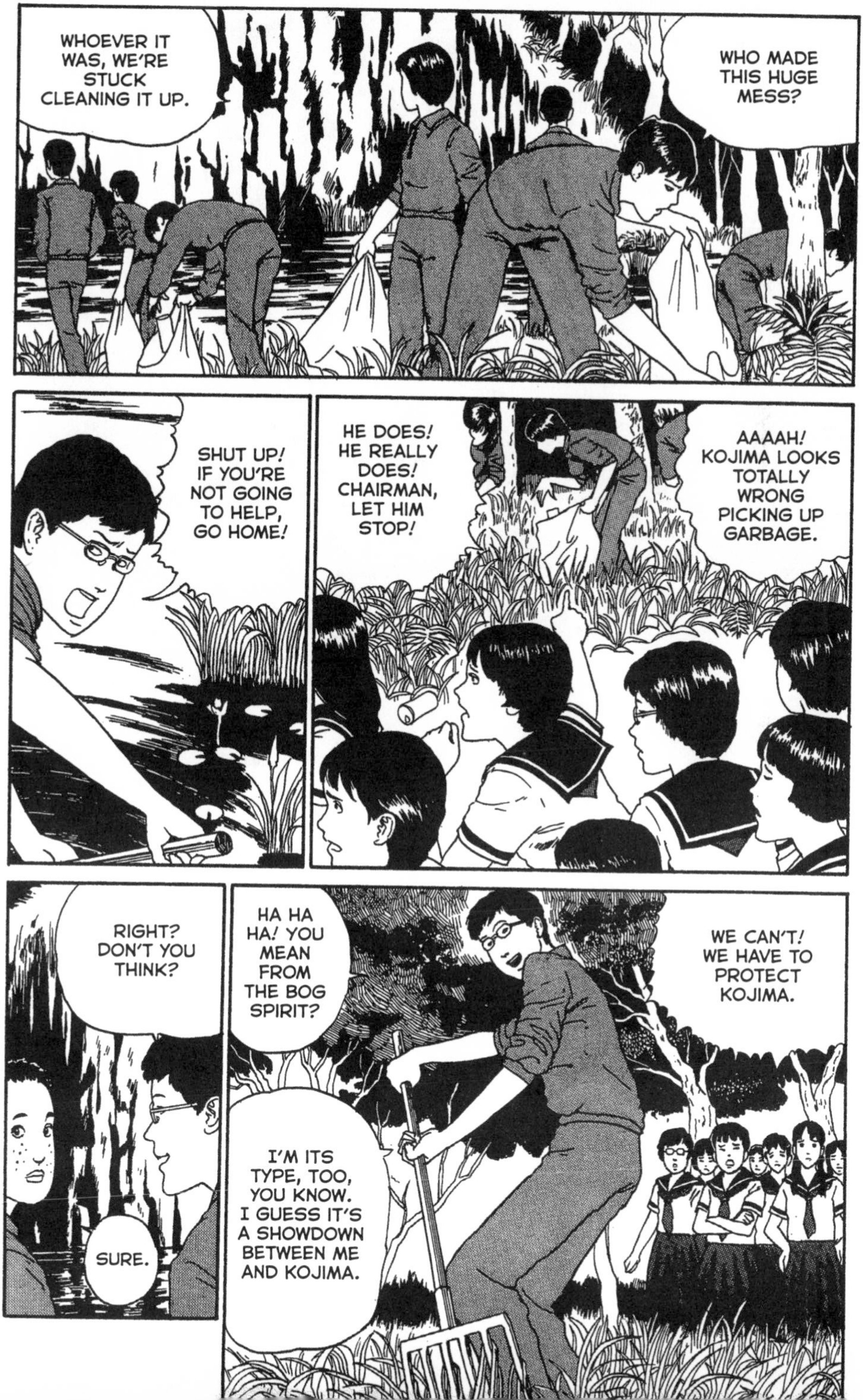
WHO MADE THIS HUGE MESS?
WHOEVER IT WAS, WE'RE STUCK CLEANING IT UP.
AAAAH! KOJIMA LOOKS TOTALLY WRONG PICKING UP GARBAGE.
HE DOES! HE REALLY DOES! CHAIRMAN, LET HIM STOP!
SHUT UP! IF YOU'RE NOT GOING TO HELP, GO HOME!
WE CAN'T! WE HAVE TO PROTECT KOJIMA.
HA HA HA! YOU MEAN FROM THE BOG SPIRIT?
I'M ITS TYPE, TOO, YOU KNOW. I GUESS IT'S A SHOWDOWN BETWEEN ME AND KOJIMA.
RIGHT? DON'T YOU THINK?
SURE.

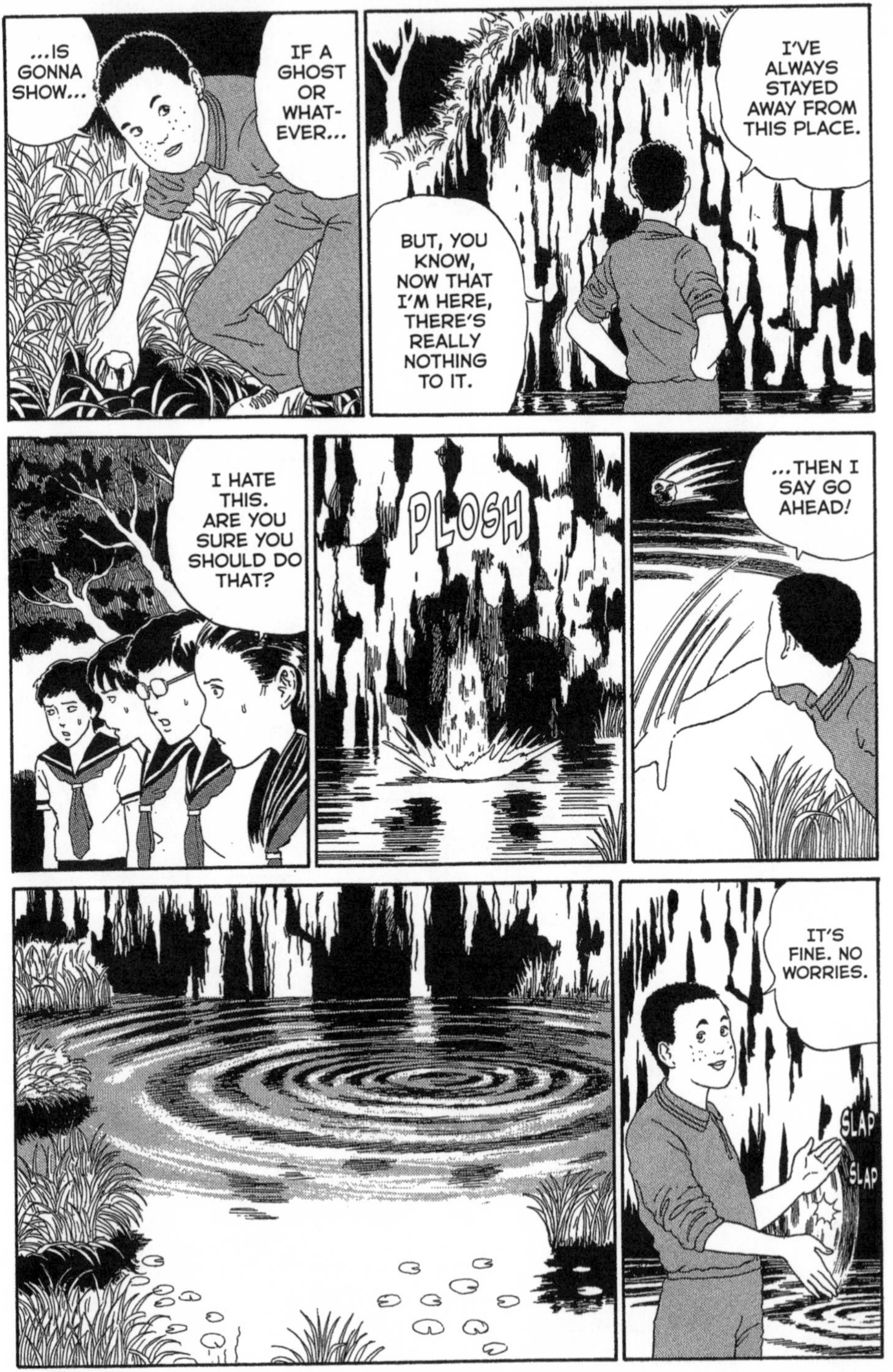
I'VE ALWAYS STAYED AWAY FROM THIS PLACE.
BUT, YOU KNOW, NOW THAT I'M HERE, THERE'S REALLY NOTHING TO IT.
IF A GHOST OR WHATEVER...
...IS GONNA SHOW...
...THEN I SAY GO AHEAD!
PLOSH
I HATE THIS. ARE YOU SURE YOU SHOULD DO THAT?
IT'S FINE. NO WORRIES.
SLAP
SLAP

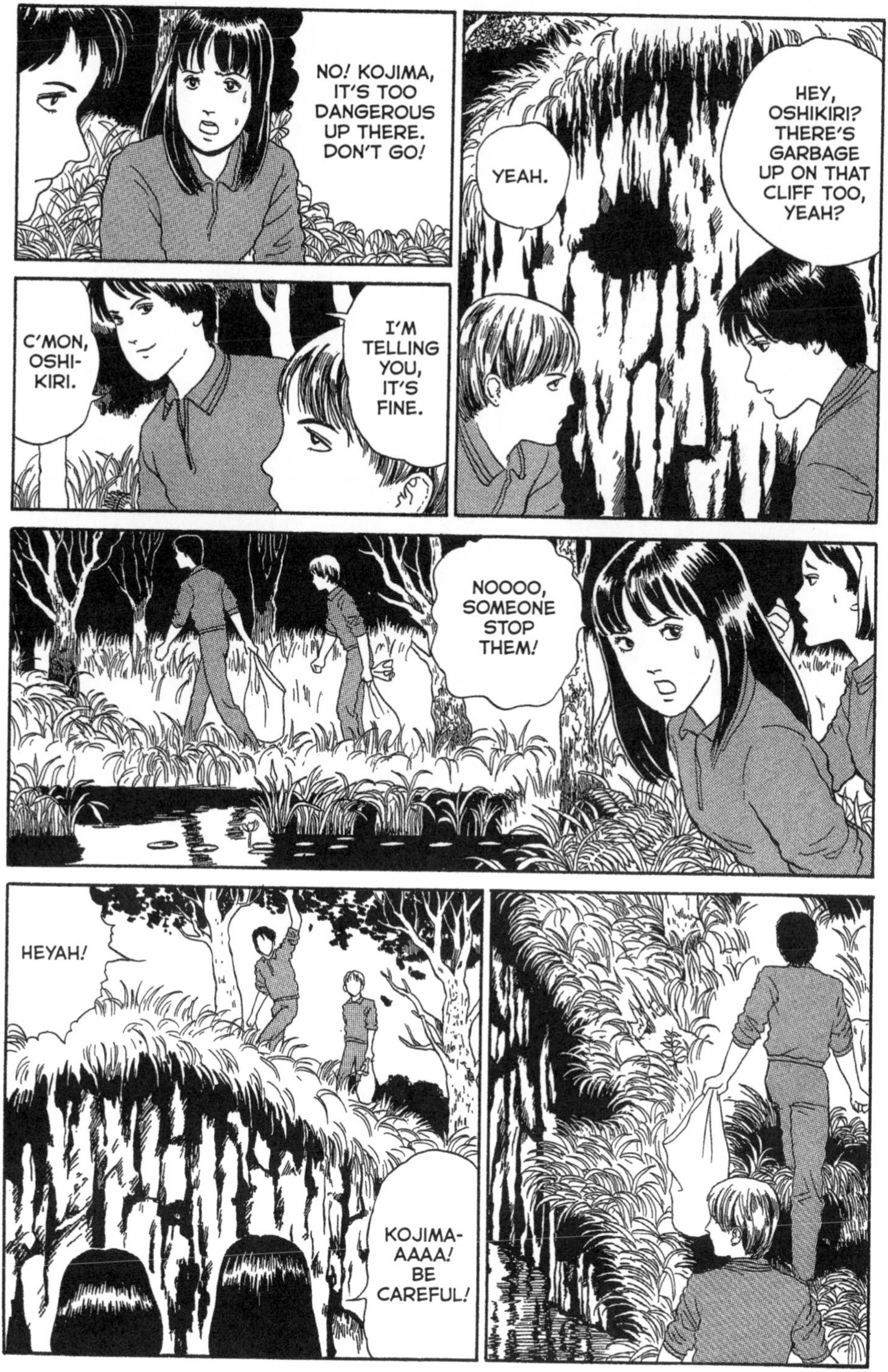
HEY, OSHIKIRI? THERE'S GARBAGE UP ON THAT CLIFF TOO, YEAH?
YEAH.
NO! KOJIMA, IT'S TOO DANGEROUS UP THERE. DON'T GO!
I'M TELLING YOU, IT'S FINE.
C'MON, OSHI-KIRI.
NOOOO, SOMEONE STOP THEM!
HEYAH!
KOJIMA-AAAA! BE CAREFUL!

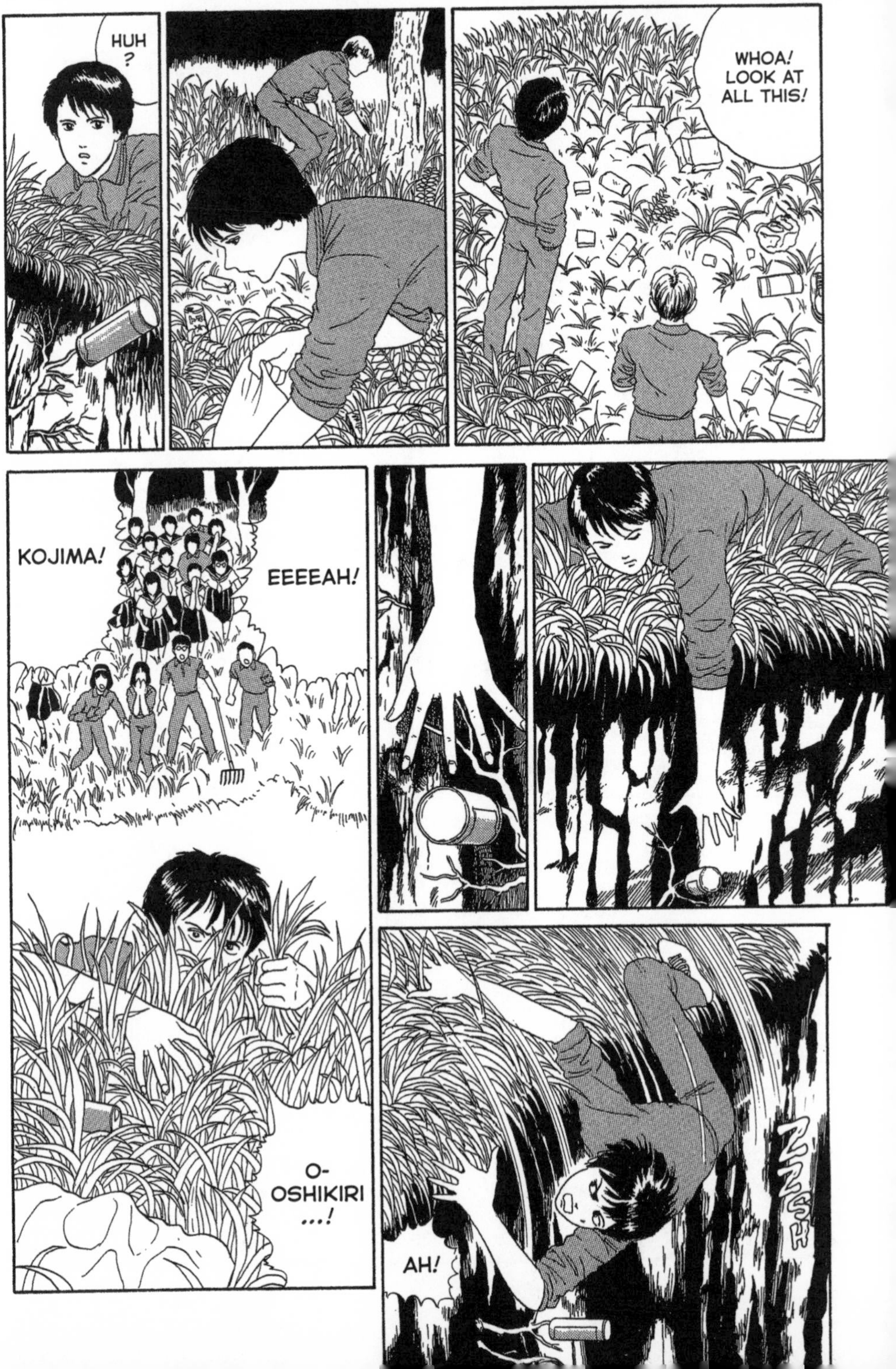
WHOA! LOOK AT ALL THIS!
HUH?
AH!
KOJIMA!
EEEEAH!
O-OSHIKIRI...!

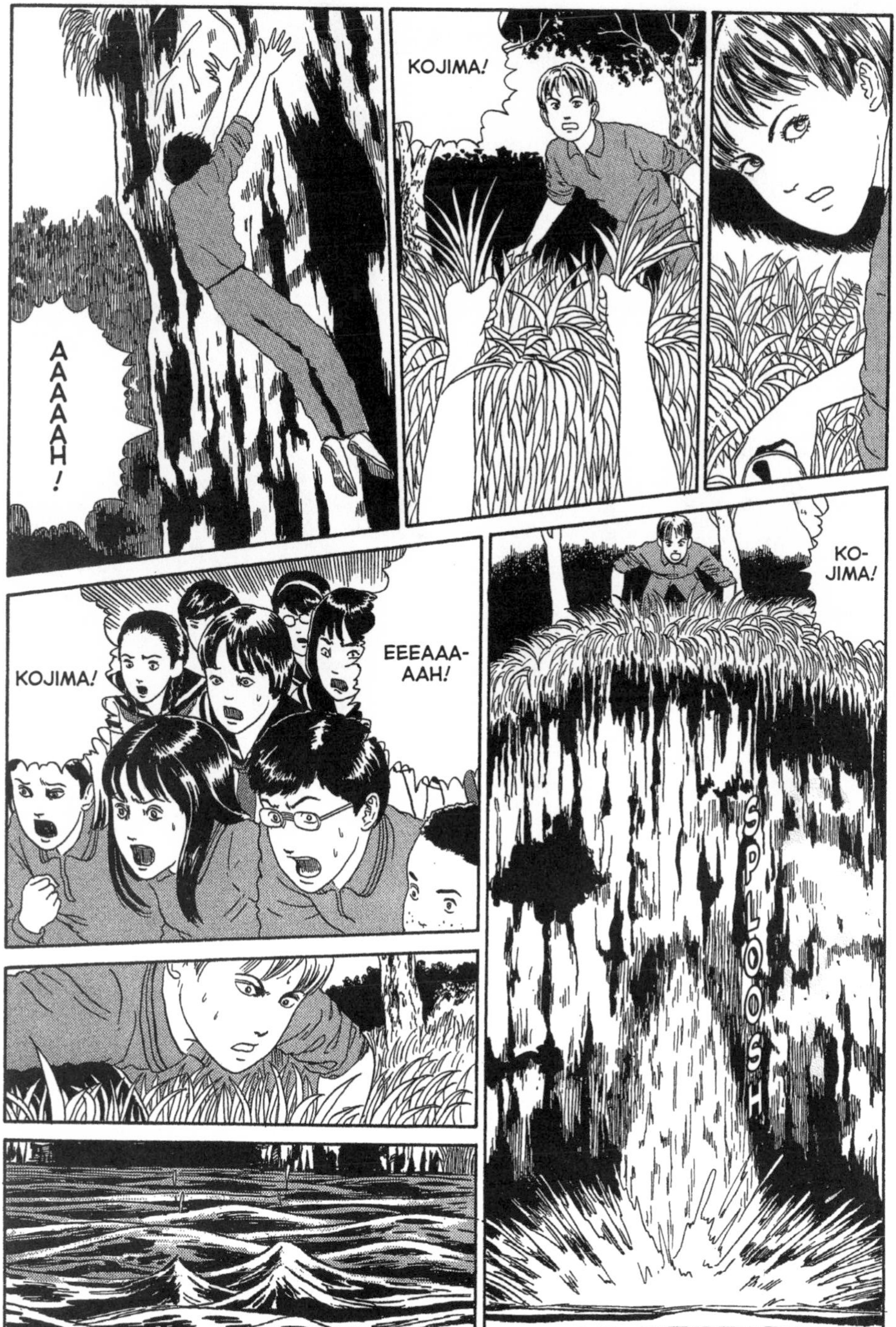
KOJIMA!
AAAAAH!
KO-
JIMA!
SPLOOSH
EEEAAA-
AAH!
KOJIMA!

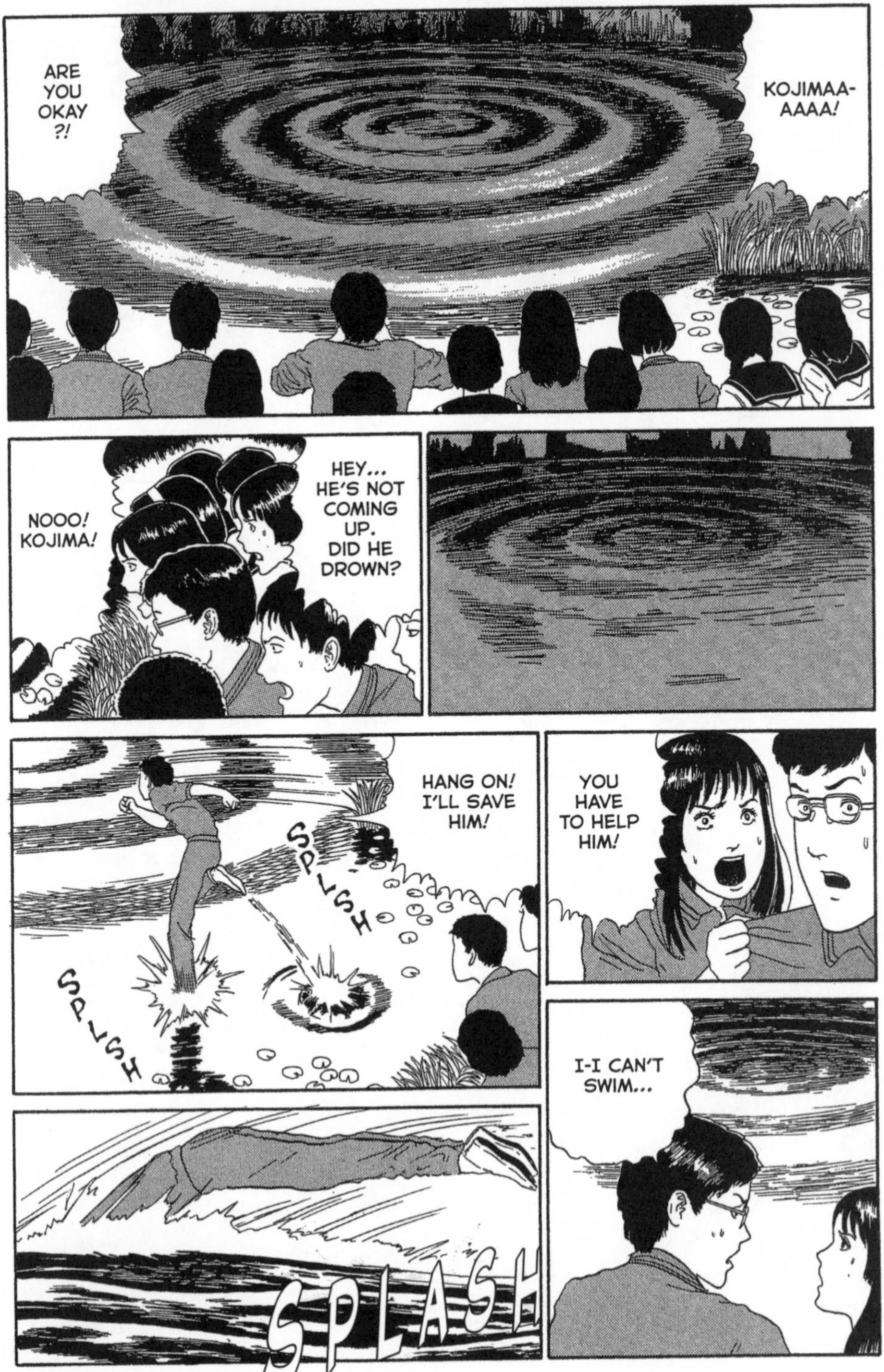
KOJIMAA-AAAA!
ARE YOU OKAY ?!
HEY... HE'S NOT COMING UP. DID HE DROWN?
NOOO! KOJIMA!
YOU HAVE TO HELP HIM!
HANG ON! I'LL SAVE HIM!
SPLSH
SPLSH
I-I CAN'T SWIM...
SPLASH

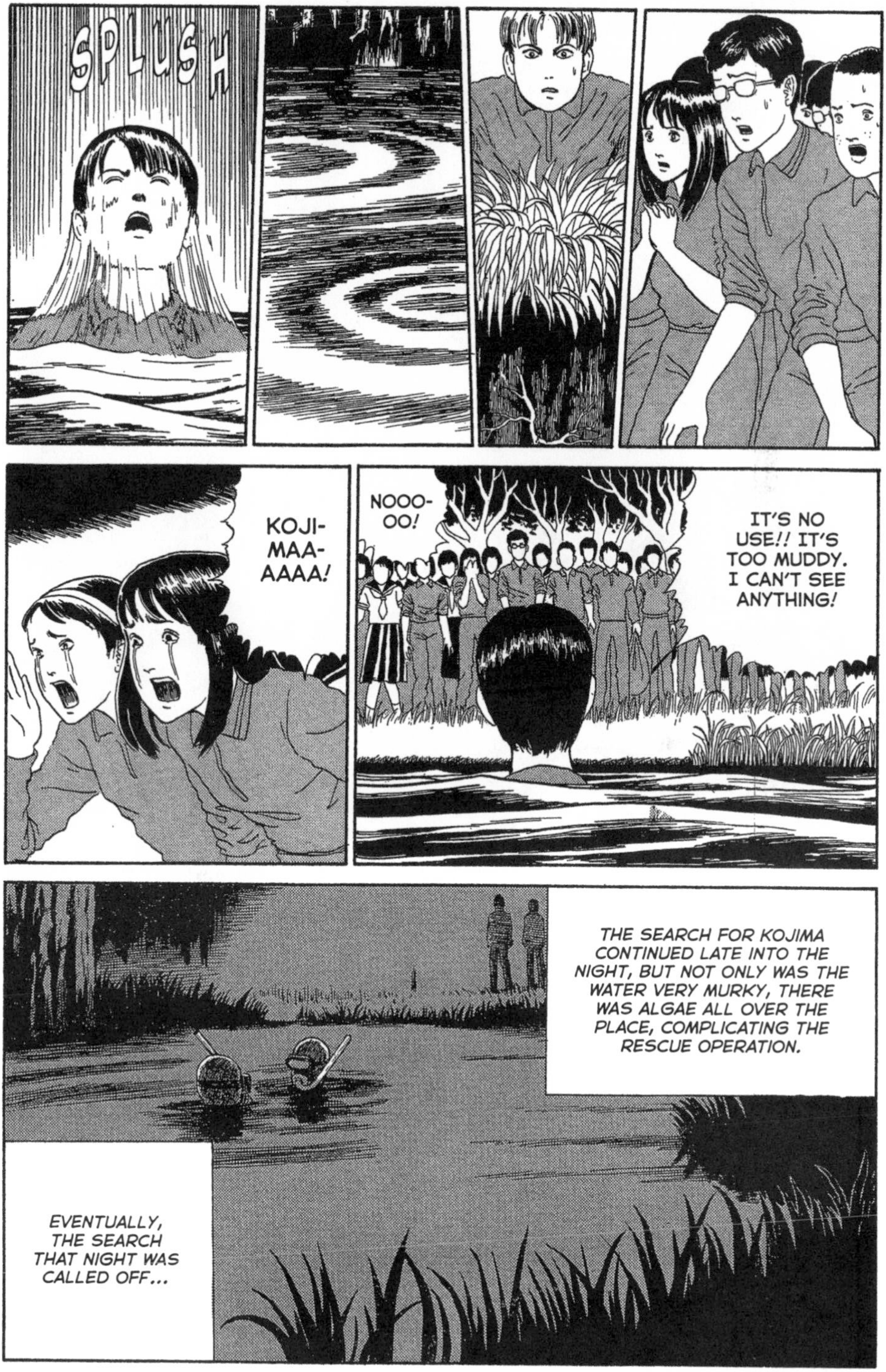
SPLUSH
IT'S NO USE!! IT'S TOO MUDDY. I CAN'T SEE ANYTHING!
NOOOO-OO!
KOJI-MAA-AAAA!
THE SEARCH FOR KOJIMA CONTINUED LATE INTO THE NIGHT, BUT NOT ONLY WAS THE WATER VERY MURKY, THERE WAS ALGAE ALL OVER THE PLACE, COMPLICATING THE RESCUE OPERATION.
EVENTUALLY, THE SEARCH THAT NIGHT WAS CALLED OFF...

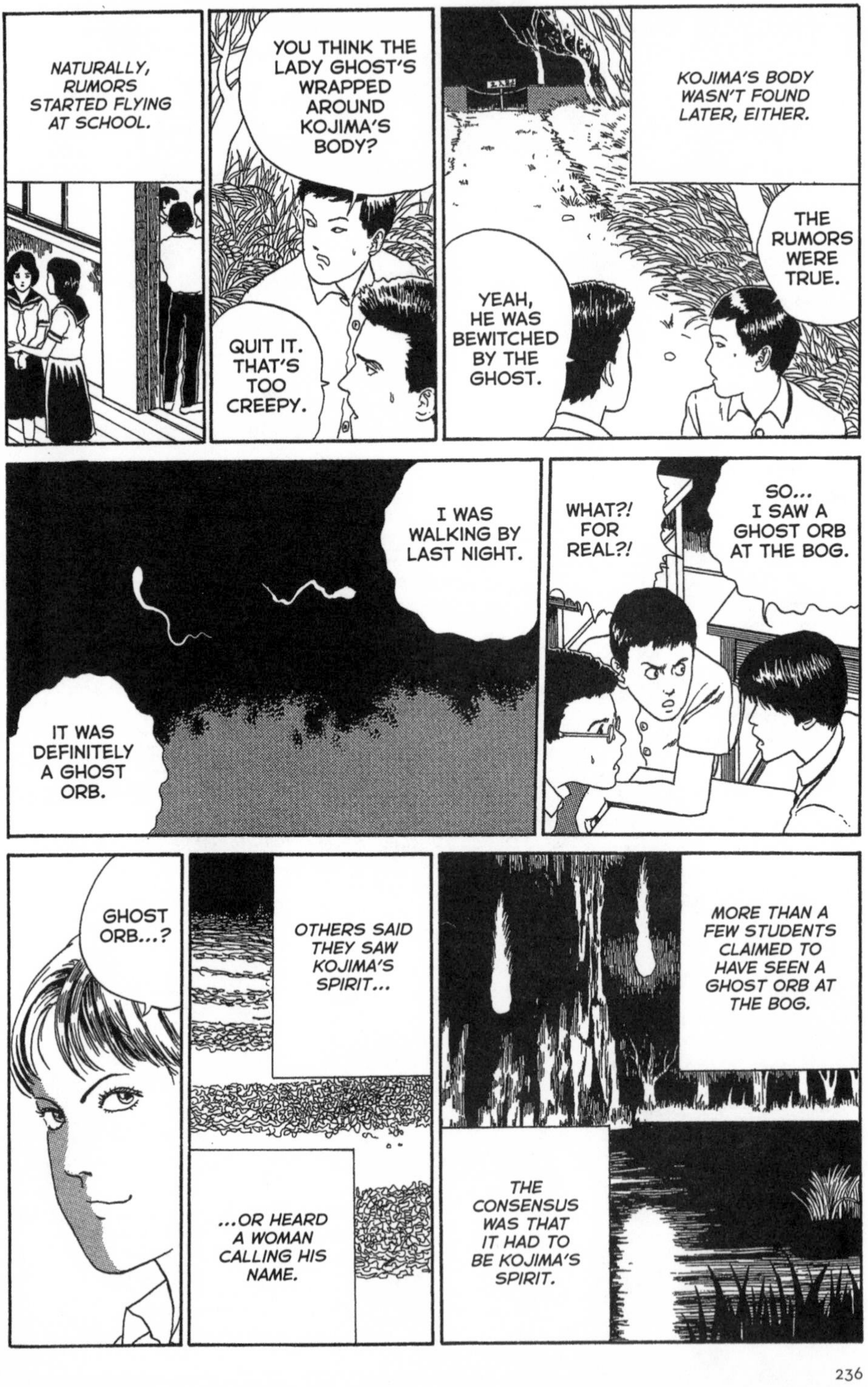
KOJIMA'S BODY WASN'T FOUND LATER, EITHER.
THE RUMORS WERE TRUE.
YEAH, HE WAS BEWITCHED BY THE GHOST.
YOU THINK THE LADY GHOST'S WRAPPED AROUND KOJIMA'S BODY?
QUIT IT. THAT'S TOO CREEPY.
NATURALLY, RUMORS STARTED FLYING AT SCHOOL.
SO... I SAW A GHOST ORB AT THE BOG.
WHAT?! FOR REAL?!
I WAS WALKING BY LAST NIGHT.
IT WAS DEFINITELY A GHOST ORB.
MORE THAN A FEW STUDENTS CLAIMED TO HAVE SEEN A GHOST ORB AT THE BOG.
THE CONSENSUS WAS THAT IT HAD TO BE KOJIMA'S SPIRIT.
OTHERS SAID THEY SAW KOJIMA'S SPIRIT...
...OR HEARD A WOMAN CALLING HIS NAME.
GHOST ORB...?

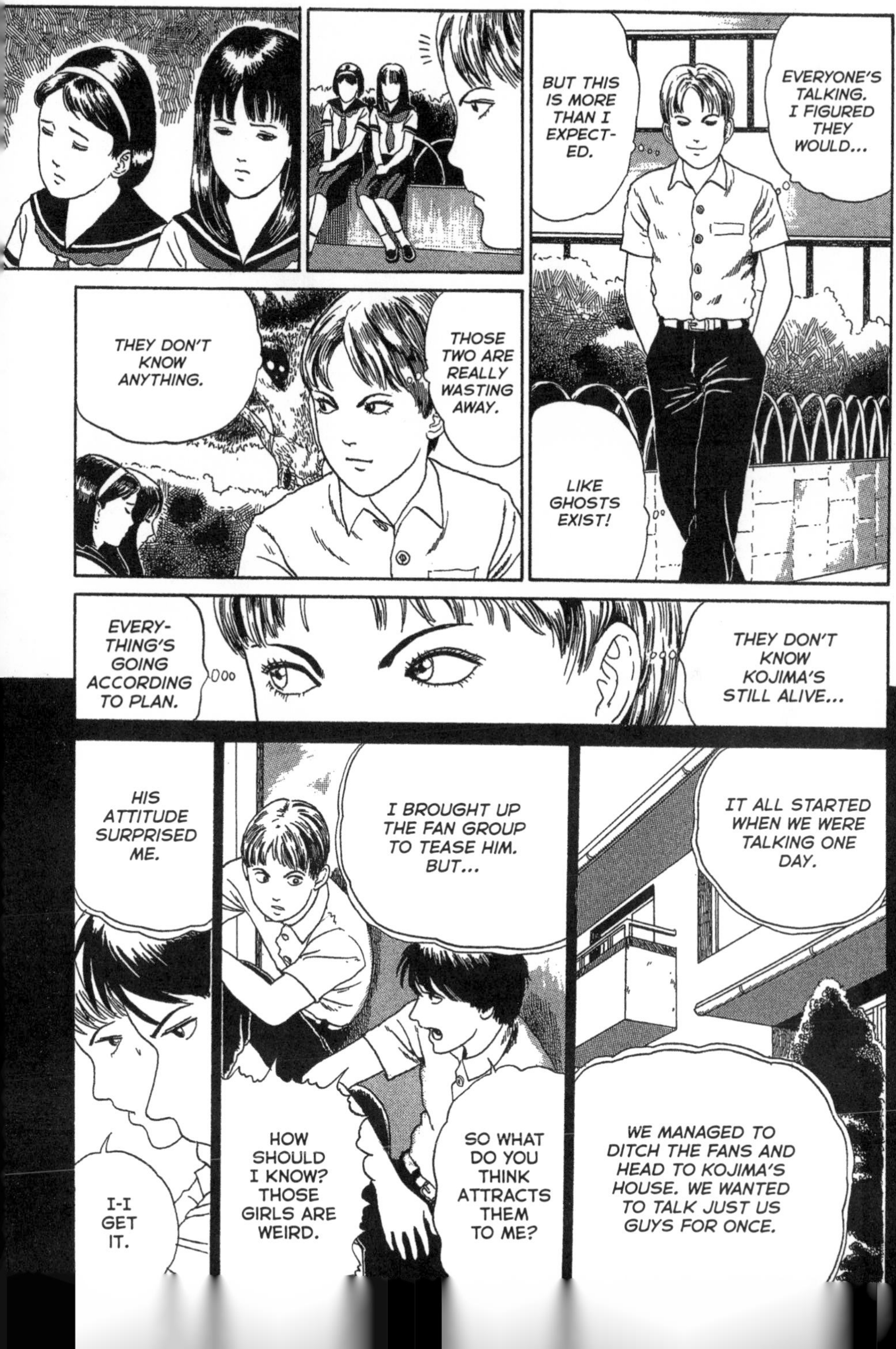
EVERYONE'S TALKING. I FIGURED THEY WOULD...
BUT THIS IS MORE THAN I EXPECT-ED.
LIKE GHOSTS EXIST!
THOSE TWO ARE REALLY WASTING AWAY.
THEY DON'T KNOW ANYTHING.
THEY DON'T KNOW KOJIMA'S STILL ALIVE...
EVERY-THING'S GOING ACCORDING TO PLAN.
IT ALL STARTED WHEN WE WERE TALKING ONE DAY.
WE MANAGED TO DITCH THE FANS AND HEAD TO KOJIMA'S HOUSE. WE WANTED TO TALK JUST US GUYS FOR ONCE.
I BROUGHT UP THE FAN GROUP TO TEASE HIM. BUT...
SO WHAT DO YOU THINK ATTRACTS THEM TO ME?
HOW SHOULD I KNOW? THOSE GIRLS ARE WEIRD.
HIS ATTITUDE SURPRISED ME.
I-I GET IT.

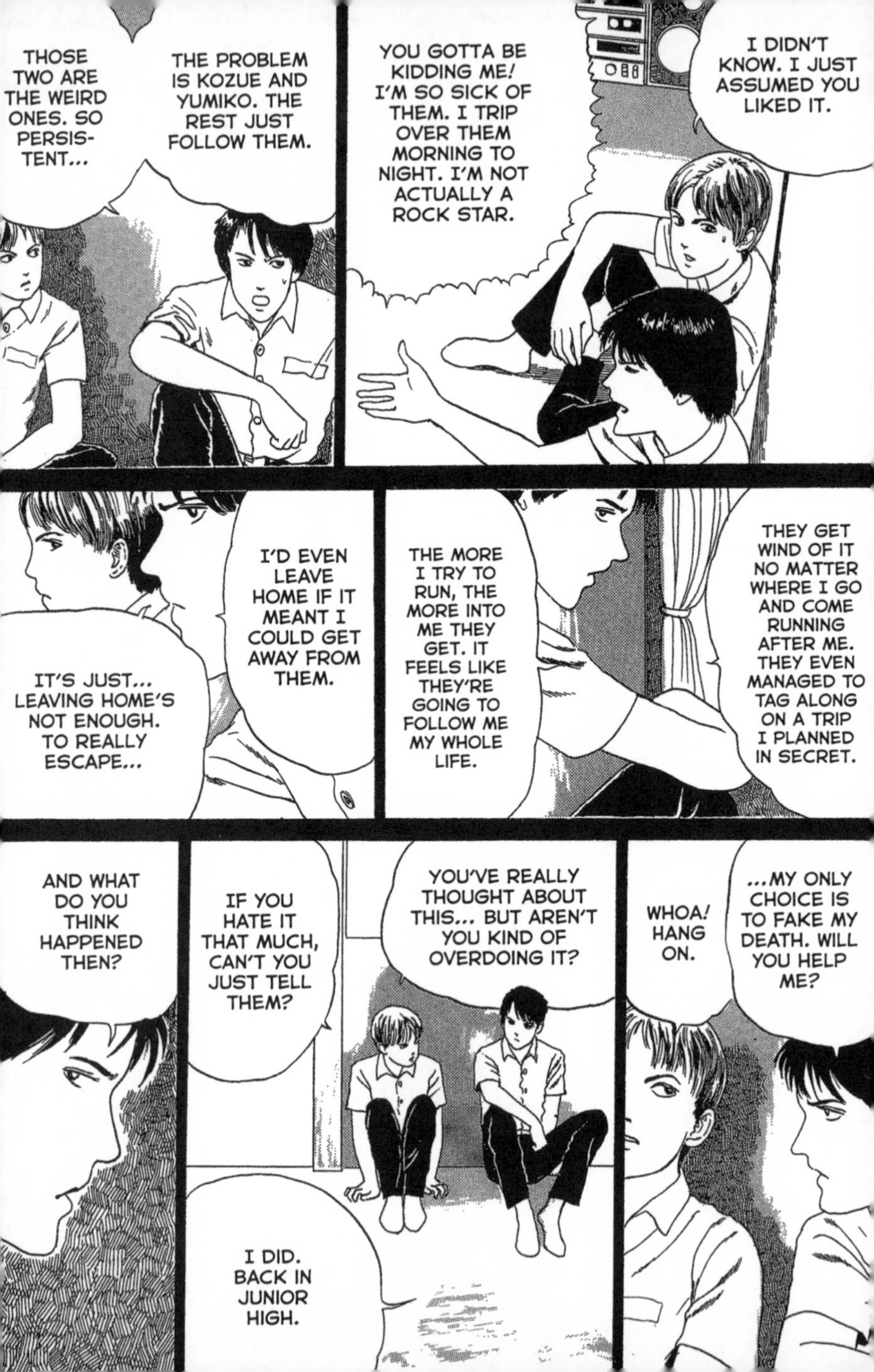
I DIDN'T KNOW. I JUST ASSUMED YOU LIKED IT.
YOU GOTTA BE KIDDING ME! I'M SO SICK OF THEM. I TRIP OVER THEM MORNING TO NIGHT. I'M NOT ACTUALLY A ROCK STAR.
THE PROBLEM IS KOZUE AND YUMIKO. THE REST JUST FOLLOW THEM.
THOSE TWO ARE THE WEIRD ONES. SO PERSIS-TENT...
THEY GET WIND OF IT NO MATTER WHERE I GO AND COME RUNNING AFTER ME. THEY EVEN MANAGED TO TAG ALONG ON A TRIP I PLANNED IN SECRET.
THE MORE I TRY TO RUN, THE MORE INTO ME THEY GET. IT FEELS LIKE THEY'RE GOING TO FOLLOW ME MY WHOLE LIFE.
I'D EVEN LEAVE HOME IF IT MEANT I COULD GET AWAY FROM THEM.
IT'S JUST... LEAVING HOME'S NOT ENOUGH. TO REALLY ESCAPE...
...MY ONLY CHOICE IS TO FAKE MY DEATH. WILL YOU HELP ME?
WHOA! HANG ON.
YOU'VE REALLY THOUGHT ABOUT THIS... BUT AREN'T YOU KIND OF OVERDOING IT?
IF YOU HATE IT THAT MUCH, CAN'T YOU JUST TELL THEM?
I DID. BACK IN JUNIOR HIGH.
AND WHAT DO YOU THINK HAPPENED THEN?

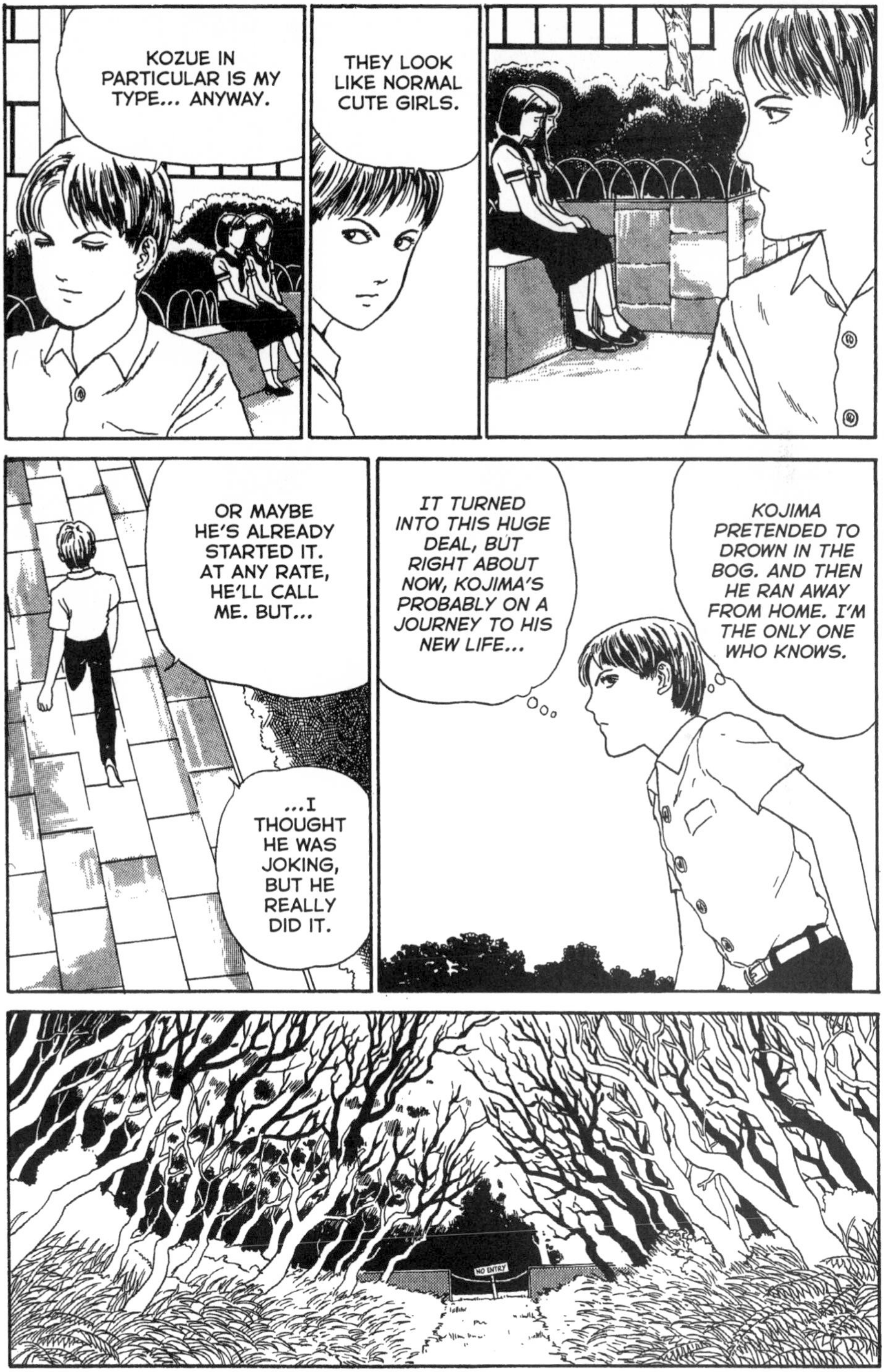
THEY LOOK LIKE NORMAL CUTE GIRLS.
KOZUE IN PARTICULAR IS MY TYPE... ANYWAY.
KOJIMA PRETENDED TO DROWN IN THE BOG. AND THEN HE RAN AWAY FROM HOME. I'M THE ONLY ONE WHO KNOWS.
IT TURNED INTO THIS HUGE DEAL, BUT RIGHT ABOUT NOW, KOJIMA'S PROBABLY ON A JOURNEY TO HIS NEW LIFE...
OR MAYBE HE'S ALREADY STARTED IT. AT ANY RATE, HE'LL CALL ME. BUT...
...I THOUGHT HE WAS JOKING, BUT HE REALLY DID IT.
NO ENTRY

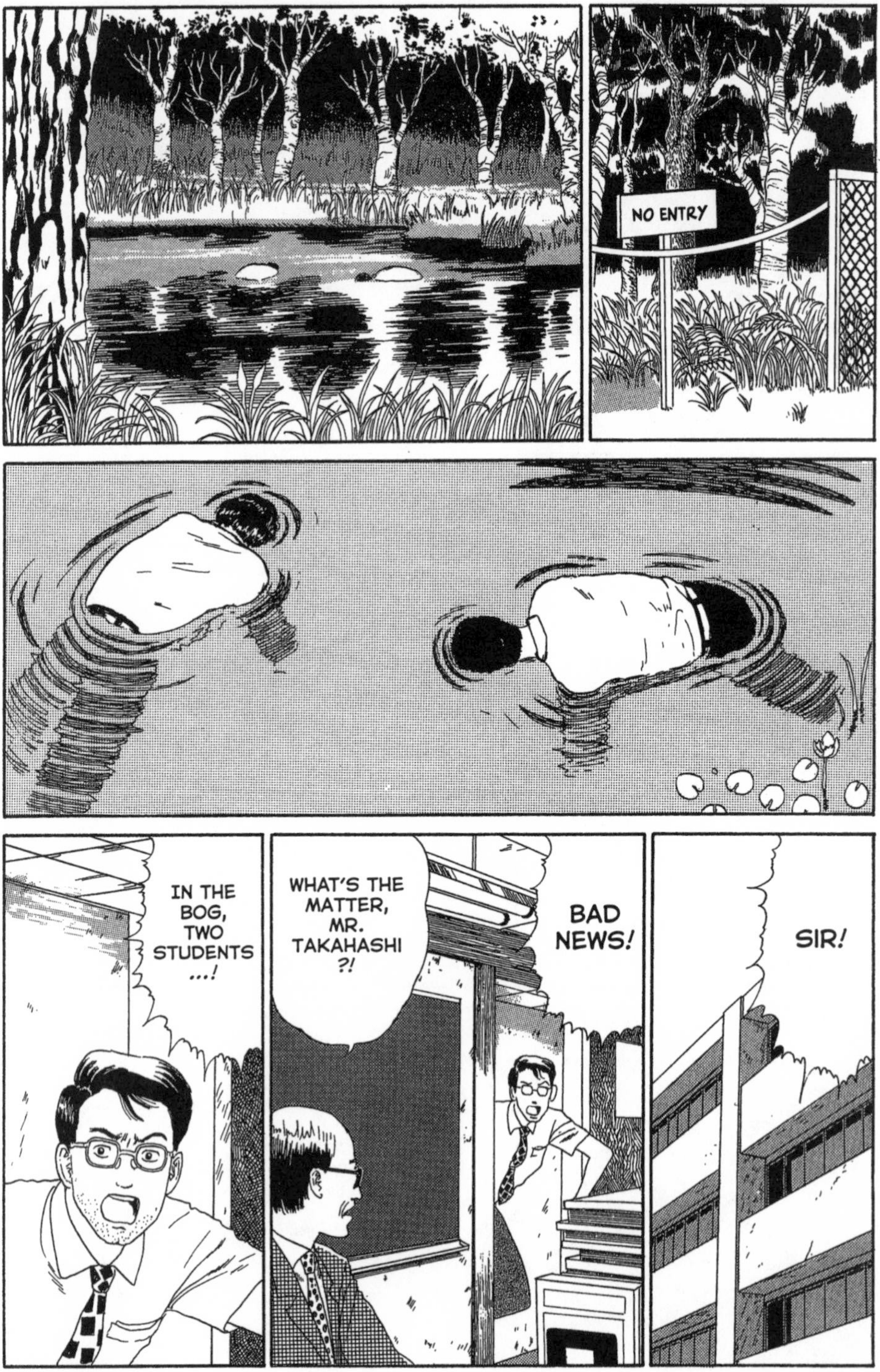
NO ENTRY
SIR!
BAD NEWS!
WHAT'S THE MATTER, MR. TAKAHASHI?!
IN THE BOG, TWO STUDENTS ...!

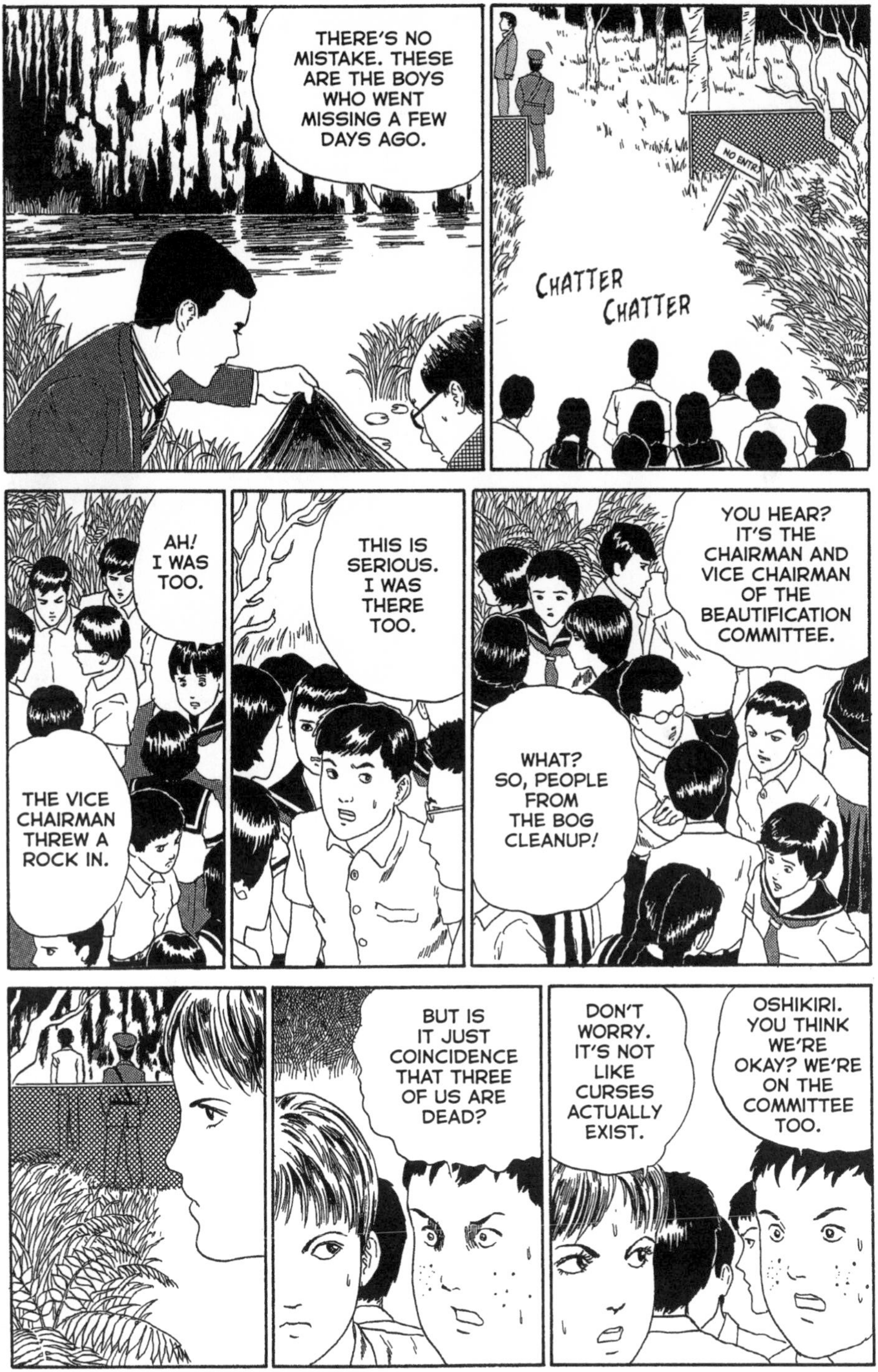
CHATTER CHATTER
THERE'S NO MISTAKE. THESE ARE THE BOYS WHO WENT MISSING A FEW DAYS AGO.
YOU HEAR? IT'S THE CHAIRMAN AND VICE CHAIRMAN OF THE BEAUTIFICATION COMMITTEE.
WHAT? SO, PEOPLE FROM THE BOG CLEANUP!
THIS IS SERIOUS. I WAS THERE TOO.
AH! I WAS TOO.
THE VICE CHAIRMAN THREW A ROCK IN.
OSHIKIRI. YOU THINK WE'RE OKAY? WE'RE ON THE COMMITTEE TOO.
DON'T WORRY. IT'S NOT LIKE CURSES ACTUALLY EXIST.
BUT IS IT JUST COINCIDENCE THAT THREE OF US ARE DEAD?

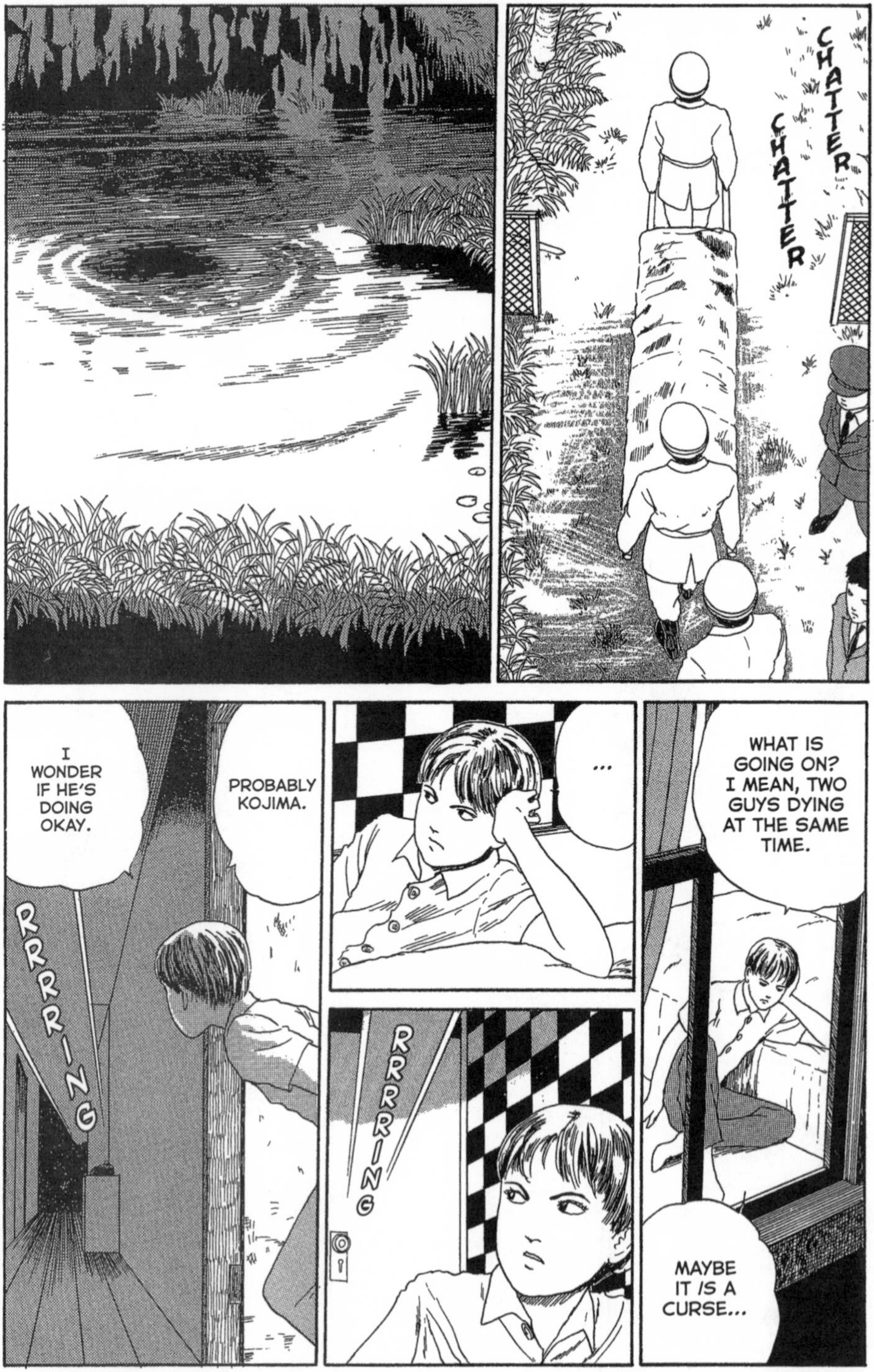

CHATTER CHATTER
WHAT IS GOING ON? I MEAN, TWO GUYS DYING AT THE SAME TIME.
MAYBE IT *IS* A CURSE...
...
RRRRING
PROBABLY KOJIMA.
I WONDER IF HE'S DOING OKAY.
RRRRING

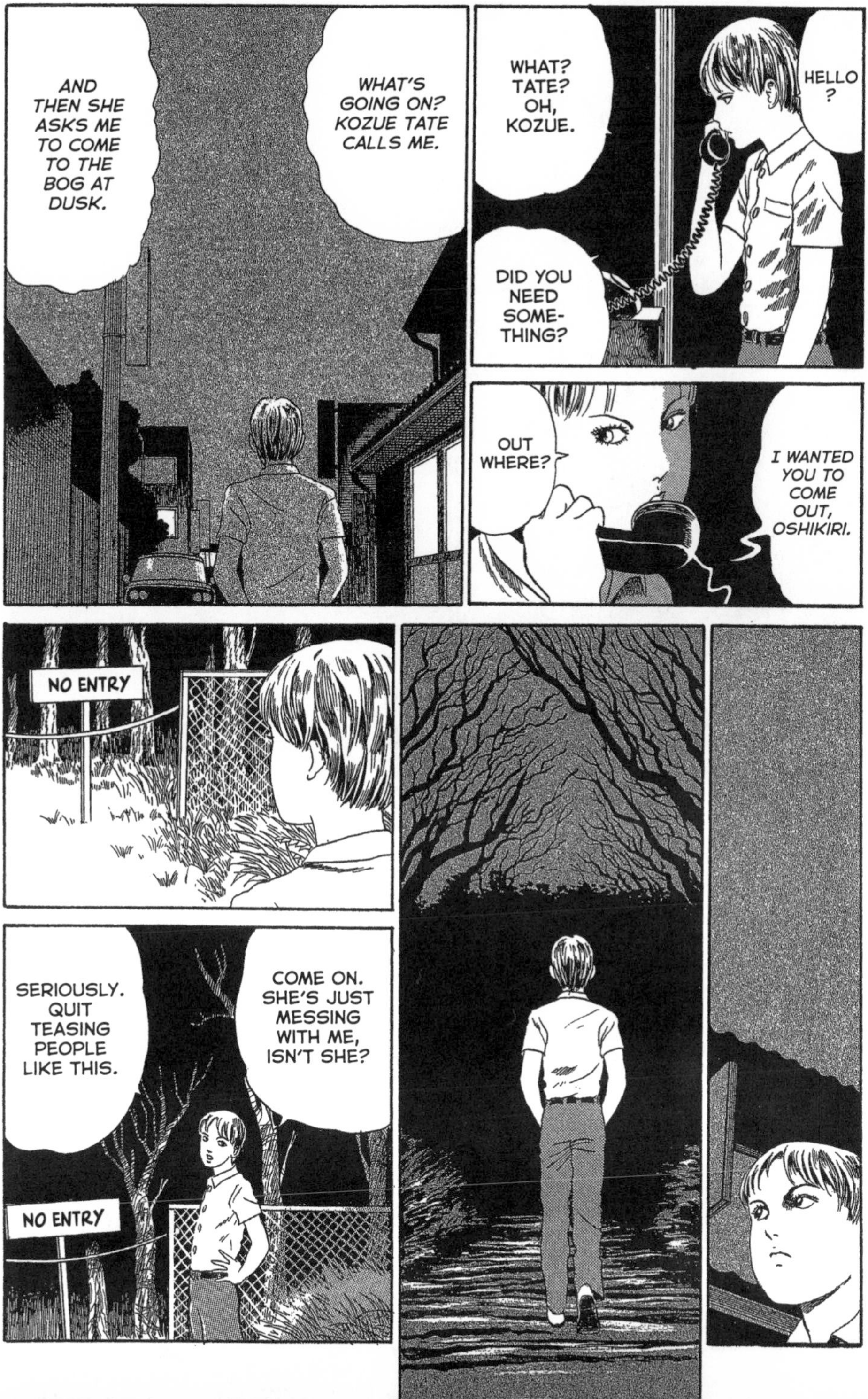
HELLO?
WHAT? TATE? OH, KOZUE.
DID YOU NEED SOMETHING?
I WANTED YOU TO COME OUT, OSHIKIRI.
OUT WHERE?
WHAT'S GOING ON? KOZUE TATE CALLS ME.
AND THEN SHE ASKS ME TO COME TO THE BOG AT DUSK.
NO ENTRY
COME ON. SHE'S JUST MESSING WITH ME, ISN'T SHE?
SERIOUSLY. QUIT TEASING PEOPLE LIKE THIS.
NO ENTRY

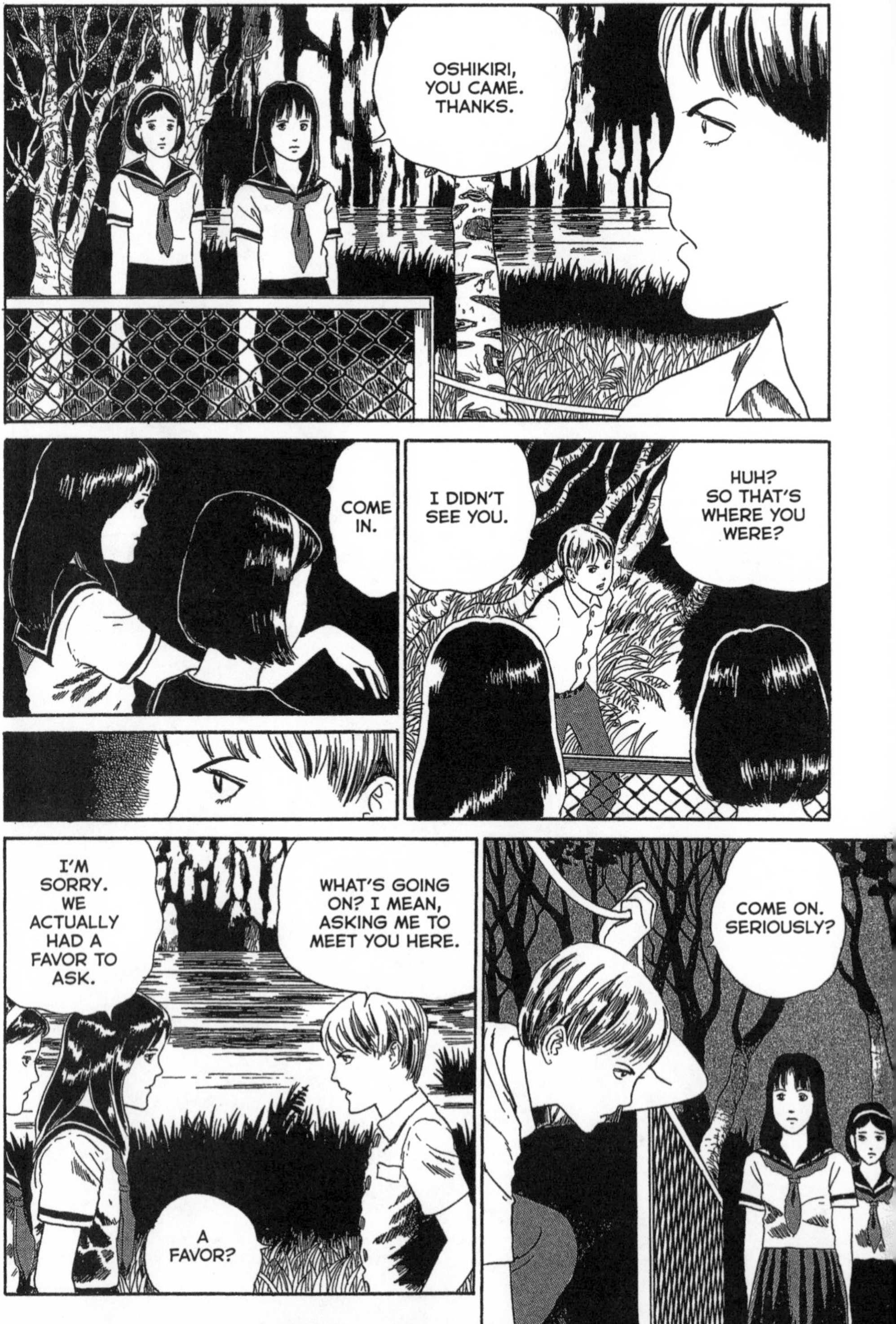
OSHIKIRI, YOU CAME. THANKS.
HUH? SO THAT'S WHERE YOU WERE?
I DIDN'T SEE YOU.
COME IN.
COME ON. SERIOUSLY?
WHAT'S GOING ON? I MEAN, ASKING ME TO MEET YOU HERE.
I'M SORRY. WE ACTUALLY HAD A FAVOR TO ASK.
A FAVOR?

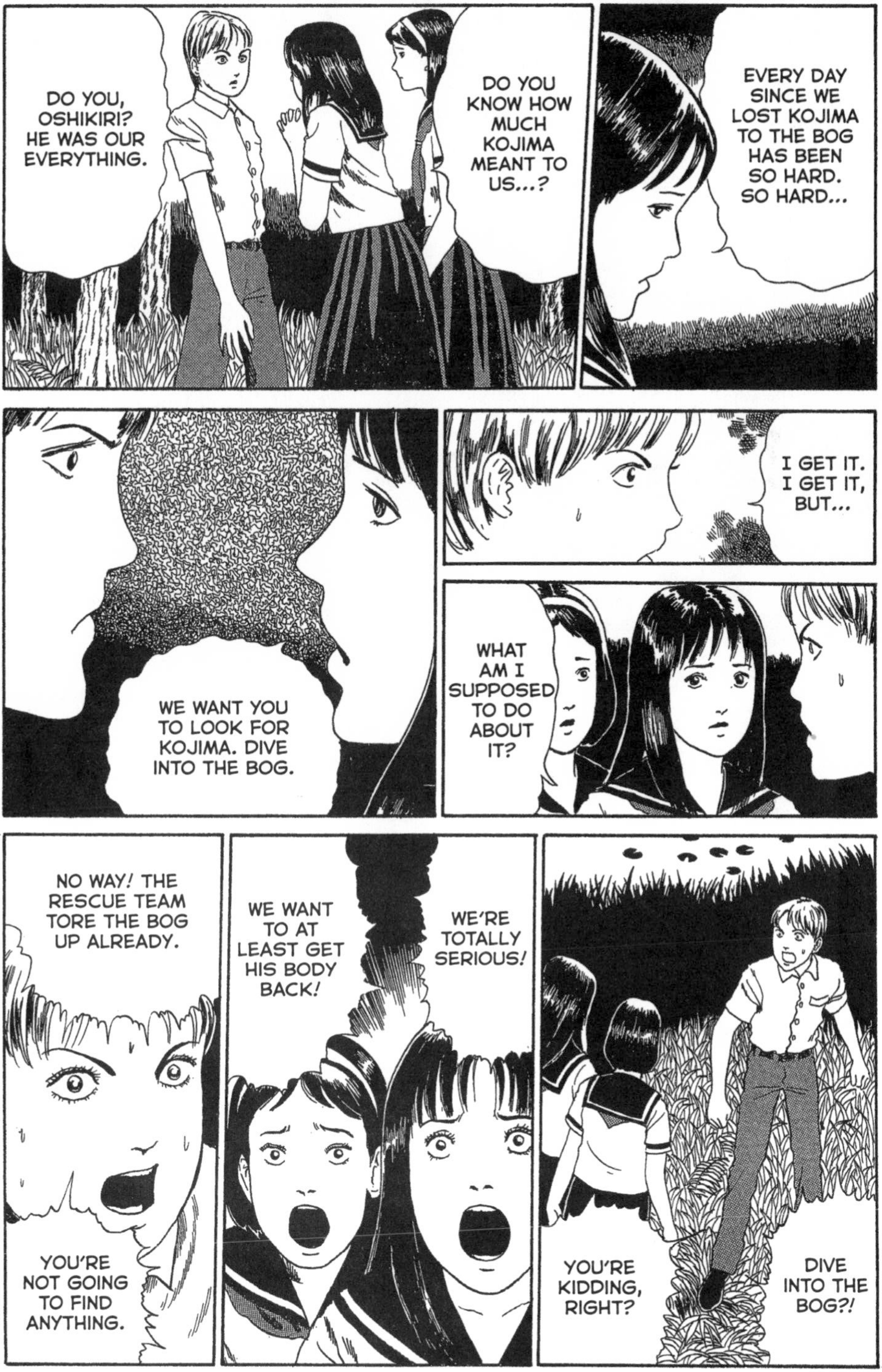
EVERY DAY SINCE WE LOST KOJIMA TO THE BOG HAS BEEN SO HARD. SO HARD...
DO YOU KNOW HOW MUCH KOJIMA MEANT TO US...?
DO YOU, OSHIKIRI? HE WAS OUR EVERYTHING.
I GET IT. I GET IT, BUT...
WHAT AM I SUPPOSED TO DO ABOUT IT?
WE WANT YOU TO LOOK FOR KOJIMA. DIVE INTO THE BOG.
DIVE INTO THE BOG?!
YOU'RE KIDDING, RIGHT?
WE'RE TOTALLY SERIOUS!
WE WANT TO AT LEAST GET HIS BODY BACK!
NO WAY! THE RESCUE TEAM TORE THE BOG UP ALREADY.
YOU'RE NOT GOING TO FIND ANYTHING.

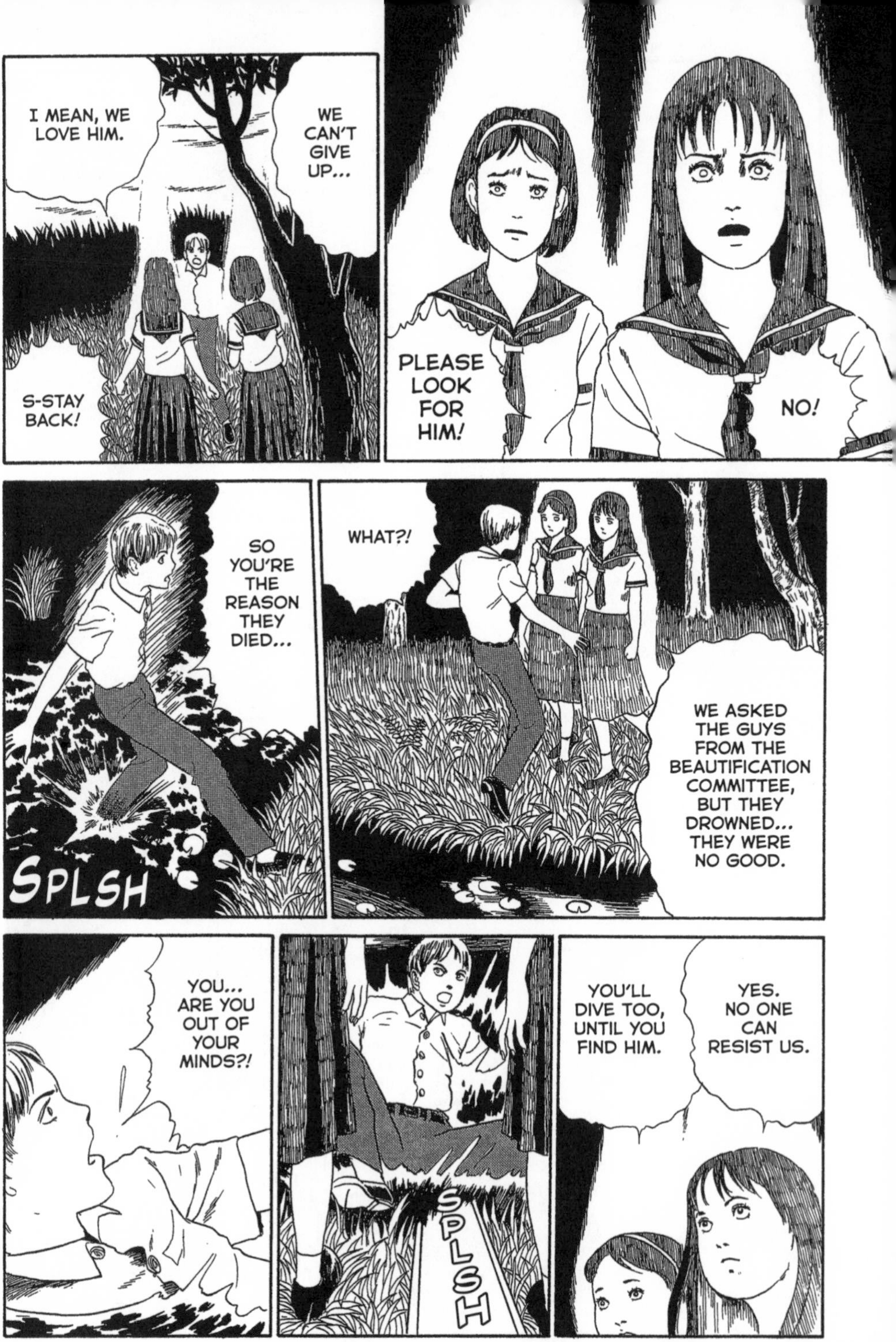
PLEASE LOOK FOR HIM!
NO!
WE CAN'T GIVE UP...
I MEAN, WE LOVE HIM.
S-STAY BACK!
WE ASKED THE GUYS FROM THE BEAUTIFICATION COMMITTEE, BUT THEY DROWNED... THEY WERE NO GOOD.
WHAT?!
SO YOU'RE THE REASON THEY DIED...
SPLSH
YES. NO ONE CAN RESIST US.
YOU'LL DIVE TOO, UNTIL YOU FIND HIM.
SPLSH
YOU... ARE YOU OUT OF YOUR MINDS?!

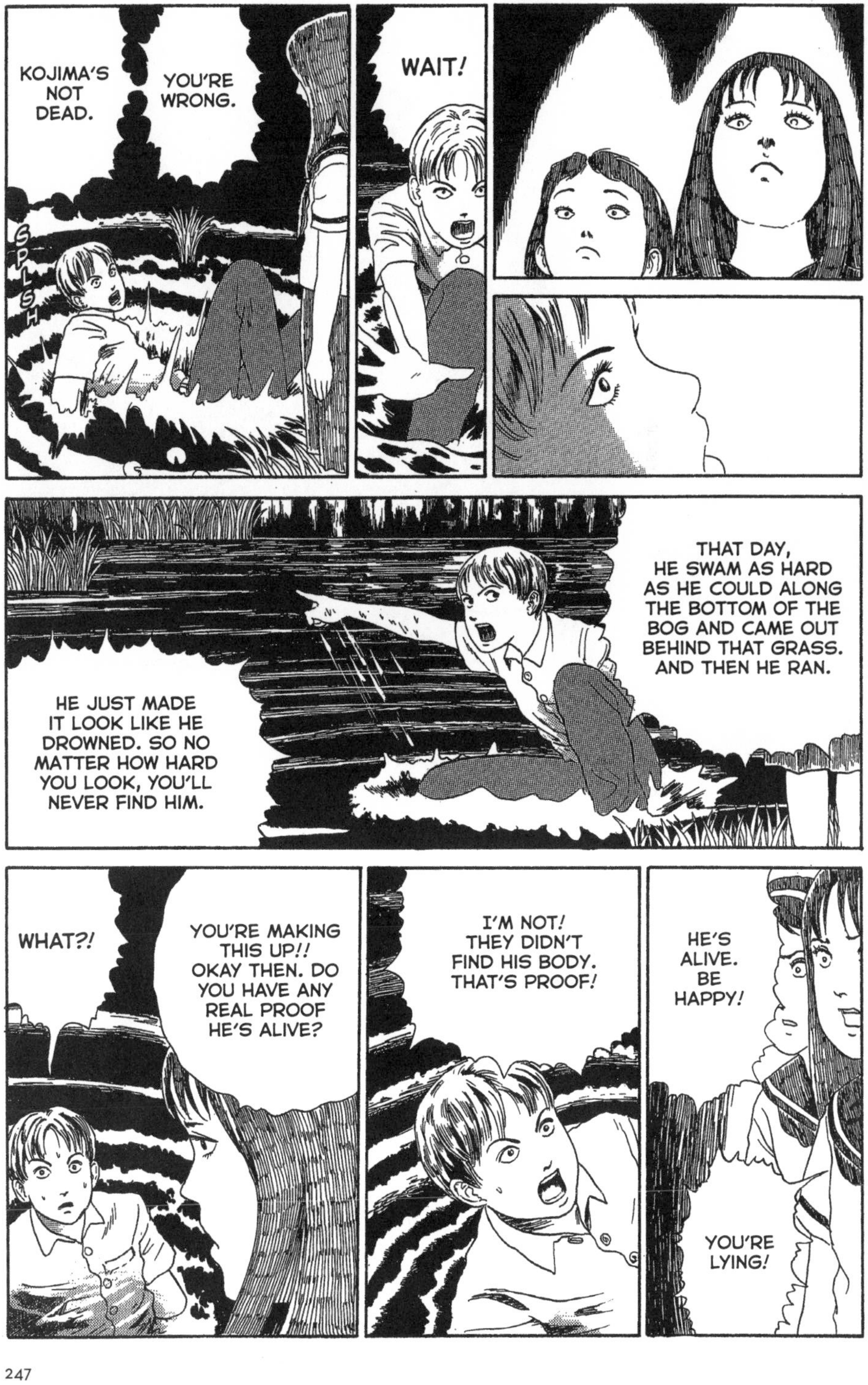

WAIT!
YOU'RE WRONG.
KOJIMA'S NOT DEAD.
SPLSH
THAT DAY, HE SWAM AS HARD AS HE COULD ALONG THE BOTTOM OF THE BOG AND CAME OUT BEHIND THAT GRASS. AND THEN HE RAN.
HE JUST MADE IT LOOK LIKE HE DROWNED. SO NO MATTER HOW HARD YOU LOOK, YOU'LL NEVER FIND HIM.
HE'S ALIVE. BE HAPPY!
YOU'RE LYING!
I'M NOT! THEY DIDN'T FIND HIS BODY. THAT'S PROOF!
YOU'RE MAKING THIS UP!! OKAY THEN. DO YOU HAVE ANY REAL PROOF HE'S ALIVE?
WHAT?!

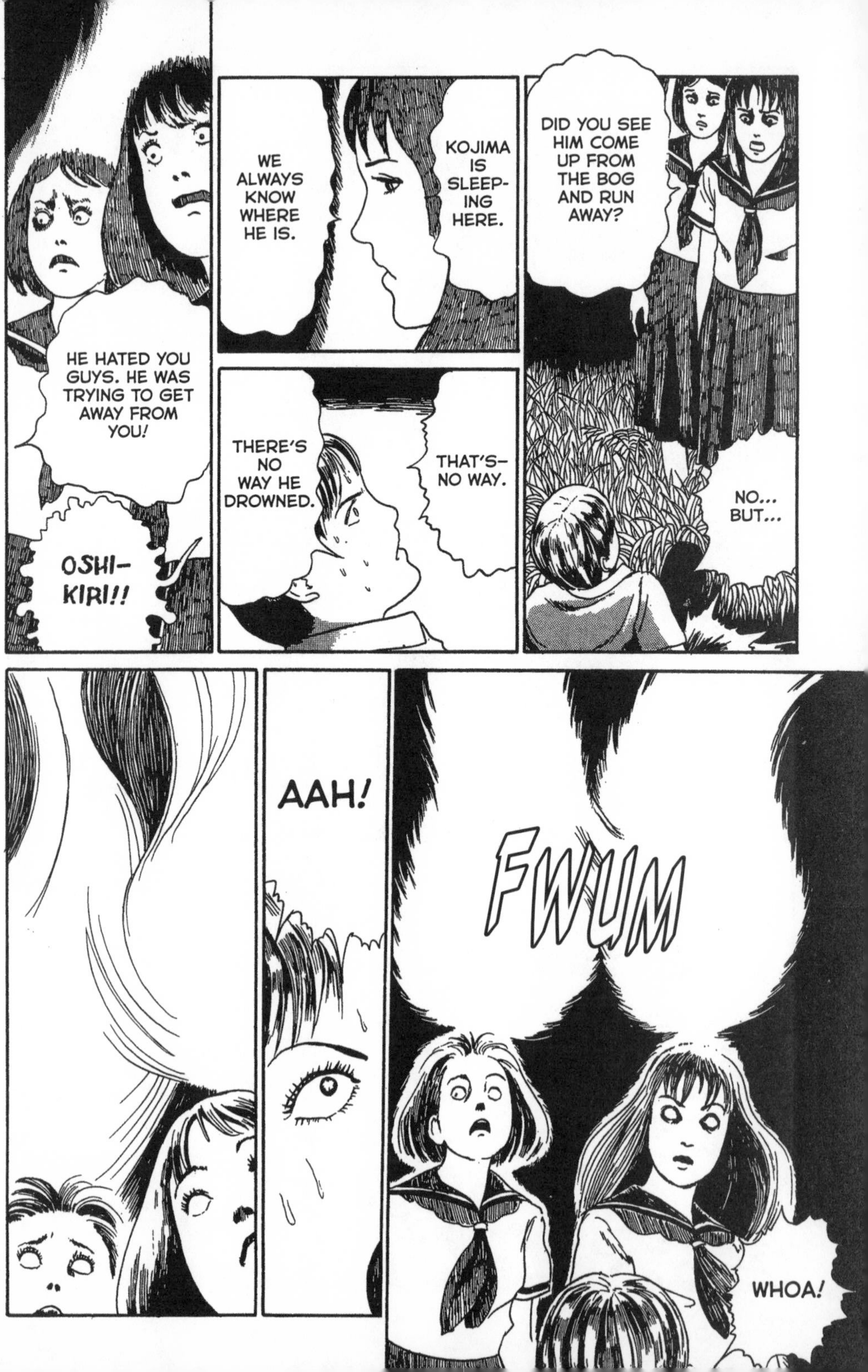
DID YOU SEE HIM COME UP FROM THE BOG AND RUN AWAY?
NO... BUT...
KOJIMA IS SLEEP-ING HERE.
WE ALWAYS KNOW WHERE HE IS.
THAT'S— NO WAY.
THERE'S NO WAY HE DROWNED.
HE HATED YOU GUYS. HE WAS TRYING TO GET AWAY FROM YOU!
OSHI-KIRI!!
FWUM
WHOA!
AAH!

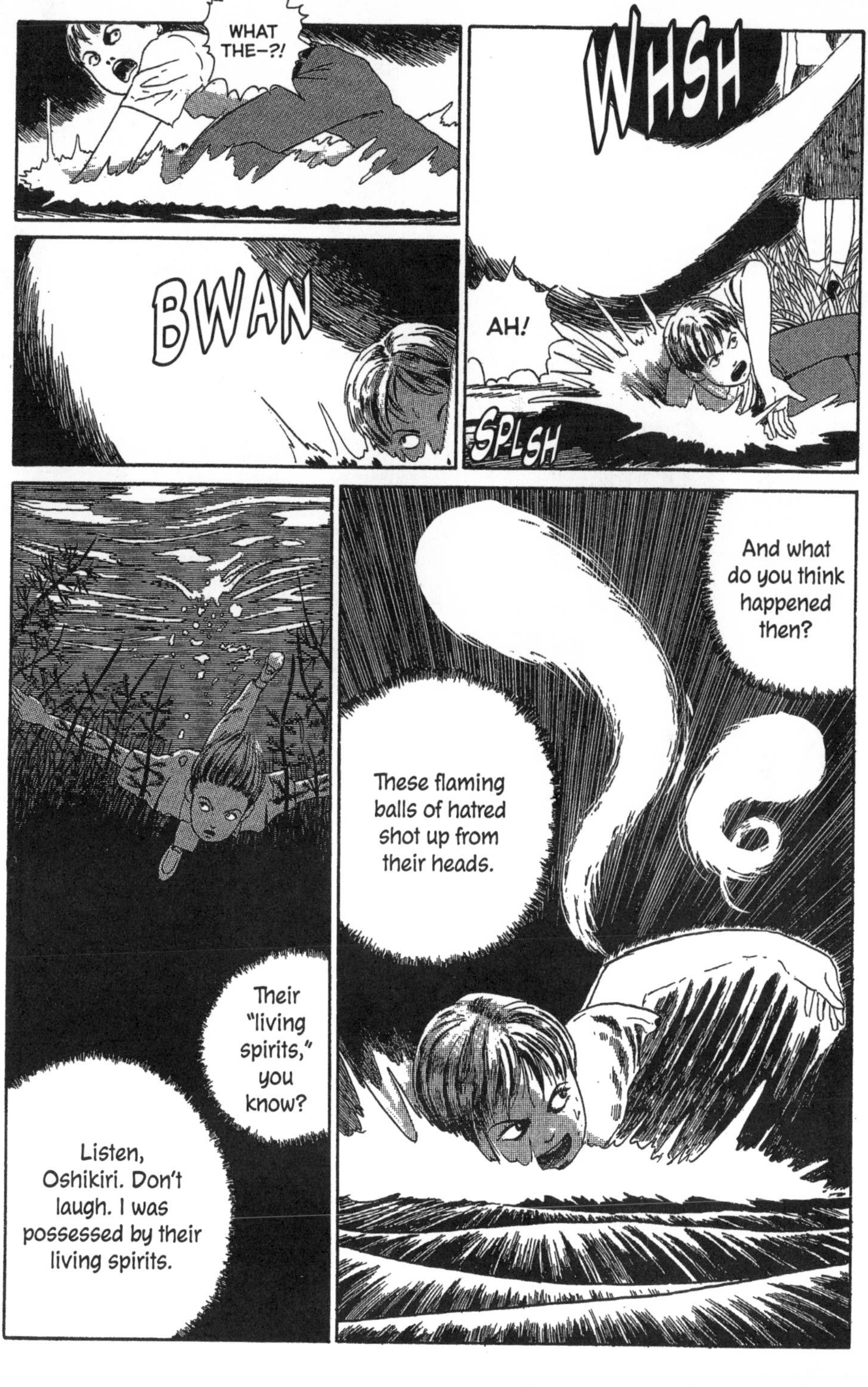
WHSH
AH!
SPLSH
WHAT THE-?!
BWAN
And what do you think happened then?
These flaming balls of hatred shot up from their heads.
Their "living spirits," you know?
Listen, Oshikiri. Don't laugh. I was possessed by their living spirits.

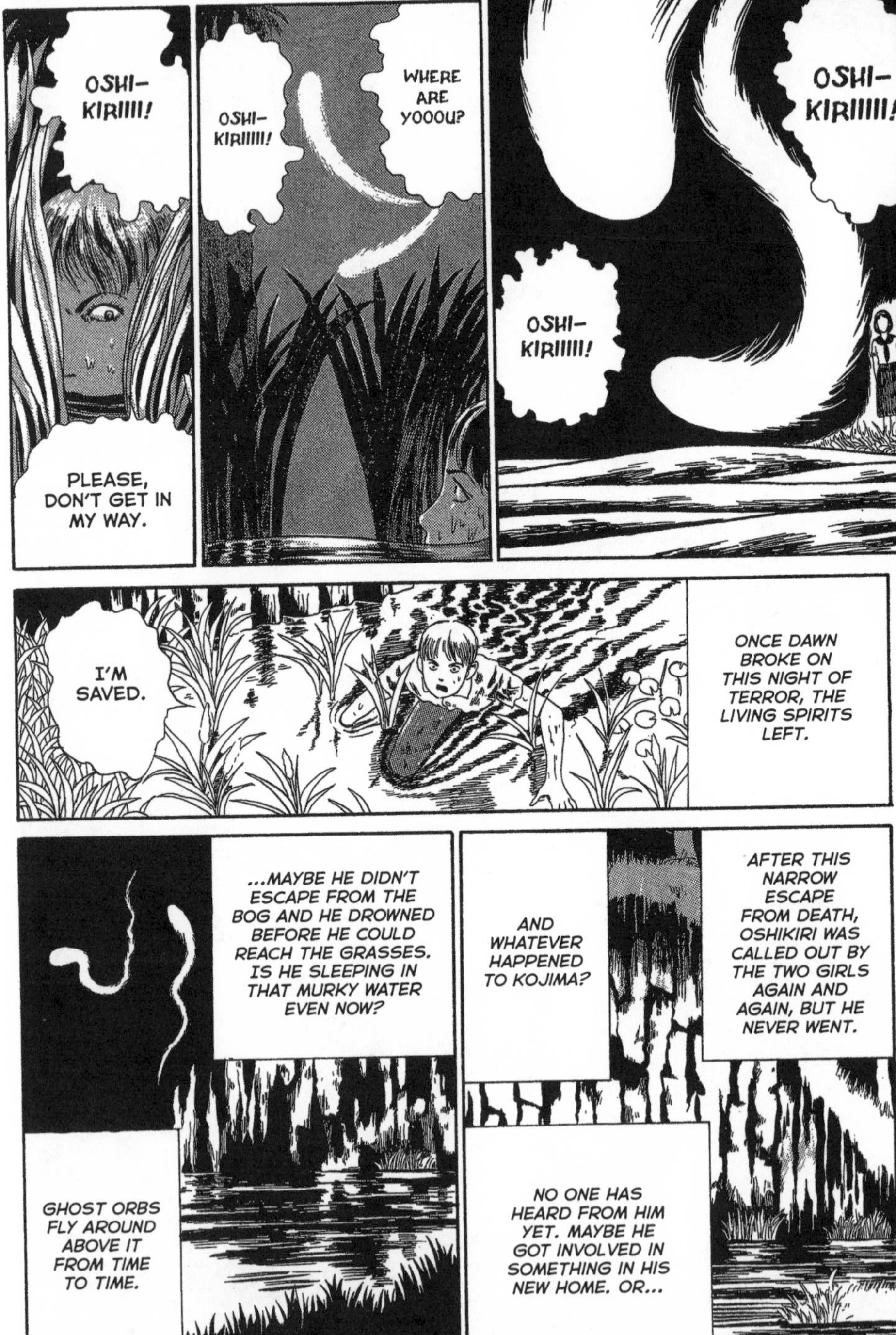
OSHI-KIRIIIIII!
OSHI-KIRIIIIII!
WHERE ARE YOOOU?
OSHI-KIRIIIIII!
OSHI-KIRIIIII!
PLEASE, DON'T GET IN MY WAY.
ONCE DAWN BROKE ON THIS NIGHT OF TERROR, THE LIVING SPIRITS LEFT.
I'M SAVED.
AFTER THIS NARROW ESCAPE FROM DEATH, OSHIKIRI WAS CALLED OUT BY THE TWO GIRLS AGAIN AND AGAIN, BUT HE NEVER WENT.
AND WHATEVER HAPPENED TO KOJIMA?
NO ONE HAS HEARD FROM HIM YET. MAYBE HE GOT INVOLVED IN SOMETHING IN HIS NEW HOME. OR...
...MAYBE HE DIDN'T ESCAPE FROM THE BOG AND HE DROWNED BEFORE HE COULD REACH THE GRASSES. IS HE SLEEPING IN THAT MURKY WATER EVEN NOW?
GHOST ORBS FLY AROUND ABOVE IT FROM TIME TO TIME.

BOG OF LIVING SPIRITS / END

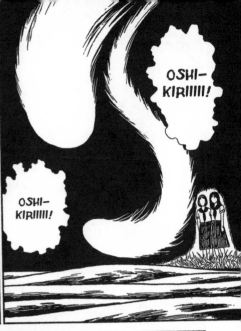

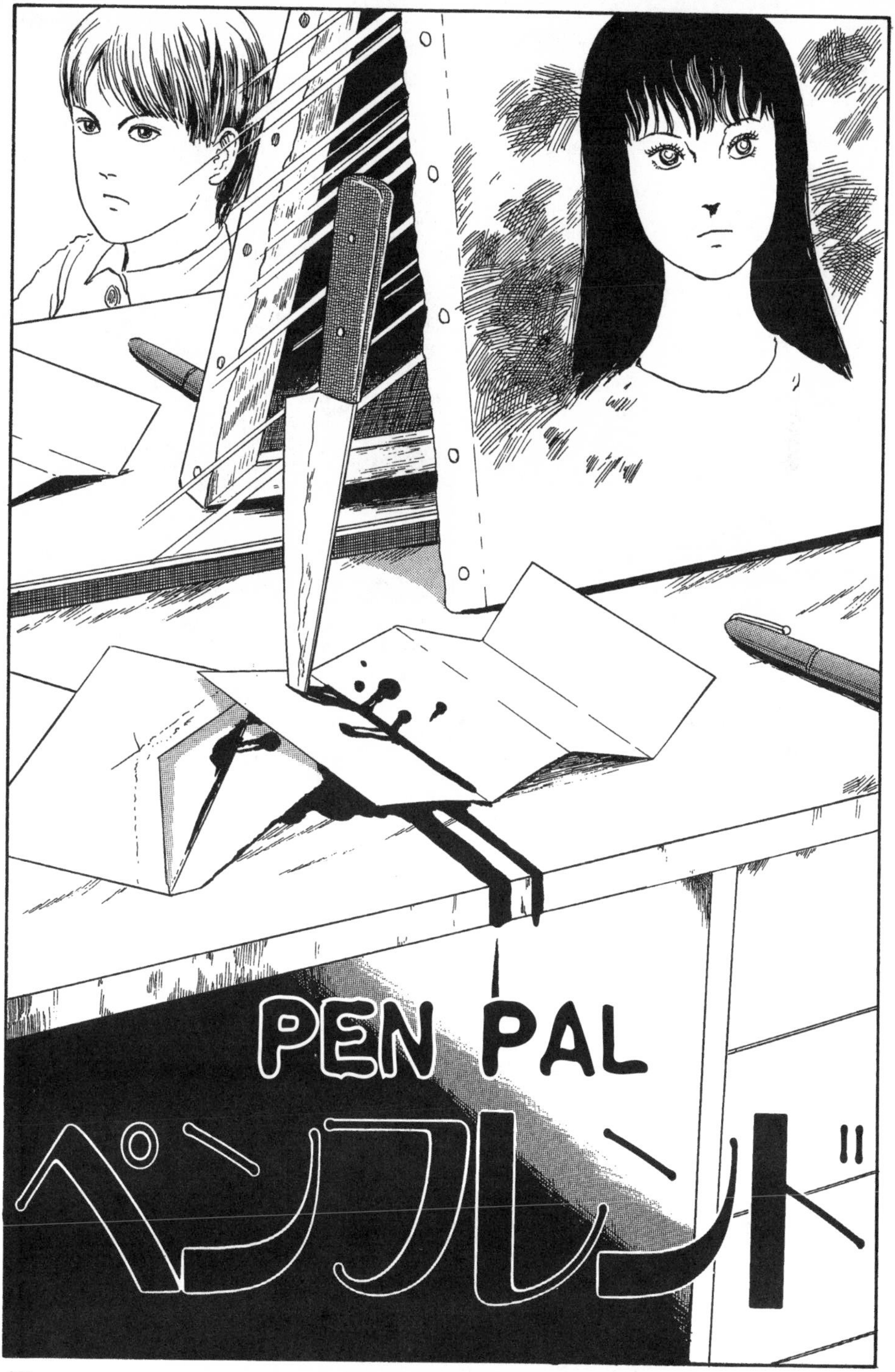
PEN PAL
ペンフレンド

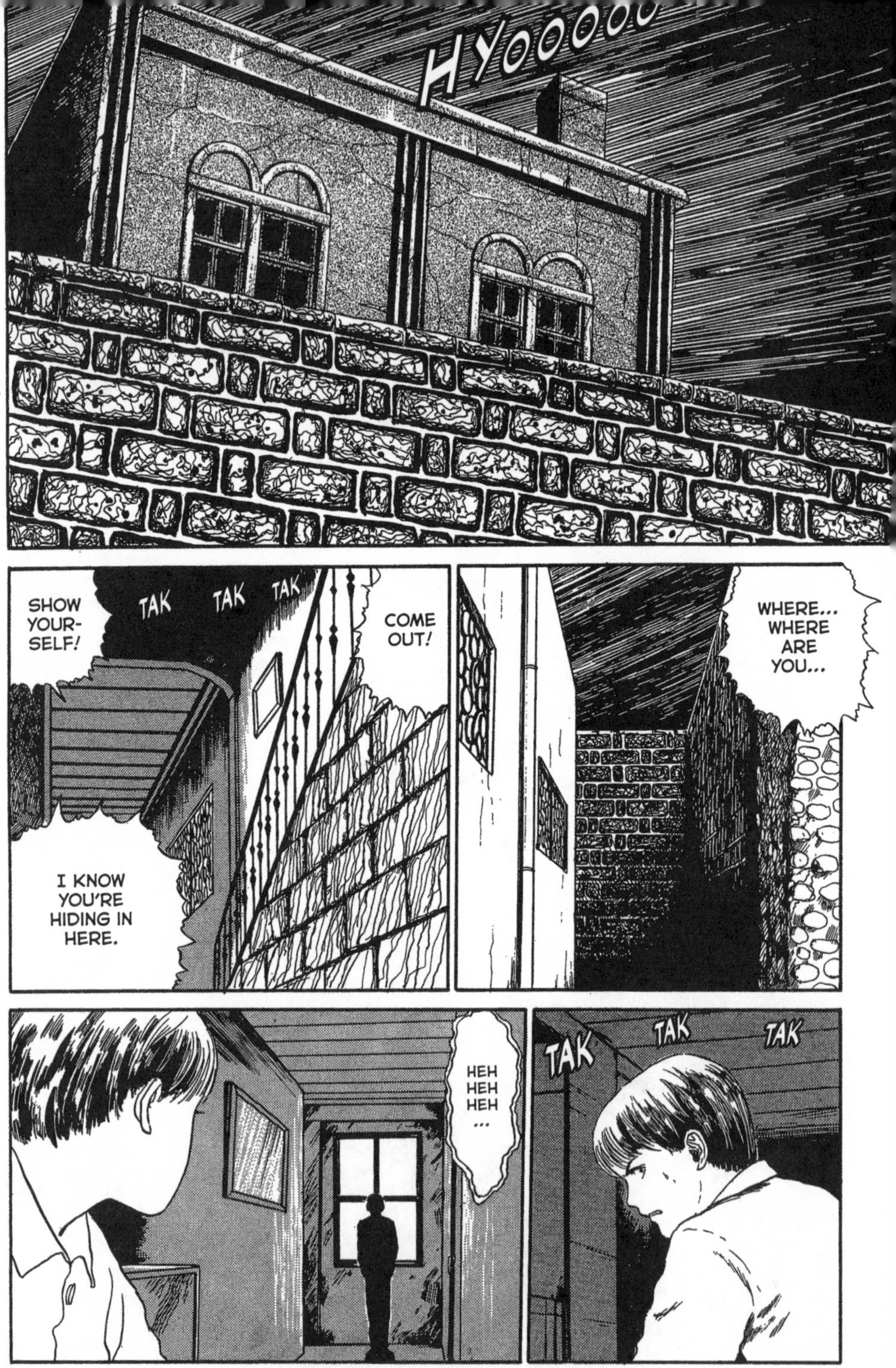
HYOOOO
WHERE... WHERE ARE YOU...
COME OUT!
TAK TAK TAK
SHOW YOUR-SELF!
I KNOW YOU'RE HIDING IN HERE.
TAK TAK TAK
HEH HEH HEH...

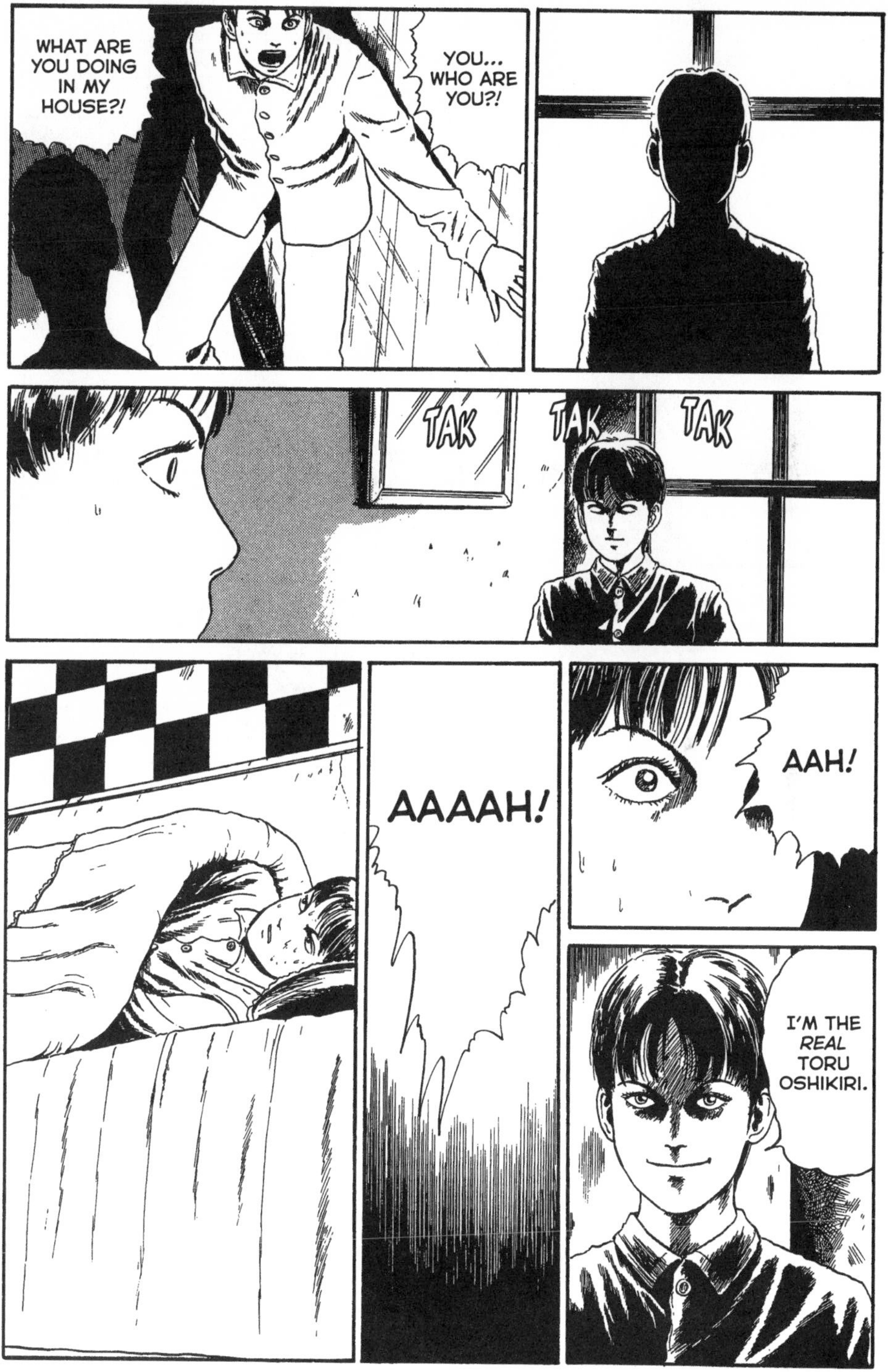
YOU... WHO ARE YOU?!
WHAT ARE YOU DOING IN MY HOUSE?!
TAK TAK TAK
AAH!
I'M THE *REAL* TORU OSHIKIRI.
AAAAH!

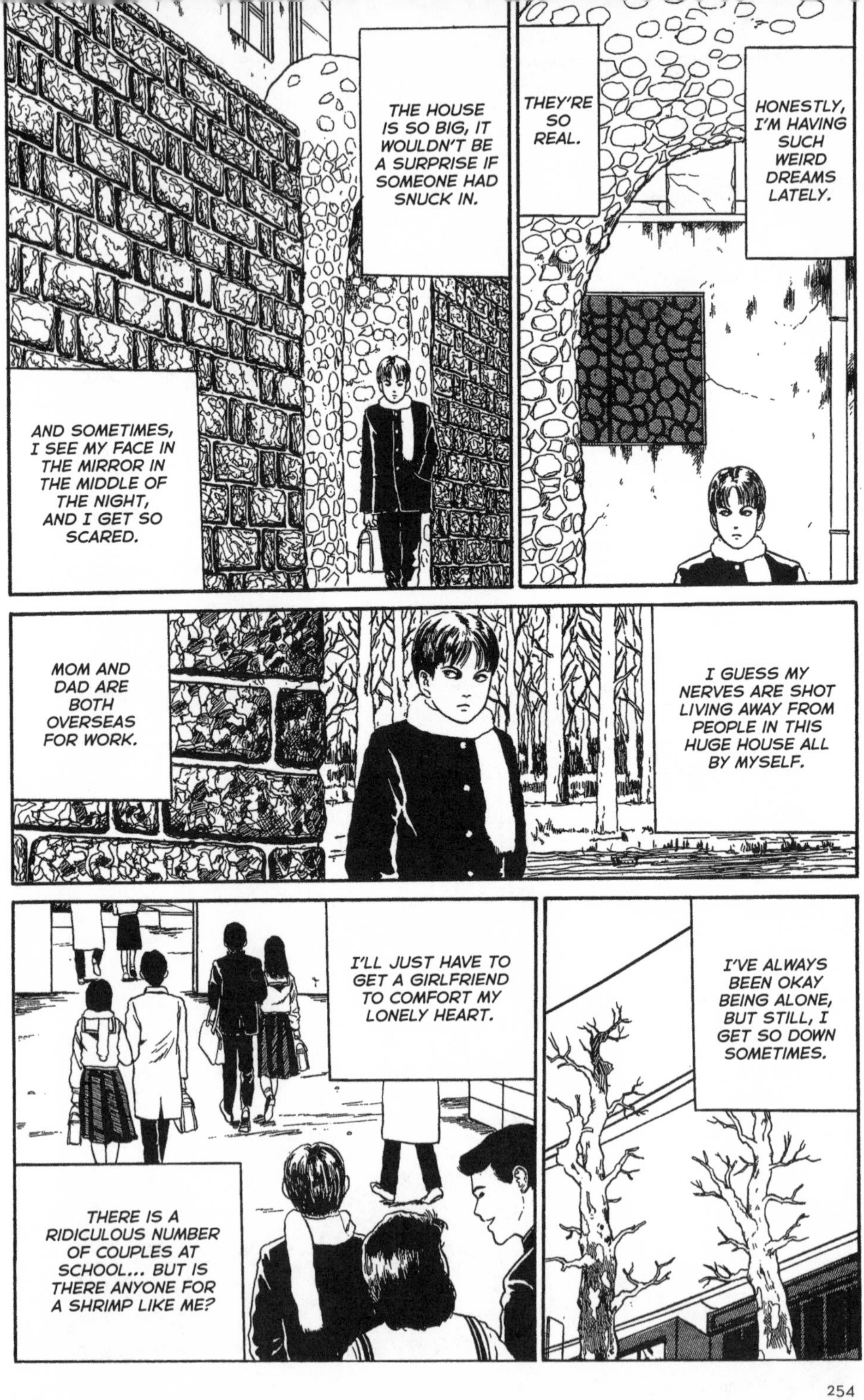
HONESTLY, I'M HAVING SUCH WEIRD DREAMS LATELY.
THEY'RE SO REAL.
THE HOUSE IS SO BIG, IT WOULDN'T BE A SURPRISE IF SOMEONE HAD SNUCK IN.
AND SOMETIMES, I SEE MY FACE IN THE MIRROR IN THE MIDDLE OF THE NIGHT, AND I GET SO SCARED.
I GUESS MY NERVES ARE SHOT LIVING AWAY FROM PEOPLE IN THIS HUGE HOUSE ALL BY MYSELF.
MOM AND DAD ARE BOTH OVERSEAS FOR WORK.
I'VE ALWAYS BEEN OKAY BEING ALONE, BUT STILL, I GET SO DOWN SOMETIMES.
I'LL JUST HAVE TO GET A GIRLFRIEND TO COMFORT MY LONELY HEART.
THERE IS A RIDICULOUS NUMBER OF COUPLES AT SCHOOL... BUT IS THERE ANYONE FOR A SHRIMP LIKE ME?

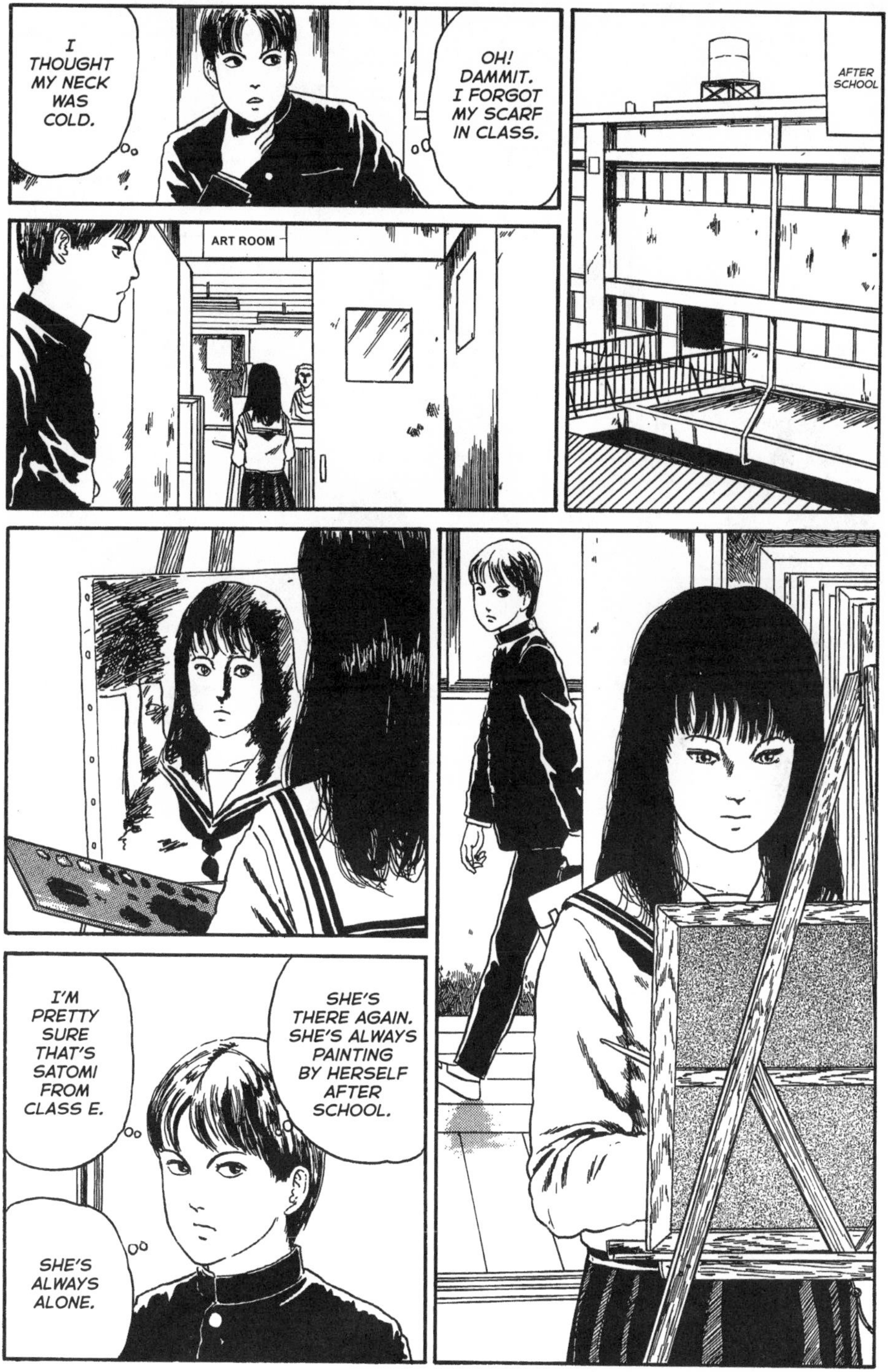
AFTER SCHOOL
OH! DAMMIT. I FORGOT MY SCARF IN CLASS.
I THOUGHT MY NECK WAS COLD.
ART ROOM
SHE'S THERE AGAIN. SHE'S ALWAYS PAINTING BY HERSELF AFTER SCHOOL.
I'M PRETTY SURE THAT'S SATOMI FROM CLASS E.
SHE'S ALWAYS ALONE.

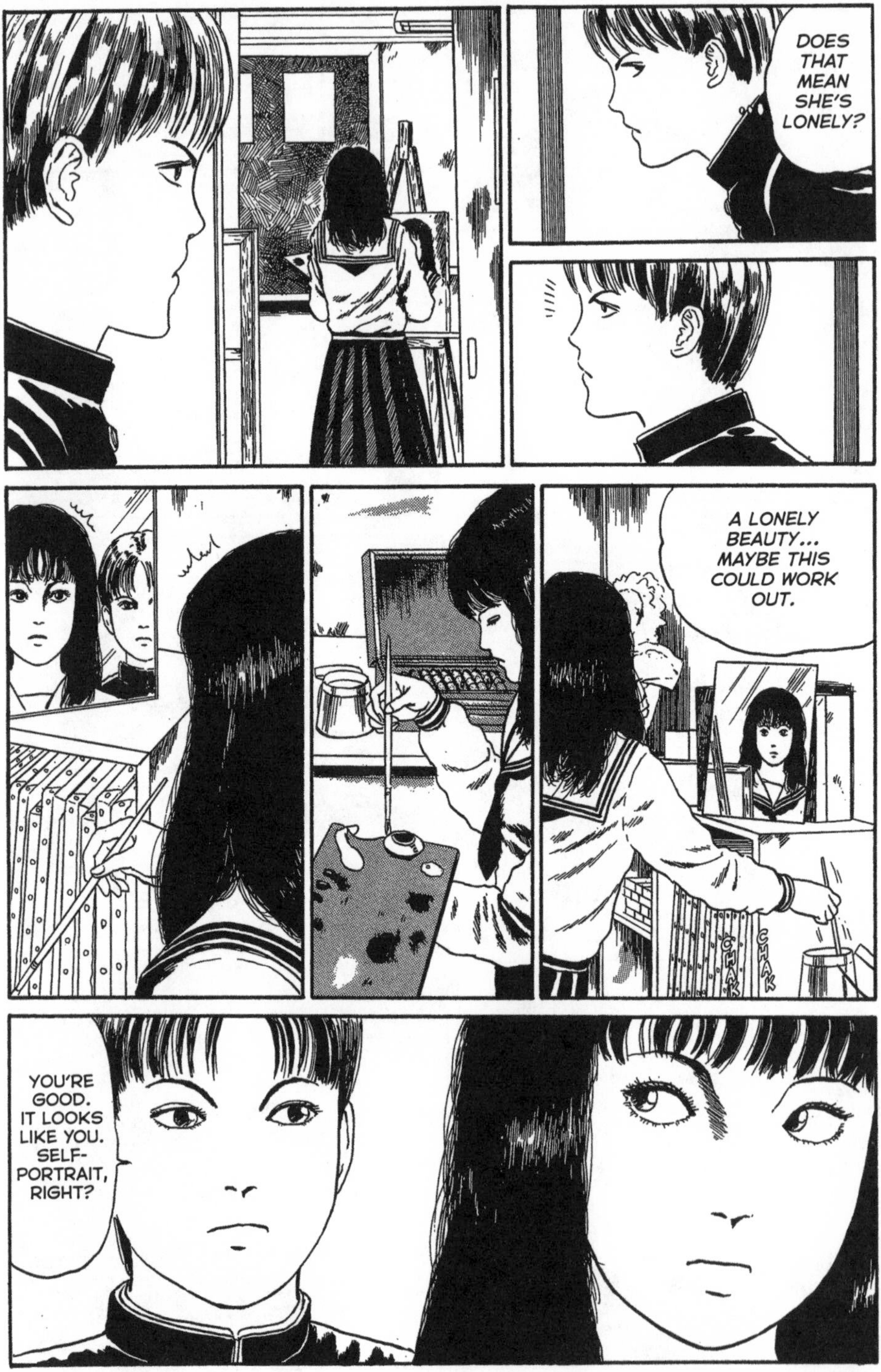
DOES THAT MEAN SHE'S LONELY?
A LONELY BEAUTY... MAYBE THIS COULD WORK OUT.
CHAK
CHAK
YOU'RE GOOD. IT LOOKS LIKE YOU. SELF-PORTRAIT, RIGHT?

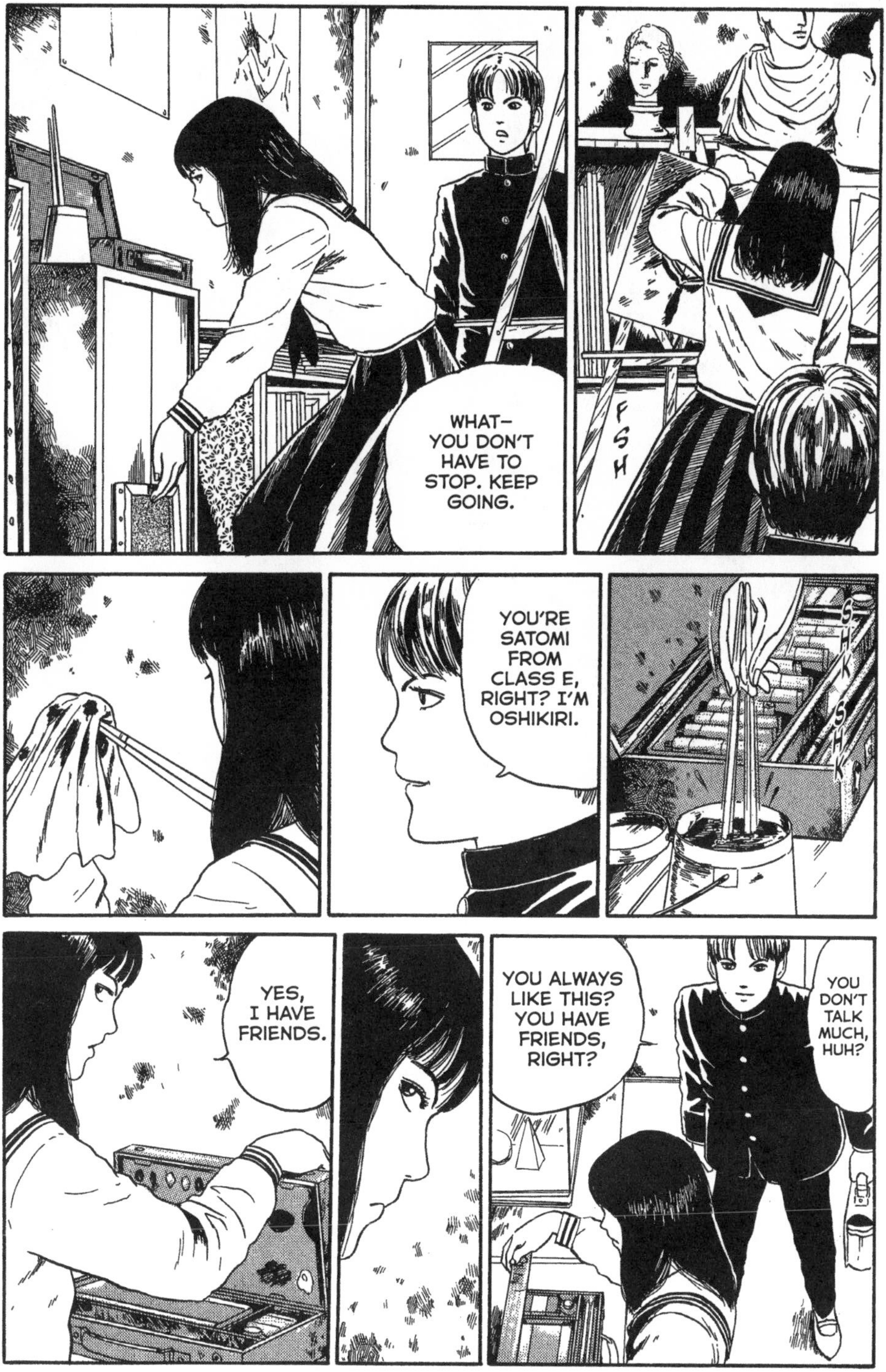
FSH
WHAT— YOU DON'T HAVE TO STOP. KEEP GOING.
SHK SHK
YOU'RE SATOMI FROM CLASS E, RIGHT? I'M OSHIKIRI.
YOU DON'T TALK MUCH, HUH?
YOU ALWAYS LIKE THIS? YOU HAVE FRIENDS, RIGHT?
YES, I HAVE FRIENDS.

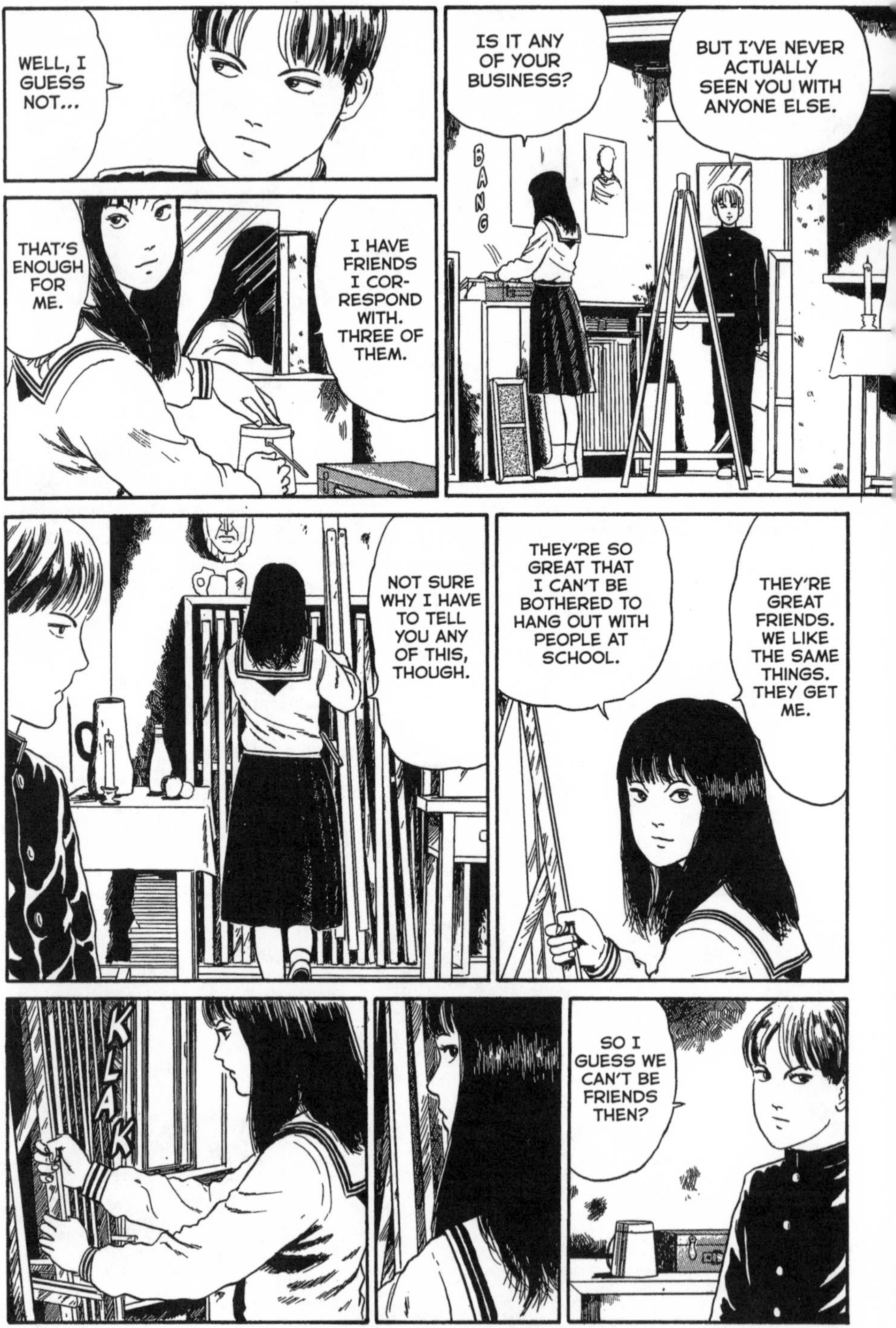
BUT I'VE NEVER ACTUALLY SEEN YOU WITH ANYONE ELSE.
IS IT ANY OF YOUR BUSINESS?
BANG
WELL, I GUESS NOT...
I HAVE FRIENDS I COR-RESPOND WITH. THREE OF THEM.
THAT'S ENOUGH FOR ME.
THEY'RE GREAT FRIENDS. WE LIKE THE SAME THINGS. THEY GET ME.
THEY'RE SO GREAT THAT I CAN'T BE BOTHERED TO HANG OUT WITH PEOPLE AT SCHOOL.
NOT SURE WHY I HAVE TO TELL YOU ANY OF THIS, THOUGH.
SO I GUESS WE CAN'T BE FRIENDS THEN?
KLAK

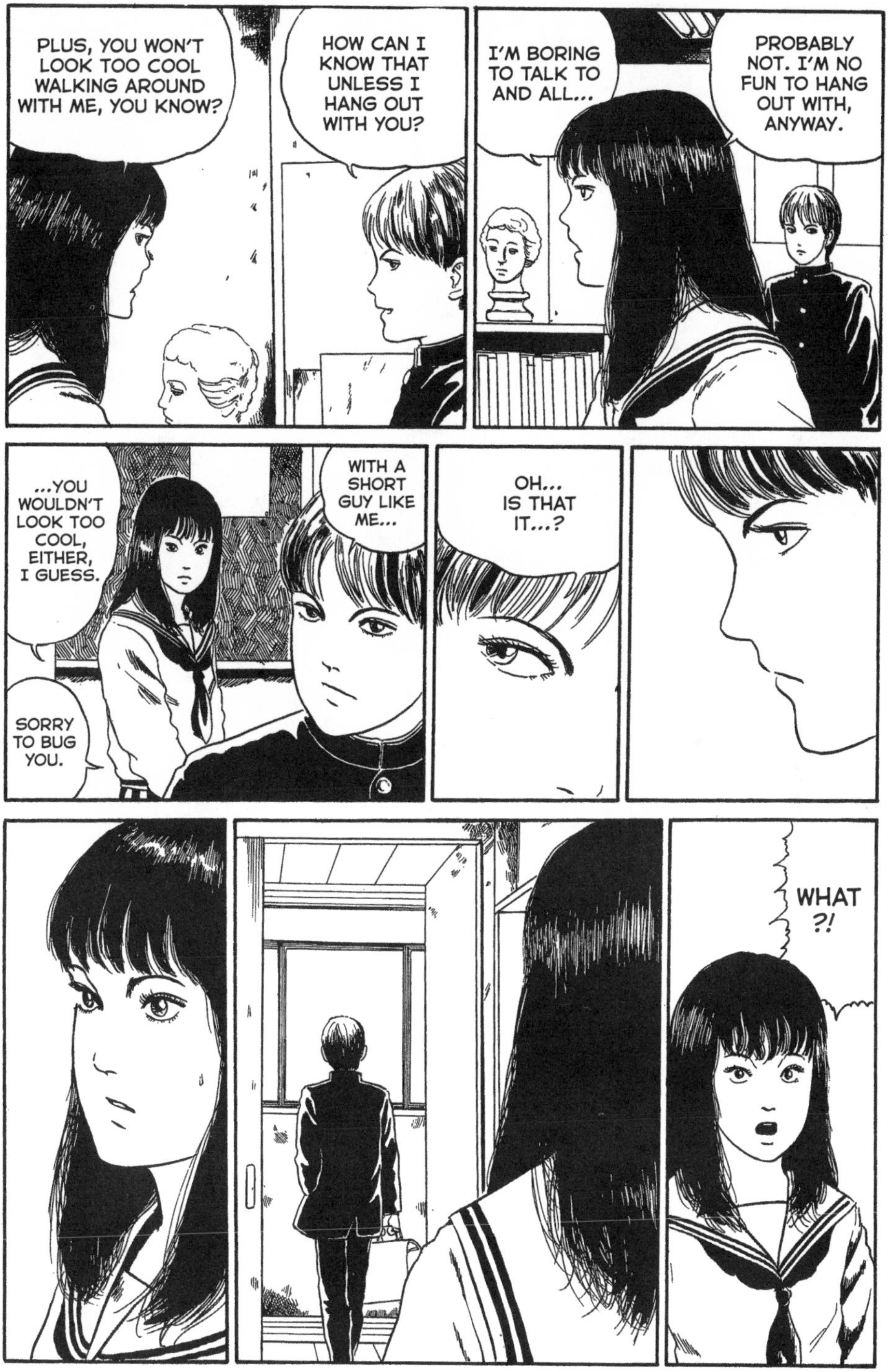
PROBABLY NOT. I'M NO FUN TO HANG OUT WITH, ANYWAY.
I'M BORING TO TALK TO AND ALL...
HOW CAN I KNOW THAT UNLESS I HANG OUT WITH YOU?
PLUS, YOU WON'T LOOK TOO COOL WALKING AROUND WITH ME, YOU KNOW?
OH... IS THAT IT...?
WITH A SHORT GUY LIKE ME...
...YOU WOULDN'T LOOK TOO COOL, EITHER, I GUESS.
SORRY TO BUG YOU.
WHAT ?!

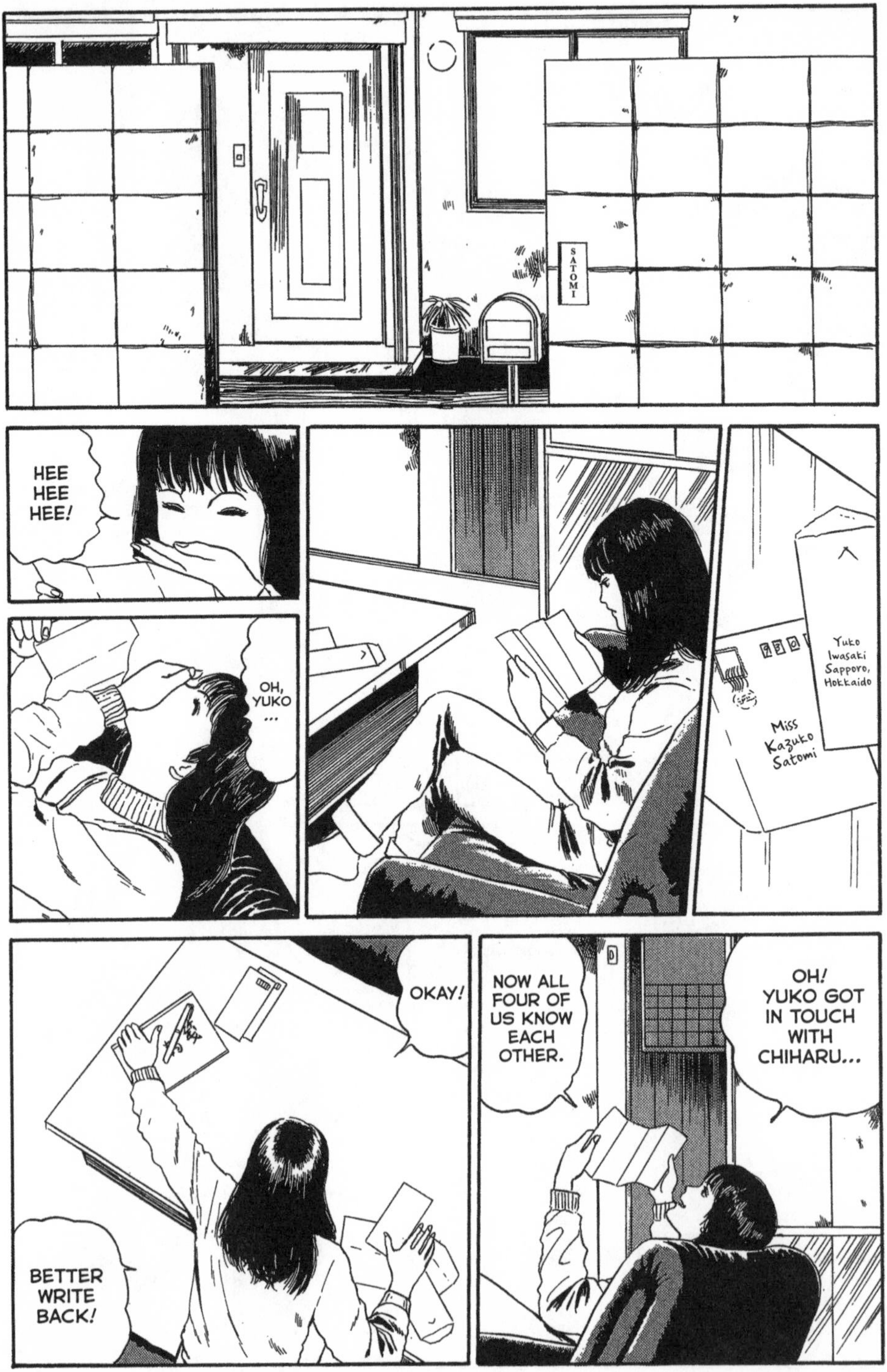
SATOMI
Yuko Iwasaki Sapporo, Hokkaido
Miss Kazuko Satomi
HEE HEE HEE!
OH, YUKO ...
OH! YUKO GOT IN TOUCH WITH CHIHARU...
NOW ALL FOUR OF US KNOW EACH OTHER.
OKAY!
BETTER WRITE BACK!

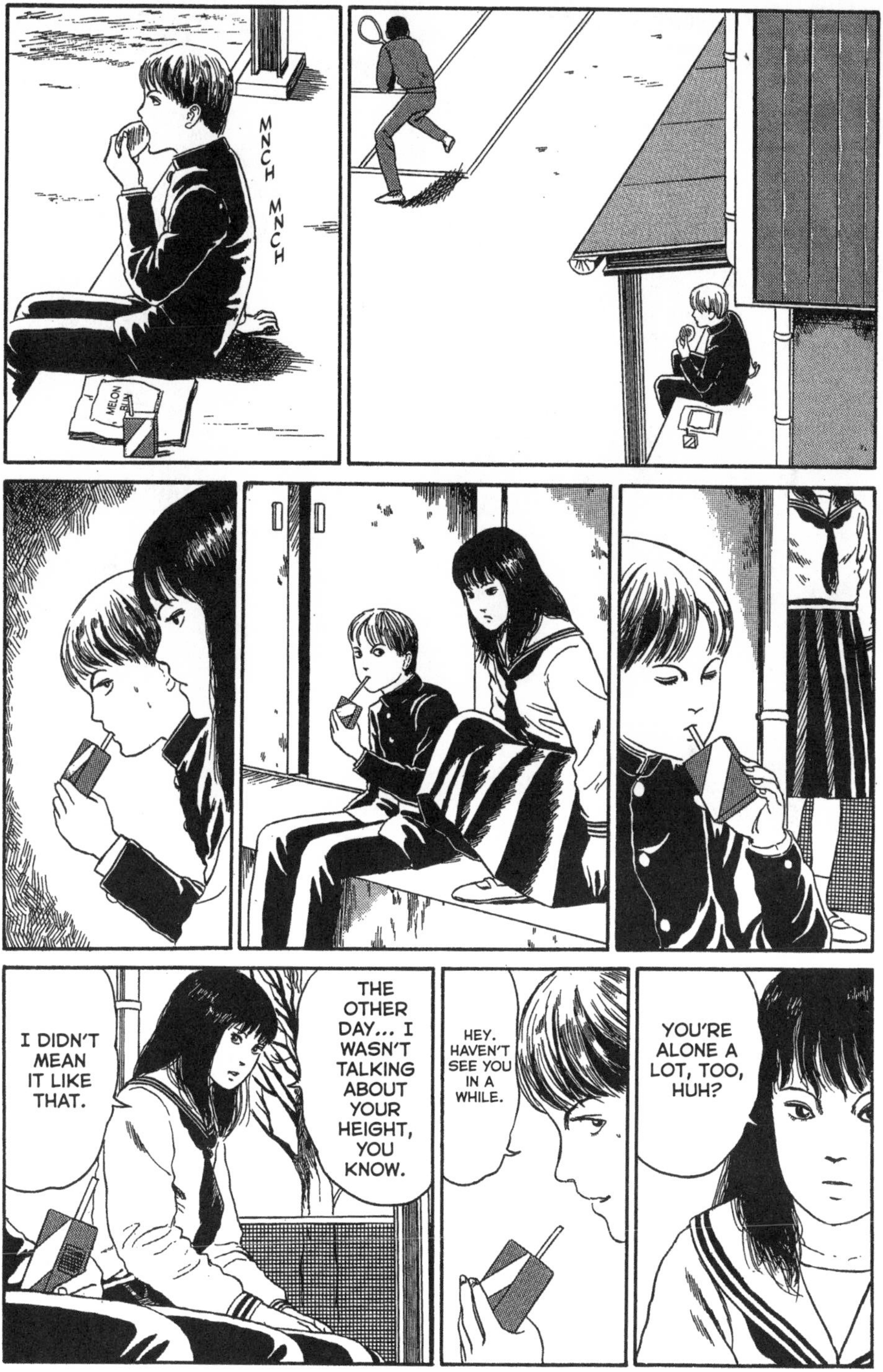
MNCH MNCH
MELON BUN
YOU'RE ALONE A LOT, TOO, HUH?
HEY. HAVEN'T SEE YOU IN A WHILE.
THE OTHER DAY... I WASN'T TALKING ABOUT YOUR HEIGHT, YOU KNOW.
I DIDN'T MEAN IT LIKE THAT.

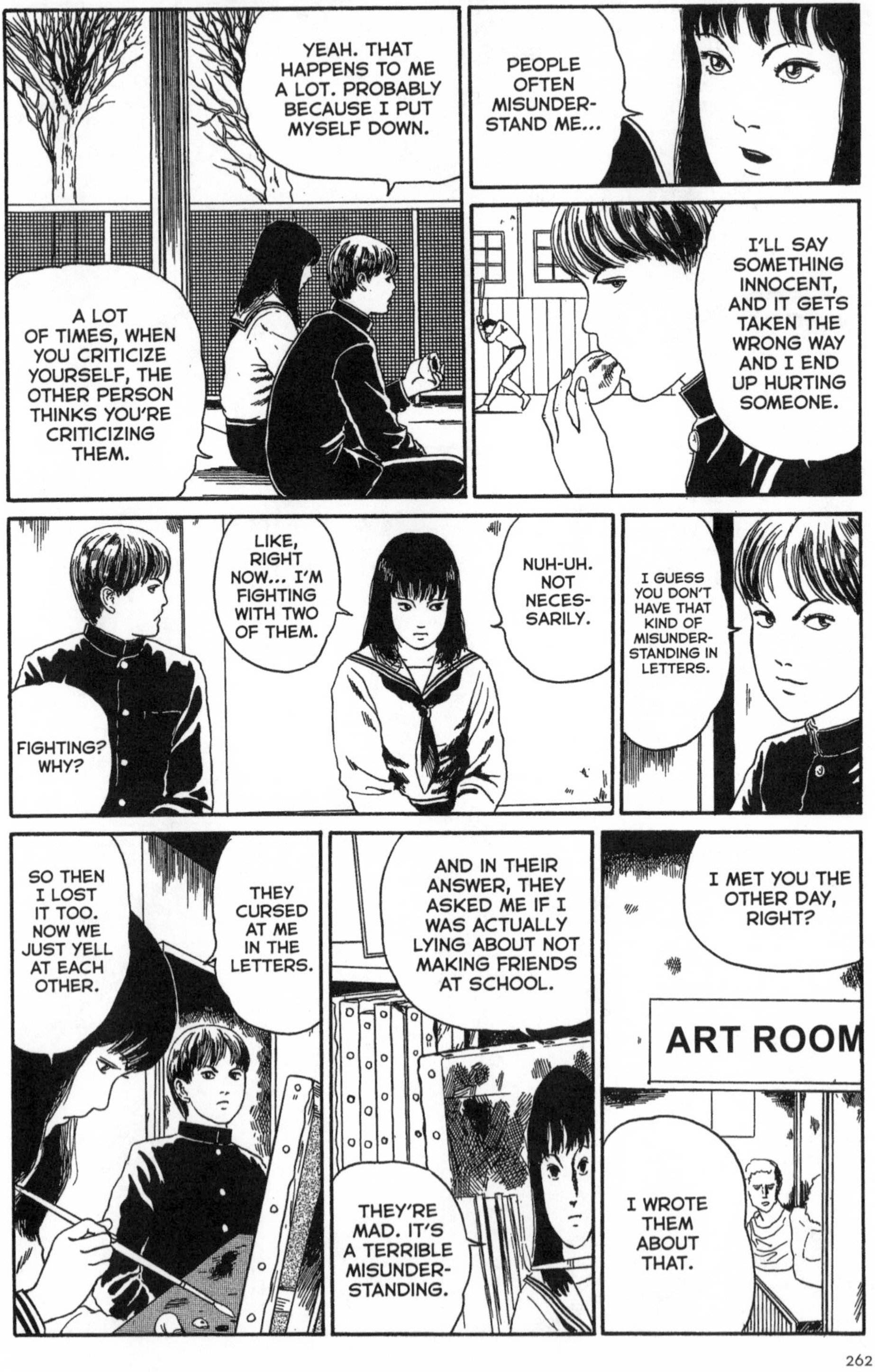
PEOPLE OFTEN MISUNDER-STAND ME...
I'LL SAY SOMETHING INNOCENT, AND IT GETS TAKEN THE WRONG WAY AND I END UP HURTING SOMEONE.
YEAH. THAT HAPPENS TO ME A LOT. PROBABLY BECAUSE I PUT MYSELF DOWN.
A LOT OF TIMES, WHEN YOU CRITICIZE YOURSELF, THE OTHER PERSON THINKS YOU'RE CRITICIZING THEM.
I GUESS YOU DON'T HAVE THAT KIND OF MISUNDER-STANDING IN LETTERS.
NUH-UH. NOT NECES-SARILY.
LIKE, RIGHT NOW... I'M FIGHTING WITH TWO OF THEM.
FIGHTING? WHY?
I MET YOU THE OTHER DAY, RIGHT?
ART ROOM
I WROTE THEM ABOUT THAT.
AND IN THEIR ANSWER, THEY ASKED ME IF I WAS ACTUALLY LYING ABOUT NOT MAKING FRIENDS AT SCHOOL.
THEY'RE MAD. IT'S A TERRIBLE MISUNDER-STANDING.
THEY CURSED AT ME IN THE LETTERS.
SO THEN I LOST IT TOO. NOW WE JUST YELL AT EACH OTHER.

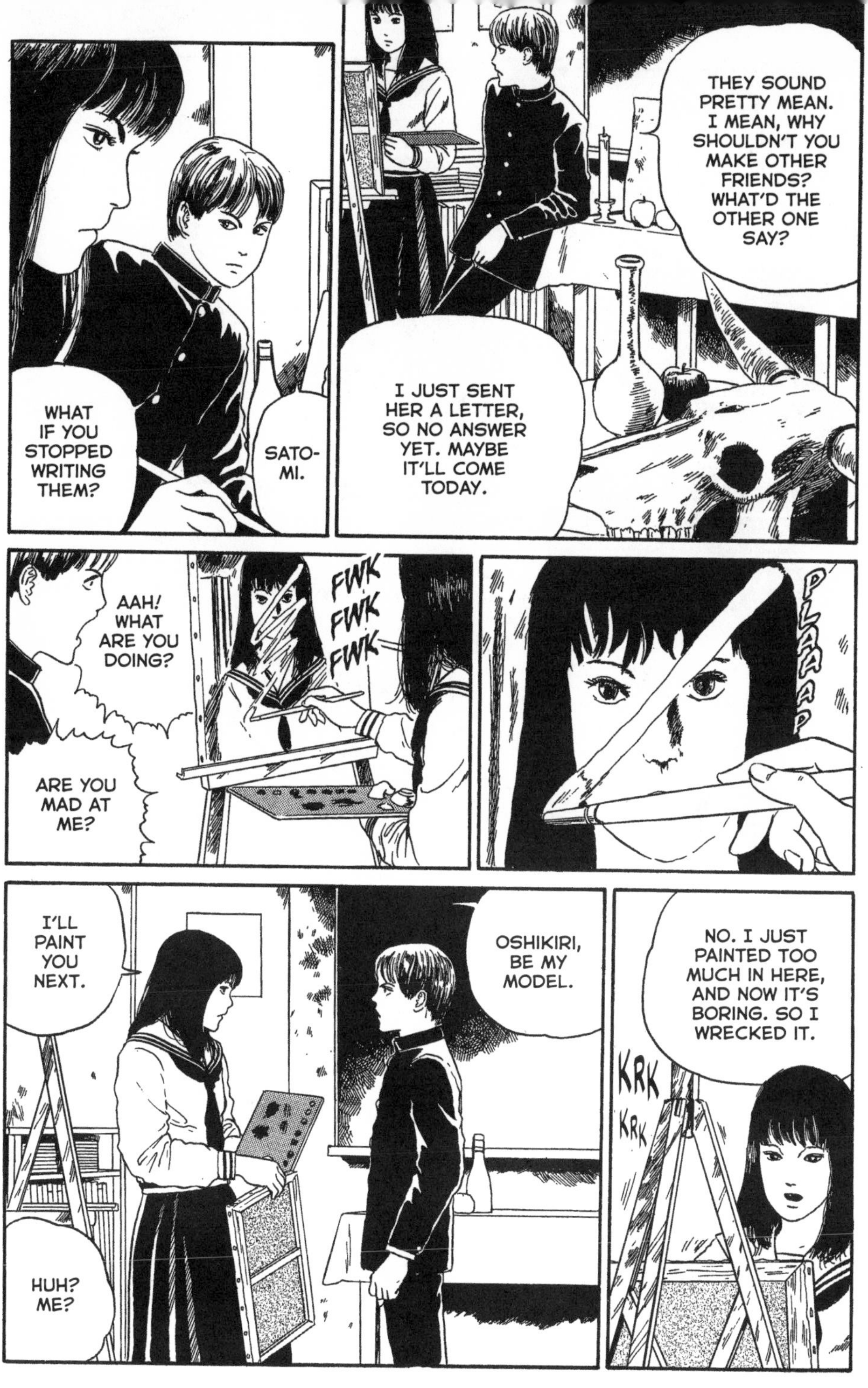
THEY SOUND PRETTY MEAN. I MEAN, WHY SHOULDN'T YOU MAKE OTHER FRIENDS? WHAT'D THE OTHER ONE SAY?
I JUST SENT HER A LETTER, SO NO ANSWER YET. MAYBE IT'LL COME TODAY.
SATO-MI.
WHAT IF YOU STOPPED WRITING THEM?
PLAAAP
FWK FWK FWK
AAH! WHAT ARE YOU DOING?
ARE YOU MAD AT ME?
NO. I JUST PAINTED TOO MUCH IN HERE, AND NOW IT'S BORING. SO I WRECKED IT.
KRK KRK
OSHIKIRI, BE MY MODEL.
I'LL PAINT YOU NEXT.
HUH? ME?

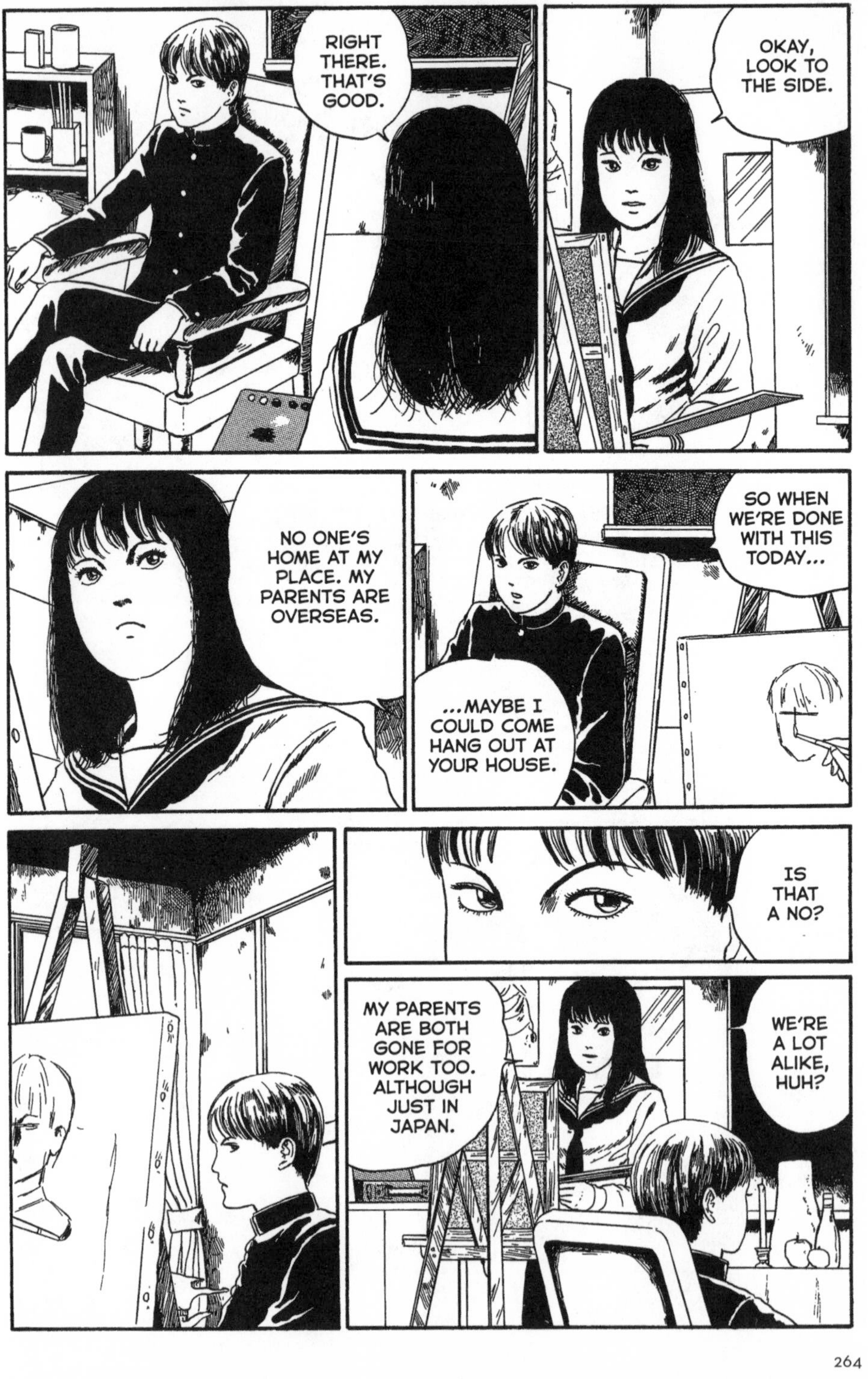
OKAY, LOOK TO THE SIDE.
RIGHT THERE. THAT'S GOOD.
SO WHEN WE'RE DONE WITH THIS TODAY...
...MAYBE I COULD COME HANG OUT AT YOUR HOUSE.
NO ONE'S HOME AT MY PLACE. MY PARENTS ARE OVERSEAS.
IS THAT A NO?
WE'RE A LOT ALIKE, HUH?
MY PARENTS ARE BOTH GONE FOR WORK TOO. ALTHOUGH JUST IN JAPAN.

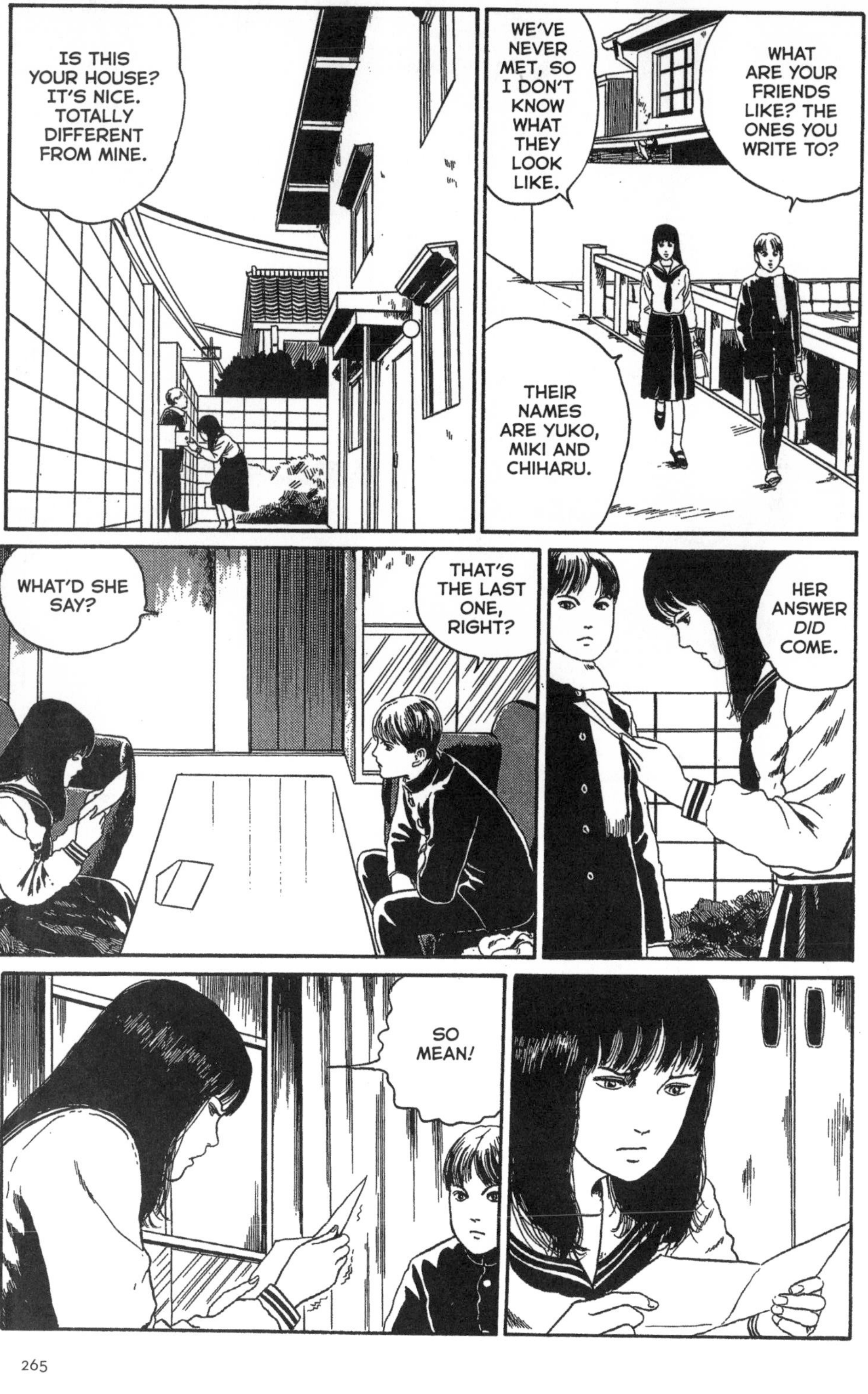
WHAT ARE YOUR FRIENDS LIKE? THE ONES YOU WRITE TO?
WE'VE NEVER MET, SO I DON'T KNOW WHAT THEY LOOK LIKE.
THEIR NAMES ARE YUKO, MIKI AND CHIHARU.
IS THIS YOUR HOUSE? IT'S NICE. TOTALLY DIFFERENT FROM MINE.
HER ANSWER *DID* COME.
THAT'S THE LAST ONE, RIGHT?
WHAT'D SHE SAY?
SO MEAN!

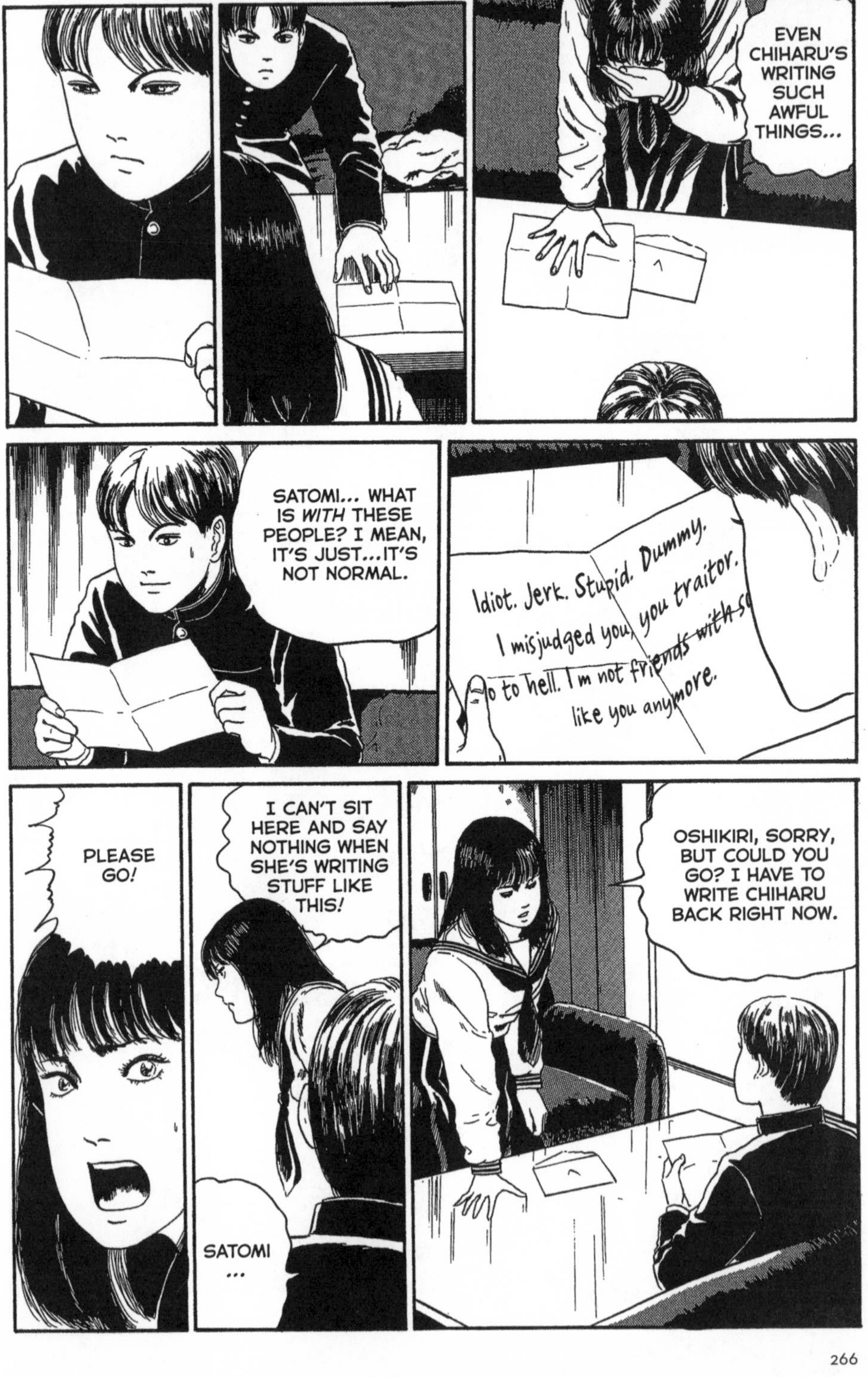
EVEN CHIHARU'S WRITING SUCH AWFUL THINGS...
Idiot. Jerk. Stupid. Dummy.
I misjudged you, you traitor.
to hell. I'm not friends with
like you anymore.
SATOMI... WHAT IS *WITH* THESE PEOPLE? I MEAN, IT'S JUST...IT'S NOT NORMAL.
OSHIKIRI, SORRY, BUT COULD YOU GO? I HAVE TO WRITE CHIHARU BACK RIGHT NOW.
I CAN'T SIT HERE AND SAY NOTHING WHEN SHE'S WRITING STUFF LIKE THIS!
SATOMI ...
PLEASE GO!

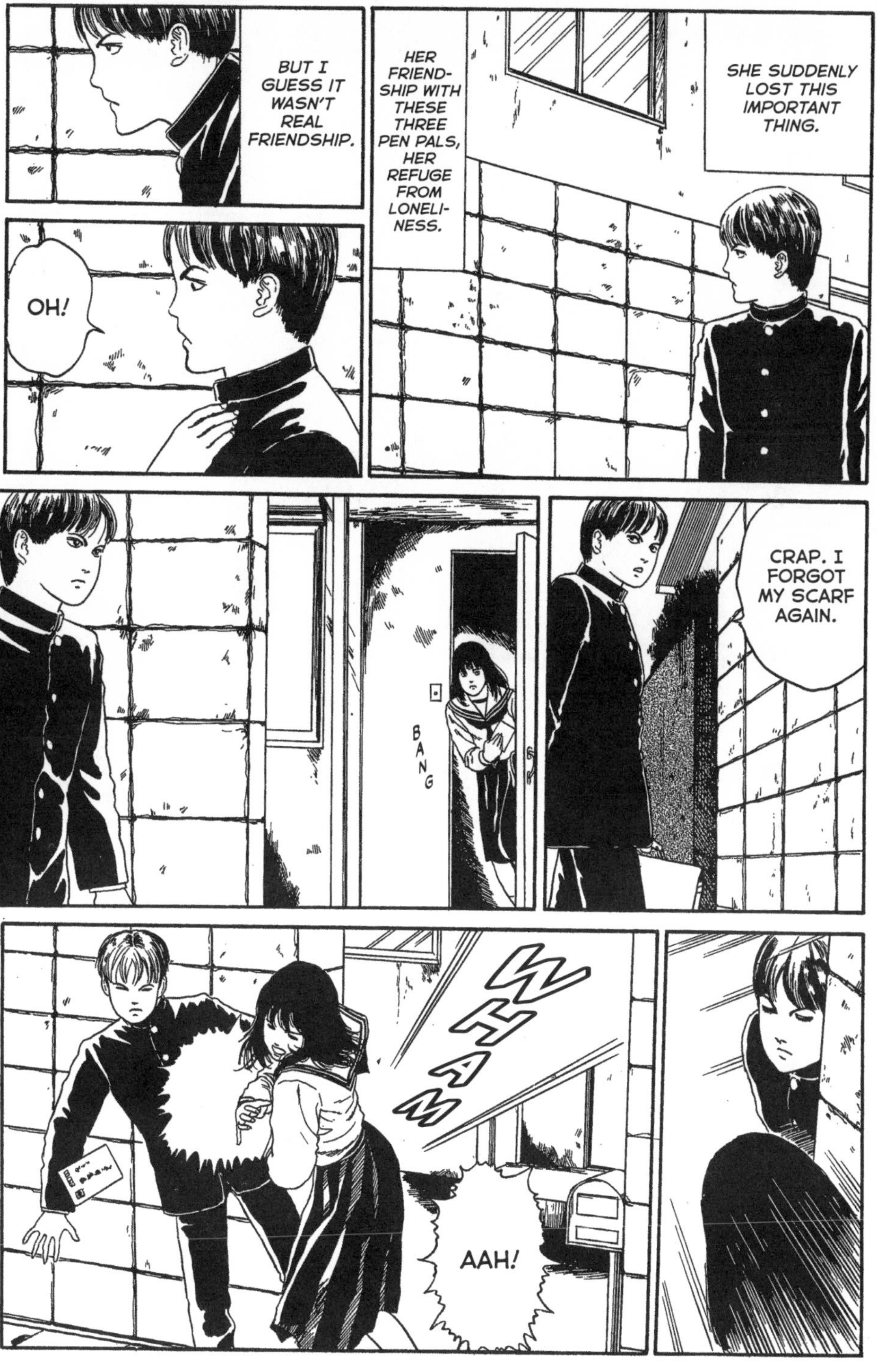
HER FRIENDSHIP WITH THESE THREE PEN PALS, HER REFUGE FROM LONELINESS.
SHE SUDDENLY LOST THIS IMPORTANT THING.
BUT I GUESS IT WASN'T REAL FRIENDSHIP.
OH!
CRAP. I FORGOT MY SCARF AGAIN.
BANG
WHAM
AAH!

THK
SORRY, SATOMI.
930
Toyama City
25-3
Miss Kazuko
Satomi
THANKS!

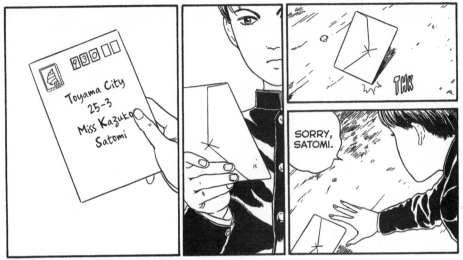

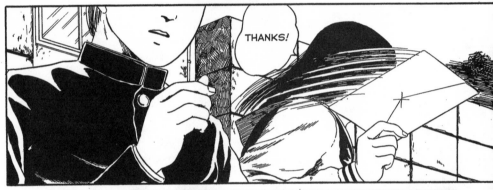

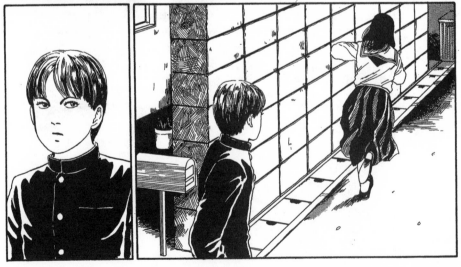

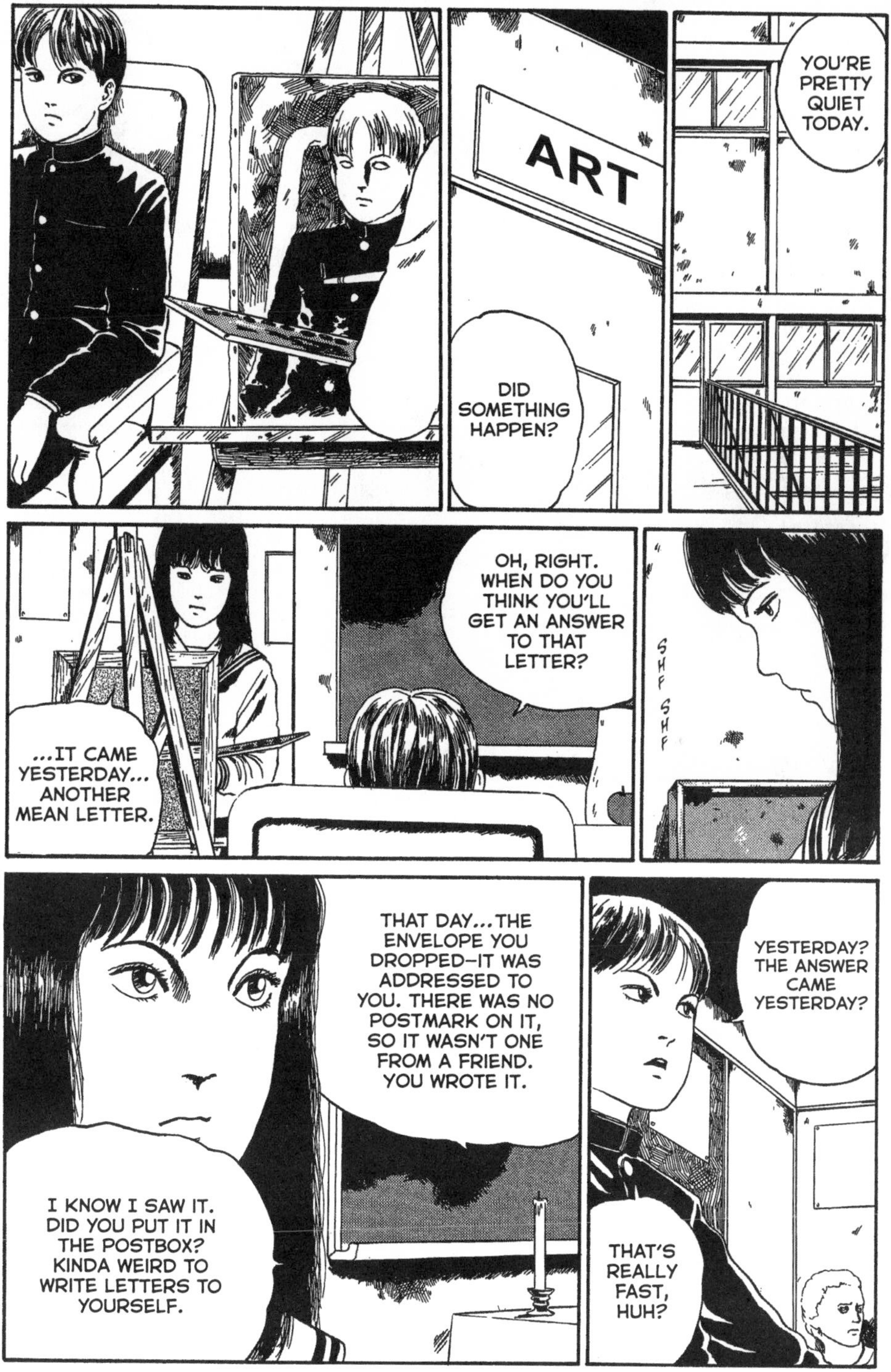
YOU'RE PRETTY QUIET TODAY.
ART
DID SOMETHING HAPPEN?
SHF SHF
OH, RIGHT. WHEN DO YOU THINK YOU'LL GET AN ANSWER TO THAT LETTER?
...IT CAME YESTERDAY... ANOTHER MEAN LETTER.
YESTERDAY? THE ANSWER CAME YESTERDAY?
THAT'S REALLY FAST, HUH?
THAT DAY...THE ENVELOPE YOU DROPPED—IT WAS ADDRESSED TO YOU. THERE WAS NO POSTMARK ON IT, SO IT WASN'T ONE FROM A FRIEND. YOU WROTE IT.
I KNOW I SAW IT. DID YOU PUT IT IN THE POSTBOX? KINDA WEIRD TO WRITE LETTERS TO YOURSELF.

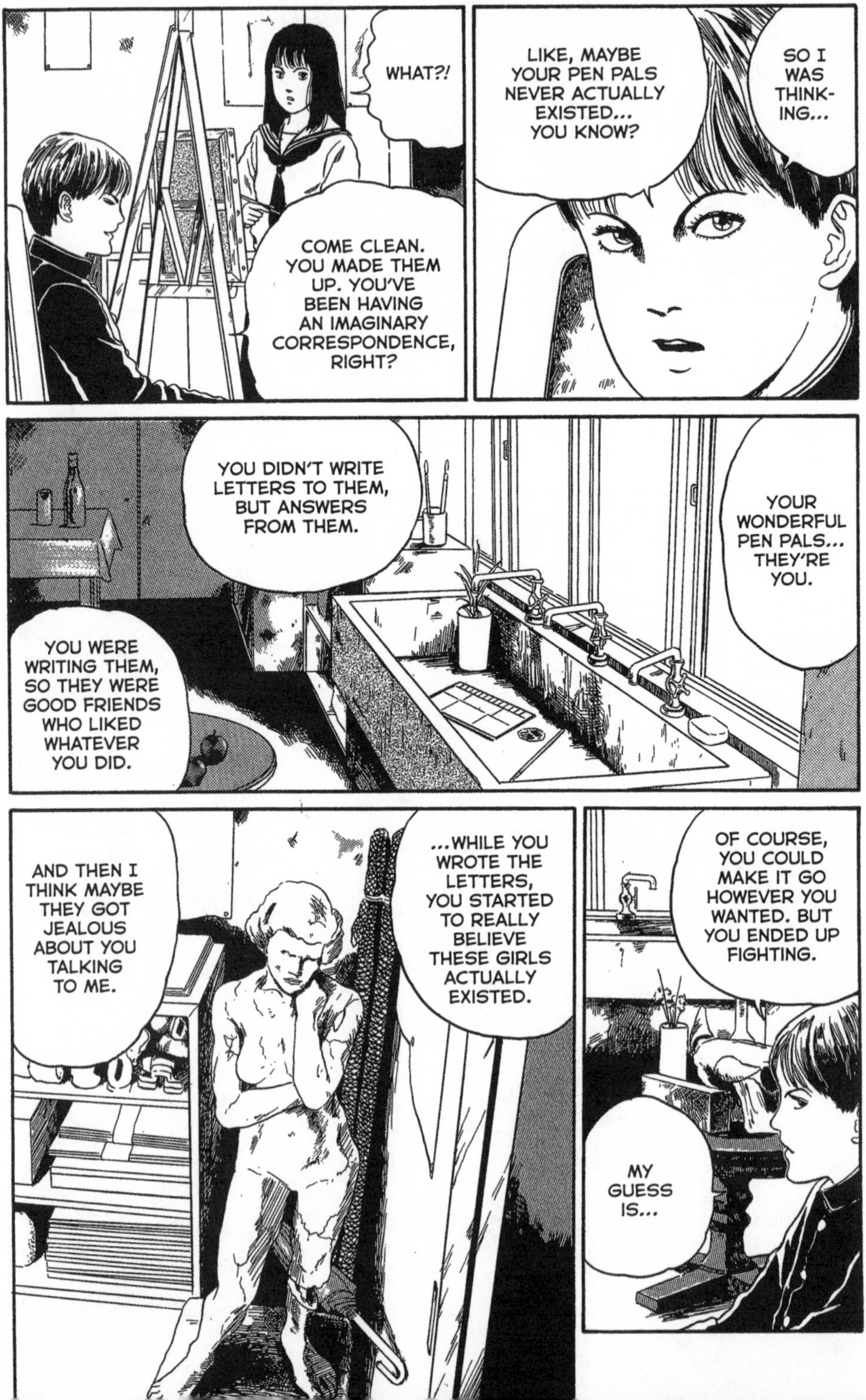
SO I WAS THINKING...
LIKE, MAYBE YOUR PEN PALS NEVER ACTUALLY EXISTED... YOU KNOW?
WHAT?!
COME CLEAN. YOU MADE THEM UP. YOU'VE BEEN HAVING AN IMAGINARY CORRESPONDENCE, RIGHT?
YOUR WONDERFUL PEN PALS... THEY'RE YOU.
YOU DIDN'T WRITE LETTERS TO THEM, BUT ANSWERS FROM THEM.
YOU WERE WRITING THEM, SO THEY WERE GOOD FRIENDS WHO LIKED WHATEVER YOU DID.
OF COURSE, YOU COULD MAKE IT GO HOWEVER YOU WANTED. BUT YOU ENDED UP FIGHTING.
MY GUESS IS...
...WHILE YOU WROTE THE LETTERS, YOU STARTED TO REALLY BELIEVE THESE GIRLS ACTUALLY EXISTED.
AND THEN I THINK MAYBE THEY GOT JEALOUS ABOUT YOU TALKING TO ME.

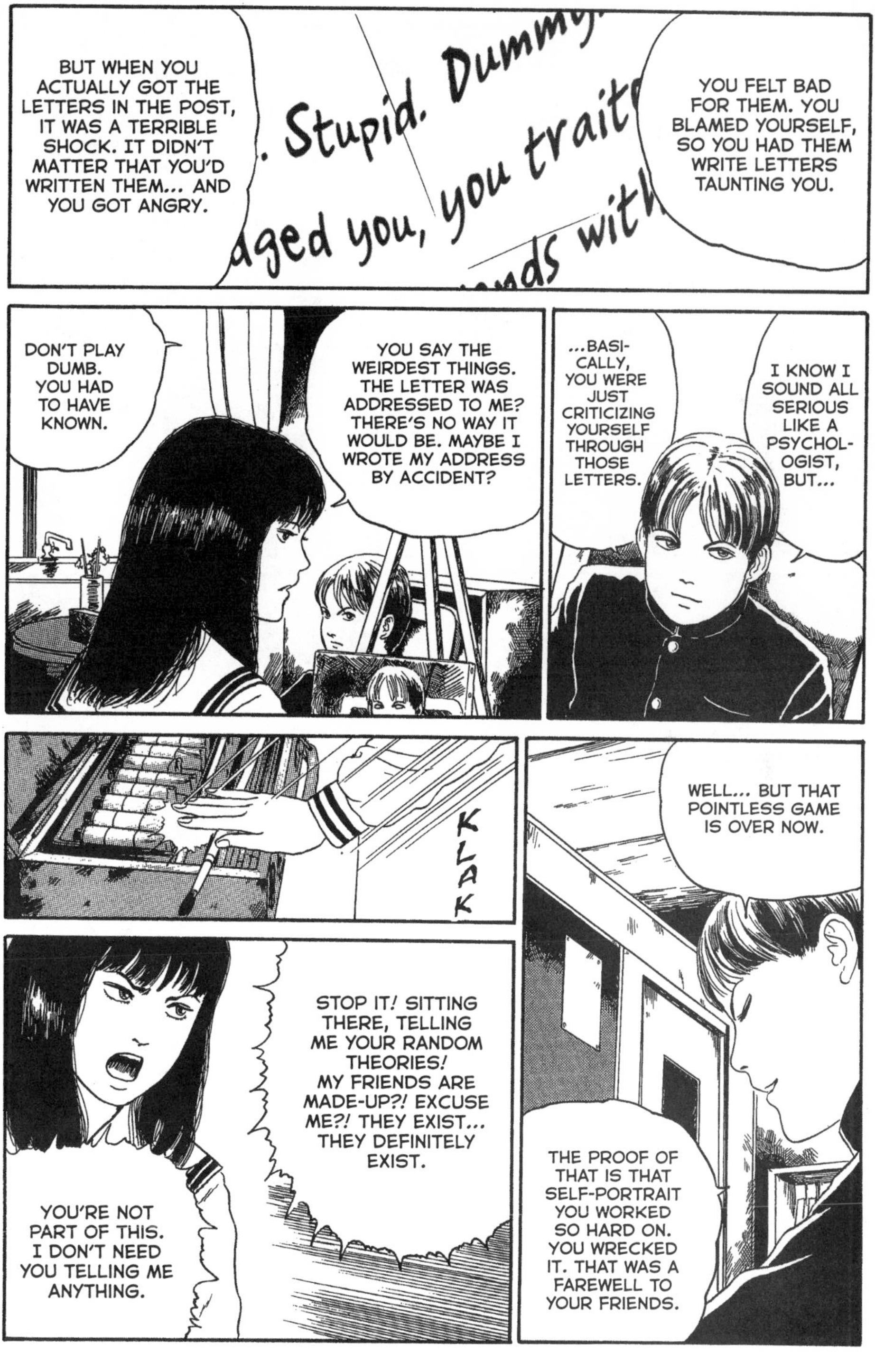
YOU FELT BAD FOR THEM. YOU BLAMED YOURSELF, SO YOU HAD THEM WRITE LETTERS TAUNTING YOU.
. Stupid. Dummy.
aged you, you traito
nds with
BUT WHEN YOU ACTUALLY GOT THE LETTERS IN THE POST, IT WAS A TERRIBLE SHOCK. IT DIDN'T MATTER THAT YOU'D WRITTEN THEM... AND YOU GOT ANGRY.
I KNOW I SOUND ALL SERIOUS LIKE A PSYCHOLOGIST, BUT...
...BASICALLY, YOU WERE JUST CRITICIZING YOURSELF THROUGH THOSE LETTERS.
YOU SAY THE WEIRDEST THINGS. THE LETTER WAS ADDRESSED TO ME? THERE'S NO WAY IT WOULD BE. MAYBE I WROTE MY ADDRESS BY ACCIDENT?
DON'T PLAY DUMB. YOU HAD TO HAVE KNOWN.
WELL... BUT THAT POINTLESS GAME IS OVER NOW.
THE PROOF OF THAT IS THAT SELF-PORTRAIT YOU WORKED SO HARD ON. YOU WRECKED IT. THAT WAS A FAREWELL TO YOUR FRIENDS.
KLAK
STOP IT! SITTING THERE, TELLING ME YOUR RANDOM THEORIES! MY FRIENDS ARE MADE-UP?! EXCUSE ME?! THEY EXIST... THEY DEFINITELY EXIST.
YOU'RE NOT PART OF THIS. I DON'T NEED YOU TELLING ME ANYTHING.

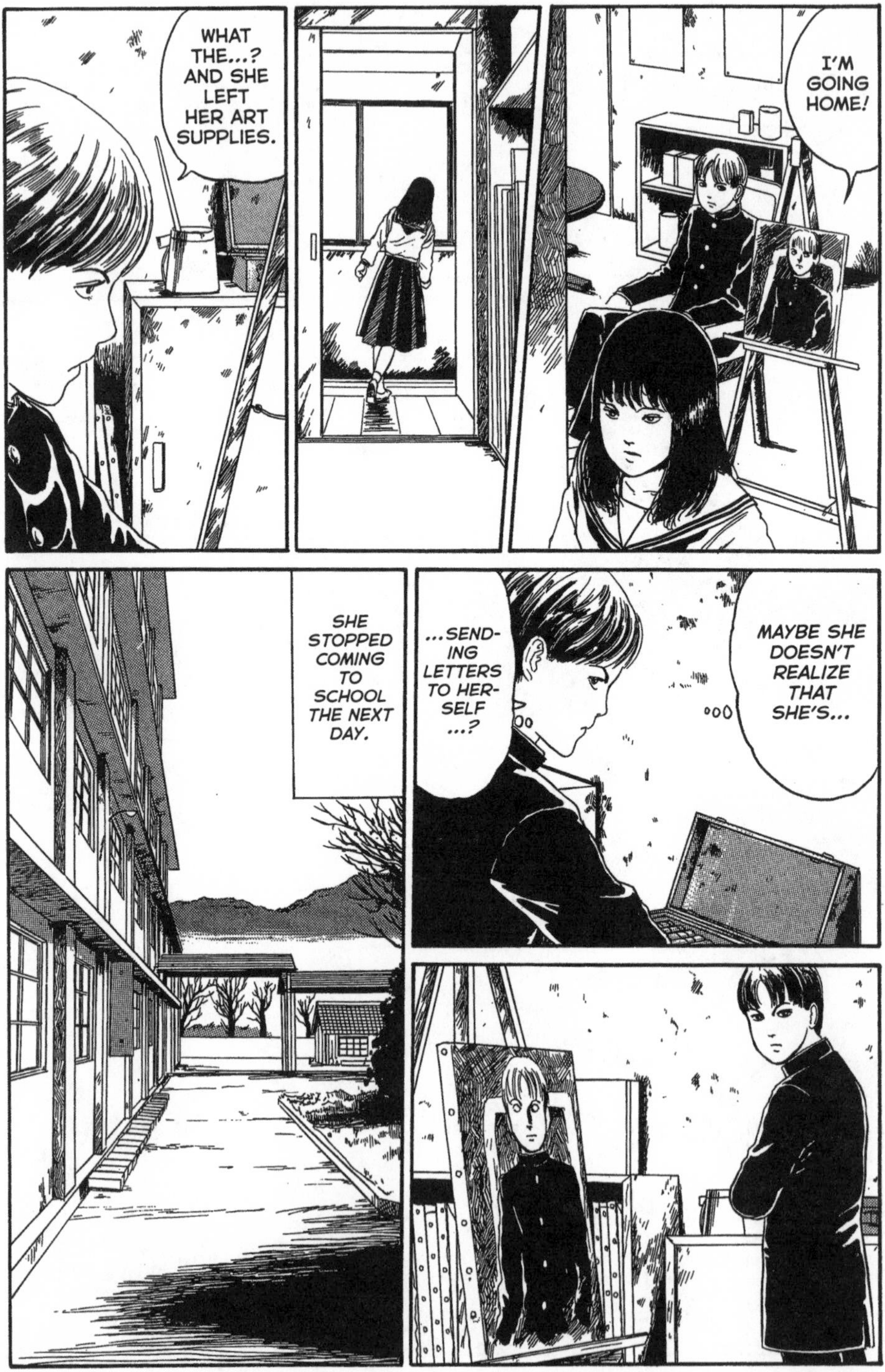
I'M GOING HOME!
WHAT THE...? AND SHE LEFT HER ART SUPPLIES.
MAYBE SHE DOESN'T REALIZE THAT SHE'S...
...SENDING LETTERS TO HERSELF ...?
SHE STOPPED COMING TO SCHOOL THE NEXT DAY.

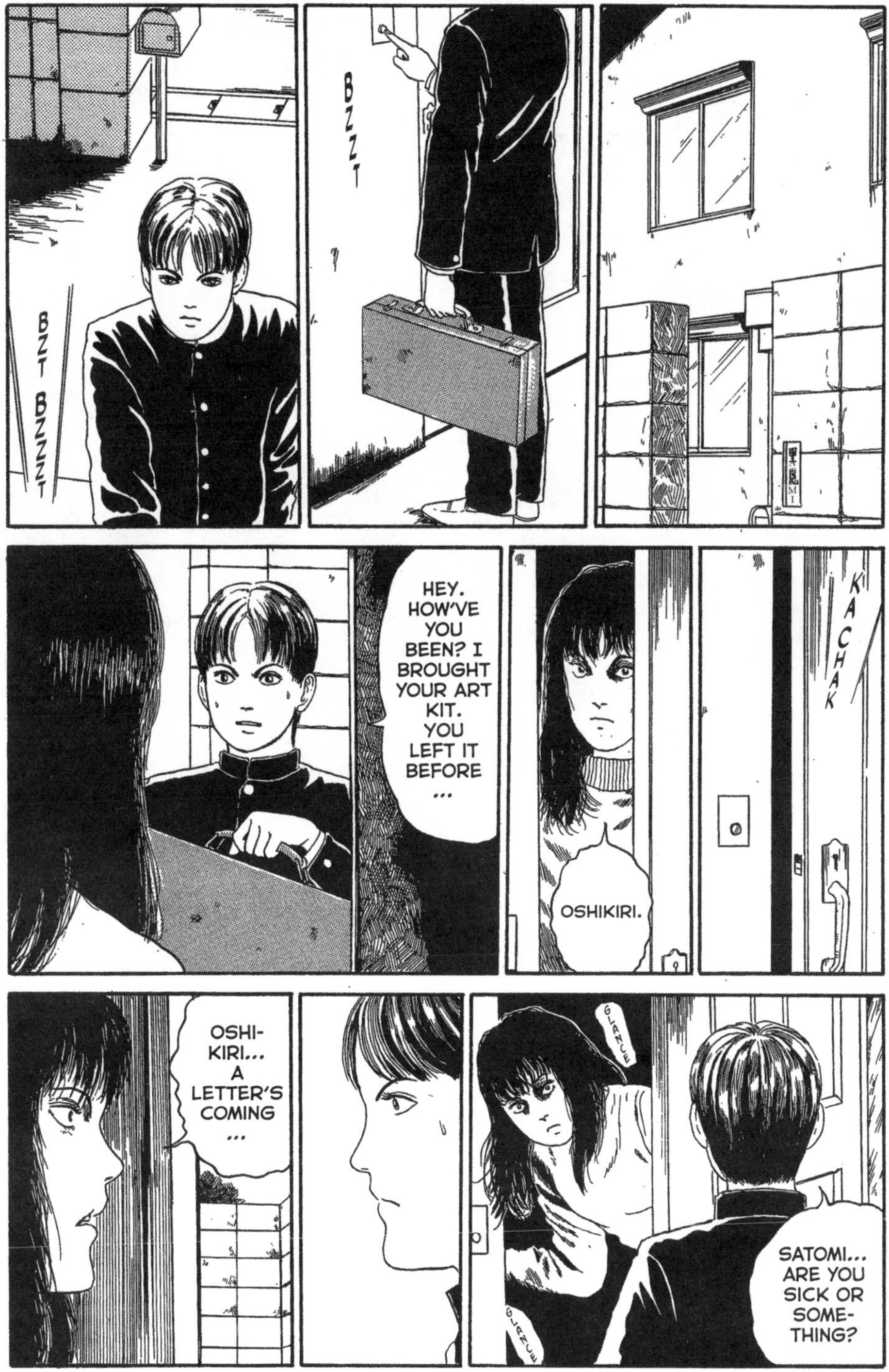
BZZT
BZT BZZZZT
KACHAK
OSHIKIRI.
HEY. HOW'VE YOU BEEN? I BROUGHT YOUR ART KIT. YOU LEFT IT BEFORE ...
GLANCE
GLANCE
SATOMI... ARE YOU SICK OR SOME-THING?
OSHI-KIRI... A LETTER'S COMING ...

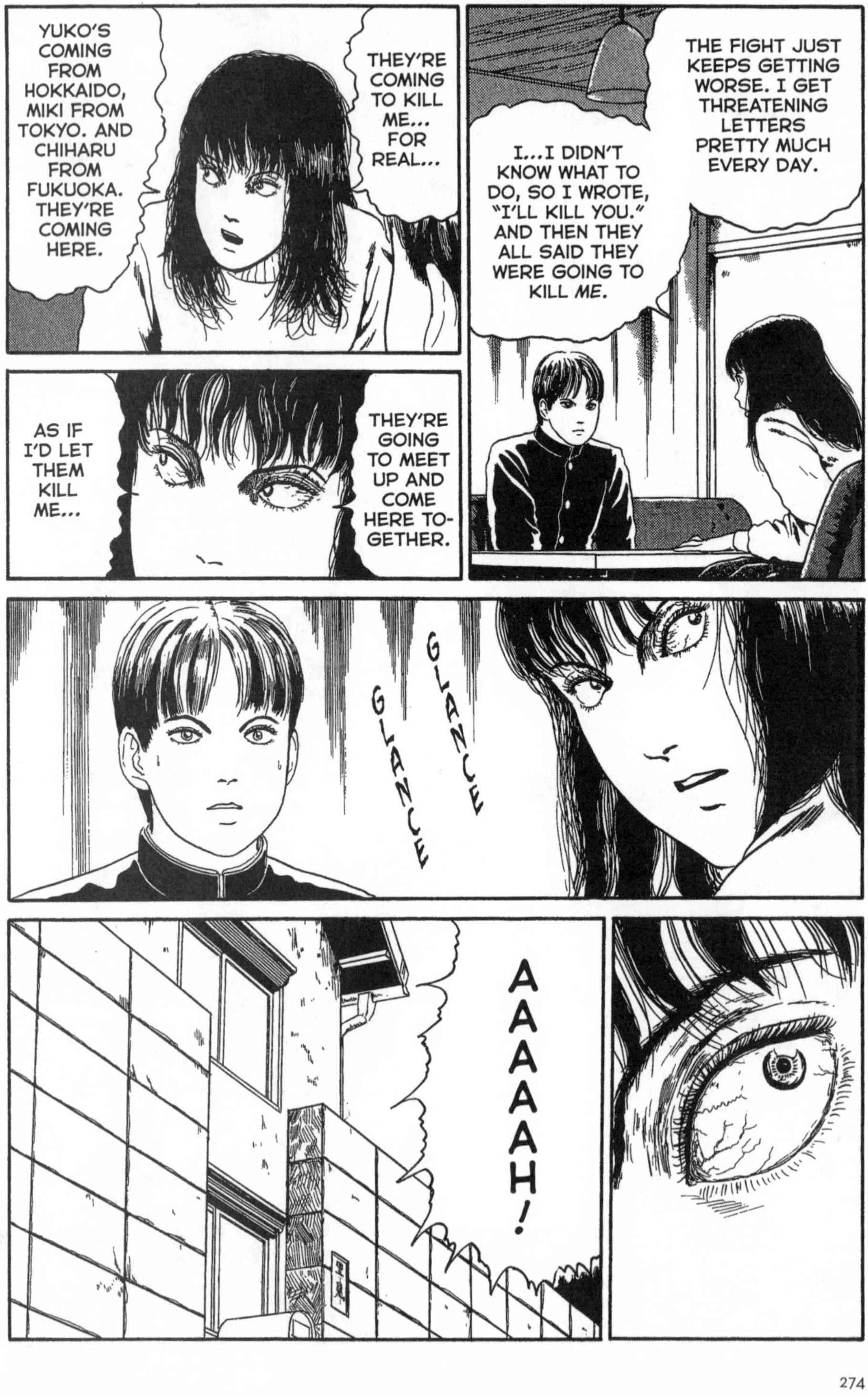
THE FIGHT JUST KEEPS GETTING WORSE. I GET THREATENING LETTERS PRETTY MUCH EVERY DAY.
I...I DIDN'T KNOW WHAT TO DO, SO I WROTE, "I'LL KILL YOU." AND THEN THEY ALL SAID THEY WERE GOING TO KILL *ME*.
THEY'RE COMING TO KILL ME... FOR REAL...
YUKO'S COMING FROM HOKKAIDO, MIKI FROM TOKYO. AND CHIHARU FROM FUKUOKA. THEY'RE COMING HERE.
THEY'RE GOING TO MEET UP AND COME HERE TO-GETHER.
AS IF I'D LET THEM KILL ME...
GLANCE
GLANCE
AAAAAH!

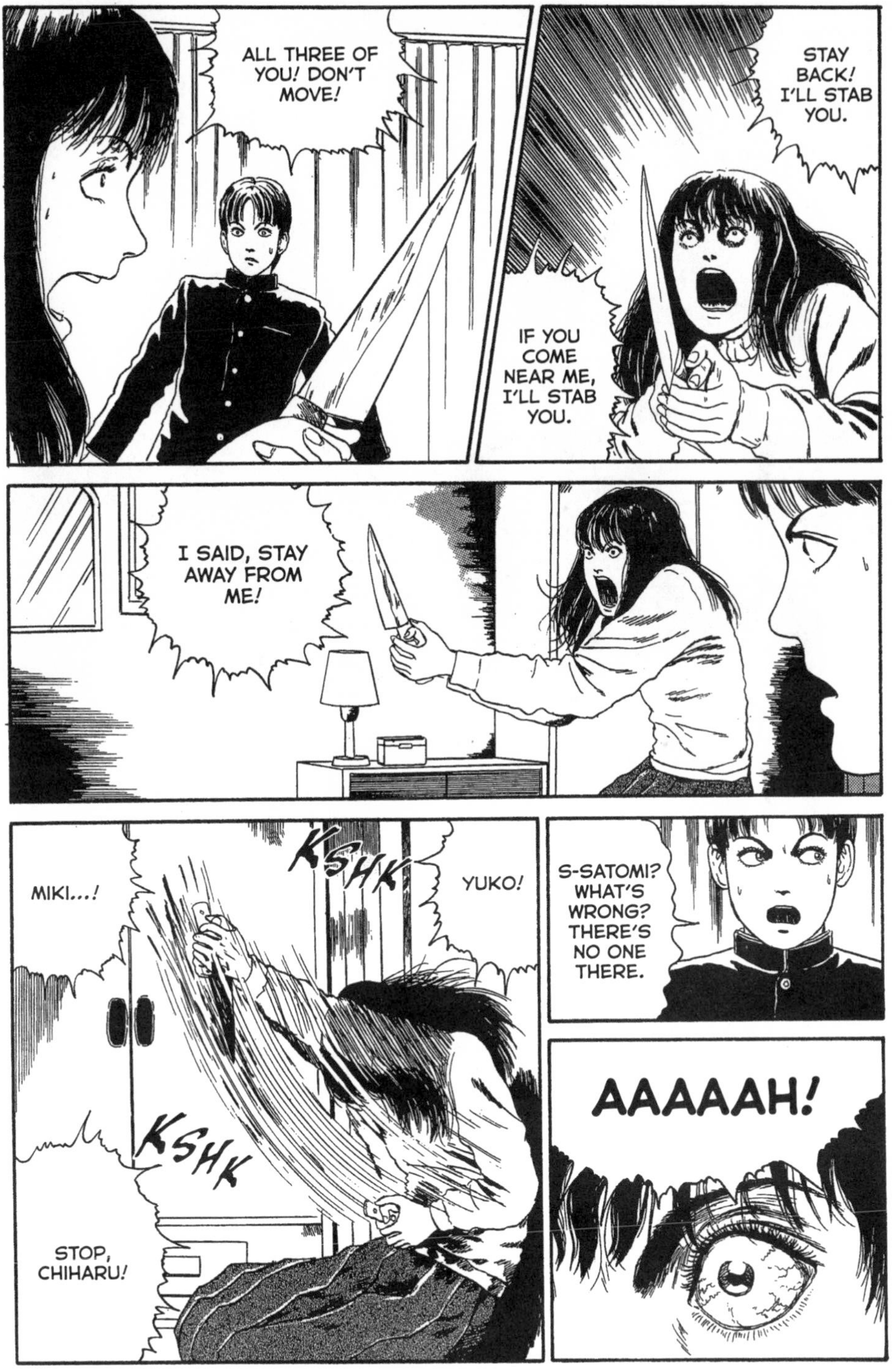
STAY BACK! I'LL STAB YOU.
IF YOU COME NEAR ME, I'LL STAB YOU.
ALL THREE OF YOU! DON'T MOVE!
I SAID, STAY AWAY FROM ME!
S-SATOMI? WHAT'S WRONG? THERE'S NO ONE THERE.
AAAAAH!
YUKO!
KSHK
MIKI...!
KSHK
STOP, CHIHARU!

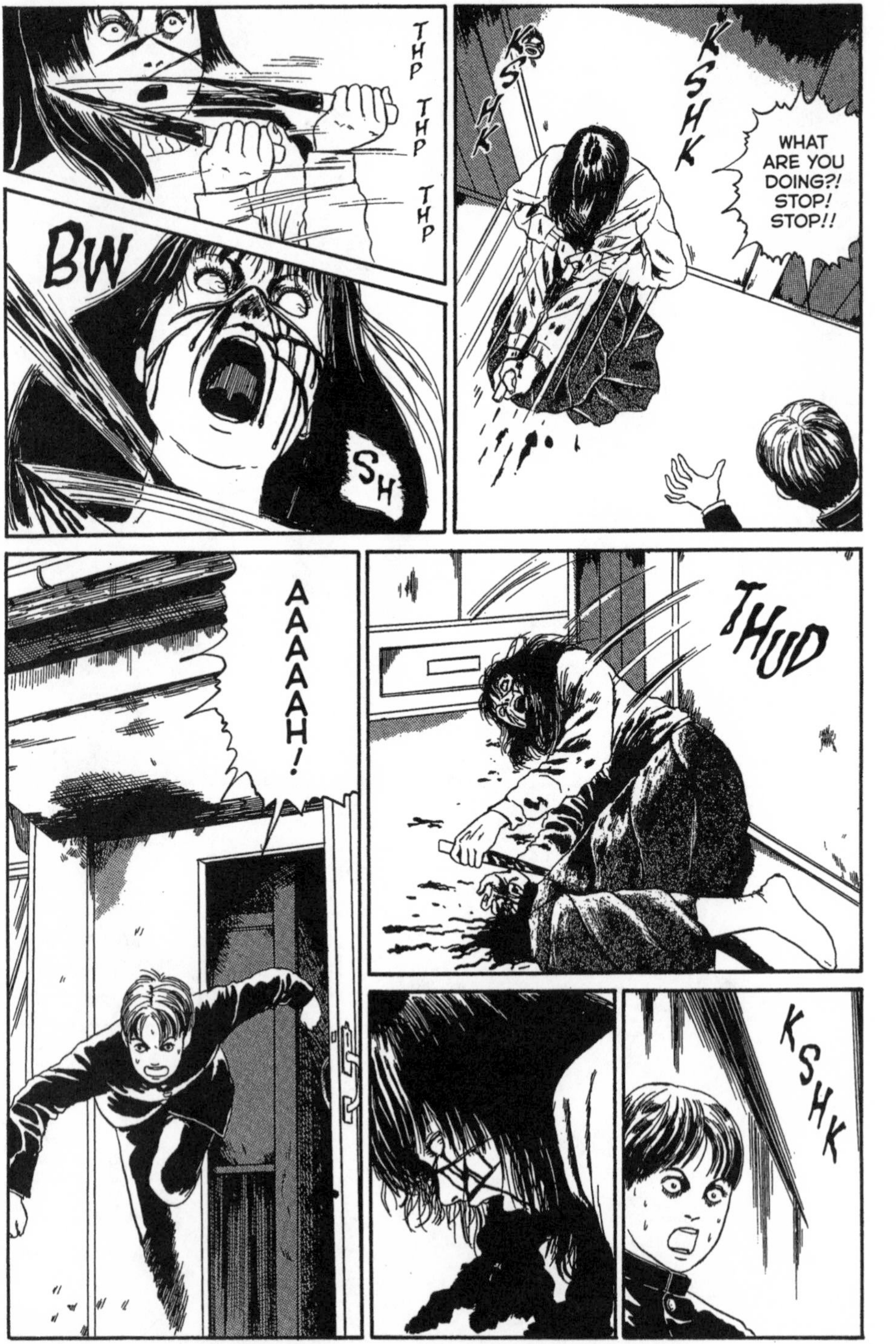
KSHK
KSHK
WHAT ARE YOU DOING?! STOP! STOP!!
THP THP THP
BW
SH
THUD
KSHK
AAAAAAH!

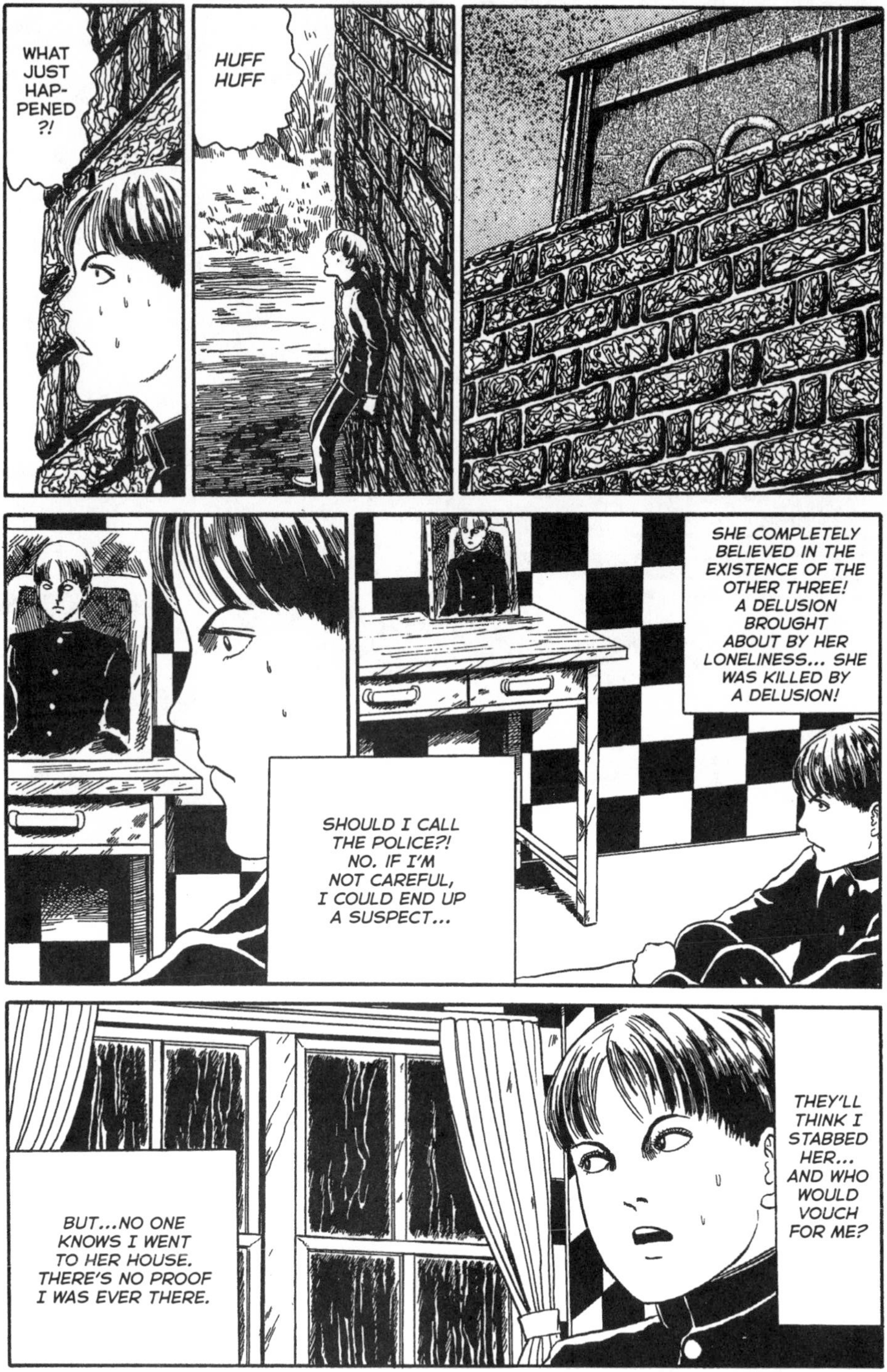
HUFF
HUFF
WHAT JUST HAP-PENED?!
SHE COMPLETELY BELIEVED IN THE EXISTENCE OF THE OTHER THREE! A DELUSION BROUGHT ABOUT BY HER LONELINESS... SHE WAS KILLED BY A DELUSION!
SHOULD I CALL THE POLICE?! NO. IF I'M NOT CAREFUL, I COULD END UP A SUSPECT...
THEY'LL THINK I STABBED HER... AND WHO WOULD VOUCH FOR ME?
BUT...NO ONE KNOWS I WENT TO HER HOUSE. THERE'S NO PROOF I WAS EVER THERE.

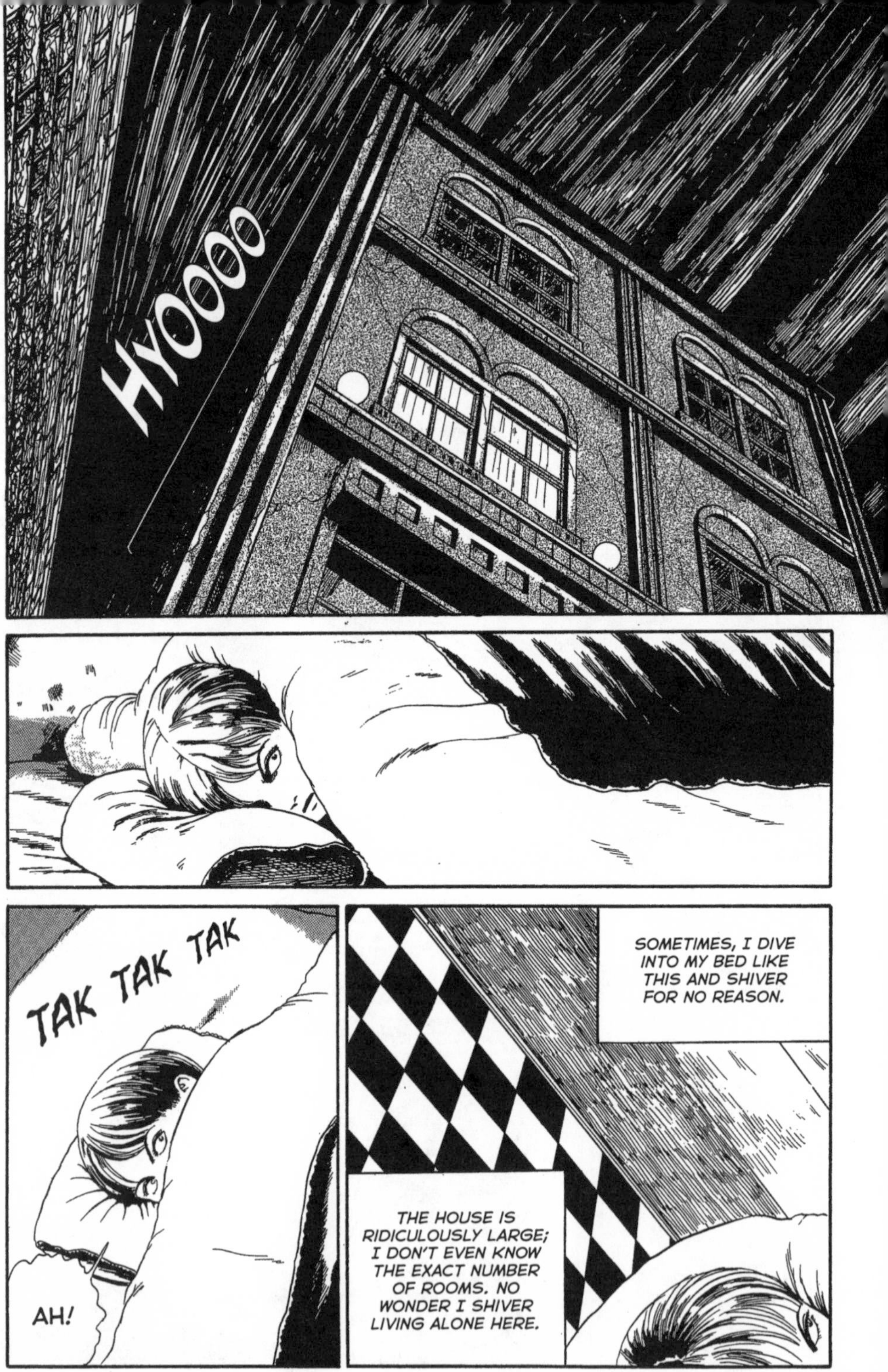
HYOOOO
SOMETIMES, I DIVE INTO MY BED LIKE THIS AND SHIVER FOR NO REASON.
THE HOUSE IS RIDICULOUSLY LARGE; I DON'T EVEN KNOW THE EXACT NUMBER OF ROOMS. NO WONDER I SHIVER LIVING ALONE HERE.
TAK TAK TAK
AH!

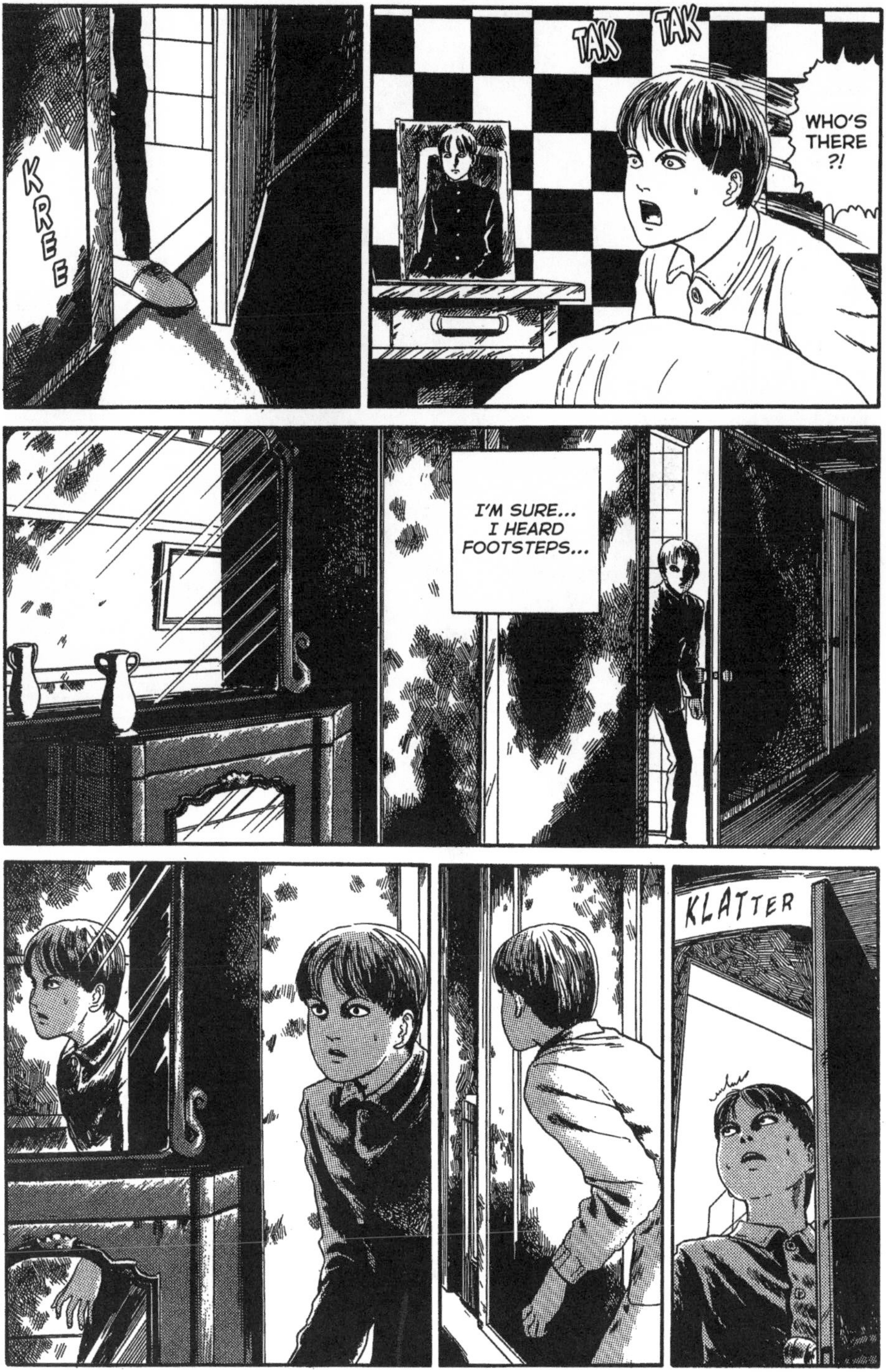
TAK TAK
WHO'S THERE ?!
KREE
I'M SURE... I HEARD FOOTSTEPS...
KLATTER

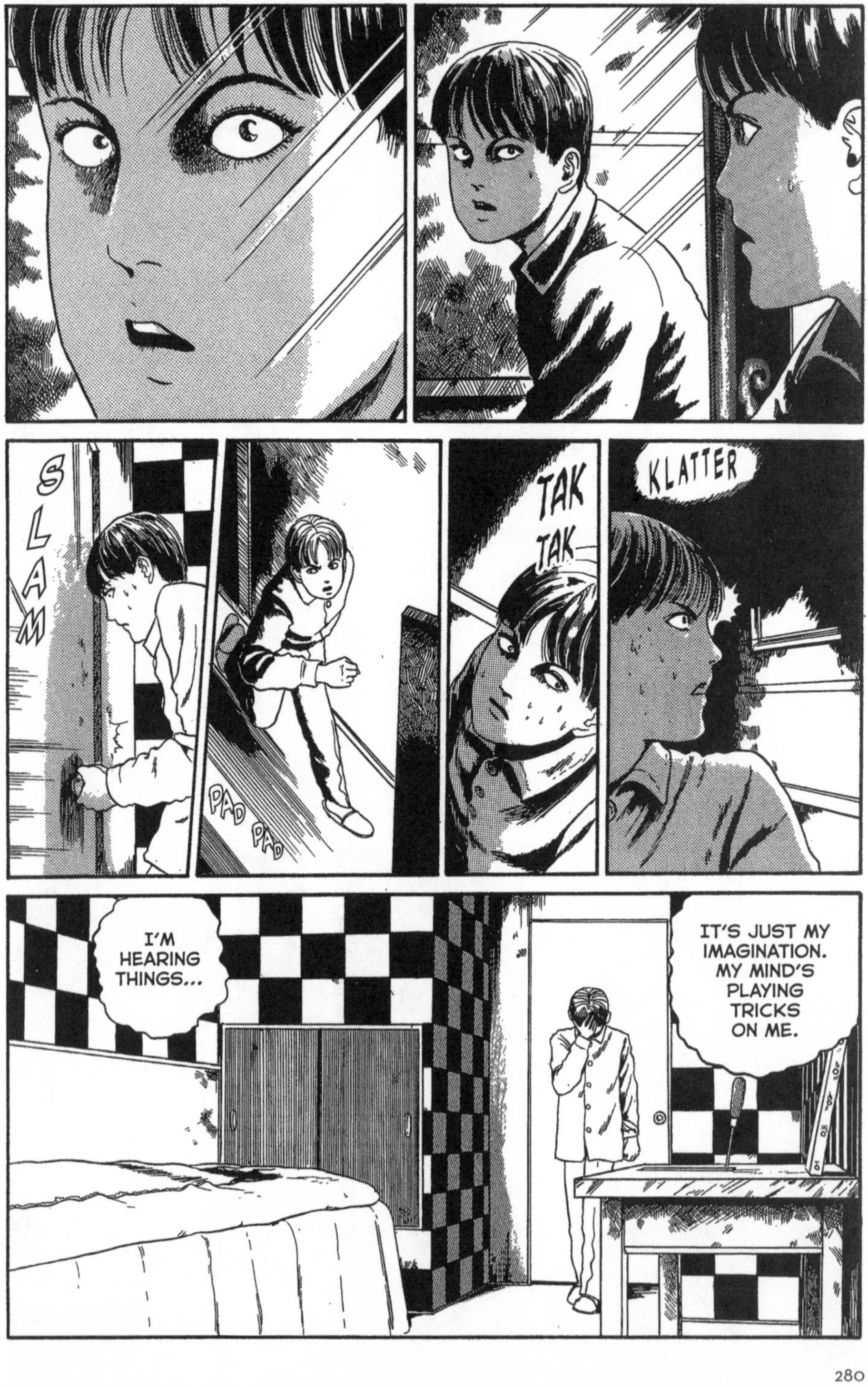
KLATTER
TAK TAK
PAD PAD
SLAM
IT'S JUST MY IMAGINATION. MY MIND'S PLAYING TRICKS ON ME.
I'M HEARING THINGS...

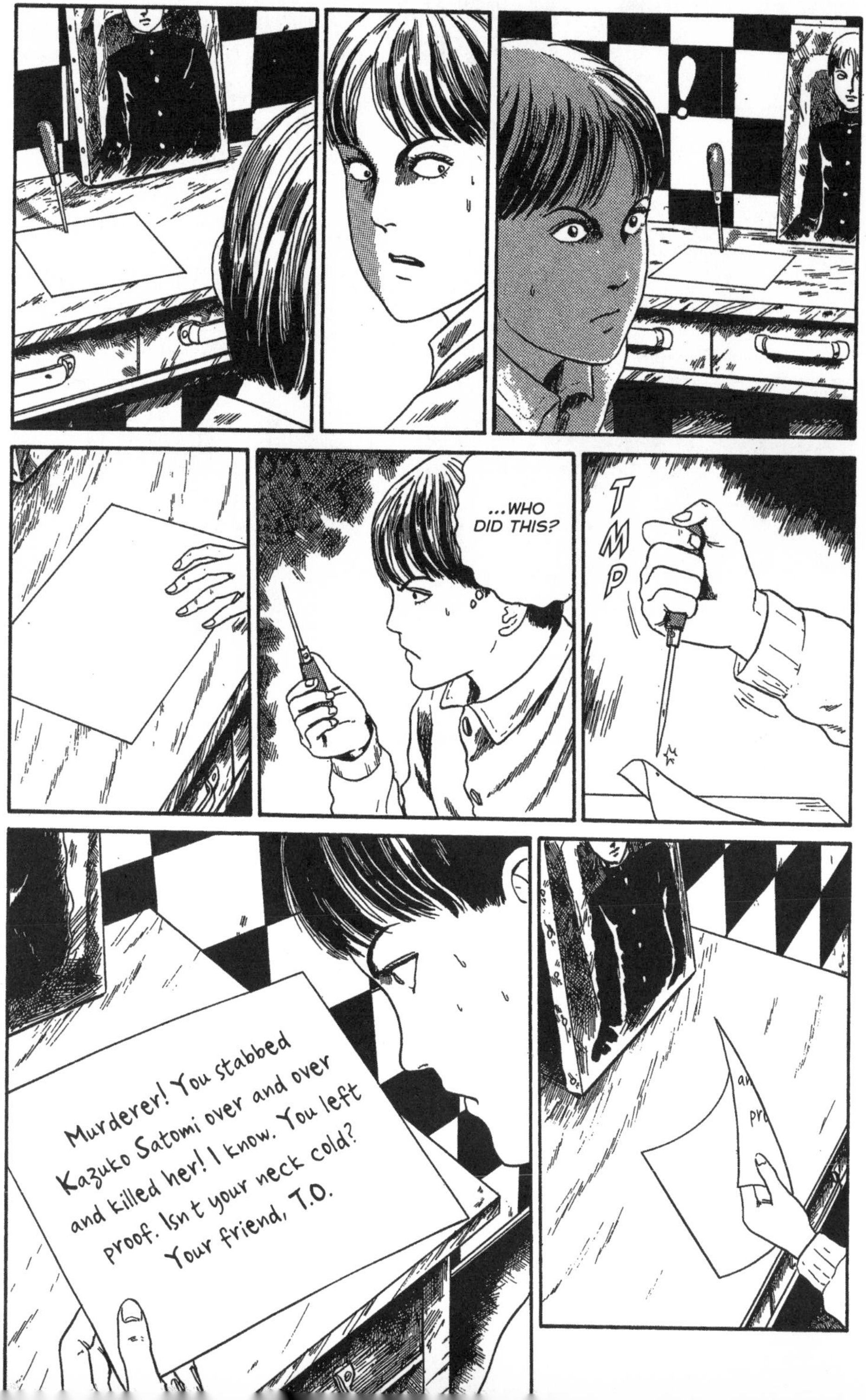
TMP
...WHO DID THIS?
Murderer! You stabbed Kazuko Satomi over and over and killed her! I know. You left proof. Isn't your neck cold? Your friend, T.O.

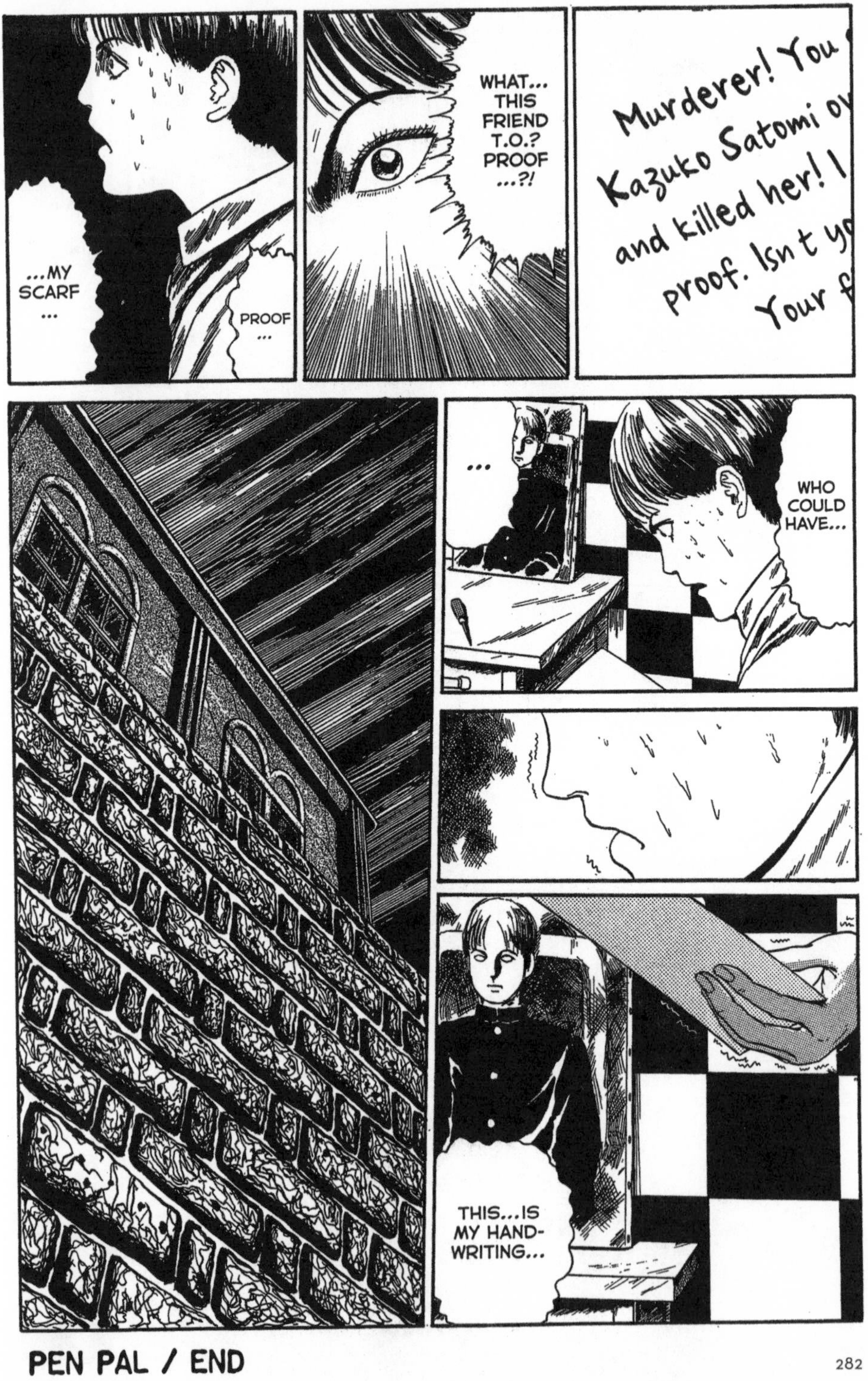
Murderer! You
Kazuko Satomi o
and killed her! I
proof. Isn t yo
Your f
WHAT... THIS FRIEND T.O.? PROOF ...?!
...MY SCARF ...
PROOF ...
...
WHO COULD HAVE...
THIS...IS MY HAND-WRITING...

PEN PAL / END

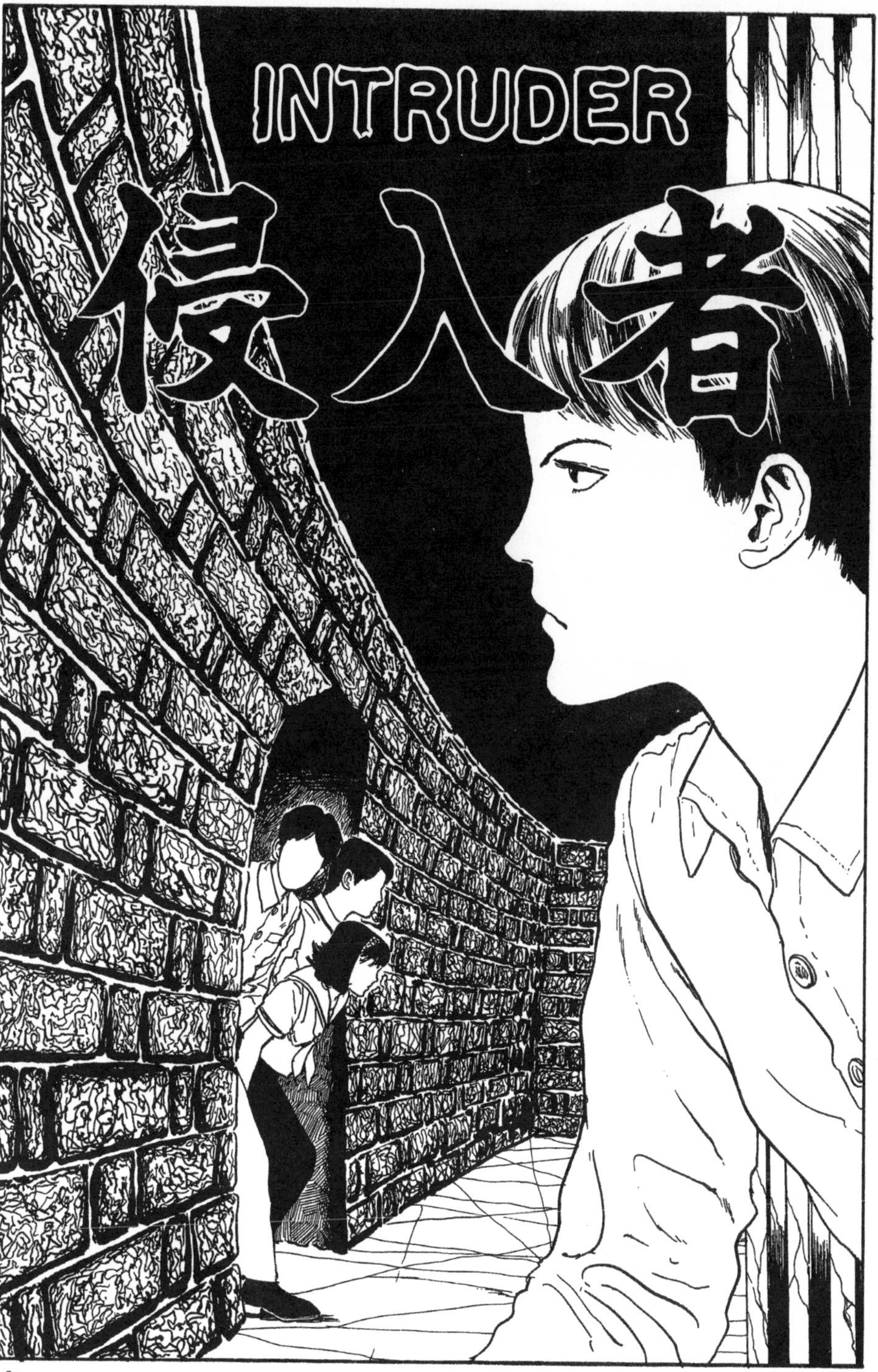
INTRUDER
侵入者

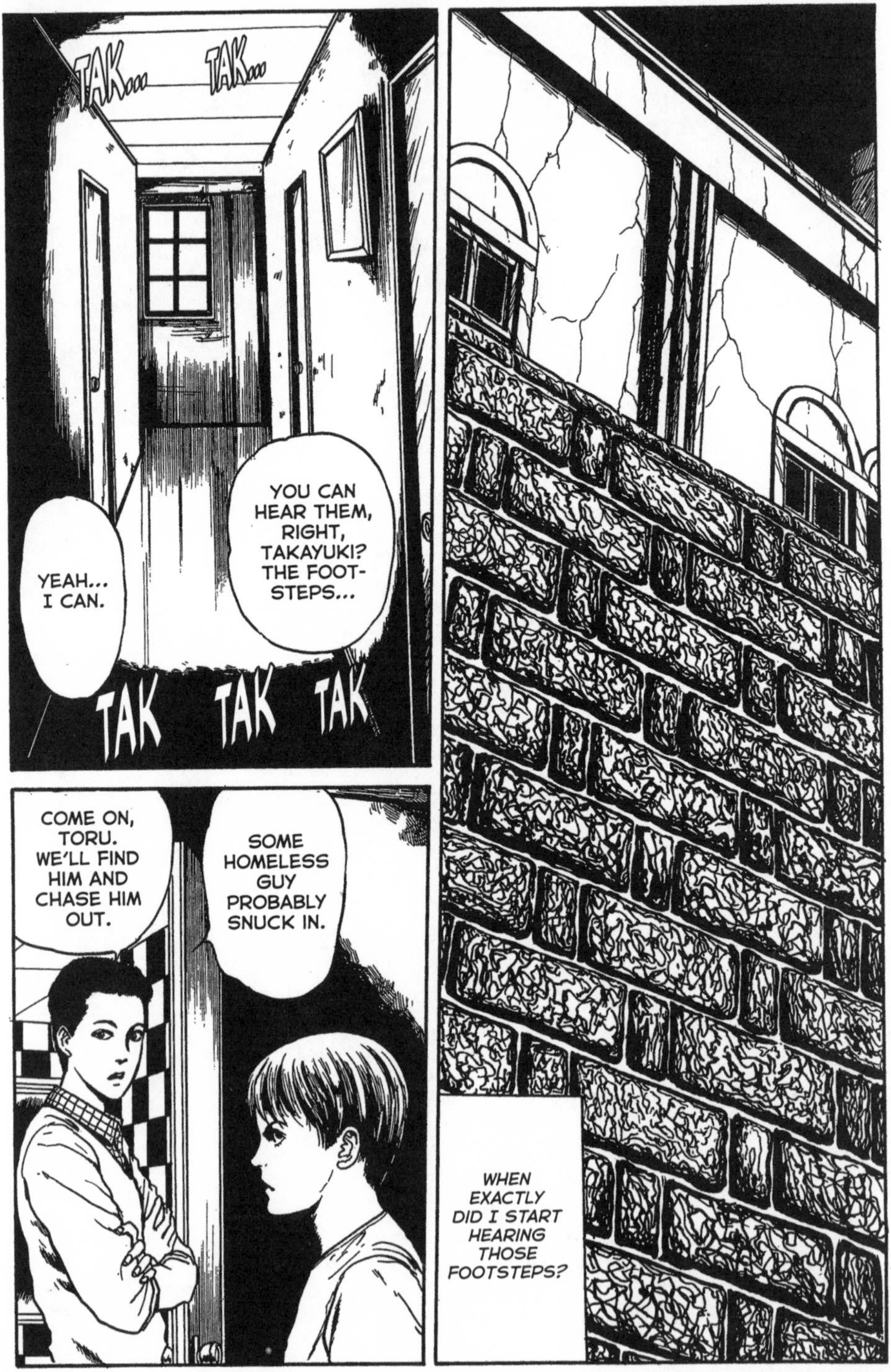
WHEN EXACTLY DID I START HEARING THOSE FOOTSTEPS?
TAK... TAK...
YOU CAN HEAR THEM, RIGHT, TAKAYUKI? THE FOOT- STEPS...
YEAH... I CAN.
TAK TAK TAK
SOME HOMELESS GUY PROBABLY SNUCK IN.
COME ON, TORU. WE'LL FIND HIM AND CHASE HIM OUT.

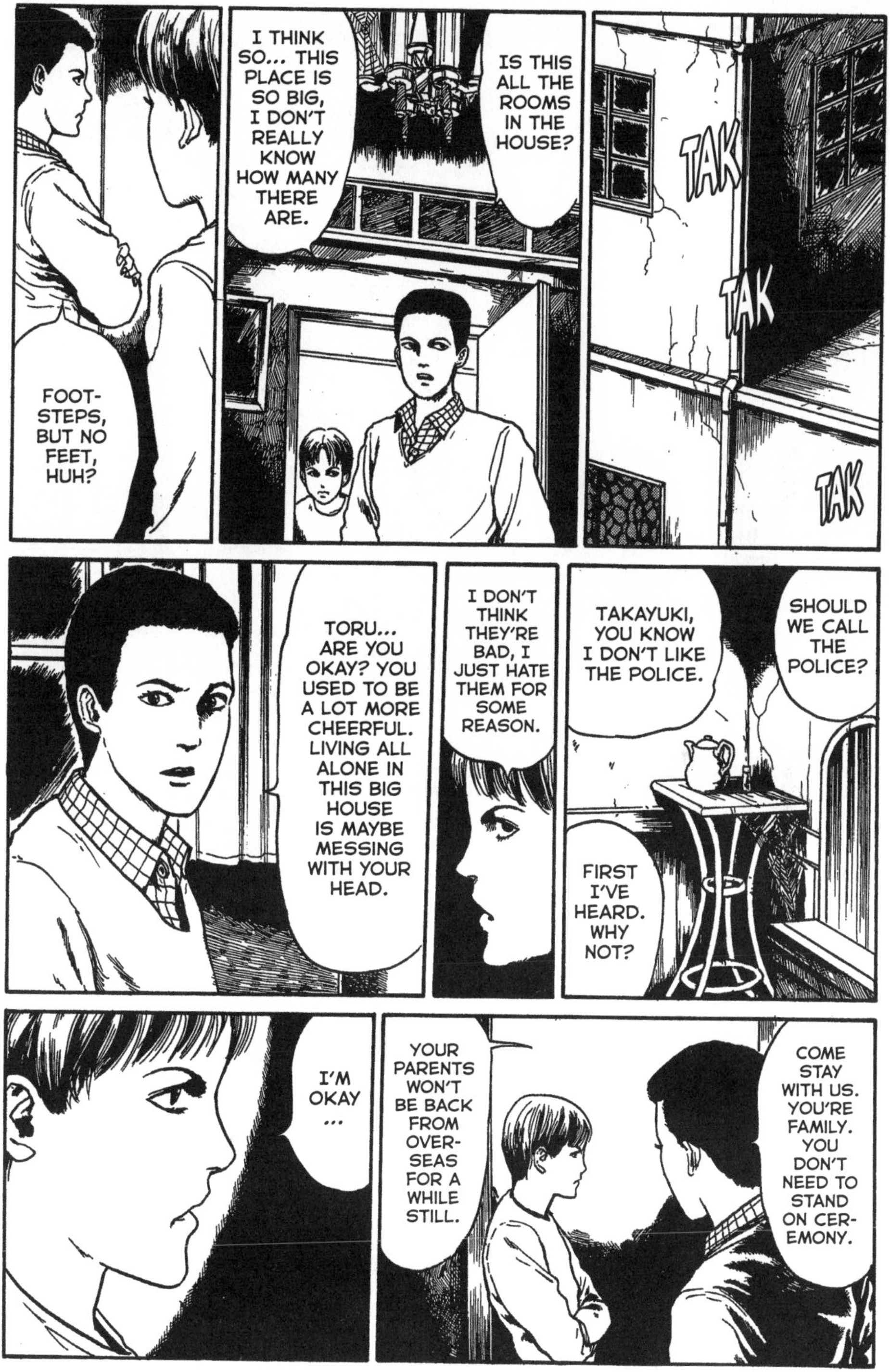
TAK
TAK
TAK
IS THIS ALL THE ROOMS IN THE HOUSE?
I THINK SO... THIS PLACE IS SO BIG, I DON'T REALLY KNOW HOW MANY THERE ARE.
FOOT-STEPS, BUT NO FEET, HUH?
SHOULD WE CALL THE POLICE?
TAKAYUKI, YOU KNOW I DON'T LIKE THE POLICE.
FIRST I'VE HEARD. WHY NOT?
I DON'T THINK THEY'RE BAD, I JUST HATE THEM FOR SOME REASON.
TORU... ARE YOU OKAY? YOU USED TO BE A LOT MORE CHEERFUL. LIVING ALL ALONE IN THIS BIG HOUSE IS MAYBE MESSING WITH YOUR HEAD.
COME STAY WITH US. YOU'RE FAMILY. YOU DON'T NEED TO STAND ON CER-EMONY.
YOUR PARENTS WON'T BE BACK FROM OVER-SEAS FOR A WHILE STILL.
I'M OKAY ...

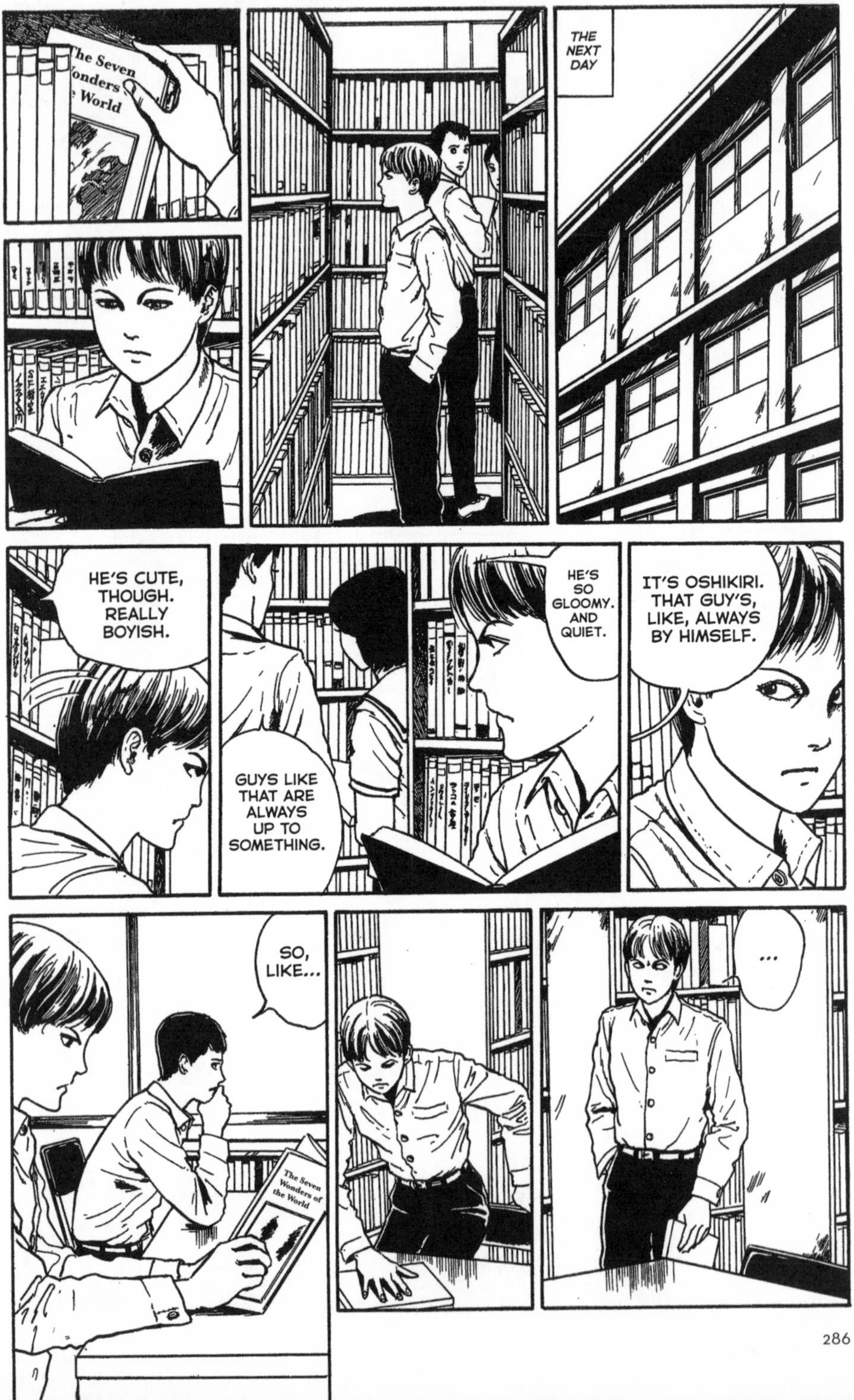
THE NEXT DAY
IT'S OSHIKIRI. THAT GUY'S, LIKE, ALWAYS BY HIMSELF.
HE'S SO GLOOMY. AND QUIET.
GUYS LIKE THAT ARE ALWAYS UP TO SOMETHING.
HE'S CUTE, THOUGH. REALLY BOYISH.
...
SO, LIKE...
The Seven Wonders of the World

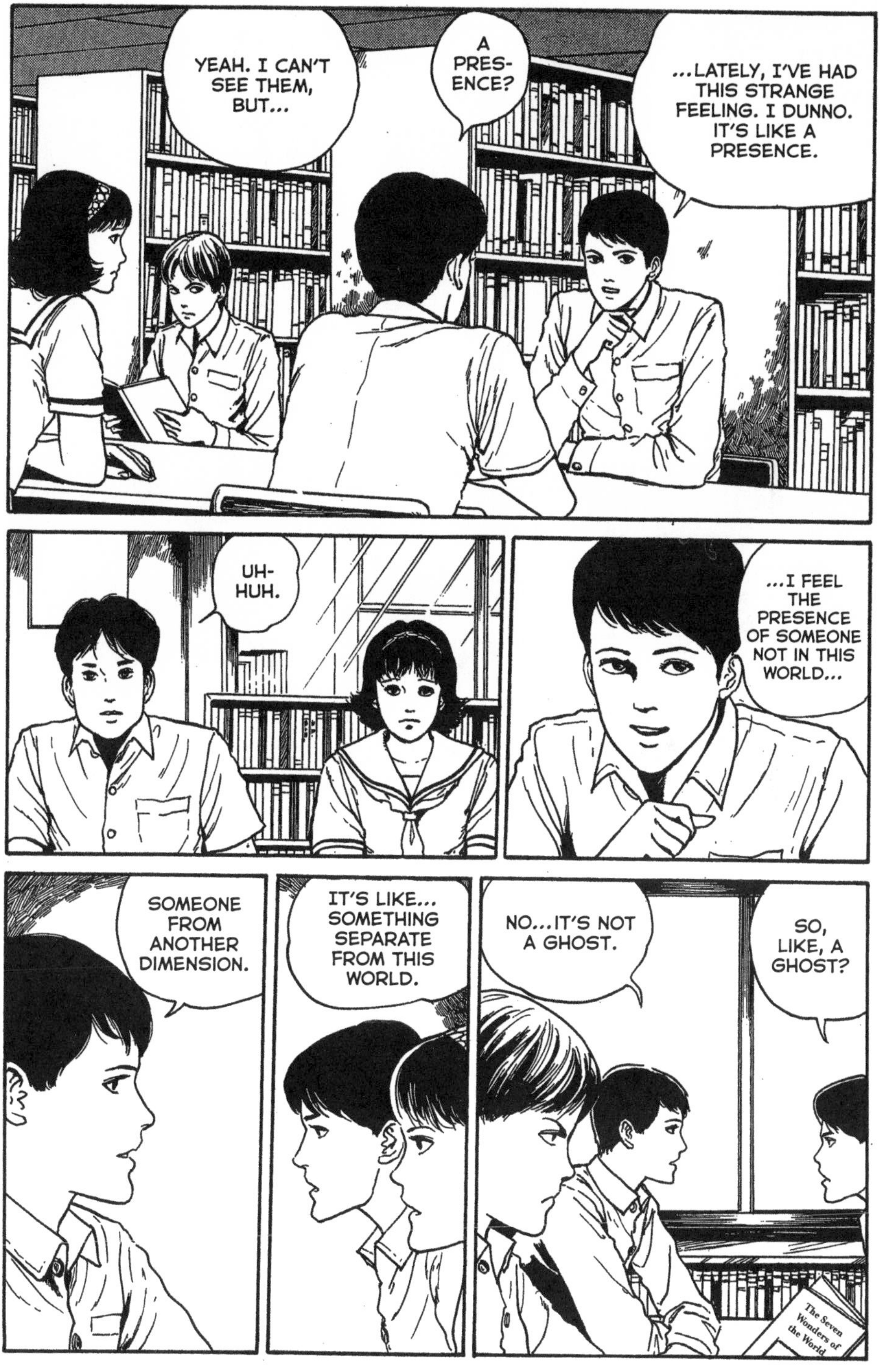
...LATELY, I'VE HAD THIS STRANGE FEELING. I DUNNO. IT'S LIKE A PRESENCE.
A PRESENCE?
YEAH. I CAN'T SEE THEM, BUT...
...I FEEL THE PRESENCE OF SOMEONE NOT IN THIS WORLD...
UH-HUH.
SO, LIKE, A GHOST?
NO...IT'S NOT A GHOST.
The Seven Wonders of the World
IT'S LIKE... SOMETHING SEPARATE FROM THIS WORLD.
SOMEONE FROM ANOTHER DIMENSION.

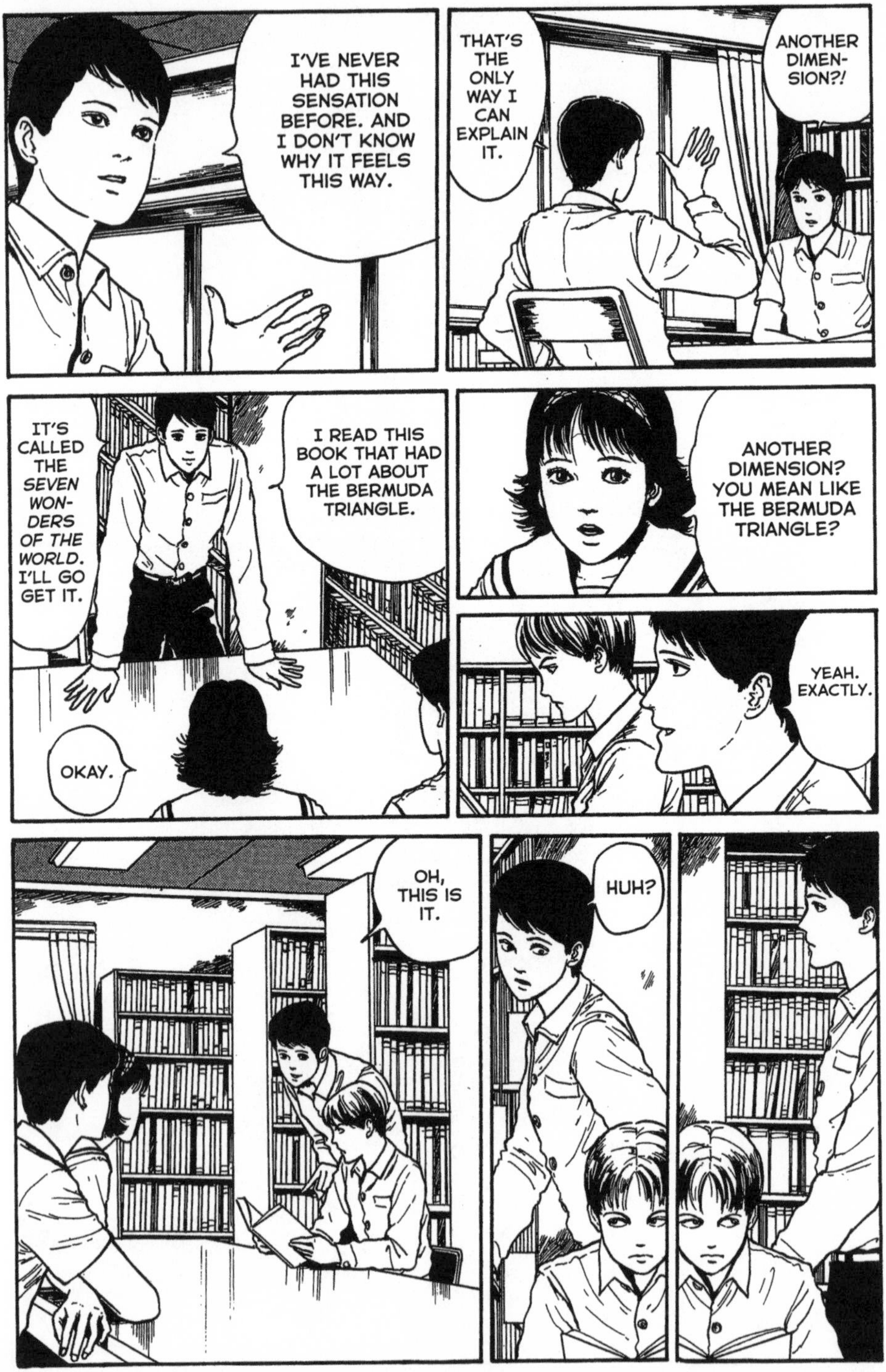
ANOTHER DIMENSION?!
THAT'S THE ONLY WAY I CAN EXPLAIN IT.
I'VE NEVER HAD THIS SENSATION BEFORE. AND I DON'T KNOW WHY IT FEELS THIS WAY.
ANOTHER DIMENSION? YOU MEAN LIKE THE BERMUDA TRIANGLE?
YEAH. EXACTLY.
I READ THIS BOOK THAT HAD A LOT ABOUT THE BERMUDA TRIANGLE.
IT'S CALLED THE *SEVEN WONDERS OF THE WORLD*. I'LL GO GET IT.
OKAY.
HUH?
OH, THIS IS IT.

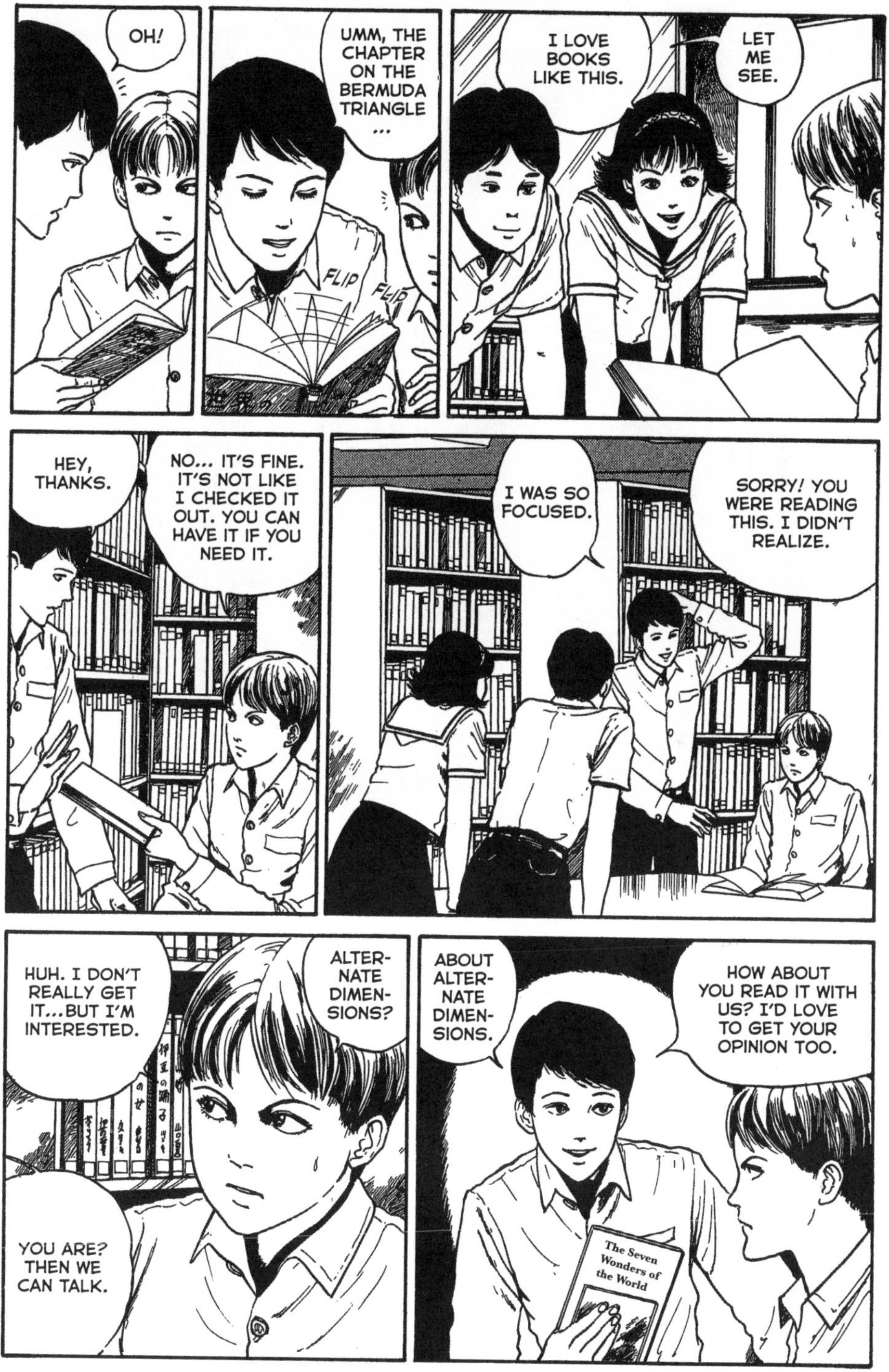
LET ME SEE.
I LOVE BOOKS LIKE THIS.
UMM, THE CHAPTER ON THE BERMUDA TRIANGLE ...
FLIP
FLIP
OH!
SORRY! YOU WERE READING THIS. I DIDN'T REALIZE.
I WAS SO FOCUSED.
NO... IT'S FINE. IT'S NOT LIKE I CHECKED IT OUT. YOU CAN HAVE IT IF YOU NEED IT.
HEY, THANKS.
HOW ABOUT YOU READ IT WITH US? I'D LOVE TO GET YOUR OPINION TOO.
ABOUT ALTERNATE DIMENSIONS.
The Seven Wonders of the World
ALTERNATE DIMENSIONS?
HUH. I DON'T REALLY GET IT...BUT I'M INTERESTED.
YOU ARE? THEN WE CAN TALK.

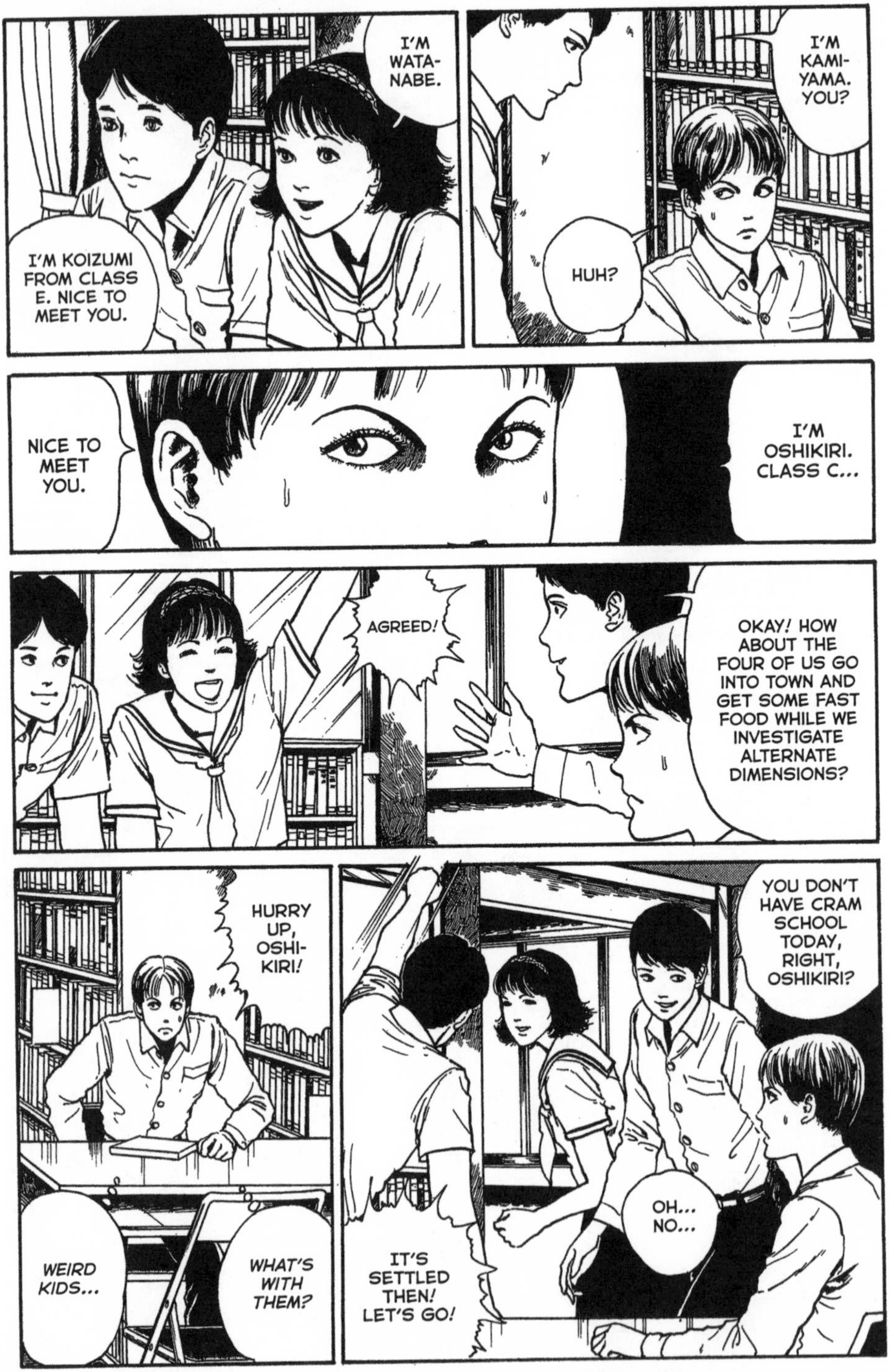
I'M KAMI-YAMA. YOU?
HUH?
I'M WATA-NABE.
I'M KOIZUMI FROM CLASS E. NICE TO MEET YOU.
I'M OSHIKIRI. CLASS C...
NICE TO MEET YOU.
OKAY! HOW ABOUT THE FOUR OF US GO INTO TOWN AND GET SOME FAST FOOD WHILE WE INVESTIGATE ALTERNATE DIMENSIONS?
AGREED!
YOU DON'T HAVE CRAM SCHOOL TODAY, RIGHT, OSHIKIRI?
OH... NO...
IT'S SETTLED THEN! LET'S GO!
HURRY UP, OSHI-KIRI!
WHAT'S WITH THEM?
WEIRD KIDS...

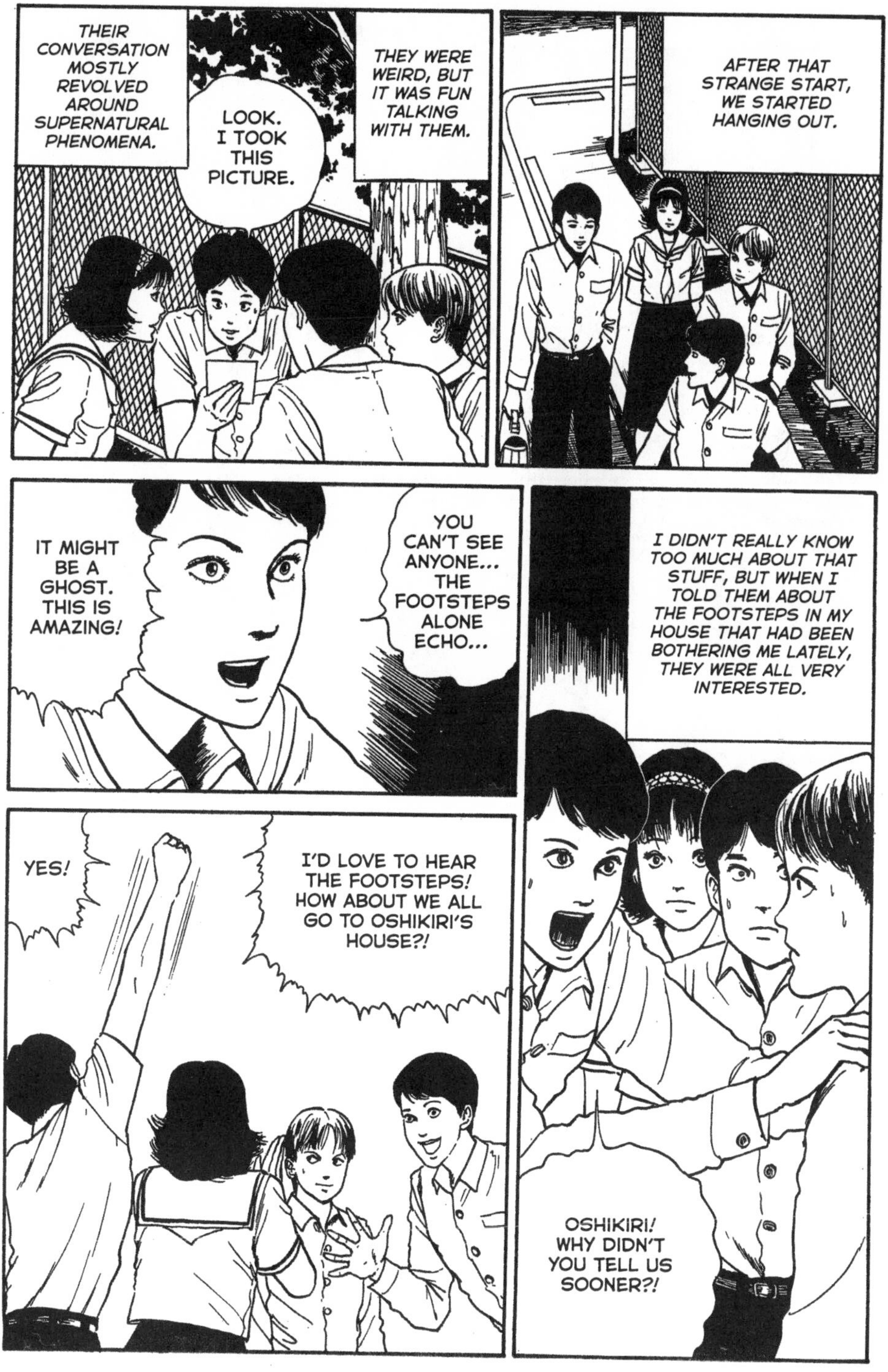
AFTER THAT STRANGE START, WE STARTED HANGING OUT.
THEY WERE WEIRD, BUT IT WAS FUN TALKING WITH THEM.
LOOK. I TOOK THIS PICTURE.
THEIR CONVERSATION MOSTLY REVOLVED AROUND SUPERNATURAL PHENOMENA.
I DIDN'T REALLY KNOW TOO MUCH ABOUT THAT STUFF, BUT WHEN I TOLD THEM ABOUT THE FOOTSTEPS IN MY HOUSE THAT HAD BEEN BOTHERING ME LATELY, THEY WERE ALL VERY INTERESTED.
OSHIKIRI! WHY DIDN'T YOU TELL US SOONER?!
YOU CAN'T SEE ANYONE... THE FOOTSTEPS ALONE ECHO...
IT MIGHT BE A GHOST. THIS IS AMAZING!
I'D LOVE TO HEAR THE FOOTSTEPS! HOW ABOUT WE ALL GO TO OSHIKIRI'S HOUSE?!
YES!

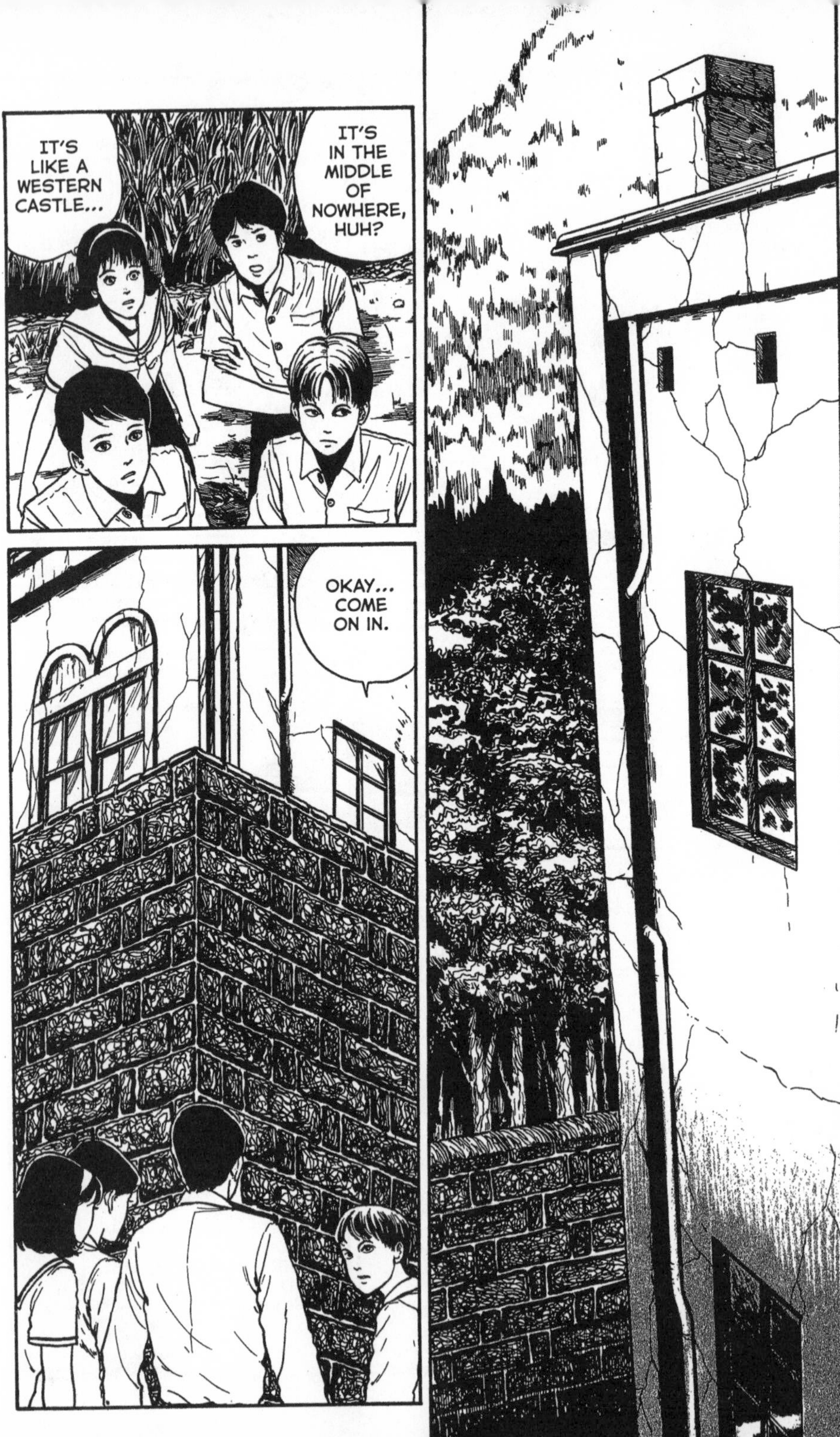
IT'S IN THE MIDDLE OF NOWHERE, HUH?
IT'S LIKE A WESTERN CASTLE...
OKAY... COME ON IN.

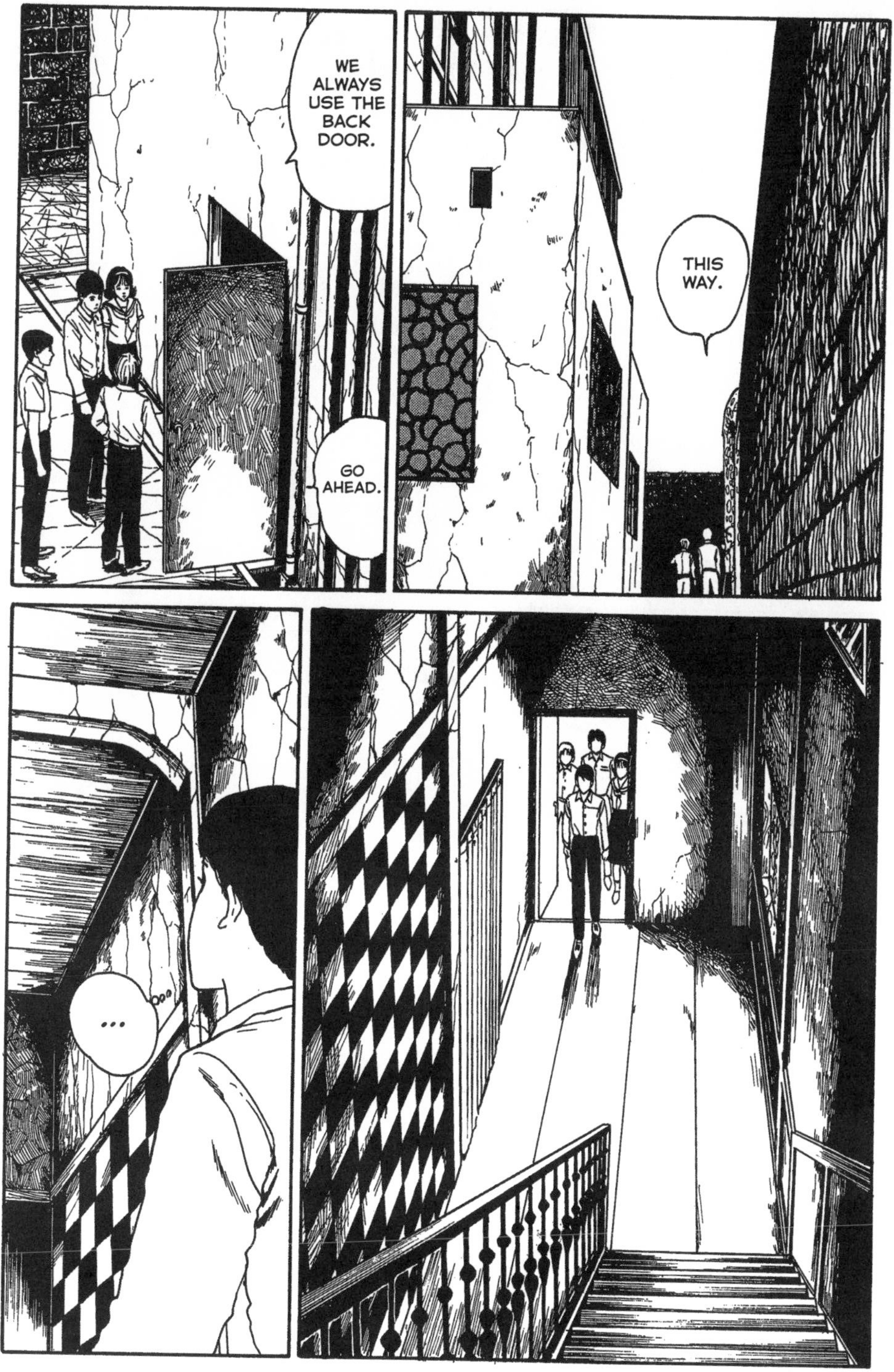
THIS WAY.
WE ALWAYS USE THE BACK DOOR.
GO AHEAD.
...

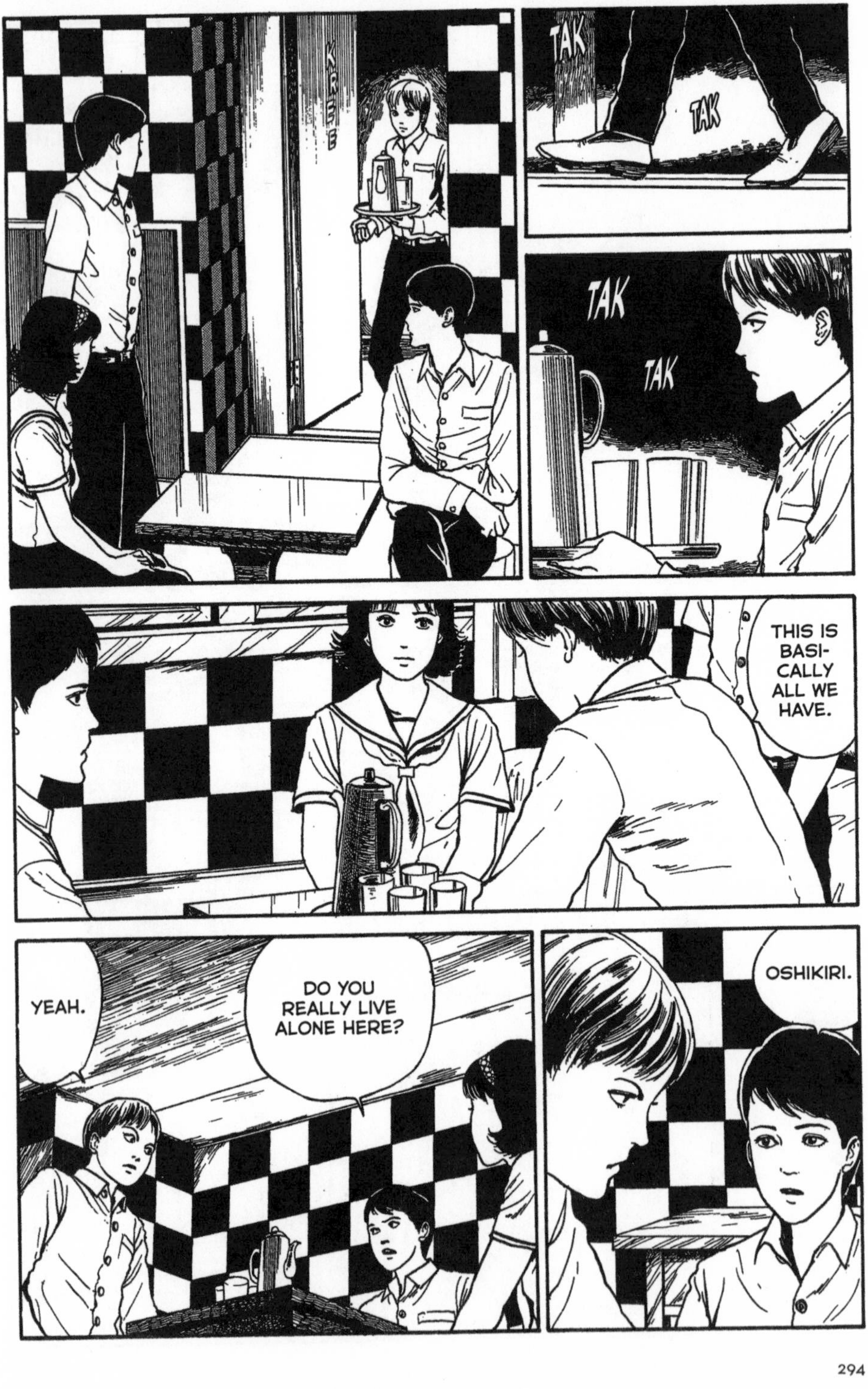
TAK
TAK
TAK
TAK
KREEE
THIS IS BASI-CALLY ALL WE HAVE.
OSHIKIRI.
DO YOU REALLY LIVE ALONE HERE?
YEAH.

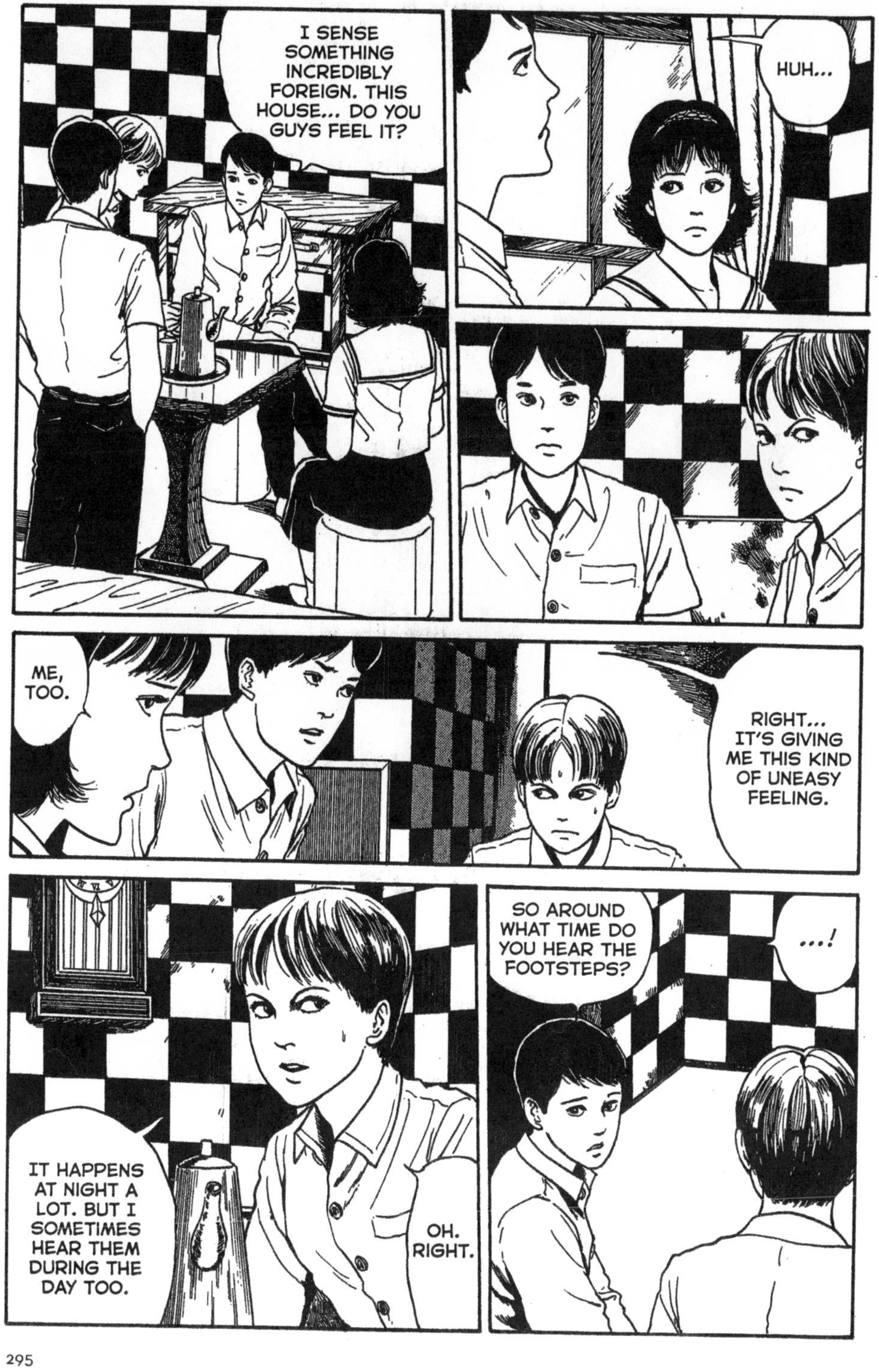

HUH...
I SENSE SOMETHING INCREDIBLY FOREIGN. THIS HOUSE... DO YOU GUYS FEEL IT?
RIGHT... IT'S GIVING ME THIS KIND OF UNEASY FEELING.
ME, TOO.
...!
SO AROUND WHAT TIME DO YOU HEAR THE FOOTSTEPS?
OH. RIGHT.
IT HAPPENS AT NIGHT A LOT. BUT I SOMETIMES HEAR THEM DURING THE DAY TOO.

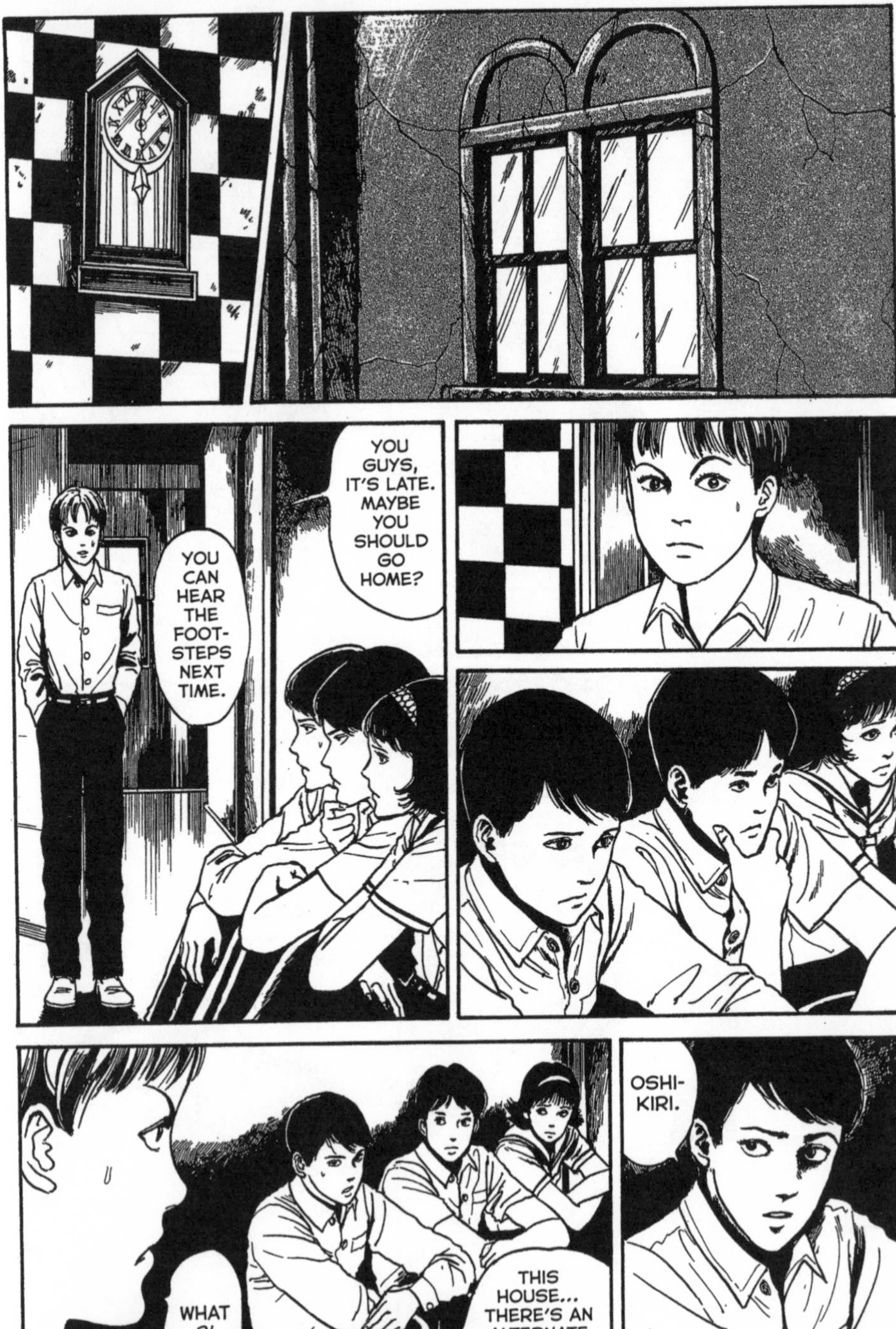
YOU GUYS, IT'S LATE. MAYBE YOU SHOULD GO HOME?
YOU CAN HEAR THE FOOT-STEPS NEXT TIME.
OSHI-KIRI.
THIS HOUSE... THERE'S AN ALTERNATE DIMENSIONAL PRESENCE...
WHAT?!

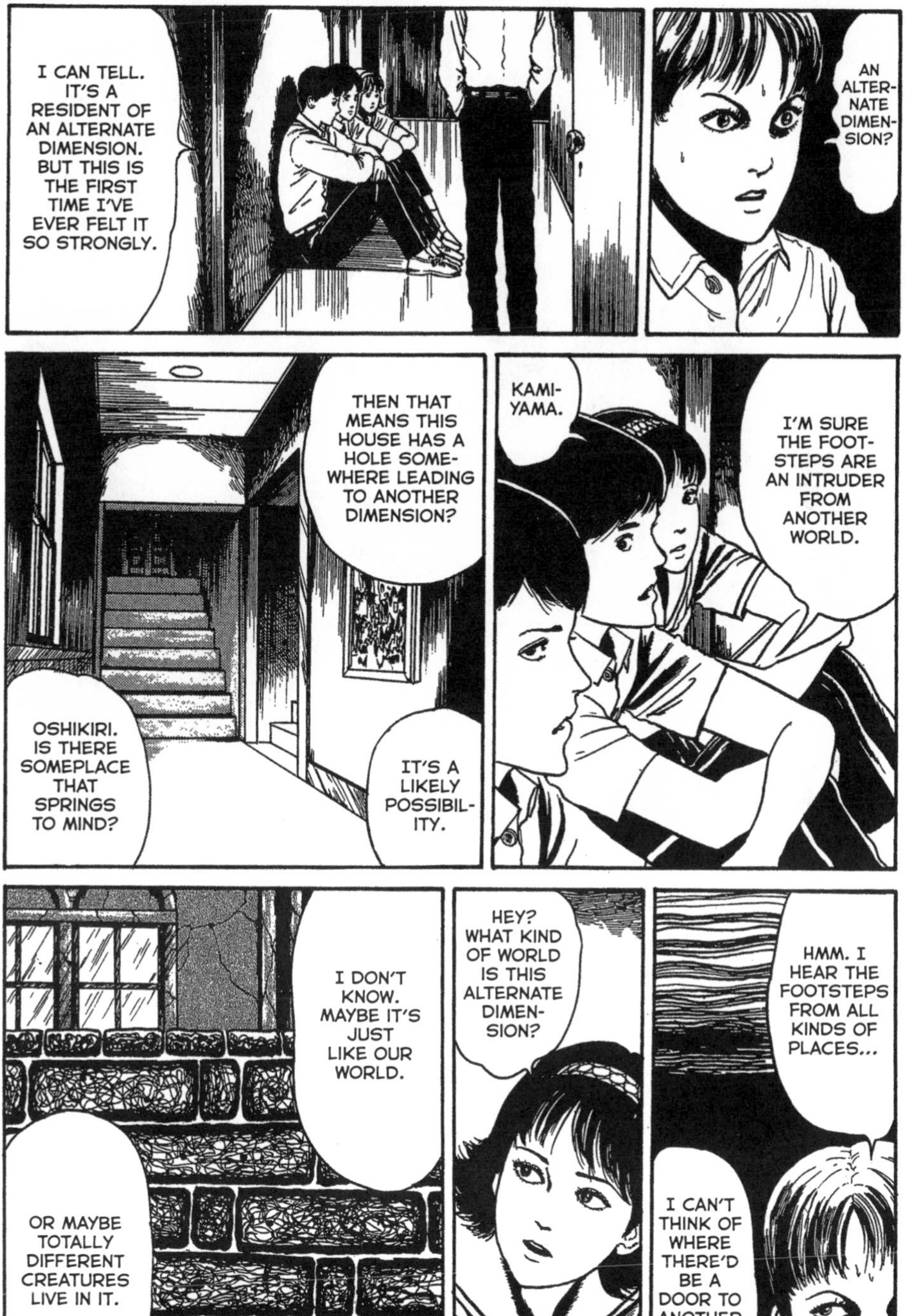
AN ALTER-NATE DIMEN-SION?
I CAN TELL. IT'S A RESIDENT OF AN ALTERNATE DIMENSION. BUT THIS IS THE FIRST TIME I'VE EVER FELT IT SO STRONGLY.
KAMI-YAMA.
I'M SURE THE FOOT-STEPS ARE AN INTRUDER FROM ANOTHER WORLD.
THEN THAT MEANS THIS HOUSE HAS A HOLE SOME-WHERE LEADING TO ANOTHER DIMENSION?
IT'S A LIKELY POSSIBIL-ITY.
OSHIKIRI. IS THERE SOMEPLACE THAT SPRINGS TO MIND?
HMM. I HEAR THE FOOTSTEPS FROM ALL KINDS OF PLACES...
I CAN'T THINK OF WHERE THERE'D BE A DOOR TO ANOTHER DIMEN-SION.
HEY? WHAT KIND OF WORLD IS THIS ALTERNATE DIMEN-SION?
I DON'T KNOW. MAYBE IT'S JUST LIKE OUR WORLD.
OR MAYBE TOTALLY DIFFERENT CREATURES LIVE IN IT.

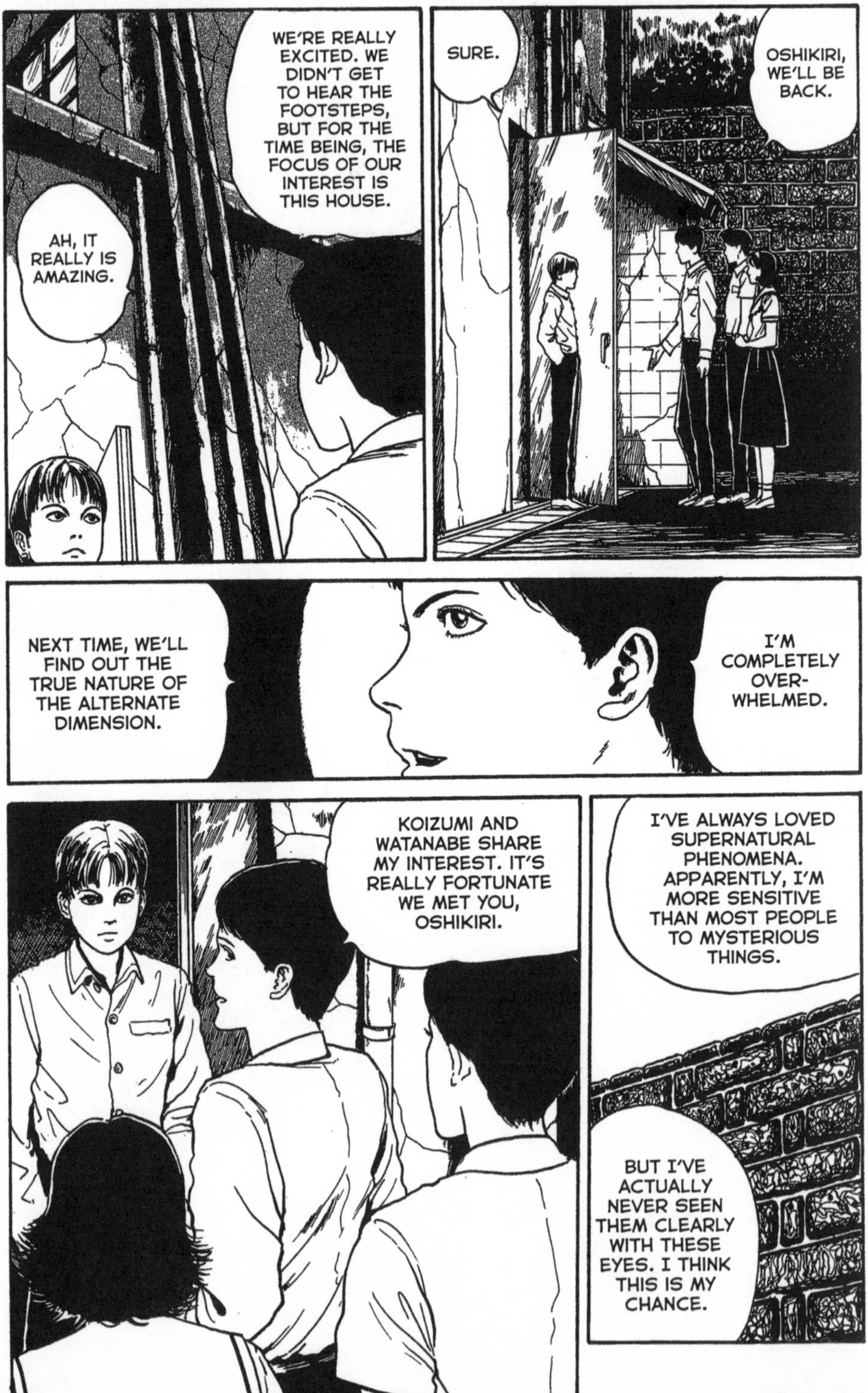
OSHIKIRI, WE'LL BE BACK.
SURE.
WE'RE REALLY EXCITED. WE DIDN'T GET TO HEAR THE FOOTSTEPS, BUT FOR THE TIME BEING, THE FOCUS OF OUR INTEREST IS THIS HOUSE.
AH, IT REALLY IS AMAZING.
I'M COMPLETELY OVER-WHELMED.
NEXT TIME, WE'LL FIND OUT THE TRUE NATURE OF THE ALTERNATE DIMENSION.
I'VE ALWAYS LOVED SUPERNATURAL PHENOMENA. APPARENTLY, I'M MORE SENSITIVE THAN MOST PEOPLE TO MYSTERIOUS THINGS.
BUT I'VE ACTUALLY NEVER SEEN THEM CLEARLY WITH THESE EYES. I THINK THIS IS MY CHANCE.
KOIZUMI AND WATANABE SHARE MY INTEREST. IT'S REALLY FORTUNATE WE MET YOU, OSHIKIRI.

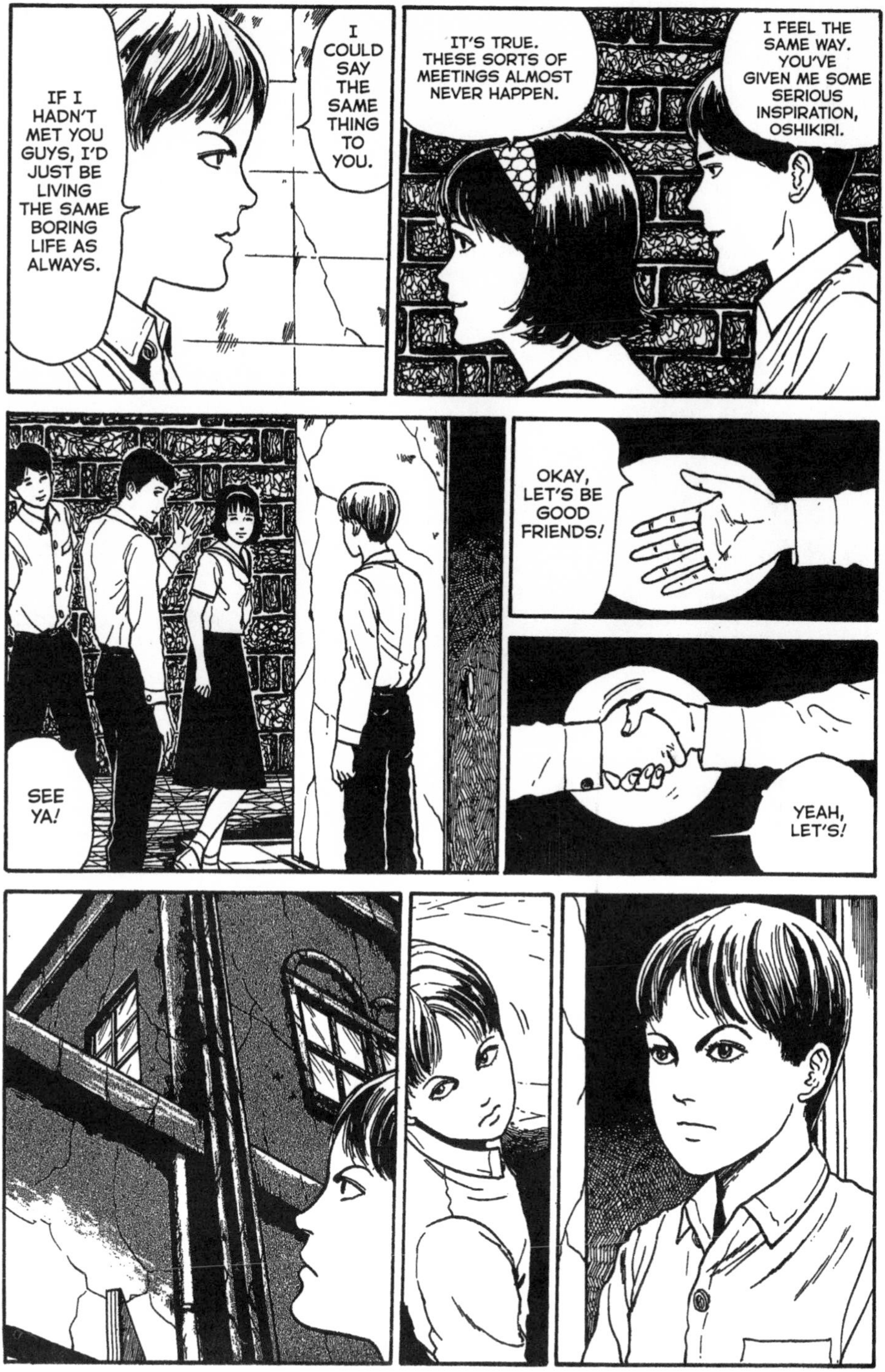
I FEEL THE SAME WAY. YOU'VE GIVEN ME SOME SERIOUS INSPIRATION, OSHIKIRI.
IT'S TRUE. THESE SORTS OF MEETINGS ALMOST NEVER HAPPEN.
I COULD SAY THE SAME THING TO YOU.
IF I HADN'T MET YOU GUYS, I'D JUST BE LIVING THE SAME BORING LIFE AS ALWAYS.
OKAY, LET'S BE GOOD FRIENDS!
YEAH, LET'S!
SEE YA!

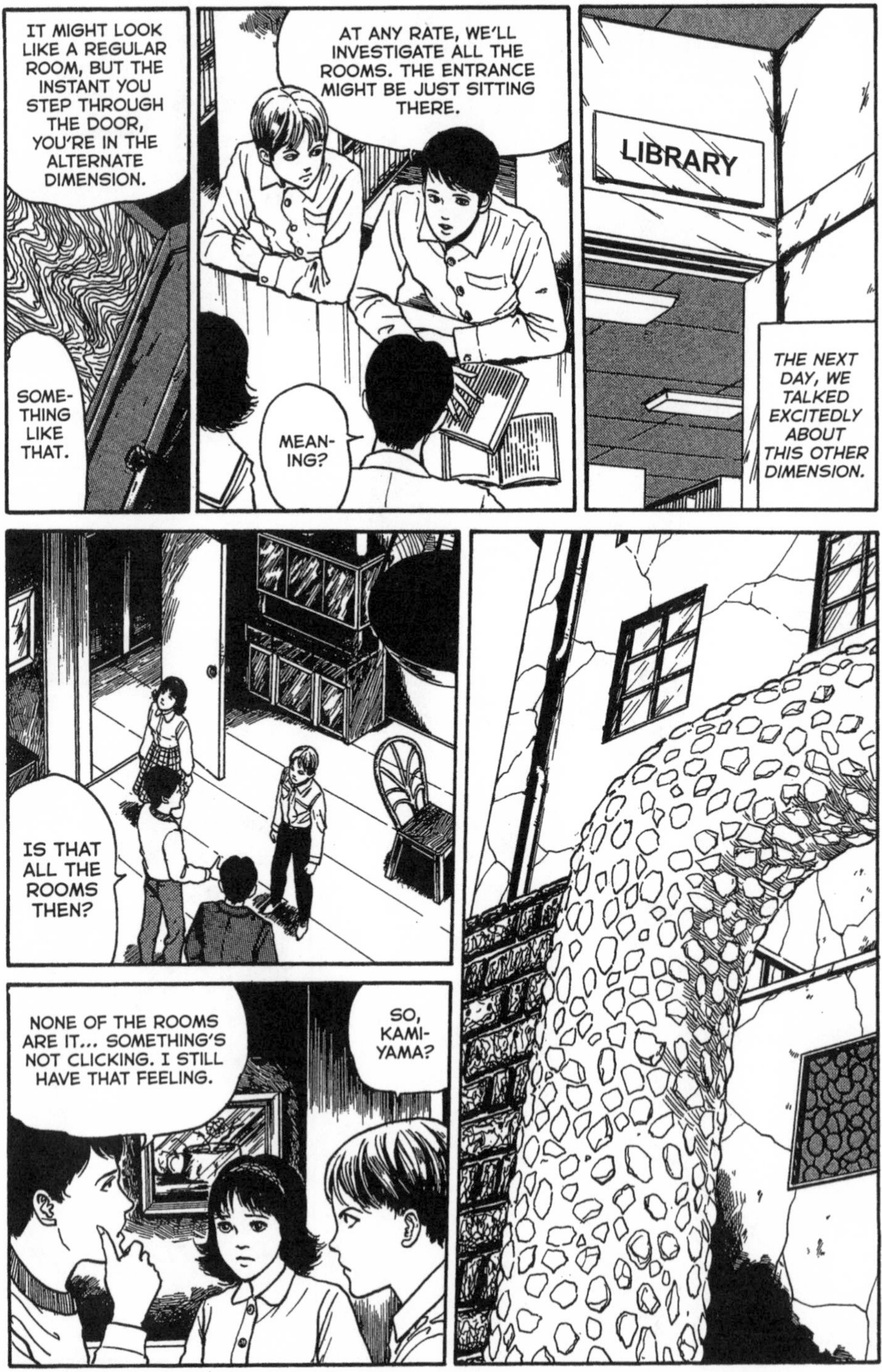
LIBRARY
THE NEXT DAY, WE TALKED EXCITEDLY ABOUT THIS OTHER DIMENSION.
AT ANY RATE, WE'LL INVESTIGATE ALL THE ROOMS. THE ENTRANCE MIGHT BE JUST SITTING THERE.
MEANING?
IT MIGHT LOOK LIKE A REGULAR ROOM, BUT THE INSTANT YOU STEP THROUGH THE DOOR, YOU'RE IN THE ALTERNATE DIMENSION.
SOMETHING LIKE THAT.
IS THAT ALL THE ROOMS THEN?
SO, KAMIYAMA?
NONE OF THE ROOMS ARE IT... SOMETHING'S NOT CLICKING. I STILL HAVE THAT FEELING.

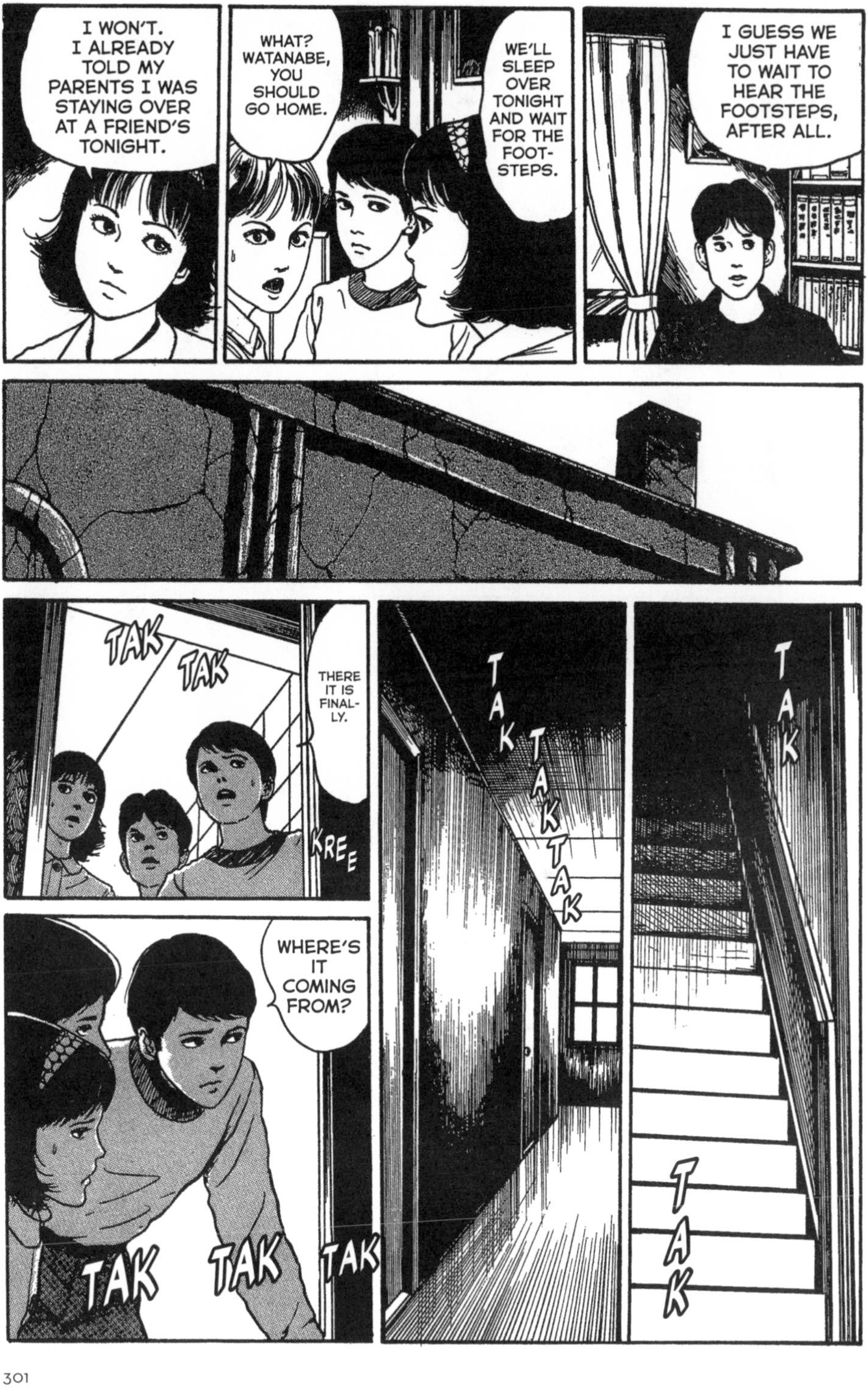
I GUESS WE JUST HAVE TO WAIT TO HEAR THE FOOTSTEPS, AFTER ALL.
WE'LL SLEEP OVER TONIGHT AND WAIT FOR THE FOOT-STEPS.
WHAT? WATANABE, YOU SHOULD GO HOME.
I WON'T. I ALREADY TOLD MY PARENTS I WAS STAYING OVER AT A FRIEND'S TONIGHT.
TAK
TAK
TAK
TAK
TAK
TAK
TAK
TAK
THERE IT IS FINAL-LY.
KREE
WHERE'S IT COMING FROM?
TAK
TAK
TAK

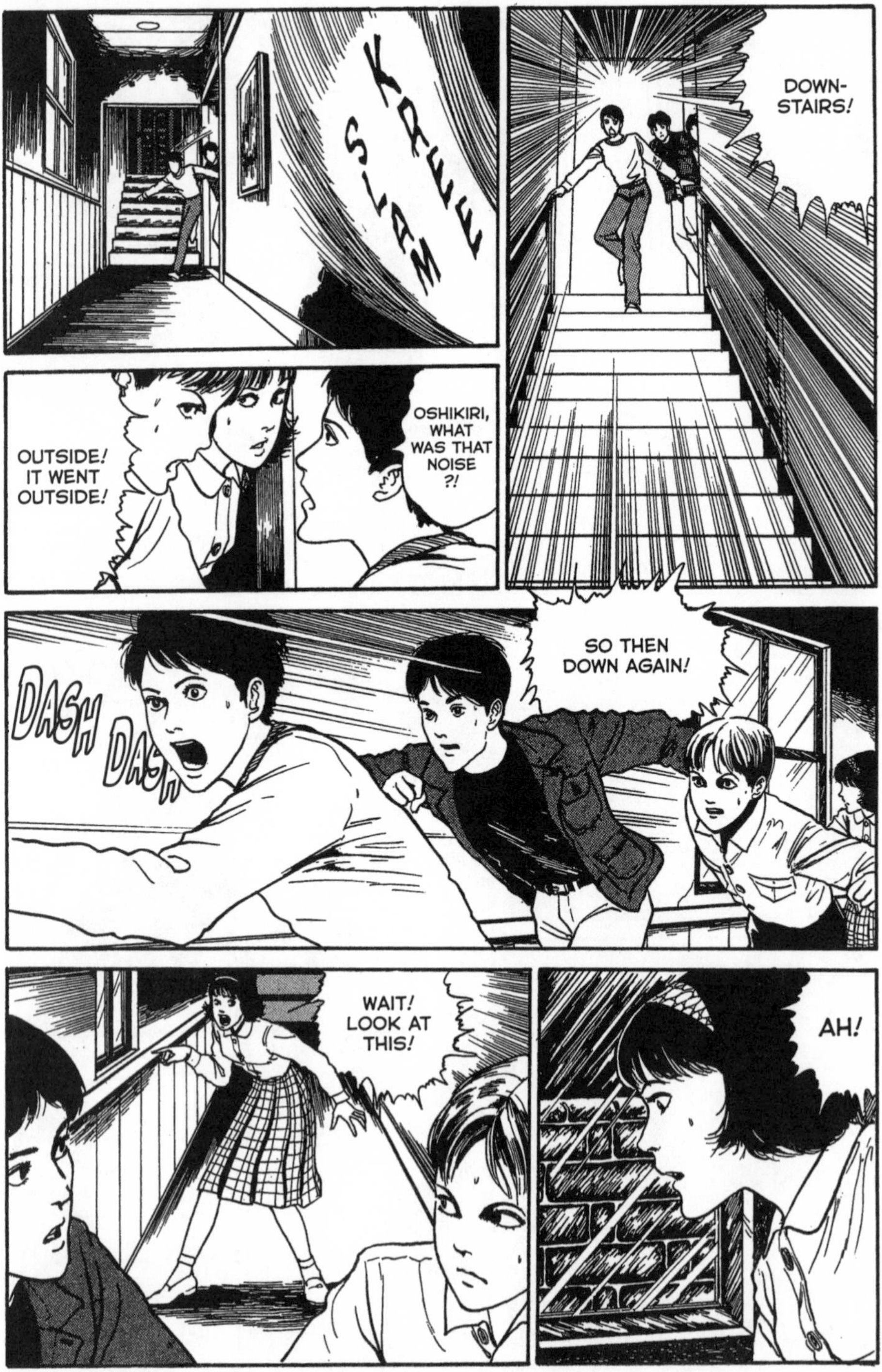
DOWN-STAIRS!
KRUMM
SLAM
OSHIKIRI, WHAT WAS THAT NOISE ?!
OUTSIDE! IT WENT OUTSIDE!
SO THEN DOWN AGAIN!
DASH DASH
AH!
WAIT! LOOK AT THIS!

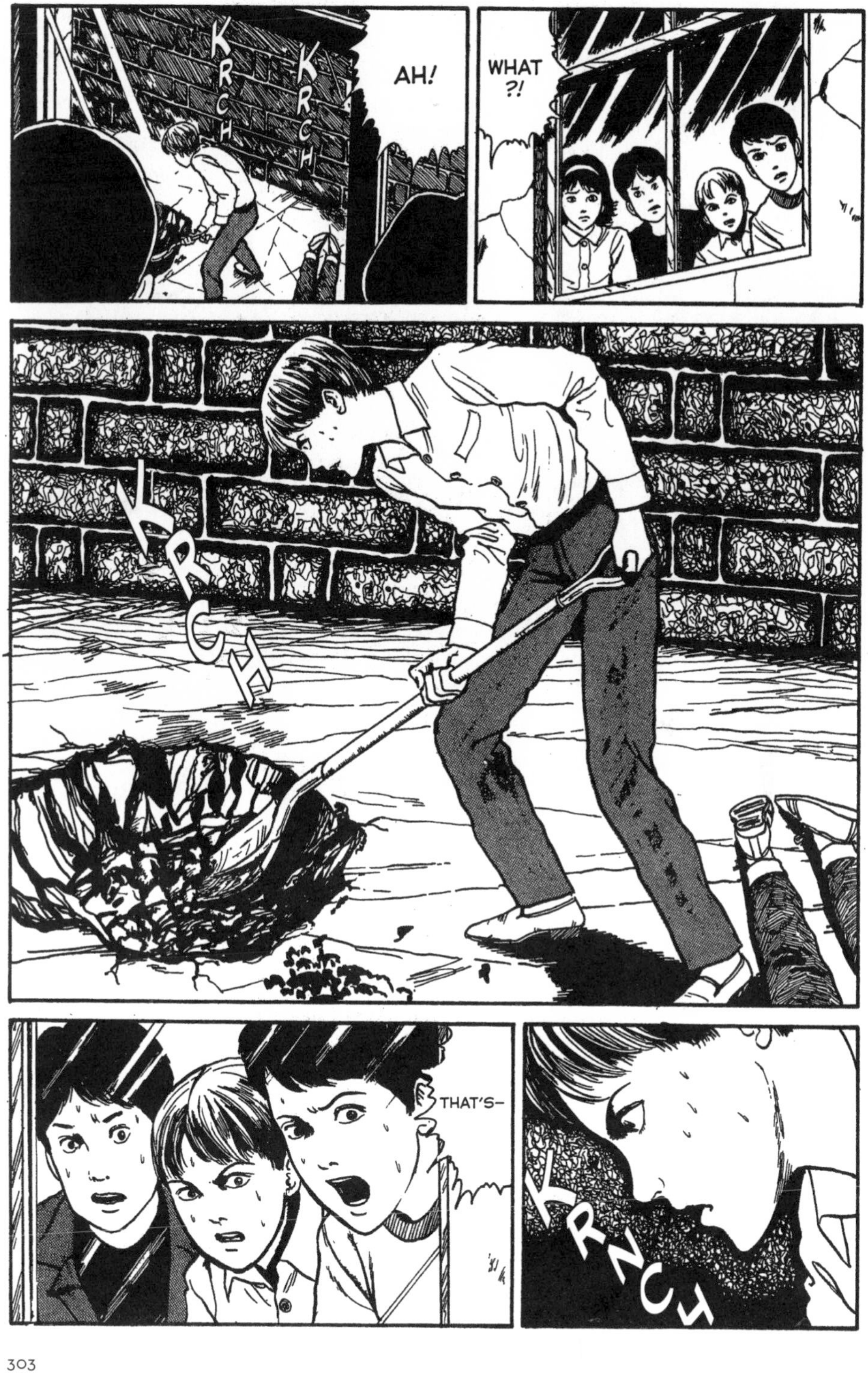
WHAT ?!
AH!
KRCH
KRCH
KRCH
KRNCH
THAT'S-

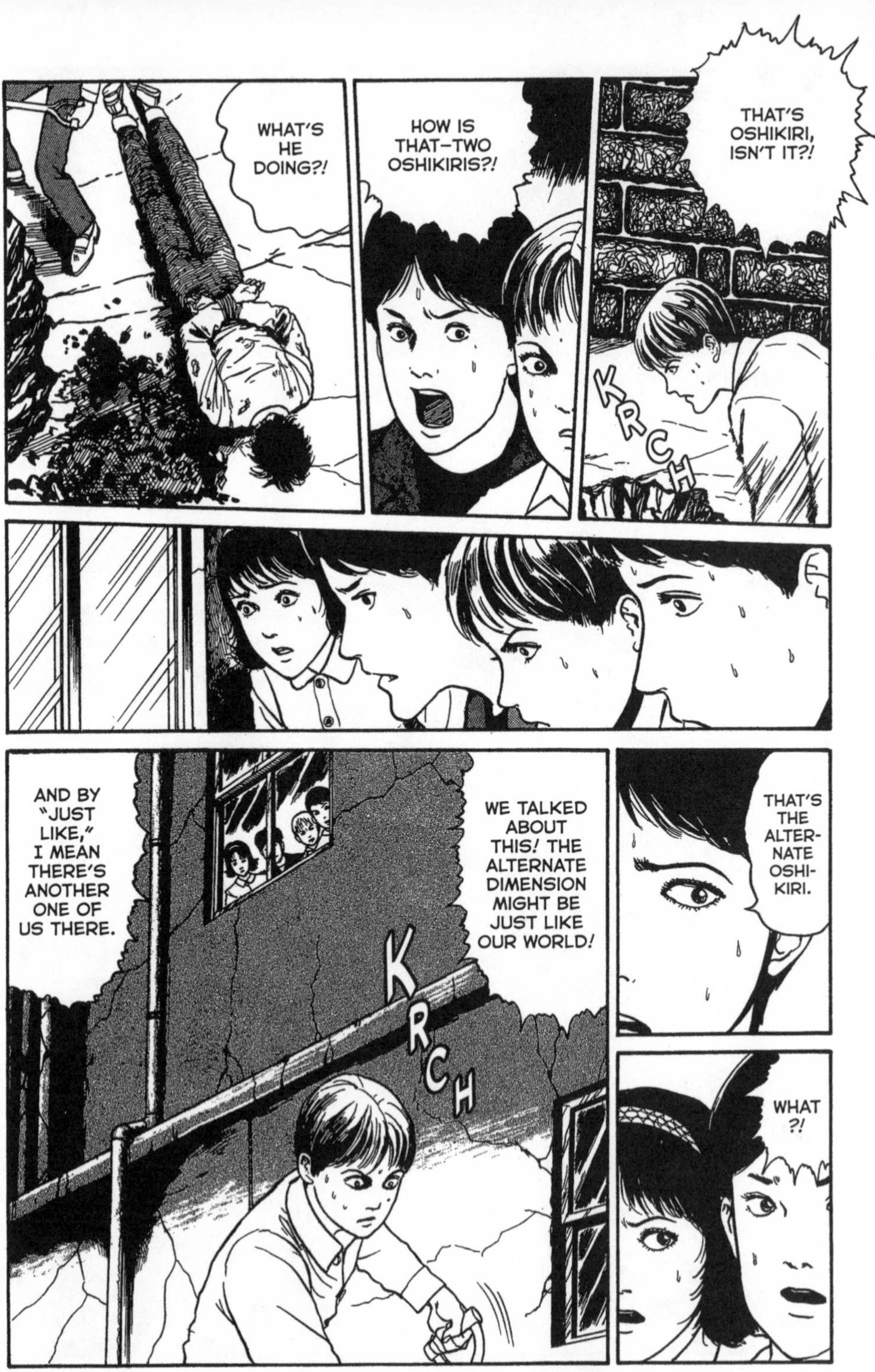
THAT'S OSHIKIRI, ISN'T IT?!
KRCH
HOW IS THAT—TWO OSHIKIRIS?!
WHAT'S HE DOING?!
THAT'S THE ALTER-NATE OSHI-KIRI.
WHAT?!
WE TALKED ABOUT THIS! THE ALTERNATE DIMENSION MIGHT BE JUST LIKE OUR WORLD!
AND BY "JUST LIKE," I MEAN THERE'S ANOTHER ONE OF US THERE.
KRCH

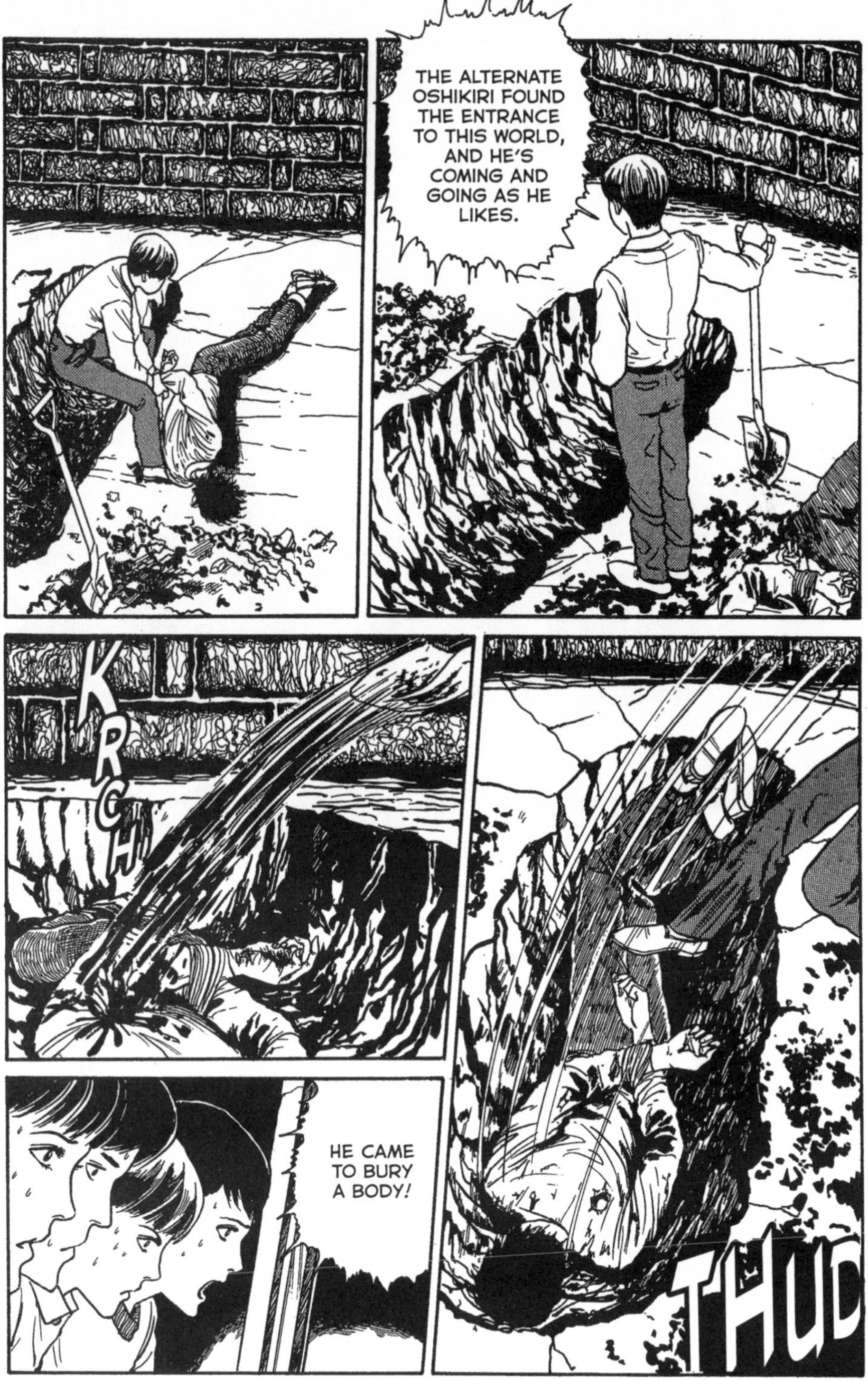
THE ALTERNATE OSHIKIRI FOUND THE ENTRANCE TO THIS WORLD, AND HE'S COMING AND GOING AS HE LIKES.
THUD
KRCH
HE CAME TO BURY A BODY!

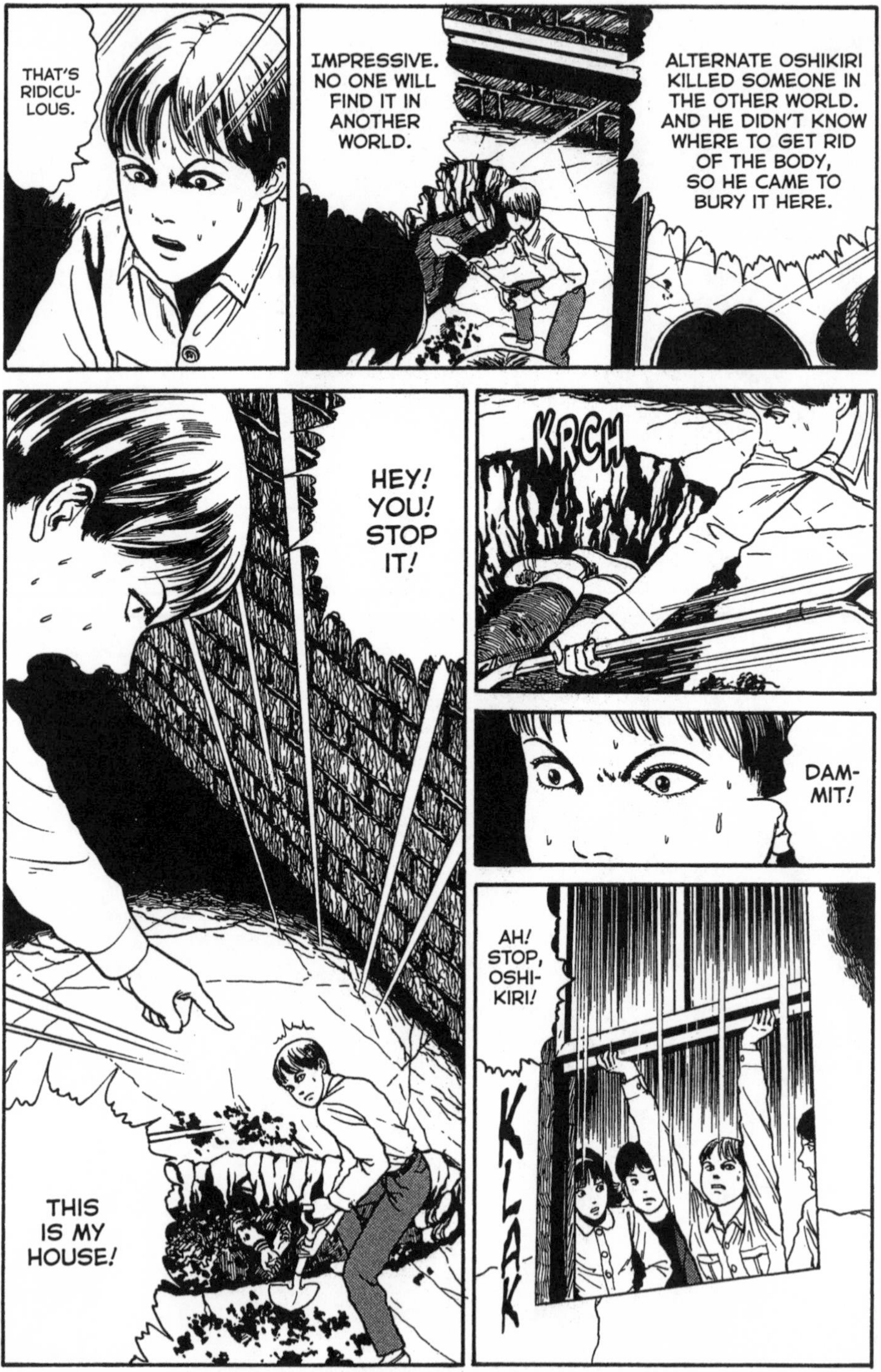
ALTERNATE OSHIKIRI KILLED SOMEONE IN THE OTHER WORLD. AND HE DIDN'T KNOW WHERE TO GET RID OF THE BODY, SO HE CAME TO BURY IT HERE.
IMPRESSIVE. NO ONE WILL FIND IT IN ANOTHER WORLD.
THAT'S RIDICU-LOUS.
KRCH
DAM-MIT!
AH! STOP, OSHI-KIRI!
KLAK
HEY! YOU! STOP IT!
THIS IS MY HOUSE!

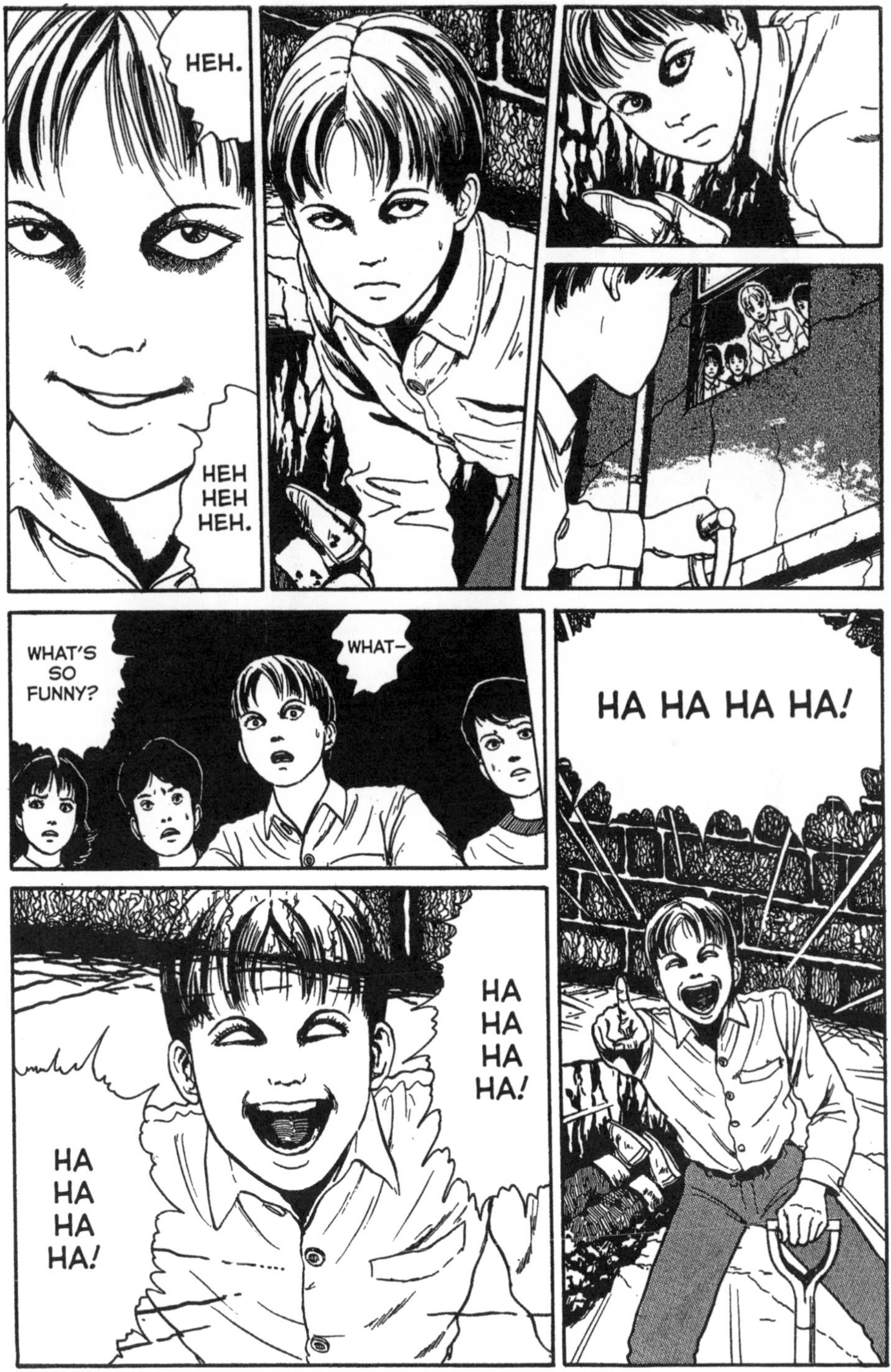

HEH.
HEH HEH HEH.
HA HA HA HA!
WHAT—
WHAT'S SO FUNNY?
HA HA HA HA!
HA HA HA HA!

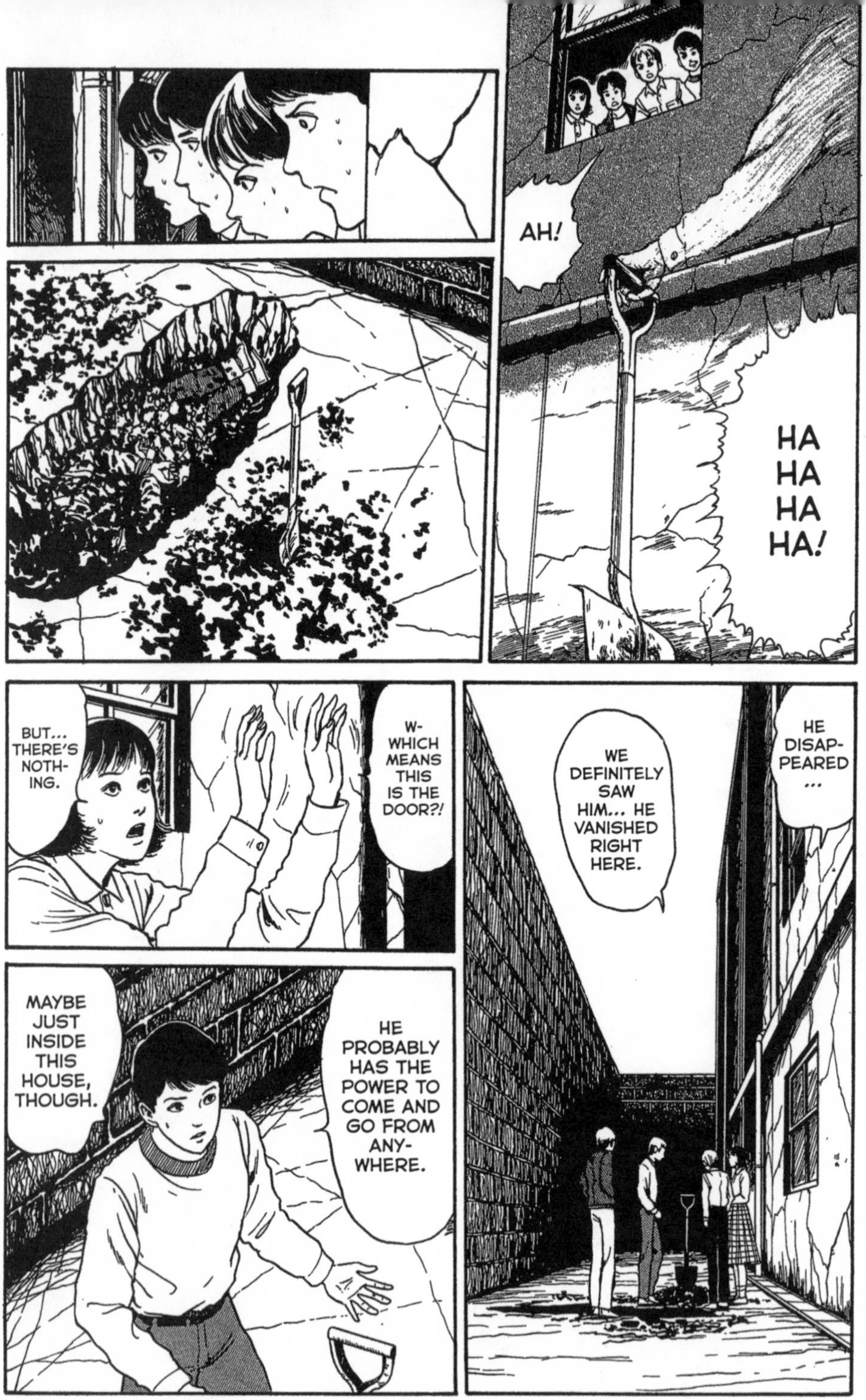
AH!
HA HA HA HA!
HE DISAPPEARED...
WE DEFINITELY SAW HIM... HE VANISHED RIGHT HERE.
W-WHICH MEANS THIS IS THE DOOR?!
BUT... THERE'S NOTHING.
HE PROBABLY HAS THE POWER TO COME AND GO FROM ANYWHERE.
MAYBE JUST INSIDE THIS HOUSE, THOUGH.

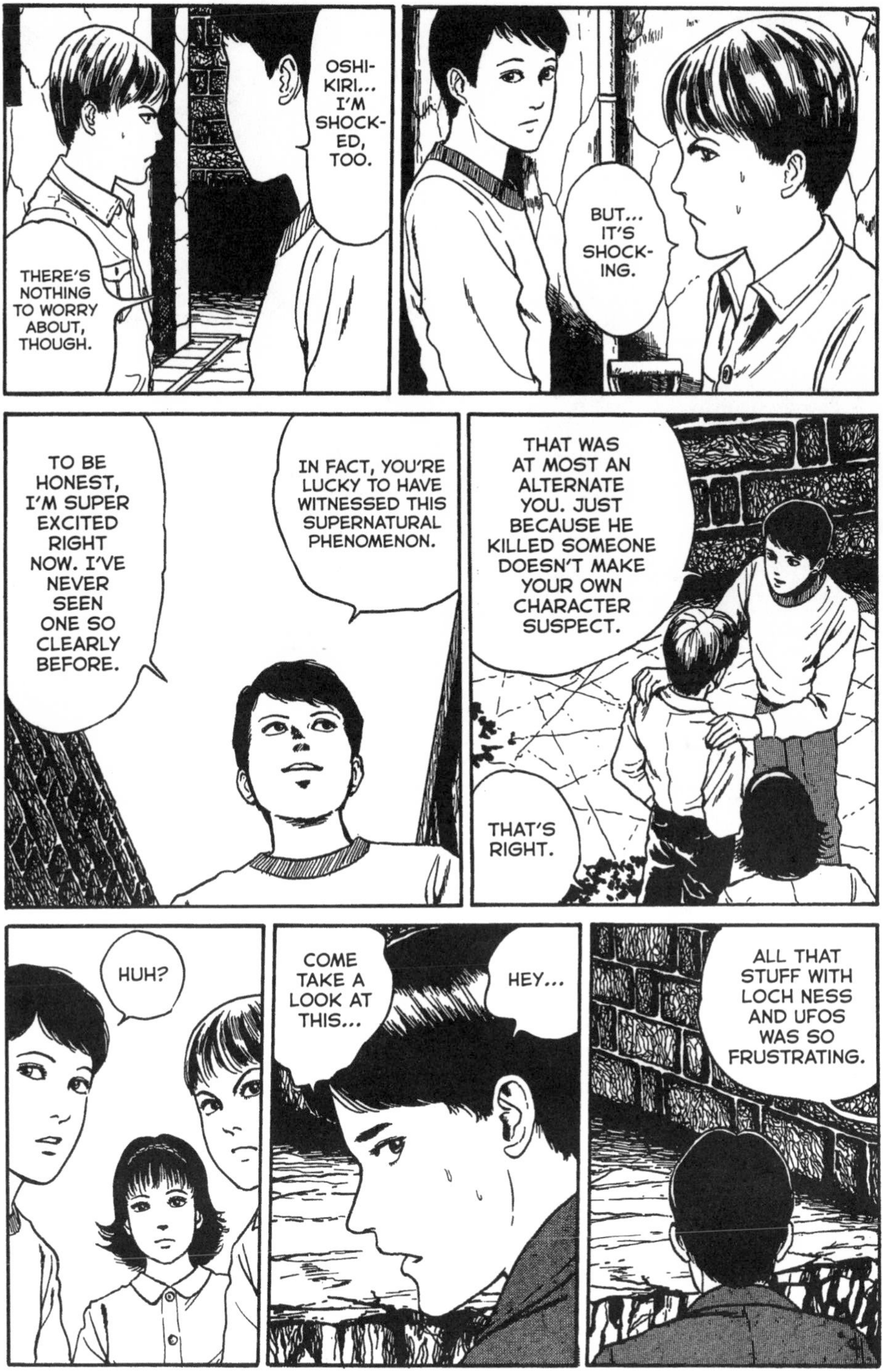
BUT... IT'S SHOCKING.
OSHIKIRI... I'M SHOCKED, TOO.
THERE'S NOTHING TO WORRY ABOUT, THOUGH.
THAT WAS AT MOST AN ALTERNATE YOU. JUST BECAUSE HE KILLED SOMEONE DOESN'T MAKE YOUR OWN CHARACTER SUSPECT.
THAT'S RIGHT.
IN FACT, YOU'RE LUCKY TO HAVE WITNESSED THIS SUPERNATURAL PHENOMENON.
TO BE HONEST, I'M SUPER EXCITED RIGHT NOW. I'VE NEVER SEEN ONE SO CLEARLY BEFORE.
ALL THAT STUFF WITH LOCH NESS AND UFOS WAS SO FRUSTRATING.
HEY...
COME TAKE A LOOK AT THIS...
HUH?

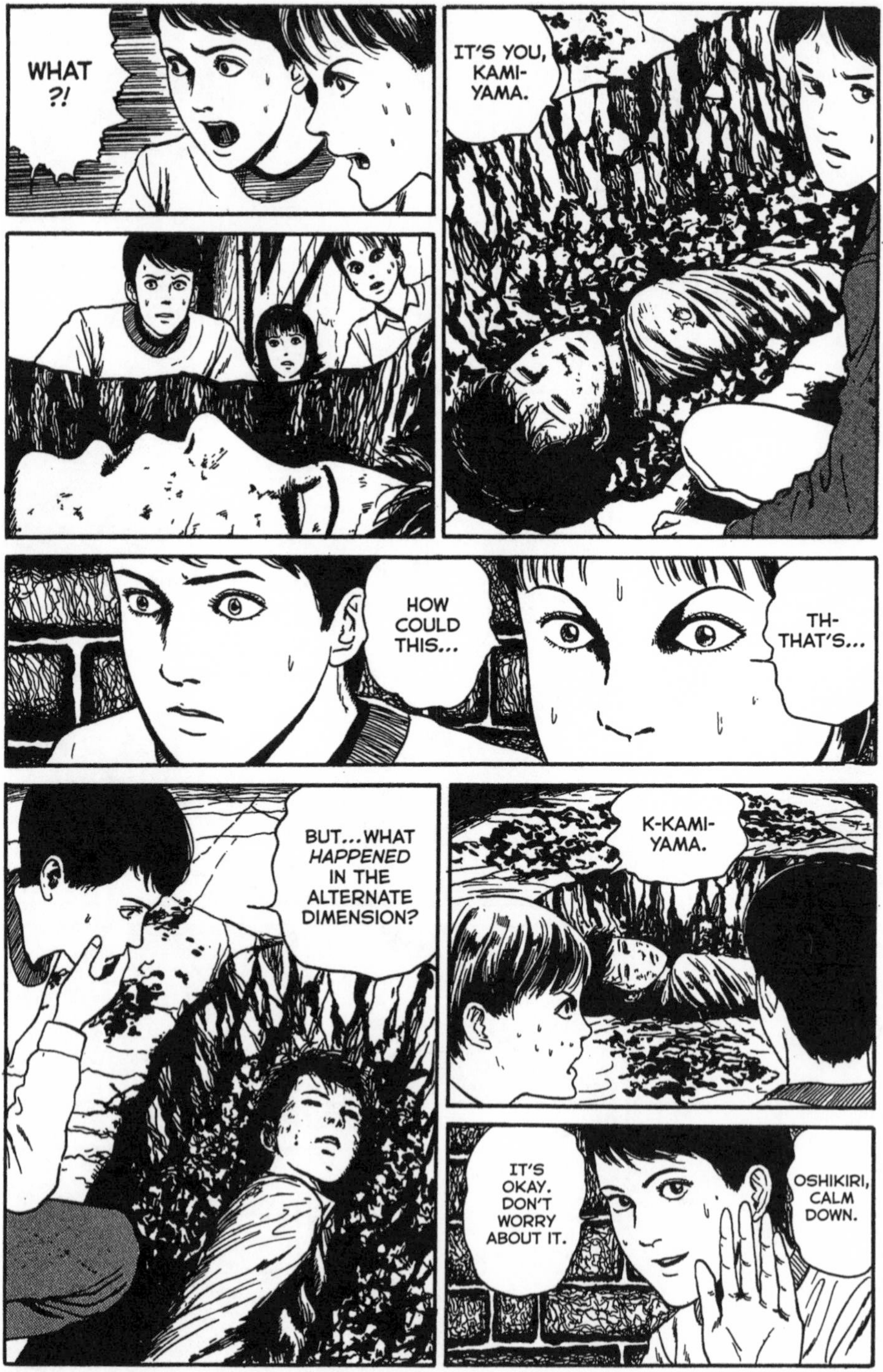
IT'S YOU, KAMI-YAMA.
WHAT ?!
TH- THAT'S...
HOW COULD THIS...
K-KAMI-YAMA.
OSHIKIRI, CALM DOWN.
IT'S OKAY. DON'T WORRY ABOUT IT.
BUT...WHAT *HAPPENED* IN THE ALTERNATE DIMENSION?

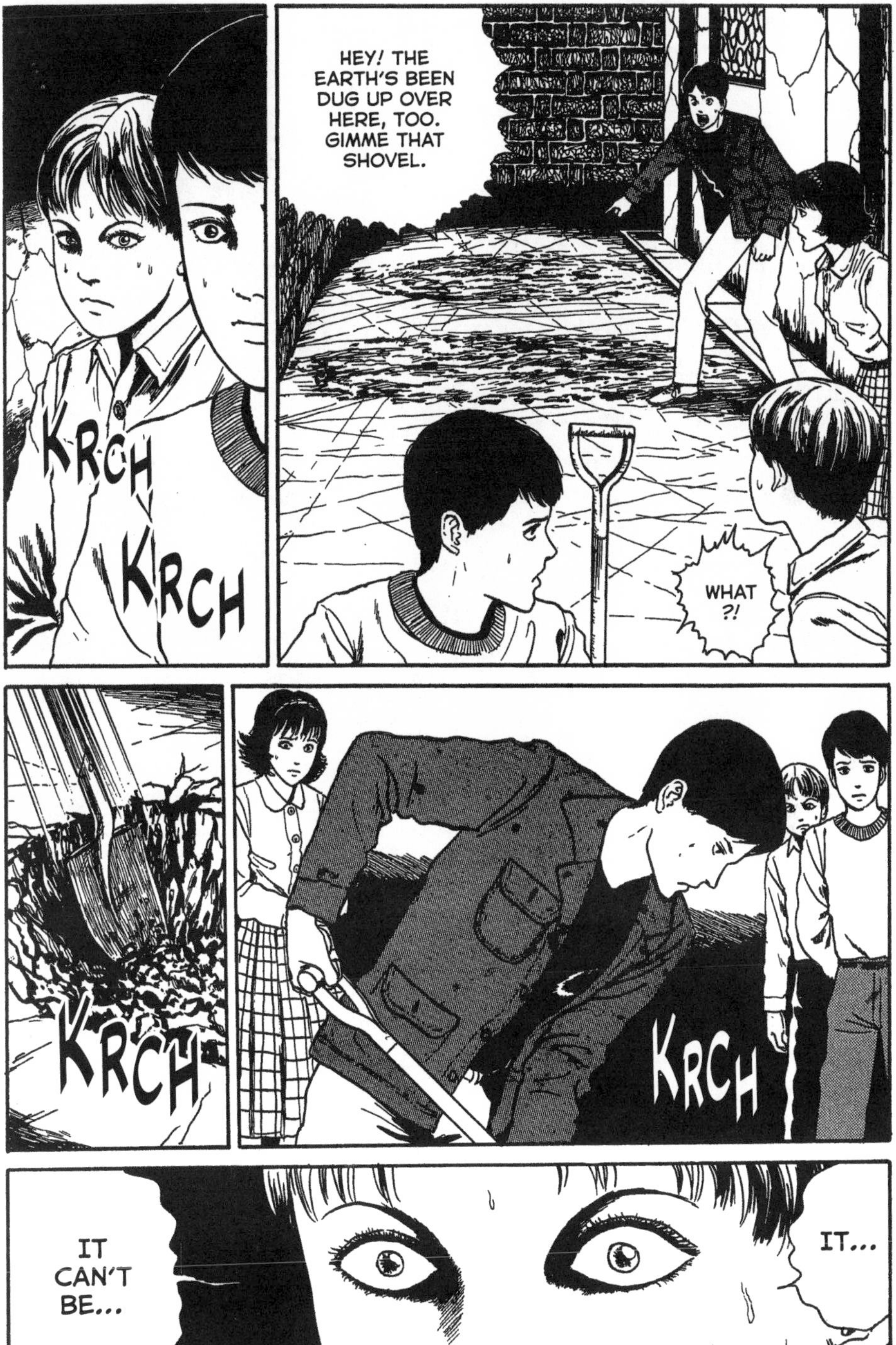
HEY! THE EARTH'S BEEN DUG UP OVER HERE, TOO. GIMME THAT SHOVEL.
WHAT ?!
KRCH
KRCH
KRCH
KRCH
IT...
IT CAN'T BE...

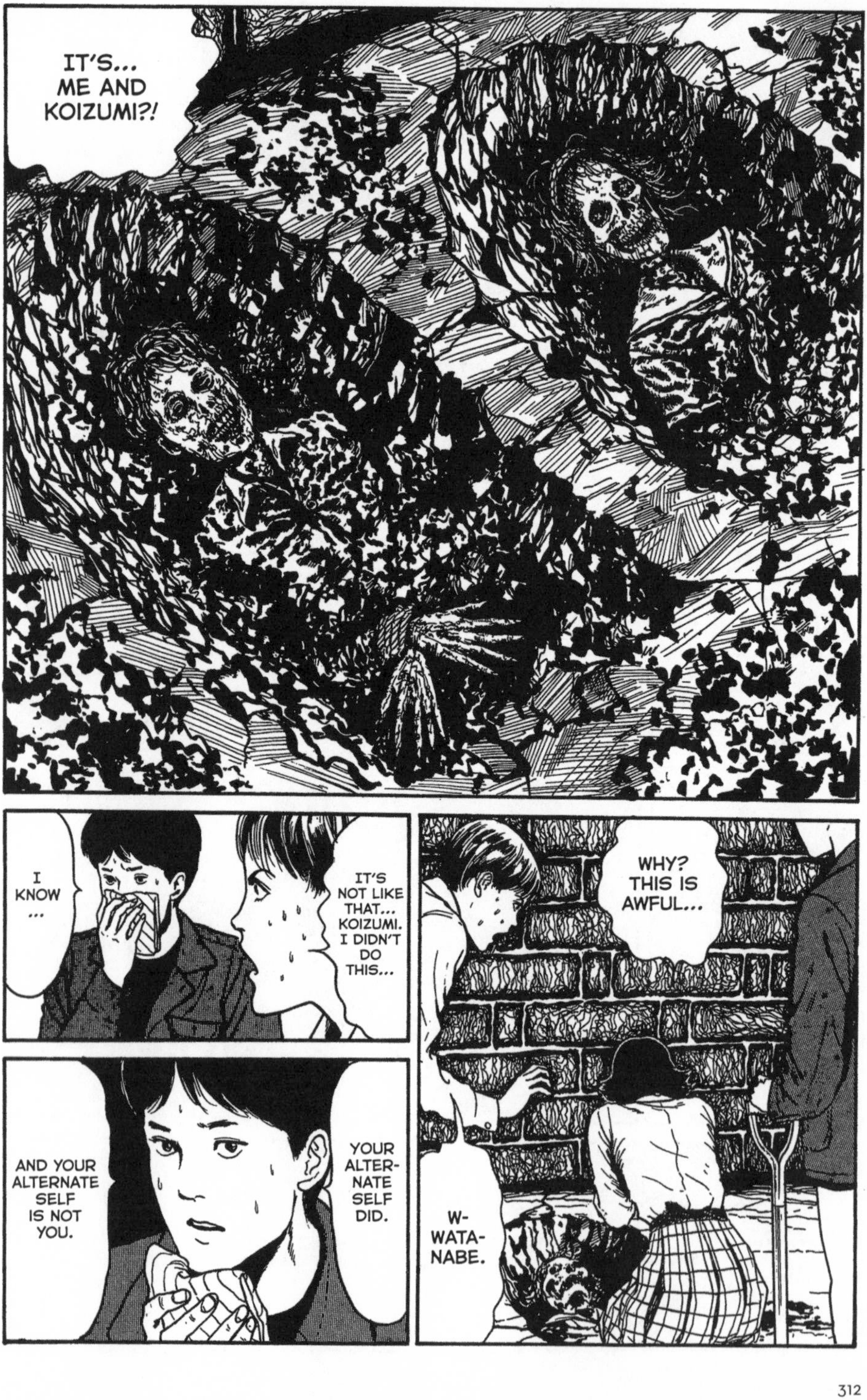
IT'S... ME AND KOIZUMI?!
WHY? THIS IS AWFUL...
W-WATANABE.
IT'S NOT LIKE THAT... KOIZUMI. I DIDN'T DO THIS...
I KNOW...
YOUR ALTERNATE SELF DID.
AND YOUR ALTERNATE SELF IS NOT YOU.

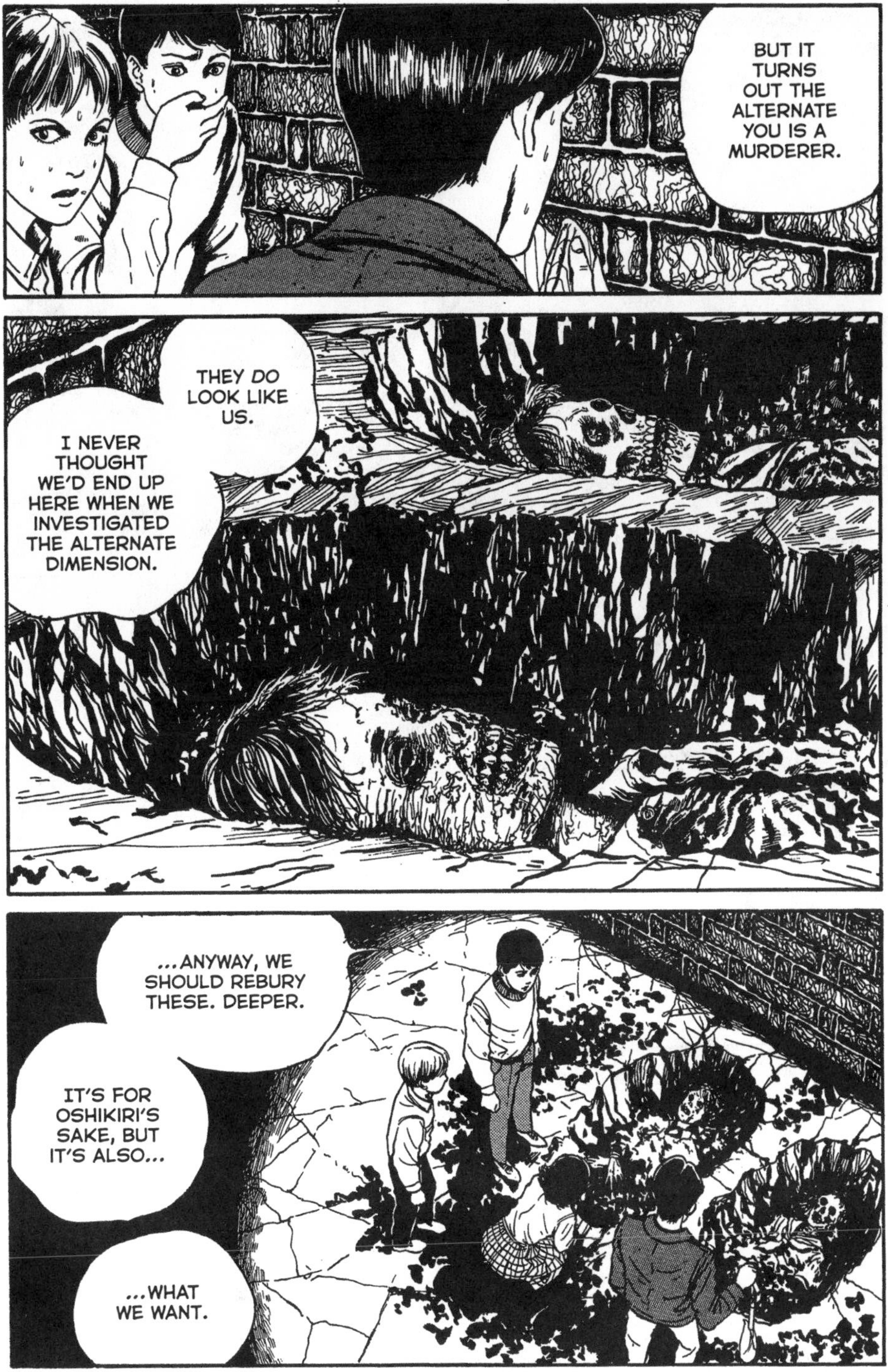
BUT IT TURNS OUT THE ALTERNATE YOU IS A MURDERER.
THEY *DO* LOOK LIKE US.
I NEVER THOUGHT WE'D END UP HERE WHEN WE INVESTIGATED THE ALTERNATE DIMENSION.
...ANYWAY, WE SHOULD REBURY THESE. DEEPER.
IT'S FOR OSHIKIRI'S SAKE, BUT IT'S ALSO...
...WHAT WE WANT.

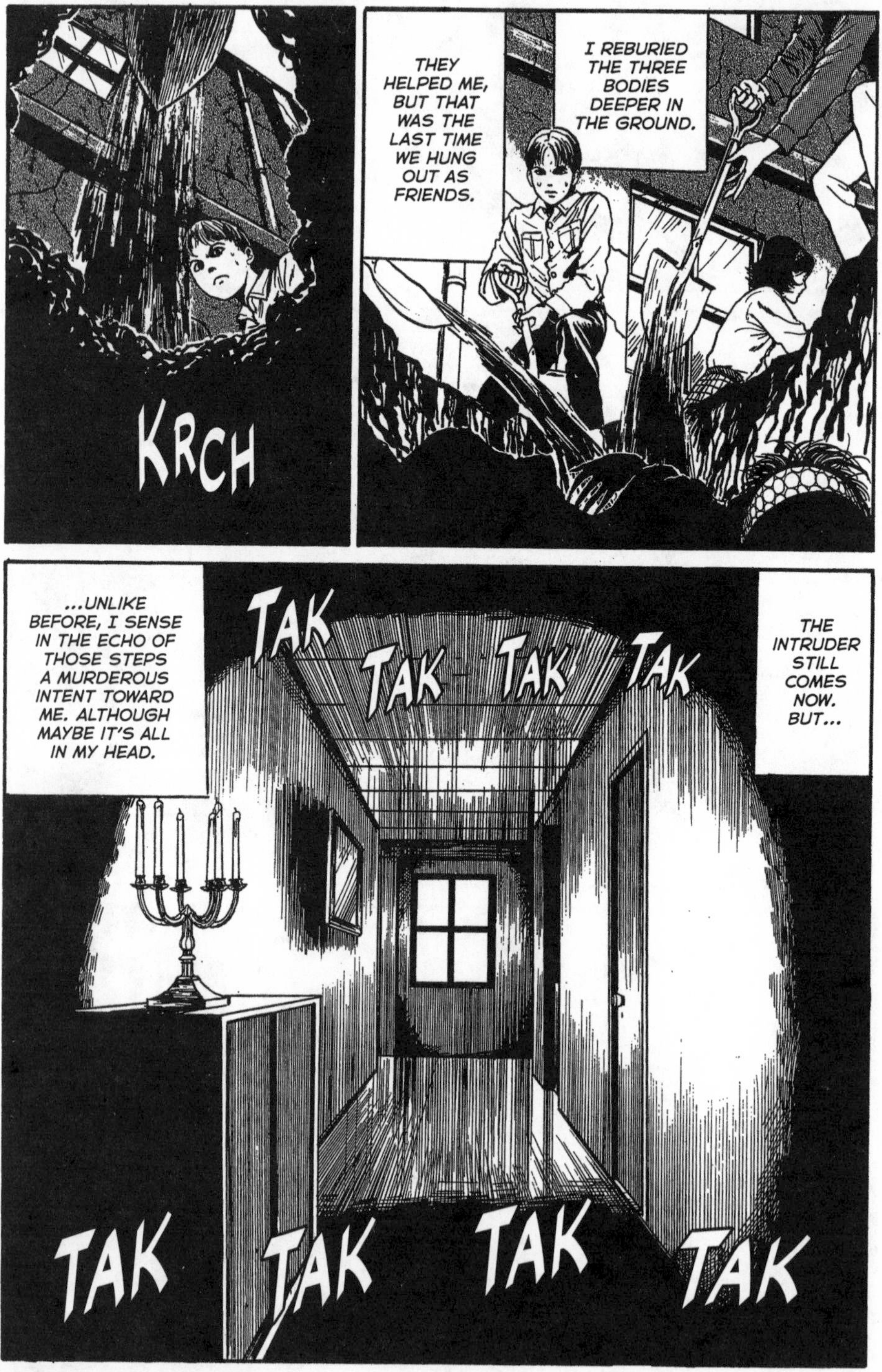
I REBURIED THE THREE BODIES DEEPER IN THE GROUND.
THEY HELPED ME, BUT THAT WAS THE LAST TIME WE HUNG OUT AS FRIENDS.
KRCH
THE INTRUDER STILL COMES NOW. BUT...
...UNLIKE BEFORE, I SENSE IN THE ECHO OF THOSE STEPS A MURDEROUS INTENT TOWARD ME. ALTHOUGH MAYBE IT'S ALL IN MY HEAD.
TAK TAK TAK TAK
TAK TAK TAK TAK

INTRUDER / END

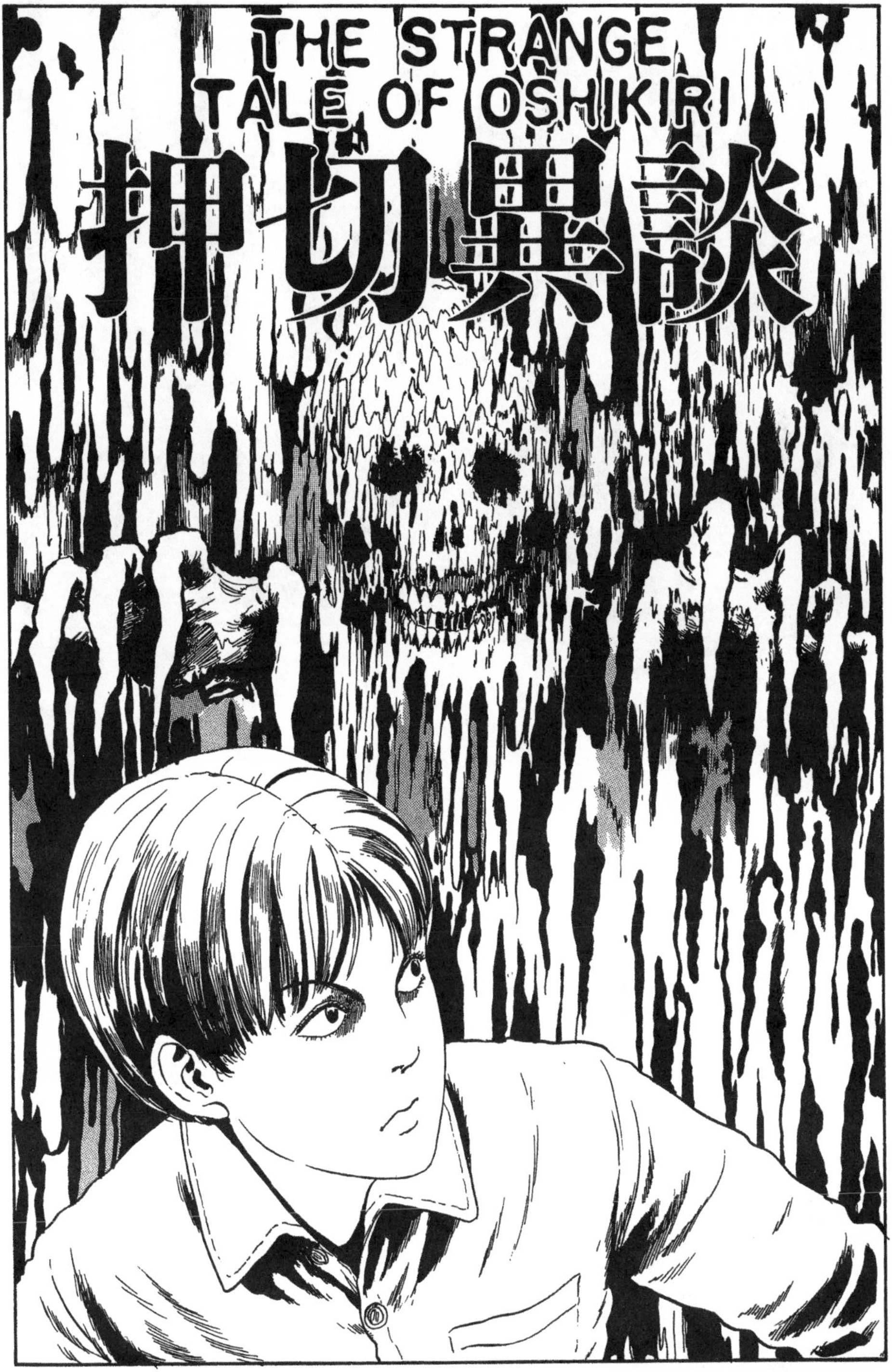
THE STRANGE
TALE OF OSHIKIRI
押切異談

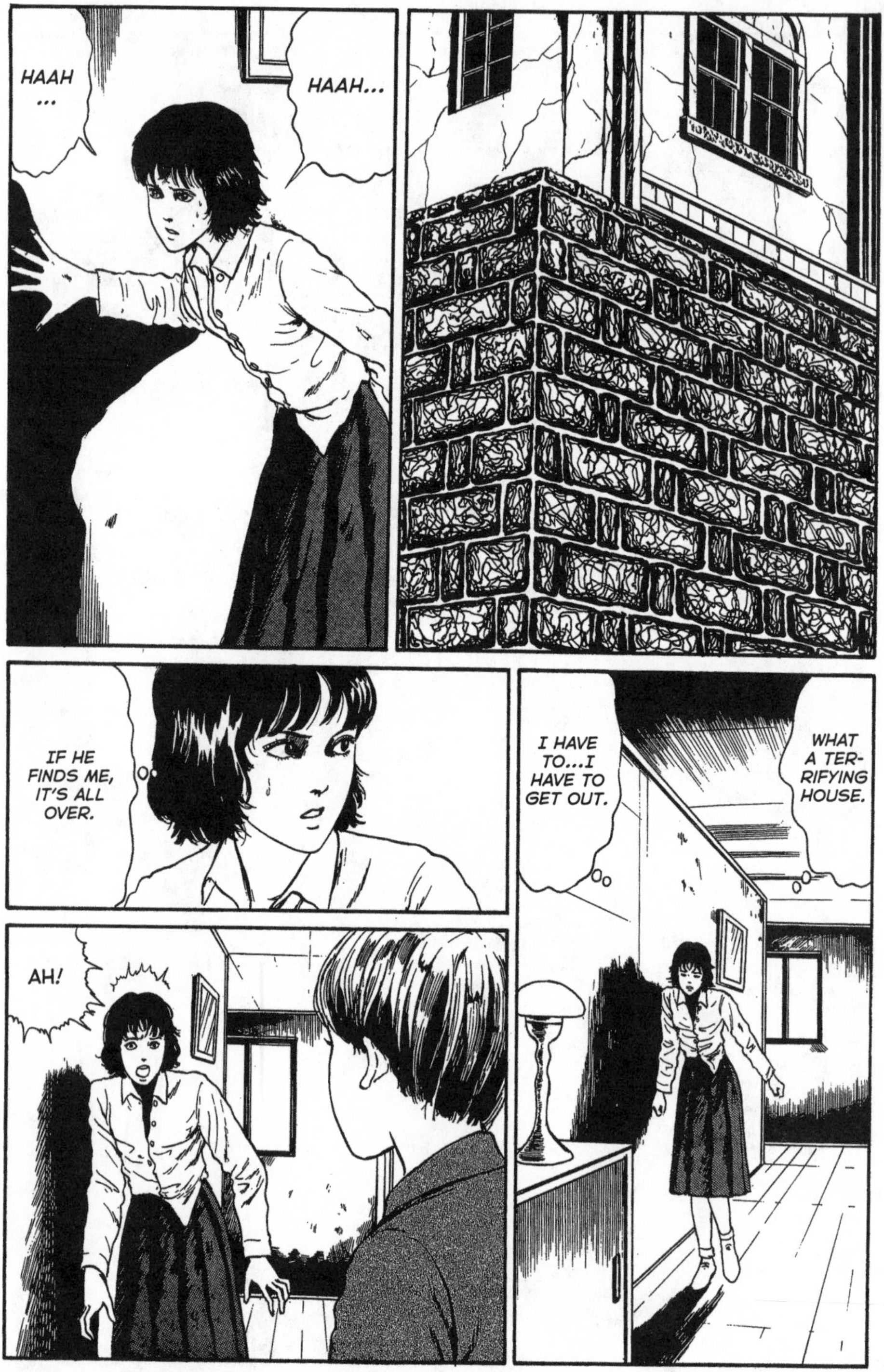
HAAH...
HAAH ...
WHAT A TER-RIFYING HOUSE.
I HAVE TO...I HAVE TO GET OUT.
IF HE FINDS ME, IT'S ALL OVER.
AH!

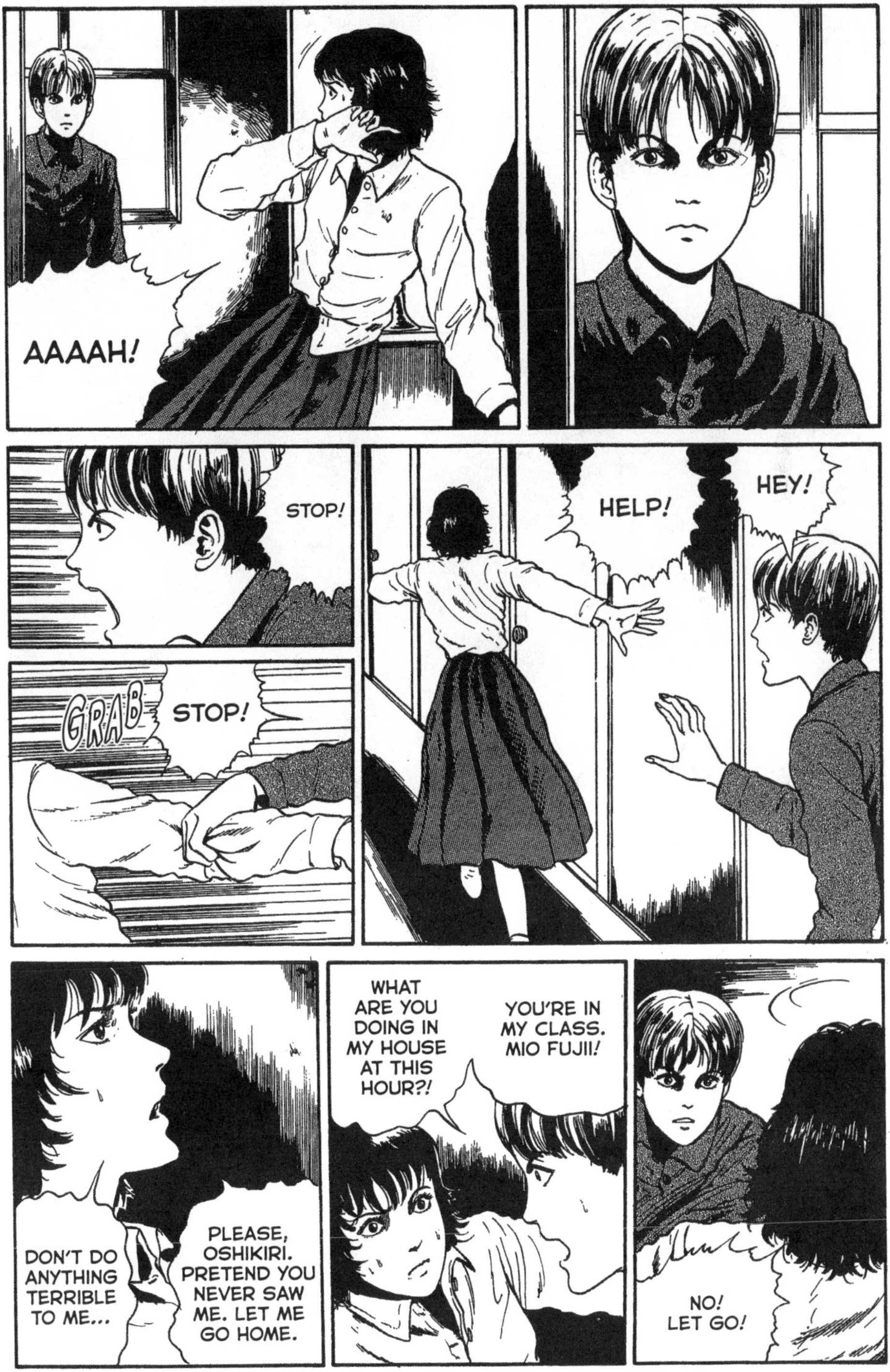
AAAAH!
HEY!
HELP!
STOP!
GRAB
STOP!
NO! LET GO!
YOU'RE IN MY CLASS. MIO FUJII!
WHAT ARE YOU DOING IN MY HOUSE AT THIS HOUR?!
PLEASE, OSHIKIRI. PRETEND YOU NEVER SAW ME. LET ME GO HOME.
DON'T DO ANYTHING TERRIBLE TO ME...

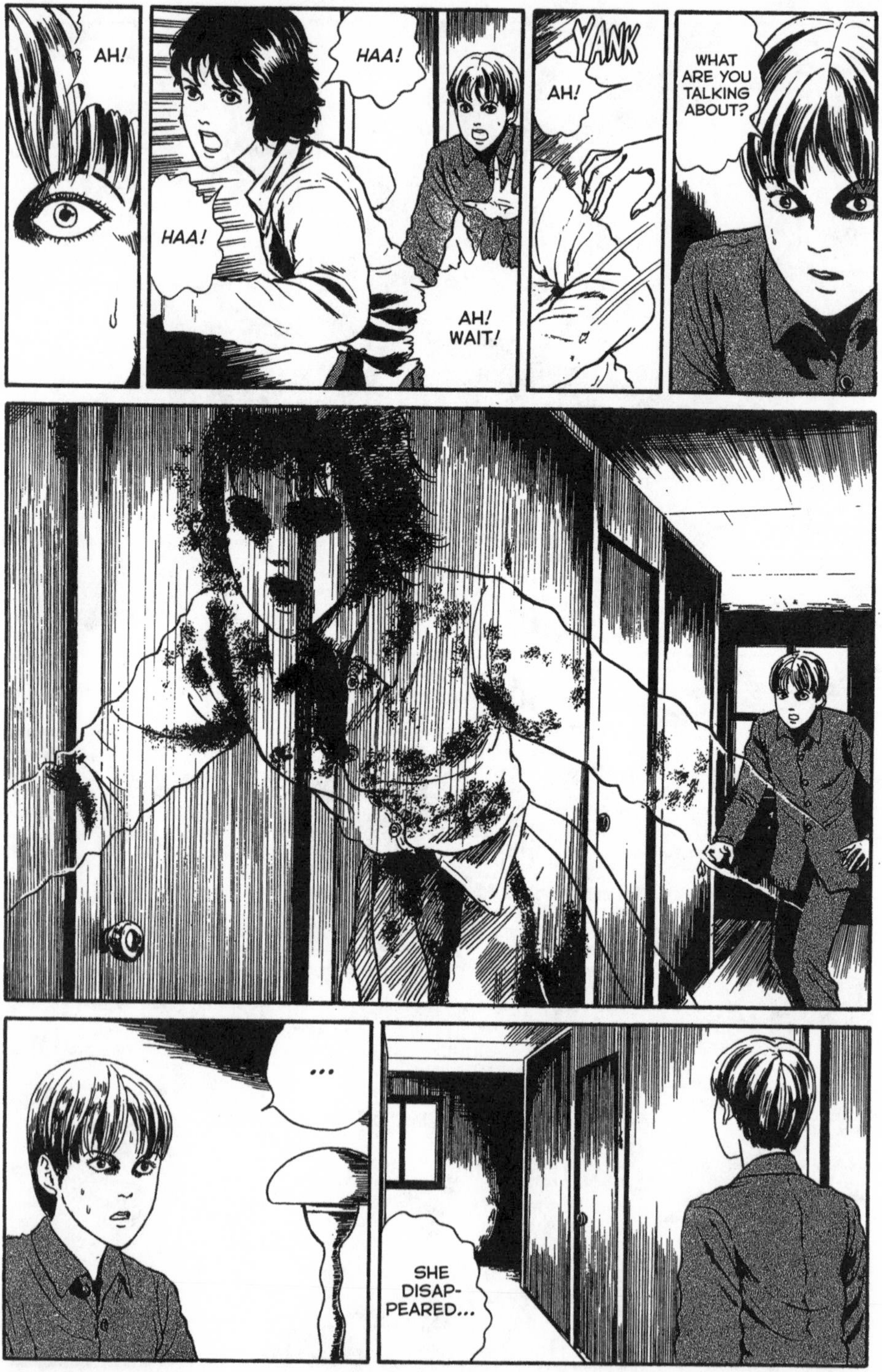
WHAT ARE YOU TALKING ABOUT?
YANK
AH!
HAA!
HAA!
AH! WAIT!
AH!
SHE DISAP-PEARED...
...

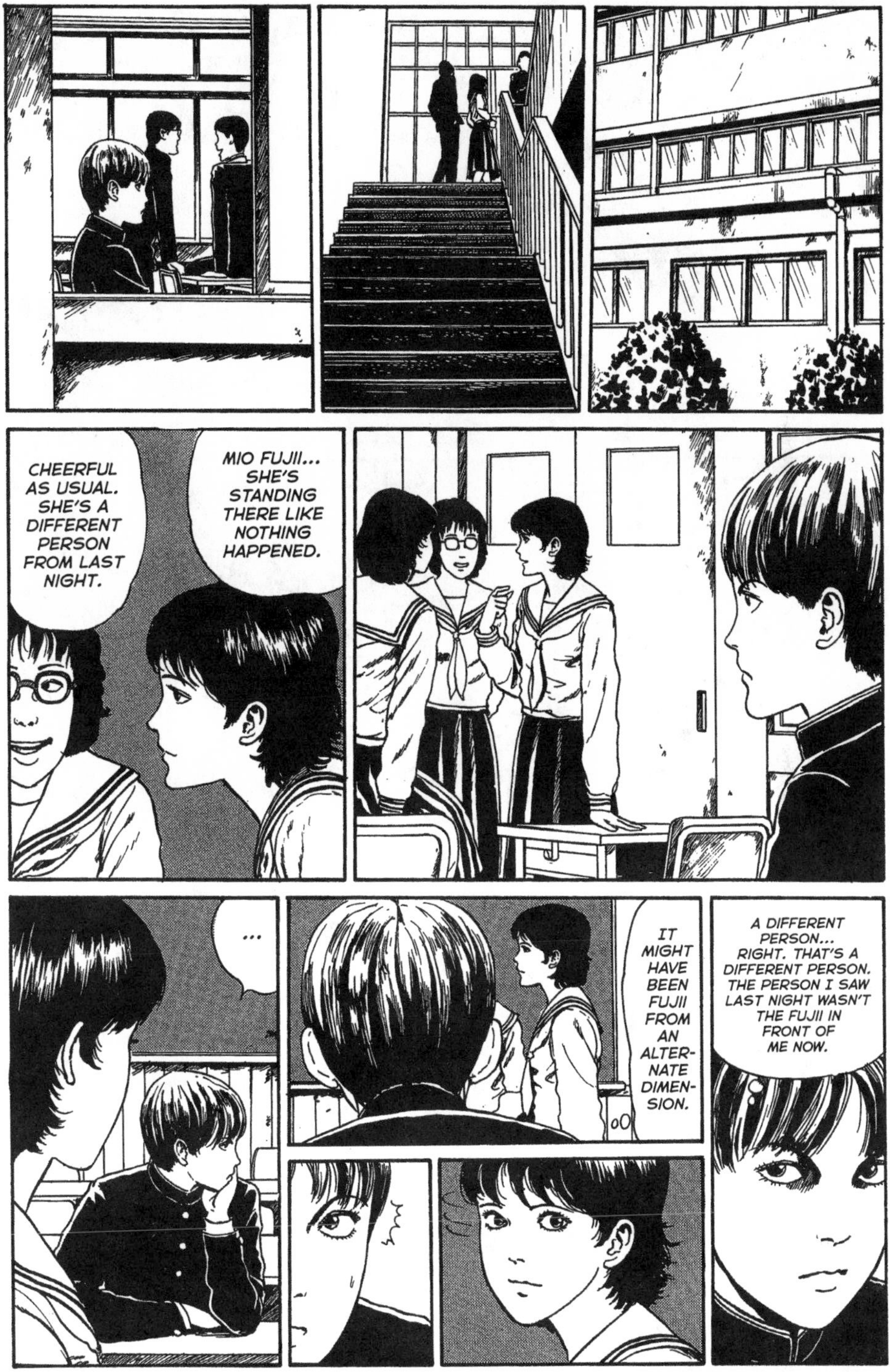
MIO FUJII... SHE'S STANDING THERE LIKE NOTHING HAPPENED.
CHEERFUL AS USUAL. SHE'S A DIFFERENT PERSON FROM LAST NIGHT.
A DIFFERENT PERSON... RIGHT. THAT'S A DIFFERENT PERSON. THE PERSON I SAW LAST NIGHT WASN'T THE FUJII IN FRONT OF ME NOW.
IT MIGHT HAVE BEEN FUJII FROM AN ALTERNATE DIMENSION.
...

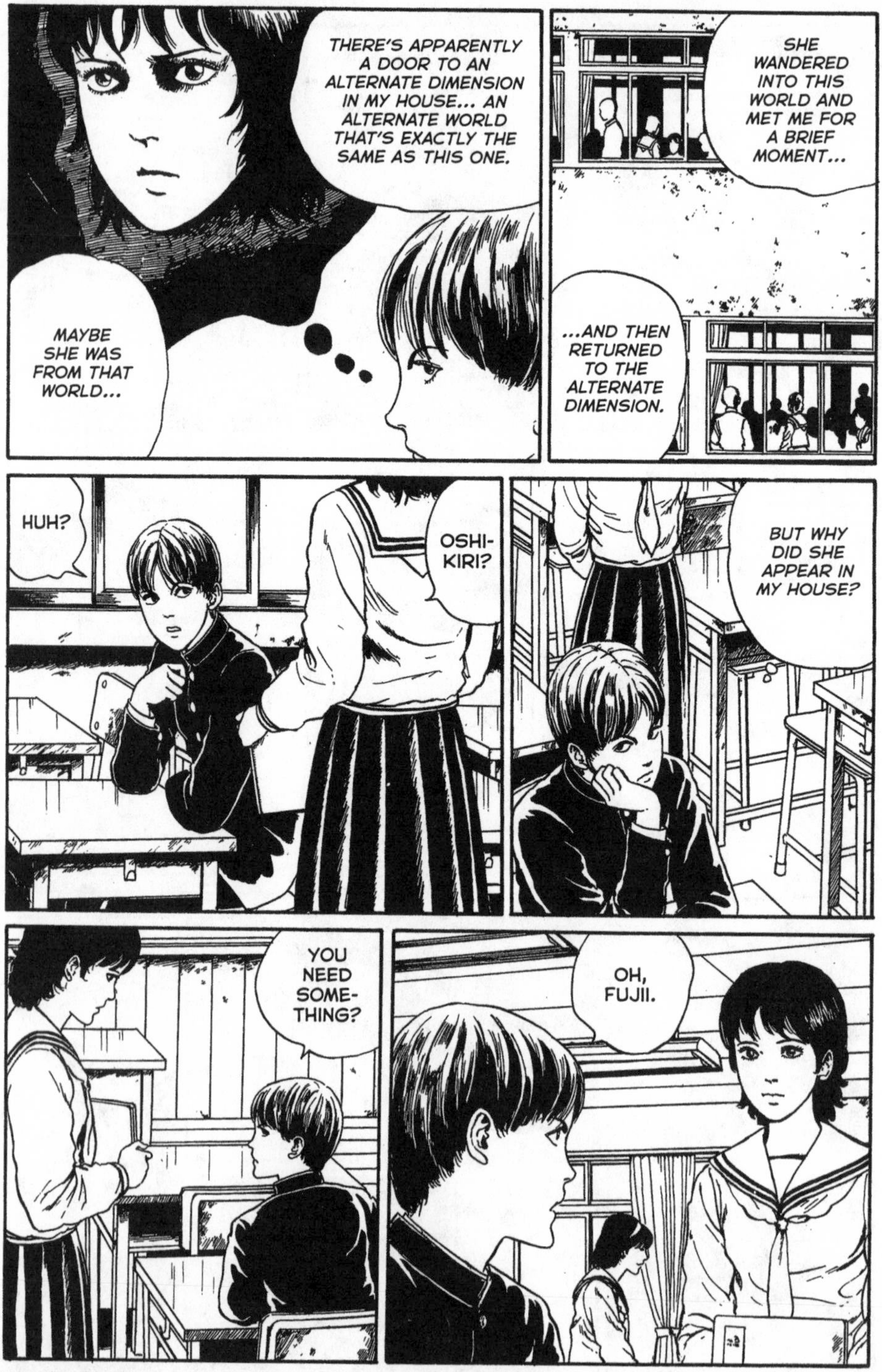
SHE WANDERED INTO THIS WORLD AND MET ME FOR A BRIEF MOMENT...
...AND THEN RETURNED TO THE ALTERNATE DIMENSION.
THERE'S APPARENTLY A DOOR TO AN ALTERNATE DIMENSION IN MY HOUSE... AN ALTERNATE WORLD THAT'S EXACTLY THE SAME AS THIS ONE.
MAYBE SHE WAS FROM THAT WORLD...
BUT WHY DID SHE APPEAR IN MY HOUSE?
OSHI-KIRI?
HUH?
OH, FUJII.
YOU NEED SOME-THING?

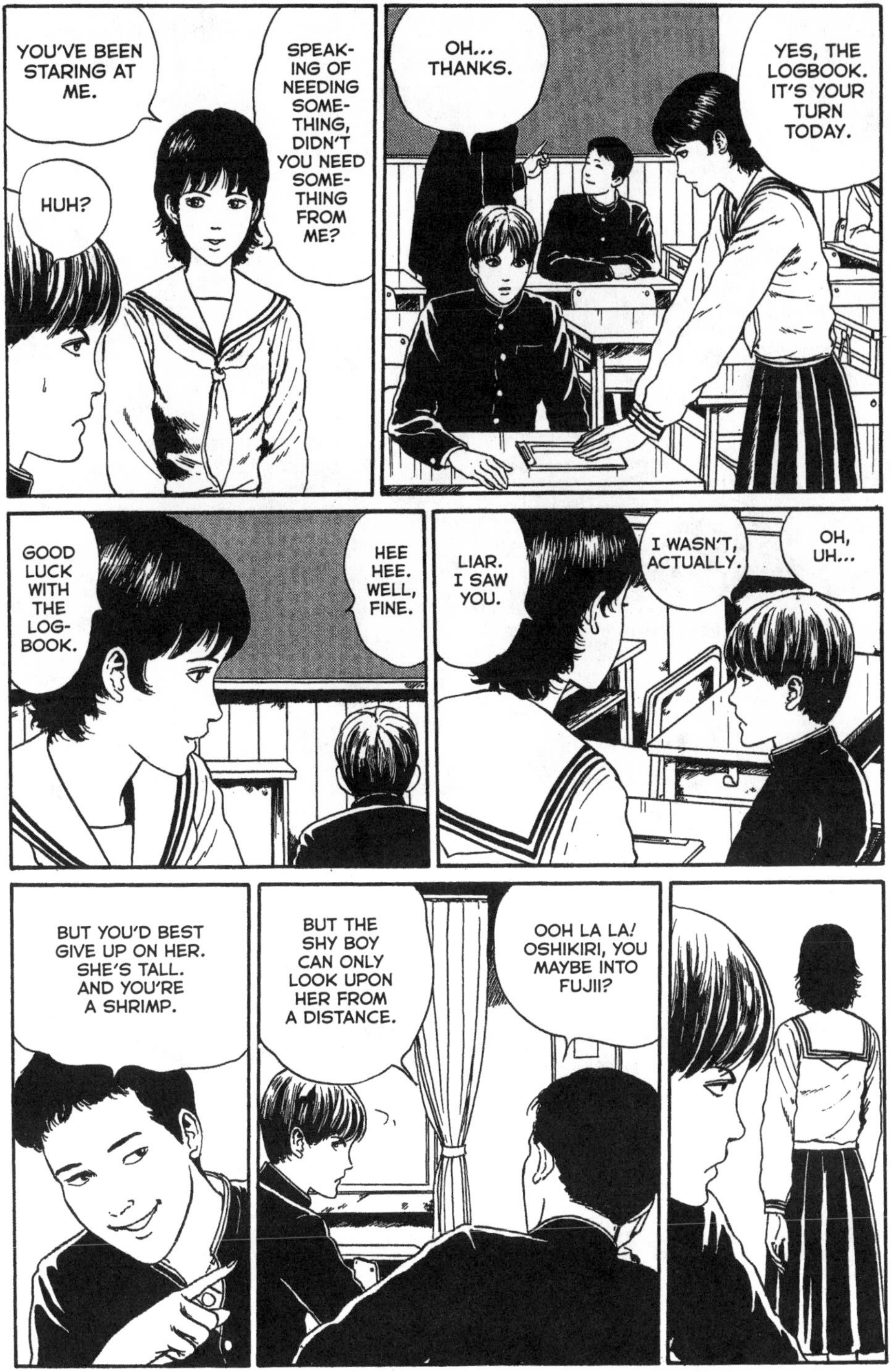
YES, THE LOGBOOK. IT'S YOUR TURN TODAY.
OH... THANKS.
SPEAKING OF NEEDING SOMETHING, DIDN'T YOU NEED SOMETHING FROM ME?
YOU'VE BEEN STARING AT ME.
HUH?
OH, UH...
I WASN'T, ACTUALLY.
LIAR. I SAW YOU.
HEE HEE. WELL, FINE.
GOOD LUCK WITH THE LOGBOOK.
OOH LA LA! OSHIKIRI, YOU MAYBE INTO FUJII?
BUT THE SHY BOY CAN ONLY LOOK UPON HER FROM A DISTANCE.
BUT YOU'D BEST GIVE UP ON HER. SHE'S TALL. AND YOU'RE A SHRIMP.

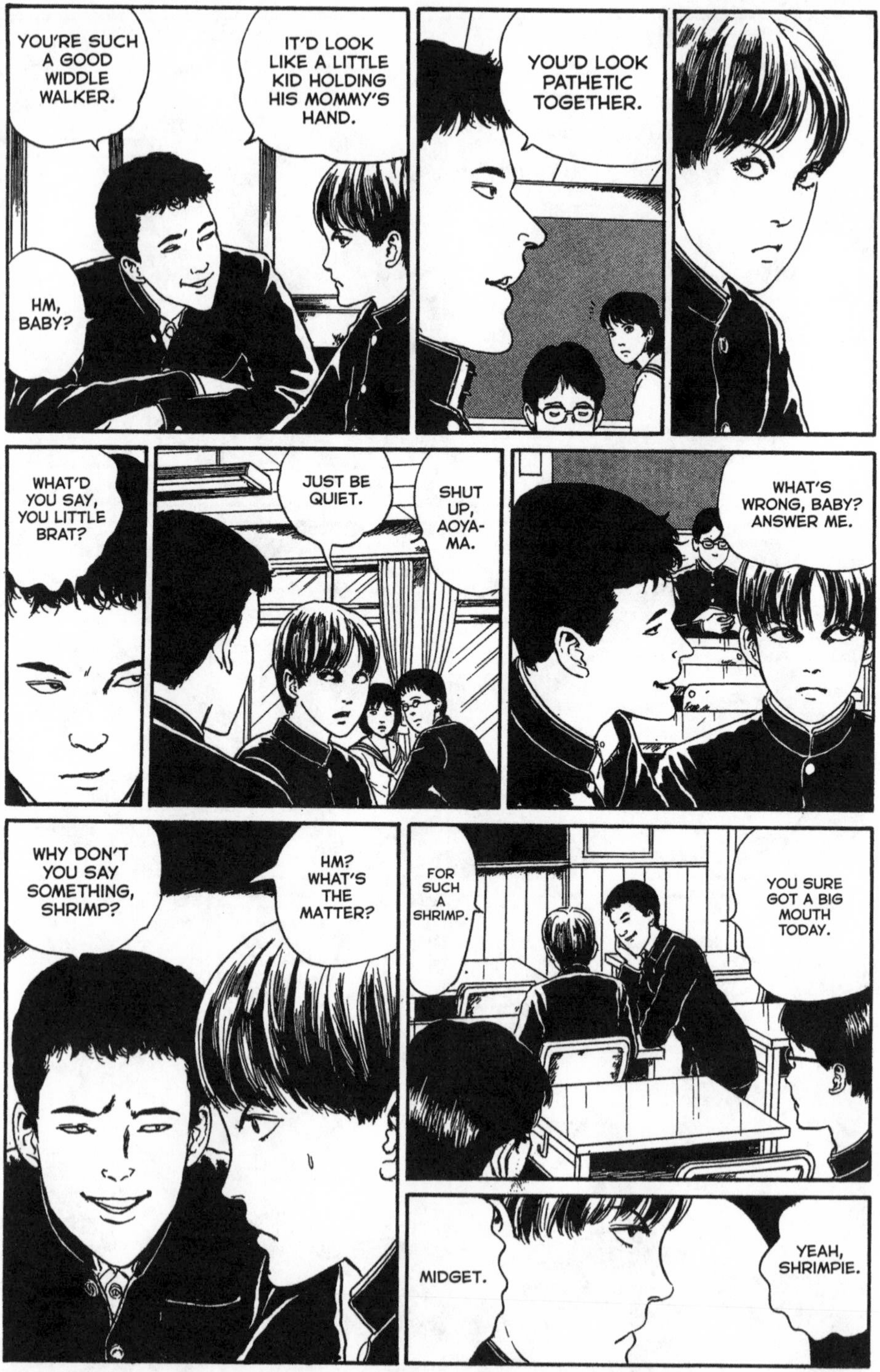
YOU'D LOOK PATHETIC TOGETHER.
IT'D LOOK LIKE A LITTLE KID HOLDING HIS MOMMY'S HAND.
YOU'RE SUCH A GOOD WIDDLE WALKER.
HM, BABY?
WHAT'S WRONG, BABY? ANSWER ME.
SHUT UP, AOYAMA.
JUST BE QUIET.
WHAT'D YOU SAY, YOU LITTLE BRAT?
YOU SURE GOT A BIG MOUTH TODAY.
FOR SUCH A SHRIMP.
YEAH, SHRIMPIE.
MIDGET.
HM? WHAT'S THE MATTER?
WHY DON'T YOU SAY SOMETHING, SHRIMP?

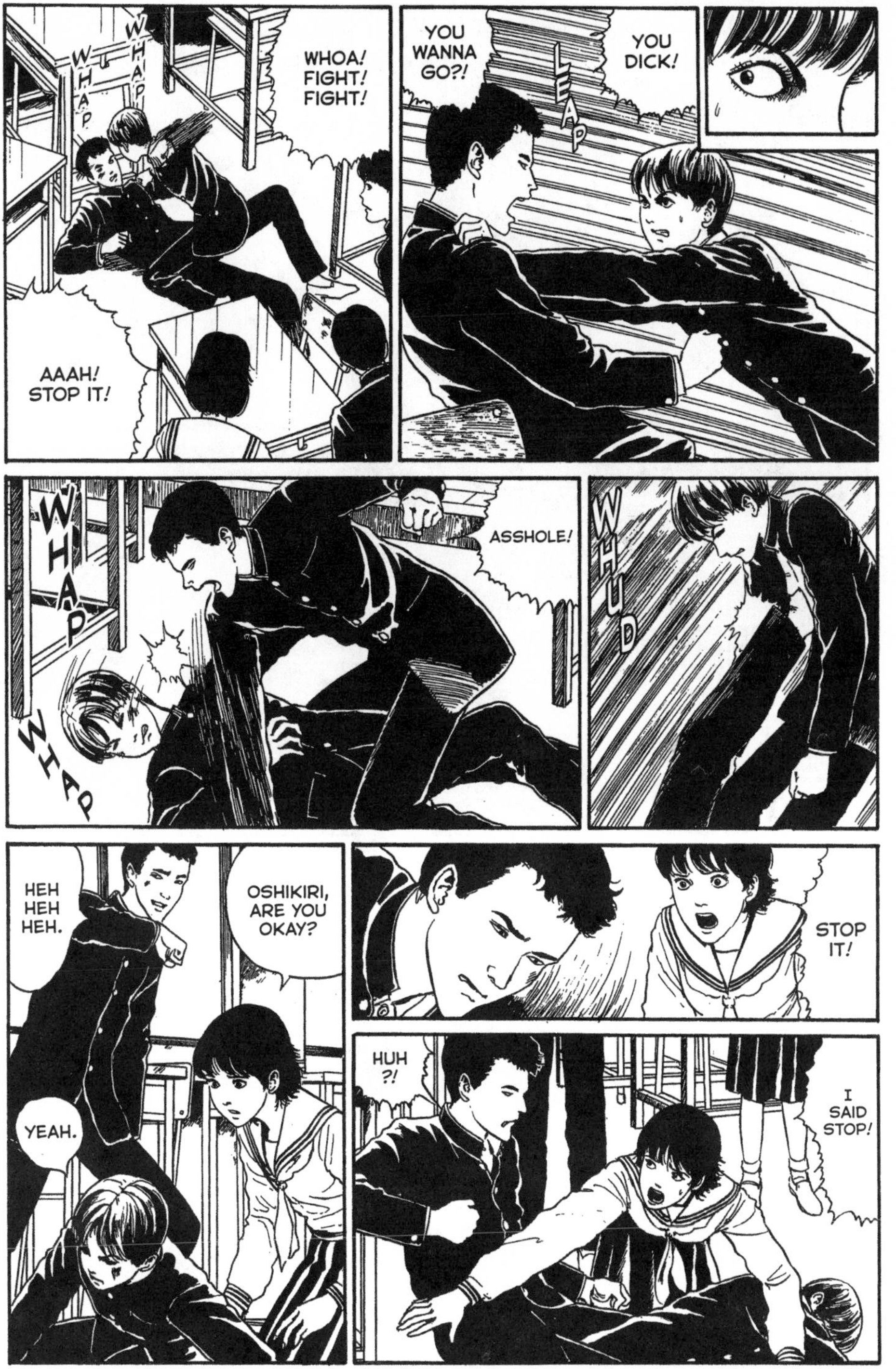
YOU DICK!
YOU WANNA GO?!
LEAP
WHOA! FIGHT! FIGHT!
WHAP
WHAP
AAAH! STOP IT!
WHUD
ASSHOLE!
WHAP
WHAP
STOP IT!
I SAID STOP!
HUH ?!
OSHIKIRI, ARE YOU OKAY?
HEH HEH HEH.
YEAH.

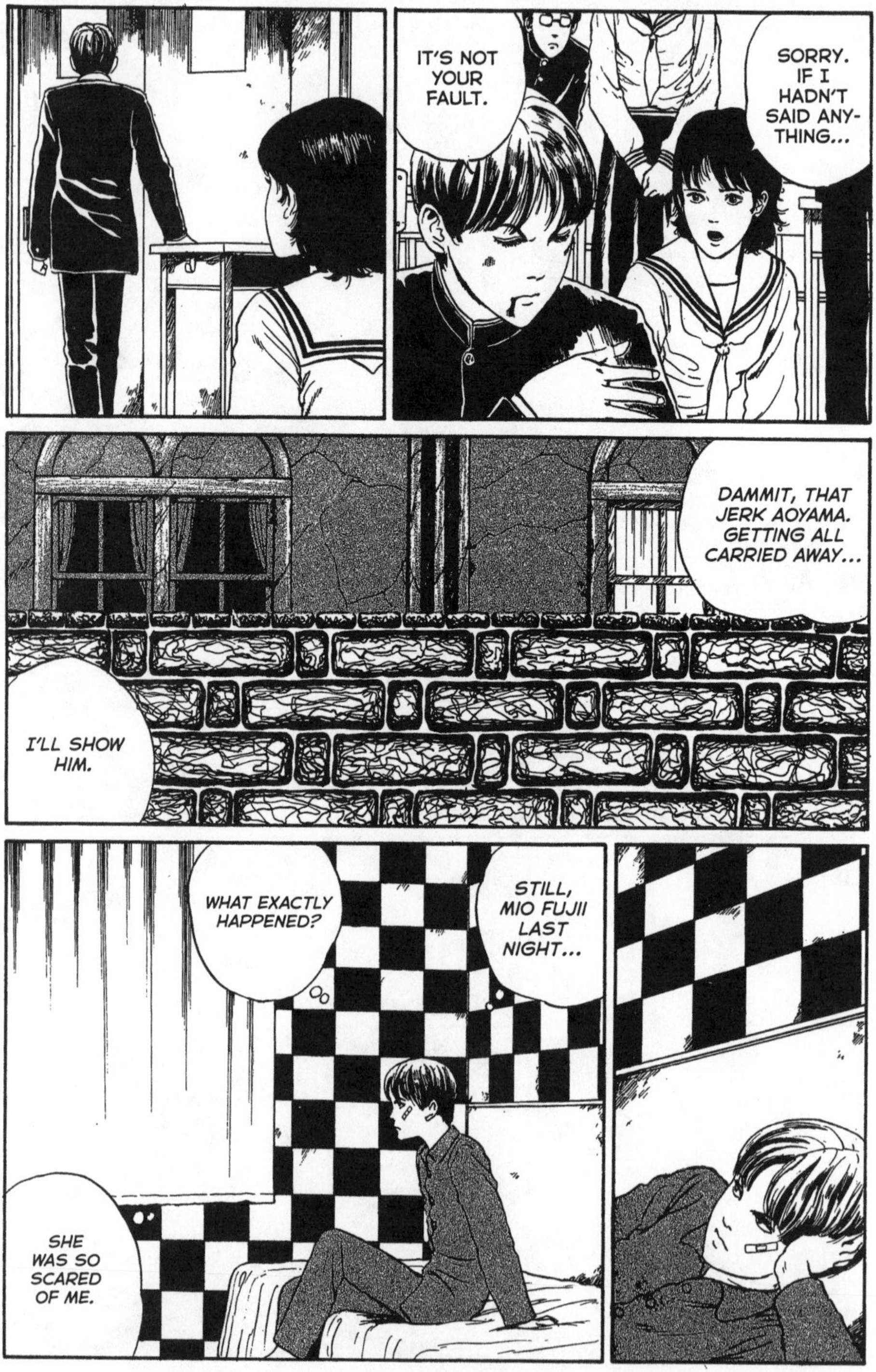
SORRY. IF I HADN'T SAID ANY-THING...
IT'S NOT YOUR FAULT.
DAMMIT, THAT JERK AOYAMA. GETTING ALL CARRIED AWAY...
I'LL SHOW HIM.
STILL, MIO FUJII LAST NIGHT...
WHAT EXACTLY HAPPENED?
SHE WAS SO SCARED OF ME.

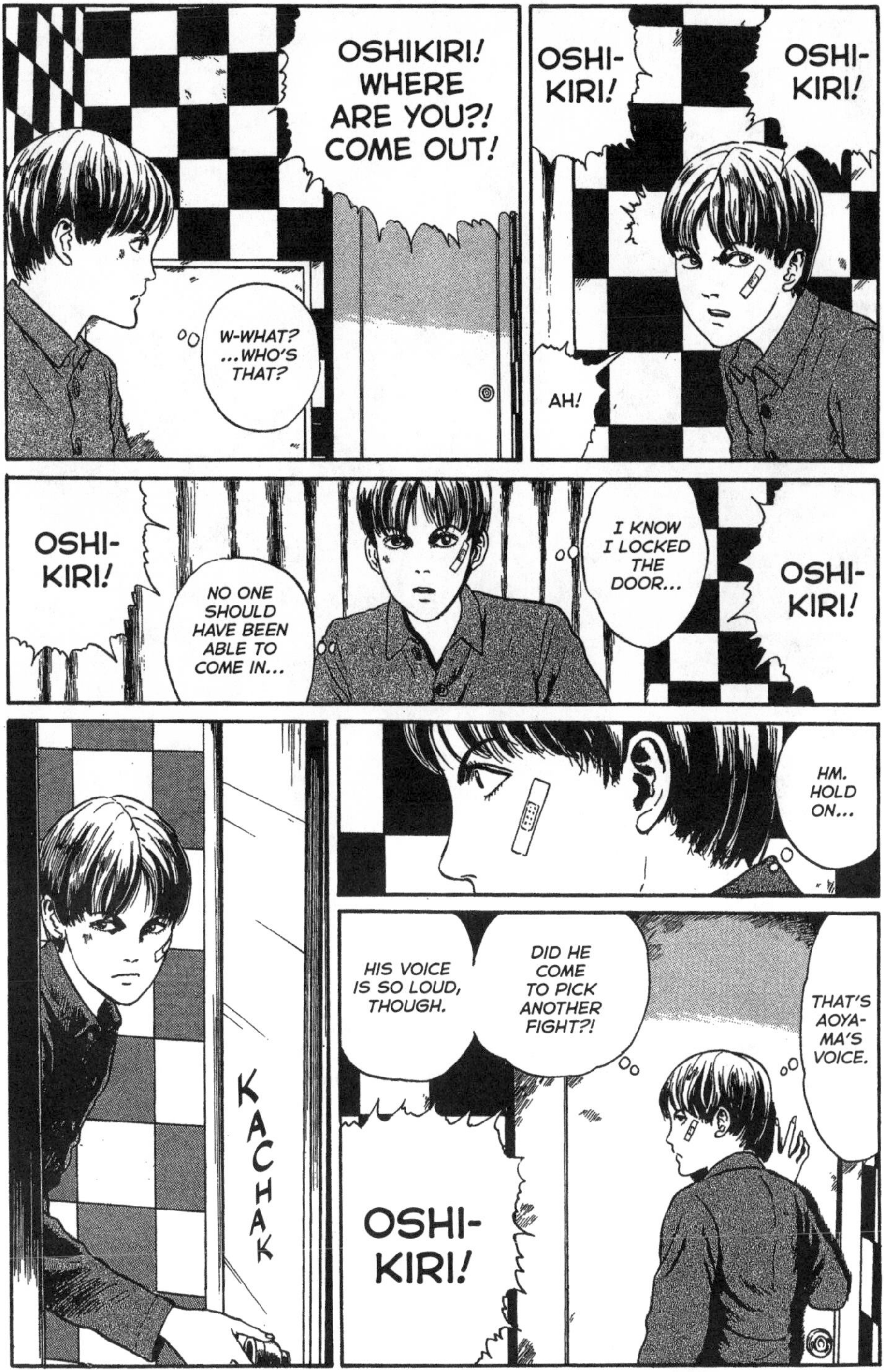
OSHI-KIRI!
OSHI-KIRI!
AH!
OSHIKIRI! WHERE ARE YOU?! COME OUT!
W-WHAT? ...WHO'S THAT?
OSHI-KIRI!
I KNOW I LOCKED THE DOOR...
NO ONE SHOULD HAVE BEEN ABLE TO COME IN...
OSHI-KIRI!
HM. HOLD ON...
THAT'S AOYAMA'S VOICE.
DID HE COME TO PICK ANOTHER FIGHT?!
HIS VOICE IS SO LOUD, THOUGH.
OSHI-KIRI!
KACHAK

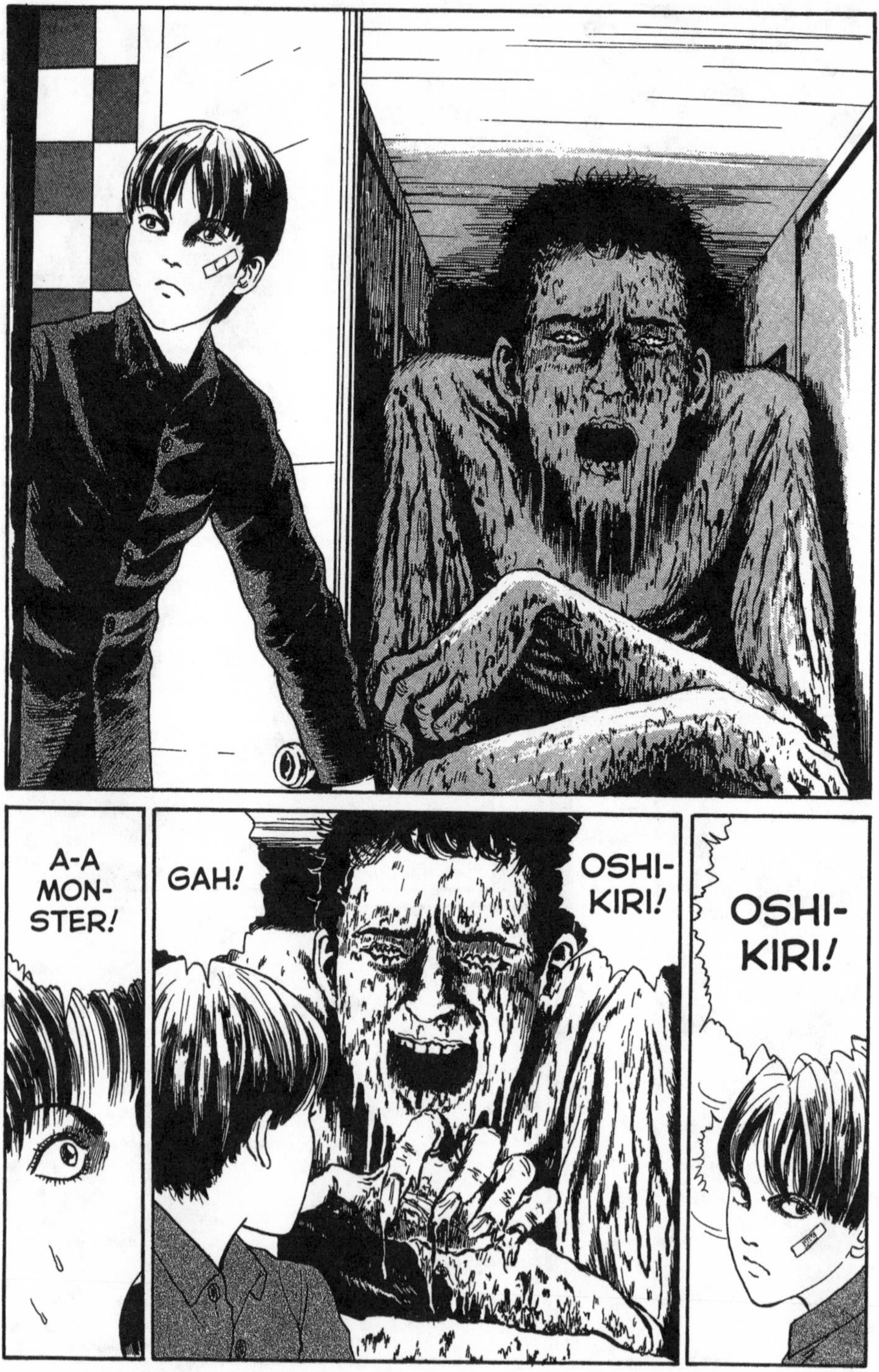
OSHI-KIRI!
OSHI-KIRI!
GAH!
A-A MON-STER!

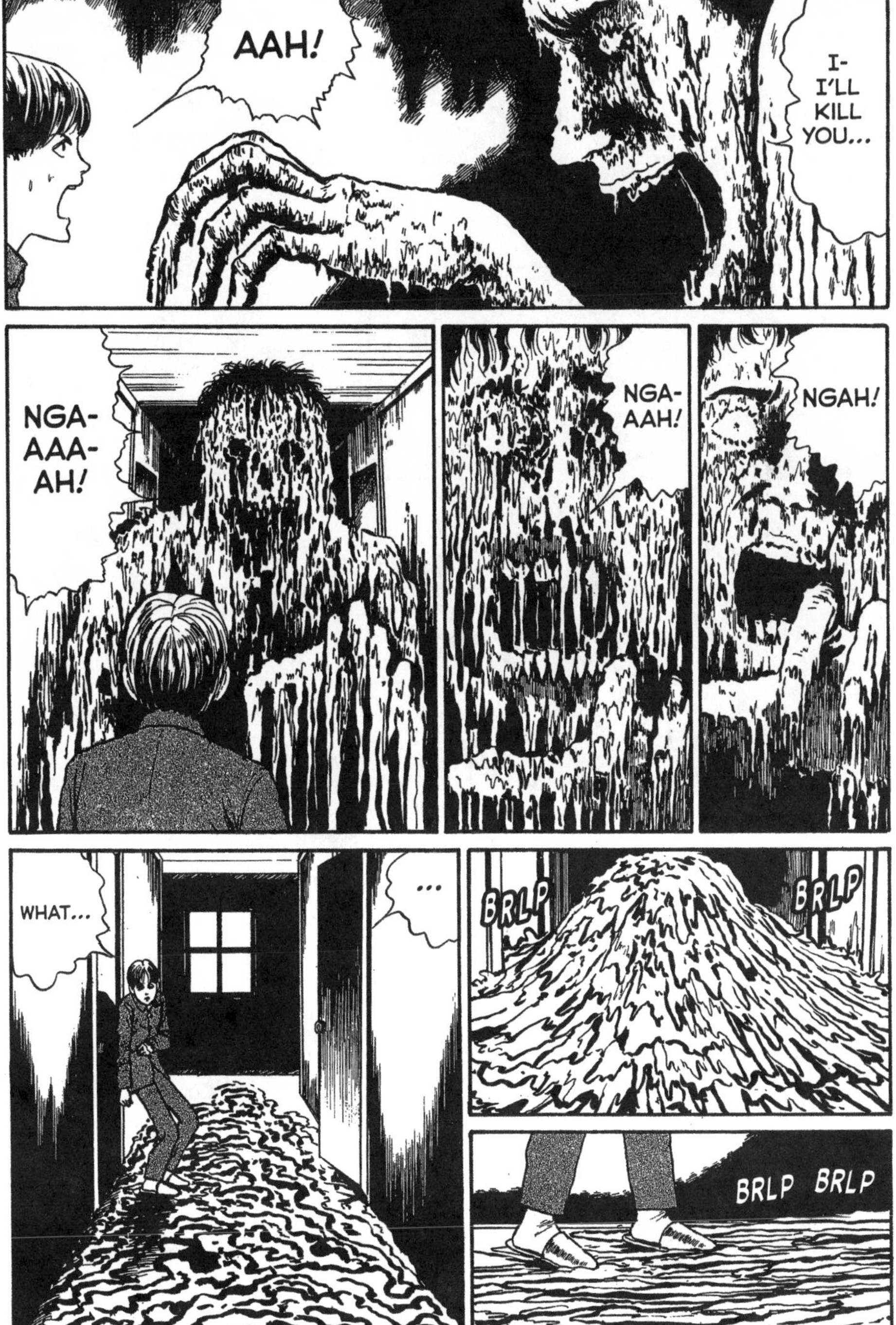
I- I'LL KILL YOU...
AAH!
NGAH!
NGA-AAH!
NGA-AAA-AH!
BRLP
BRLP
BRLP BRLP
...
WHAT...

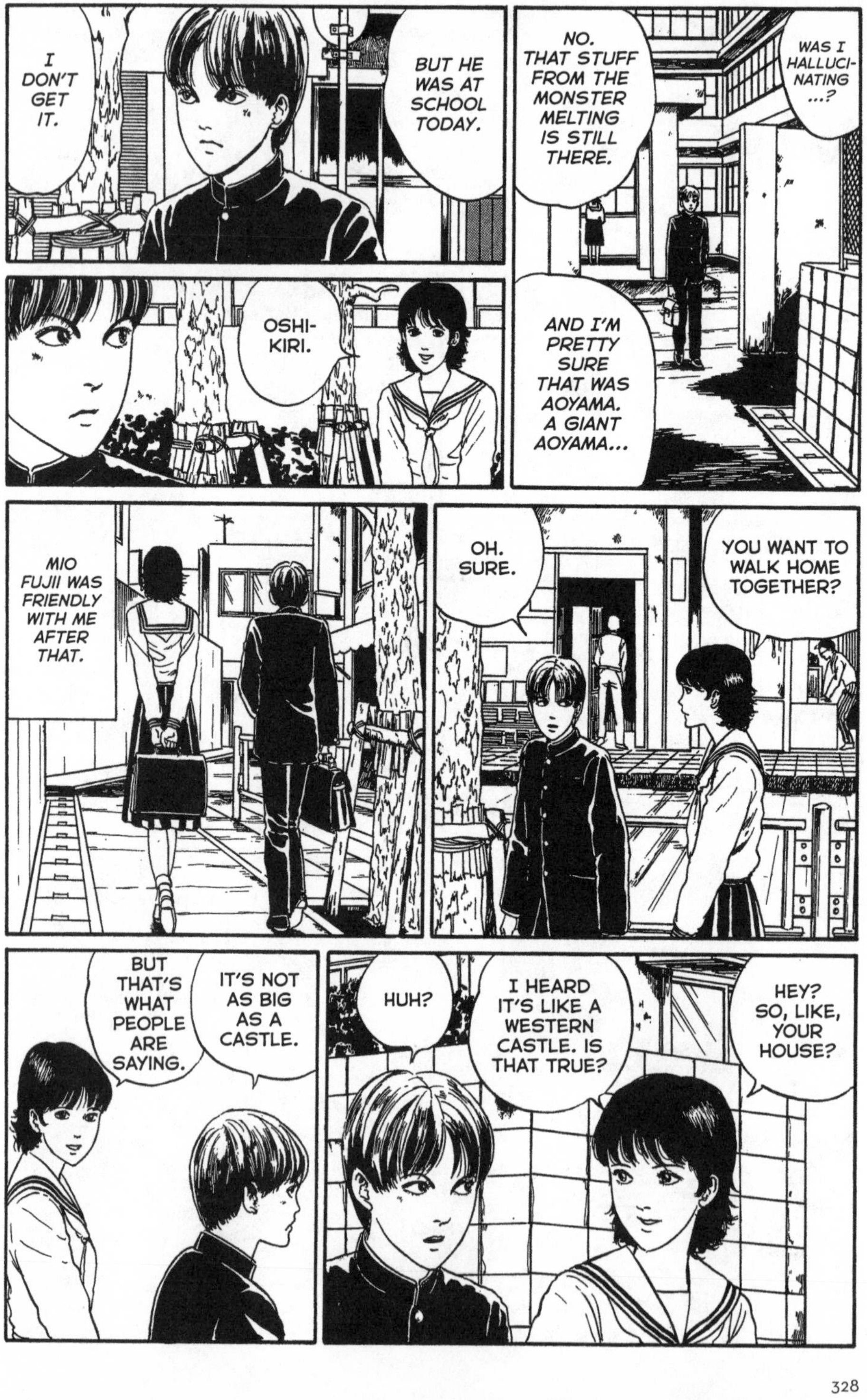
WAS I HALLUCI-NATING ...?
NO. THAT STUFF FROM THE MONSTER MELTING IS STILL THERE.
AND I'M PRETTY SURE THAT WAS AOYAMA. A GIANT AOYAMA...
BUT HE WAS AT SCHOOL TODAY.
I DON'T GET IT.
OSHI-KIRI.
YOU WANT TO WALK HOME TOGETHER?
OH. SURE.
MIO FUJII WAS FRIENDLY WITH ME AFTER THAT.
HEY? SO, LIKE, YOUR HOUSE?
I HEARD IT'S LIKE A WESTERN CASTLE. IS THAT TRUE?
HUH?
IT'S NOT AS BIG AS A CASTLE.
BUT THAT'S WHAT PEOPLE ARE SAYING.

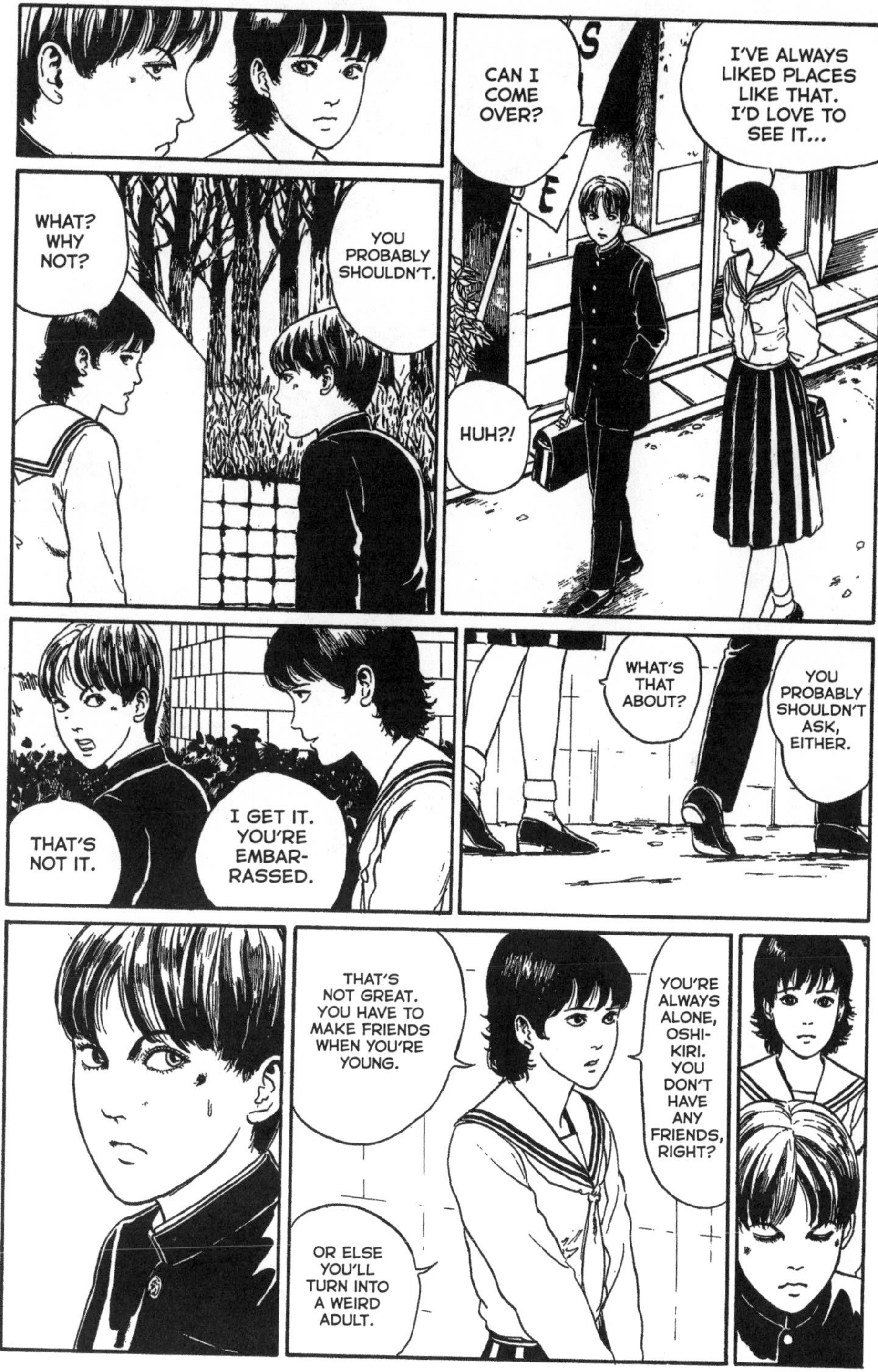
I'VE ALWAYS LIKED PLACES LIKE THAT. I'D LOVE TO SEE IT...
CAN I COME OVER?
HUH?!
YOU PROBABLY SHOULDN'T.
WHAT? WHY NOT?
YOU PROBABLY SHOULDN'T ASK, EITHER.
WHAT'S THAT ABOUT?
I GET IT. YOU'RE EMBAR-RASSED.
THAT'S NOT IT.
YOU'RE ALWAYS ALONE, OSHI-KIRI. YOU DON'T HAVE ANY FRIENDS, RIGHT?
THAT'S NOT GREAT. YOU HAVE TO MAKE FRIENDS WHEN YOU'RE YOUNG.
OR ELSE YOU'LL TURN INTO A WEIRD ADULT.

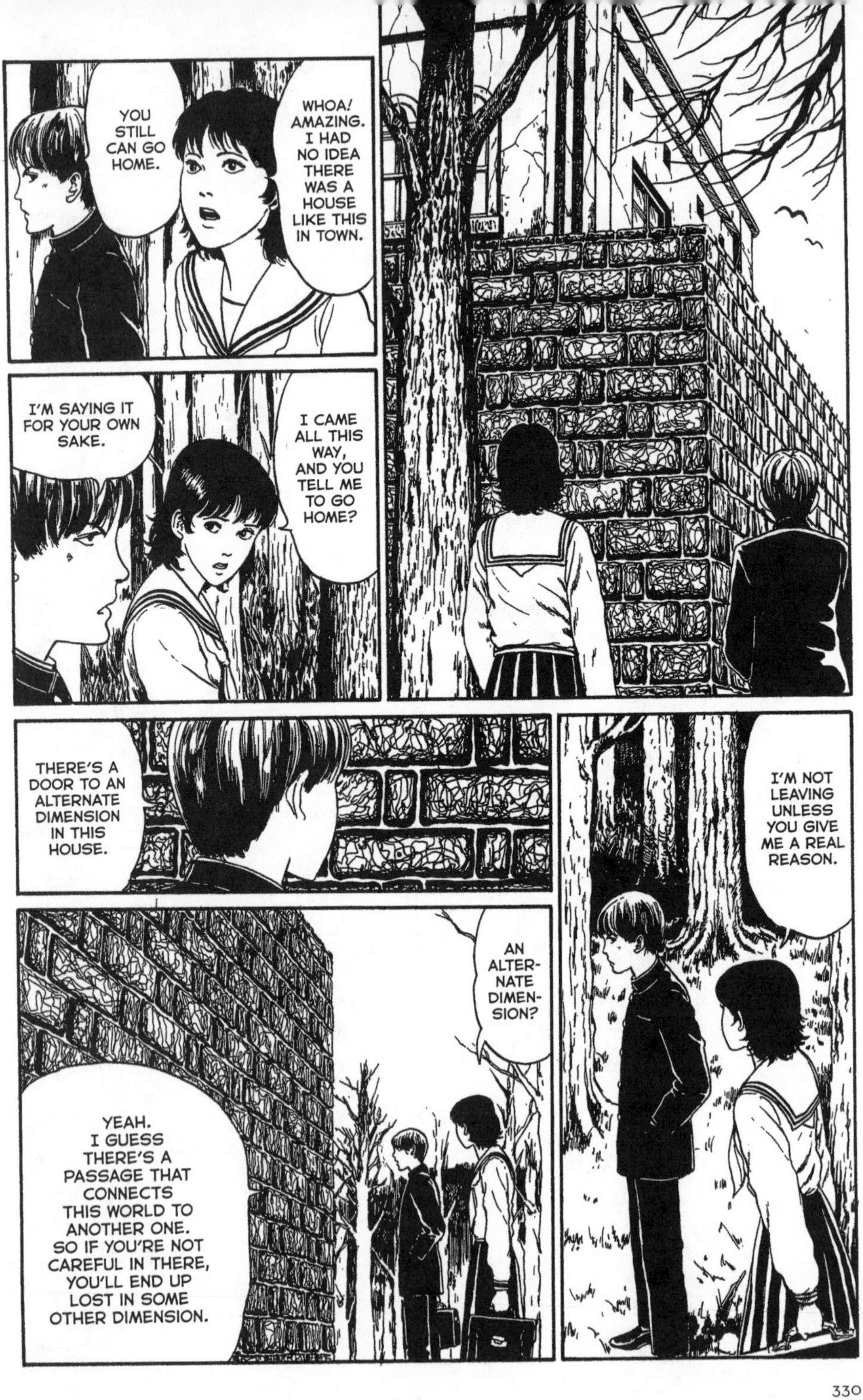
WHOA! AMAZING. I HAD NO IDEA THERE WAS A HOUSE LIKE THIS IN TOWN.
YOU STILL CAN GO HOME.
I CAME ALL THIS WAY, AND YOU TELL ME TO GO HOME?
I'M SAYING IT FOR YOUR OWN SAKE.
I'M NOT LEAVING UNLESS YOU GIVE ME A REAL REASON.
THERE'S A DOOR TO AN ALTERNATE DIMENSION IN THIS HOUSE.
AN ALTER-NATE DIMEN-SION?
YEAH. I GUESS THERE'S A PASSAGE THAT CONNECTS THIS WORLD TO ANOTHER ONE. SO IF YOU'RE NOT CAREFUL IN THERE, YOU'LL END UP LOST IN SOME OTHER DIMENSION.

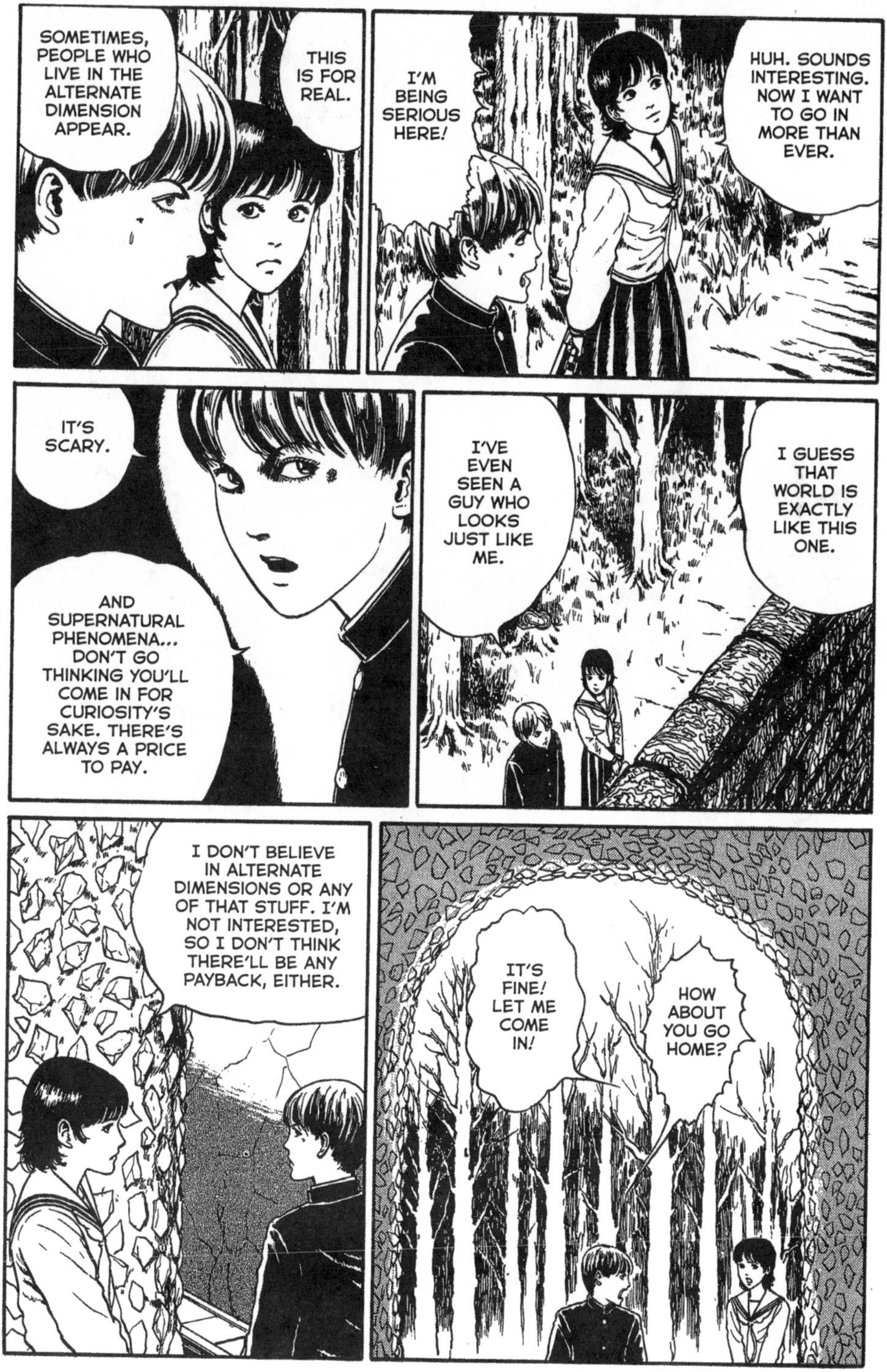
HUH. SOUNDS INTERESTING. NOW I WANT TO GO IN MORE THAN EVER.
I'M BEING SERIOUS HERE!
THIS IS FOR REAL.
SOMETIMES, PEOPLE WHO LIVE IN THE ALTERNATE DIMENSION APPEAR.
I GUESS THAT WORLD IS EXACTLY LIKE THIS ONE.
I'VE EVEN SEEN A GUY WHO LOOKS JUST LIKE ME.
IT'S SCARY.
AND SUPERNATURAL PHENOMENA... DON'T GO THINKING YOU'LL COME IN FOR CURIOSITY'S SAKE. THERE'S ALWAYS A PRICE TO PAY.
HOW ABOUT YOU GO HOME?
IT'S FINE! LET ME COME IN!
I DON'T BELIEVE IN ALTERNATE DIMENSIONS OR ANY OF THAT STUFF. I'M NOT INTERESTED, SO I DON'T THINK THERE'LL BE ANY PAYBACK, EITHER.

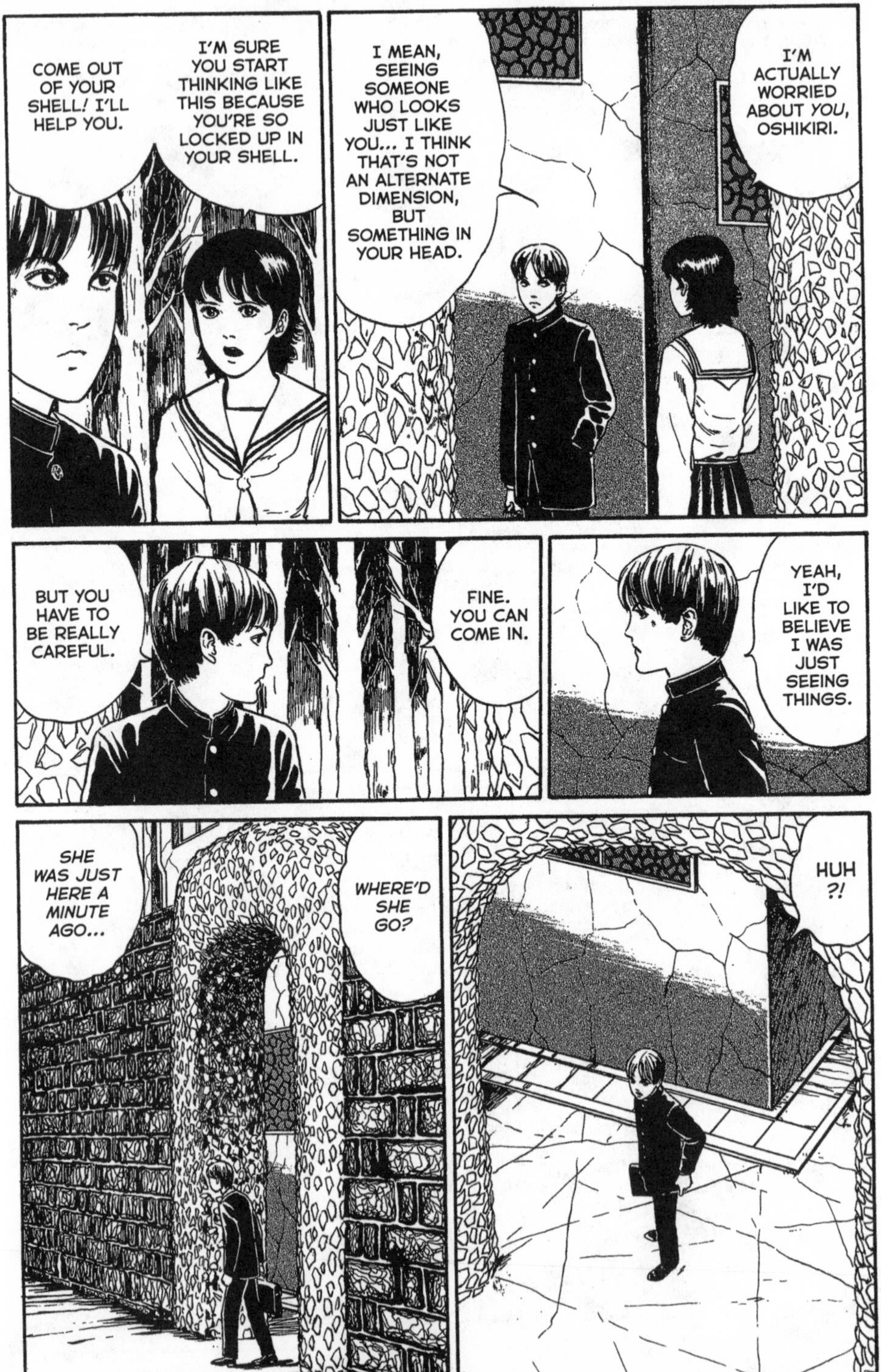
I'M ACTUALLY WORRIED ABOUT *YOU*, OSHIKIRI.
I MEAN, SEEING SOMEONE WHO LOOKS JUST LIKE YOU... I THINK THAT'S NOT AN ALTERNATE DIMENSION, BUT SOMETHING IN YOUR HEAD.
I'M SURE YOU START THINKING LIKE THIS BECAUSE YOU'RE SO LOCKED UP IN YOUR SHELL.
COME OUT OF YOUR SHELL! I'LL HELP YOU.
YEAH, I'D LIKE TO BELIEVE I WAS JUST SEEING THINGS.
FINE. YOU CAN COME IN.
BUT YOU HAVE TO BE REALLY CAREFUL.
HUH ?!
WHERE'D SHE GO?
SHE WAS JUST HERE A MINUTE AGO...

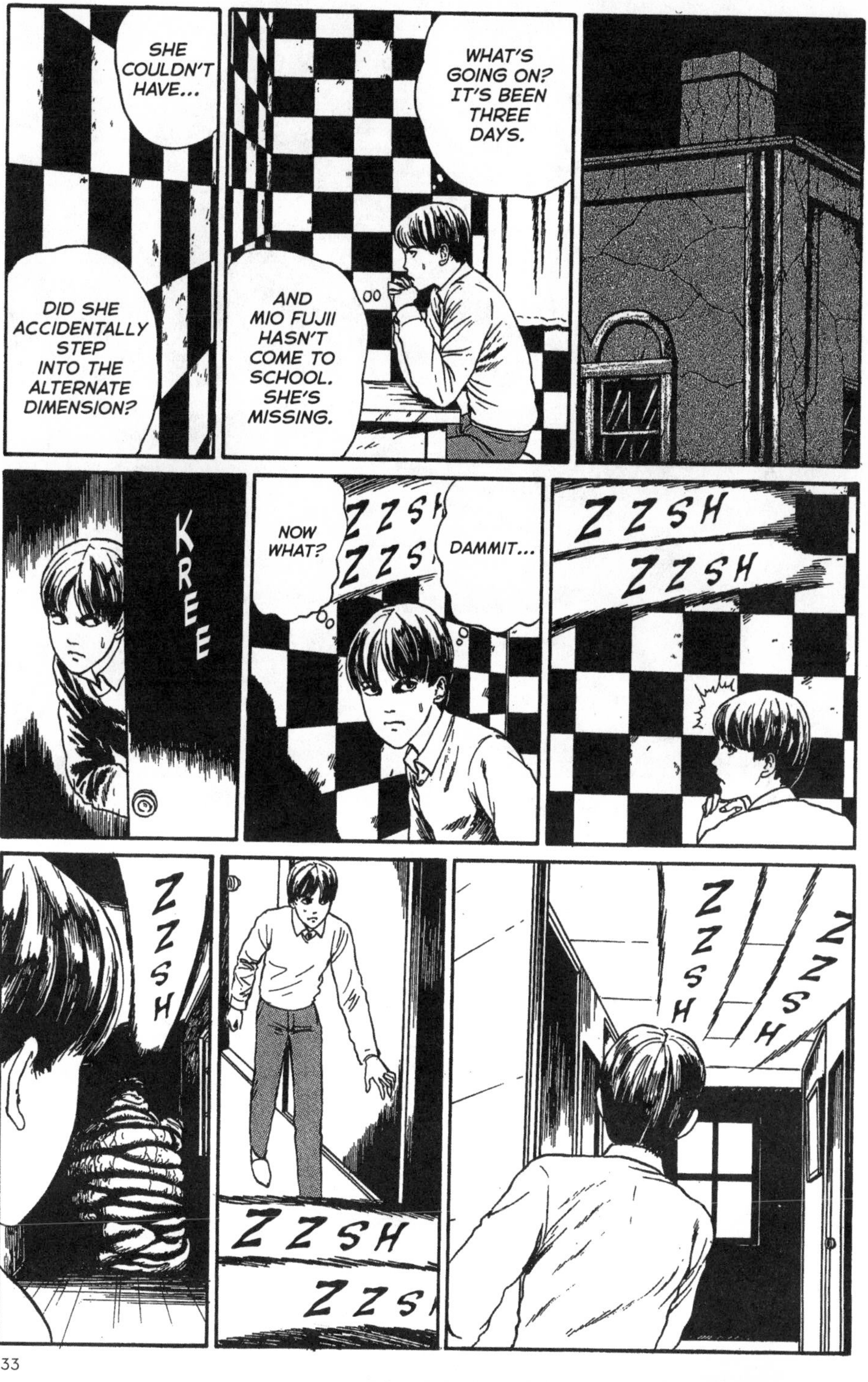
WHAT'S GOING ON? IT'S BEEN THREE DAYS.
AND MIO FUJII HASN'T COME TO SCHOOL. SHE'S MISSING.
SHE COULDN'T HAVE...
DID SHE ACCIDENTALLY STEP INTO THE ALTERNATE DIMENSION?
ZZSH
ZZSH
DAMMIT...
ZZS
ZZS
NOW WHAT?
KREE
ZZSH
ZZSH
ZZSH
ZZS
ZZSH

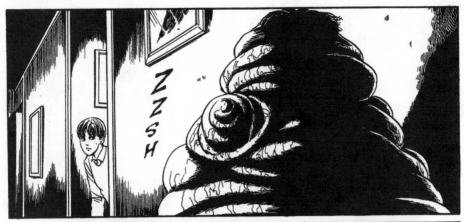

ZZSH
O-OSHIKI-RIIIII.
I FOUND YOUUU-UUU.
OSHIKIRI. PUT MY BODY BACK THE WAY IT WAAAAS!
THAT VOICE ...
MIO FUJII!

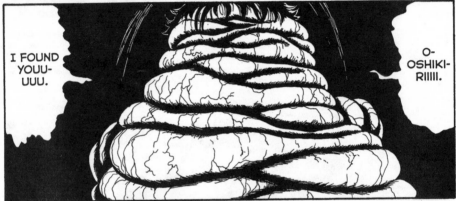

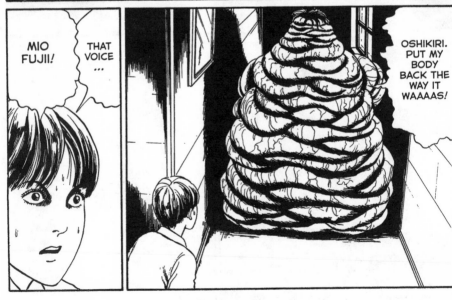

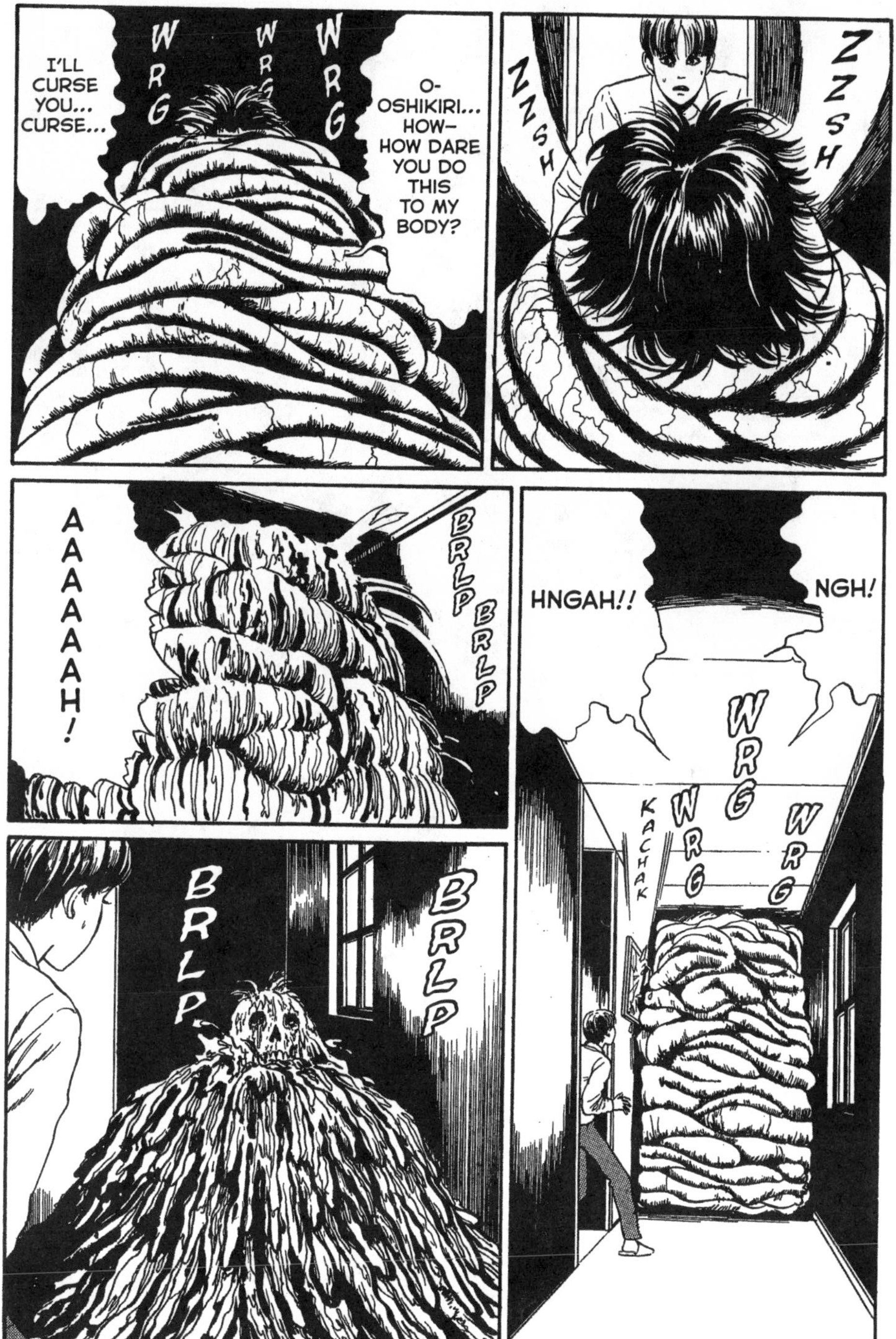
ZZSH
ZZSH
O-OSHIKIRI... HOW— HOW DARE YOU DO THIS TO MY BODY?
WRG
WRG
WRG
I'LL CURSE YOU... CURSE...
NGH!
HNGAH!!
WRG
WRG
WRG
WRG
KACHAK
BRLP
BRLP
AAAAAAAH!
BRLP
BRLP

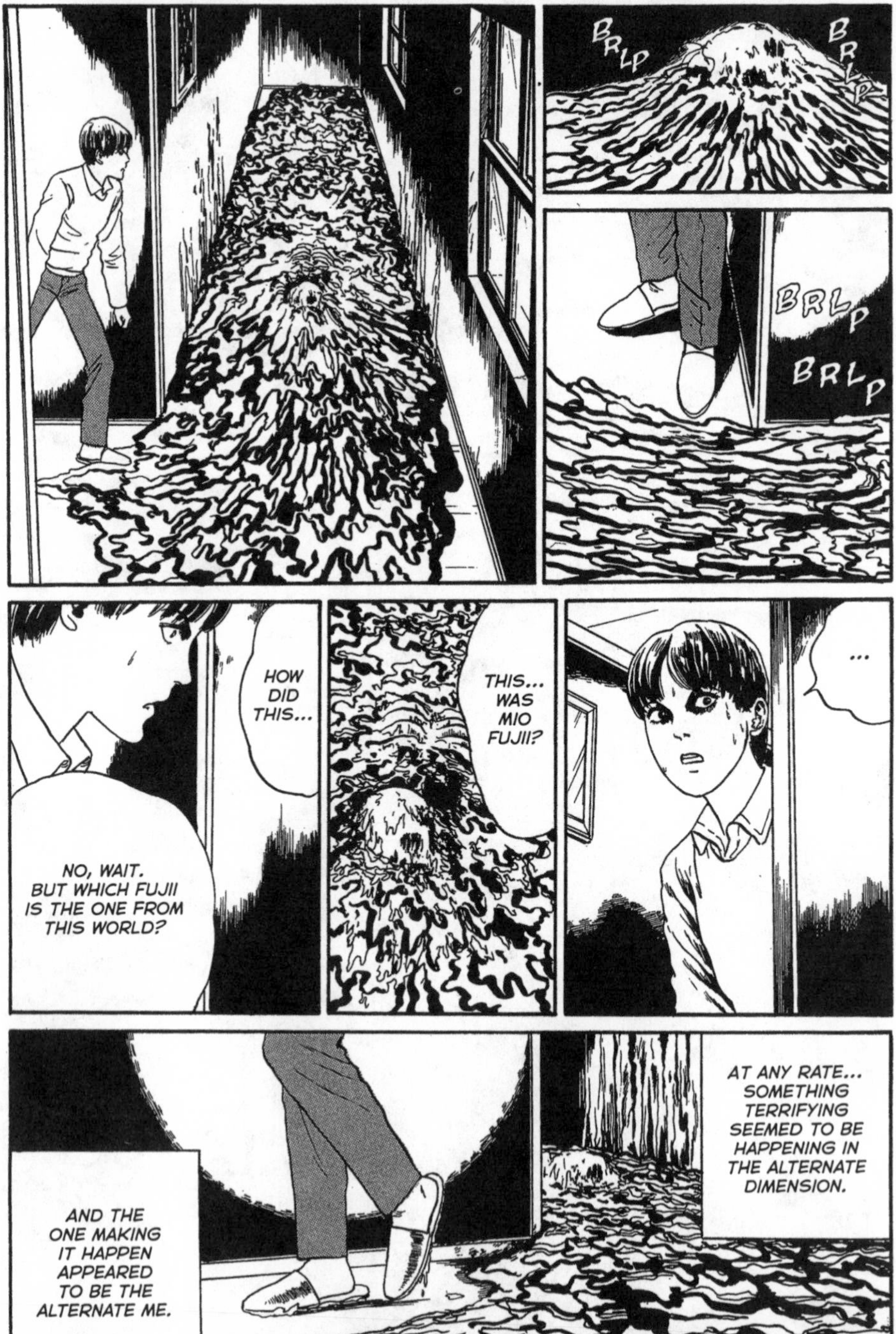

BRLP
BRLP
BRLP
BRLP
...
THIS... WAS MIO FUJII?
HOW DID THIS...
NO, WAIT. BUT WHICH FUJII IS THE ONE FROM THIS WORLD?
AT ANY RATE... SOMETHING TERRIFYING SEEMED TO BE HAPPENING IN THE ALTERNATE DIMENSION.
AND THE ONE MAKING IT HAPPEN APPEARED TO BE THE ALTERNATE ME.

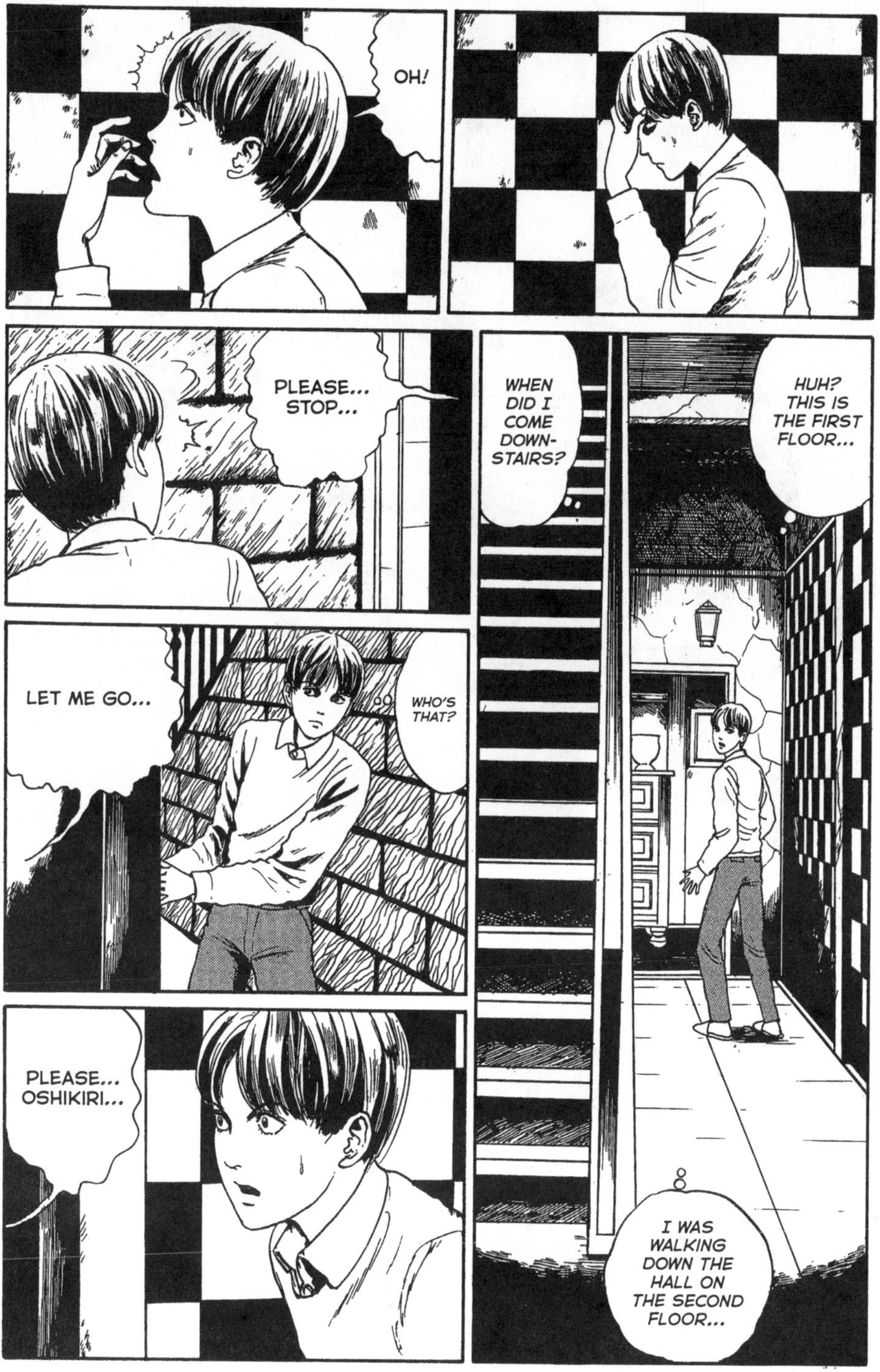
OH!
HUH? THIS IS THE FIRST FLOOR...
WHEN DID I COME DOWN-STAIRS?
I WAS WALKING DOWN THE HALL ON THE SECOND FLOOR...
PLEASE... STOP...
WHO'S THAT?
LET ME GO...
PLEASE... OSHIKIRI...

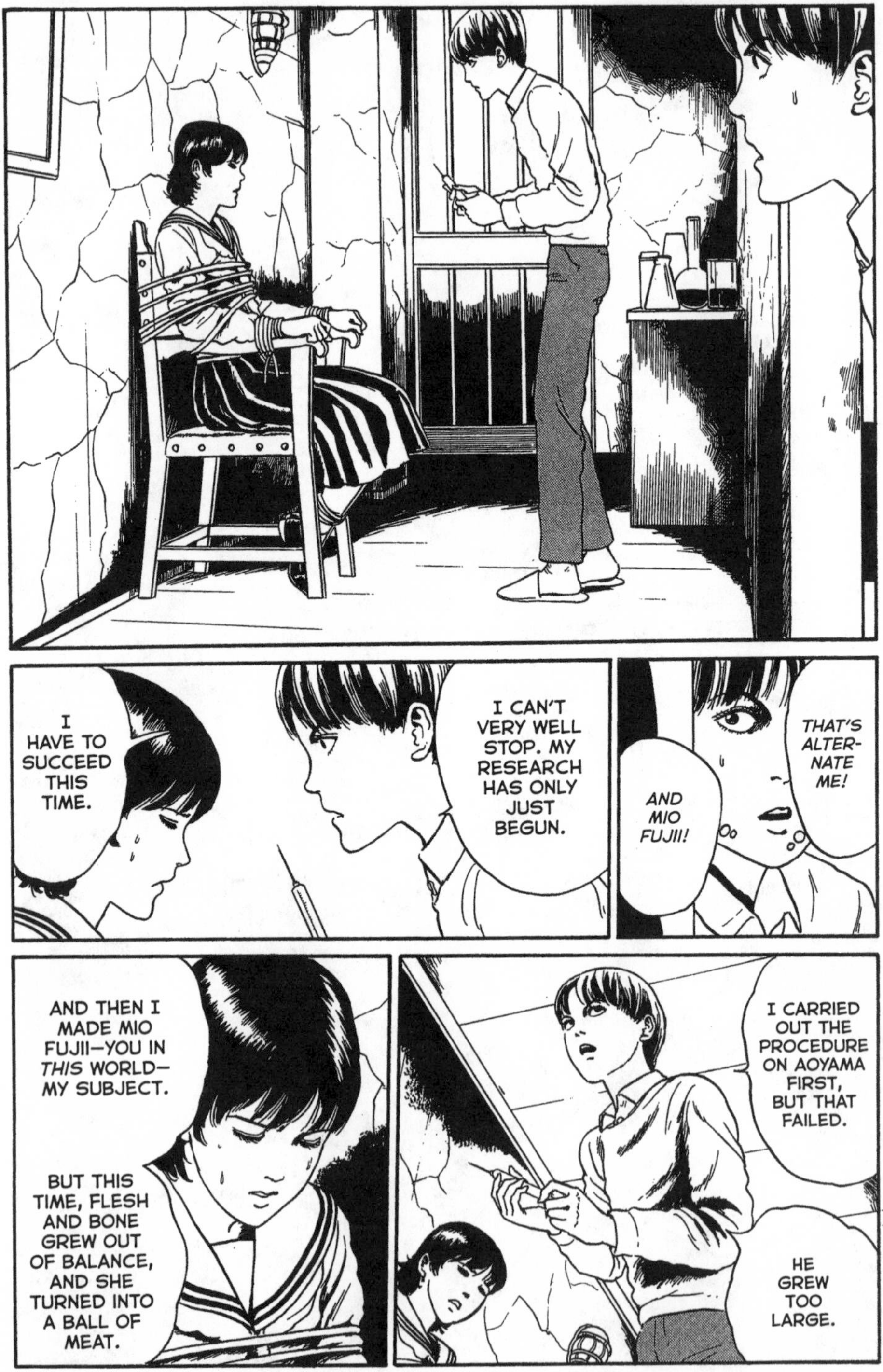
THAT'S ALTERNATE ME!
AND MIO FUJII!
I CAN'T VERY WELL STOP. MY RESEARCH HAS ONLY JUST BEGUN.
I HAVE TO SUCCEED THIS TIME.
I CARRIED OUT THE PROCEDURE ON AOYAMA FIRST, BUT THAT FAILED.
HE GREW TOO LARGE.
AND THEN I MADE MIO FUJII—YOU IN *THIS* WORLD—MY SUBJECT.
BUT THIS TIME, FLESH AND BONE GREW OUT OF BALANCE, AND SHE TURNED INTO A BALL OF MEAT.

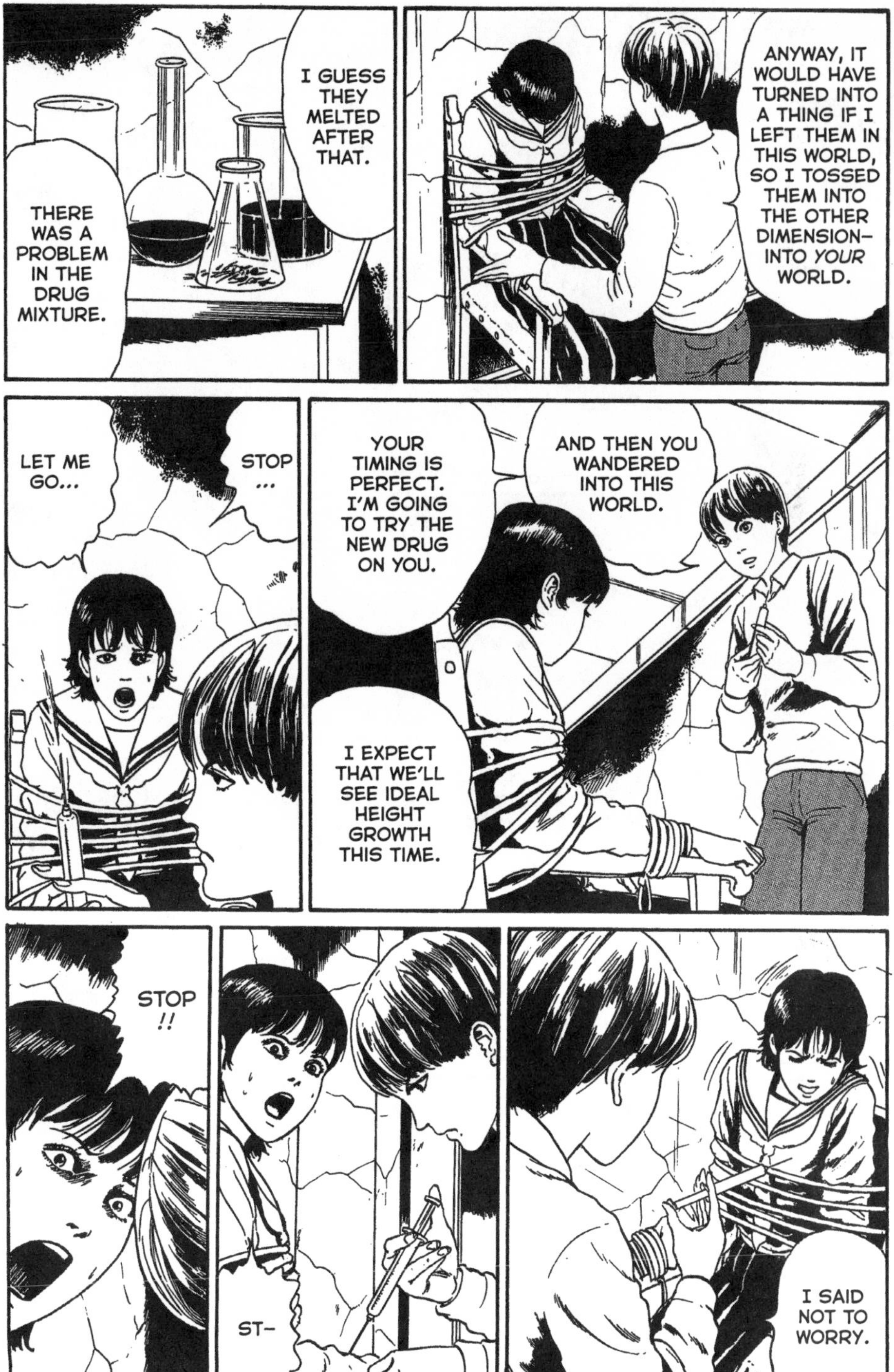
ANYWAY, IT WOULD HAVE TURNED INTO A THING IF I LEFT THEM IN THIS WORLD, SO I TOSSED THEM INTO THE OTHER DIMENSION–INTO *YOUR* WORLD.
I GUESS THEY MELTED AFTER THAT.
THERE WAS A PROBLEM IN THE DRUG MIXTURE.
AND THEN YOU WANDERED INTO THIS WORLD.
YOUR TIMING IS PERFECT. I'M GOING TO TRY THE NEW DRUG ON YOU.
I EXPECT THAT WE'LL SEE IDEAL HEIGHT GROWTH THIS TIME.
STOP ...
LET ME GO...
I SAID NOT TO WORRY.
ST–
STOP !!

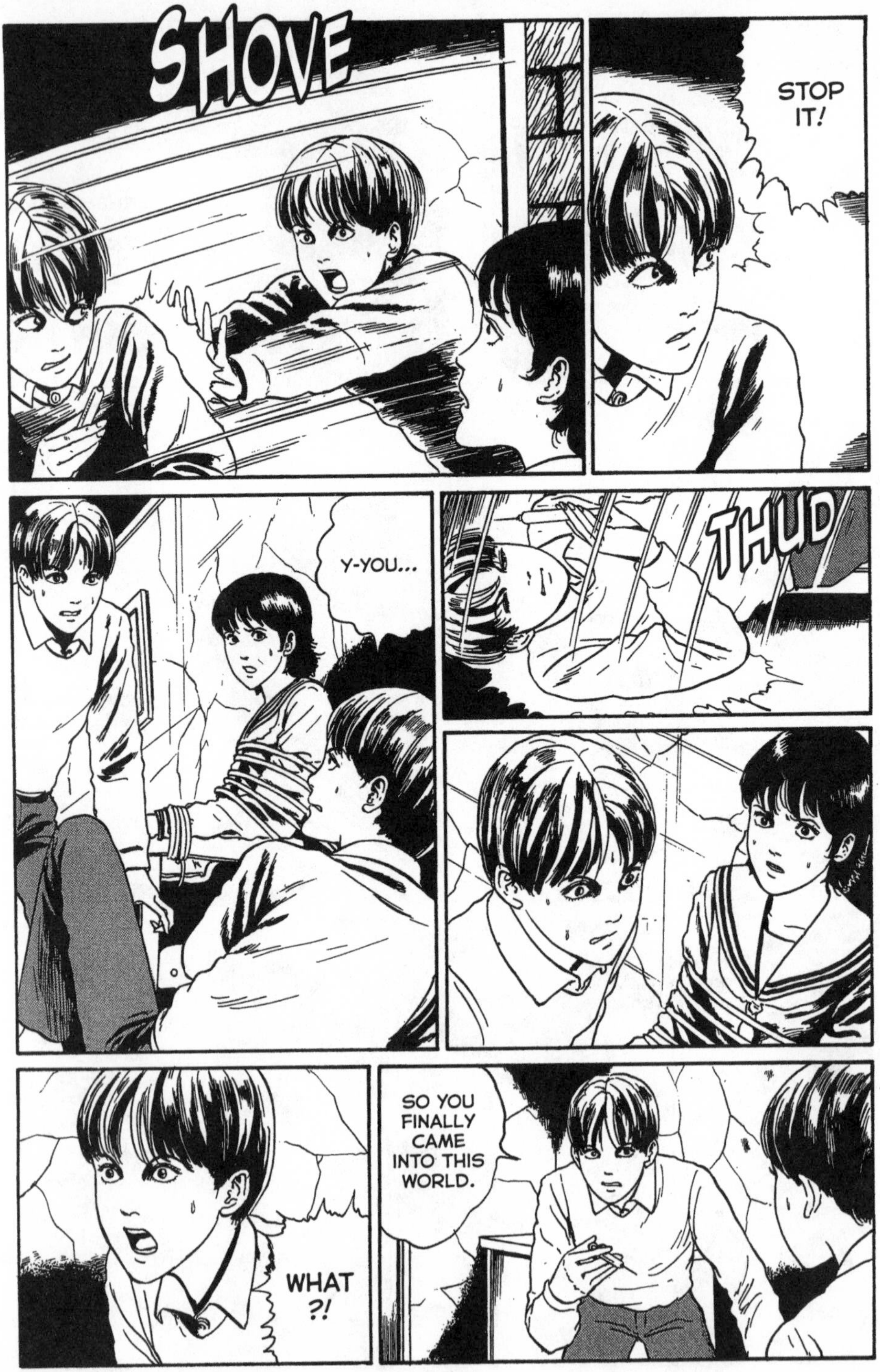
STOP IT!
SHOVE
THUD
Y-YOU...
SO YOU FINALLY CAME INTO THIS WORLD.
WHAT ?!

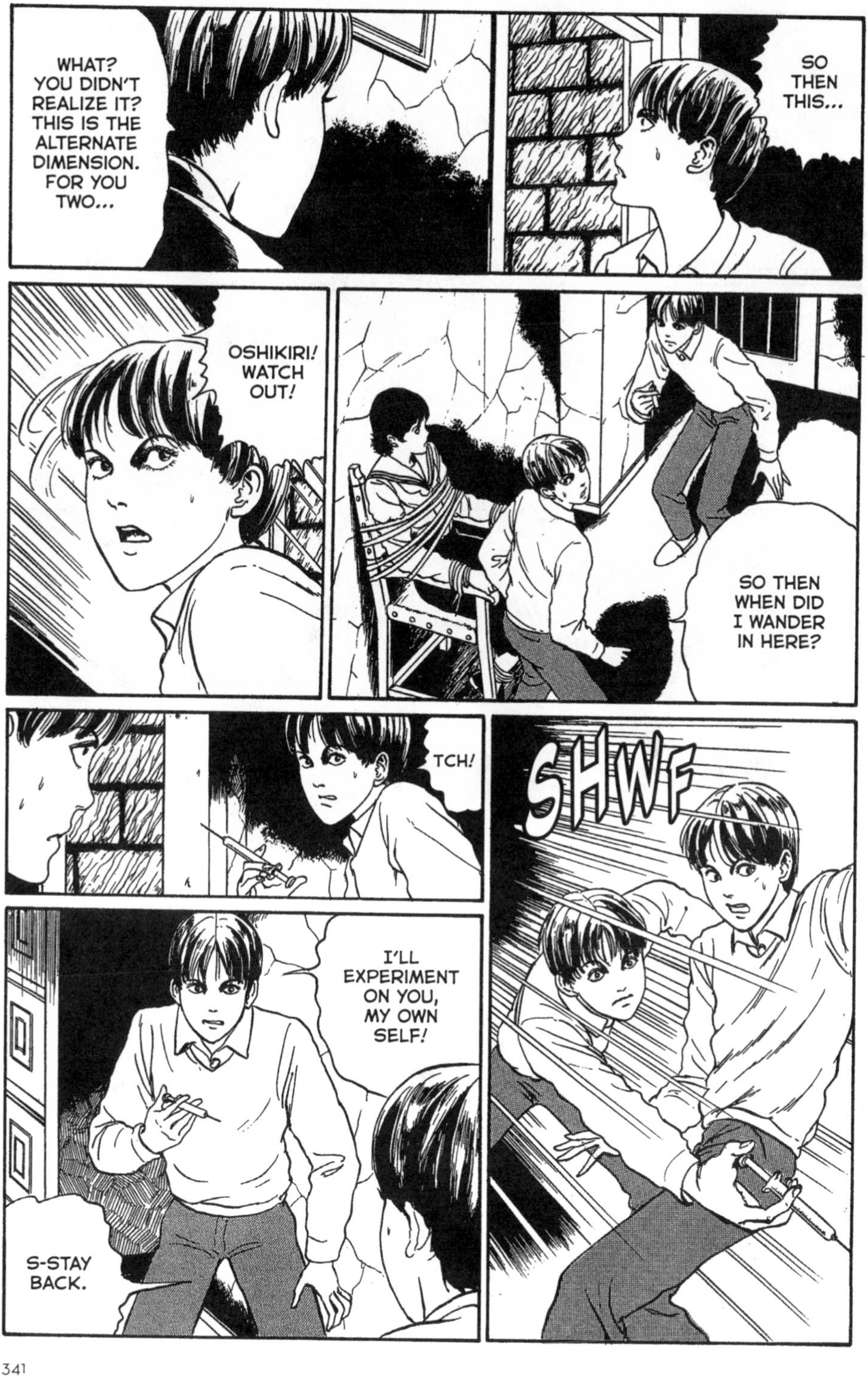
SO THEN THIS...
WHAT? YOU DIDN'T REALIZE IT? THIS IS THE ALTERNATE DIMENSION. FOR YOU TWO...
SO THEN WHEN DID I WANDER IN HERE?
OSHIKIRI! WATCH OUT!
SHWF
TCH!
I'LL EXPERIMENT ON YOU, MY OWN SELF!
S-STAY BACK.

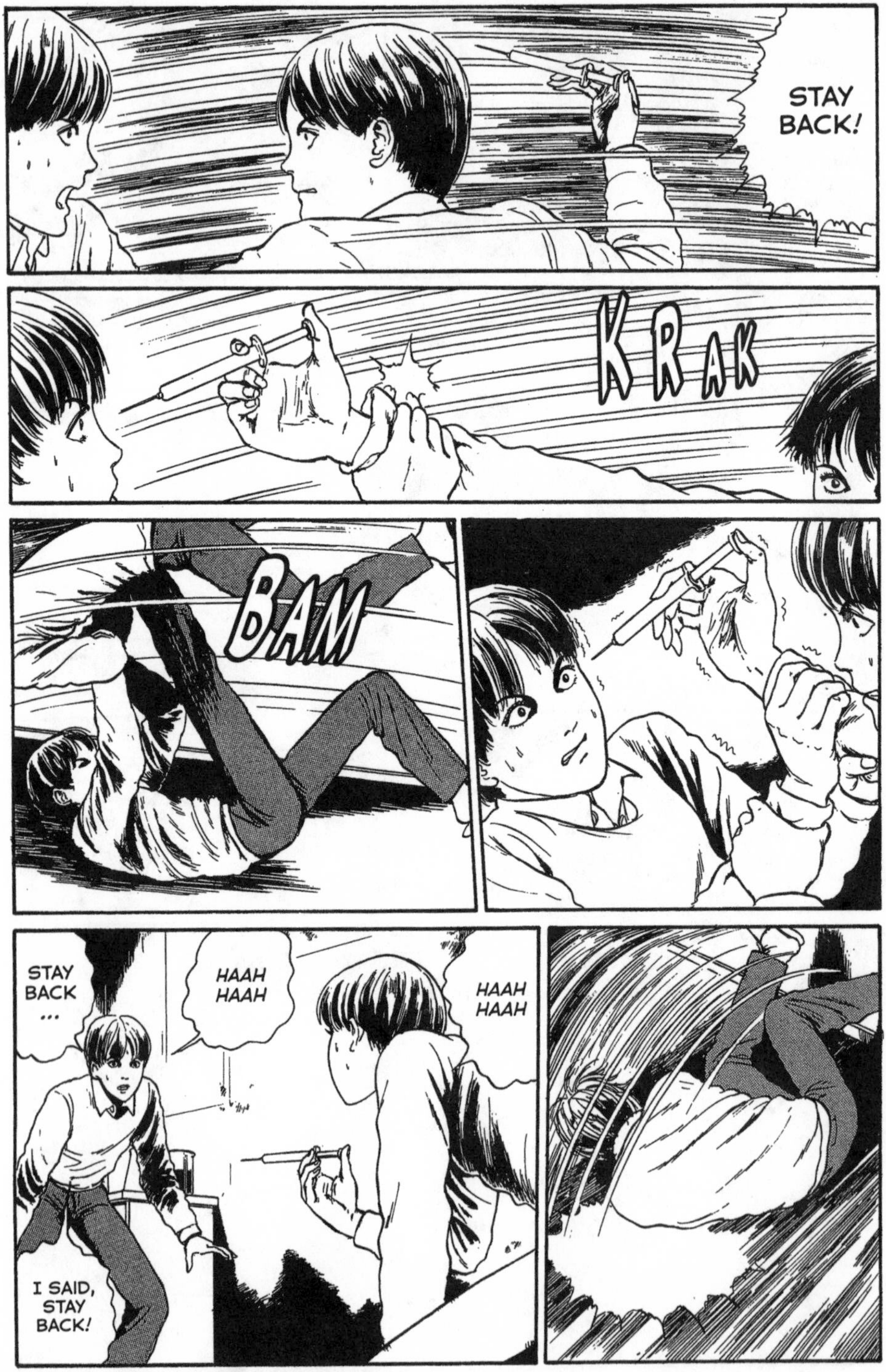
STAY BACK!
KRAK
BAM
HAAH HAAH
HAAH HAAH
STAY BACK ...
I SAID, STAY BACK!

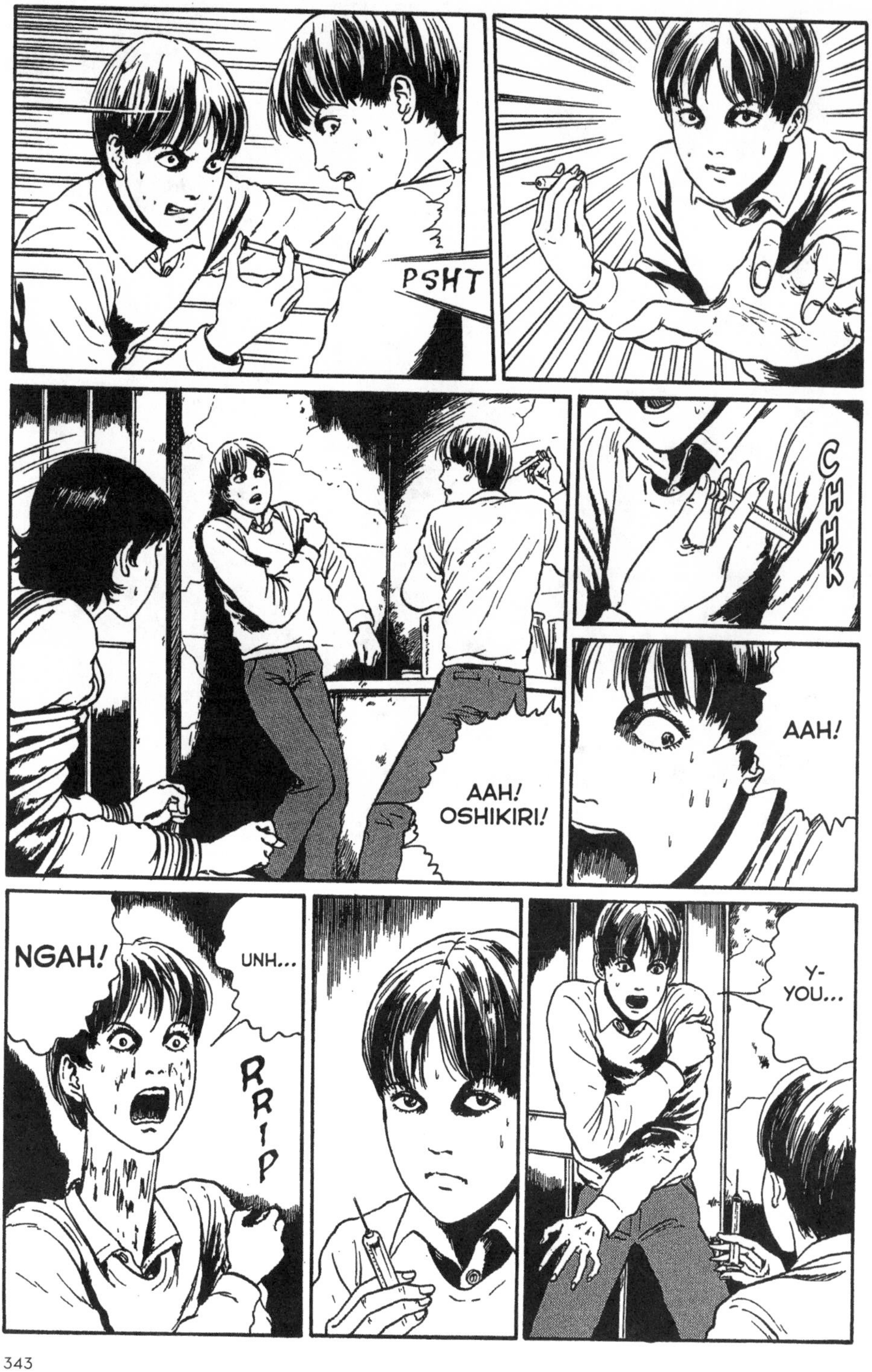
PSHT
CHHK
AAH!
AAH! OSHIKIRI!
Y- YOU...
UNH...
NGAH!
RRIP

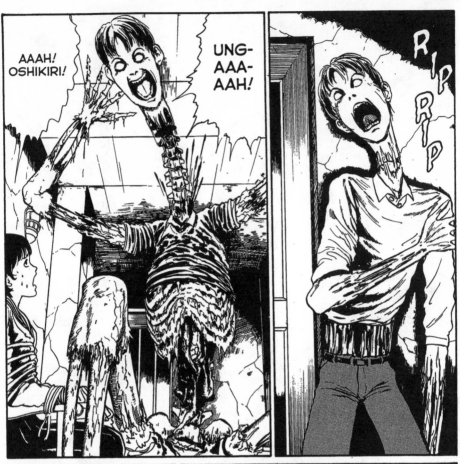

RIP RIP RIP
UNG-AAA-AAH!
AAAH! OSHIKIRI!
EEEEEEE!
THE EXPERIMENT'S A FAILURE! THE GROWTH OF BONE AND MUSCLE IS UNBALANCED!
THE BONES ALONE ARE GROWING ABNORMALLY.

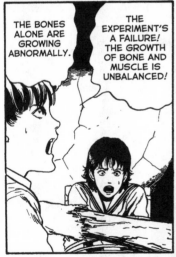

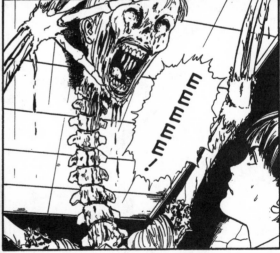

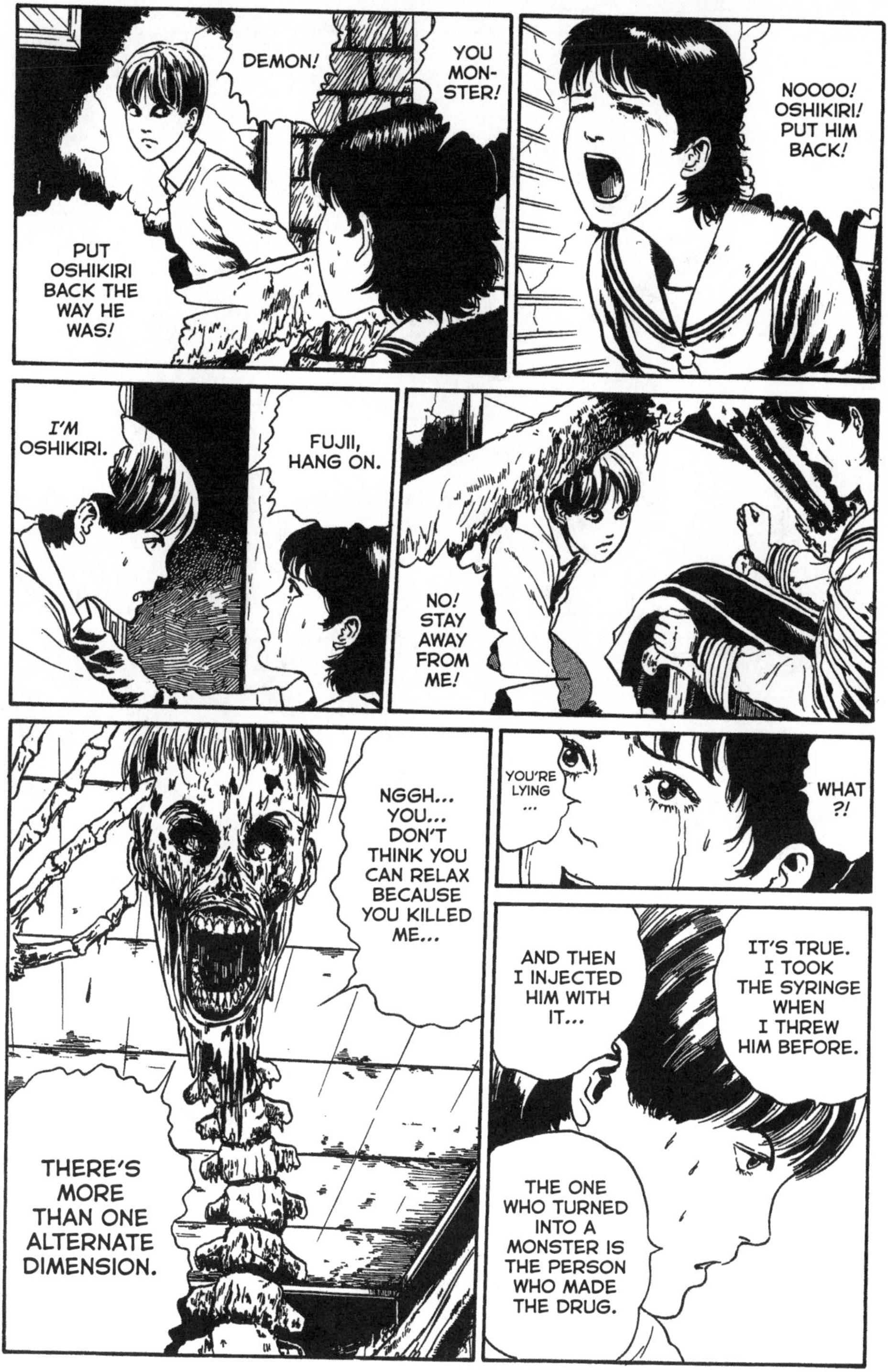
NOOOO! OSHIKIRI! PUT HIM BACK!
YOU MONSTER!
DEMON!
PUT OSHIKIRI BACK THE WAY HE WAS!
NO! STAY AWAY FROM ME!
FUJII, HANG ON.
I'M OSHIKIRI.
WHAT?!
YOU'RE LYING...
IT'S TRUE. I TOOK THE SYRINGE WHEN I THREW HIM BEFORE.
AND THEN I INJECTED HIM WITH IT...
THE ONE WHO TURNED INTO A MONSTER IS THE PERSON WHO MADE THE DRUG.
NGGH... YOU... DON'T THINK YOU CAN RELAX BECAUSE YOU KILLED ME...
THERE'S MORE THAN ONE ALTERNATE DIMENSION.

UNGAAAAH!

BRLP BRLP

UNH...

DON'T FORGET THAT THERE ARE INFINITE OSHIKIRIS. THERE HAS TO BE AN EVEN MORE EVIL OSHIKIRI...

THERE ARE INFINITE DIMEN-SIONS.

PLSH PLSH

YOU THINK WE'LL BE ABLE TO GET BACK TO OUR OWN WORLD?

OSHIKIRI ...

...

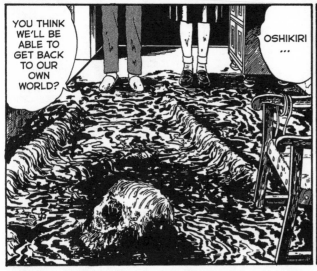

THE STRANGE TALE OF OSHIKIRI / END

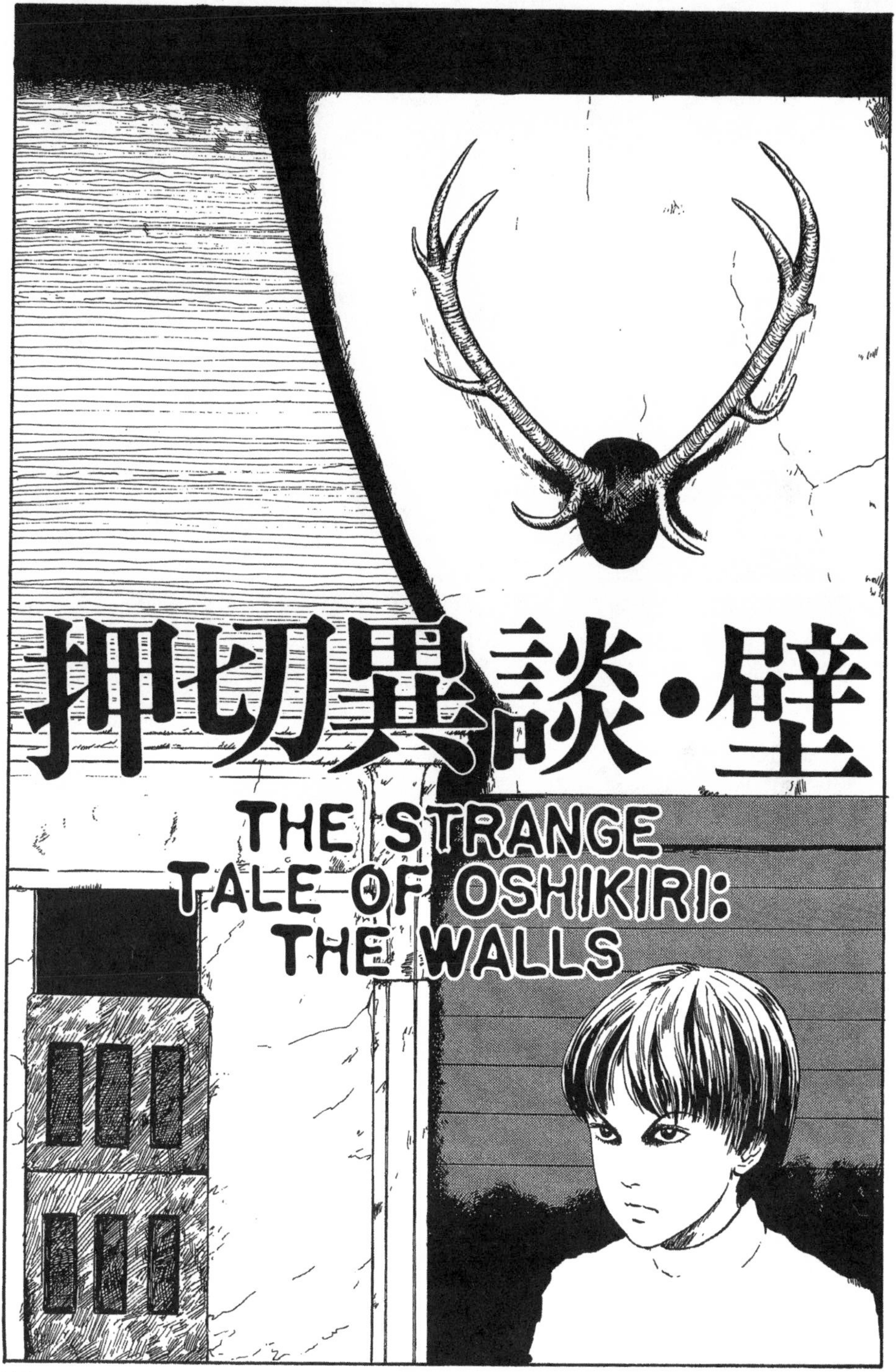
押切異談・壁
THE STRANGE TALE OF OSHIKIRI: THE WALLS

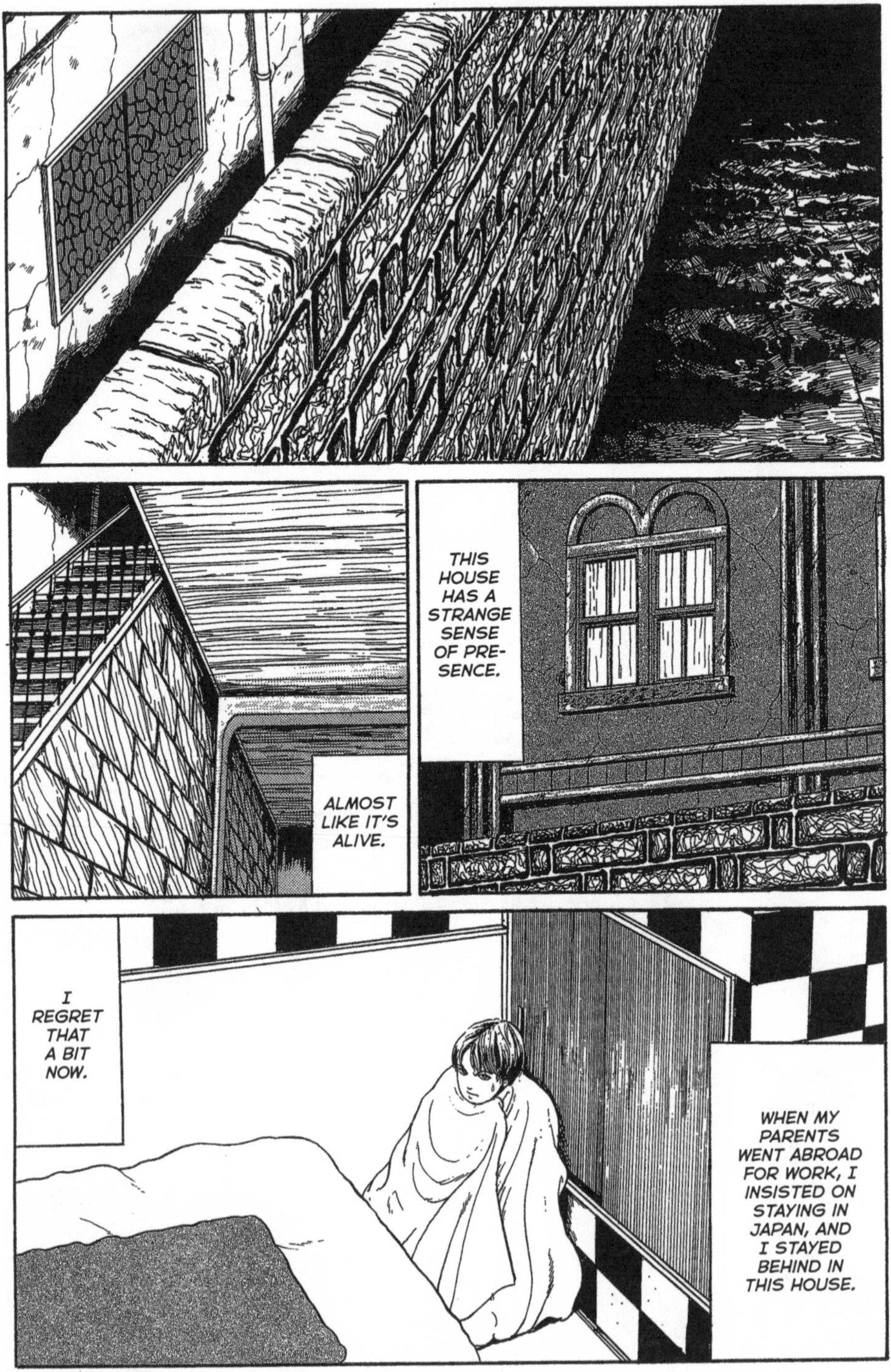
THIS HOUSE HAS A STRANGE SENSE OF PRE-SENCE.
ALMOST LIKE IT'S ALIVE.
WHEN MY PARENTS WENT ABROAD FOR WORK, I INSISTED ON STAYING IN JAPAN, AND I STAYED BEHIND IN THIS HOUSE.
I REGRET THAT A BIT NOW.

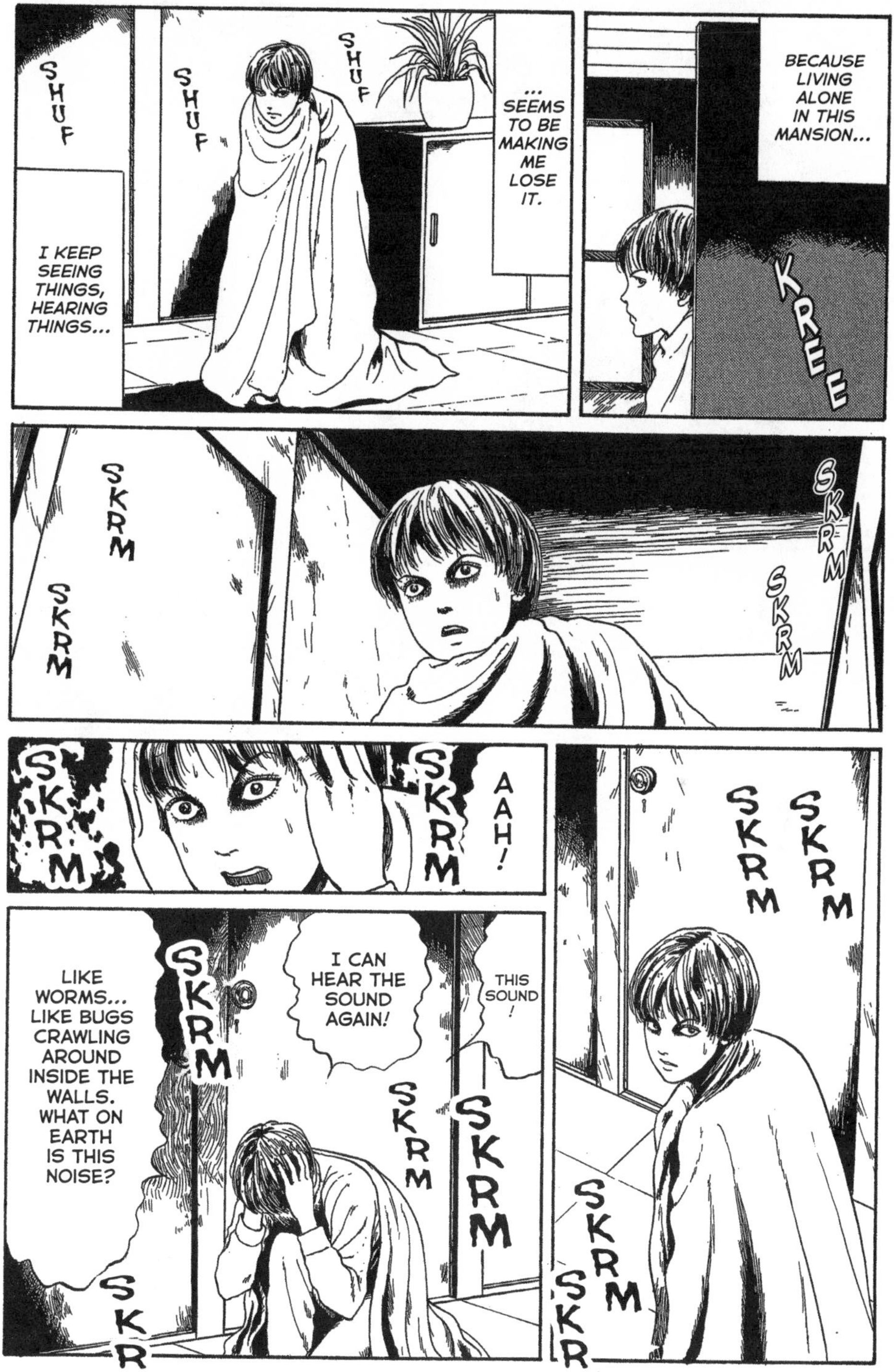
BECAUSE LIVING ALONE IN THIS MANSION...
KREE
...SEEMS TO BE MAKING ME LOSE IT.
SHUF
SHUF
SHUF
I KEEP SEEING THINGS, HEARING THINGS...
SKRM
SKRM
SKRM
SKRM
SKRM
SKRM
SKRM
SKRM
AAH!
SKRM
SKRM
THIS SOUND!
I CAN HEAR THE SOUND AGAIN!
LIKE WORMS... LIKE BUGS CRAWLING AROUND INSIDE THE WALLS. WHAT ON EARTH IS THIS NOISE?
SKRM
SKRM
SKRM
SKRM

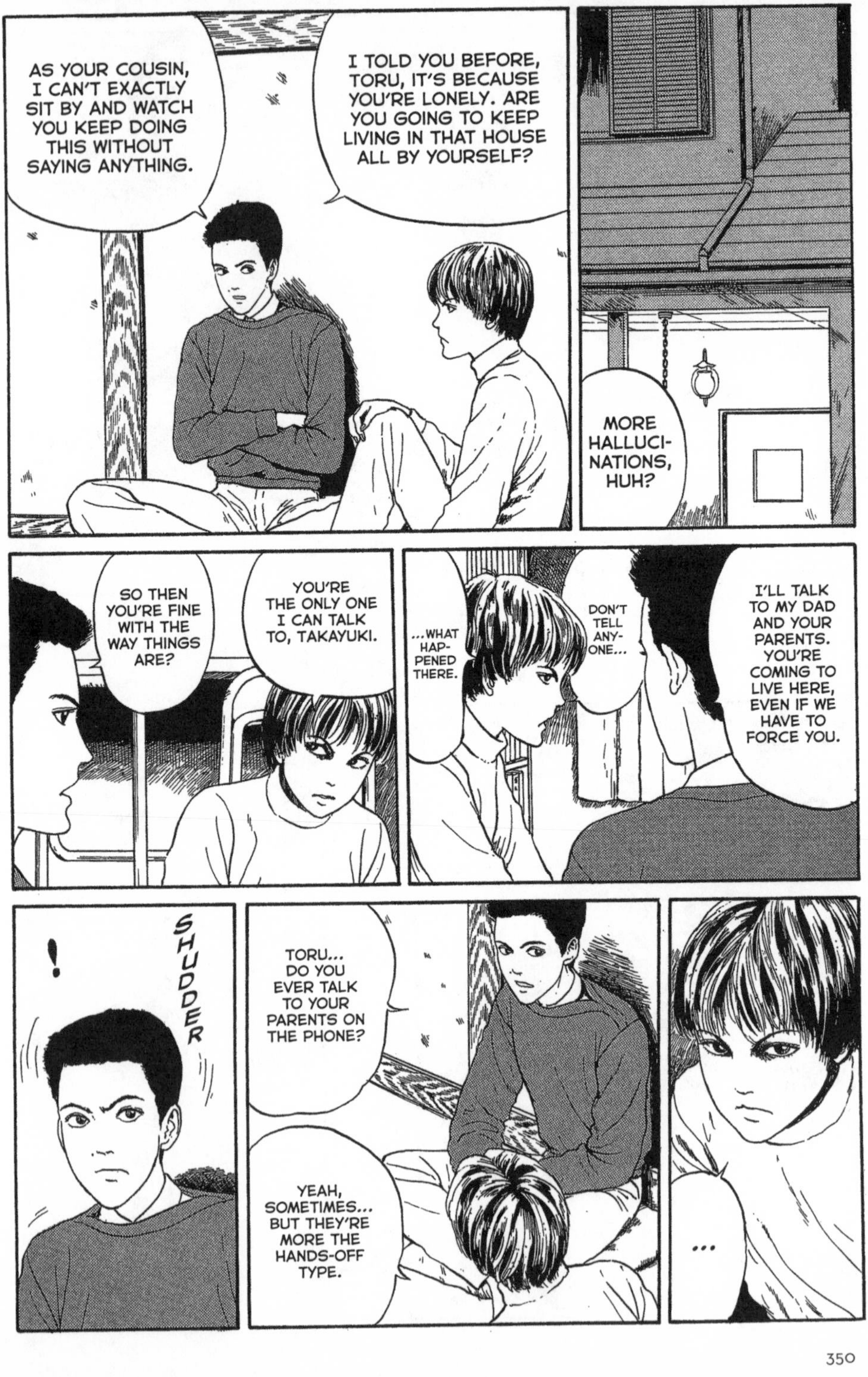
MORE HALLUCI-NATIONS, HUH?
I TOLD YOU BEFORE, TORU, IT'S BECAUSE YOU'RE LONELY. ARE YOU GOING TO KEEP LIVING IN THAT HOUSE ALL BY YOURSELF?
AS YOUR COUSIN, I CAN'T EXACTLY SIT BY AND WATCH YOU KEEP DOING THIS WITHOUT SAYING ANYTHING.
I'LL TALK TO MY DAD AND YOUR PARENTS. YOU'RE COMING TO LIVE HERE, EVEN IF WE HAVE TO FORCE YOU.
DON'T TELL ANY-ONE...
...WHAT HAP-PENED THERE.
YOU'RE THE ONLY ONE I CAN TALK TO, TAKAYUKI.
SO THEN YOU'RE FINE WITH THE WAY THINGS ARE?
...
TORU... DO YOU EVER TALK TO YOUR PARENTS ON THE PHONE?
YEAH, SOMETIMES... BUT THEY'RE MORE THE HANDS-OFF TYPE.
SHUDDER
!

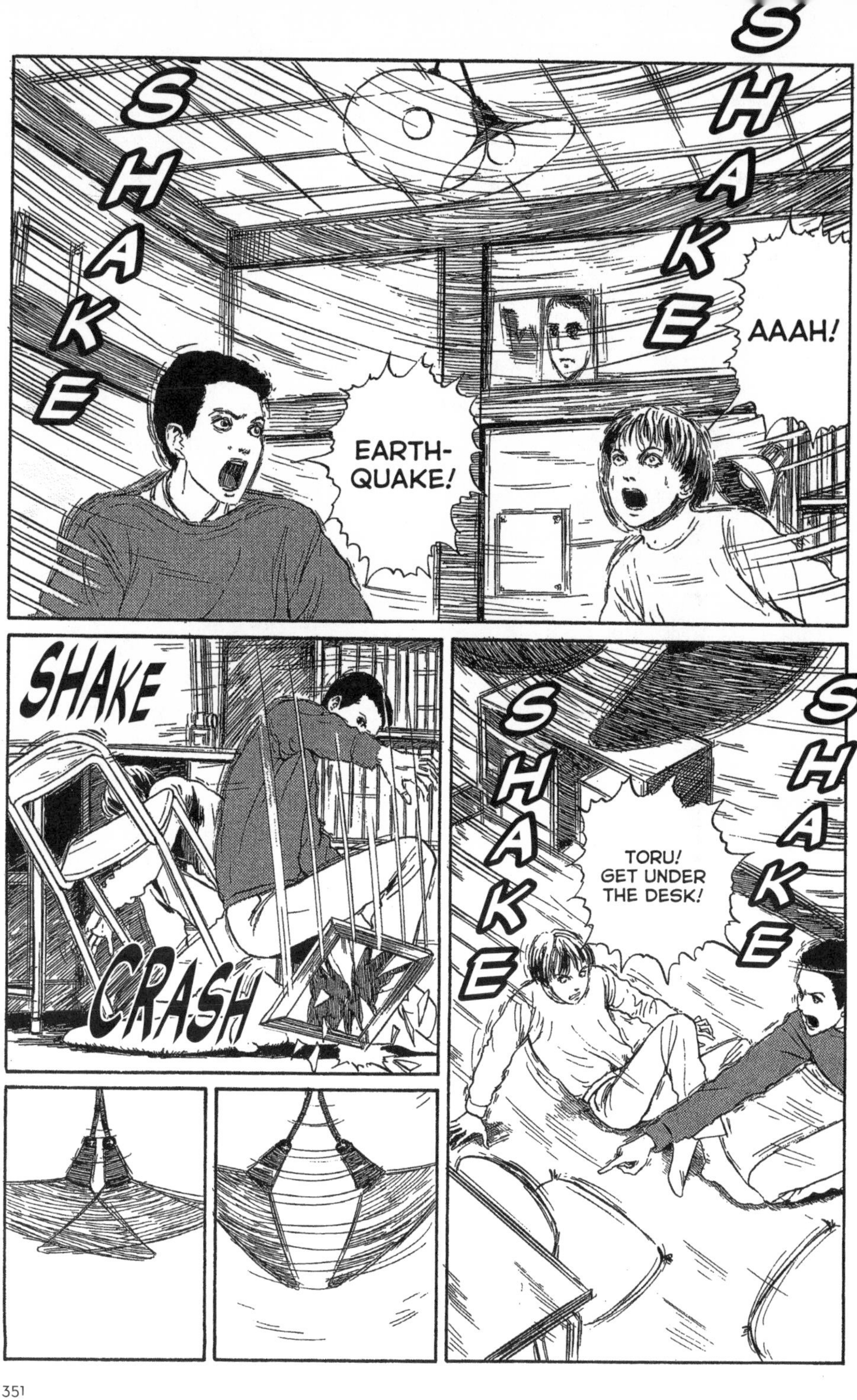
SHAKE
AAAH!
SHAKE
EARTH-QUAKE!
SHAKE
SHAKE
TORU! GET UNDER THE DESK!
SHAKE
CRASH

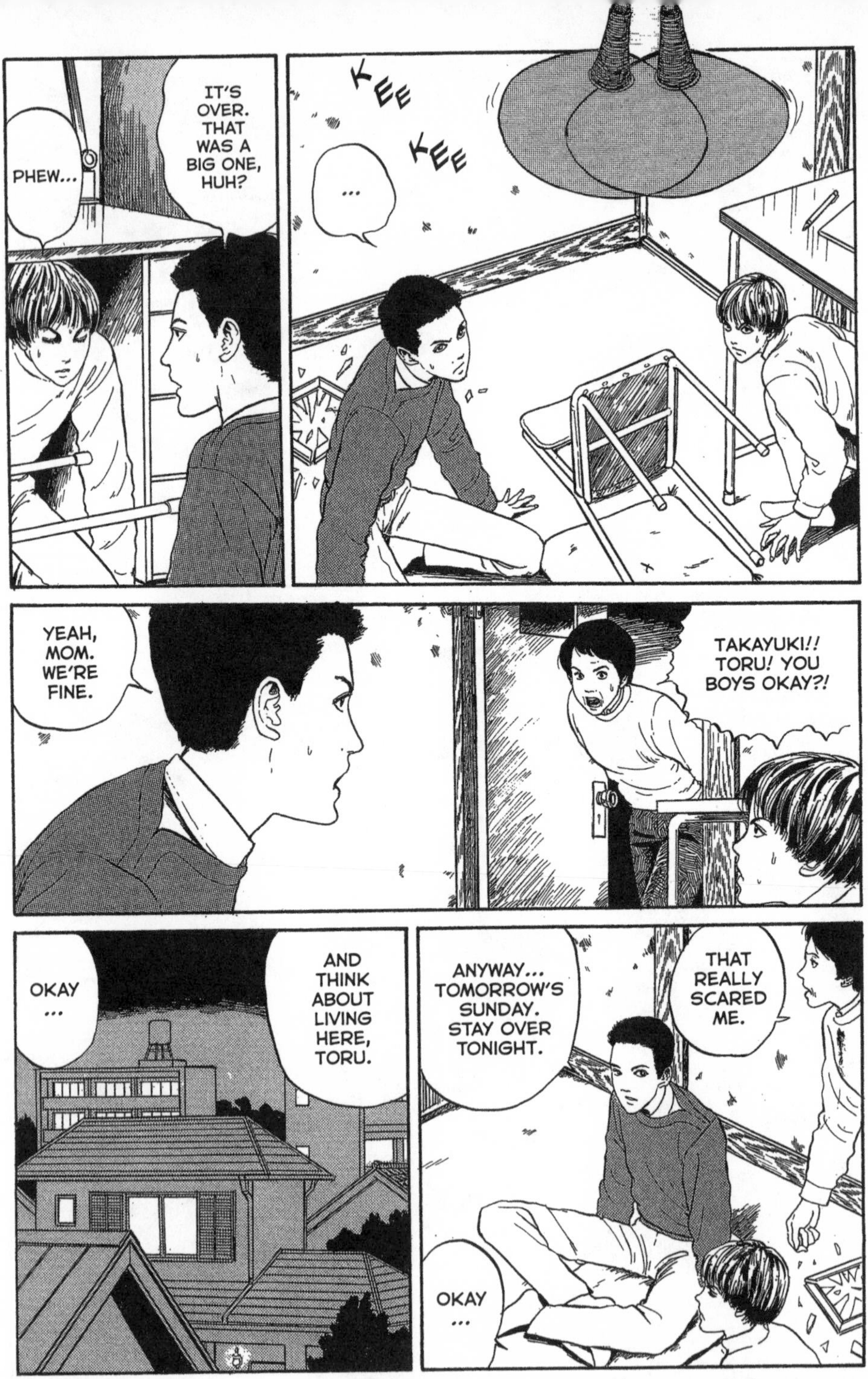
KEE
KEE
...
IT'S OVER. THAT WAS A BIG ONE, HUH?
PHEW...
TAKAYUKI!! TORU! YOU BOYS OKAY?!
YEAH, MOM. WE'RE FINE.
THAT REALLY SCARED ME.
ANYWAY... TOMORROW'S SUNDAY. STAY OVER TONIGHT.
OKAY...
AND THINK ABOUT LIVING HERE, TORU.
OKAY...

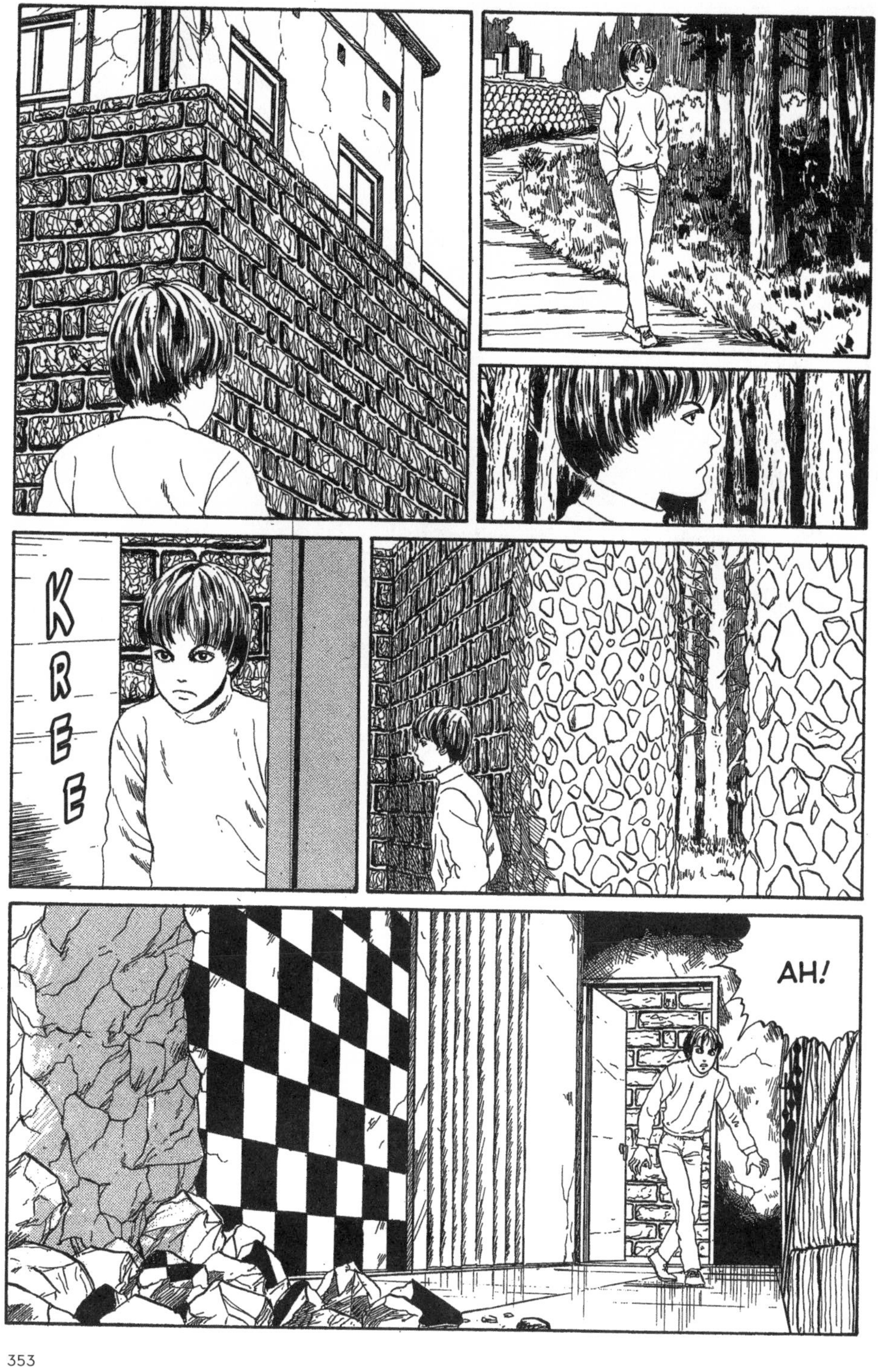
KREE
AH!

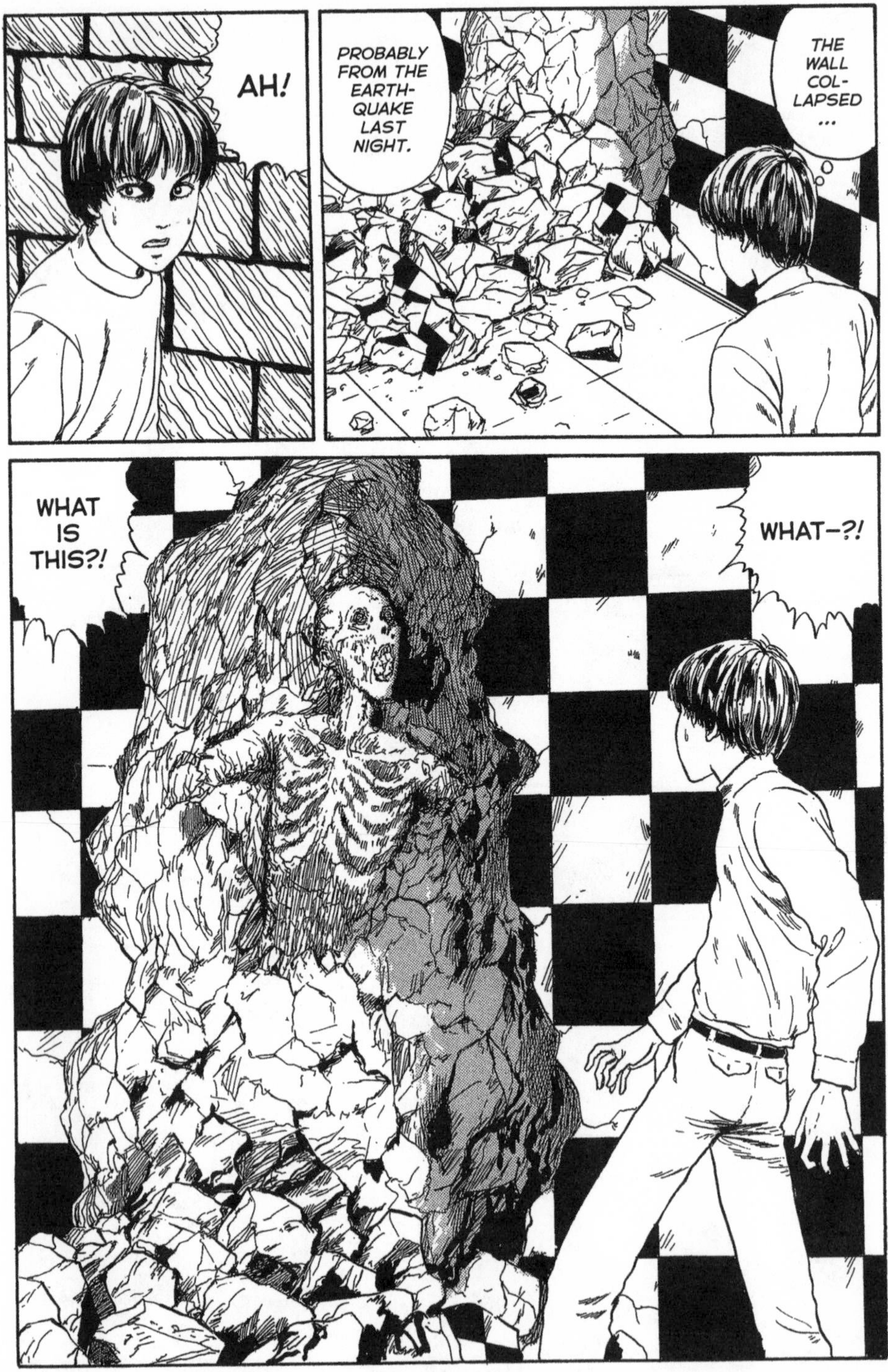
THE WALL COL-LAPSED...
PROBABLY FROM THE EARTH-QUAKE LAST NIGHT.
AH!
WHAT-?!
WHAT IS THIS?!

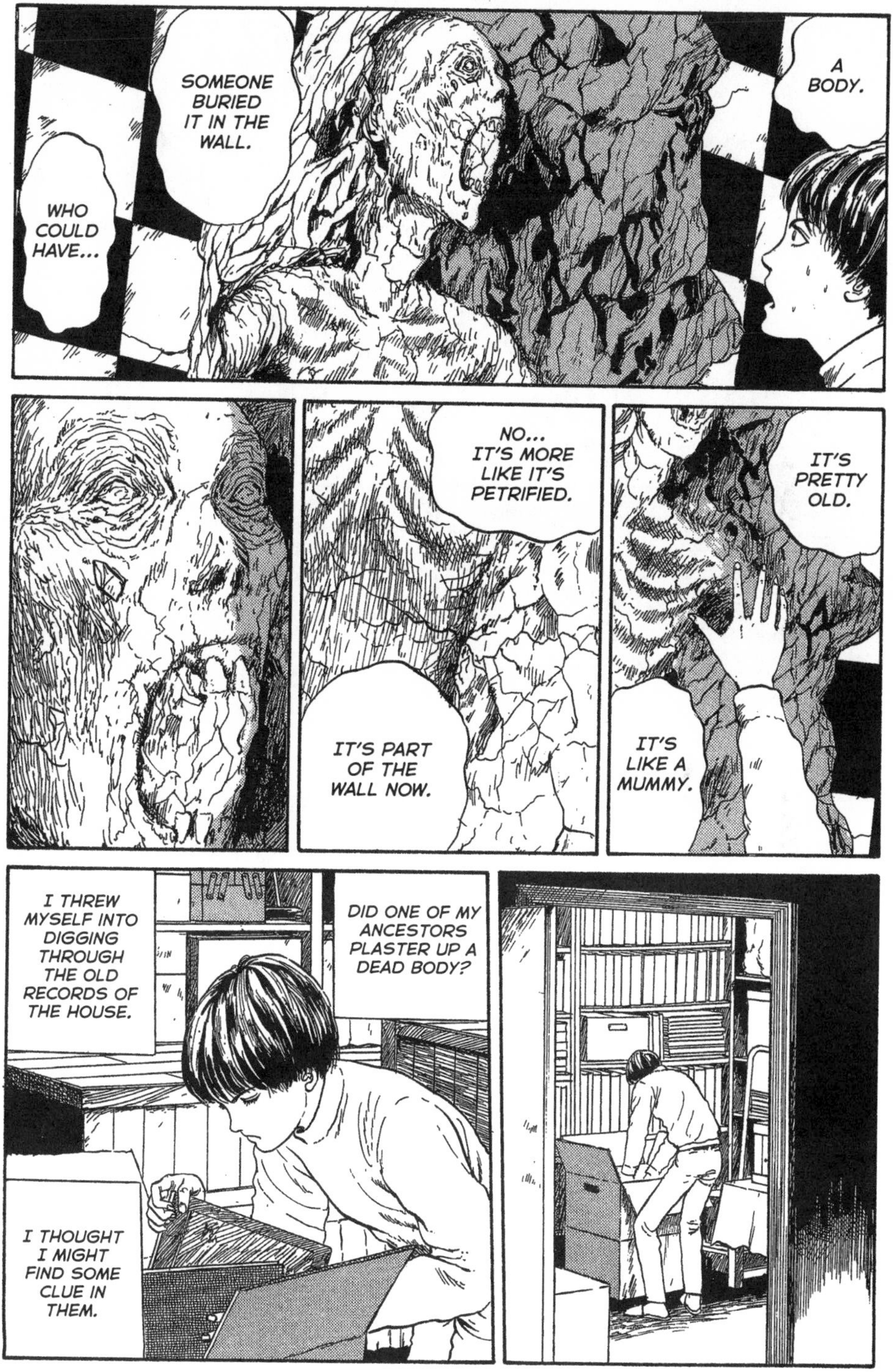
A BODY.
SOMEONE BURIED IT IN THE WALL.
WHO COULD HAVE...
IT'S PRETTY OLD.
IT'S LIKE A MUMMY.
NO... IT'S MORE LIKE IT'S PETRIFIED.
IT'S PART OF THE WALL NOW.
DID ONE OF MY ANCESTORS PLASTER UP A DEAD BODY?
I THREW MYSELF INTO DIGGING THROUGH THE OLD RECORDS OF THE HOUSE.
I THOUGHT I MIGHT FIND SOME CLUE IN THEM.

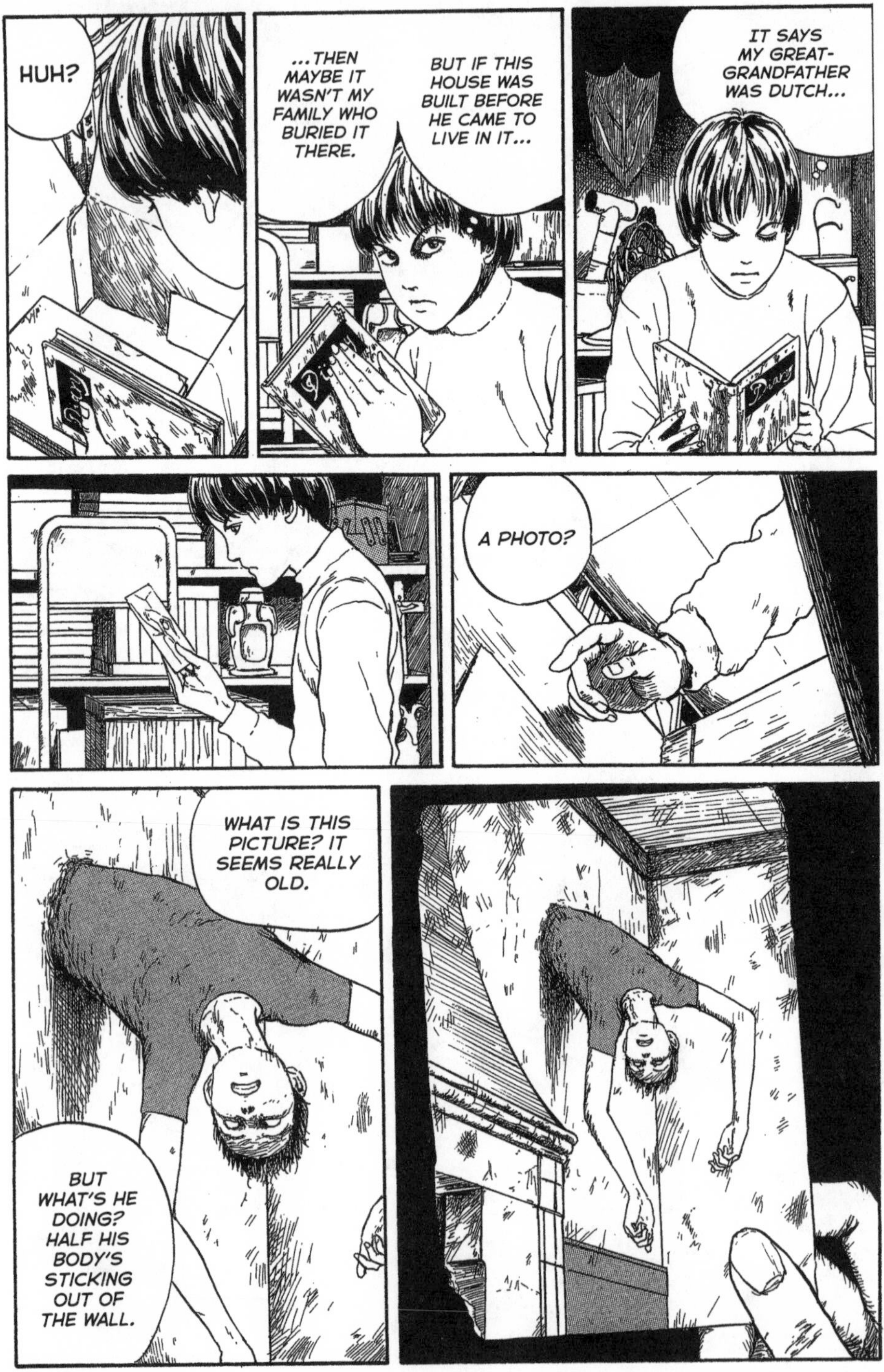
IT SAYS MY GREAT-GRANDFATHER WAS DUTCH...
BUT IF THIS HOUSE WAS BUILT BEFORE HE CAME TO LIVE IN IT...
...THEN MAYBE IT WASN'T MY FAMILY WHO BURIED IT THERE.
HUH?
A PHOTO?
WHAT IS THIS PICTURE? IT SEEMS REALLY OLD.
BUT WHAT'S HE DOING? HALF HIS BODY'S STICKING OUT OF THE WALL.

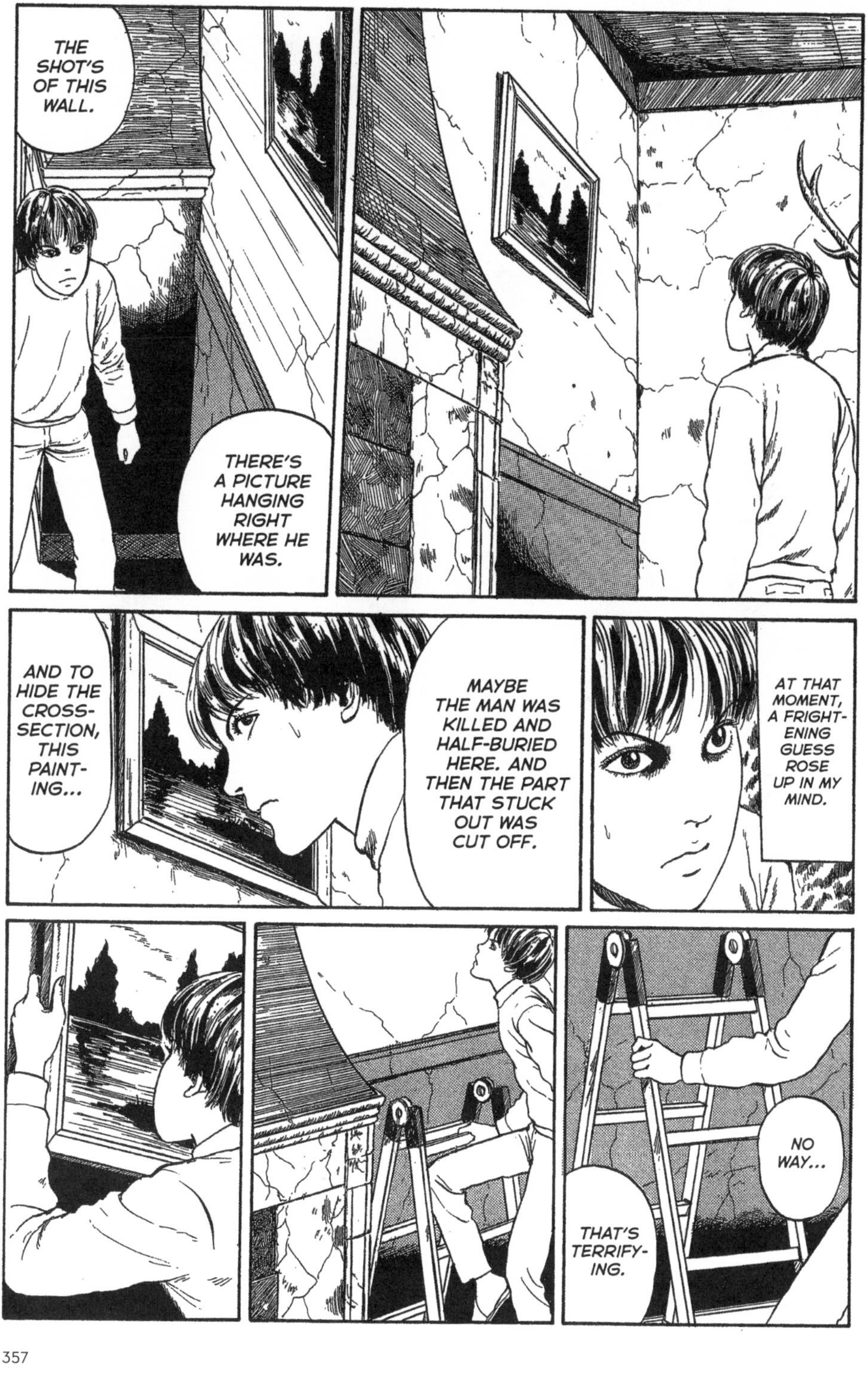
THE SHOT'S OF THIS WALL.
THERE'S A PICTURE HANGING RIGHT WHERE HE WAS.
AT THAT MOMENT, A FRIGHTENING GUESS ROSE UP IN MY MIND.
MAYBE THE MAN WAS KILLED AND HALF-BURIED HERE. AND THEN THE PART THAT STUCK OUT WAS CUT OFF.
AND TO HIDE THE CROSS-SECTION, THIS PAINTING...
NO WAY...
THAT'S TERRIFYING.

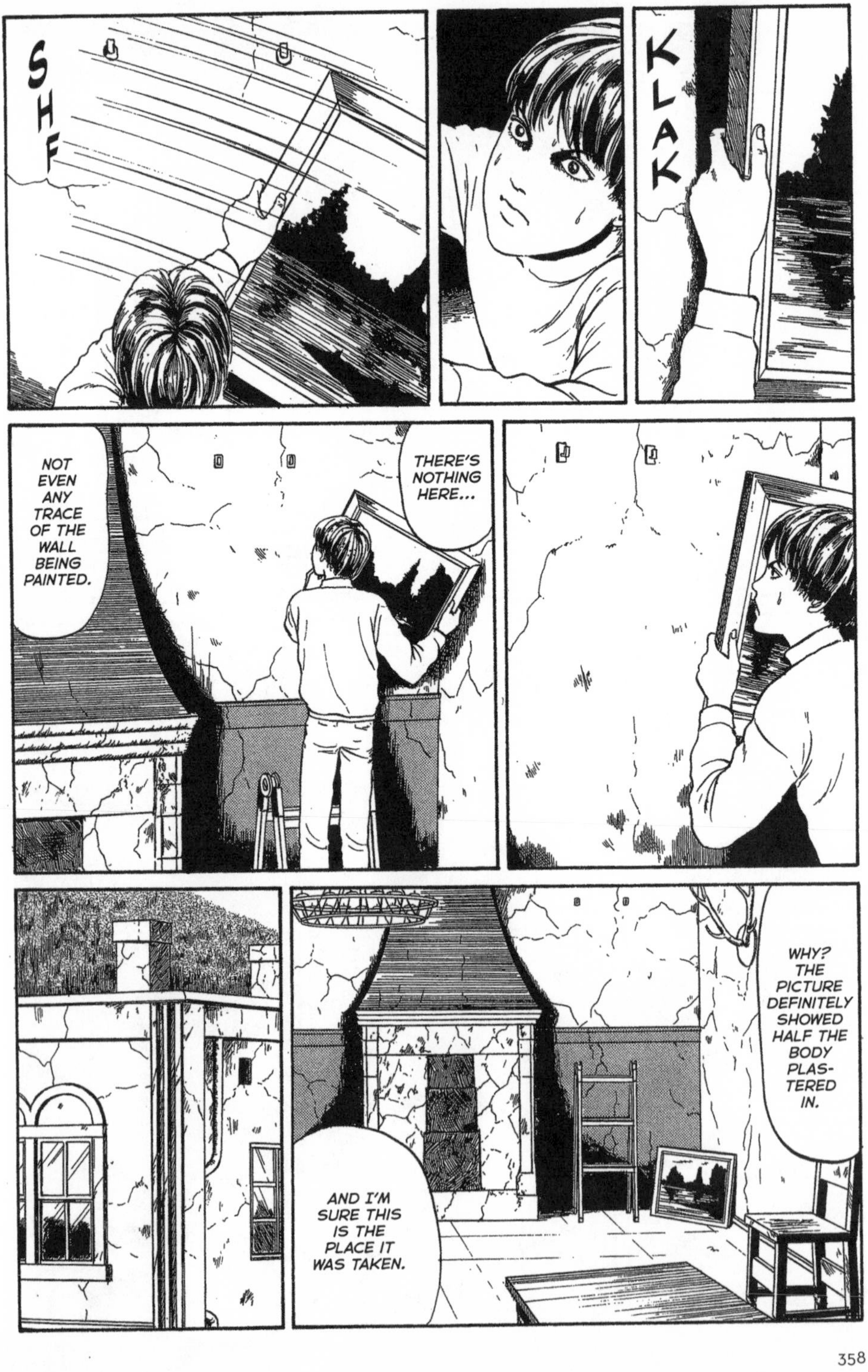
KLAK
SHF
THERE'S NOTHING HERE...
NOT EVEN ANY TRACE OF THE WALL BEING PAINTED.
WHY? THE PICTURE DEFINITELY SHOWED HALF THE BODY PLAS-TERED IN.
AND I'M SURE THIS IS THE PLACE IT WAS TAKEN.

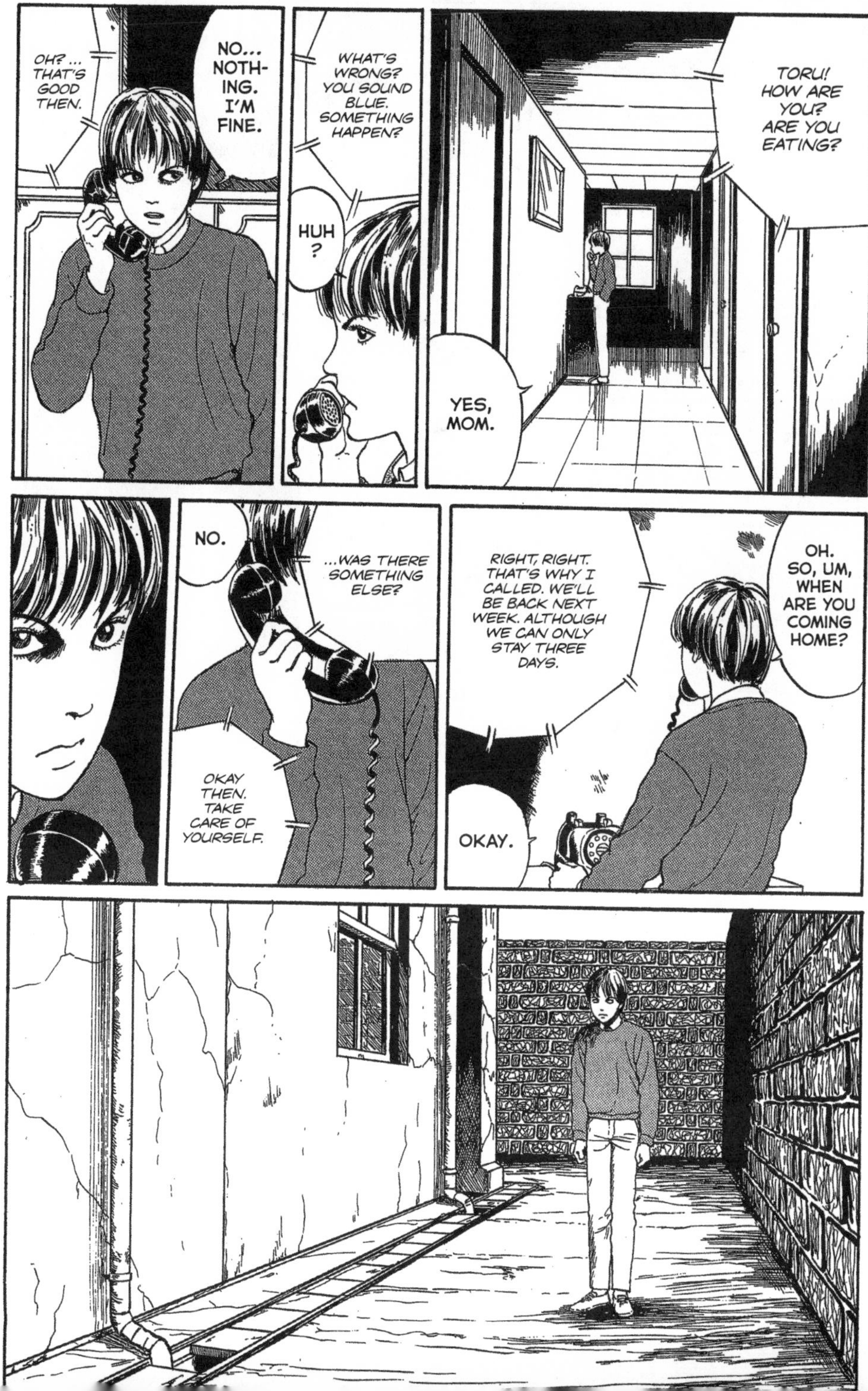
TORU! HOW ARE YOU? ARE YOU EATING?
YES, MOM.
WHAT'S WRONG? YOU SOUND BLUE. SOMETHING HAPPEN?
HUH?
NO... NOTHING. I'M FINE.
OH? ... THAT'S GOOD THEN.
OH. SO, UM, WHEN ARE YOU COMING HOME?
RIGHT, RIGHT. THAT'S WHY I CALLED. WE'LL BE BACK NEXT WEEK. ALTHOUGH WE CAN ONLY STAY THREE DAYS.
OKAY.
...WAS THERE SOMETHING ELSE?
NO.
OKAY THEN. TAKE CARE OF YOURSELF.

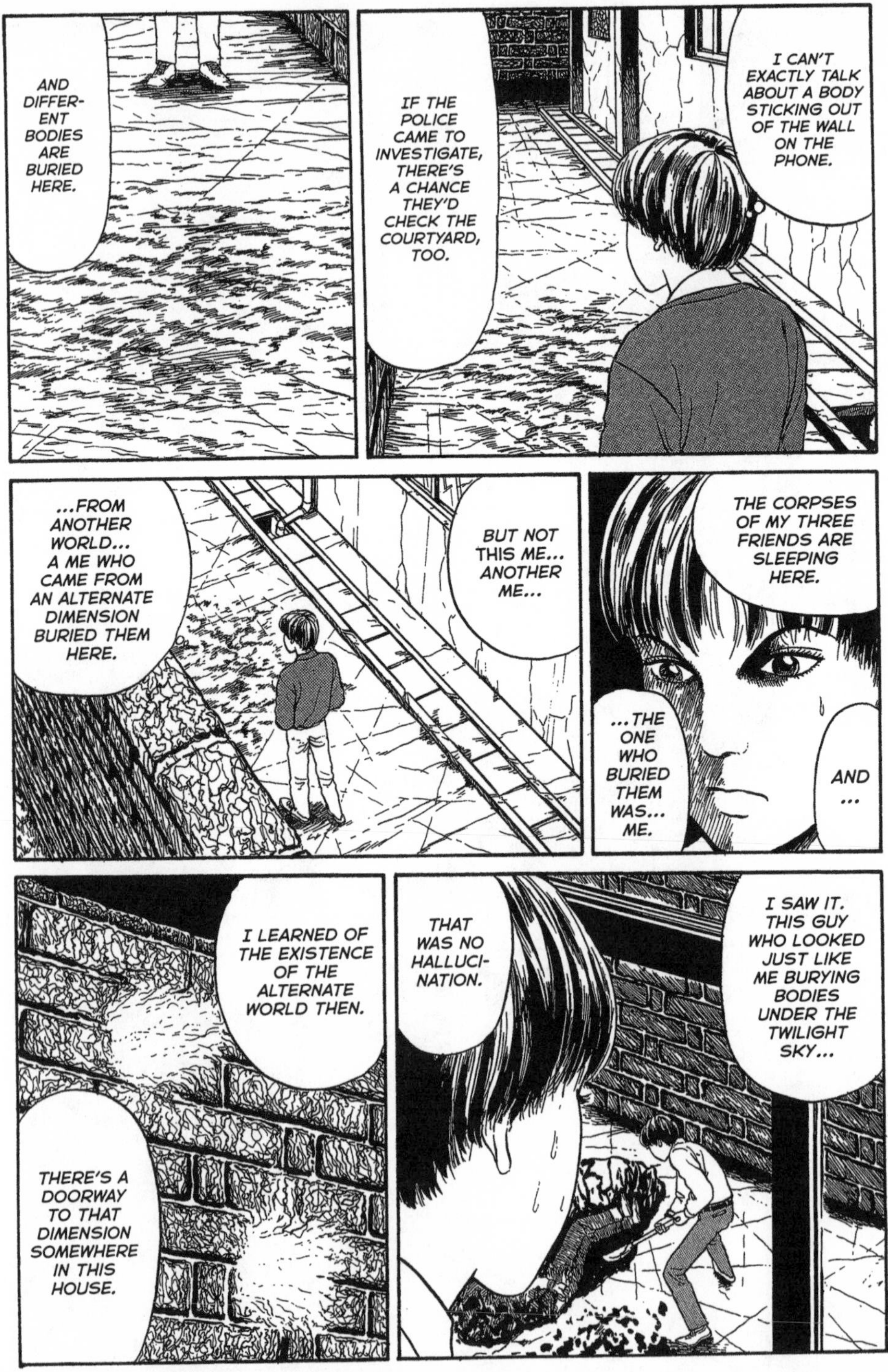

I CAN'T EXACTLY TALK ABOUT A BODY STICKING OUT OF THE WALL ON THE PHONE.
IF THE POLICE CAME TO INVESTIGATE, THERE'S A CHANCE THEY'D CHECK THE COURTYARD, TOO.
AND DIFFERENT BODIES ARE BURIED HERE.
THE CORPSES OF MY THREE FRIENDS ARE SLEEPING HERE.
AND ...
...THE ONE WHO BURIED THEM WAS... ME.
BUT NOT THIS ME... ANOTHER ME...
...FROM ANOTHER WORLD... A ME WHO CAME FROM AN ALTERNATE DIMENSION BURIED THEM HERE.
I SAW IT. THIS GUY WHO LOOKED JUST LIKE ME BURYING BODIES UNDER THE TWILIGHT SKY...
THAT WAS NO HALLUCINATION.
I LEARNED OF THE EXISTENCE OF THE ALTERNATE WORLD THEN.
THERE'S A DOORWAY TO THAT DIMENSION SOMEWHERE IN THIS HOUSE.

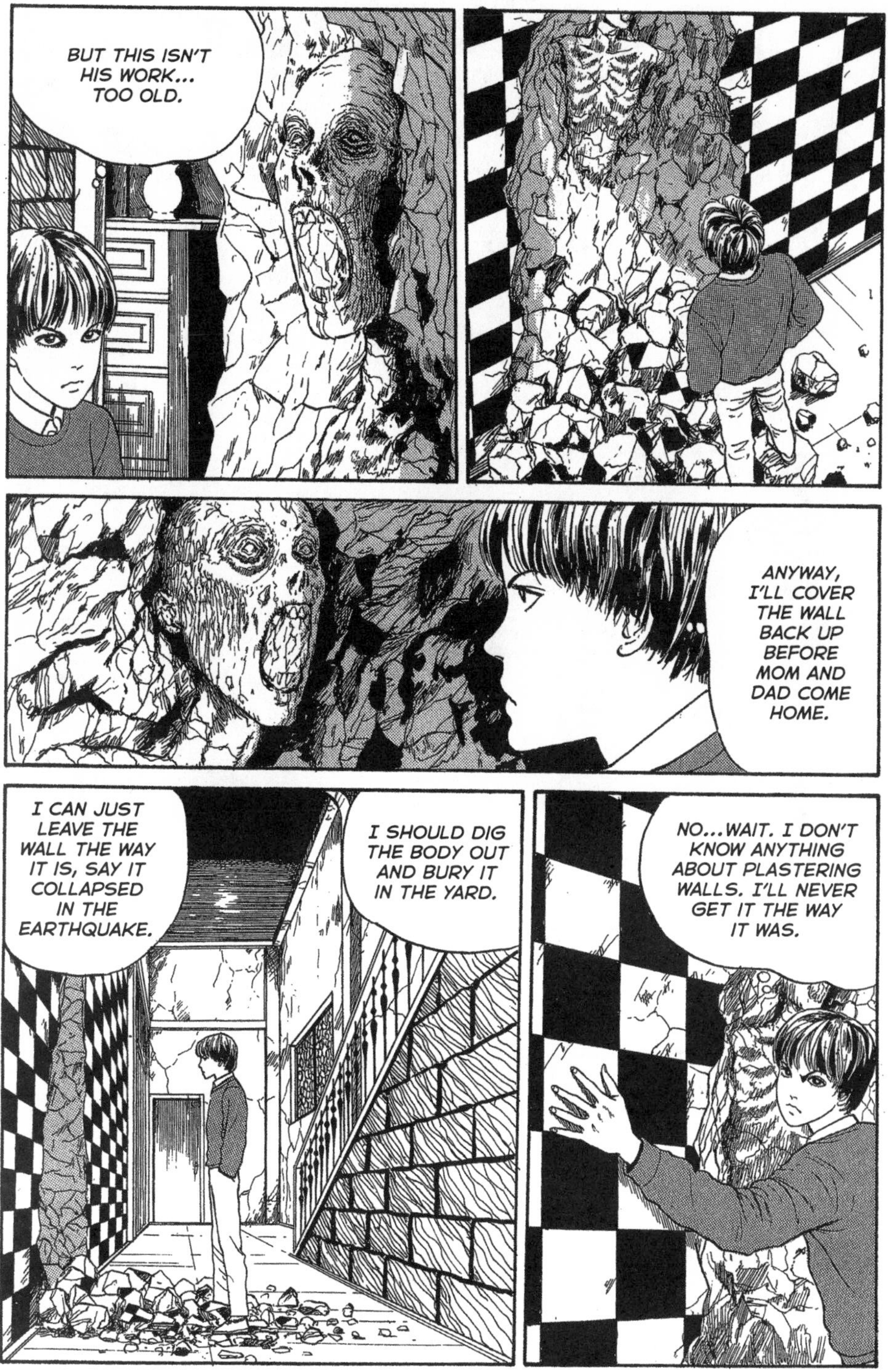
BUT THIS ISN'T HIS WORK... TOO OLD.
ANYWAY, I'LL COVER THE WALL BACK UP BEFORE MOM AND DAD COME HOME.
NO...WAIT. I DON'T KNOW ANYTHING ABOUT PLASTERING WALLS. I'LL NEVER GET IT THE WAY IT WAS.
I SHOULD DIG THE BODY OUT AND BURY IT IN THE YARD.
I CAN JUST LEAVE THE WALL THE WAY IT IS, SAY IT COLLAPSED IN THE EARTHQUAKE.

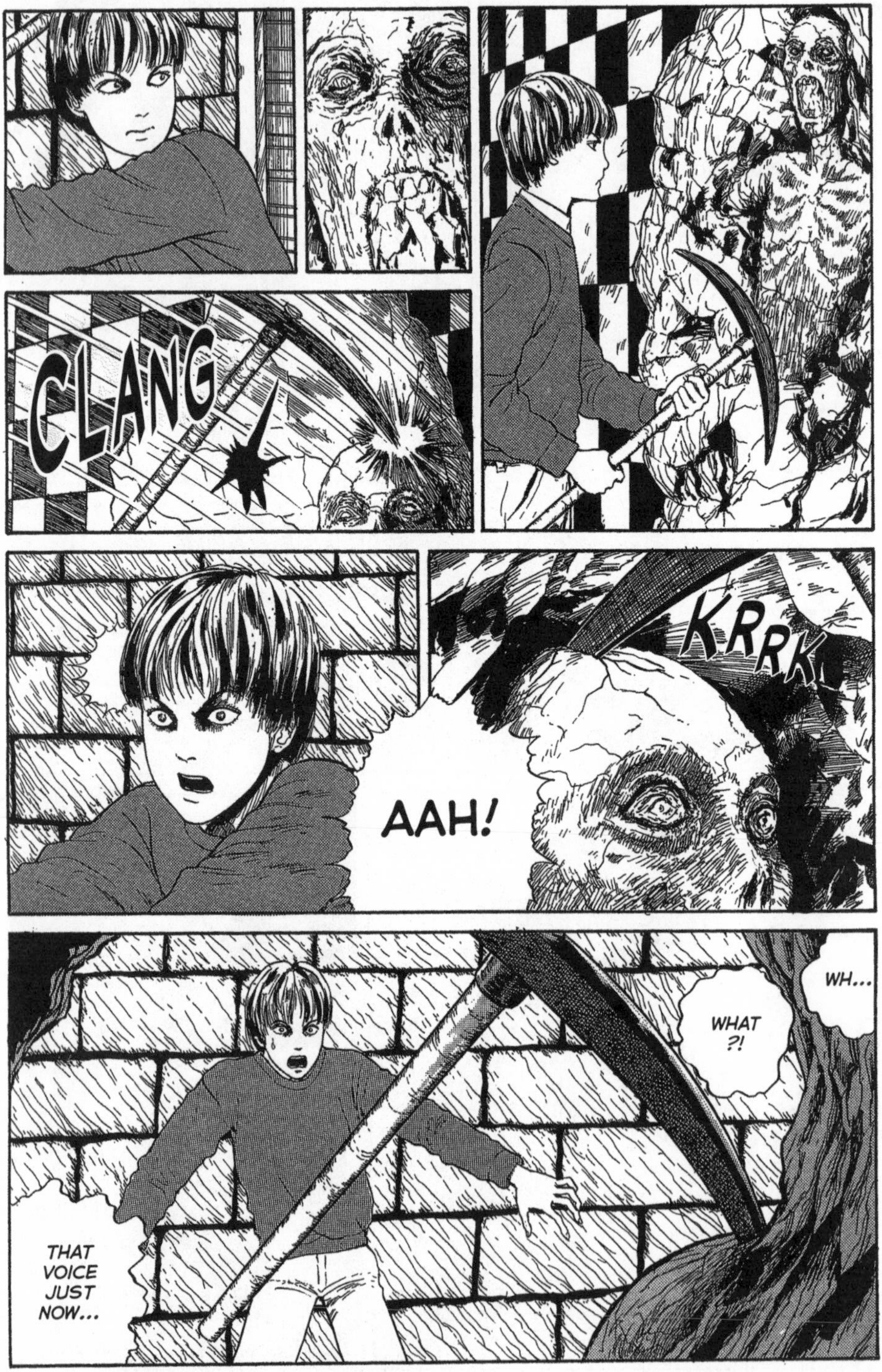
CLANG
KRRK
AAH!
WH...
WHAT ?!
THAT VOICE JUST NOW...

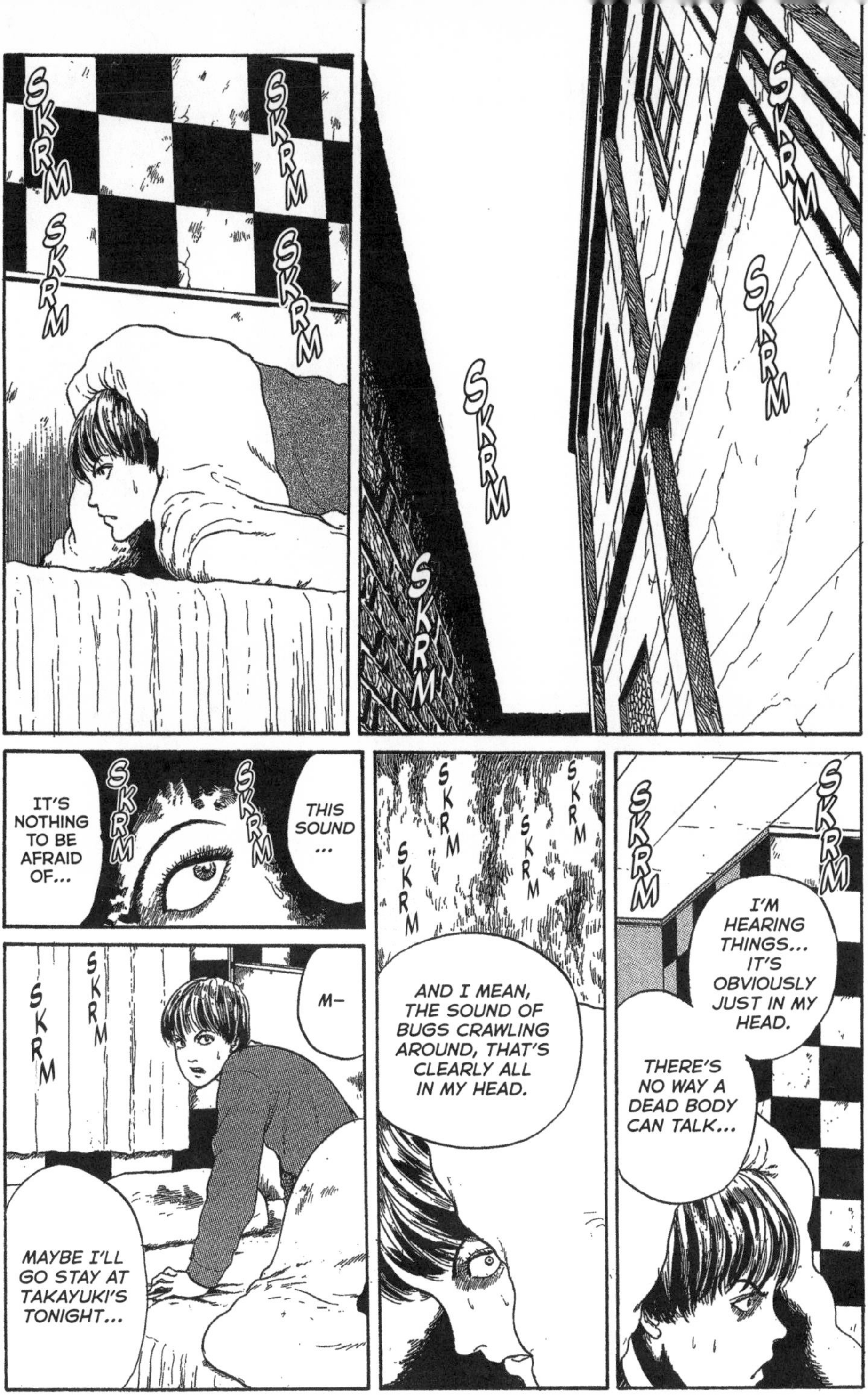
SKRM
SKRM
SKRM
SKRM
SKRM
SKRM
SKRM
SKRM
SKRM
SKRM
I'M HEARING THINGS... IT'S OBVIOUSLY JUST IN MY HEAD.
THERE'S NO WAY A DEAD BODY CAN TALK...
SKRM
SKRM
SKRM
SKRM
AND I MEAN, THE SOUND OF BUGS CRAWLING AROUND, THAT'S CLEARLY ALL IN MY HEAD.
SKRM
SKRM
THIS SOUND ...
IT'S NOTHING TO BE AFRAID OF...
SKRM
SKRM
M–
MAYBE I'LL GO STAY AT TAKAYUKI'S TONIGHT...

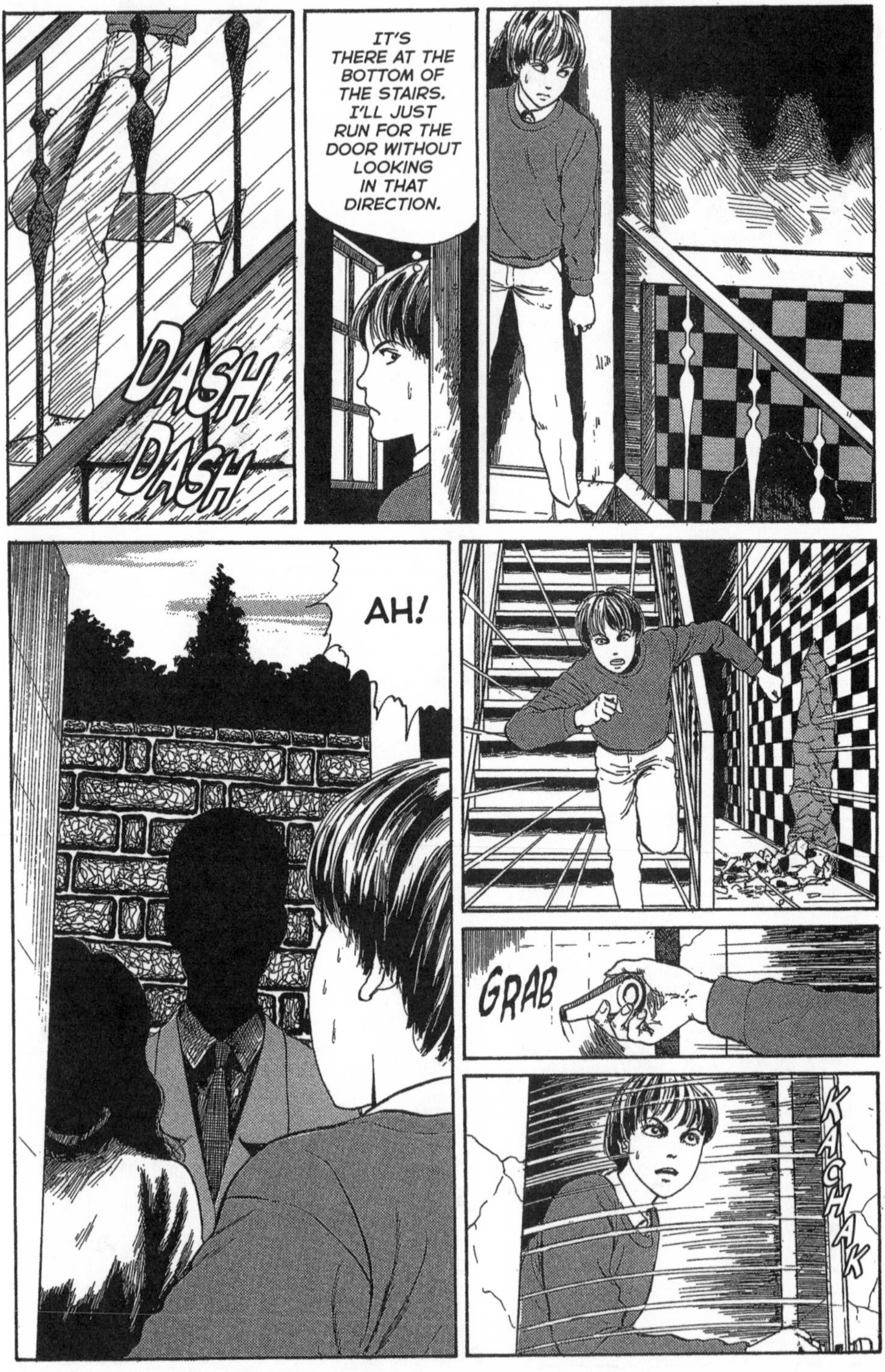
IT'S THERE AT THE BOTTOM OF THE STAIRS. I'LL JUST RUN FOR THE DOOR WITHOUT LOOKING IN THAT DIRECTION.
DASH DASH
GRAB
KACHAK
AH!

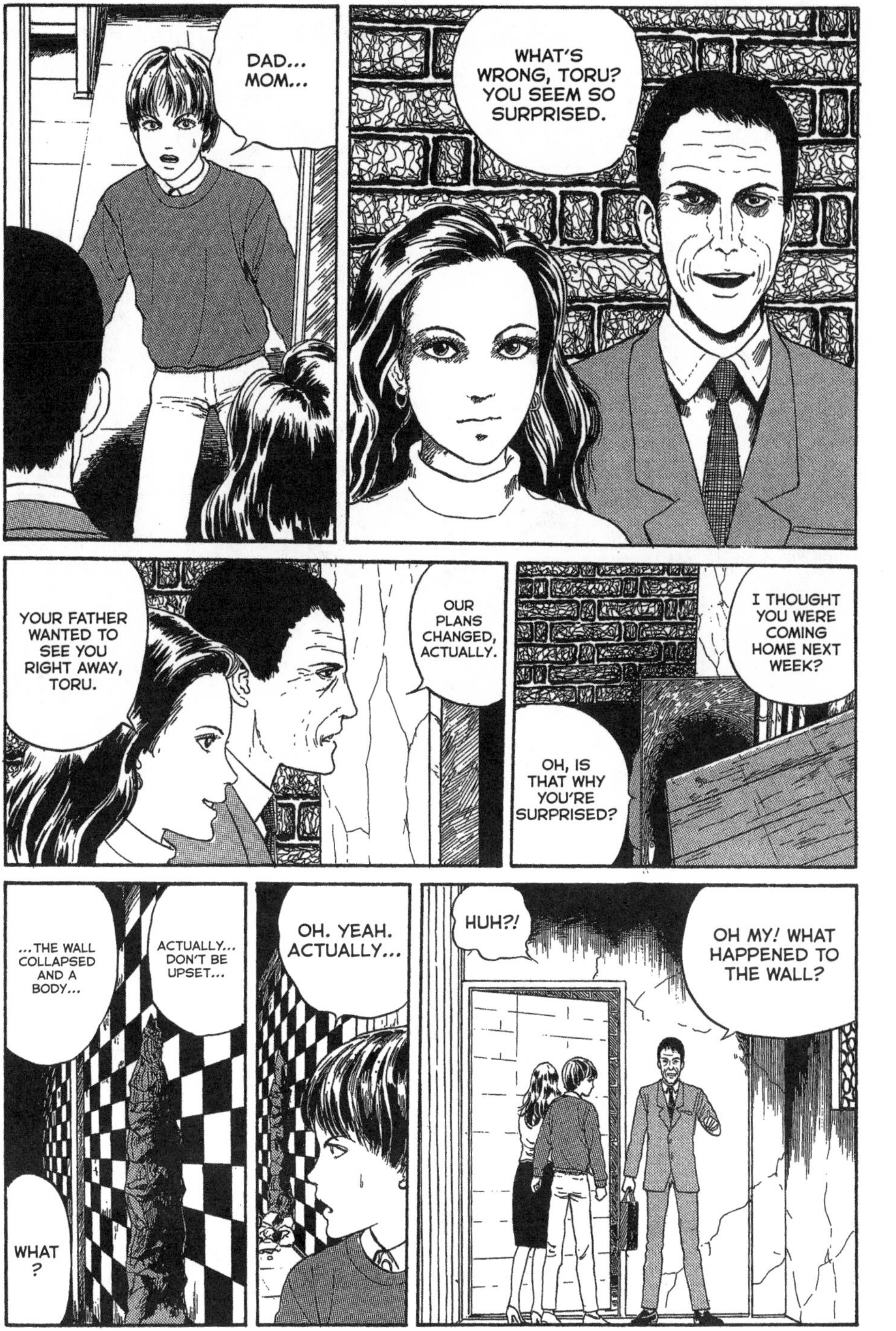
WHAT'S WRONG, TORU? YOU SEEM SO SURPRISED.
DAD... MOM...
I THOUGHT YOU WERE COMING HOME NEXT WEEK?
OH, IS THAT WHY YOU'RE SURPRISED?
OUR PLANS CHANGED, ACTUALLY.
YOUR FATHER WANTED TO SEE YOU RIGHT AWAY, TORU.
OH MY! WHAT HAPPENED TO THE WALL?
HUH?!
OH. YEAH. ACTUALLY...
ACTUALLY... DON'T BE UPSET...
...THE WALL COLLAPSED AND A BODY...
WHAT?

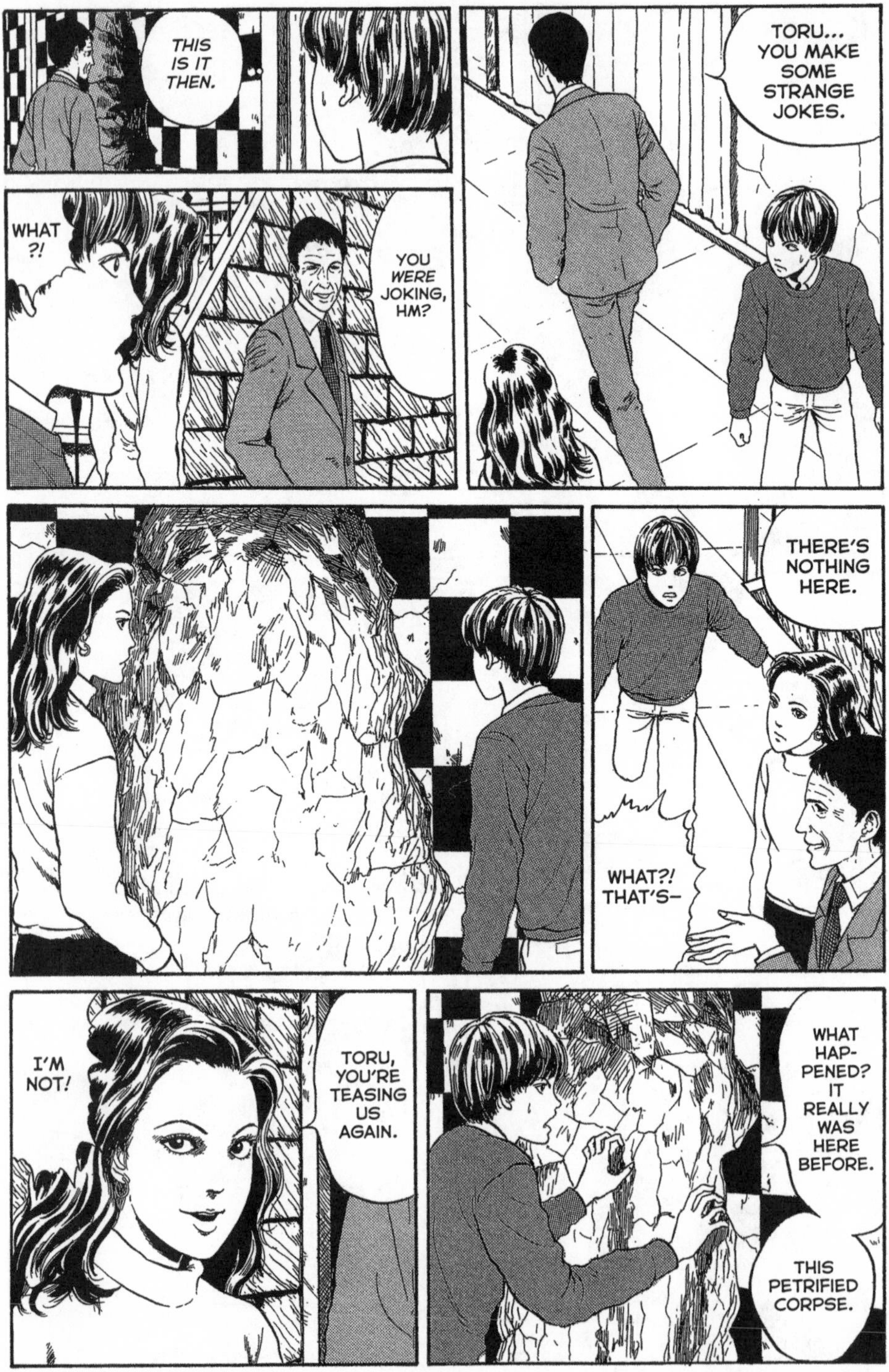
TORU... YOU MAKE SOME STRANGE JOKES.
THIS IS IT THEN.
YOU *WERE* JOKING, HM?
WHAT ?!
THERE'S NOTHING HERE.
WHAT?! THAT'S—
WHAT HAP-PENED? IT REALLY WAS HERE BEFORE.
THIS PETRIFIED CORPSE.
TORU, YOU'RE TEASING US AGAIN.
I'M NOT!

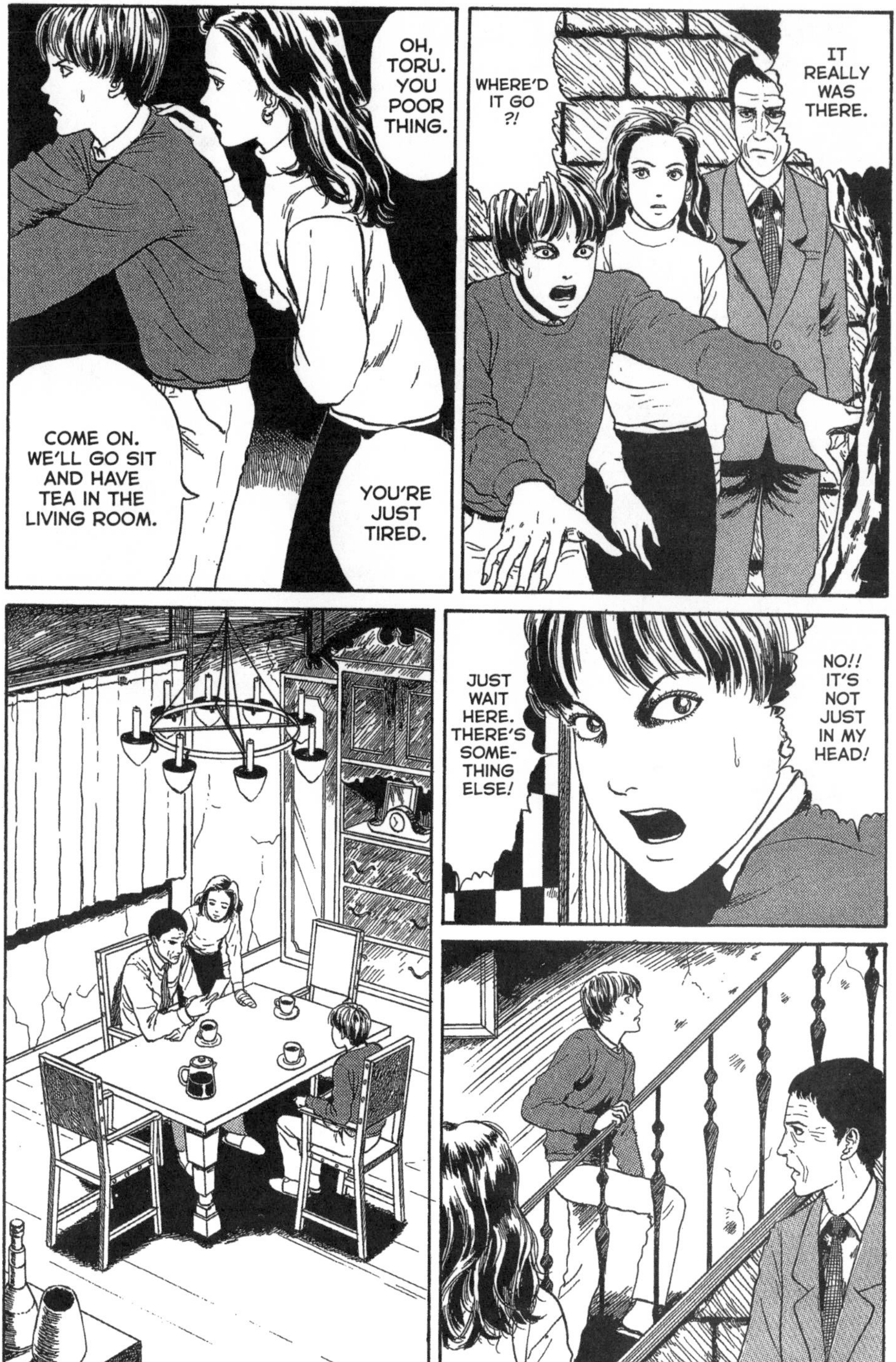
IT REALLY WAS THERE.
WHERE'D IT GO ?!
OH, TORU. YOU POOR THING.
YOU'RE JUST TIRED.
COME ON. WE'LL GO SIT AND HAVE TEA IN THE LIVING ROOM.
NO!! IT'S NOT JUST IN MY HEAD!
JUST WAIT HERE. THERE'S SOME-THING ELSE!

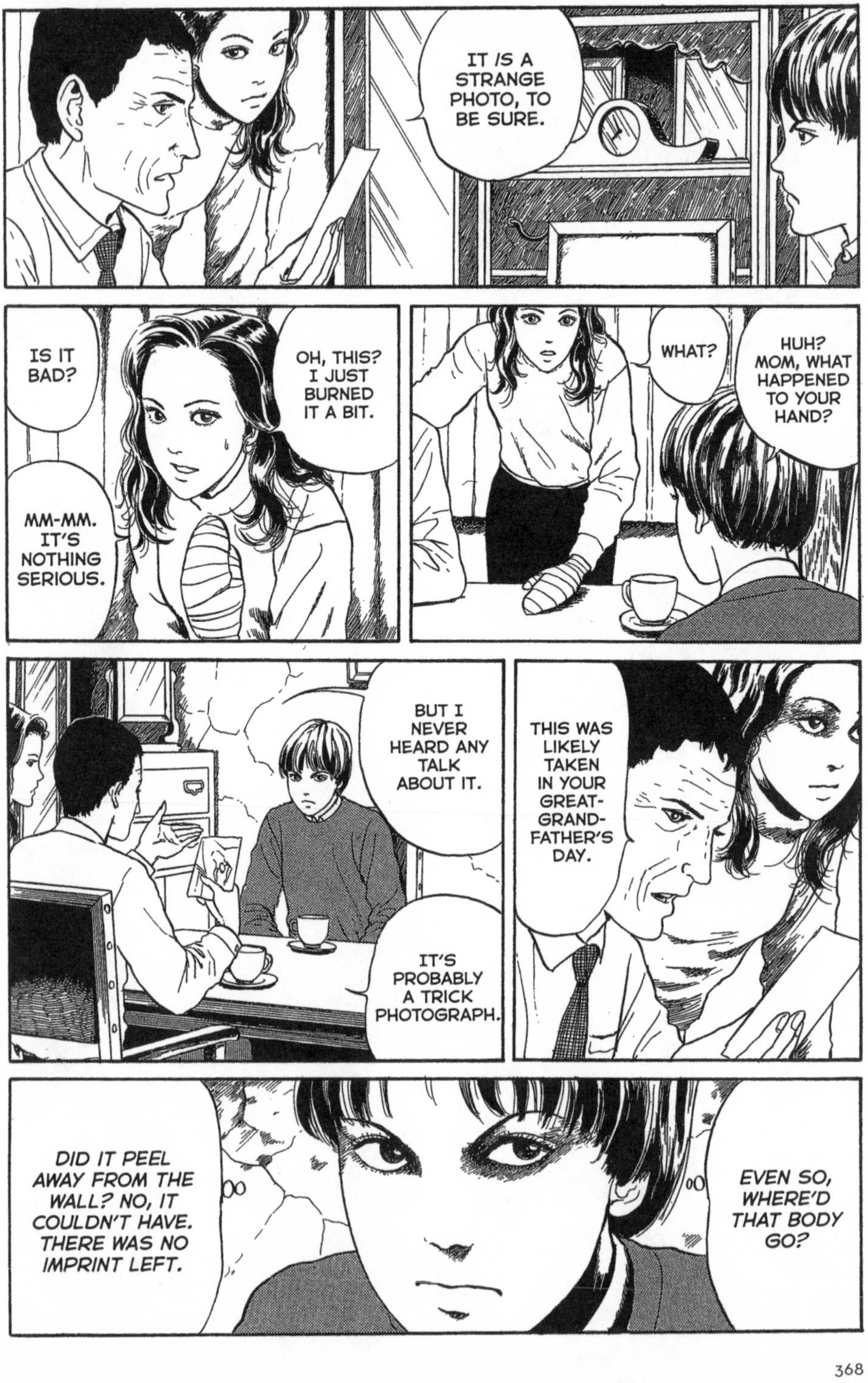
IT *IS* A STRANGE PHOTO, TO BE SURE.
HUH? MOM, WHAT HAPPENED TO YOUR HAND?
WHAT?
OH, THIS? I JUST BURNED IT A BIT.
IS IT BAD?
MM-MM. IT'S NOTHING SERIOUS.
THIS WAS LIKELY TAKEN IN YOUR GREAT-GRANDFATHER'S DAY.
BUT I NEVER HEARD ANY TALK ABOUT IT.
IT'S PROBABLY A TRICK PHOTOGRAPH.
EVEN SO, WHERE'D THAT BODY GO?
DID IT PEEL AWAY FROM THE WALL? NO, IT COULDN'T HAVE. THERE WAS NO IMPRINT LEFT.

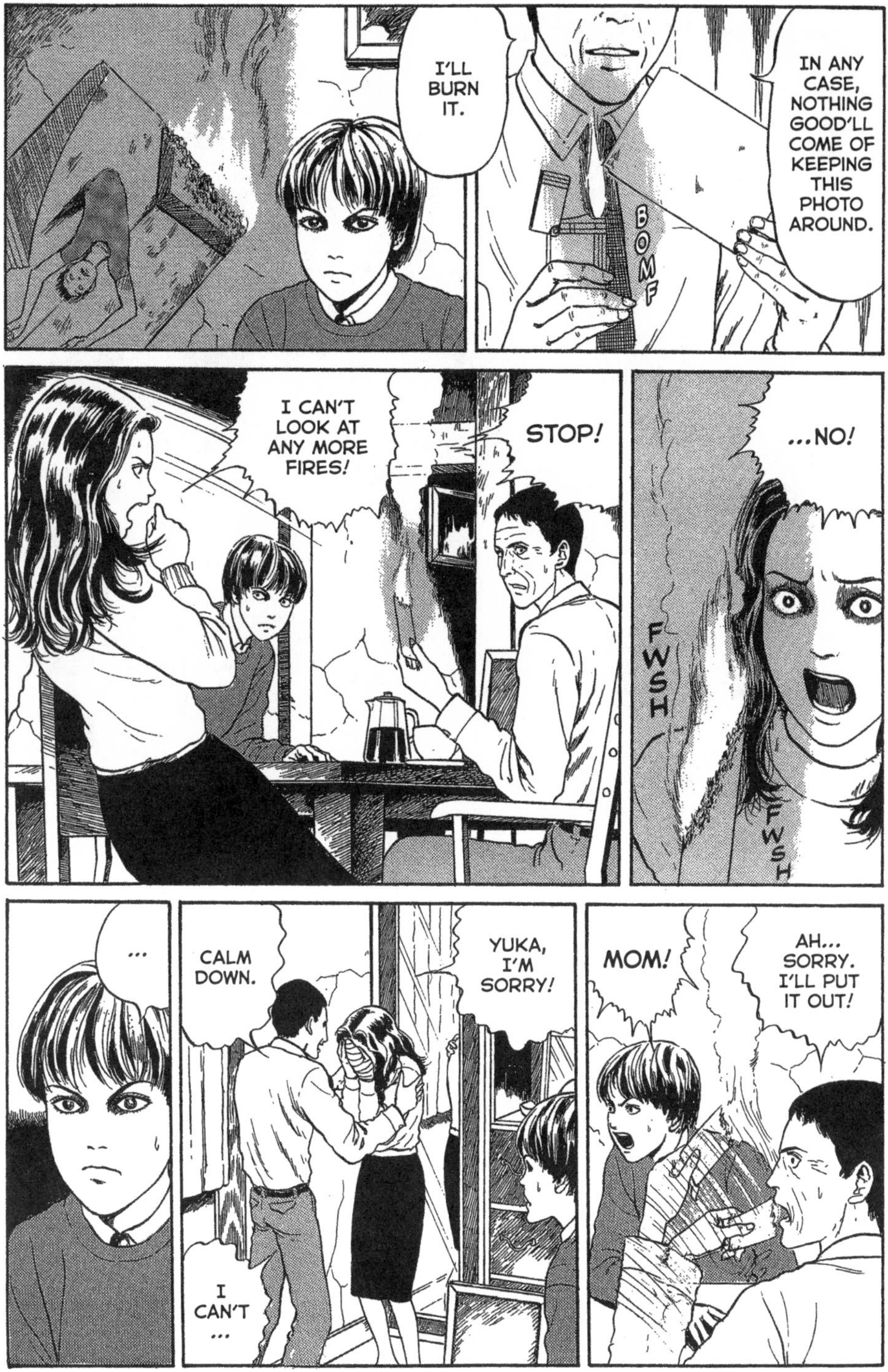
IN ANY CASE, NOTHING GOOD'LL COME OF KEEPING THIS PHOTO AROUND.
BOMF
I'LL BURN IT.
...NO!
FWSH
FWSH
STOP!
I CAN'T LOOK AT ANY MORE FIRES!
AH... SORRY. I'LL PUT IT OUT!
MOM!
YUKA, I'M SORRY!
CALM DOWN.
I CAN'T ...
...

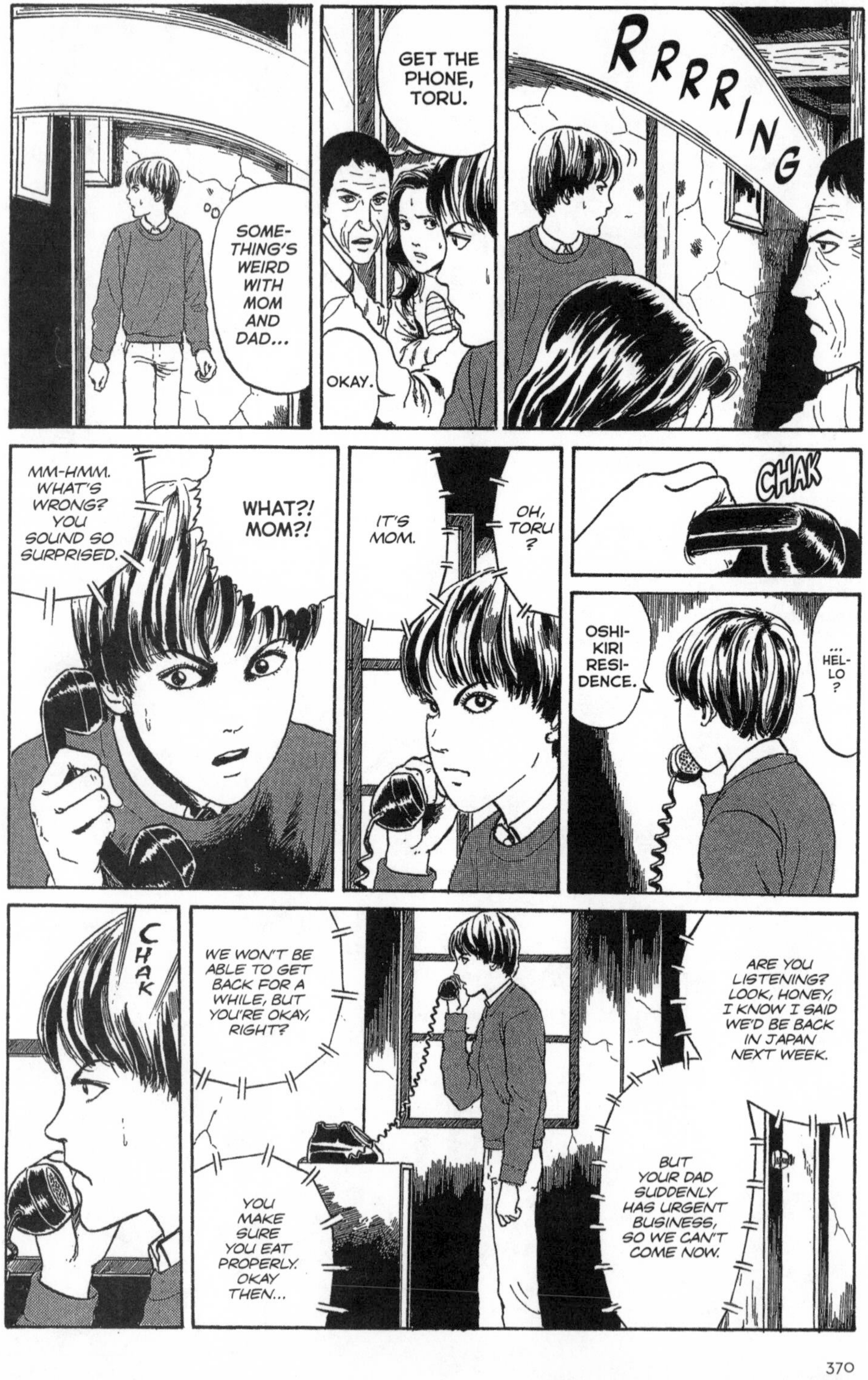
RRRRING
GET THE PHONE, TORU.
OKAY.
SOME-THING'S WEIRD WITH MOM AND DAD...
CHAK
...HEL-LO?
OSHI-KIRI RESI-DENCE.
OH, TORU?
IT'S MOM.
WHAT?! MOM?!
MM-HMM. WHAT'S WRONG? YOU SOUND SO SURPRISED.
ARE YOU LISTENING? LOOK, HONEY, I KNOW I SAID WE'D BE BACK IN JAPAN NEXT WEEK.
BUT YOUR DAD SUDDENLY HAS URGENT BUSINESS, SO WE CAN'T COME NOW.
WE WON'T BE ABLE TO GET BACK FOR A WHILE, BUT YOU'RE OKAY, RIGHT?
YOU MAKE SURE YOU EAT PROPERLY. OKAY THEN...
CHAK

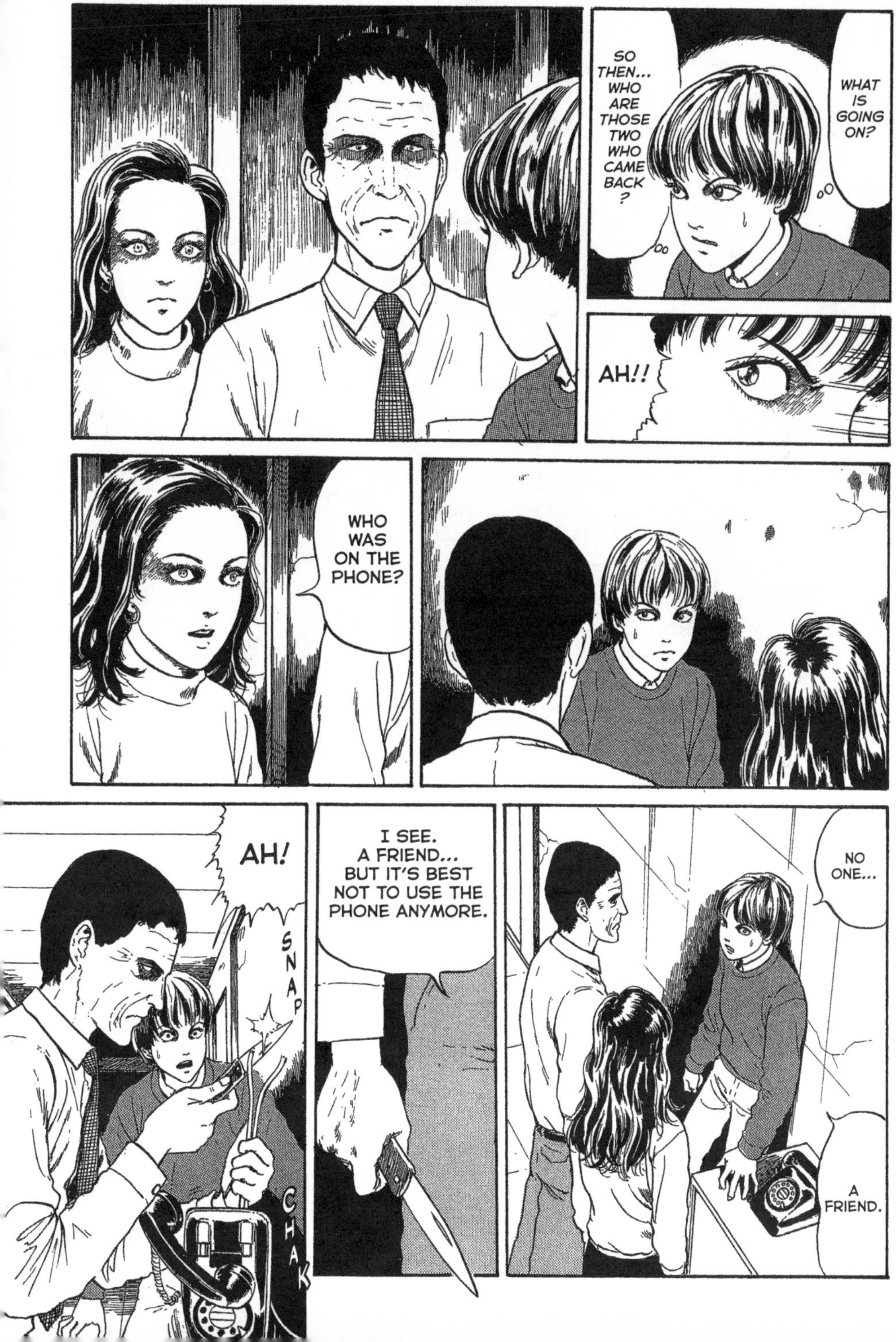
WHAT IS GOING ON?
SO THEN... WHO ARE THOSE TWO WHO CAME BACK?
AH!!
WHO WAS ON THE PHONE?
NO ONE...
A FRIEND.
I SEE. A FRIEND... BUT IT'S BEST NOT TO USE THE PHONE ANYMORE.
AH!
SNAP
CHAK

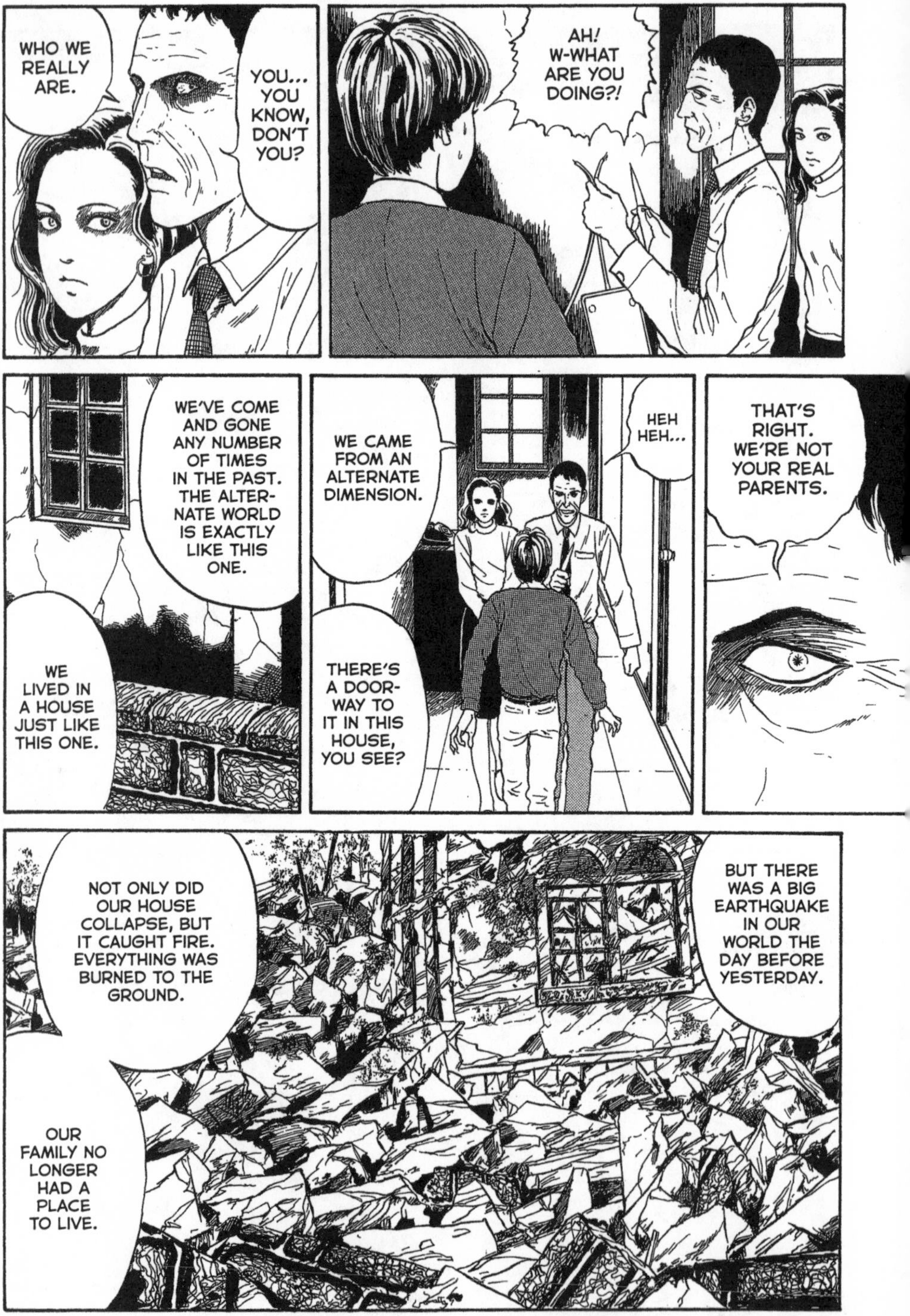
AH! W-WHAT ARE YOU DOING?!
YOU... YOU KNOW, DON'T YOU?
WHO WE REALLY ARE.
THAT'S RIGHT. WE'RE NOT YOUR REAL PARENTS.
HEH HEH...
WE CAME FROM AN ALTERNATE DIMENSION.
THERE'S A DOORWAY TO IT IN THIS HOUSE, YOU SEE?
WE'VE COME AND GONE ANY NUMBER OF TIMES IN THE PAST. THE ALTERNATE WORLD IS EXACTLY LIKE THIS ONE.
WE LIVED IN A HOUSE JUST LIKE THIS ONE.
BUT THERE WAS A BIG EARTHQUAKE IN OUR WORLD THE DAY BEFORE YESTERDAY.
NOT ONLY DID OUR HOUSE COLLAPSE, BUT IT CAUGHT FIRE. EVERYTHING WAS BURNED TO THE GROUND.
OUR FAMILY NO LONGER HAD A PLACE TO LIVE.

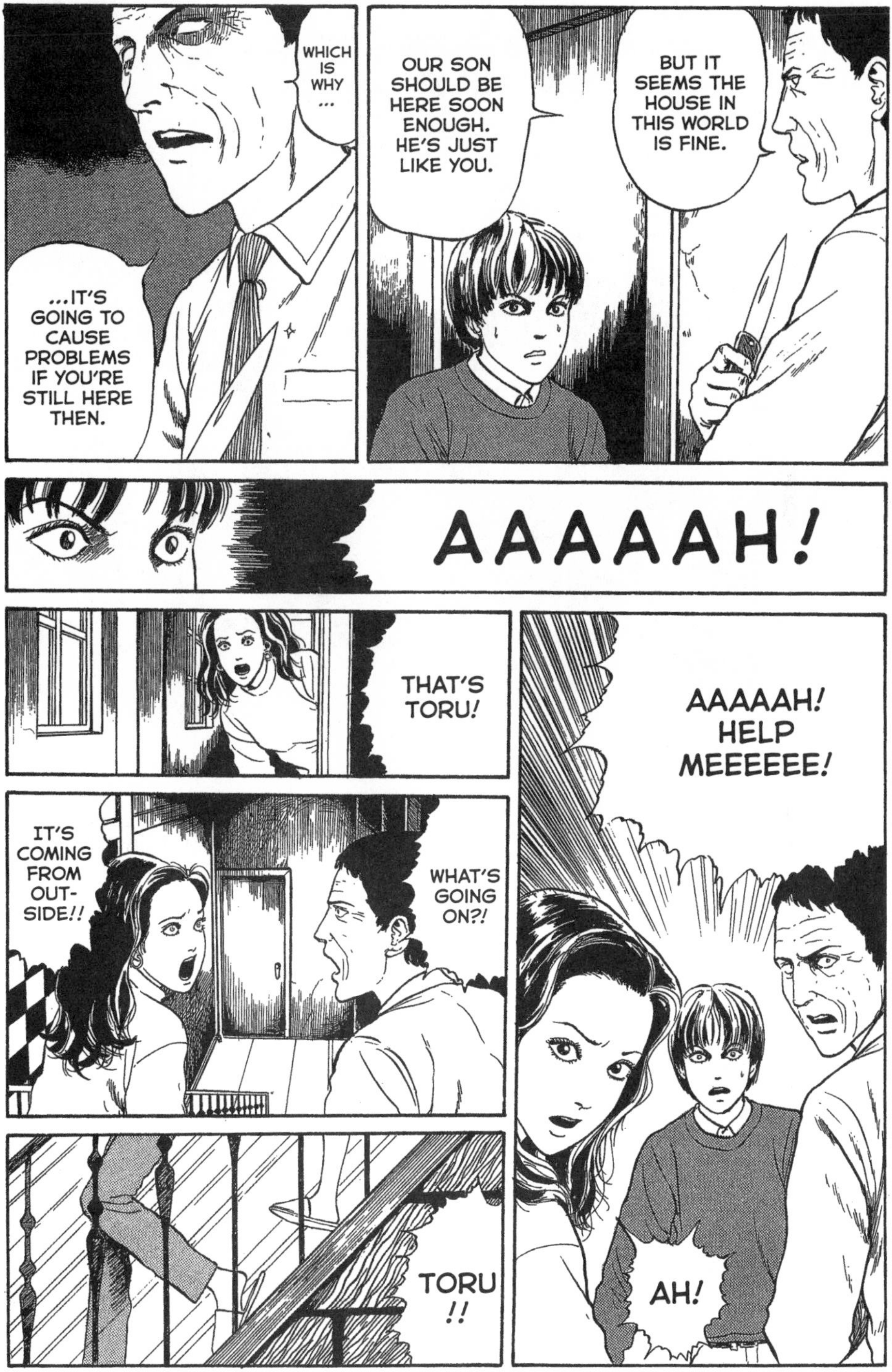
BUT IT SEEMS THE HOUSE IN THIS WORLD IS FINE.
OUR SON SHOULD BE HERE SOON ENOUGH. HE'S JUST LIKE YOU.
WHICH IS WHY ...
...IT'S GOING TO CAUSE PROBLEMS IF YOU'RE STILL HERE THEN.
AAAAAH!
AAAAAH! HELP MEEEEEE!
AH!
THAT'S TORU!
WHAT'S GOING ON?!
IT'S COMING FROM OUTSIDE!!
TORU!!

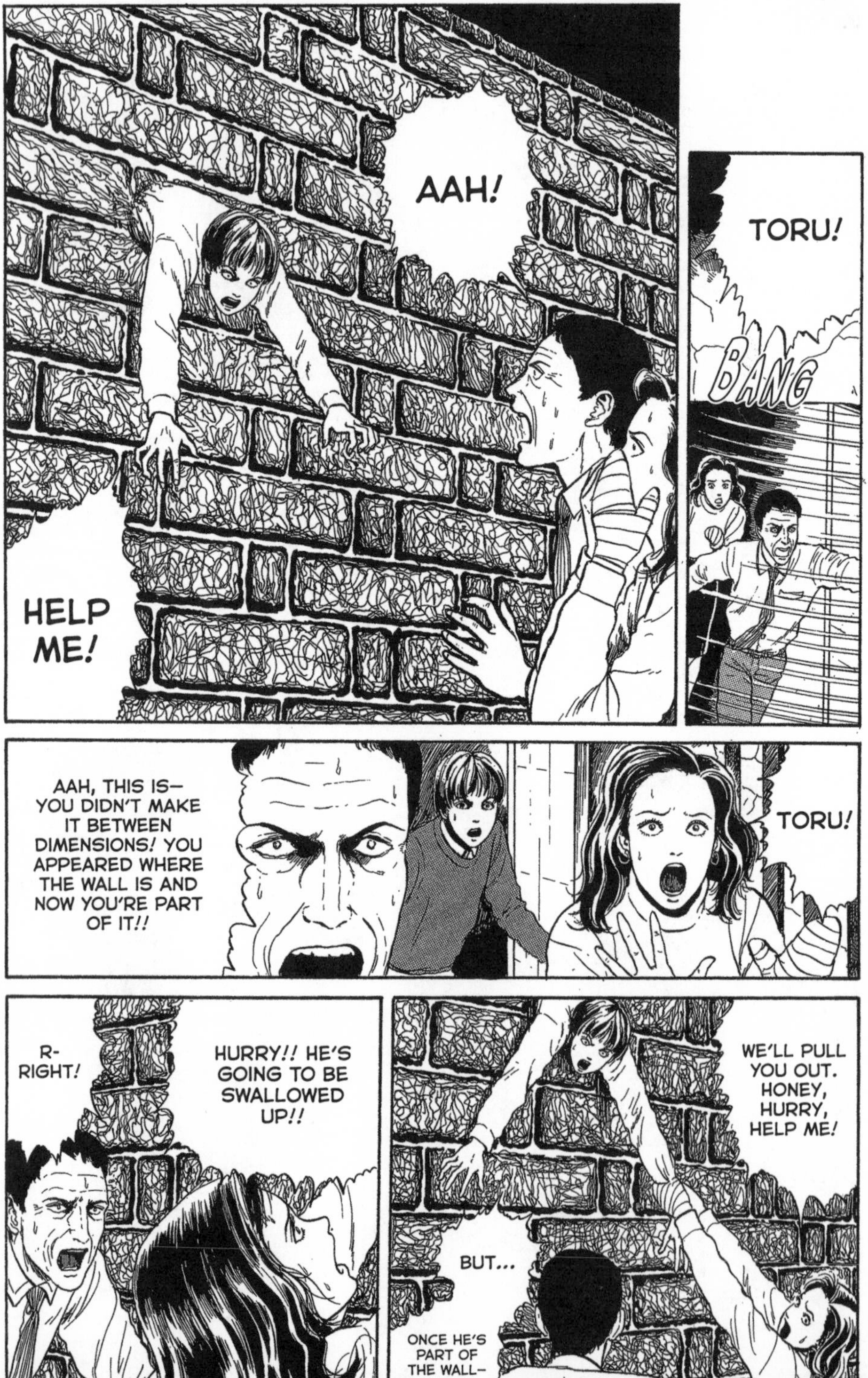
TORU!
BANG
AAH!
HELP ME!
TORU!
AAH, THIS IS— YOU DIDN'T MAKE IT BETWEEN DIMENSIONS! YOU APPEARED WHERE THE WALL IS AND NOW YOU'RE PART OF IT!!
WE'LL PULL YOU OUT. HONEY, HURRY, HELP ME!
BUT...
ONCE HE'S PART OF THE WALL—
HURRY!! HE'S GOING TO BE SWALLOWED UP!!
R-RIGHT!

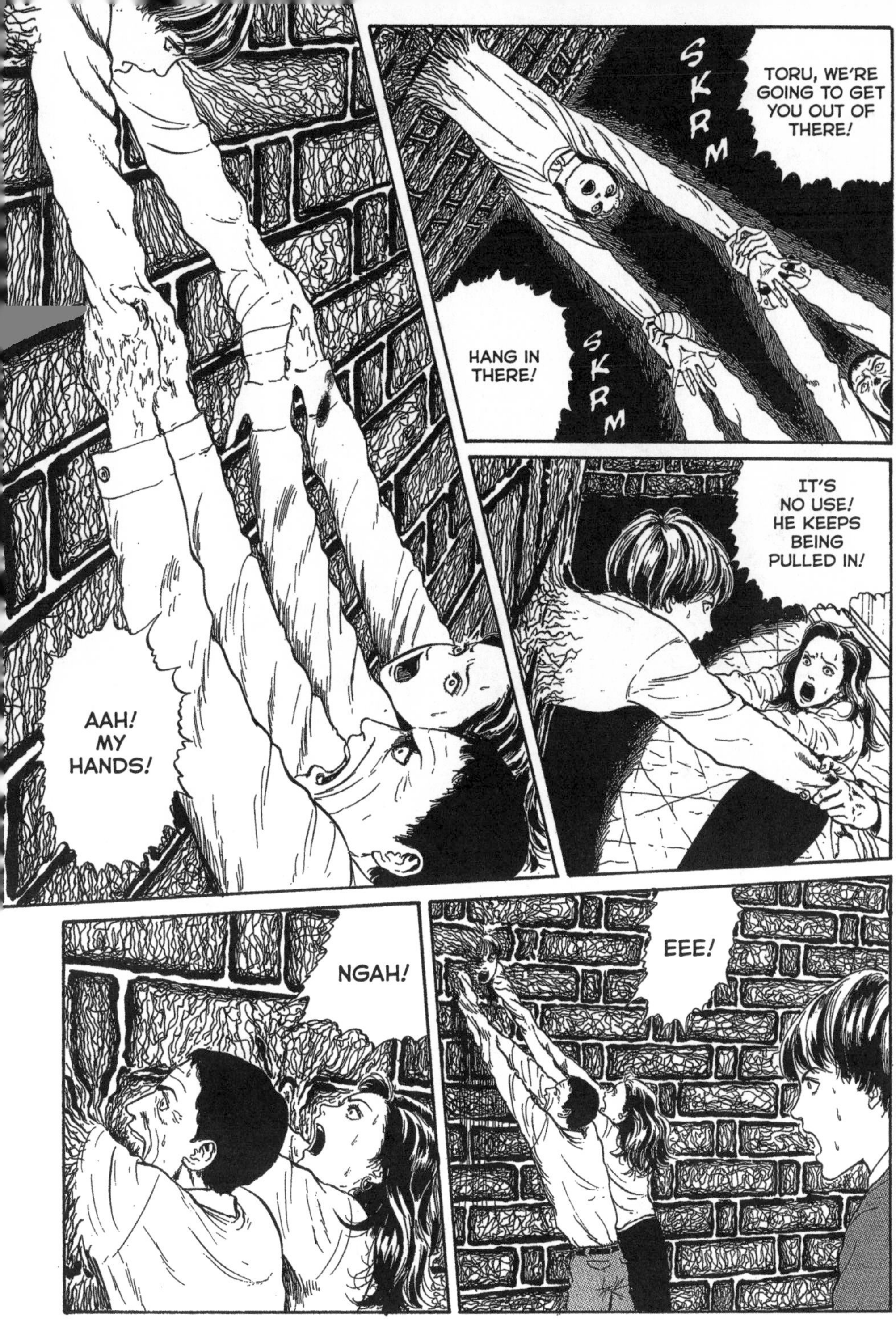
SKRM
TORU, WE'RE GOING TO GET YOU OUT OF THERE!
HANG IN THERE!
SKRM
IT'S NO USE! HE KEEPS BEING PULLED IN!
AAH! MY HANDS!
EEE!
NGAH!

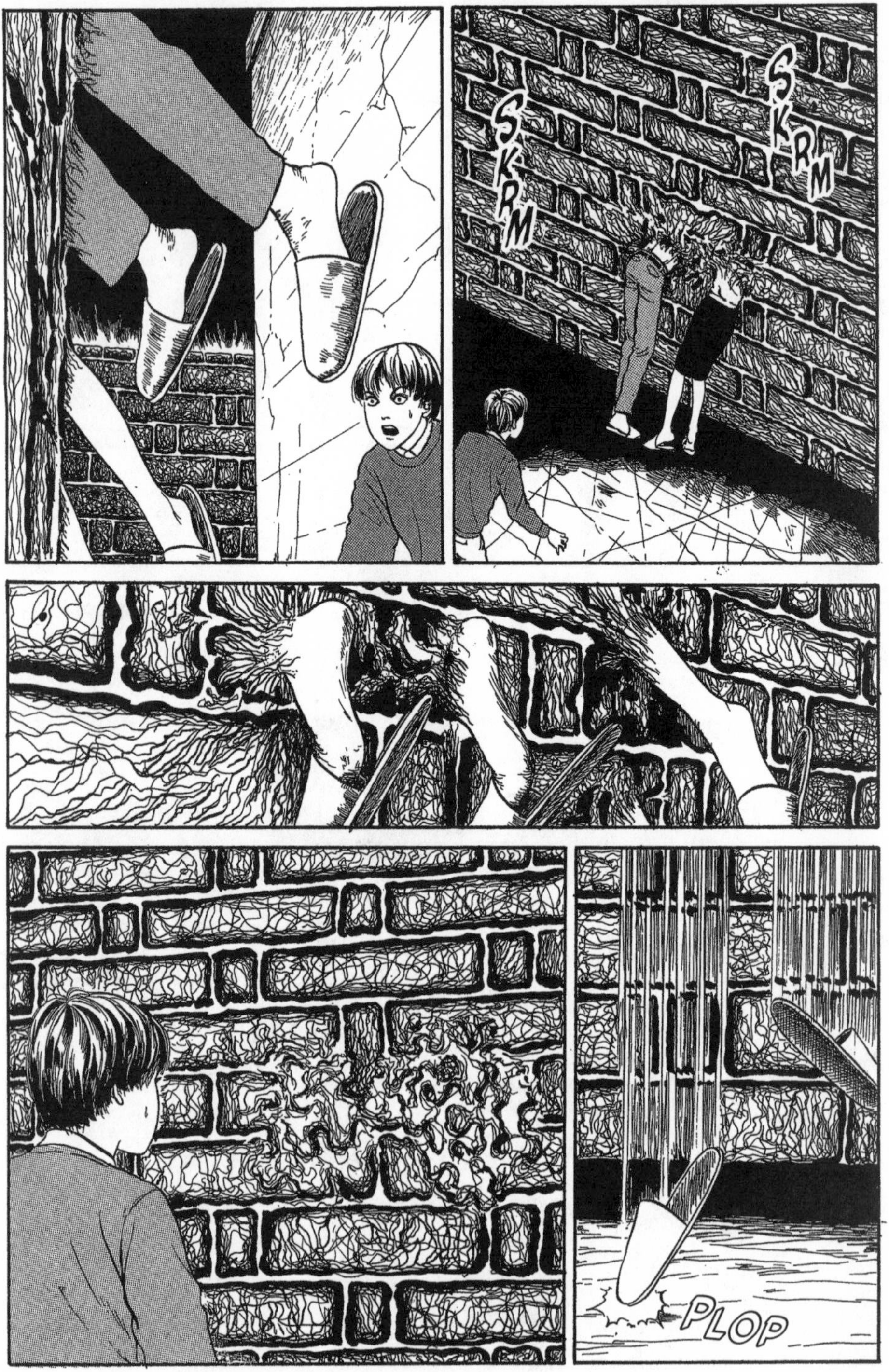
SKRM
SKRM
PLOP

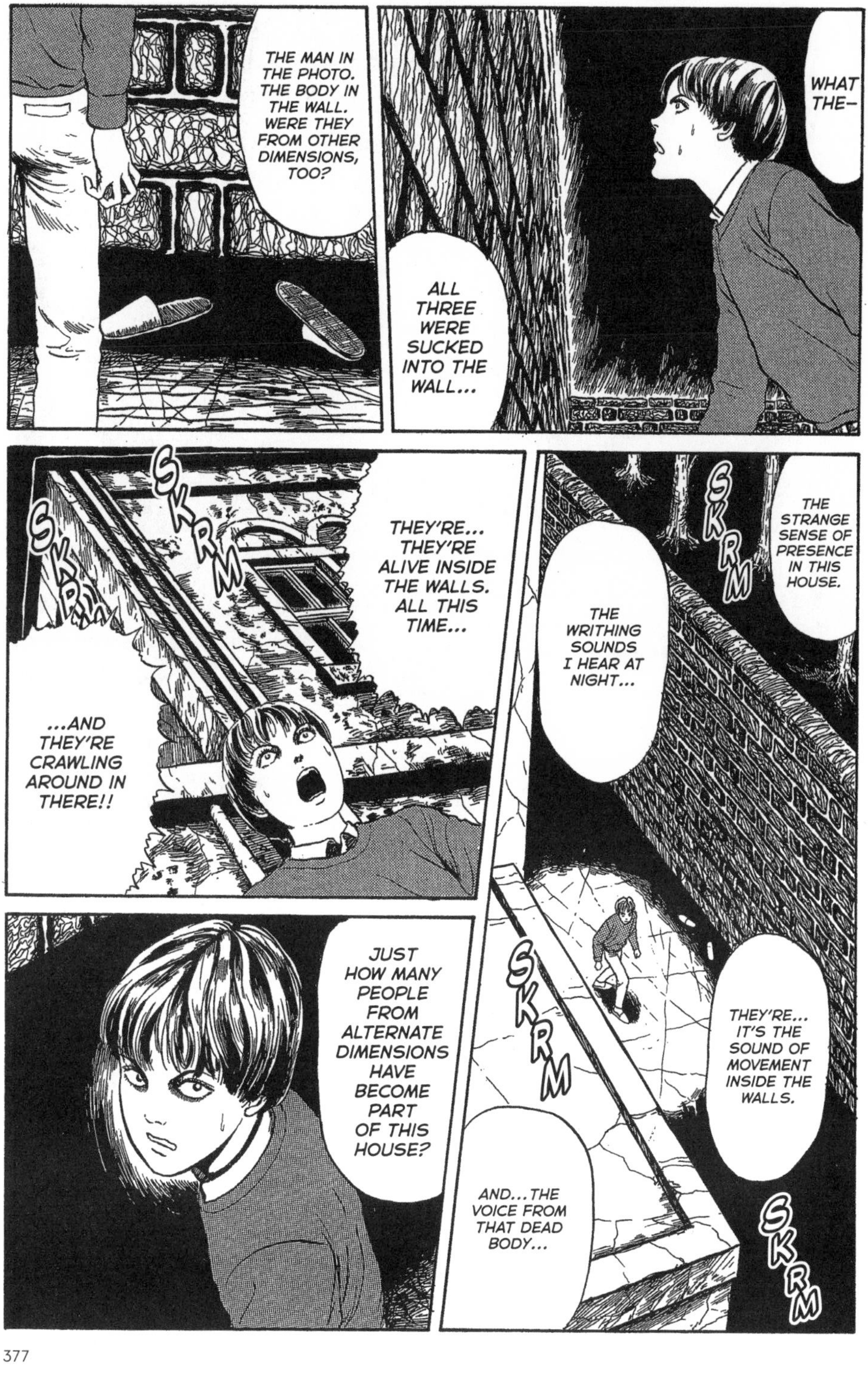
WHAT THE–
ALL THREE WERE SUCKED INTO THE WALL...
THE MAN IN THE PHOTO. THE BODY IN THE WALL. WERE THEY FROM OTHER DIMENSIONS, TOO?
SKRM
THE STRANGE SENSE OF PRESENCE IN THIS HOUSE.
THE WRITHING SOUNDS I HEAR AT NIGHT...
SKRM
THEY'RE... IT'S THE SOUND OF MOVEMENT INSIDE THE WALLS.
SKRM
AND...THE VOICE FROM THAT DEAD BODY...
THEY'RE... THEY'RE ALIVE INSIDE THE WALLS. ALL THIS TIME...
SKRM
...AND THEY'RE CRAWLING AROUND IN THERE!!
JUST HOW MANY PEOPLE FROM ALTERNATE DIMENSIONS HAVE BECOME PART OF THIS HOUSE?

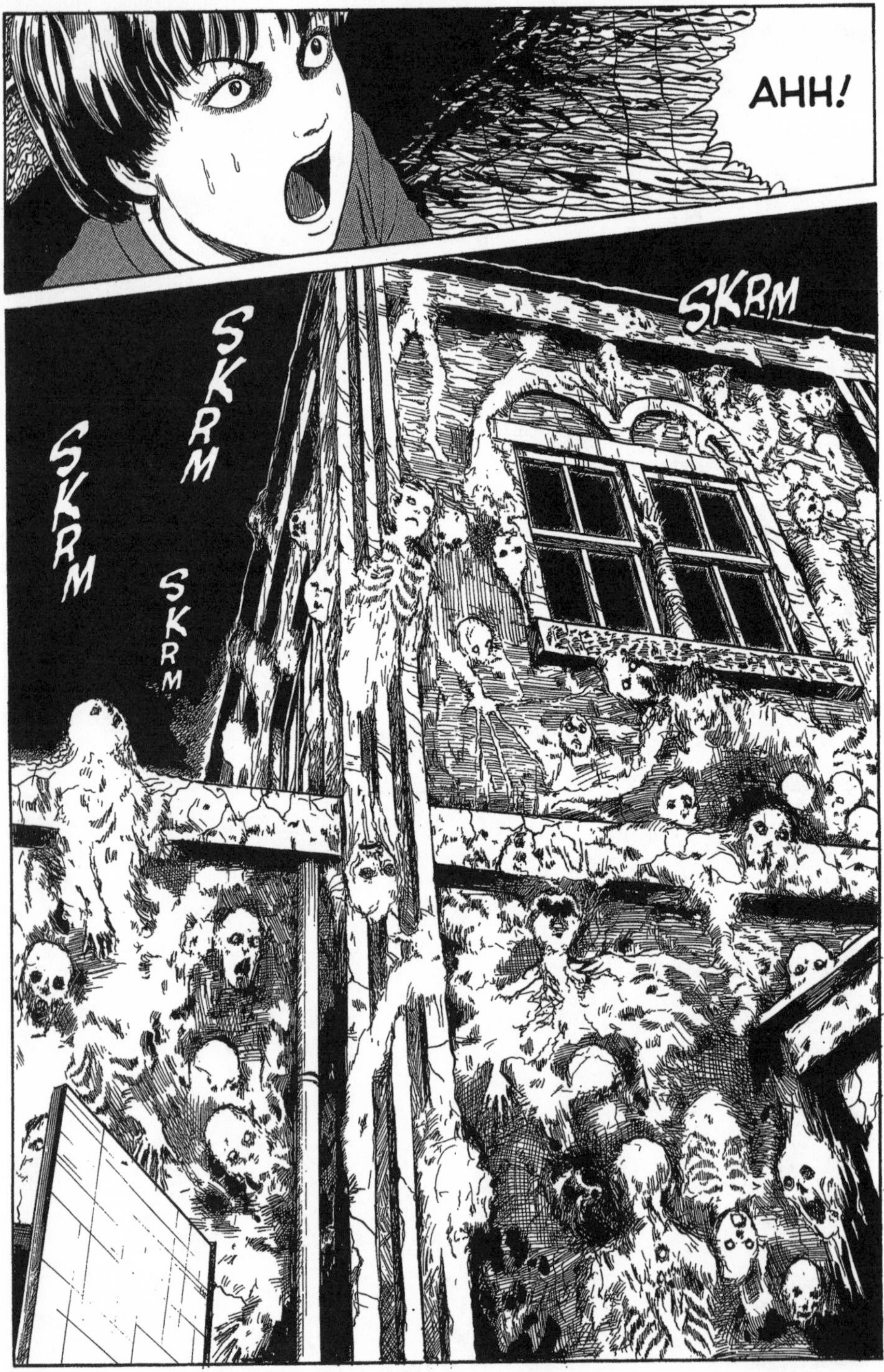
AHH!
SKRM
SKRM
SKRM
SKRM

THE STRANGE TALE OF OSHIKIRI: THE WALLS / END

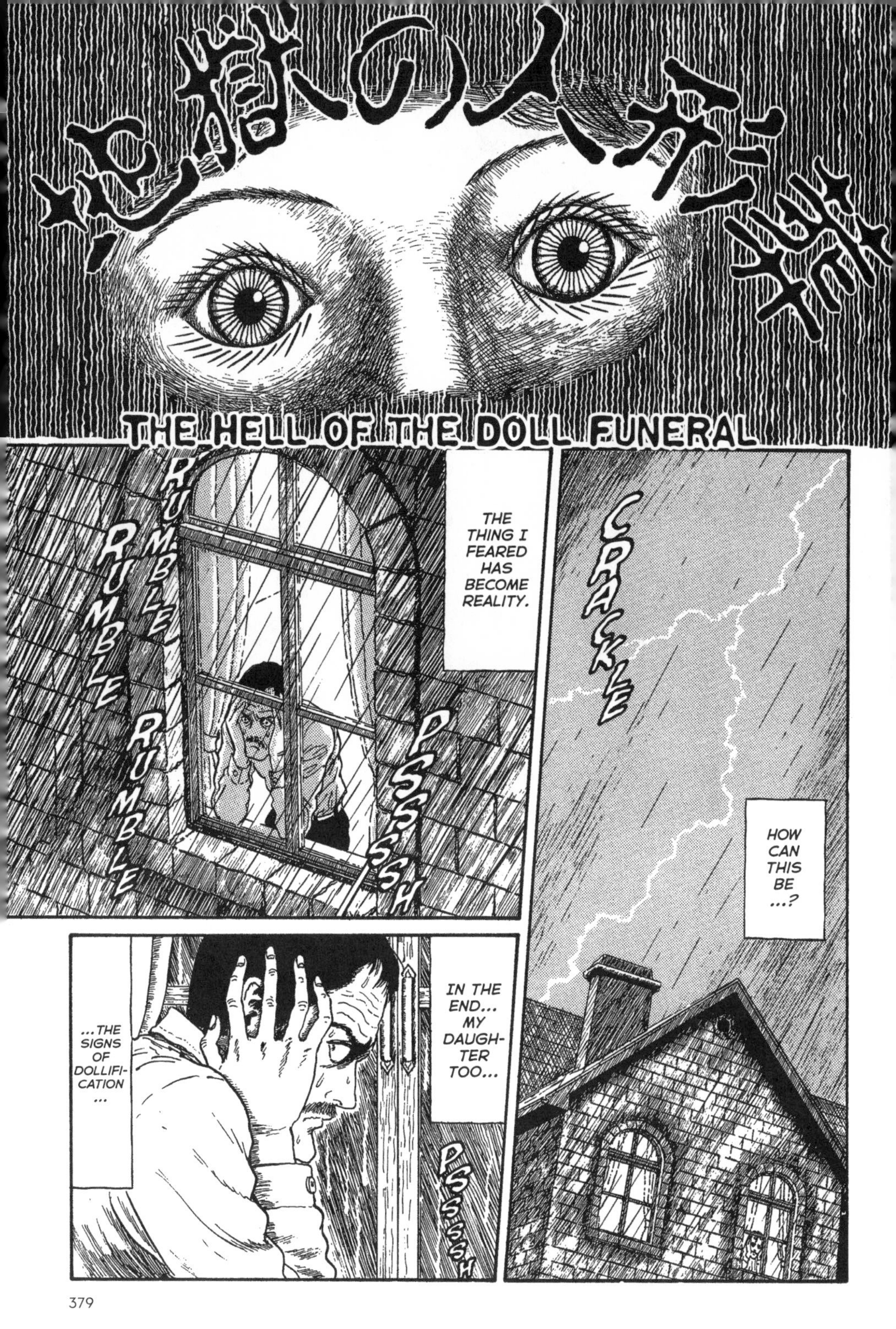
地獄の人形葬
THE HELL OF THE DOLL FUNERAL
CRACKLE
HOW CAN THIS BE ...?
RUMBLE RUMBLE
RUMBLE RUMBLE
PSSSSH
THE THING I FEARED HAS BECOME REALITY.
IN THE END... MY DAUGHTER TOO...
...THE SIGNS OF DOLLIFICATION ...
PSSSSH

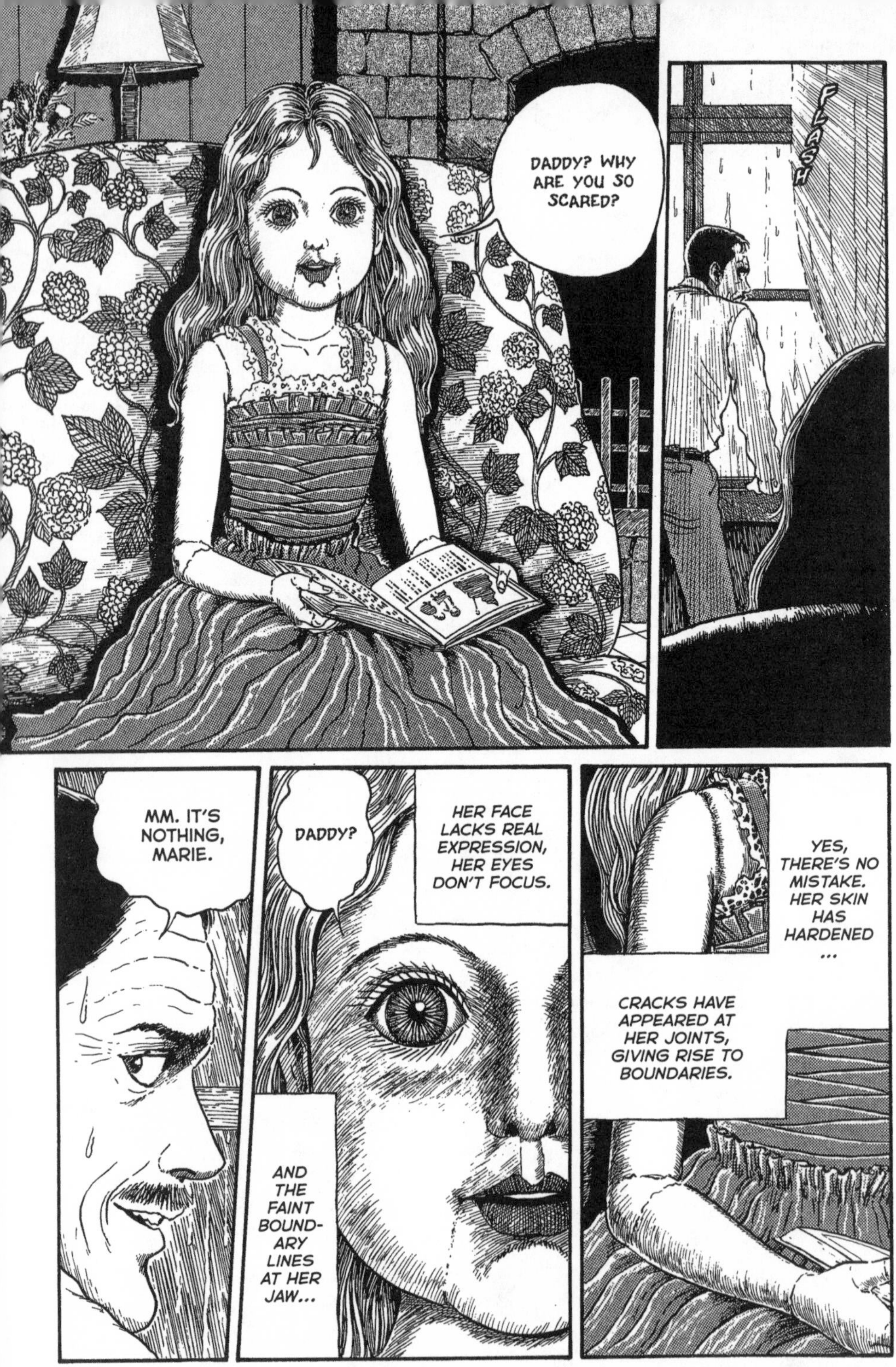
FLASH
DADDY? WHY ARE YOU SO SCARED?
YES, THERE'S NO MISTAKE. HER SKIN HAS HARDENED ...
CRACKS HAVE APPEARED AT HER JOINTS, GIVING RISE TO BOUNDARIES.
HER FACE LACKS REAL EXPRESSION, HER EYES DON'T FOCUS.
DADDY?
AND THE FAINT BOUNDARY LINES AT HER JAW...
MM. IT'S NOTHING, MARIE.

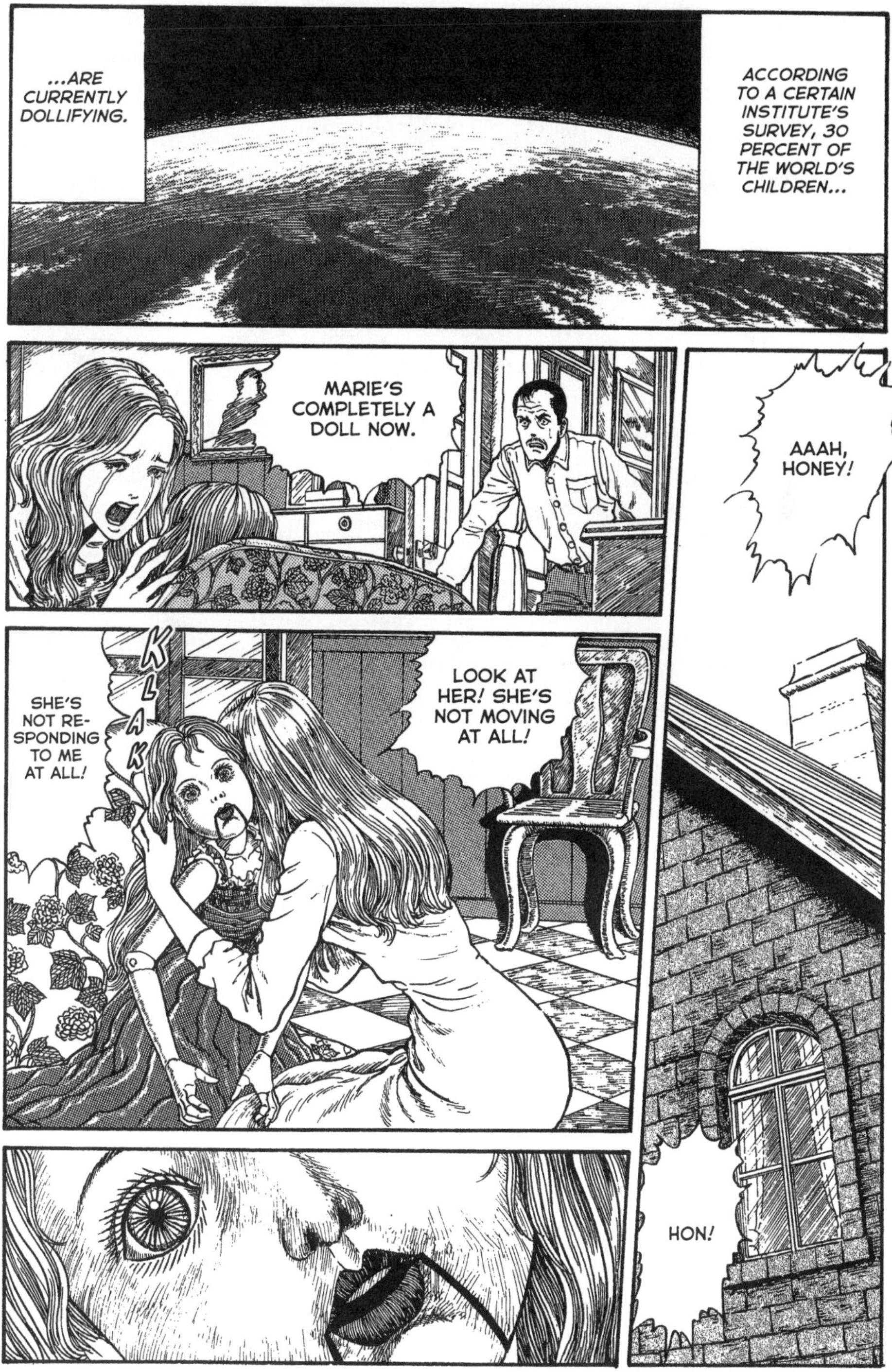
ACCORDING TO A CERTAIN INSTITUTE'S SURVEY, 30 PERCENT OF THE WORLD'S CHILDREN...
...ARE CURRENTLY DOLLIFYING.
AAAH, HONEY!
HON!
MARIE'S COMPLETELY A DOLL NOW.
LOOK AT HER! SHE'S NOT MOVING AT ALL!
KLAK
SHE'S NOT RE-SPONDING TO ME AT ALL!

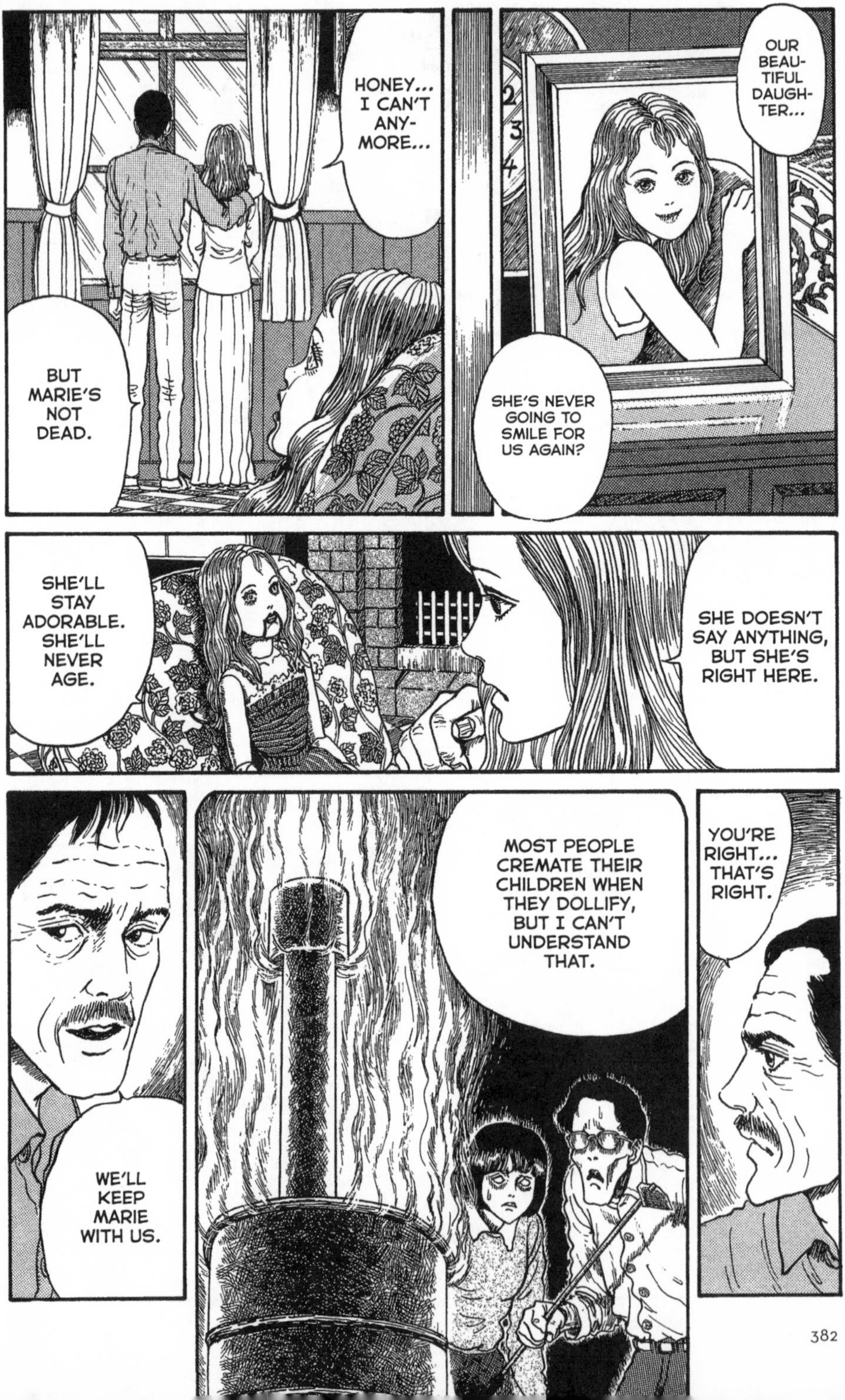
OUR BEAUTIFUL DAUGHTER...
SHE'S NEVER GOING TO SMILE FOR US AGAIN?
HONEY... I CAN'T ANYMORE...
BUT MARIE'S NOT DEAD.
SHE DOESN'T SAY ANYTHING, BUT SHE'S RIGHT HERE.
SHE'LL STAY ADORABLE. SHE'LL NEVER AGE.
YOU'RE RIGHT... THAT'S RIGHT.
MOST PEOPLE CREMATE THEIR CHILDREN WHEN THEY DOLLIFY, BUT I CAN'T UNDERSTAND THAT.
WE'LL KEEP MARIE WITH US.

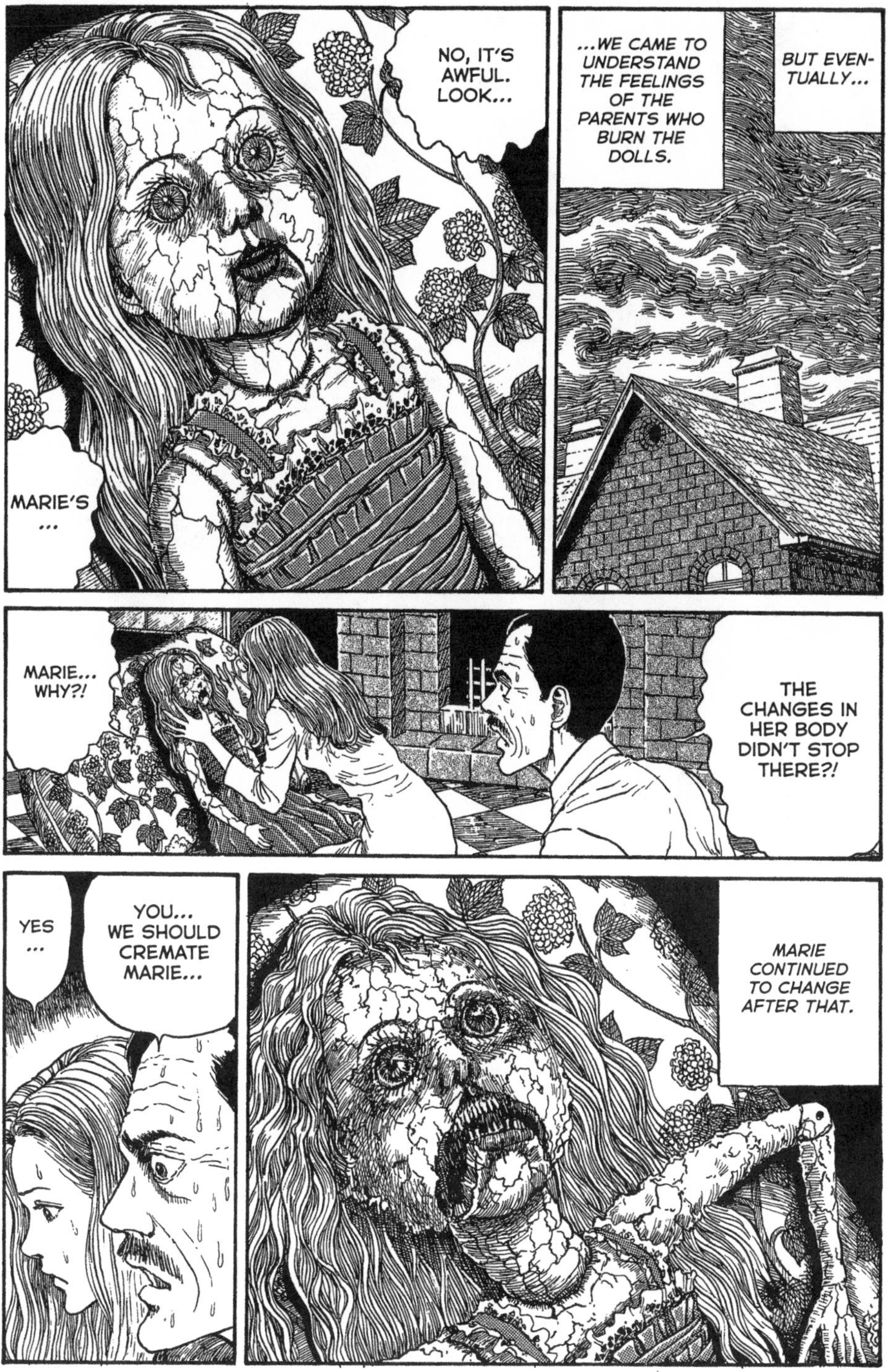
BUT EVENTUALLY...
...WE CAME TO UNDERSTAND THE FEELINGS OF THE PARENTS WHO BURN THE DOLLS.
NO, IT'S AWFUL. LOOK...
MARIE'S ...
THE CHANGES IN HER BODY DIDN'T STOP THERE?!
MARIE... WHY?!
MARIE CONTINUED TO CHANGE AFTER THAT.
YOU... WE SHOULD CREMATE MARIE...
YES ...

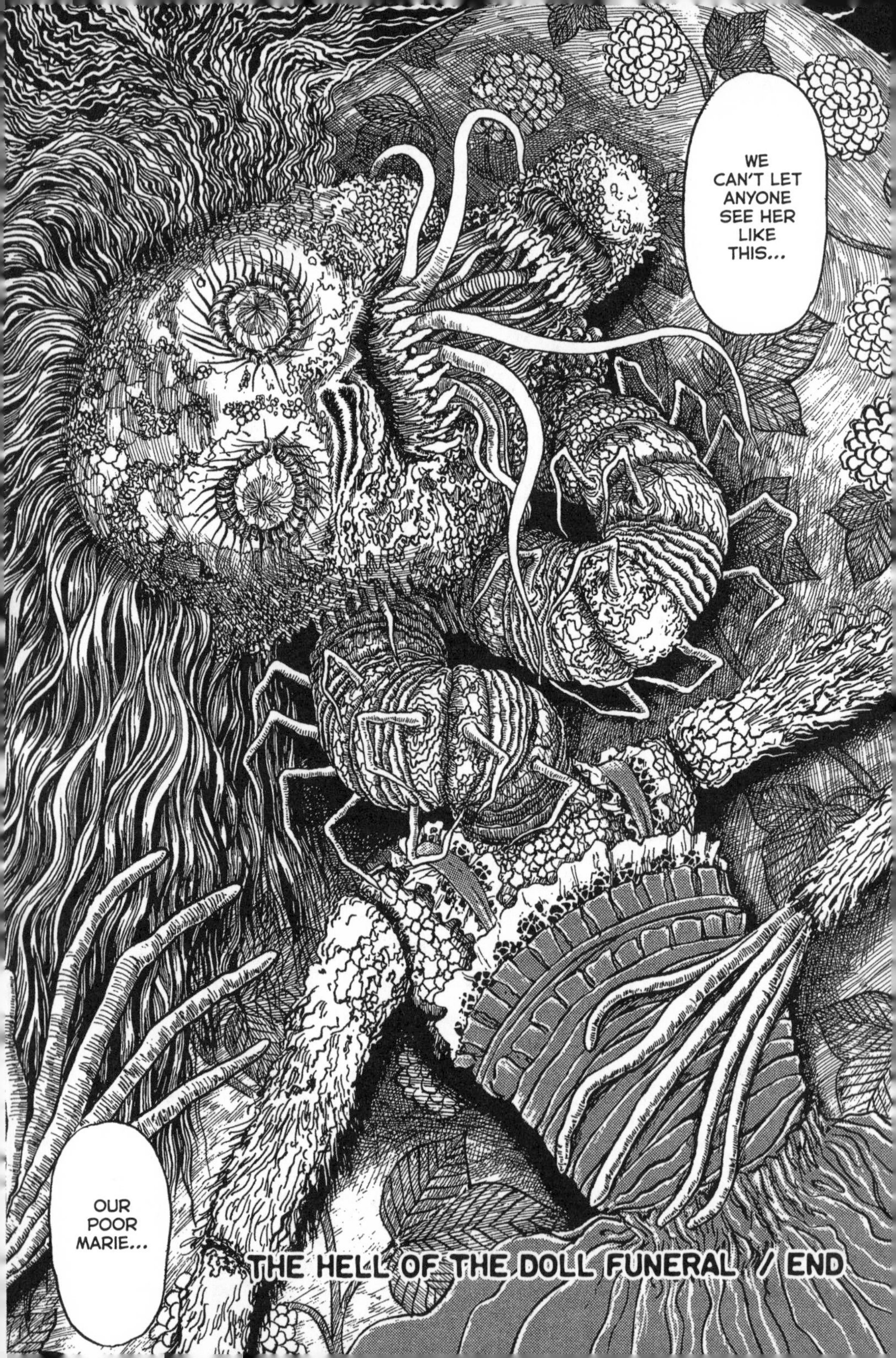
WE CAN'T LET ANYONE SEE HER LIKE THIS...
OUR POOR MARIE...
THE HELL OF THE DOLL FUNERAL / END

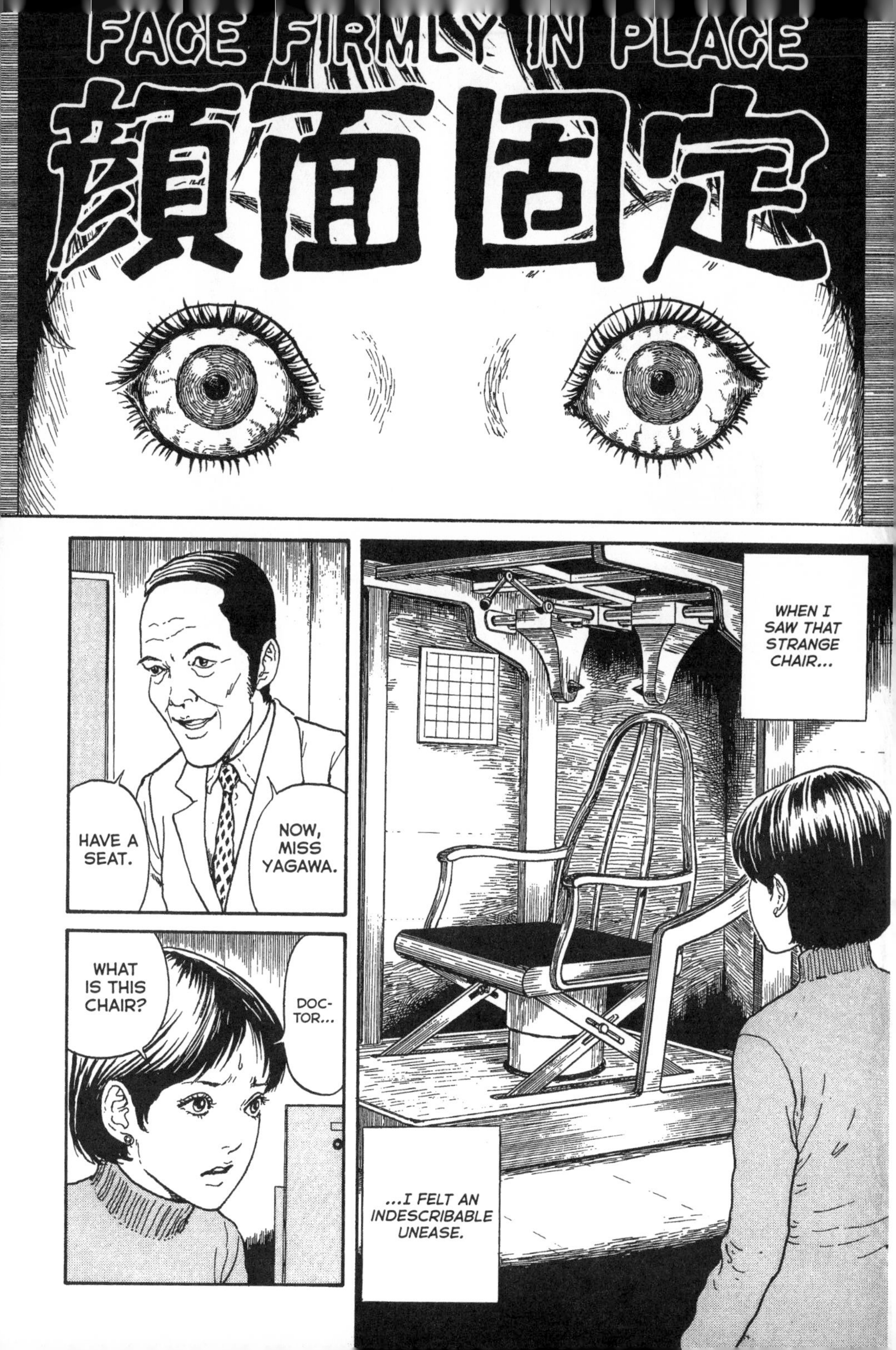
FACE FIRMLY IN PLACE
顔面固定
WHEN I SAW THAT STRANGE CHAIR...
...I FELT AN INDESCRIBABLE UNEASE.
NOW, MISS YAGAWA.
HAVE A SEAT.
DOC-TOR...
WHAT IS THIS CHAIR?

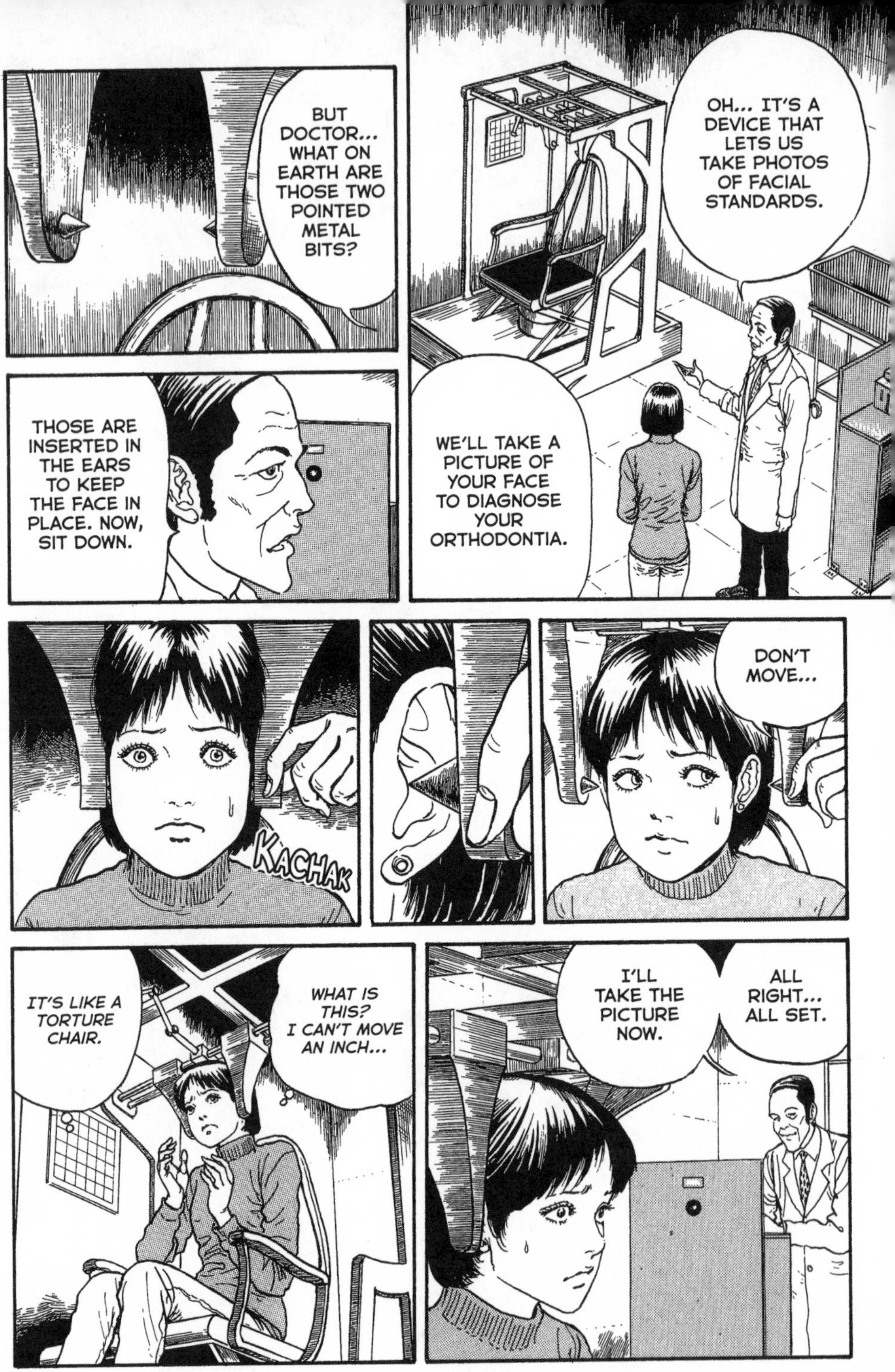
OH... IT'S A DEVICE THAT LETS US TAKE PHOTOS OF FACIAL STANDARDS.
WE'LL TAKE A PICTURE OF YOUR FACE TO DIAGNOSE YOUR ORTHODONTIA.
BUT DOCTOR... WHAT ON EARTH ARE THOSE TWO POINTED METAL BITS?
THOSE ARE INSERTED IN THE EARS TO KEEP THE FACE IN PLACE. NOW, SIT DOWN.
DON'T MOVE...
KACHAK
ALL RIGHT... ALL SET.
I'LL TAKE THE PICTURE NOW.
WHAT IS THIS? I CAN'T MOVE AN INCH...
IT'S LIKE A TORTURE CHAIR.

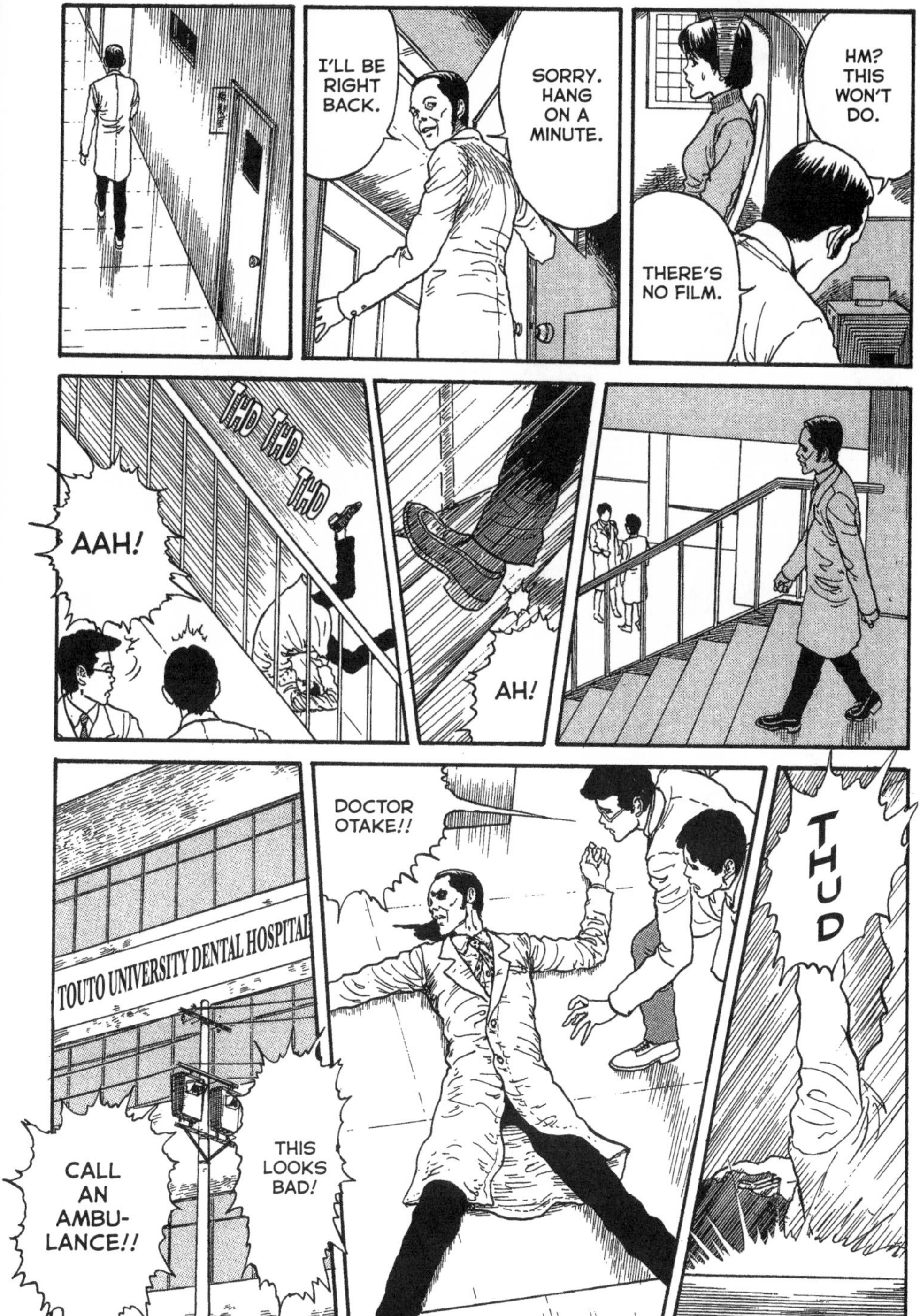
HM? THIS WON'T DO.
THERE'S NO FILM.
SORRY. HANG ON A MINUTE.
I'LL BE RIGHT BACK.
AH!
THD THD THD
AAH!
THUD
DOCTOR OTAKE!!
THIS LOOKS BAD!
TOUTO UNIVERSITY DENTAL HOSPITAL
CALL AN AMBULANCE!!

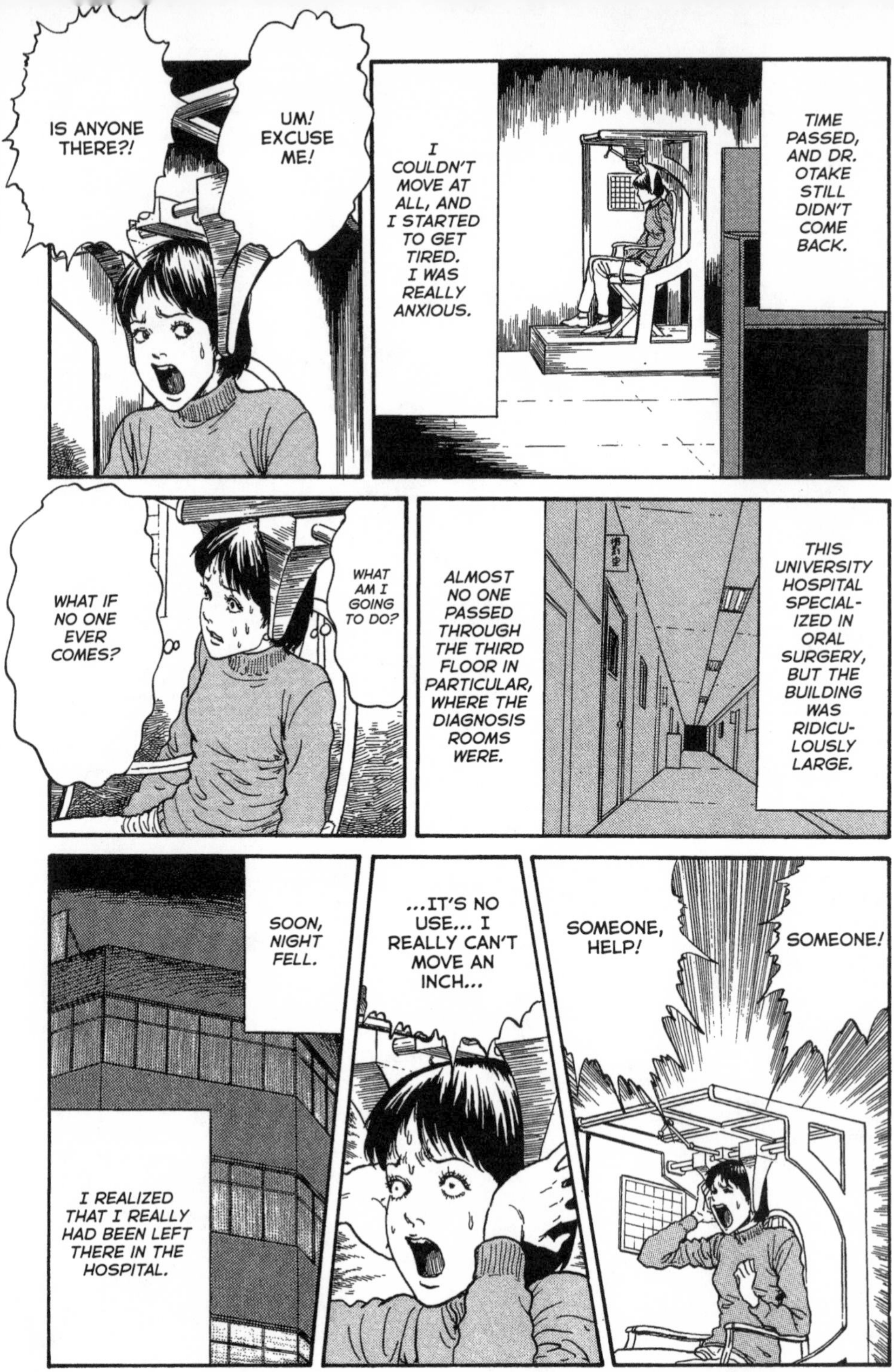
TIME PASSED, AND DR. OTAKE STILL DIDN'T COME BACK.
I COULDN'T MOVE AT ALL, AND I STARTED TO GET TIRED. I WAS REALLY ANXIOUS.
UM! EXCUSE ME!
IS ANYONE THERE?!
THIS UNIVERSITY HOSPITAL SPECIAL-IZED IN ORAL SURGERY, BUT THE BUILDING WAS RIDICU-LOUSLY LARGE.
ALMOST NO ONE PASSED THROUGH THE THIRD FLOOR IN PARTICULAR, WHERE THE DIAGNOSIS ROOMS WERE.
WHAT AM I GOING TO DO?
WHAT IF NO ONE EVER COMES?
SOMEONE!
SOMEONE, HELP!
...IT'S NO USE... I REALLY CAN'T MOVE AN INCH...
SOON, NIGHT FELL.
I REALIZED THAT I REALLY HAD BEEN LEFT THERE IN THE HOSPITAL.

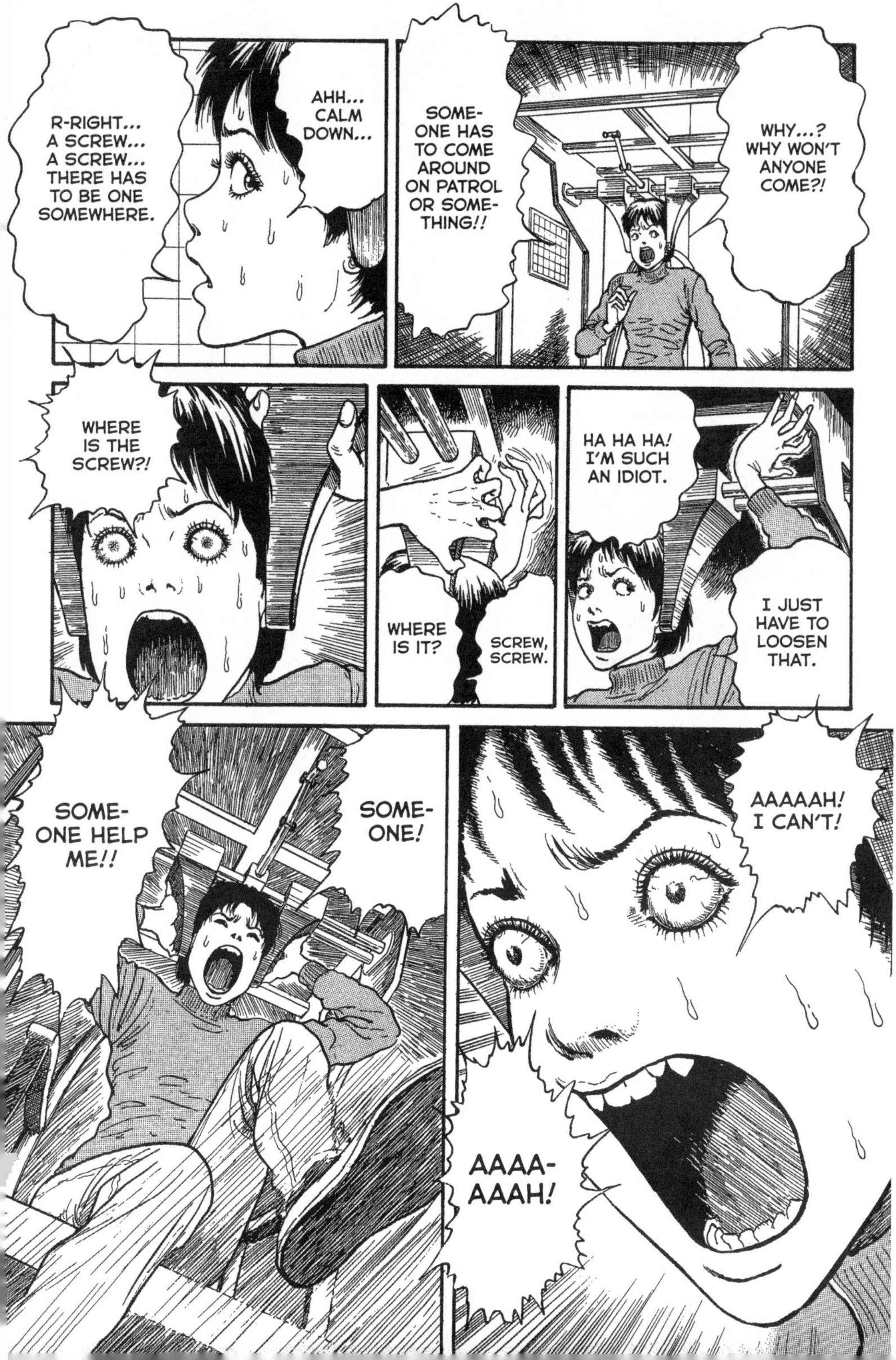
WHY...? WHY WON'T ANYONE COME?!
SOME-ONE HAS TO COME AROUND ON PATROL OR SOME-THING!!
AHH... CALM DOWN...
R-RIGHT... A SCREW... A SCREW... THERE HAS TO BE ONE SOMEWHERE.
HA HA HA! I'M SUCH AN IDIOT.
I JUST HAVE TO LOOSEN THAT.
SCREW, SCREW.
WHERE IS IT?
WHERE IS THE SCREW?!
AAAAAH! I CAN'T!
AAAA-AAAH!
SOME-ONE!
SOME-ONE HELP ME!!

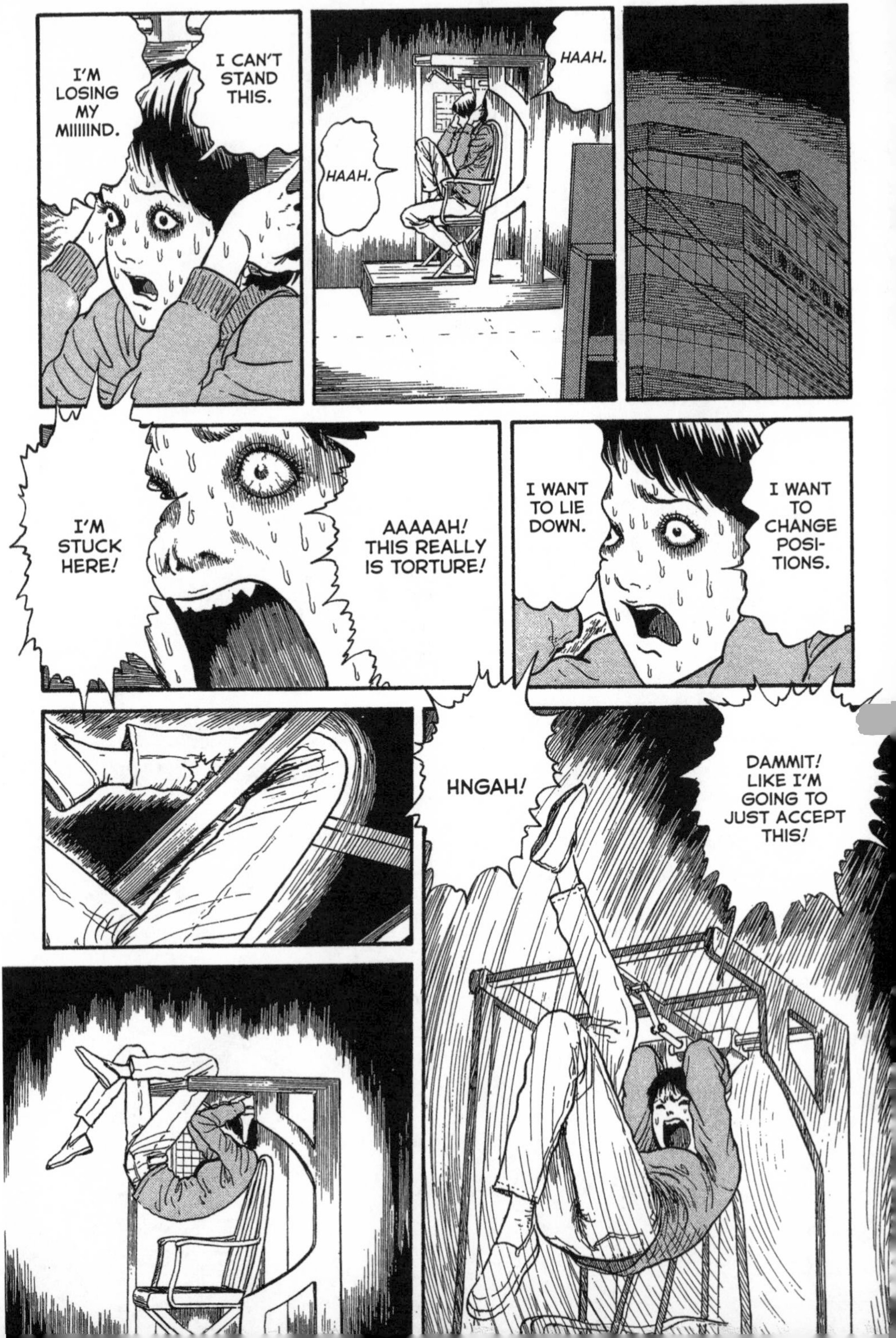
HAAH.
HAAH.
I CAN'T STAND THIS.
I'M LOSING MY MIIIIIND.
I WANT TO CHANGE POSI-TIONS.
I WANT TO LIE DOWN.
AAAAAH! THIS REALLY IS TORTURE!
I'M STUCK HERE!
DAMMIT! LIKE I'M GOING TO JUST ACCEPT THIS!
HNGAH!

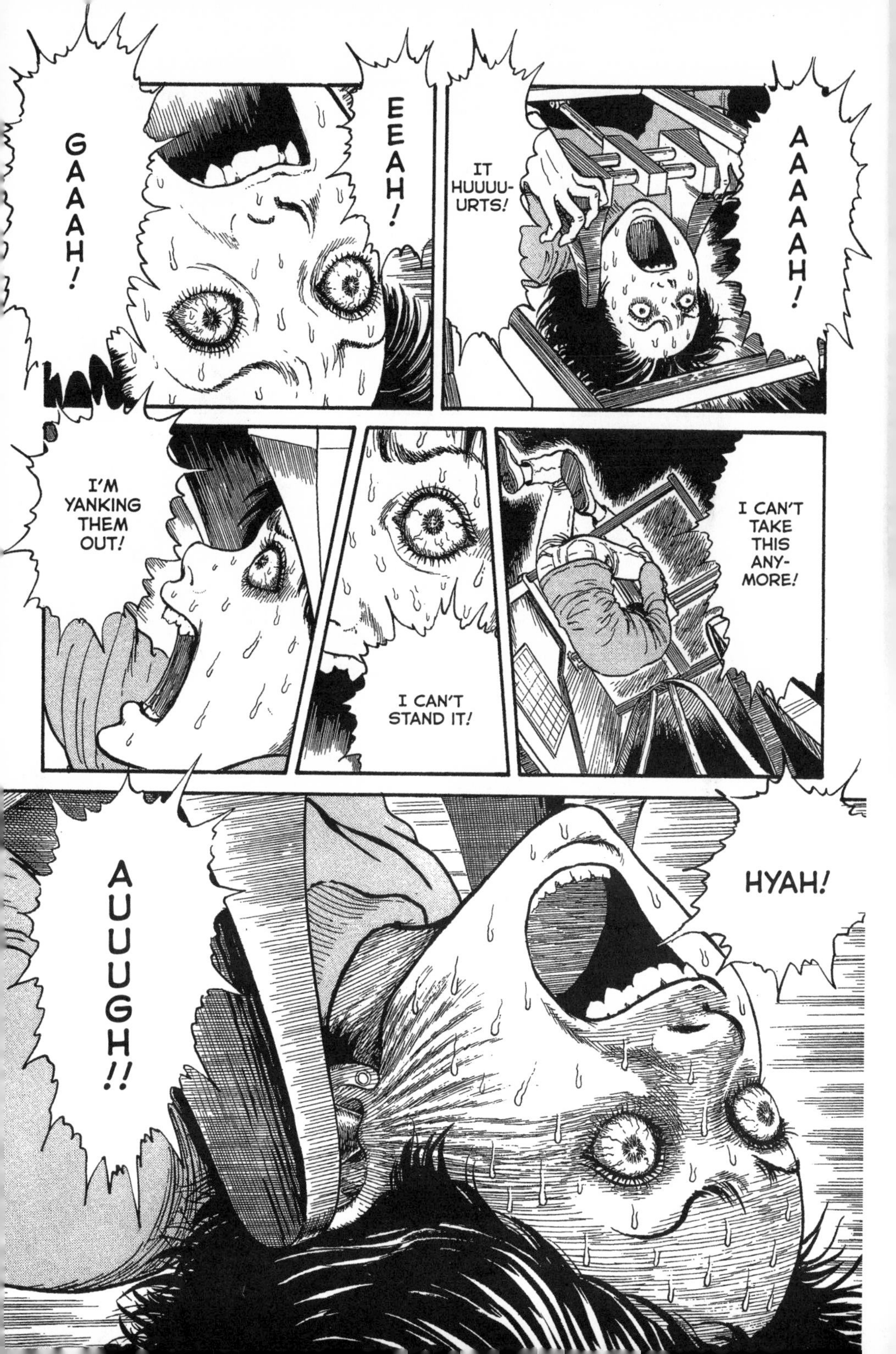
AAAAAAH!
IT HUUUU-URTS!
EEAH!
GAAAH!
I CAN'T TAKE THIS ANY-MORE!
I CAN'T STAND IT!
I'M YANKING THEM OUT!
HYAH!
AUUUGH!!

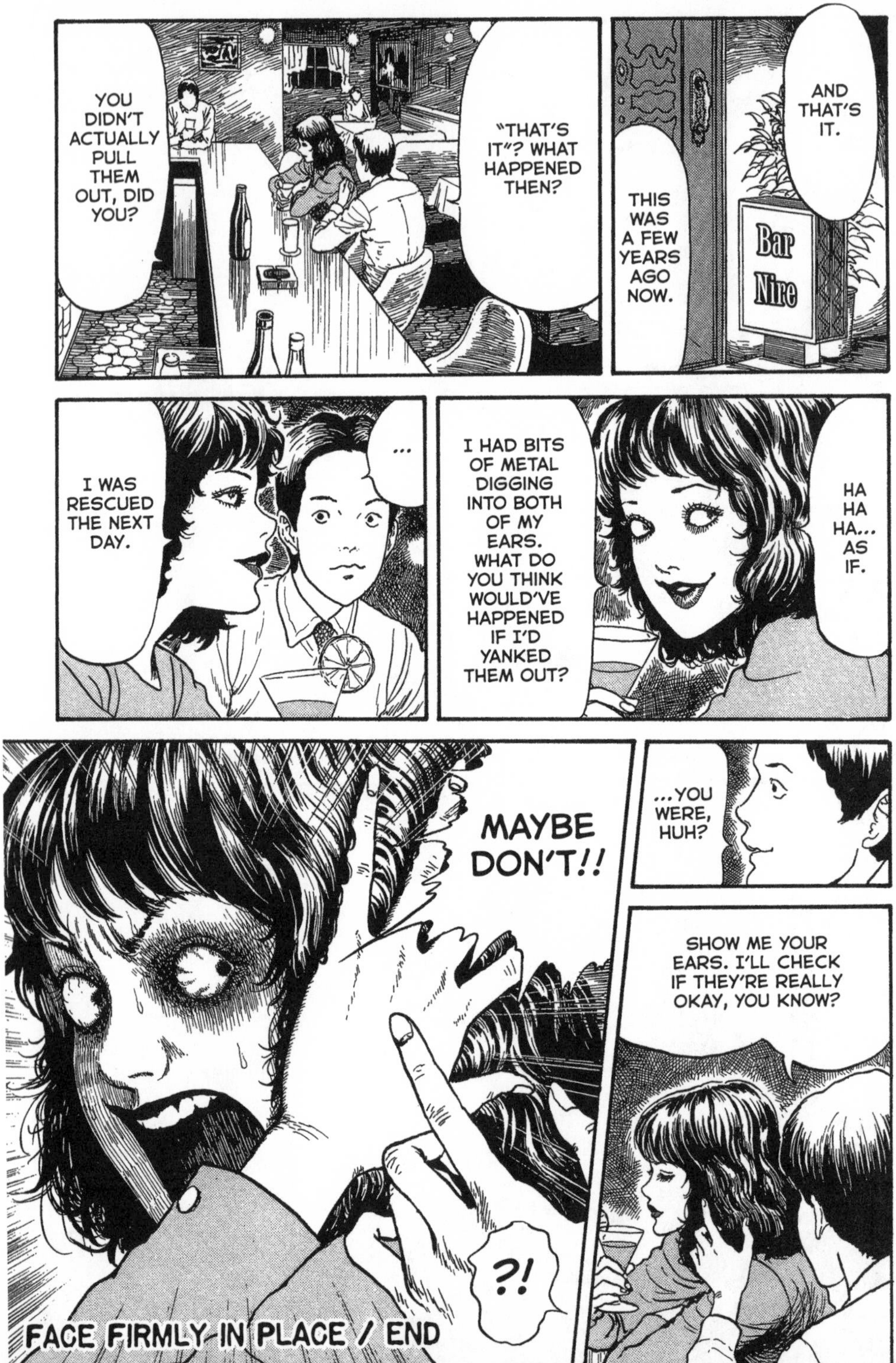
AND THAT'S IT.
THIS WAS A FEW YEARS AGO NOW.
Bar Nire
"THAT'S IT"? WHAT HAPPENED THEN?
YOU DIDN'T ACTUALLY PULL THEM OUT, DID YOU?
HA HA HA... AS IF.
I HAD BITS OF METAL DIGGING INTO BOTH OF MY EARS. WHAT DO YOU THINK WOULD'VE HAPPENED IF I'D YANKED THEM OUT?
...
I WAS RESCUED THE NEXT DAY.
...YOU WERE, HUH?
SHOW ME YOUR EARS. I'LL CHECK IF THEY'RE REALLY OKAY, YOU KNOW?
MAYBE DON'T!!
?!
FACE FIRMLY IN PLACE / END

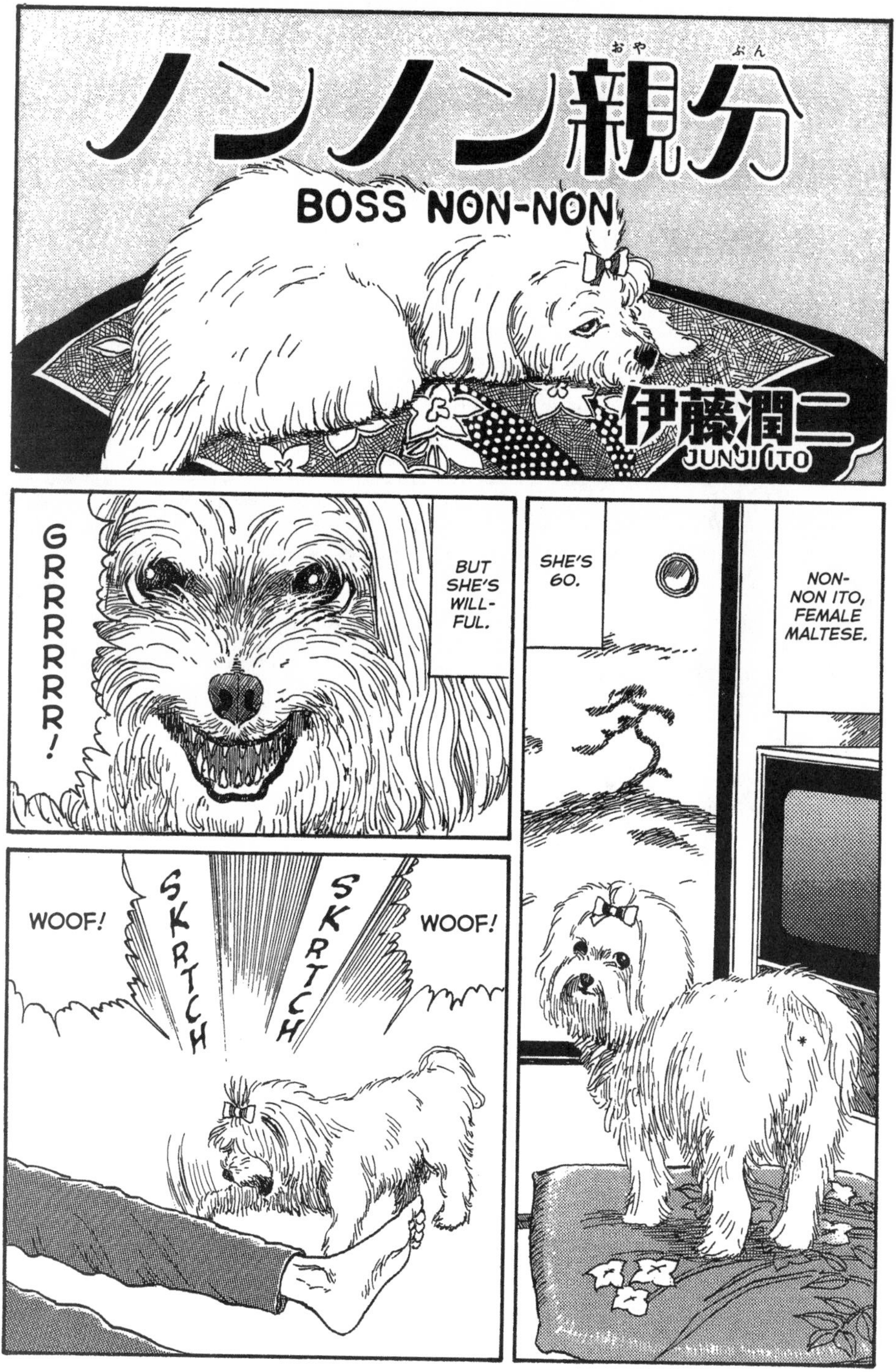
ノンノン親分
BOSS NON-NON
伊藤潤二
JUNJI ITO
NON-NON ITO, FEMALE MALTESE.
SHE'S 60.
BUT SHE'S WILLFUL.
GRRRRRRR!
WOOF!
SKRTCH
SKRTCH
WOOF!

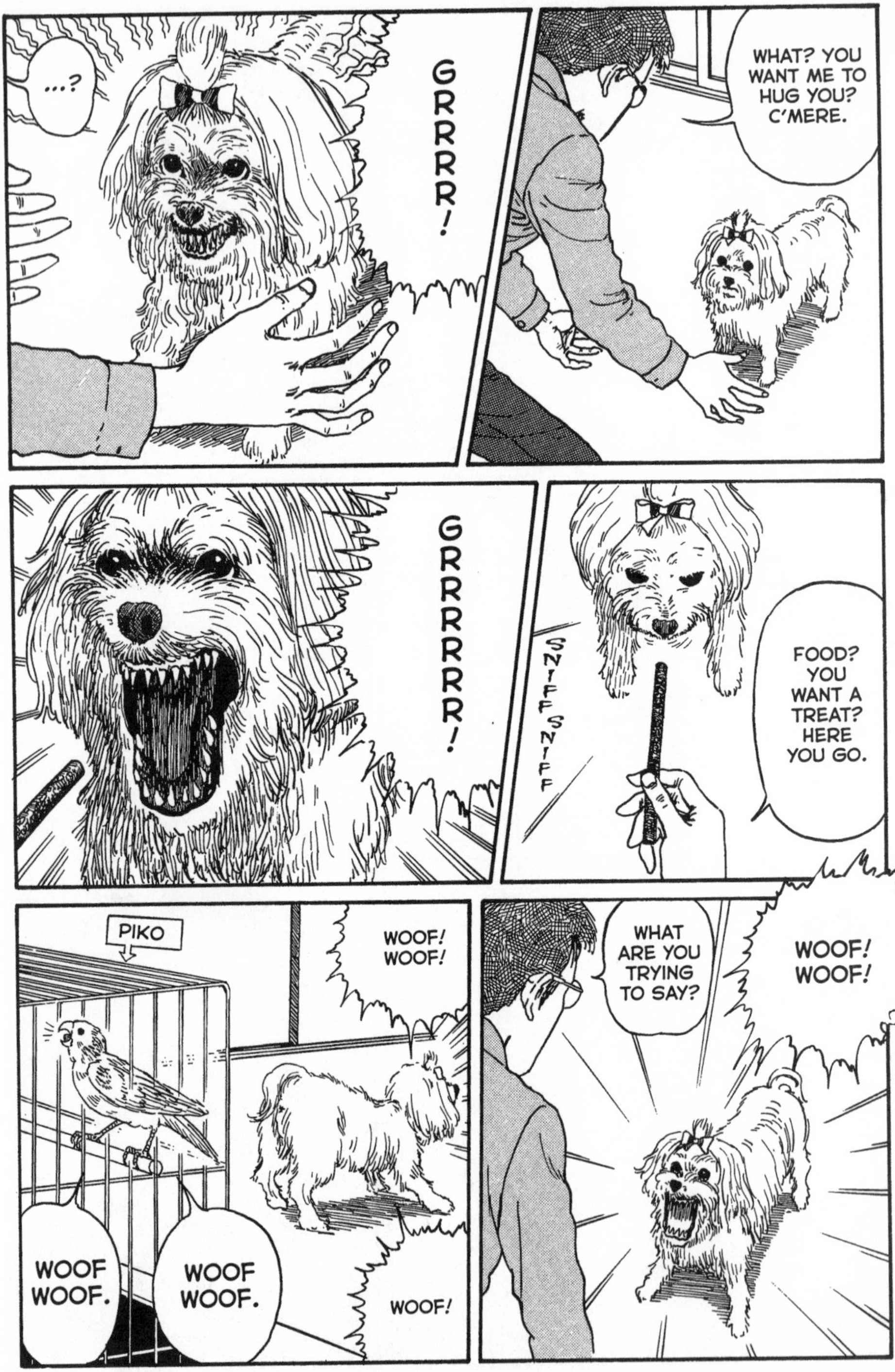
WHAT? YOU WANT ME TO HUG YOU? C'MERE.
GRRRR!
...?
FOOD? YOU WANT A TREAT? HERE YOU GO.
SNIFF SNIFF
GRRRRRRR!
WOOF! WOOF!
WHAT ARE YOU TRYING TO SAY?
WOOF! WOOF!
PIKO
WOOF!
WOOF WOOF.
WOOF WOOF.

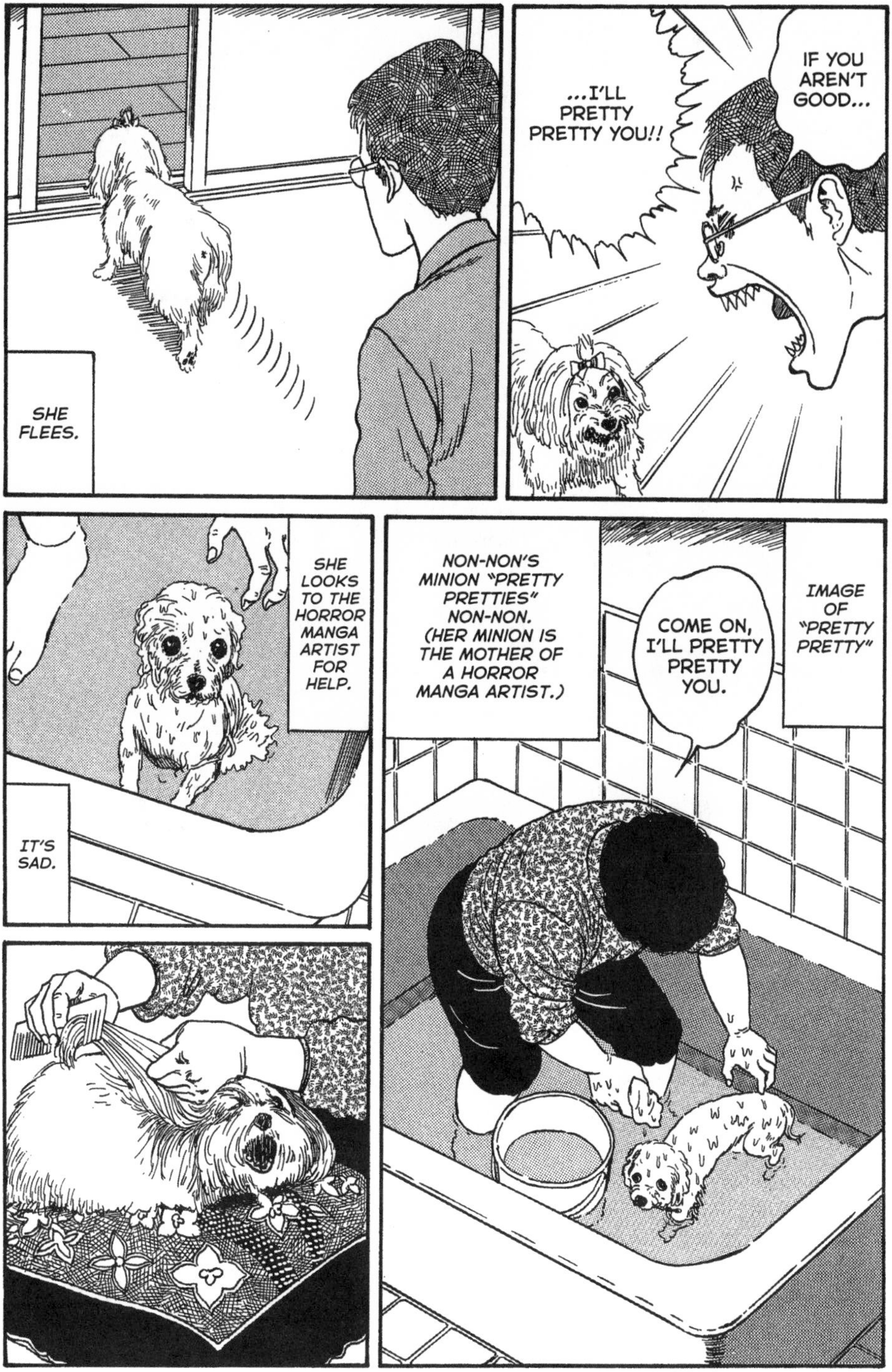
IF YOU AREN'T GOOD...
...I'LL PRETTY PRETTY YOU!!
SHE FLEES.
IMAGE OF "PRETTY PRETTY"
COME ON, I'LL PRETTY PRETTY YOU.
NON-NON'S MINION "PRETTY PRETTIES" NON-NON. (HER MINION IS THE MOTHER OF A HORROR MANGA ARTIST.)
SHE LOOKS TO THE HORROR MANGA ARTIST FOR HELP.
IT'S SAD.

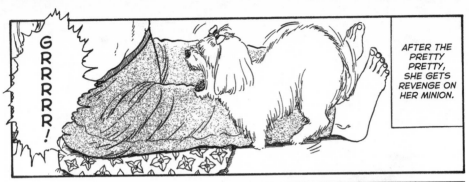

AFTER THE PRETTY PRETTY, SHE GETS REVENGE ON HER MINION.
GRRRRRR!
THE BOSS IS ALREADY 60.
SO SHE HAS WARTS ALL OVER HER BODY.
SHE HAS HEMORRHOIDS, TOO.
SHE SCRATCHES AT HER NECK AND MAKES IT OOZE.
SO HER MINION PUTS A LARGE BANDAGE OVER IT.
AGAIN TONIGHT...
...THE BOSS SLEEPS WITH HER MINION.
SNRRRRR
SNRRRRR
SHE ALSO SNORES.

BOSS NON-NON / END

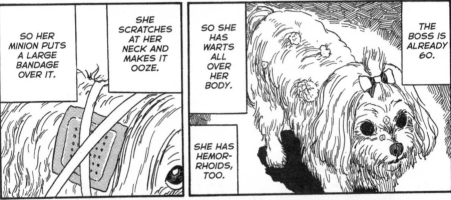

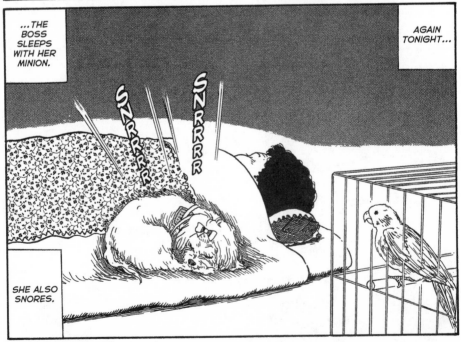

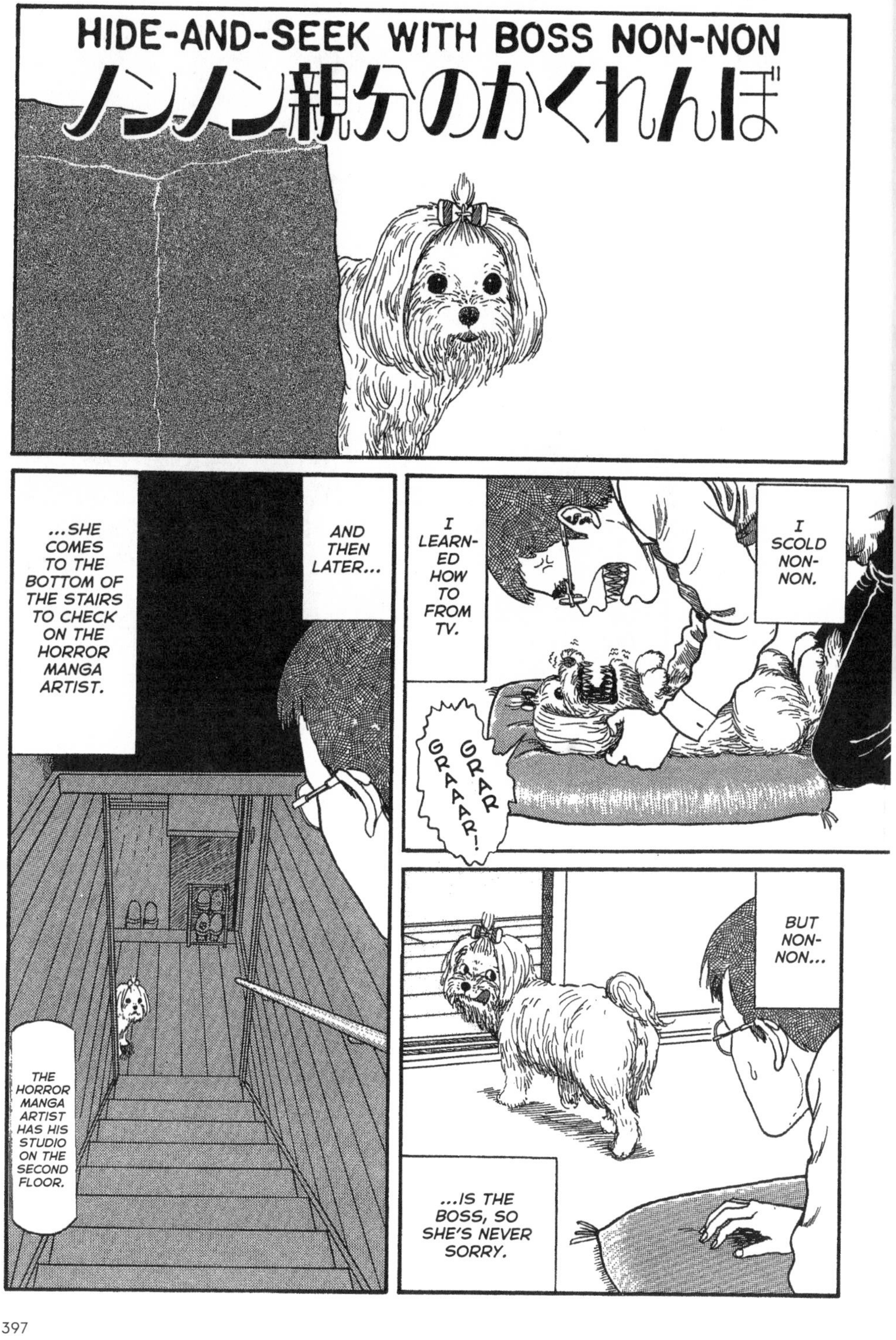
HIDE-AND-SEEK WITH BOSS NON-NON
ノンノン親分のかくれんぼ
I SCOLD NON-NON.
I LEARNED HOW TO FROM TV.
GRAR GRAAAR!
BUT NON-NON...
...IS THE BOSS, SO SHE'S NEVER SORRY.
AND THEN LATER...
...SHE COMES TO THE BOTTOM OF THE STAIRS TO CHECK ON THE HORROR MANGA ARTIST.
THE HORROR MANGA ARTIST HAS HIS STUDIO ON THE SECOND FLOOR.

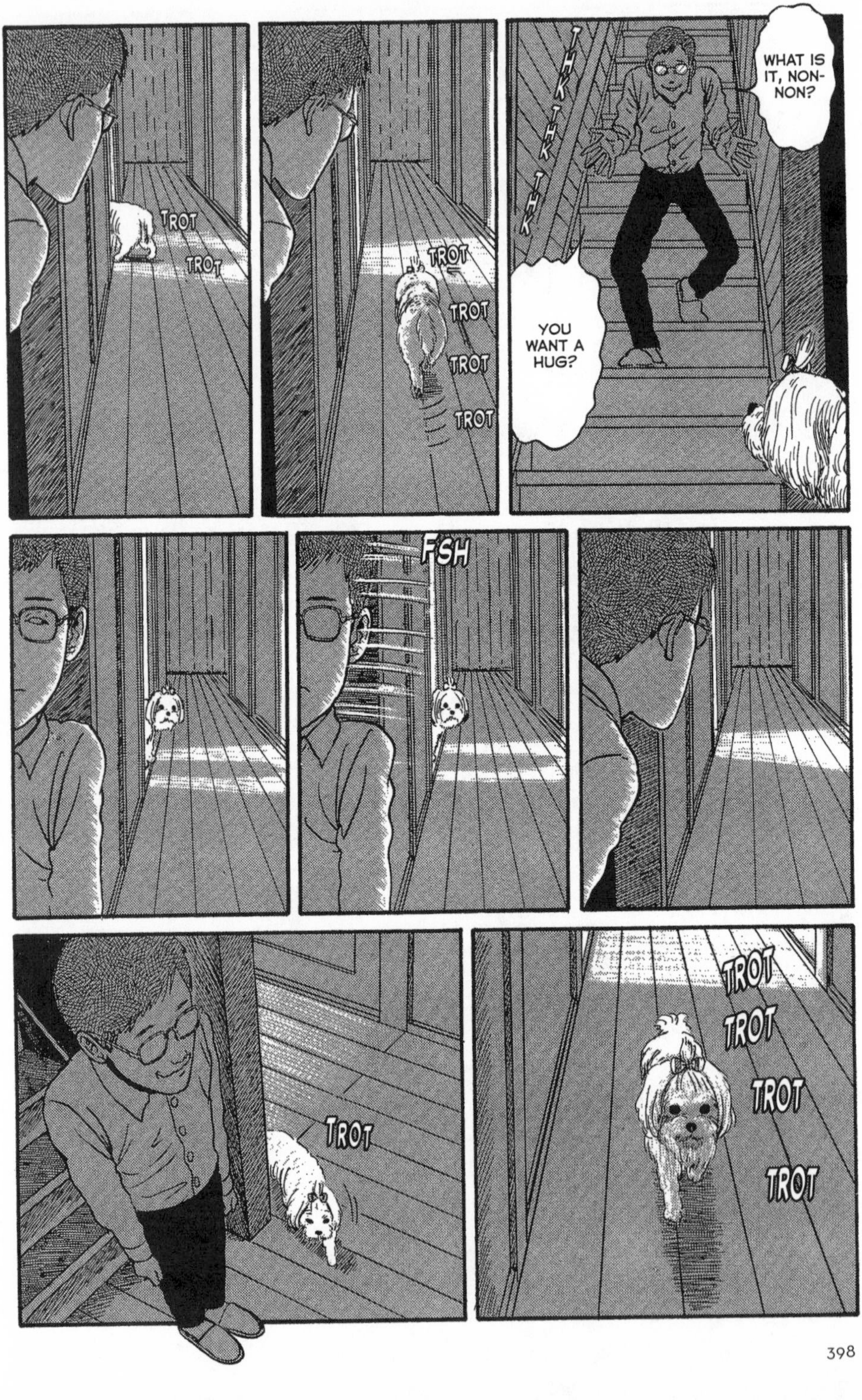
THK THK THK
WHAT IS IT, NON-NON?
YOU WANT A HUG?
TROT
TROT
TROT
TROT
TROT
TROT
FSH
TROT
TROT
TROT
TROT
TROT

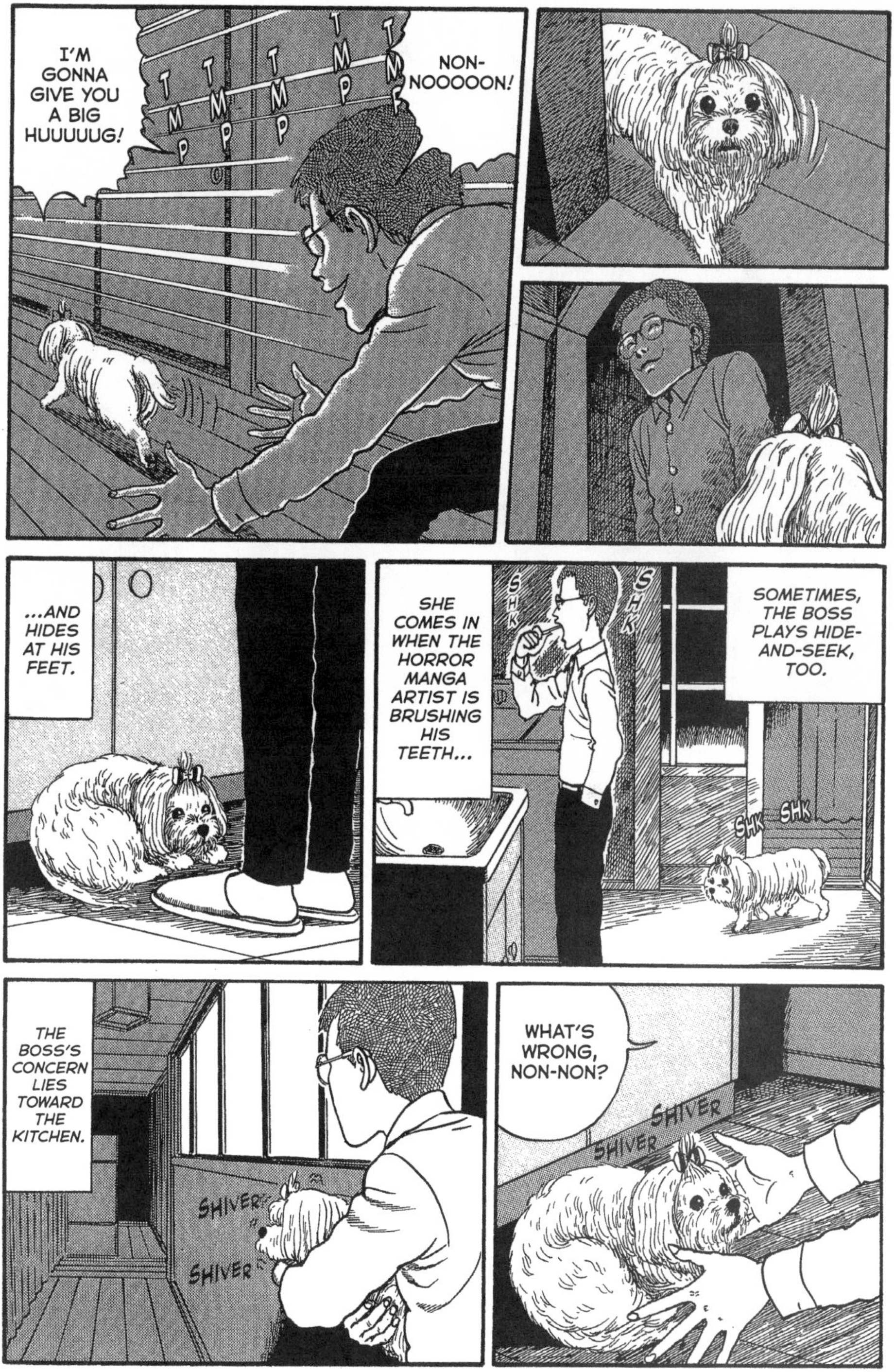
NON-NOOOOON!
TMP TMP TMP TMP TMP
I'M GONNA GIVE YOU A BIG HUUUUUG!
SOMETIMES, THE BOSS PLAYS HIDE-AND-SEEK, TOO.
SHK SHK
SHK SHK
SHE COMES IN WHEN THE HORROR MANGA ARTIST IS BRUSHING HIS TEETH...
...AND HIDES AT HIS FEET.
WHAT'S WRONG, NON-NON?
SHIVER SHIVER
THE BOSS'S CONCERN LIES TOWARD THE KITCHEN.
SHIVER SHIVER

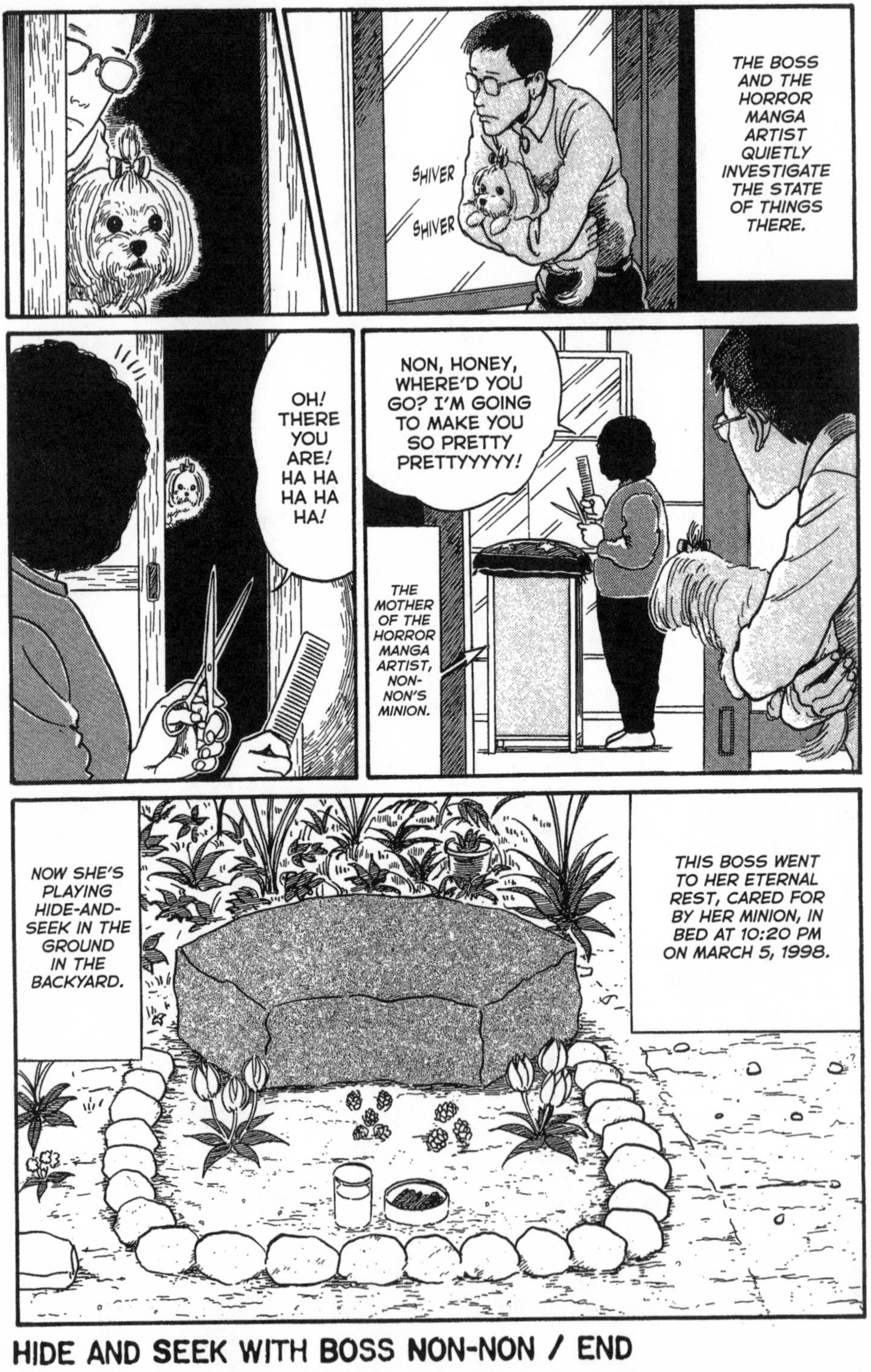
THE BOSS AND THE HORROR MANGA ARTIST QUIETLY INVESTIGATE THE STATE OF THINGS THERE.
SHIVER
SHIVER
NON, HONEY, WHERE'D YOU GO? I'M GOING TO MAKE YOU SO PRETTY PRETTYYYYY!
THE MOTHER OF THE HORROR MANGA ARTIST, NON-NON'S MINION.
OH! THERE YOU ARE! HA HA HA HA HA!
THIS BOSS WENT TO HER ETERNAL REST, CARED FOR BY HER MINION, IN BED AT 10:20 PM ON MARCH 5, 1998.
NOW SHE'S PLAYING HIDE-AND-SEEK IN THE GROUND IN THE BACKYARD.

HIDE AND SEEK WITH BOSS NON-NON / END

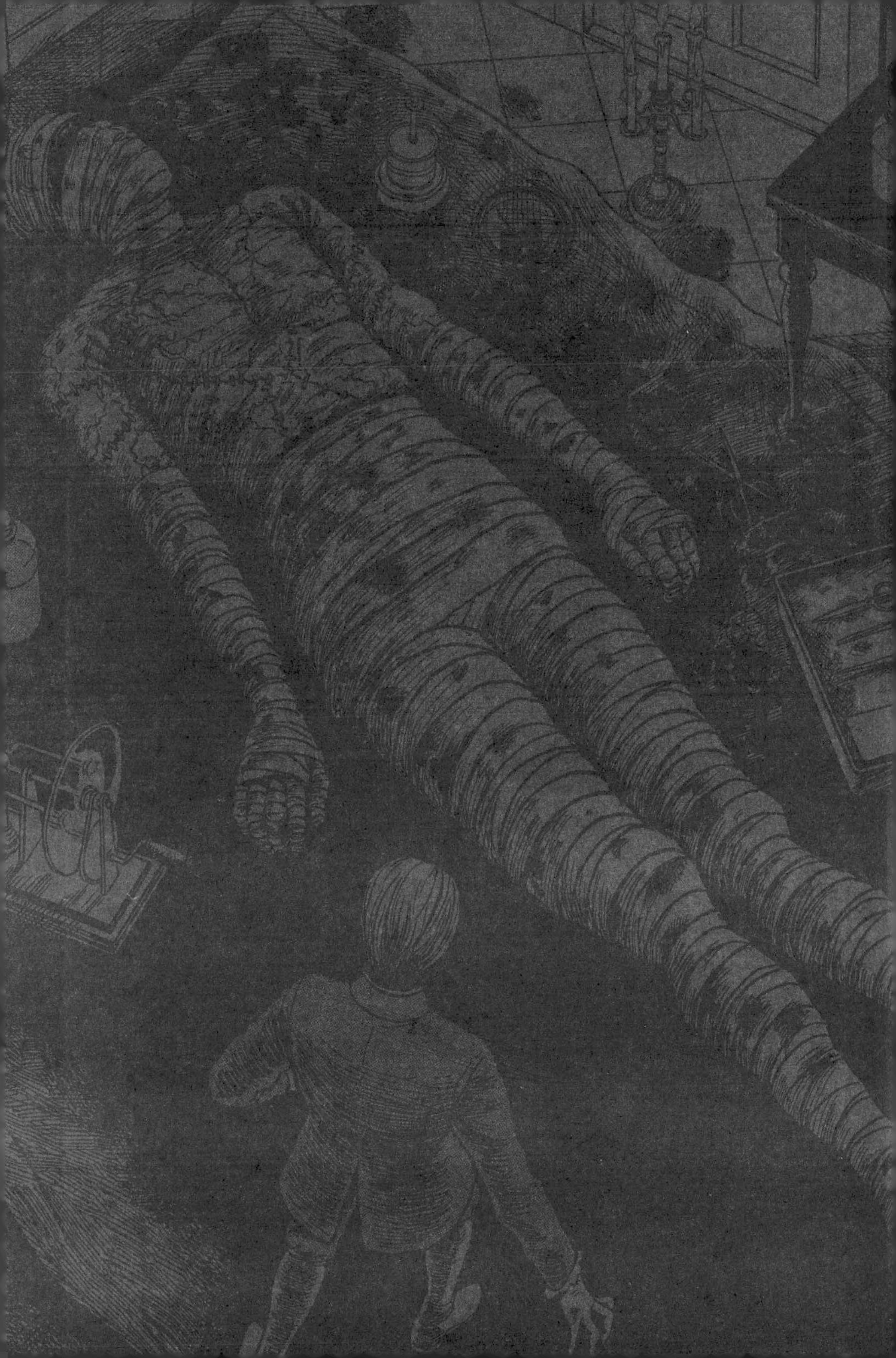

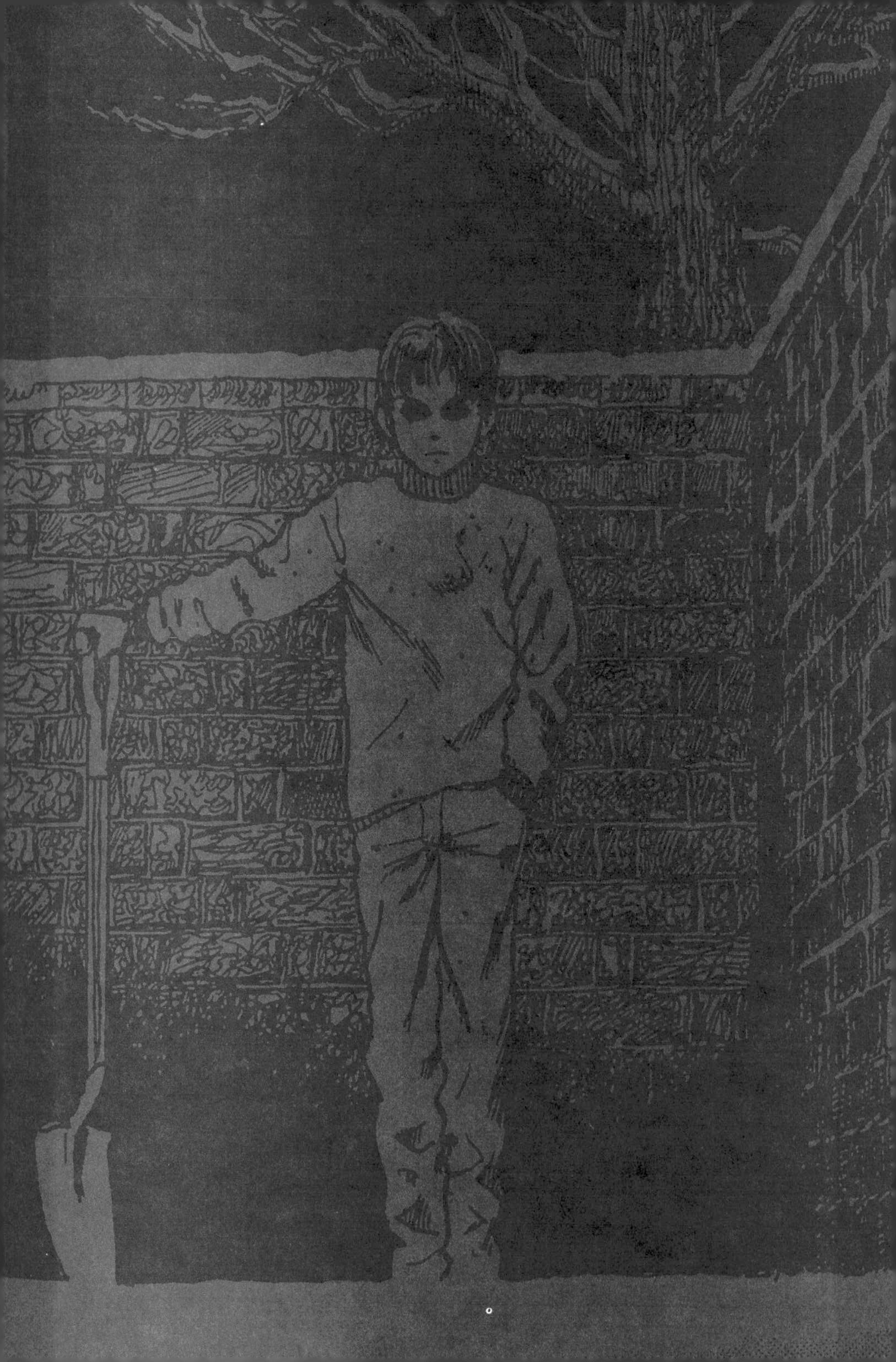

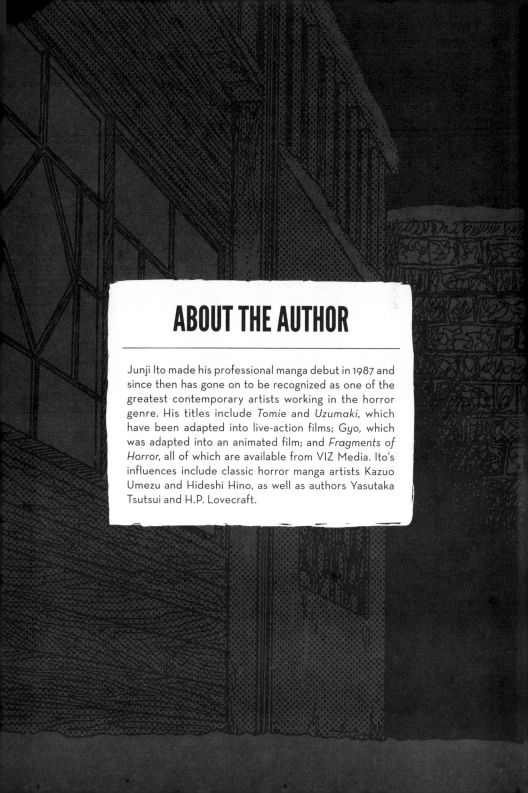

ABOUT THE AUTHOR

Junji Ito made his professional manga debut in 1987 and since then has gone on to be recognized as one of the greatest contemporary artists working in the horror genre. His titles include *Tomie* and *Uzumaki,* which have been adapted into live-action films; *Gyo,* which was adapted into an animated film; and *Fragments of Horror,* all of which are available from VIZ Media. Ito's influences include classic horror manga artists Kazuo Umezu and Hideshi Hino, as well as authors Yasutaka Tsutsui and H.P. Lovecraft.

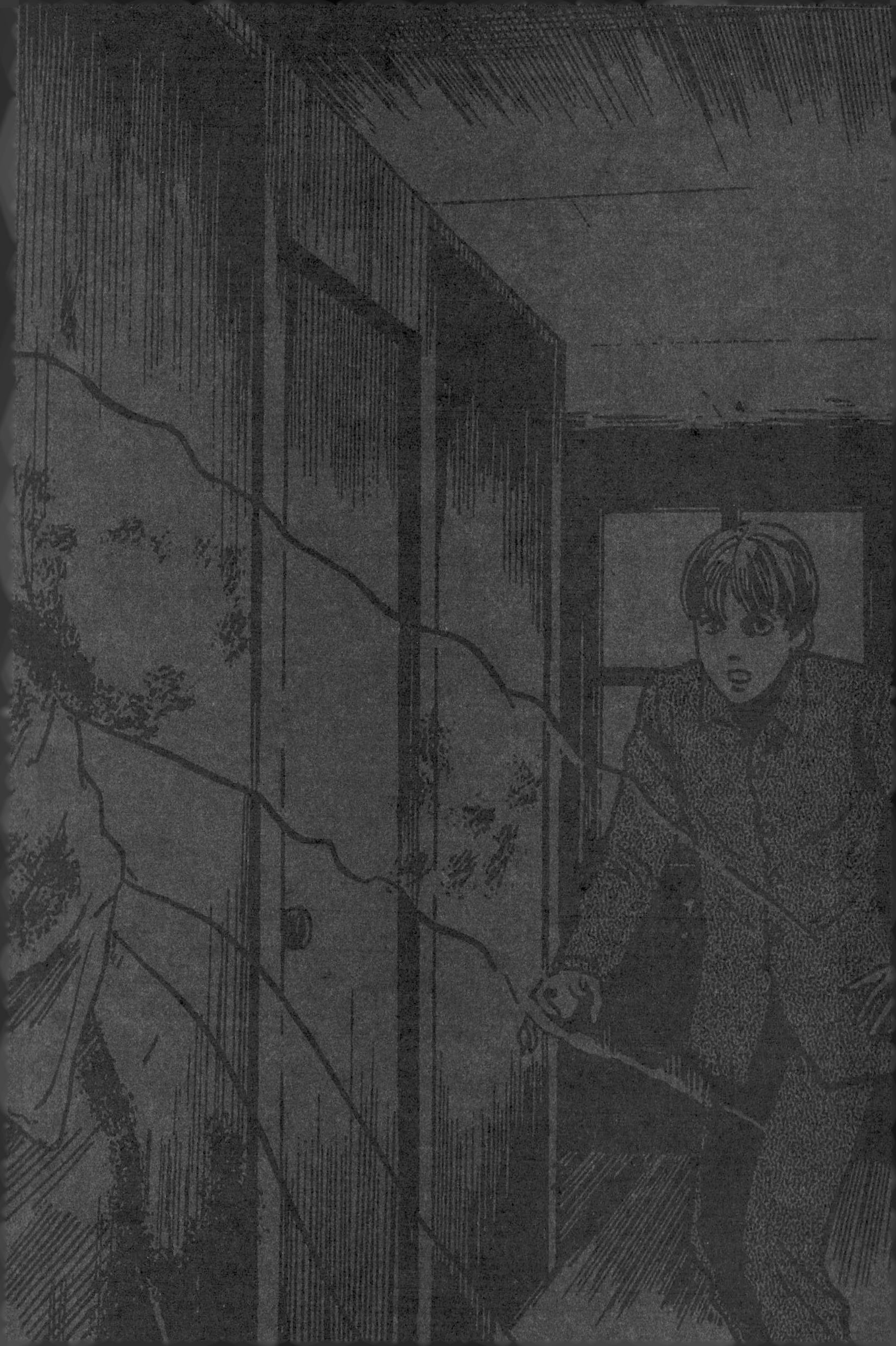

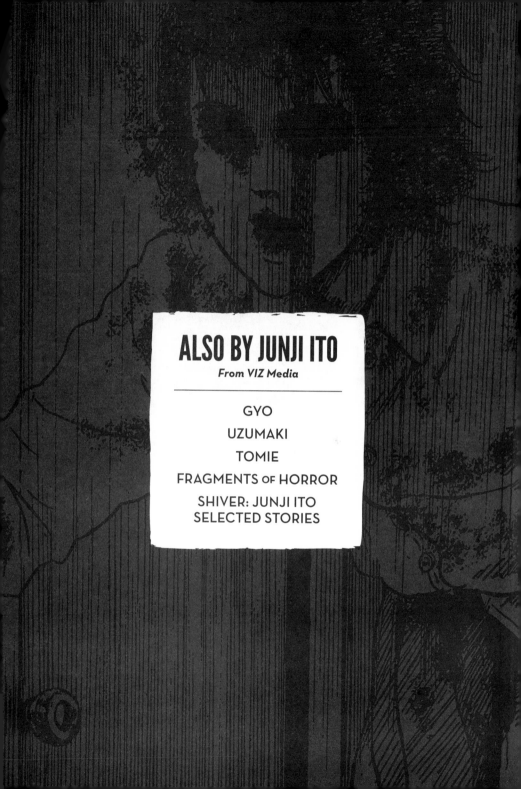

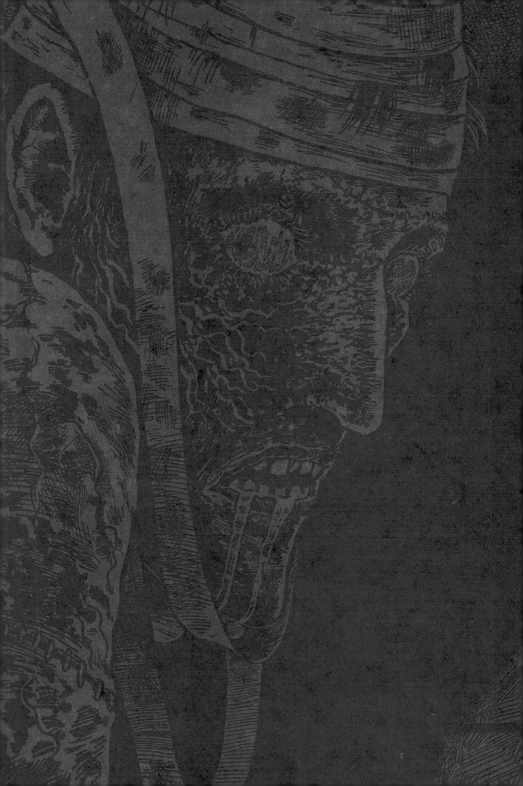

Frankenstein

JUNJI ITO STORY COLLECTION

Story & Art by Junji Ito

Ito Junji Kessakushu 10: Frankenstein

Originally published in Japan in 2013 by Asahi Shimbun Publications Inc., Tokyo. English translation rights arranged with Asahi Shimbun Publications Inc., Tokyo through TOHAN CORPORATION, Tokyo.

"Frankenstein"
Based on *Frankenstein: Or, the Modern Prometheus* by Mary Shelley, published in 1831
Translation: Jocelyne Allen
English Adaptation: Nick Mamatas

Other Stories
Translation & Adaptation: Jocelyne Allen

Touch-Up Art & Lettering: James Dashiell
Cover & Graphic Design: Adam Grano
Editor: Masumi Washington

Printed in the U.S.A.

Published by VIZ Media, LLC
P.O. Box 77010
San Francisco, CA 94107

10 9 8 7 6 5
First printing, October 2018
Fifth printing, October 2021

VIZ SIGNATURE

PARENTAL ADVISORY
FRANKENSTEIN is rated T+ for Older Teen and is recommended for ages 16 and up. This volume contains graphic violence and mature themes.

VIZ MEDIA
viz.com

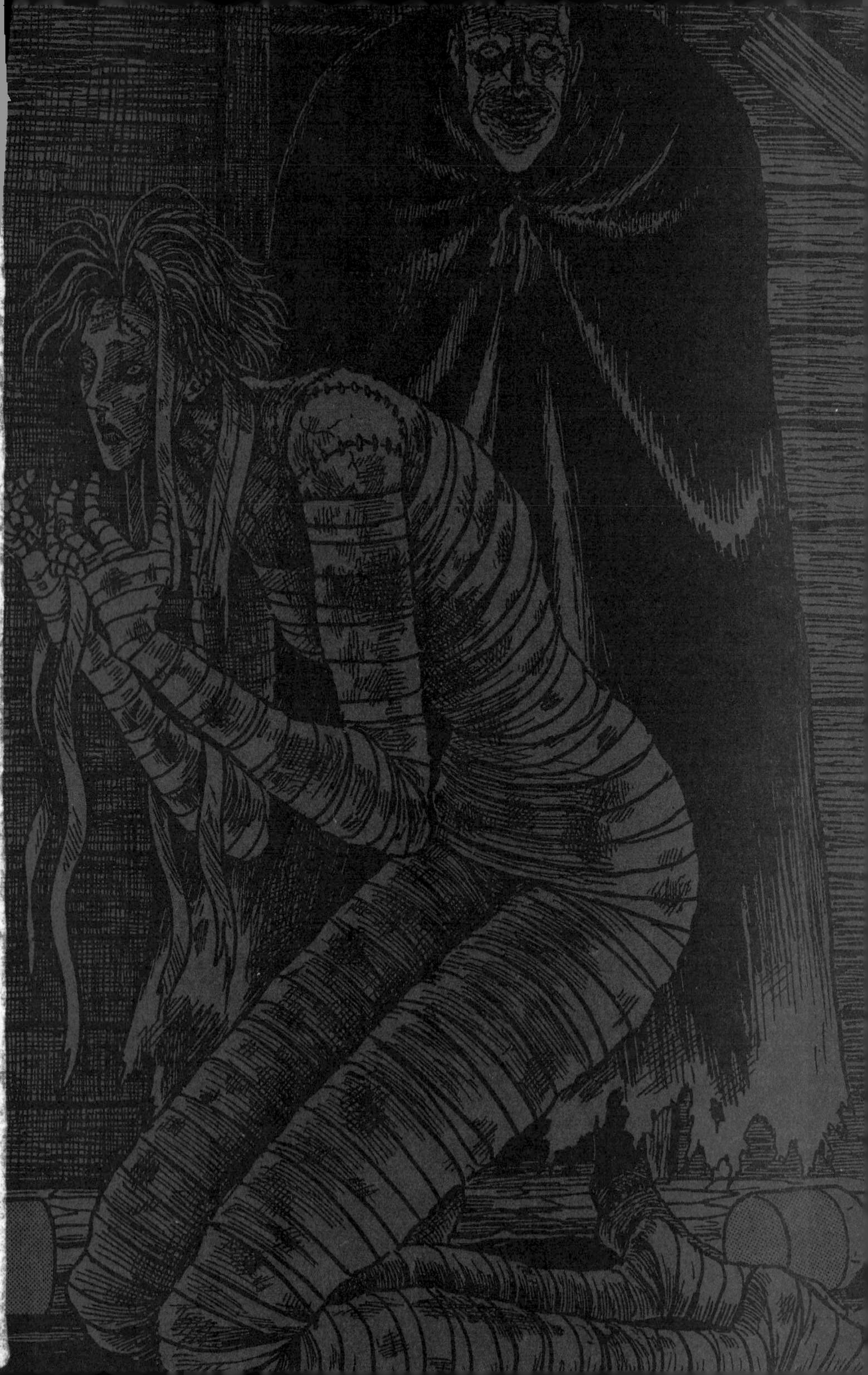